Sources of

Global History
Since 1900

Sources of

Global History
Since 1900

Second Edition

James H. Overfield
University of Vermont

WADSWORTH
CENGAGE Learning·

Australia • Brazil • Japan • Korea • Mexico • Singapore • Spain • United Kingdom • United States

WADSWORTH
CENGAGE Learning®

Sources of Global History Since 1900,
Second Edition
James H. Overfield

Publisher/Executive Editor: Suzanne Jeans

Acquiring Sponsoring Editor: Brooke Barbier

Development Editor: Lauren Athmer, LEAP
Publishing Services, Inc.

Editorial Assistant: Katie Coaster

Media Editor: Lisa Ciccolo

Marketing Program Manager: Caitlin Green

Manufacturing Planner: Sandee Milewski

Rights Acquisitions Specialist: Jennifer
Meyer Dare

Design Direction, Production Management,
and Composition: PreMediaGlobal

Cover Image: Martin Puddy

For product information and technology assistance, contact us at
Cengage Learning Customer & Sales Support, 1-800-354-9706
For permission to use material from this text or product,
submit all requests online at **www.cengage.com/permissions.**
Further permissions questions can be emailed to
permissionrequest@cengage.com.

Library of Congress Control Number: 2011946212

ISBN-13: 978-1-111-83538-5

ISBN-10: 1-111-83538-1

Wadsworth
20 Channel Center Street
Boston, MA 02210
USA

Cengage Learning is a leading provider of customized learning solutions
with office locations around the globe, including Singapore, the United
Kingdom, Australia, Mexico, Brazil and Japan. Locate your local office at
international.cengage.com/region

Cengage Learning products are represented in Canada by
Nelson Education, Ltd.

For your course and learning solutions, visit **www.cengage.com.**

Purchase any of our products at your local college store or at our preferred
online store **www.cengagebrain.com.**

Instructors: Please visit **login.cengage.com** and log in to access
instructor-specific resources.

Printed in the United States of America
1 2 3 4 5 6 7 16 15 14 13 12

Contents

Preface

Several goals and principles have guided the writing of *Sources of Global History Since 1900*. Primary among them is the conviction that history students at every level need to meet the challenge of analyzing primary sources, thereby becoming active inquirers into the past. Involvement with primary-source evidence accomplishes what is beyond the capacity of even the best textbooks and the most stirring lectures: it reveals to students that historical scholarship is more than memorizing facts and the conclusions of others; it is an intellectual process of drawing inferences and discovering patterns from clues—primary sources—yielded by the past.

Structure and Themes

At a time when this project was just getting started, a reviewer of a very preliminary outline of the proposed book stated that the author would undoubtedly find it an "interesting" challenge to choose a little over one hundred sources that would capture the richness and complexity of global history since 1900. Several years and many outlines later, I can state unequivocally that this outside reviewer was correct. Choosing the sources to include in this edition has been interesting, as well as frustrating, humbling, and at times overwhelming.

From start to finish, however, my decisions were guided by a number of considerations:

- First, I wanted to produce a book that was truly global in scope. Without an appreciation of the experiences of *all* the world's major regions and peoples, no true understanding of recent world history is possible.

- Second, I wanted to show the book's student readers that history is more than the study of past wars, politics, and diplomacy. Although these topics are amply covered in *Sources of Global History Since 1900*, the arts, popular culture, social change, intellectual developments, economics, technology, and the environment are also represented. Special efforts have been made to include sources pertaining to the experiences of women.

- Third, I was interested in introducing students to a variety of sources. The collection contains speeches, private letters, treaties, poems, memoirs, magazine illustrations, government documents, newspaper accounts, and diplomatic correspondence.

- Fourth, I never lost sight of the fact that the book's ultimate test would be its classroom effectiveness. I have tried to include sources that will hold our students' interest, while also providing instructors with material that can be woven into lectures and can serve as the basis for class discussions and a variety of written assignments.

The result is a book of more than one hundred sources, divided into four parts.

The choice of sources in **Part I**, "Seeds of Change: Politics, Society, and Culture, 1900–1914," was driven by an appreciation of the challenges faced by instructors at the beginning of courses on recent world history, a time in the semester when they must convey to their students the broad outlines of world political and economic relationships while simultaneously introducing them to a host of significant ideologies and movements. Chapter 1 concentrates on developments in the West and includes sources on imperialism, political ideologies, and feminism. Chapter 2 includes sources on the world's other remaining regions—sub-Saharan Africa, the Middle East and North Africa, East Asia, Latin America, and South Asia. It touches on many topics, most of which relate to the question of how non-Western peoples responded to the realities of Western global dominance.

Part II, "Decades of War, Economic Upheaval, and Revolution, 1914–1939," begins with a chapter on World War I. This is followed by four chapters on the Western world and the Soviet Union (Chapter 4), Latin America (Chapter 5), Africa (Chapter 6), and Asia (Chapter 7) in the 1920s and 1930s.

Part III, "From World War II to the Early 1970s: Decades of Conflict, Decolonization, and Economic Recovery," is organized around the concept of the "three worlds" (first, second, and third), a way of viewing the world that originated and gained wide currency in the 1950s, 1960s, and 1970s. Chapter 8, on World War II and the origins of the Cold War, is followed by chapters on the industrialized, capitalistic West (Chapter 9); the Soviet bloc and Communist China (Chapter 10); and Latin America, Africa, and those parts of Asia emerging from colonialism (Chapter 11).

Part IV, "The Recent Past: the late 1970s to the Present," consists of two chapters, both of which are global in scope. Chapter 12, "The 1970s and 1980s: Years of Challenge and Change," touches on political changes in the West, the Soviet Union, China, and Latin America; economic developments in the Middle East and Japan; and the role of religion, especially the growing importance of religious fundamentalism. One section is devoted to women in non-Western societies. Chapter 13, "The World Since 1990," includes sources on some of the most important developments in the recent past (intensified globalization, the Internet revolution, and terrorism).

The sources have been chosen and organized so that each of them is connected thematically with others in the book. No source exists in isolation. Each chapter is divided into several smaller sections in which two or three sources that center on a common theme are grouped together. In some cases, the sources in these sections complement one another, and in other cases they present different perspectives on the same phenomenon. Many sources, especially those dealing with key topics such as nationalism, colonialism, gender relations, race, and warfare, are linked with sources in other chapters. Such linkages give students a sense of change and development, and also provide opportunities to make cross-cultural comparisons.

Learning Aids

Every effort has been made to make these sources as accessible as possible to our students by providing a variety of aids.

- The *Prologue* defines primary sources, discusses their importance, and provides guidelines for their analysis.

- Extensive *part, chapter, section,* and *individual source introductions* help the reader place each selection in historical context and understand its significance.

- Suggested *Questions for Analysis* precede each source. Their purpose is to help students make sense of each piece of evidence and wrest from it as much insight as possible. They are also intended to resemble the historian's approach to source analysis and to help students make historical and cross-cultural comparisons. Some specific questions are intended to assist the reader in picking out important pieces of information. Questions of this type require the student to address two issues: What does the document or artifact say, and what meaningful facts can I garner from it? This prepares students for the next, level of analysis: drawing inferences. Questions that require inferential conclusions follow the fact-oriented questions. Other questions require students to make comparisons between two or more sources.

- Many of the sources have *extensive footnotes.* These explain words and allusions that most college students cannot reasonably be expected to know.

In summary, the goal of this book is to prepare the student-reader for success—comfort with historical analysis, proficiency in critical thinking, greater understanding of recent global history, and a greater awareness of the rich varieties, as well as shared characteristics, of the world's peoples.

Feedback

If you have questions or comments about the book, please address them to james.overfield@uvm.edu.

Acknowledgments

I am in debt to many individuals who provided help, assistance, and encouragement during the preparation of *Sources of Global History Since 1900.* They include editors at Cengage Learning, especially Brooke Barbier, and at LEAP Publishing Services, Inc., especially Lauren Athmer; many reference and circulation librarians at the University of Vermont; and scholars and colleagues at the University of Vermont, especially my friend, Alfred J. Andrea, who provided much of the inspiration for the Prologue to *Sources of Global History Since 1900.*

I would also like to thank the following historians who read and commented on the book at various stages in its development: Laura Bergstrom, Ivy Tech

Community College—Southern Indiana Region; Marjorie Berman, Red Rocks
Community College; and Martin Wilson, East Stroudsburg University.

Thanks, finally, to my wife Susan, for her constant support on this project and
much else.

James H. Overfield
Essex Center, Vermont
March 30, 2012

PROLOGUE

Primary Sources and How to Read Them

Imagine a course in organic chemistry in which students never set foot in a laboratory; or a literature course in which they read commentaries on Shakespeare's plays but none of the plays themselves; or a course on the history of jazz in which they never listen to a note of music. Most students would consider such courses strange and deficient, and many would soon be beating a path to the door of their academic advisor or college dean with complaints about flawed teaching methods and wasted tuition payments. One cannot understand chemistry without doing experiments. Nor can one understand literature without reading plays, poetry, and fiction; or music without listening to performances.

In much the same way, one cannot truly understand history without reading and analyzing *primary sources*. Primary sources are historical records produced at a time that is contemporary with the event or period that is being studied. They are distinct from *secondary sources*—books, articles, television documentaries, and historical films—that were produced after the events they describe have occurred. Secondary sources, or "histories" in the conventional sense of the term, organize the jumble of past events into understandable narratives; provide interpretations; make comparisons; and discuss questions of motive and causation. When they are well done, they provide pleasure and insight to their readers. But such works are still *secondary*, in that they are written after the fact and, more importantly, derive their evidence and information from primary sources.

History is an ambitious discipline that deals with all aspects of past human activity and belief. This means that the primary sources that historians use to re-create the past are equally wide-ranging and diverse. Most of the primary sources they use are written sources, such as government records, law codes, private correspondence, literary works, religious texts, merchants' account books, memoirs, and an almost endless list of others. So important are written records to the study of history that past societies with no alphabet or writing system are called "prehistoric"—not because they lack histories, but because there is no way of retrieving those histories due to the lack of records. Nonwritten records can also be primary sources for historians. Important insights about the past have been derived from humble objects that are part of everyday life—fabrics, tools, kitchen implements, weapons, farm equipment, jewelry, pieces of furniture—as well as from paintings, buildings, sculpture, musical compositions, photographs, and film.

To be a historian is to work with primary sources. But to do so effectively is not easy. Each source provides only one glimpse of reality, and no single source can possibly give us the whole picture of past events and developments. Many sources are difficult to understand, and can be interpreted accurately only after the precise meaning of their words has been deciphered and their backgrounds thoroughly investigated. Many sources contain distortions and errors that can be discovered only by rigorous internal analysis and comparison with evidence from other sources. Only after all these source-related difficulties have been overcome can a historian hope to achieve a coherent and accurate understanding of the past.

"Understanding" history involves much more than memorizing dates and facts. By the time you complete your course on recent global history, you will undoubtedly have learned many historical facts. For example, on June 28, 1914, Gavrilo Princip assassinated the archduke and archduchess of Austria-Hungary in the Bosnian city of Sarajevo; on March 6, 1957, the former British colony of the Gold Coast became the independent state of Ghana; and in 1962 and 1963 Rachel Carson's book about insecticides, *Silent Spring*, topped the bestseller charts in the United States. But knowing these facts will be of little value unless it contributes to your understanding of the past. What motivated Princip, and why did his murder of the archduke and archduchess bring about World War I? What caused Ghanaian independence, and what was its significance in the history of imperialism? Why did Carson's book become a bestseller, and how did it affect environmentalism? Finding answers to such questions are the historian's ultimate goal, and these answers can be found in primary sources.

One noted historian, Robin Winks, wrote a book entitled *The Historian as Detective*, and the image is appropriate although inexact. Like a detective, the historian examines evidence to reconstruct events. Like a detective, the historian is interested in discovering "what happened, who did it and why." Like a detective interrogating witnesses, the historian also must carefully examine available sources to determine their accuracy and usefulness, and both investigators must ask similar questions.

First and foremost, the historian must evaluate the *validity* of the source. Is it what it claims to be? Clever forgeries have misled many historians. Even authentic sources can be misleading if the author lied or deliberately misrepresented reality. In addition, historians can easily be led astray when they fail to consider the *perspective* reflected in a document. As any detective soon learns, eyewitnesses to the same event often disagree on what they saw. The detective has the opportunity to reexamine witnesses and offer them the opportunity to change their testimony in the light of new evidence and deeper reflection. The historian is not so fortunate. Even when the historian compares a piece of documentary evidence with other evidence in order to uncover its flaws, there is no way to cross-examine its author. Given this fact, it is necessary for the historian to understand as fully as possible the source's perspective. Thus, the historian must ask several key questions:

- *What* kind of document is this?

- *Who* wrote it?

- *Why* was it written, and for *whom?*

- *Where* was it composed and *when?*

What is important because understanding the nature of a source will give the historian an idea of what kind of information he or she can expect to find in it. Many sources simply do not address the questions a historian would like to ask of them, and knowing this can save a great deal of frustration. A future historian writing about the academic quality of your school's courses in the early twenty-first century would be foolish to think that anything useful could be learned from a study of the registrar's class lists or grade reports. Student and faculty class notes, copies of syllabi, examinations, student papers, and textbooks would be far more useful.

Who, for whom, and *why* are equally important questions. Thinking about a future historian writing about student social life at your school in the early twenty-first century, he or she would be unwise to rely very heavily on letters, pamphlets, and other statements prepared by the admissions office. Documents like these—designed to attract potential students and to place the school in the best possible light—cannot be accepted uncritically. They must be tested against student testimony contained in private letters, memoirs, posters, the student newspaper, and yearbook.

Where and *when* are also important questions to ask of any primary source. As a rule, distance from an event in space and time colors perceptions and can diminish the reliability of a source's testimony. Your school's future historian might very well wish to consult the recollections of a person celebrating a twenty-fifth class reunion. Conceivably, this graduate would have a perspective and information that he or she lacked a quarter of a century earlier. Just as conceivably, however, this person's memory of what college was like might have faded to the point where his or her recollections have little value.

You and the Sources

This book will actively involve you in the work of historical inquiry by asking you to draw inferences based on your analysis of primary source evidence. This may prove difficult at first, but it is well within your capability.

You will analyze two types of evidence: documents and artifacts. Each source will be authentic, so you do not have to worry about validating it. Editorial material in this book also supplies you with the information necessary to place each piece of evidence into its proper context and will suggest questions you legitimately can and should ask of each source.

It is important to keep in mind that historians approach each source they consider with questions, even though they might be vaguely formulated. Like detectives, historians want to discover some particular truth or shed light on a particular issue. This requires asking specific questions of the witnesses or, in the historian's case, of the evidence. These questions should not be prejudgments. One of the worst errors a historian can make is setting out to prove a point or to defend an ideological position. Questions are simply starting points, nothing else, but they are essential. Therefore, as you approach a source, have your question or questions fixed in your mind and remind yourself as you work your way through a source what issue or issues you are investigating. Each source in this anthology is preceded by a number of suggested Questions for Analysis. You or your professor may want to ask other questions. In any case, focus on your questions and issues, and take notes as you read. Without written outlines or summaries of what you have read, insights and information you have acquired will tend to quickly fade from your memory. Above all, *you must be honest and thorough as you study a source*. Read each footnote carefully to avoid misunderstanding a word or allusion. Try to understand exactly what the source is saying and what its author's perspective is. Be careful not to distort words or ideas by wrenching them out of context. Above all, read the entire source so that you understand as fully as possible what it says and does not say.

This is not as difficult as it sounds. But it does take concentration and work. And do not let the word *work* mislead you. True, primary source analysis demands attention to detail and mental effort, but it is also rewarding. There is great satisfaction in developing a deeper and truer understanding of the past based on an exploration of the evidence.

PART ONE

Seeds of Change: Politics, Society, and Culture, 1900–1914

In the summer of 1914, Europe went to war. Painstakingly planned for, and even welcomed by some, the war was not expected to last long. Generals and politicians believed that the outcome would be decided in just a few short months or even within weeks. They promised that the "boys would be home by Christmas." The war, however, turned out quite differently. It became World War I, a four–year exercise of slaughter that resulted in close to ten million battlefield deaths, twice that many wounded, and almost seven million civilian deaths. And in the end, it settled very little.

World War I's legacy went far beyond lost lives and broken bodies. It led to the overthrow of Russia's tsarist government and the establishment of the world's first communist state. It resulted in the breakup of the Austro-Hungarian Empire in central Europe and the demise of the Ottoman Empire in the Middle East. It undermined faith in leaders, and contributed to the defeat of liberal, democratic governments in much of Europe in the 1920s and 1930s. It was a major factor in the rise of dangerous demagogues like Mussolini in Italy and Hitler in Germany. Wartime destruction, massive government borrowing, and the punitive reparations payments imposed on defeated Germany distorted financial markets and contributed to the onset of the Great Depression in the 1930s. Beyond Europe, the war stoked nationalism and undermined colonialism. The Japanese, Chinese, Middle Eastern Arabs, and colonial subjects of Britain and France, all of whom had contributed to the war against Germany and its allies, were angered when the victors, especially France and Great Britain, reneged on wartime promises of greater independence or territorial gains.

So great were the costs and consequences of World War I—clearly one of the turning points in modern history—that it is easy to underestimate the importance of events and developments that occurred in the immediate prewar years. The first transatlantic radio broadcast was made in 1901, and the first successful airplane flight occurred in 1903. In the early 1900s Europeans and Americans could entertain themselves by playing recordings on their gramophones and watching films at a local cinema. In 1903 the German state of Prussia became the first government entity to require drivers' licenses for the operation of motor vehicles; in 1908 the world's first affordable automobile, the Ford Model T, rolled off an assembly line in Detroit. New intellectual currents such as Freudian psychology, quantum physics, and the theory of relativity challenged long-established views of human nature, matter, and the universe. In Europe, avant-garde artists, choreographers, and composers shocked viewers and listeners by their embrace of new modernist movements which threatened to cast aside longstanding traditions and standards.

Profound political changes occurred. Europe and the United States entered fully into the age of mass politics, and for the first time left-wing socialist parties made significant electoral gains. Revolutions occurred in Russia in 1905, Persia in 1906, Ottoman Turkey in 1908, Mexico in 1910, and China in 1911. In many parts of Africa and Asia, even though Europe's overseas empires reached their greatest extent in the early 1900s, anticolonial movements were stirring. Rebellions against colonial rule occurred in parts of Africa, Vietnam, the Dutch East Indies, and the Philippines, but the most important changes occurred in India, "the jewel in the crown" of the British Empire, where populist leaders drew widespread support for a campaign to boycott British goods and force the British to "quit India."

The international landscape was changing in other ways. The United States was beginning to emerge as a major force in world affairs. By the early 1900s it had the world's largest economy, with an annual gross domestic product almost twice as large as those of Great Britain and Germany. Between 1898 and 1903, the United States joined the imperialist club when it annexed Hawaii, took possession of Guam, the Samoan Islands, the Philippines, and Puerto Rico, and established a protectorate over Cuba. Another new power was emerging in East Asia. In 1905 Japan, which had been forced out of its self-imposed isolation only fifty years earlier, defeated Russia in the Russo-Japanese War. Europeans were shocked that a small Asian nation was capable of conquering a major European state, while millions of Asians and Africans drew inspiration from Japan's rapid modernization. The time when a few European "Great Powers" dominated international relations as well as the world economy was beginning to draw to a close.

Meanwhile, diplomatic tensions in Europe grew. Newly united Germany had Europe's most powerful army, built a formidable navy, and established colonies in Africa and Asia; its businessmen aggressively competed with Great Britain and France in world markets. France continued to brood over its loss to Germany in the Franco-Prussian War (1870–1871), and while waiting for revenge, sought to bolster its status by maintaining an overseas empire second in size only to that of Great Britain. Great Britain resented Germany's economic success, military power, and diplomatic bluster, but until the early 1900s also competed with Russia and France for territories in Africa and Asia. Statesmen worried about Russian expansion into the Balkans and Asia Minor if the Hapsburg Empire of Austria-Hungary disintegrated or if Ottoman Turkey continued to decline.

In response, European statesmen sought security through alliance systems, and politicians approved huge military budgets to pay for new weapons and ever-expanding armies and navies. Generals developed strategies and drew up time-tables to fight a war that everyone viewed as inevitable. That war finally came in 1914, setting in motion events that accelerated the disintegration of the European-dominated world of the early 1900s.

CHAPTER I

The Western World on the
Eve of the Great War

The concept of the "West" has never been static. Originally applied to Europe to differentiate the people who lived on the western tip of Eurasia from the non-Christian, mostly nonwhite peoples to their east and south, the meaning of the term was expanded at the end of the nineteenth century to include areas which had experienced extensive European settlement and whose economies, cultures, and political institutions drew on European models. Thus, by the early 1900s when people referred to the "Western world," they were thinking not just of Europe but also of the United States, Canada, Australia, and New Zealand. Despite their historic ties to Europe, states in Central and South America were not considered part of "the West," perhaps because of their large indigenous populations and relatively backward economies.

Profound and rapid change had been the dominant theme in Western history for more than a century, and in the early 1900s changes, especially in cities, were coming more quickly than ever. On the eve of World War I, metropolitan London had 7 million inhabitants, having doubled in size since 1870 to make it the world's largest city. Berlin, Vienna, and Paris had populations of 2 million; Moscow and St. Petersburg had approximately 1.5 million each. In 1870, only two American cities had populations over 500,000; by 1910, there were eight, and one of them, New York, with almost 4.8 million inhabitants, was second in size only to London. In these cities, the fruits of recent technological breakthroughs were on full display. Electricity lighted streets, businesses, and homes and provided power for factories, trams, and subways. Telephones connected business offices and increasing numbers of private homes. Nickelodeons and movie theaters provided cheap entertainment.

Urbanization was accompanied by significant economic and social changes. After a slump that began in the 1870s, most Western nations experienced a surge of economic growth beginning in the 1890s, spurred by population growth, new construction, and new industries (chemicals, motor vehicles, electricity, and a host of new consumer products). International trade flourished, and agricultural prices steadied and showed some increases. In Europe and the United States the number of farmers declined, and city-based blue-collar workers— wage-earners who did physical labor to earn a salary—became the largest single part of the work force. As a result, socialist political parties, trade unions, and consumer cooperatives began to play key roles in society and politics. It was also a time when increasing numbers of women, who benefited from increased educational opportunities, entered the paid work force as office workers, teachers, nurses, and sales personnel.

The early 1900s also saw discernable shifts in the political landscape on both sides of the Atlantic. In the United States, progressive reformers crusaded against urban political bosses and corporate robber barons in the name of greater democracy, social justice, and honest government. In Europe, liberal political parties continued to support legal equality, constitutional government, and education, but they dropped their opposition to expanding the electorate, government intervention in the economy, and social welfare programs. On the right, traditional conservatives, who were skeptical of democracy, supportive of organized churches, and open to social reform, were challenged by more radical conservatives who were drawn to racist and antisemitic ideas and supported militarism, relentless opposition to the labor movement, and a total rejection of parliamentary government.

Along with nationalism, socialism was the most successful new political movement of the early twentieth century. Although some socialists still looked to violent revolution as the only way to end capitalism and achieve a just society, most threw their energies into organizing labor unions and political parties, winning elections, and passing laws that improved the lot of workers. They made impressive gains, especially in Germany, where in 1912 the Social Democratic Party became the largest single party in the Reichstag with 110 members.

Striking cultural and intellectual innovations also occurred in the early 1900s. The discovery of X-rays in 1895 and investigations of radioactivity by Ernest Rutherford and Pierre and Marie Curie provided the background for two groundbreaking scientific developments: the quantum theory of the German Max Planck, which stated that energy was emitted not in waves but in discrete particles or quanta, and the theory of relativity by the Swiss-born Albert Einstein, which provided a mathematical model for the electrodynamics of moving bodies. Whereas the work of Planck, Einstein, and others challenged centuries-old understandings of the physical world, the writings of Sigmund Freud on the role of the subconscious in human behavior called into question humanity's basic rationality. Meanwhile, scores of Western artists, writers, and composers concluded, seemingly all at once, that old forms of artistic and musical expression were no longer adequate to express the reality of the new century. They launched dozens of new movements—post-impressionism, expressionism, cubism, fauvism, primitivism, futurism, atonalism, and symbolism, to name the most prominent—that unsettled and challenged, as well as occasionally infuriated their viewers and audiences.

The most important changes resulted from choices made by politicians, diplomats, and generals about alliances, war plans, war aims, naval construction projects, the size of armies, and the potential costs and benefits of peace and warfare. As a result of their decisions, when the archduke and archduchess of Austria-Hungary were assassinated by a Bosnian Serb nationalist in Sarajevo on June 28, 1914, the outcome was not a diplomatic compromise, not a brief and localized conflict, but a general war involving all the Great Powers of Europe, their colonies, and ten other states including the Ottoman Empire, China, Japan, and the United States. A new era had begun.

The Pros and Cons of Empire: Two British Perspectives

By the early 1900s, the greatest land-grab in history was complete. In the previous three decades, the imperialist powers—primarily Great Britain, France, and Germany but also Italy, Belgium, the United States, Portugal, and the Netherlands—brought almost all of Africa under their control and extended their authority in Southeast Asia and Oceania. Great Britain added 4.25 million square miles of territory and 66 million people to its empire; France added 3.5 million square miles and 26 million people; Germany added 1 million square miles and 13 million people. When these new acquisitions were added to older colonial holdings in Asia, Africa, and the Caribbean, approximately 80 percent of the world's landmass consisted of Europe, lands under the direct control of a Western power, or lands populated and dominated by people of European descent.

Western imperialism was controversial from the start. Missionary groups, certain business interests, the military, conservatives, and nationalists tended to support it. Left-leaning political groups were skeptical of its benefits. Some of the latter believed that imperialism went against basic principles of social justice and freedom; others argued that money spent on foreign ventures could better be used for social programs. Although by the early 1900s the division of the world among a small number of Western powers was a *fait accompli*, imperialism continued to be a controversial subject, as the writings in this section clearly show.

The Benefits of Imperialism

◆

1 ◆ Joseph Chamberlain, *"WANT OF EMPLOYMENT AND THE DEVELOPMENT OF FREE MARKETS"* and *"THE TRUE CONCEPTION OF EMPIRE"*

Joseph Chamberlain (1836–1914), British imperialism's' most ardent defender in the 1890s and early 1900s, was the son of a London shoemaker. When he was in his late teens, his family moved to the industrial city of Birmingham, where he became a wealthy businessman and an advocate of educational reform, public health initiatives, and expansion of the franchise to working-class men. After serving three years as mayor of Birmingham, in 1876 he was elected to Parliament, in which he served until 1914, the year of his death. In the 1890s, he became one of Britain's most prominent politicians as leader of the Liberal Unionists (Liberals who opposed self-rule for Ireland); he served as president of the Board of Trade before becoming secretary of state for the colonies from 1895 to 1906. Known as the "Prime Minister of the British Empire," Chamberlain defended the empire as beneficial to the home country and the colonies alike. His speech "Want of Employment and the Development of Free Markets" was delivered at a banquet of the West Birmingham Relief Association, a philanthropic organization, in January 1894; "The True Conception of Empire" was delivered in March 1897 at the annual dinner of the Royal Colonial Institute, a London club founded in 1868 "for gentlemen interested in colonial and Indian affairs."

QUESTIONS FOR ANALYSIS

1. According to Chamberlain, what economic benefits accrue to Britain from its overseas colonies?
2. What plan does Chamberlain propose to develop the newly acquired colony of Uganda? How will this plan benefit the British and the people of Uganda?
3. When Chamberlain refers to Great Britain's "work of civilization," what specifically does he have in mind?
4. How does Chamberlain represent the racial characteristics of the peoples that have recently come under British dominion?

"WANT OF EMPLOYMENT AND THE DEVELOPMENT OF FREE MARKETS"

I am convinced that it is a necessity as well as a duty for us to uphold the dominion and empire which we now possess. . . .

I would never lose the hold which we now have over our great Indian dependency—by far the greatest and most valuable of all the customers we have or ever shall have in this country. I approve of the continued occupation of Egypt . . . I have urged . . . the necessity for using every legitimate opportunity to extend our influence and control in that great African continent which is now being opened up to civilisation

Source: "Employment and the Development of Empire" and "The True Conception of Empire" from *Joseph Chamberlain, Foreign and Colonial Speeches* (London: Routledge, 1897).

and to commerce; and, lastly, it is for the same reasons that I hold that our navy should be strengthened until its supremacy is so assured that we cannot be shaken in any of the possessions which we hold or may hold hereafter.

Believe me, if in any one of the places to which I have referred any change took place which deprived us of control and influence . . . the first to suffer would be the working-men of this country. Then, indeed, we should see a distress which would . . . be chronic, and we should find that England was entirely unable to support the enormous population which is now maintained by the aid of her foreign trade. If the working-men of this country . . . understand their own interests, they will never lend any countenance to the doctrines of those politicians who never lose an opportunity of pouring contempt . . . upon the brave Englishmen, who . . . in all parts of the world are carving out new dominions for Britain, and are opening up fresh markets for British commerce, and laying out fresh fields for British labour.

A few years ago Uganda[1], was only known to us by the reports of . . . travellers, or by the accounts which were given by those self-denying missionaries who have gone through all these wild and savage lands, endeavouring to carry to the people inhabiting them the blessings of Christianity and civilisation. But within very recent times English authority has been established in Uganda, and an English sphere of influence has been declared. Uganda is a most fertile country. It contains every variety of climate; in a large portion of it European colonisation is perfectly feasible; . . . there is hardly anything which is of value or use to us in our commerce which cannot be grown there; but in spite of these natural advantages, during the past generation the country has been desolated by civil strife and by the barbarities of its rulers. . . .

All that is wanted to restore this country to a state of prosperity, to a commercial position which it has never attained before, is settled peace and order. . . .

But I will go further than that. This rich country should be developed. . . .

What we want is to give to this country the means of communication by a railway from the coast which would bring to that population—which is more intelligent than the ordinary populations in the heart of Africa—our iron, and our cloths, and our cotton, and even our jewellery, because I believe that savages are not at all insensible to the delights of personal adornment. (Laughter.) It would bring to these people the goods which they want and which they cannot manufacture, and it would bring to us the raw materials, of which we should be able to make further use.

"THE TRUE MEANING OF EMPIRE"

But the British Empire is not confined to the self-governing colonies and the United Kingdom. It includes a much greater area, a much more numerous population in tropical climes, where no considerable European settlement is possible, and where the native population must always vastly outnumber the white inhabitants . . . We feel now that our rule over these territories can only be justified if we can show that it adds to the happiness and prosperity of the people—and I maintain that our rule does, and has, brought security and peace and comparative prosperity to countries that never knew these blessings before.

In carrying out this work of civilisation we are fulfilling what I believe to be our national mission, and we are finding scope for the exercise of those faculties and qualities which have made of us a great governing race. I do not say that our success has been perfect in every case, I do not say that all our methods have been beyond reproach; but I do say that in almost every instance in which the rule of the Queen has been established and the great *Pax Britannica* [British peace] has been enforced, there has come with it greater security to life and property, and a material improvement to the condition of the bulk of the population. No doubt, in the first instance, when these conquests have been made, there has been bloodshed, there has been loss of life among the native populations,

[1] A landlocked region of east Africa.

loss of still more precious lives among those who have been sent out to bring these countries into some kind of disciplined order, but it must be remembered that that is the condition of the mission we have to fulfil....

You cannot have omelettes without breaking eggs; you cannot destroy the practices of barbarism, of slavery, of superstition, which for centuries have desolated the interior of Africa, without the use of force; but if you will fairly contrast the gain to humanity with the price which we are bound to pay for it, I think you may well rejoice in the result of such expeditions as those which have recently been conducted with such signal success—in Nyassaland, Ashanti, Benin, and Nupe[2]—expeditions which may have, and indeed have, cost valuable lives, but as to which for...one life lost a hundred will be gained, and the cause of civilisation and the prosperity of the people will in the long run be eminently advanced.

In the wide dominions of the Queen...it is a gigantic task that we have undertaken when we have determined to wield the sceptre of empire. Great is the task, but great is the honour—and I am convinced that the conscience and the spirit of the country will rise to the height of its obligations, and that we shall have the strength to fulfil the mission which our history and our national character have imposed on us....

The mother country is still vigorous and fruitful, is still able to send forth troops of stalwart sons to people and occupy the waste spaces of the earth;...let it be our endeavour, let it be our task, to keep alight the torch of Imperial patriotism, to hold fast the affection and the confidence of our kinsmen across the seas, so that in every vicissitude of fortune the British Empire may present an unbroken front to all her foes, and may carry on even to distant ages the glorious traditions of the British flag.

---

[2]These are all recently colonized regions of Africa.

Imperialist Delusions

❖

2 ❖ John A. Hobson, *IMPERIALISM: A STUDY*

The leading British critic of imperialism in the early 1900s was Oxford-educated economist J. A. Hobson (1858–1940), who wrote *Imperialism: A Study* in 1902 following his experiences as a correspondent covering the Second Boer War, or South African War, for the *Manchester Guardian.* This was an imperialist war directed not against native Africans but against the Boers, white descendants of mainly Dutch immigrants who lived in two independent South African republics, Transvaal and the Orange Free State. At issue were access to the republics' rich diamond and gold deposits and the political rights of the *uitlanders*, non-Dutch (mainly English) immigrants to the republics. The British won the war and incorporated the Boer republics into the Union of South Africa, but at great costs. The war dragged on from 1899 to 1902, cost the lives of 22,000 British soldiers and 42,000 Boers (26,000 of whom were women and children who died in British concentration camps after their farms had been burned), and cost the British dearly in terms of world opinion. To Hobson it epitomized the hypocrisy and failures of colonialism, which he spelled out in his widely read book.

Source: J. A. Hobson, *Imperialism: A Study* (London: James Nisbet and Co., Ltd., 1902).

QUESTIONS FOR ANALYSIS

1. On what basis does Hobson reject Chamberlain's arguments about the economic benefits of Britain's overseas empire?
2. What arguments does Hobson develop to justify his skepticism about the "civilizing mission" of imperialism?
3. How, according to Hobson, does imperialism affect British and international politics?
4. What are Hobson's views of the recently colonized people of Asia and Africa? How do his views compare to those of Chamberlain?

No mere array of facts and figures...will suffice to dispel the popular delusion that the use of national force to secure new markets by annexing fresh tracts of territory is a sound and a necessary policy for an advanced industrial country like Great Britain. It has indeed been proved that recent annexations of tropical countries, procured at great expense, have furnished poor and precarious markets, that our aggregate trade with our colonial possessions is virtually stationary, and that our most profitable...trade is with rival industrial nations, whose territories we have no desire to annex, whose markets we cannot force, and whose active antagonism we are provoking by our expansive policy....

The political effects...of the new Imperialism...may be thus summarised. It is a constant menace to peace, by furnishing continual temptations to further aggression upon lands occupied by lower races and by embroiling our nation with other nations of rival imperial ambitions; to the sharp peril of war it adds the chronic danger and degradation of militarism, which not merely wastes the current physical and moral resources of the nations, but checks the very course of civilization. It consumes to an illimitable and incalculable extent the financial resources of a nation by military preparation, stopping the expenditure of the current income of the State upon productive public projects and burdening posterity with heavy loads of debt. Absorbing the public money, time, interest and energy on costly and unprofitable work

of territorial aggrandisement, it thus wastes those energies of public life in the governing classes...which are needed for internal reforms and for the cultivation of the arts of material and intellectual progress at home. Finally, the spirit, the policy, and the methods of Imperialism are hostile to the institutions of popular self-government, favouring forms of political tyranny and social authority which are the deadly enemies of effective liberty and equality.

Seeing that the Imperialism...is clearly condemned...we may ask, "How is the British nation induced to embark upon such unsound business?" The only possible answer is that the business interests of the nation as a whole are subordinated to those of certain sectional interests that usurp control of the national resources and use them for their private gain....

Certain definite business and professional interests feeding upon imperialistic expenditure, or upon the results of that expenditure, are thus set up in opposition to the common good, and, instinctively feeling their way to one another, are found united in strong sympathy to support every new imperialist exploit.

If the £60,000,000 which may now be taken as a minimum expenditure on armaments in time of peace were subjected to a close analysis, most of it would be traced directly to the tills of certain big firms engaged in building warships and transports, equipping and coaling them, manufacturing guns, rifles, ammunition, supplying horses, waggons, saddlery, food, clothing for the services, contracting for barracks, and for other large irregular needs. Through these main channels the millions flow to feed many subsidiary trades, most of which are quite aware that they are engaged in executing contracts for the services. Here we have an important nucleus of commercial Imperialism....

With them stand the great manufacturers for export trade, who gain a living by supplying the real or artificial wants of the new countries we annex or open up. Manchester, Sheffield, Birmingham, to name three representative cases, are full of firms which compete in pushing textiles and hardware, engines, tools, machinery, spirits, guns, upon new markets....

The making of railways, canals, and other public works, the establishment of factories, the development of mines, the improvement of agriculture in new countries, stimulate a definite interest in important manufacturing industries which feeds a very firm imperialist faith in their owners....

The shipping trade has a very definite interest which makes for Imperialism. This is well illustrated by the policy of State subsidies now claimed by shipping firms as a retainer, and in order to encourage British shipping for purposes of imperial safety and defence.

The military services are, of course, imperialist by conviction and by professional interest, and every increase enhances the political power they exert....

The direct professional influence of the services carries with it a less organised but powerful sympathetic support on the part of the aristocracy and the wealthy classes, who seek in the services careers for their sons.

To the military services we may add the Indian Civil Service and the numerous official and semi-official posts in our colonies and protectorates. Every expansion of the Empire is also regarded by these same classes as affording new openings for their sons as ranchers, planters, engineers, or missionaries.

From this standpoint our colonies still remain what James Mill[1] cynically described them as being, "a vast system of outdoor relief for the upper classes."

There exists in a considerable though not a large proportion of the British nation a genuine desire to spread Christianity among the heathen, to diminish the cruelty and other sufferings which they believe exist in countries less fortunate than their own, and to do good work about the world in the cause of humanity. Most of the churches contain a small body of men and women deeply, even passionately, interested in such work. Ill-trained for the most part in psychology and history, these people believe that religion and other arts of civilization are portable commodities which it is our duty to convey to the backward nations, and that a certain amount of compulsion is justified in pressing their benefits upon people too ignorant at once to recognize them.

Is it surprising that the selfish forces which direct Imperialism should utilize the protective colours of these disinterested movements? Imperialist politicians, soldiers, or company directors...do not deliberately and consciously work up these motives in order to incite British public. They simply and instinctively attach to themselves any strong, genuine elevated feeling which is of service, fan it and feed it until it assumes fervour, and utilize it for their ends....

The actual history of Western relations with lower races occupying lands on which we have settled throws a curious light upon the theory of a "trust for civilization." When the settlement approaches the condition of genuine colonization, it has commonly implied the extermination of the lower races, either by war or by private slaughter, as in the case of Australian Bushmen, African Bushmen and Hottentots, Red Indians, and Maoris, or by forcing upon them the habits of a civilization equally destructive to them.[2] This is what is meant by saying that "lower races" in contact with "superior races" naturally tend to disappear. How much of "nature" or "necessity" belongs to the

---

[1] James Mill (1773–1836) was a Scottish economist, political theorist, and philosopher. He was the father of the illustrious philosopher and civil servant John Stuart Mill (1806–1873).

[2] This is a reference to the native peoples in colonies of white settlement: Australia, South Africa, Canada, the United States, and New Zealand.

process is seen from the fact that only those "lower races" tend to disappear who are incapable of profitable exploitation either because they are too "savage" for effective industrialism or because the demand for labour does not require their presence.

Whenever superior races settle on lands where lower races can be profitably used for manual labour in agriculture, mining, and domestic work, the latter do not tend to die out, but to form a servile class.

This is the root fact of Imperialism so far as it relates to the control of inferior races; when the latter are not killed out they are subjected by force to the ends of their white superiors.

◆

Europe's Changing Political Landscape: Nationalism and Socialism

A major development in the political life of nineteenth-century Europe was the emergence of ideologies—integrated bodies of sociopolitical doctrines, assumptions, and aims that form the basis for a political, economic, or social philosophy or program. Between the 1810s and the 1840s, all of the following words, each representing a different ideology, appeared in the English language: liberalism, radicalism, socialism, republicanism, conservatism, monarchism, nationalism, and communism. The ideas behind these ideologies were not necessarily new. Love of one's nation existed before "nationalism" became a word in the 1840s, and reverence for tradition predated the entry of "conservatism" into the English language in the 1830s. What these new words signify is that the political divisions and heightened political activism of the early nineteenth century were forcing people to define their beliefs more systematically and coherently.

Every ideology that emerged in the early 1800s changed over time. Liberalism, with support mainly from the middle class, maintained its commitment to free trade, parliamentary government, and the protection of individual freedoms, but by the end of the 1800s its supporters were more willing to extend the franchise to workers and women and use government to solve social issues.

Emerging in the 1820s and 1830s, socialism at first appealed to a small number of idealists who were appalled by the coldblooded competition of early industrial capitalism and outlined plans for alternative communities and new ways of governing based on cooperation, harmony, and the communal ownership of property. From midcentury onward, socialism came to be identified with the doctrines of Karl Marx, who dismissed his socialist predecessors as "utopian," and sought to make socialism "scientific" by grounding it on the study of history and economics. He saw a future in which the impoverished working class would rise up in revolution, overthrow capitalism, end the class struggle, and create a classless society. Beginning in the 1890s, however, "revisionist" socialists challenged Marxist orthodoxy, especially in their belief that socialism could and should be attained through the ballot box, not violent revolution.

Nationalism also changed in the nineteenth century. It emerged during the French Revolution, when the French people came to see the wars against Austria, Great Britain, Prussia, and Russia as a patriotic crusade to save the revolution and spread its ideals across the continent. In 1792 and 1793, the fervor of French troops saved the revolution, and in the early 1800s it contributed to

Napoleon's victories and the extension of French control over much of Europe. French conquests in turn aroused nationalism among Germans, Italians, Poles, and Russians who fought to gain their independence from the French. Nationalists had their hopes dashed in 1815 at the Congress of Vienna, when diplomats ignored their aspirations in redrawing the map of Europe. But nationalism could not be eradicated. From the 1820s to the 1840s, nationalists allied themselves with liberalism and republicanism, and espoused the principle of national self-determination for all peoples. After the liberal/nationalist revolutions of 1848 failed, nationalism came to be identified with pragmatic and conservative politicians who orchestrated the unification of Italy and Germany in the following two decades. By century's end nationalism was increasingly associated with conservative, if not reactionary, groups that used it to lure the masses away from socialism and democracy and to justify militarism, imperialism, aggressive foreign policies, and antisemitism. In the web of events that led to World War I, nationalism played a central role.

Racism, Militarism, and the New Nationalism

3 ◆ Heinrich von Treitschke, extracts from *HISTORY OF GERMANY IN THE NINETEENTH CENTURY* and *HISTORICAL AND POLITICAL WRITINGS*

German historian Heinrich von Treitschke (1834–1896) represents the increasingly strong link in the late 1800s between nationalism and militarism, racism, and authoritarianism. The son of a Prussian general, Treitschke taught history at several universities, including the University of Berlin. He was also a member of the German parliament, the Reichstag, from 1871 to 1884. His best-known work is his seven-volume *History of Germany in the Nineteenth Century.* In this and his numerous other writings, lectures, and speeches, Treitschke disparaged Jews, socialists, and the two nations he saw as Germany's principal rivals, France and England. For Germany he advocated militarism, authoritarianism, and war as the paths to national greatness. Well after his death in 1896, his views struck a responsive chord among many Germans who feared socialism and democracy and yearned for the day when Germany would be recognized as the world's most powerful nation.

QUESTIONS FOR ANALYSIS

1. According to Treitschke, what is the relationship between the state and the individual?
2. In Treitschke's view, why is monarchy superior to democracy?
3. What qualities do Germans have that set them apart from other peoples, especially the English and the Jews, according to Treitschke?

Source: Von Treitschke, Extracts. . . . From Louis Snyder, ed., *Documents of German History* (New Brunswick, Rutgers University Press, 1958), 258–262.

4. Early-nineteenth-century nationalists believed that all nations had a contribution to make to human progress. What is Treitschke's view?
5. According to Treitschke, what is the value of war for a nation?

ON THE GERMAN CHARACTER

Depth of thought, idealism, cosmopolitan views; a transcendent philosophy which boldly oversteps (or freely looks over) the separating barriers of finite existence, familiarity with every human thought and feeling, the desire to traverse the world-wide realm of ideas in common with the foremost intellects of all nations and all times. All that has at all times been held to be characteristic of the Germans and has always been praised as the essence of German character and breeding.

The simple loyalty of the Germans contrasts remarkably with the lack of chivalry in the English character. This seems to be due to the fact that in England physical culture is sought, not in the exercise of noble arms, but in sports like boxing, swimming, and rowing, sports which undoubtedly have their value, but which obviously tend to encourage a brutal and purely athletic point of view, and the single and superficial ambition of getting a first prize.[1]

ON THE STATE

The state is a moral community, which is called upon to educate the human race by positive achievement. Its ultimate object is that a nation should develop in it, a nation distinguished by a real national character. To achieve this state is the highest moral duty for nation and individual alike. All private quarrels must be forgotten when the state is in danger.

At the moment when the state cries out that its very life is at stake, social selfishness must cease and party hatred be hushed. The individual must forget his egoism, and feel that he is a member of the whole body...

Only the truly great and powerful states ought to exist. Small states are unable to protect their subjects against external enemies; moreover, they are incapable of producing genuine patriotism or national pride and are sometimes incapable of *Kultur*[2] in great dimensions. Weimar produced a Goethe and a Schiller;[3] still these poets would have been greater had they been citizens of a German national state.

ON MONARCHY

The will of the state is, in a monarchy, the expression of the will of one man who wears the crown by virtue of the historic right of a certain family; with him the final authority rests. Nothing in a monarchy can be done contrary to the will of the monarch. In a democracy, plurality, the will of the people, expresses the will of the state. A monarchy excels any other form of government, including the democratic, in achieving unity and power in a nation. It is for this reason that monarchy seems so natural, and that it makes such an appeal to the popular understanding. We Germans had an experience of this in the first years of our new empire.[4] How wonderfully the idea of a united Fatherland was embodied for us in the person of the venerable Emperor! How much it meant to us that we could feel once more: "That man is Germany; there is no doubting it!"

---

[1]Treitschke is correct in drawing a distinction between English and German sports. The English prized competitive athletic contests, whereas the Germans favored group calisthenics and exercises.

[2]German for "culture" or "civilization."

[3]Johann Wolfgang von Goethe (1749–1832) and Johann von Schiller (1759–1805) were poets and dramatists who lived before German unification. They both spent much of their adult lives in Weimar, the capital of the Duchy of Saxe-Weimar.

[4]With German unification (1871), the king of Prussia, Wilhelm I, became emperor of Germany.

ON WAR

The idea of perpetual peace is an illusion supported only by those of weak character. It has always been the weary, spiritless, and exhausted ages which have played with the dream of perpetual peace. A thousand touching portraits testify to the sacred power of the love which a righteous war awakes in noble nations. It is altogether impossible that peace be maintained in a world bristling with arms, and even God will see to it that war always recurs as a drastic medicine for the human race. Among great states the greatest political sin and the most contemptible is feebleness....

War is elevating because the individual disappears before the great conception of the state. The devotion of the members of a community to each other is nowhere so splendidly conspicuous as in war.

Modern wars are not waged for the sake of goods and resources. What is at stake is the sublime moral good of national honor, which has something in the nature of unconditional sanctity, and compels the individual to sacrifice himself for it....

The grandeur of war lies in the utter annihilation of puny man in the great conception of the State, and it brings out the full magnificence of the sacrifice of fellow-countrymen for one another. In war the chaff is winnowed from the wheat. Those who have lived through 1870 cannot fail to understand Niebuhr's[5] description of his feelings in 1813, when he speaks of how no one who has entered into the joy of being bound by a common tie to all his compatriots, gentle and simple alike, can ever forget how he was up-lifted by the love, the friendliness, and the strength of that mutual sentiment.

It is war which fosters the political idealism which the materialist rejects. What a disaster for civilization it would be if mankind blotted its heroes from memory. The heroes of a nation are the figures which rejoice and inspire the spirit of its youth, and the writers whose words ring like trumpet blasts become the idols of our boyhood and our early manhood. He who feels no answering thrill is unworthy to bear arms for his country. To Aryan[6] races, who are before all things courageous, the foolish preaching of everlasting peace has always been in vain. They have always been man enough to maintain with the sword what they have attained through the spirit....

ON THE ENGLISH

The hypocritical Englishman, with the Bible in one hand and a pipe of opium[7] in the other, possesses no redeeming qualities. The nation was an ancient robber-knight, in full armor, lance in hand, on every one of the world's trade routes.

The English possess a commercial spirit, a love of money which has killed every sentiment of honor and every distinction of right and wrong.... In England all notions of honor and class prejudices vanish before the power of money. The newspapers, in their accounts of aristocratic weddings, record in exact detail how much each wedding guest has contributed in the form of presents or in cash; even the youth of the nation have turned their sports into a business, and contend for valuable prizes, whereas the German students wrought havoc

---

[5]Barthold Georg Niebuhr (1776–1831) was a Prussian civil servant and historian. He lectured for a time at the University of Berlin and is best known for his three-volume history of Rome.

[6]Today, the term *Aryan*, or Indo-Iranian, refers to a branch of the Indo-European family of languages, which also includes Baltic, Slavic, Armenian, Greek, Celtic, Latin, and Germanic. Indo-Iranian includes Bengali, Persian, Punjabi, and Hindi. In Treitschke's day, *Aryan* was used to refer not only to the prehistoric language

from which all these languages derive but also to the racial group that spoke the language and migrated from its base in central Asia to Europe and India in the distant past. In the racial mythology that grew in connection with the term and that later Hitler and the Nazis embraced, the Aryans provided Europe's original racial stock.

[7]Treitschke is making a point about what he considers the hypocrisy of the British, professed Christians who nonetheless sell opium to the Chinese.

on their countenances for the sake of a real or imaginary honor.[8]

ON JEWS

The Jews at one time played a necessary role in German history, because of their ability in the management of money. But now that the Aryans have become accustomed to the idiosyncrasies of finance, the Jews are no longer necessary. The international Jew, hidden in the mask of different nationalities, is a disintegrating influence; he can be of no further use to the world. It is necessary to speak openly about the Jews, undisturbed by the fact that the Jewish press befouls what is purely historical truth.

---

[8]Treitschke again uses examples from sports to underscore the differences between the Germans and the English. English sports such as rugby and football (American soccer) were organized into professional leagues; the Germans were still willing to be scarred in duels to defend their honor.

The Tasks of Socialism

4 ◆ Vladimir Ilyich Lenin, *"WHAT IS TO BE DONE?"*

From its beginning, socialism was marked by doctrinal disagreements. Early utopian socialists produced widely dissimilar plans to deal with society's imperfections. Later in the century Karl Marx became socialism's leading theoretician, but the First International, an international socialist organization founded in 1864, included not just disciples of Marx but also anarchists, union leaders, radical republicans, and utopians. Marx managed to bring about the expulsion of most of his rivals before the First International disbanded in 1876, and Marxism remained the inspiration for socialist political parties founded in the 1880s and 1890s. Nonetheless, ideological struggles continued to divide the movement in the late nineteenth and early twentieth centuries. The sharpest division was between orthodox Marxists, who believed in the inevitability of class conflict, rejected cooperation with bourgeoisie governments, and considered revolution to be the only path to socialism, and revisionist socialists, who believed that Marx had misread history and socialism's future. Most importantly, revisionists rejected violent revolution. Now that most workers had the vote and their own political party, revisionists were convinced that socialists could reach their goals by winning elections and passing laws in their favor.

Two events in 1899, the publication *Evolutionary Socialism* by the German theoretician Eduard Bernstein and the decision of the French socialist Alexandre Millerand to accept a ministerial position in a French cabinet, intensified the debate over revisionism. Millerand was expelled from the Socialist Party of France for identifying himself with the enemy bourgeois state, and Bernstein's book was attacked by dozens of critics. Among them was Vladimir Ilyich Lenin (1870–1924), who at the time was a relatively obscure Russian Marxist who had joined the recently founded Russian Social Democratic Party in 1900 after having spent five years in prison and Siberian exile. While living in Munich following his return from Siberia, Lenin wrote "What is to be Done," in which he attacked

---

Source: "What is to be Done?" from *V. I. Lenin, Collected Works*, vol. 5 (Moscow: Progress Publishers, 1973), 352–353, 375–376, 399–401, 413–414, 425, 454, 463–467.

both revisionism and the doctrines of other Russian Social Democrats who believed that because of Russia's autocratic government and limited industrialization, the prospect of a socialist revolution lay in the distant future. After the party's meeting in 1903 (held in exile in Brussels and London), Lenin assumed leadership of the Bolsheviks, who in opposition to the Mensheviks demanded highly centralized party leadership, noncooperation with bourgeois liberals, and single-minded devotion to revolution. He returned to Russia during the Revolution of 1905, but resumed his life of exile in Western Europe in 1907. Living in poverty and obscurity, Lenin continued to plot and plan for Russia's socialist revolution, which under his leadership occurred in 1917.

QUESTIONS FOR ANALYSIS

1. According to Lenin, how does the "critical Marxism" of men such as Bernstein endanger the socialist movement?
2. In Lenin's view, how are the goals and purposes of trade unionism similar to and different from those of the Social-Democratic Party?
3. Why, according to Lenin, have the workers been unable to develop true revolutionary consciousness? What does he believe must be done to change this?
4. What advantages does Lenin see in restricting the party to a small corps of dedicated revolutionaries?
5. What kinds of activities will these professional revolutionaries carry on to further the cause of revolution?

[SOCIALIST DIVISIONS]

In fact, it is no secret for anyone that two trends have taken form in present-day international Social-Democracy.... The essence of the "new" trend, which adopts a "critical" attitude towards "obsolete dogmatic" Marxism, has been clearly enough *presented* by Bernstein and *demonstrated* by Millerand.

Social-Democracy must change from a party of social revolution into a democratic party of social reforms. Bernstein has surrounded this political demand with a whole battery of well-attuned "new" arguments and reasonings. Denied was the possibility of putting socialism on a scientific basis and of demonstrating its necessity and inevitability.... Denied was the fact of growing impoverishment, the process of proletarization, and the intensification of capitalist contradictions; the very concept, "*ultimate aim*," was declared to be unsound, and the idea of the dictatorship of the proletariat was completely rejected. Denied was the antithesis in principle between liberalism and socialism.

Denied was *the theory of the class struggle*, on the alleged grounds that it could not be applied to a strictly democratic society governed according to the will of the majority, etc....

[THE WORKERS AND REVOLUTION]

The history of all countries shows that the working class, exclusively by its own effort, is able to develop only trade-union consciousness, i.e., the conviction that it is necessary to combine in unions, fight the employers, and strive to compel the government to pass necessary labor legislation, etc....

The overwhelming majority of Russian Social-Democrats have of late been almost entirely absorbed by this work of organising the exposure of factory conditions.... —so much so, indeed, that they have lost sight of the fact that this, *taken by itself*, is in essence still not Social-Democratic work, but merely trade union work.... These exposures could have served as a beginning and a component part of Social-Democratic activity; but they could also have led...to a "purely trade union" struggle and to a non-Social-Democratic working-class movement. Social-Democracy leads the struggle of the working class, not only for better terms for the sale of labor-power, but for the abolition of the social system that compels the propertyless to sell themselves to the rich. Social-Democracy represents the working class, not in its relation to a given group of employers alone, but in its relation to all classes of modern society and to the state as an organised political force....

Why do the Russian workers still manifest little revolutionary activity in response to the brutal treatment of the people by the police, the persecution of religious sects, the flogging of peasants, the outrageous censorship, the torture of soldiers, the persecution of the most innocent cultural undertakings, etc.? Is it because the "economic struggle" does not "stimulate" them to this, because such activity does not "promise palpable results," because it produces little that is "positive"?...[Social Democrats] must blame ourselves, our lagging behind the mass movement, for still being unable to organize sufficiently wide, striking, and rapid exposures of all the shameful outrages. When we do that (and we must and can do it), the most backward worker will understand, *or will feel*, that the students and religious sects, the peasants and the authors are being abused and outraged by those same dark forces that are oppressing and crushing him at every step of his life. Feeling that, he himself will be filled with an irresistible desire to react, and he will know how to heckle the censors one day, on another day to demonstrate outside the house of a governor who has brutally suppressed a peasant uprising...etc. As yet we have done very little, almost nothing, *to bring* before the working masses prompt exposures on all possible issues. Many of us as yet do not recognize this as our *bounden duty* but trail spontaneously in the wake of the "drab everyday struggle," in the narrow confines of factory life....

[THE PARTY AND ITS PURPOSES]

If we begin with the solid foundation of a strong organisation of revolutionaries, we can ensure the stability of the movement as a whole and carry out the aims both of Social-Democracy and of trade unions proper. If, however, we begin with a broad workers' organisation, which is supposedly most "accessible" to the masses (but which is actually most accessible to the gendarmes and makes revolutionaries most accessible to the police), we shall achieve neither the one aim nor the other;...

"A dozen wise men can be more easily wiped out than a hundred fools." This wonderful truth (for which the hundred fools will always applaud you) appears obvious only because in the very midst of the argument you have skipped from one question to another. You [the skeptical reader] began by talking and continued to talk of the unearthing of a "committee," of the unearthing of an "organization," and now you skip to the question of unearthing the movement's "roots" in their "depths." The fact is, of course, that our movement cannot be unearthed, for the very reason that it has countless thousands of roots deep down among the masses....But since you raise the question of *organizations* being unearthed...I assert that it is far more difficult to unearth a dozen wise men than a hundred fools. This position I will defend, no matter how much you instigate the masses against me for my "anti-democratic" views, etc. As I have stated repeatedly, by "wise men," in connection with organization, I mean *professional revolutionaries.*...I assert: (1) that no revolutionary movement can endure without a stable organization of leaders maintaining continuity; (2) that the broader the popular mass drawn spontaneously into the struggle, which forms the basis of the movement and participates in it, the more urgent the need for such an organization, and the more solid this organization must be (for it is much easier for all sorts of demagogues to side-track the more backward sections of the masses); (3) that such an organization must consist chiefly of people professionally engaged in revolutionary activity; (4) that in an autocratic state, the more we *confine* the membership of such an organization to people who are professionally engaged in revolutionary activity and who have been professionally trained in the art of combating the political police, the more difficult will it be to unearth the organization; and (5) the *greater* will be the number of people from the working class and from the other social classes who will be able to join the movement and perform active work in it.

I shall deal only with the last two points. The question as to whether it is easier to wipe out "a dozen wise men" or "a hundred fools" reduces itself to the question, above considered, whether it is possible to have a mass *organization* when the maintenance of strict secrecy is essential.... To concentrate all secret functions in the hands of as small a number of professional revolutionaries as possible does not mean that the latter will "do the thinking for all" and that the rank and file will not take an active part in the *movement*. ...

The active and widespread participation of the masses will not suffer; on the contrary, it will benefit by the fact that a "dozen" experienced revolutionaries, trained professionally no less than the police, will centralize all the secret aspects of the work—the drawing up of leaflets, the working out of approximate plans; and the appointing of bodies of leaders for each urban district, for each factory district, and for each educational institution.... Centralization of the most secret functions in an organization of revolutionaries will not diminish, but rather increase the extent and enhance the quality of the activity of a large number of other organizations, that are intended for a broad public and are therefore as loose and as non-secret as possible, such as workers' trade unions; workers' self-education circles[1] and circles for reading illegal literature; and socialist, as well as democratic, circles among *all* other sections of

the population; etc., etc. We must have such circles, trade unions, and organizations everywhere in *as large a number as possible* and with the widest variety of functions; but it would be absurd and harmful *to confound* them with the organization of *revolutionaries*; ... in order to "serve" the mass movement we must have people who will devote themselves exclusively to Social-Democratic activities, and such people must *train* themselves patiently and steadfastly to be professional revolutionaries.

Yes, this recognition is incredibly dim. Our worst sin with regard to organization consists in the fact that *by our primitiveness we have lowered the prestige of revolutionaries in Russia.* A person who is flabby and shaky on questions of theory, who has a narrow outlook, who pleads the spontaneity of the masses as an excuse for his own sluggishness, who resembles a trade-union secretary more than a spokesman of the people, who is unable to conceive of a broad and bold plan that would command the respect even of opponents, and who is inexperienced and clumsy in his own professional art—the art of combating the political police—such a man is not a revolutionary, but a wretched amateur! ...

I used to work in a study circle that set itself very broad, all-embracing tasks; and all of us, members of that circle, suffered painfully and acutely from the realization that we were acting as amateurs at a moment in history when we might have been able to say, varying a well-known statement: "Give us an organization of revolutionaries, and we will overturn Russia!" The more I recall the burning sense of shame I then experienced, the bitterer become my feelings towards those pseudo-Social-Democrats whose preachings "bring disgrace on the calling of a revolutionary," who fail to understand that our task is not to champion the degrading of the revolutionary to the level of an amateur, but *to raise* the amateurs to the level of revolutionaries.

---

[1]Regular meetings of workers, intellectuals, or students to discuss and plan strategies to overcome Russia's social and political problems.

The New Voice of Women in the Early Twentieth Century

Although debates about women's place in society are centuries old and took place in many parts of the world, only during the French Revolution in the 1790s did women's political and legal rights become matters of public debate and controversy. Although the revolution's leaders (all male) ultimately rebuffed appeals for female political rights, early in the revolution women won the right to own property, marry without parental consent, initiate divorce, and take legal action against fathers of illegitimate children. This legislation was rescinded in the late 1790s and early 1800s, and in the conservative atmosphere of the 1820s and 1830s women's political activism diminished. Prevailing opinion consigned middle- and upper-class women to a domestic role centered on child care, housekeeping, supervising servants, and providing husbands with a tranquil haven where they could escape the rigors of politics and business.

By midcentury, women on both sides of the Atlantic, many of whom had been active in temperance and antislavery campaigns, once more began to speak out and organize on behalf of women's rights. A landmark was the women's rights convention held in Seneca Falls, New York, in 1848, at which participants adopted resolutions proclaiming the equality of men and women and demanding for women the vote, divorce and property rights, and equal employment and educational opportunities. By the late 1800s, some gains had been made, especially in the areas of women's legal status and access to higher education. In addition, professions such as nursing and teaching provided new opportunities for many middle-class women, and a few women established careers as doctors, lawyers, and scientists. Efforts to gain full political rights met stiff resistance, however, and by 1914, only Australia, New Zealand, Finland, Norway, and several western U.S. states had granted women full voting privileges. The stage was set for the epic battles over women's suffrage that took place in many Western countries, especially the United States and Great Britain, in the years before the outbreak of World War.

"Race Decadence" and the U.S. Women's Movement

5 ◆ Anna Howard Shaw, *PRESIDENTIAL ADDRESSES AT THE CONVENTIONS OF THE NATIONAL AMERICAN WOMAN SUFFRAGE ASSOCIATION, 1905, 1906*

For many opponents of women's rights in Europe and the United States around the year 1900, feminism's most disturbing figure was not Elizabeth Cady Stanton, a founder of the U.S. women's rights movement who insisted that "obey" be left

Source: Anna Howard Shaw, "1905 Presidential Address" from *The Woman's Journal*, 36, no, 28 (July 22, 1905), 114–115; "1906 Presidential Address" from *The Woman's Journal*, 37 (February 17, 1906, p. 26).

out of her marriage vows; it was not Margaret Sanger, who pioneered the birth control movement in the United States; it was not even Emmeline Pankhurst and her daughters, Sylvia and Christabel, who led the militant fight for women's suffrage in England. It was not a real woman at all. It was Nora, the fictional heroine of the Norwegian playwright Henrik Ibsen's *A Doll's House*, which was performed throughout Europe and the United States after its premiere in 1880. Having endured a childhood dominated by a stifling father and then eight years of an empty marriage, Nora slams the door on her husband and three children to begin a quest for self-enlightenment and fulfillment.

To opponents of women's rights, Nora's rejection of domesticity epitomized the unhealthy self-centeredness that underlay women's search for equality, meaningful work, and independence. Such self-centeredness, they feared, threatened to consign woman's traditional role as wife and mother to oblivion. Anxieties over the incompatibility of motherhood and female emancipation were deepened in the 1880s by declining birth rates in industrialized nations, especially within the middle class. This troubled European nationalists, who feared manpower shortages for the military. It also worried many Americans of northern European stock, who feared inundation by the millions of new immigrants from southern and eastern Europe.

Never one to skirt such issues, U.S. President Theodore Roosevelt (1858–1919) discussed women's duties and true calling in a speech to the National Congress of Mothers in Washington, DC, in 1905. Although a supporter of women's suffrage, Roosevelt was an advocate of "equality in difference." He believed men should run the government, manage businesses, and earn a living; women should marry, become mothers, and raise children. In his speech, he expressed contempt for women who out of "viciousness, coldness, shallow-heartedness, or self-indulgence" neglected their duty to raise families. He further stated that "the existence of women of this type was one of the most unpleasant and unwholesome features of modern life."

The president's remarks gained a quick response from Anna Howard Shaw (1847–1919), president of the National American Woman Suffrage Association from 1904 to 1915. Born in England and raised in Michigan, she obtained degrees in divinity and medicine from Boston University. She chose a life of political action, however, first through the Women's Christian Temperance Union and then on behalf of women's suffrage. She remained single to better accomplish her life's work.

The following excerpts are from her presidential addresses to the annual meetings of the National American Woman Suffrage Association in 1905 and 1906. In both excerpts, she discusses women's work and its relationship to motherhood and the family.

QUESTIONS FOR ANALYSIS

1. What evidence is there that Shaw accepts Roosevelt's premise that "race decadence" is a problem in the United States? How does her view of its causes differ from that of the president?
2. What ulterior motives does she ascribe to those who blame women for "race-suicide"? What does she feel are the flaws in their arguments?
3. How does Shaw link the problems she describes in U.S. society to women's lack of political rights?

[1905]

When the cry of race-suicide is heard, and men arraign women for race decadence, it would be well for them to examine conditions and causes, and base their attacks upon firmer foundations of fact. Instead of attacking women for their interest in public affairs and relegating them to their children, their kitchen, and their church, they will learn that the kitchen is in politics; that the children's physical, intellectual, and moral well-being is controlled and regulated by law; that the real cause of race decadence is not the fact that fewer children are born, but to the more fearful fact that, of those born, so few live, not primarily because of the neglect of the mother, but because men themselves neglect their duty as citizens and public officials. If men honestly desire to prevent the causes of race decadence, let them examine the accounts of food adulteration, and learn that from the effect of impure milk alone, in one city 5,600 babies died in a single year. Let them examine the water supply, so impregnated with disease that in some cities there is continual epidemic of typhoid fever. Let them gaze upon the filthy streets, from which perpetually arises contagion of scarlet fever and diphtheria. Let them examine the plots of our great cities, and find city after city with no play places for children, except the streets, alleys, and lanes. Let them examine the school buildings, many of them badly lighted, unsanitary, and without yards. Let them turn to the same cities, and learn that from five to a score or thousand children secure only half-day tuition because there are not adequate schoolhouse facilities. Let them watch these half-day children playing in the streets and alleys and viler places, until they have learned the lessons which take them to ever-growing numbers of reformatories, whose inmates are increasing four times as rapidly as the population. Let them follow the children who survive all these ills of early childhood, until they enter the sweat-shops and factories, and behold there the maimed, dwarfed, and blighted little ones, 500,000 of whom under 14 years of age are employed in these pestilential places. Let them behold the legalized saloons and the dens of iniquity where so many of the voting population spend the money that should be used in feeding, housing, and caring for their children.

Then, if these mentors of women's clubs and mothers' meetings do not find sufficient cause for race degeneracy where they have power to control conditions, let them turn to lecturing women.... That which is desirable is not that the greatest possible number of children should be born into the world; the need is for more intelligent motherhood and fatherhood, and for better born and better educated children....

The great fear that the participation of women in public affairs will impair the quality and character of home service is irrational and contrary to the tests of experience. Does an intelligent interest in the education of a child render a woman less a mother? Does the housekeeping instinct of woman, manifested in a desire for clean streets, pure water, and unadulterated food, destroy her efficiency as a home-maker? Does a desire for an environment of moral and civic purity show neglect of the highest good of the family? It is the "men must fight and women must weep" theory of life which makes men fear that the larger service of women will impair the high ideal of home. The newer ideal, that men must cease fighting and thus remove one prolific cause for women's weeping, and that they shall together build up a more perfect home and a more ideal government, is infinitely more sane and desirable....

[1906]

...To draw sweeping and universal conclusions in regard to a matter upon which there is an "almost complete dearth of data" is never wise. While it is true that marriage and the birth-rate have decreased within recent years, before the results are charged to the participation of women in industry, one must answer many questions.

Is it true that there is more "domestic infelicity" to-day than in times past? Is it true that there is greater "domestic infelicity" in homes where women are engaged in gainful pursuits than in those homes in which the strength of women is never taxed by toil, even to the extent of self-service? Is it true that there is a lower birth-rate among working women than among those of the wealthy class? Are not the effects of over-work and long hours in the household as great as are those of the factory or of the office?

...Is the birth-rate less among women who are engaged in the new pursuits or occupations unknown to women of the past? Or is the decline alike marked among those who are pursuing the ancient occupations which women have followed from time immemorial, but under different conditions?...

Woman as an industrial factor and wage-earner is not new. But woman as an industrial competitor and wage-collector with man is new, not because of woman's revolt against her own industrial slavery, but because changed economic conditions through inventive genius and industrial centralization have laid their hands upon the isolated labors and products of woman's toil, and brought them forth from the tent, the cottage, and the farm house, to the shop, the factory, and the marketplace.

If conditions surrounding their employment are such as to make it a "social question of the first importance" it is unfortunate the President had not seen that women, the most deeply interested factor in the problem, should constitute at least a part of any commission authorized to investigate it. No body of men, unaided by women, can be qualified to do so "in a sane and scientific spirit."...

But if the required investigations were made, even with women upon the committee, what power would the five millions of disfranchised women possess to enact beneficent laws or enforce needed reform?

One cannot but wish that with his recognized desire for "fair play" and his policy of "a square deal," it had occurred to the President that, if five millions of American women are employed in gainful occupations, every principle of justice known to a Republic would demand that these five millions of toiling women should be enfranchised to enable them to secure enforced legislation for their own protection.

The Women's Suffrage Campaign in England—In Pictures

◆

6 ◆ *English Posters and Postcards, 1908–1914*

Organized efforts by English women to gain the vote began in 1847, when a group of Sheffield women founded the Female Political Association and presented a pro-suffrage petition to the House of Lords. Four years later, in 1851, Harriet Hardy Mill (1807–1858), the wife of philosopher John Stuart Mill, wrote a widely read pamphlet titled "Enfranchisement of Women." In 1867, nine years after her death, John Stuart Mill, then a member of the House of Commons, proposed an amendment to a voting reform bill that would have given women the vote. It was rejected 194 to 73, a setback that led to the founding of the National Society for Women's Suffrage in 1868. In the following decades, women made resolutions, publicized their views, and performed symbolic acts such as appearing at polling places and requesting the vote, knowing they would be turned away; as a result of their efforts, by 1900, English women could vote in local elections and stand for election to school boards and municipal offices.

This was not enough for Emmeline Pankhurst (1858–1928), who since the 1870s had been a strong advocate for women's suffrage and better treatment of working-class women. In 1903, she founded the Women's Social and Political Union (WSPU). Led by Pankhurst and her daughters, Christabel and Sylvia, the WSPU tried to advance the cause of women's suffrage by heckling politicians, organizing mass demonstrations, and then by smashing windows, slashing paintings in museums, and burning letters in mailboxes. They finally resorted to martyrdom, when in May 1913 a young woman threw herself under the hooves of the king's racehorse at Epsom Downs and was killed before thousands of shocked spectators. When arrested, many suffragettes, as they came to be called, went on hunger strikes. The government responded by approving the force-feeding of prisoners in 1909 and the Prisoners Act of 1913, by which fasting women were released from prison until they had eaten and then rearrested. Between 1910 and 1914, Parliament on three occasions considered but failed to pass women's suffrage bills.

In the midst of these events, all sides, including moderate suffragists who opposed the WSPU's militancy, held rallies, wrote books, published magazine articles, and sent endless letters to newspaper editors. They also sought to win supporters through art. This was especially true for the suffragists, who founded the Artists' Suffrage League in 1907 and the Suffrage Atelier (workshop) in 1909. Both groups produced numerous posters, postcards, banners, and illustrated leaflets. Opponents of women's suffrage could not equal their output in terms of quantity, but they certainly matched their zeal. The following selections provide an opportunity to analyze both sides' work.

The first examples were produced by opponents of suffrage, all in 1912. The first, "No Votes, Thank You," is a poster published under the auspices of the National League for Opposing Women's Suffrage (NLOWS), an organization founded in 1910. It shows a figure representing "true womanhood," with a supporter of women's suffrage brandishing a hammer for breaking windows behind her. This is followed by "Hear Some Plain Things," a postcard by an anonymous artist. The third selection, "A Suffragette's Home," is the most famous of all the anti-suffrage posters. It shows a worker returning to his home, where his pro-suffrage wife has left a note, "Be back in an hour."

The first pro-suffrage poster, "Convicts and Lunatics," was published in 1908 by the Artists' Suffrage League. It reflects the fact that the first women's colleges were founded at Oxford and Cambridge beginning in the 1860s. The next poster, "Handicapped!" shows an exhausted young woman rowing toward the Houses of Parliament in heavy seas, while the nonchalant young man with the wind at his back looks down at her condescendingly. The poster, "The Appeal of Womanhood" was a direct response to "No Votes, Thank You." The female figure stands up to defend the oppressed women behind her: a laundress, a mother, a prostitute, a widow, and a young girl holding chains in her hand. On her banner, "white slavery" refers to the practice of kidnapping young girls and then forcing them into prostitution; "sweated labour" refers to women or girls who work in sweatshops—small industrial establishments where employees are forced to work long hours, in poor conditions for low wages.

QUESTIONS FOR ANALYSIS

1. How do the anti-suffrage posters characterize women who favored the cause of votes for women?
2. What counterimages are presented in the suffragists' posters?
3. What will be the social implications of giving women the vote, according to the posters of each side?
4. How might Theodore Roosevelt and Anna Howard Shaw have viewed these posters and postcards?

The Art Archive / Museum of London/Picture Desk

"No Votes, Thank you"

University of Chicago Press

"Hear Some Plain Things"

A Suffragette's Home

Convicts, Lunatics, and Women! Have No Vote

Handicapped! - The Artists' Suffrage League

"The Appeal of Womanhood"

CHAPTER 2

Asia, Africa, and Latin America
in the Early 1900s

At the dawn of the twentieth century, Asia, Africa, and Latin America all bore witness to the same undeniable fact: the gap between the West and the rest of the world had never been wider. Western nations maintained the largest and most lethal armies and navies; had the most advanced and efficient industries; controlled world capital markets; monopolized world shipping; and alone had the technological expertise and scientific knowledge to generate electricity, build and maintain telegraph and telephone systems, and manufacture newly invented radios, automobiles, and airplanes. The standards of living, educational levels, and life spans of Europeans and Americans were all higher than those of people who lived in Asia, Africa, and Latin America.

As a result of these disparities, Africa was one large European colony. Asia contained large areas of European colonization; one state, Japan, which had transformed itself along Western lines and had become a major regional power; and three once formidable states, Persia, Ottoman Turkey, and China, that maintained their independence but were at the point of collapse because of internal problems and Western pressures. Latin America had won its political independence from Spain and Portugal in the early 1800s, but its economy was still "semicolonial." Like the colonized peoples of Africa and Asia, Latin Americans supplied the industrialized West with agricultural products, raw materials, and minerals; bought their manufactured goods from Europe and the United States; and depended on Western firms for banking, shipping, and major construction projects.

The spectacular expansion of European and U.S. power in the nineteenth century brought forth a wide range of responses. In colonized areas, many Asians and Africans chose to cooperate with their new Western masters. African chieftains and Indian princes collected taxes and enforced laws at the village level. Common people served in colonial armies and police forces, competed for low-level administrative jobs, and shifted to growing crops such as cacao and coffee for export. Some gladly took advantage of the schools and medical clinics that came with colonialism. Many others, however, deeply resented the authoritarianism, racism, land confiscations, forced labor, and new taxes that also were part of colonialism. Rebellions were frequent, and one of them, the Indian Rebellion of 1857, shook the foundations of the colonial order in South Asia. In the end, however, they all failed.

The pattern of rebellion and harsh responses continued in the early 1900s. In India and the Philippines, however, something new occurred—the emergence of anticolonial movements that sought more than piecemeal changes and drew support from more than a single region or single social group. Their goal was independence, not gradual reform. In these movements, one can see that nationalism, a transforming force in Europe for more than a century, was beginning to take root in the colonial world.

Western economic and military power also elicited different responses in the independent nations of Latin America, Asia, and Africa. In Latin America, landowners, businesspeople, and politicians who benefited from the region's semicolonial economy welcomed Western investments and tried to keep Western governments and businesspeople happy by maintaining law and order and keeping taxes and tariffs low. Leaders of China, Persia, and Ottoman Turkey all understood the extent to which their countries had fallen behind the West and sponsored programs to make their governments more efficient, raise revenue, strengthen the military, and encourage economic development. But their reforming efforts were tentative, inconsistent, and ultimately unable to halt their countries' downward slides. Japan is the great exception. Humiliated by the nation's inability to stand up to the Western nations following its forced opening by U.S. Commodore Matthew Perry in 1853–1854, a faction of patriotic aristocrats in 1867–1868 overthrew the ruling shogun and restored the emperor in what is known as the Meiji Restoration. The new leaders then launched a series of Western-inspired reforms that introduced constitutional government, revamped the social order, established a system of state-sponsored schools and universities, and transformed Japan into an industrial and military power.

As the Japanese had done in the 1860s, non-Western peoples in other regions came to realize in the early 1900s that moderate, half-measures of reform would never bring parity with the West or solve long-standing social and political problems. In a brief five-year period, revolutions occurred in Persia in 1906, Ottoman Turkey in 1908, Mexico in 1910, and China in 1911. These events, along with many others, affirmed that in the opening years of the twentieth century the world was entering a new era.

The European Assault on Africa

Paradoxically, the century that saw the near-total submission of Africa to European rule began with an effort by Europeans to outlaw their main business in Africa, the slave trade. Responding to religious, humanitarian, and economic arguments, Denmark passed a law in 1792 that ended all involvement in the slave trade by 1802. Great Britain and the United States banned the slave trade in 1807, followed by the Netherlands, Portugal, Spain (with some exceptions), and France. Unexpectedly, this step was a prelude to more, not less, European involvement in Africa. Palm oil, ivory, cocoa, coffee, rubber, and other goods replaced slaves as items of trade, and by the 1850s this "legitimate" trade was more profitable than the old slave trade had been. Then, in the closing decades of the nineteenth century, African-European relations underwent a radical transformation, and by 1914 the entire African continent except Liberia and Ethiopia had been divided up among the European powers.

The takeover began in earnest in the 1870s, a decade that saw the intensification of Catholic and Protestant missionary activity in many parts of the continent; the discovery of gold and diamonds in South Africa; heightened commercial competition among British, French, German, and African merchants in West Africa and the Niger delta region; and growing public interest in Africa because of explorers' and missionaries' writings. Most important, in 1878 King Leopold II of Belgium dispatched the Welsh-American explorer Henry M. Stanley (1841–1904) to the Congo River basin, where he secured treaties with Africans that led to the founding of the Congo Free State, a territory of 900,000 square miles that was the monarch's personal property. In 1880, the Italian-born explorer Pierre Savorgnan de Brazza (1853–1905) signed the first of hundreds of treaties with African chieftains that provided the foundation for the French colonies in equatorial Africa. In 1881, the French established a protectorate over Tunisia and in 1882 the British occupied Egypt. The Germans annexed Togo in 1883 and Cameroon in 1884. In 1884 and 1885, eleven European nations, Ottoman Turkey, and the United States attended the Berlin West Africa Conference, which established guidelines for what came to be known as the "scramble for Africa."

Africans did not passively acquiesce to the European onslaught. Many Africans fought back, but the Europeans' artillery, high-explosive shells, and machine guns doomed their efforts. In 1898, the Battle of Omdurman in present-day Sudan resulted in some eleven thousand battlefield deaths for the Sudanese and forty for the British and their Egyptian troops.

Imperialism at Its Darkest

❖

7 ◆ A. E. Scrivener, *JOURNAL*

Among the assertions made by supporters of nineteenth-century imperialism, none had more appeal than the claim that Western expansion was a "civilizing

Source: Scrivener Diary: from Edmund Morel, King Leopold's Rule in Africa (London: Heinemann Ltd., 1904), pp. 183–186.

mission" to bring law, order, literacy, modern medicine, Christianity, and a host of other benefits to the colonized. Thousands of Europeans and Americans— missionaries for the most part, but also doctors and some administrators—believed deeply in the mission of imperialism and experienced great hardship in Africa and Asia in order to fulfill its promise. On the whole, however, the results of their efforts fell short of expectations. Instead, one is struck by the immense gap between the professed altruism of imperialism's advocates and imperialism's actual record. Nowhere was the gap greater than in the Congo of King Leopold II of Belgium.

In 1876, King Leopold presided over a meeting of several dozen noted explorers, geographers, military men, and church leaders in Brussels, where they agreed to form, ostensibly for scientific and humanitarian purposes, the International African Association. Two years later, however, Leopold's true intent was revealed when he dispatched the American explorer Henry M. Stanley and other agents to the Congo River basin, where they obtained the treaties that gave the king and his business associates effective control over the region's resources. In 1879 he founded and placed under his personal control the International Association of the Congo, an organization designed to make him rich by exploiting the region's ivory, rubber, and minerals.

Beginning in the 1890s, as world demand for rubber tires, gaskets, hoses, and insulation materials soared, the collection of raw rubber became the focus of Leopold's money-making schemes. Agents of private companies and officials of the Congo Free State forced villagers into the forest to collect sap from rubber vines and maimed, whipped, or killed them if they failed to reach their quotas. Leopold tried to keep his gruesome system of forced labor a secret, but missionaries' reports and journalists' investigations gradually revealed its full horror. In 1908, after a thorough investigation, Belgium's parliament took away the Congo Free State from its king and placed it under state control.

A. E. Scrivener, an American Baptist missionary who had labored in the Congo since the late 1880s, recorded his observations of Leopold's rubber-collecting operations after a guilt-ridden Belgian official gave him permission to observe them firsthand in a number of villages. In 1904, Edmund Morel, a bitter opponent of African imperialism, published excerpts from Scrivener's journal in his book *King Leopold's Rule in Africa*. The excerpt here begins with Scrivener's first impressions of rubber collecting in a village.

QUESTIONS FOR ANALYSIS

1. What incentives and what forms of coercion did the Belgians and their agents use to "encourage" rubber collection?
2. Aside from the collection of rubber sap, what other forms of forced labor does Scrivener describe?
3. Aside from their punishments for failing to reach their quotas, why did rubber sap collection create special hardships for the African villagers?
4. How do the Africans describe their first reactions to the Belgians?
5. What was the overall impact of the rubber-collecting operation on the region that Scrivener visited?

Everything was on a military basis, but so far as I could see, the one and only reason for it all was rubber. It was the theme of every conversation, and it was evident that the only way to please one's superiors was to increase the output somehow. I saw a few men come in, and the frightened look on their faces tells only too eloquently of the awful time they have passed through. As I saw it brought in, each man had a little basket, containing say, four or five pounds of rubber. This was emptied into a larger basket and weighed, and being found sufficient, each man was given a cupful of coarse salt, and to some of the headmen a fathom [two yards] of calico....

I heard from the white men and some of the soldiers[1] some most gruesome stories. The former white man (overseer of the station) ... would stand at the door of the store to receive the rubber from the poor trembling wretches, who after, in some cases, weeks of privation in the forests, had ventured in with what they had been able to collect. A man bringing rather under the proper amount, the white man flies into a rage, and seizing a rifle from one of the guards, shoots him dead on the spot. Very rarely did rubber come in, but one or more were shot in that way at the door of the store "to make the survivors bring more next time." Men who had tried to run from the country and had been caught, were brought to the station and made to stand one behind the other, and a bullet sent through them....

On—[2]removing from the station, his successor almost fainted [leaving] on attempting to enter the station prison, in which were numbers of poor wretches so reduced by starvation and the awful stench from weeks of accumulation of filth, that they were not able to stand. Some of the stories are unprintable.... Under the present régime a list is kept of all the people. Every town is known and visited at stated intervals. Those stationed near the posts are required to do the various tasks, such as the bringing in of timber and other material. A little payment is made, but that it is in any respect an equivalent it would be absurd to suppose. The people are regarded as the property of the State for any purpose for which they may be needed. That they have any desires of their own, or any plans worth carrying out in connection with their own lives, would create a smile among the officials. It is one continual grind, and the native intercourse [communication] between one district and another in the old style is practically non-existent. Only the roads to and from the various posts are kept open, and large tracts of country are abandoned to the wild beasts. The white man himself told me that you could walk on for five days in one direction and not see a single village or a single human being. And this where formerly there was a big tribe!

[Scrivener continues his journey and joins a group of refugees who have fled from their village; his party has just arrived in the town of Ngongo.]

As one by one the surviving relatives of my men arrived, some affecting scenes were enacted. There was no falling on necks and weeping, but very genuine joy was shown and tears were shed as the losses death had made were told.... So far as the State post was concerned, it was in a very dilapidated condition.... On three sides of the usual huge quadrangle there were abundant signs of a former population, but we only found three villages—bigger indeed than any we had seen before, but sadly diminished from what had been but recently the condition of the place.... Soon we began talking, and, without any encouragement on my part, they began the tales I had become so accustomed to. They were living in peace and quietness when the white men came in ... with all sorts of requests to do this and to

---

[1]The soldiers referred to were mercenaries recruited from other parts of Africa.

[2]This is a reference to the "former white man" referred to in the previous paragraph.

do that, and they thought it meant slavery. So they attempted to keep the white men out of their country, but without avail. The rifles were too much for them. So they submitted, and made up their minds to do the best they could under the altered circumstances. First came the command to build houses for the soldiers, and this was done without a murmur. Then they had to feed the soldiers, and all the men and women—hangers-on who accompanied them. Then they were told to bring in rubber. This was quite a new thing for them to do. There was rubber in the forest several days away from their home, but that it was worth anything was news to them. A small reward was offered, and a rush was made for the rubber; "What strange white men to give us cloth and beads for the sap of a wild vine." They rejoiced in what they thought was their good fortune. But soon the reward was reduced until they were told to bring in the rubber for nothing. To this they tried to demur [object to], but to their great surprise several were shot by the soldiers, and the rest were told, with many curses and blows, to go at once or more would be killed. Terrified, they began to prepare their food for the fortnight's absence from the village, which the collection of the rubber entailed. The soldiers discovered them sitting about. "What, not gone yet!" Bang! bang! bang! And down fell one and another dead, in the midst of wives and companions. There is a terrible wail, and an attempt made to prepare the dead for burial, but this is not allowed. All must go at once to the forest. And off the poor wretches had to go without even their tinder-boxes to make fires. Many died in the forests from exposure and hunger, and still more from the rifles of the ferocious soldiers in charge of the post. In spite of all their efforts, the amount fell off,[3] and more and more were killed. . . .

I was shown round the place, and the sites of former big chiefs' settlements were pointed out. A careful estimate made the population of, say, seven years ago, to be 2000 people in and about the post, within the radius of, say, a quarter of a mile. All told they would not muster 200 now, and there is so much sadness and gloom that they are fast decreasing. . . . Lying about in the grass, within a few yards of the house I was occupying, were numbers of human bones, in some cases complete skeletons. I counted thirty-six skulls, and saw many sets of bones from which the skulls were missing. I called one of the men, and asked the meaning of it. "When the rubber palaver[4] began," said he, "the soldiers shot so many we grew tired of burying, and very often we were not allowed to bury, and so we just dragged the bodies out into the grass and left them. There are hundreds all round if you would like to see them." But I had seen more than enough, and was sickened by the stories that came from men and women alike of the awful time they had passed through. . . . In due course we reached Ibali. There was hardly a sound building in the place. . . . Why such dilapidation? The Commandant away for a trip likely to extend into three months, the sub-lieutenant away in another direction on a punitive expedition. In other words, the station must be neglected and rubber-hunting carried out with all vigor. I stayed here two days, and the one thing that impressed itself upon me was the collection of rubber. I saw long files of men come as at Mbongo with their little baskets under their arms, saw them paid their milk-tin-full of salt, and the two yards of calico flung to the head men; saw their trembling timidity, and in fact a great deal more, to prove the state of terrorism that exists, and the virtual slavery in which the people are held.

---

[3]Tapping and cutting the vines often killed them, which meant that villagers had to go deeper and deeper into the forest to find fresh vines.

[4]Literally, "discussion."

A Sampling of African Treaties and Agreements

❖

8 ❖ *Treaty Between the International Association of the Congo and Tonki, Chief of Ngombi and Mampuya, Senior Chief of Mafela; Royal Niger Company Standard Treaty Number 5; Agreement Between King Lobengula and Charles Rudd, Rochfort Maguire, and Francis Thompson; Letter of King Lobengula to Queen Victoria*

During the 1800s African kings and chiefs signed well over a thousand treaties and agreements with representatives of European states or trading companies, the cumulative effect of which was the near total subjection of Africa to colonial rule. In the early 1800s, such treaties mainly involved British efforts to suppress the slave trade. In midcentury their purpose was to guarantee Europeans access to products such as palm oil, peanuts, indigo and ivory. By the late 1800s, with the scramble for Africa in full swing, such treaties resulted in the transfer to European states of territory, sweeping political powers, and exclusive access to minerals and other raw materials.

Most of these agreements were hardly treaties in the dictionary sense of an "arrangement or agreement made by negotiation." Vague and frequently misleading discussions of a proposed treaty's content, often accompanied by threats of force, were followed by the drawing up of a legalistic document in a European language that no African signee understood. Not surprisingly, months or years after an African leader affixed his "X" to a treaty, he and his people learned that the document he had signed had provisions he had never discussed and implications he had never imagined. In the selections that follow, we present excerpts from three such treaties along with a letter written in response to one of them by an African king to Queen Victoria of Great Britain.

The first treaty is one of the several hundred treaties signed in the early 1880s by which chiefs in the Congo River basin transferred various rights and powers to the International Association of the Congo, a consortium founded in 1878 by King Leopold II of Belgium and his associates. Supposedly a subgroup of the International African Association, a philanthropic organization founded by Leopold in 1876, the International Association of the Congo was meant to enrich the king by giving him personal control over a vast African colony. Leopold did his best to disguise the organization's true purpose by identifying it with the cause of bringing peace and civilization to Africa. The task of turning this huge region into a viable colony was given to the Welsh-American journalist/explorer Henry M. Stanley, whose agents used force and trickery to coerce chiefs into signing.

The second treaty is an example of the "standard treaties" used by the agents of two British trading companies, the Royal Niger Company (f. 1886) and its predecessor, the National African Company (f. 1882), to establish their commercial privileges and political authority in the region of the lower and middle Niger River. Depending on circumstances, they could choose from a number of brief "standard treaties" in which they needed only to fill in the blanks. Between 1884 and 1892, no fewer than

373 such treaties were signed, with more than half of them utilizing Standard Treaty Number Five, which is printed below. Cumulatively, these treaties were the basis for British colony of Nigeria, which came into existence in 1900 after the Royal Niger Company sold its rights in the region to the government for £865,000.

The third treaty, signed in 1888, involved King Lobengula of Matabeleland, a region in present-day Zimbabwe, and business associates of Cecil Rhodes, the relentless British imperialist who, having already enriched himself through his ownership of the diamond mines around Kimberly, South Africa, was now was intent on extending his business interests and British authority farther north. Lobengula ruled over a kingdom founded by the Ndebele people earlier in the century after they had migrated north to escape political turmoil in southern Africa. After rejecting requests of various Europeans to grant them concessions to mine gold in his territory, in 1888 he accepted the terms offered by Rhodes' group.

Lobengula realized he had been duped after learning he had given the British businessmen the rights to all the minerals in his kingdom, not, as he had thought, the right to dig "one big hole" in his territory with just ten men. In response, he ordered the execution of several of his councilors and sent a note of protest to Queen Victoria. Some months later, he received a response from one of the queen's advisors, who informed him that after looking into the matter, the queen had concluded that the men who had signed the treaty "may be trusted to carry out the working for gold in the chief's country without molesting his people." The king formally repudiated the treaty, but the British never recognized his repudiation.

QUESTIONS FOR ANALYSIS

1. What specific powers will the rulers surrender by signing the treaties? What powers, if any, will they maintain?
2. What benefits do the rulers themselves receive as a result of signing the agreements?
3. What benefits will accrue to the European signatories of the treaties?
4. What benefits do the treaties promise for the subjects of the signatories of the treaties?
5. How, according to Lobengula, has he been misled in the agreement he signed?

Treaty Between the International Association of the Congo[1] and Tonki, Chief of Ngombi and Mampuya, Senior Chief of Mafela

I.   The chiefs . . . recognize that it is highly desirable that the International African Association should, for the advancement of civilization and trade, be firmly established in their country. They therefore . . . for themselves and their heirs and successors forever, do give up to the Association all sovereign and governing rights to all their territories. They also promise to assist the said Association in its work of governing and civilizing this country, and to use their influence with all the other inhabitants, with whose unanimous approval they make this treaty, to secure obedience to all the laws made by the Association, and

---

[1]Although this and other similar treaties listed the European contracting party as the International African Association, the philanthropic society of explorers and geographers founded by Leopold in 1876, the actual beneficiary was the International Association of the Congo, the political and business arm of Leopold's enterprise in the Congo. This is one example of how Leopold attempted to fool the world about his aims in Africa.

to assist by labor or otherwise, any works, improvements, or expeditions which the said Association shall cause at any time to be carried out . . .

II. The chiefs . . . promise to join their forces with those of the said Association, and to resist the forcible intrusion or repulse the attacks of foreigners of any nationality or color.

III. The country thus ceded has about the following boundaries, viz., the whole of the Ngombi and Mafela countries . . . All roads and waterways running through this country, the right of collecting tolls on the same, and all game, fishing, mining and forest rights, are to be the absolute property of the Association, together with any unoccupied lands as may at any time hereafter be chosen.

IV. The Association agrees to pay to the chiefs . . . the following articles, viz., one piece of cloth per month to each . . . , besides present cloth in hand; and the said chiefs accept this bounty and monthly subsidy as full settlement of all their claims . . .

V. The Association promises:

1. To take from the natives . . . no occupied or cultivated lands, except by mutual agreement.

2. To promote to its utmost the prosperity of the said country.

3. To protect the inhabitants from all oppression or foreign intrusion.

4. It authorizes the chiefs to hoist its [the Association's] flag; to settle all local disputes or palavers [discussions] and to maintain its authority with the natives.

Agreed to and signed this first day of April, 1884.

Henry M. Stanley
Tonki, his X mark
Mampuya, his X mark

Source: Henry M. Stanley, *The Congo and the Founding of its Free State*, vol. 2 (New York: Harper and Brothers, 1885), 195–197.

Royal Niger Company, Standard Treaty Number Five

We, the undersigned Chiefs of _____, with the view to the bettering of the condition of our country and people, do this day cede to the Royal Niger Company, for ever, the whole of our territory extending from _____.

We also give the Royal Niger Company full power to settle all native disputes arising from any cause whatsoever, and we pledge ourselves not to enter into any war with other tribes without the sanction of the Royal Niger Company.

We understand that the said Royal Niger Company have full power to mine, farm, and build in any portion of the country.

We bind ourselves not the have any intercourse with any strangers or foreigners except through the said Royal Niger Company.

In consideration of the foregoing, the said Royal Niger Company bind themselves not to interfere with any of the native laws or customs of the country, consistently with the maintenance of good order and good government.

The Royal Niger Company agree to pay native owners of land a reasonable amount for any portion they may require.

The said Royal Niger Company bind themselves to protect the said Chiefs from the attacks of neighbouring aggressive tribes.

The said Royal Niger Company also agree to pay the Chiefs _____ measures of native value.

We, the undersigned witnesses, do hereby solemnly declare that the _____ Chiefs whose names are placed opposite their respective crosses have in our presence affixed their crosses of their own free will and consent, and that the said _____ has in our presence affixed his signature.

Done in triplicate at _____, this _____ day of _____, 188_____.

Declaration of the Interpreter: I, _____, of _____, do hereby solemnly declare that I am well acquainted with the language of the country, and that on the _____ day of _____, I truly and faithfully explained the above Agreement to all the Chiefs present, and that they understood its meaning.

———

Source: Edward Hertslet, *The Map of Africa by Treaty*, vol. 1 (London: Her Majesty's Stationery Office, 1894), pp. 467–468.

Agreement Between King Lobengula and Charles Rudd, Rochfort Maguire, and Francis Thompson, 1891

Whereas Charles Dunell Rudd of Kimberley; Rochfort Maguire of London; and Francis Robert Thompson of Kimberley, hereinafter known as the grantees . . . covenant and agree to pay to me, my heirs, and successors the sum of one hundred pounds sterling British Currency on the first day of every lunar month and further to deliver at my Royal Kraal [homestead] one thousand Martini-Henry breech-loading rifles[2] together with one hundred thousand rounds of suitable ball cartridge, five hundred of the said rifles and fifty thousand of the said cartridges to be ordered from England forthwith and delivered with reasonable despatch, and the remainder . . . to be delivered as soon as the grantees shall have commenced to work mining machinery within my territory; and further to deliver on the Zambesi [Zambezi] River a steamboat with guns . . . , or in lieu of the said steamboat, the sum of five hundred pounds sterling. On the execution of these presents, I Lobengula, King of Matabeleland, Mashonaland and certain adjoining territories . . . do hereby grant and assign unto the grantees . . . the compete and exclusive charge over all metals and minerals contained in my Kingdoms, Principalities and Dominions, together with full power to do all things that they may deem necessary to win and procure the same and to hold, collect and enjoy the profits and revenue, if any, derivable from the said metals and minerals . . . , and whereas I have been much molested of late by diverse persons seeking

and desiring to obtain grants and concessions of land and mining rights in my territories, I do hereby authorize the said grantees to take all necessary and lawful steps to exclude from my Kingdoms, Principalities, and Dominions all persons seeking land, metals, minerals, or mining rights therein and I do hereby undertake to render them such needful assistance as they may from time to time require for the exclusion of such persons, and to grant no concessions of land or mining rights from and after this date without their consent and concurrence . . .

This given under my hand this thirtieth day of October in the year of our Lord 1888, at my royal kraal.

Lobengula

X

his mark

———

Source: Lewis Mitchell, *The Life of the Right Hon. Cecil John Rhodes, 1853–1902*, vol. 2 (London: Edward Arnold, 1910), pp. 244–245.

Letter of King Lobengula to Queen Victoria

Some time ago a party of men came to my country, the principal one appearing to be a man called Rudd. They asked me for a place to dig for gold, and said they would give me certain things for the right to do so. I told them to bring what they could give and I would show them what I would give. A document was written and presented to me for signature. I asked what it contained, and was told that in it were my words and the words of those men. I put my hand to it. About three months afterward I heard from other sources that I had given by the document the right to all the minerals of my country. I called a meeting of my Indunas [councilors], and also of the white men and demanded a copy of the document. It was proved to me that I had signed away the mineral rights of my whole country to Rudd and his friends. I have since had a meeting of my Indunas and they will not recognize the paper, as it contains neither my words nor the words of those who got it . . . I write you that you may know the truth about this thing.

———

[2]The Martini-Henry rifle, first produced in 1871, had been standard issue for British troops, but in 1888, the year in which this agreement was signed, it was replaced with the Lee-Metford magazine rifle. Production of the Martini-Henry rifle ended in 1889. After he repudiated the agreement with Rudd, Lobengula refused to accept the first shipment of rifles the English had agreed to give him.

Source: Quoted in Edmund Morel, *Black Man's Burden* (London: Arnold, 1920), 34–35.

Imperialism and Reform
in the Middle East

At the beginning of the twentieth century, the Middle East was approaching the end of a long period in its history marked on the one hand by political decline and economic stagnation, and on the other by persistent but largely futile efforts to reform and adapt its institutions to withstand foreign pressures. The two dominant states in the region were Ottoman Turkey, which once ruled an empire that included Southwest Asia, northern Africa, and southeastern Europe, and Persia, which had been a major power in the sixteenth and seventeenth centuries. Persia, however, never recovered from the fall of the Safavid dynasty in 1736. After decades of civil war, the Qajar dynasty took power in 1794, presiding over a weak central government unable to halt a downward spiral of territorial loss, indebtedness, military weakness, and ever greater Western dominance of its economic and political life.

Signs of weakness in the Ottoman Empire appeared in the seventeenth and eighteenth centuries, when the sultans lost control of their North African provinces and their army fell behind those of the European powers. During the nineteenth century, the pattern of military defeat and territorial loss continued, so that by 1913 the empire had been reduced to Turkey itself, a small bit of European territory, and the Arab provinces of Syria and Palestine. Meanwhile, three former Ottoman provinces in North Africa—Algeria (to the French), Egypt (to the English), and Libya (to the Italians)—all became part of European colonial empires.

During the nineteenth century, the region's intellectuals, military men, and religious leaders debated the causes and significance of these developments, and government officials implemented policies to halt the decline. At first this meant modernizing the military, ending corruption, improving tax collection, and guaranteeing the rights of religious and ethnic minorities while preserving the authority of traditional rulers and the centrality of Islam. From the 1870s onward, reformers pursued a more ambitious agenda that included parliamentary government, greater individual freedom, secularism, and fundamental changes in education.

Reformers faced formidable obstacles: resistance from religious conservatives; the indifference of the largely illiterate masses; opposition from well-placed families and officeholders who benefited from the status quo; and erratic support from autocratic rulers. Foreign interference added to their challenges. When Muhammad Ali, the ruler of Egypt from 1805 to 1849, sponsored an ambitious program of military, economic, and educational reform, his efforts were undermined by the French and English, who feared that a powerful Egyptian state would weaken the Ottoman Empire and invite greater Russian involvement in the region. The reformers' greatest problem was lack of money. The costs of modern armies, larger bureaucracies, schools, roads, and telegraph lines outstripped revenues, forcing governments to rely on European loans and investments and even to accept European control of taxes, expenditures, and trade policies. Thus many "reforms" led to greater dependency on the West, one of the things reformers most wanted to avoid.

While government officials wrestled with budgets and military planning, the region was undergoing broad cultural and intellectual changes. Its population grew, especially in cities such as Istanbul, Cairo, Baghdad, and Aleppo; foreign trade increased; a banking system emerged; new schools were founded and literacy rose, along with a burgeoning publishing industry; and a few new industrial enterprises were built or projected. Contacts with the West increased. Junior army officers were sent to Europe for training; Western languages, history, and science were taught in new missionary schools; and major cities had large European expatriate communities.

As a result, the Middle East was full of tensions in the years around 1900. As Turkey entered its third decade of rule under autocratic Sultan Abdulhamid II and Persia endured the reign of the uneducated, sickly, and apathetic Shah Muzaffar al-Din, discontent deepened and boiled over to cause constitutional revolutions in Persia in 1906 and Turkey in 1908. Neither revolution was able to stave off further political disasters, however. In 1907, the division of Persia between a Russian-controlled north and a British-controlled south (leaving only the central region under Persian government control) weakened the revolutionary movement and enabled the shah to end the parliamentary experiment in 1911. The Ottomans lost all but a tiny remnant of their European holdings as a result of the Balkan Wars of 1912–1913 and lost their Arab provinces as a result of World War I. The Ottoman state disappeared altogether when Turkish nationalists overthrew the sultan's government in 1920.

Economic Imperialism in Persia

❖

9 ◆ *The D'Arcy Oil Concession*

European imperialism did not always involve gunboats, armies, and political control by colonial administrators. In many instances it was more economic than political. In Persia, economic imperialism was epitomized by the numerous concessions granted to foreign businessmen in the late nineteenth and early twentieth centuries. These agreements gave foreigners control over a sector of the nation's economy in return for a one-time payment and a percentage of annual profits. Viewed as a painless way to raise capital, solve budget problems, and generate bribes, such arrangements were irresistible to Persian shahs and their ministers. The most sweeping concession was the De Reuter concession, which in 1872 granted a British businessman control of Persia's factories, minerals, irrigation works, agricultural improvements, and almost any other economic activity that had to do with the country's economic modernization. The Russians and many Persians were outraged by the arrangement, and their complaints forced the shah to withdraw the concessions. Even more controversial was the

Source: D'Arcy Oil Concession: *League of Nations, Official Journal*, Vol. 13 (December 1932), pp. 2305–2308.

concession granted in 1891 to the British Imperial Tobacco Company for the purchase, processing, and sale of all tobacco products. In this case, the concession was withdrawn after public demonstrations and a nationwide boycott of all tobacco products.

The concession that most affected the country's future was the sixty-year oil concession granted in 1901 to William Knox D'Arcy, a British subject who had become a multimillionaire in Australian gold mining. Although French archeologists had reported the existence of oil in eastern Persia in 1892, D'Arcy's engineers did not discover oil in commercial quantities until 1908. In 1909, D'Arcy organized the Anglo-Persian Oil Company, the ancestor of present-day petroleum giant BP (formerly British Petroleum). Its success was ensured when, in 1914, the British government bought an interest in the company and the company agreed to supply the Royal Navy with oil at a discounted price. This arrangement continued until the Iranian oil industry was nationalized in 1951.

QUESTIONS FOR ANALYSIS

1. What risks were involved for D'Arcy (the concessionaire) in agreeing to these arrangements?
2. What short- and long-term benefits did the shah's government hope to accrue from this agreement?
3. What, if any, provisions were made to protect Persians whose property or economic activities were affected by the undertakings of the concessionaire's company?
4. How, if at all, might the Persian people have benefited from the arrangements agreed to in the concession?
5. What control over D'Arcy's oil operations did the Persian government retain according to the provisions of the agreement?

Between the Government of His Imperial Majesty the Shah of Persia, of the one part, and William Knox d'Arcy, of independent means, residing in London at No. 42. Grosvenor Square (hereinafter called "the Concessionnaire"), of the other part;

The following has by these presents been agreed on and arranged—viz.:

ART. 1. The Government of His Imperial Majesty the Shah grants to the concessionnaire by these presents a special and exclusive privilege to search for, obtain, exploit, develop, render suitable for trade, carry away and sell natural gas petroleum, asphalt and ozokerite[1]

throughout the whole extent of the Persian Empire for a term of sixty years as from the date of these presents.

ART. 2. This privilege shall comprise the exclusive right of laying the pipe-lines necessary from the deposits where there may be found one or several of the said products up to the Persian Gulf, as also the necessary distributing branches. It shall also comprise the right of constructing and maintaining all and any wells, reservoirs, stations and pump services, factories and other works and arrangements that may be deemed necessary.

[1]A hydrocarbon used in making candles and electrical insulation.

ART. 3. The Imperial Persian Government grants gratuitously to the concessionnaire all uncultivated lands belonging to the State which the concessionnaire's engineers may deem necessary for the construction of the whole or any part of the above-mentioned works. As for the cultivated lands belonging to the State, the concessionnaire must purchase them at the fair and current price of the province.

The Government also grants to the concessionnaire the right of acquiring all and any other lands or buildings necessary for the said purpose, with the consent of the proprietors, on such conditions as may be arranged between him and them without their being allowed to make demands of a nature to surcharge the price ordinarily current for lands situate in their respective localities.

Holy places with all their dependencies within a radius of 200 Persian archines[2] are formally excluded....

ART. 5. The course of the pipe-lines shall be fixed by the concessionnaire and his engineers.

ART. 6. Notwithstanding what is above set forth, the privilege granted by these presents shall not extend to the provinces of Azerbadjan, Ghilan, Mazendaran, Asdrabad and Khorassan,[3] but on the express condition that the Persian Imperial Government shall not grant to any other person the right of constructing a pipe-line to the southern rivers or to the South Coast of Persia.

ART. 7. All lands granted by these presents to the concessionnaire or that may be acquired by him in the manner provided for in Articles 3 and 4 of these presents, as also all products exported shall be free of all imposts and taxes during the term of the present concession. All material and apparatuses necessary for the exploration, working and development of the deposits, and for the construction and development of the pipe-lines, shall enter Persia free of all taxes and Custom House duties.

ART. 8. The concessionnaire shall immediately send out to Persia and at his own cost one or several experts with a view to their exploring the region in which there exist, as he believes, the said products, and, in the event of the report of the expert being in the opinion of the concessionnaire of a satisfactory nature, the latter shall immediately send to Persia and at his own cost all the technical staff necessary, with the working plant and machinery required for boring and sinking wells and ascertaining the value of the property.

ART. 9. The Imperial Persian Government authorises the concessionnaire to found one or several companies for the working of the concession.

ART. 10. It shall be stipulated in the contract between the concessionnaire, of the one part, and the company, of the other part, that the latter is, within the term of one month as from the date of the formation of the first exploitation company, to pay the Imperial Persian Government the sum of £20,000 sterling in cash, and an additional sum of £20,000 sterling in paid-up shares of the first company founded by virtue of the foregoing article. It shall also pay the said Government annually a sum equal to 16 percent of the annual net profits of any company or companies that may be formed in accordance with the said article.

ART. 11. The said Government shall be free to appoint an Imperial Commissioner, who shall be consulted by the concessionnaire and the directors of the companies to be formed. He shall supply all and any useful information at his disposal, and he shall inform them of the best course to be adopted in the interest of the undertaking. He shall establish, by agreement with the concessionnaire, such supervision as he may deem expedient to safeguard the interests of the Imperial Government.

ART. 12. The workmen employed in the service of the company shall be subject to His Imperial

---

[2]An archine equals twenty-eight inches. Two hundred archines would be one hundred fifty yards.

[3]Provinces in the north and west in the Russian sphere of influence.

Majesty the Shah, except the technical staff, such as the managers, engineers, borers and foremen.

ART. 13. At any place in which it may be proved that the inhabitants of the country now obtain petroleum for their own use, the company must supply them gratuitously with the quantity of petroleum that they themselves got previously.

ART. 14. The Imperial Government binds itself to take all and any necessary measures to secure the safety and the carrying out of the object of this concession of the plant, and of the apparatuses, of which mention is made, for the purposes of the undertaking of the company, and to protect the representatives, agents, and servants of the company....

ART. 15. On the expiration of the term of the present concession, all materials, buildings and apparatuses then used by the company for the exploitation of its industry shall become the property of the said Government, and the company shall have no right to any indemnity in this connection.

ART. 16. If within the terms of two years as from the present date the concessionnaire shall not have established the first of the said companies authorized by Article 9 of the present agreement, the present concession shall become null and void.

ART. 17. In the event of there arising between the parties to the present concession any dispute or difference in respect of its interpretation or the rights or responsibilities of one or the other of the parties therefrom resulting, such dispute or difference shall be submitted to two arbitrators at Teheran, one of whom shall be named by each of the parties, and to an umpire who shall be appointed by the arbitrators before they proceed to arbitrate. The decision of the arbitrators or, in the event of the latter disagreeing, that of the umpire shall be final.

ART. 18. This Act of Concession, made in duplicate, is written in the French language and translated into Persian with the same meaning.

But, in the event of there being any dispute in relation to such meaning, the French text shall alone prevail.

Feminism in the Middle East

❖

10 ◆ Bahithat al-Badiya, *LECTURE IN THE CLUB OF THE UMMA PARTY, 1909*

Much in the Quran, Islam's holy book, taught that men and women were spiritual equals, but by the tenth century negative views of women had come to dominate Islamic law and theology. Although single adult women had the right to approve or reject an arranged marriage, and married women could exercise some control over their property and had certain rights in divorce cases, women were seen as intellectually and morally inferior to men and lost their roles in religious and public life. Women's lives were closely regulated to protect their chastity and prevent them from tempting men to sin. They were expected to adhere to a strict code of behavior that emphasized obedience to men, modesty, and avoidance of contacts with men

Source: Bahithat al-Badiya, "A Lecture in the Club of the Umma Party, 1909," as appeared in *Margot Badran and Miriam Cooke, Opening the Gates*, by Margot Badran and Miriam Cooke. Copyright © 1990 Indiana University Press. Reprinted with permission of Indiana University Press.

who were not related to them. Upper-class women were virtually secluded in their homes, and on the rare occasions they appeared in public they were required to wear clothing that covered their faces and bodies. Although such restrictions were less stringent among Turks than Arabs, as was true in most premodern societies, gender inequality was taken for granted throughout the region.

Such views were challenged in the nineteenth century, in part as a result of increased contact with the West. Rifa'a al-Tahtawi (1801–1873), for example, became an advocate for educating girls after his return from France, where he had been a mentor and adviser to Egyptian university students in Paris. His efforts resulted in the founding of a state-supported school for female medical practitioners in 1832. Similar steps were taken in Turkey, where a school for midwives was founded in 1842, followed by a secondary school for girls in 1858 and a teacher training school in 1870. Missionary schools and private tutors hired by upper-class families also contributed to the rise of female literacy. By the late 1800s, novelists who explored the issue of female inequality had a significant following, and periodicals that catered to women began to appear.

In the early 1900s, the debate over women's place in Islamic societies intensified after the prominent jurist and educator Qasim Amin published *The Liberation of Women* (1900) and *The New Woman* (1901), two brief treatises that argued that the mistreatment of women was an embarrassment to Islamic societies and an impediment to progress. Among the women who played a role in the debate, Malak Hifni Nasif, better known by her pen name, Bahithat al-Badiya (Arabic for "Seeker in the Desert"), stands out. Born into a prosperous Cairo family, she was educated at home and then at the Saniyya School in Cairo, a school for girls. On graduating, al-Badiya became a teacher at the school and a contributor of essays and poems to Cairo literary journals. Her writings and speeches, which were published in 1910 under the title *Al-Nisaiyat* (Feminist Pieces), address issues pertaining to Egyptian women, including education, paid work, and especially proper public attire. Al-Badiya delivered the following remarks in 1909 as part of a weekly lecture series that catered to well-to-do Cairo women. The lecture series was held in the hall of the Umma Party, a moderate Egyptian nationalist party founded in 1906.

Al-Badiya's life abruptly changed in 1911 when at the age of twenty-four she moved to an oasis west of Cairo following an arranged marriage to a Bedouin chief. To her chagrin, she discovered that the chief already had a wife and a daughter, whom she was expected to tutor. Despite disappointment and anger, she remained with her husband until she died of influenza in 1918.

QUESTIONS FOR ANALYSIS

1. What does the source tell us about the arguments being made by opponents of women entering the paid work force? How does the author counter these arguments?

2. What does the source reveal about relations between males and females in Egypt in the early 1900s?

3. What are the shortcomings of upper-class Egyptian women, according to al-Badiya?

4. How does she view European women? Why does she consider them poor role models for Egyptian women?

5. How much of what al-Badiya says relates to the experiences of lower- and middle-class Egyptian women?

6. If the provisions of the author's program had been carried out, how would Egyptian women's lives have changed?

Our meeting today is not simply for getting acquainted or for displaying our finery but it is a serious meeting.... At the moment there is a semi-feud between us and men because of the low level of agreement between us. Men blame the discord on our poor upbringing and haphazard education while we claim it is due to men's arrogance and pride. This mutual blame which has deepened the antagonism between the sexes is something to be regretted and feared....

Men say when we become educated we shall push them out of work and abandon the role for which God has created us. But, isn't it rather men who have pushed women out of work? Before, women used to spin and to weave cloth for clothes for themselves and their children, but men invented machines for spinning and weaving and put women out of work. In the past, women sewed clothes for themselves and their households but men invented the sewing machine. Then men took up the profession of tailoring and began to make clothes for our men and children. Before women winnowed the wheat and ground flour on grinding stones for the bread they used to make with their own hands, sifting flour and kneading dough. Then men established bakeries employing men. They gave us rest but at the same time pushed us out of work....

Since male inventors and workers have taken away a lot of our work should we waste our time in idleness or seek other work to occupy us? Of course, we should do the latter. Work at home now does not occupy more than half the day. We must pursue an education in order to occupy the other half of the day but that is what

men wish to prevent us from doing under the pretext of taking their jobs away. Obviously, I am not urging women to neglect their home and children to go out and become lawyers or judges or railway engineers. But if any of us wish to work in such professions our personal freedom should not be infringed.... Is it just to prevent women from doing what they believe is good for themselves and their support? If pregnancy impedes work outside the house it also impedes work inside the house. Furthermore, how many able-bodied men have not become sick from time to time and have had to stop work?

Men say to us categorically, "You women have been created for the house and we have been created to be breadwinners." Is this a God-given dictate? How are we to know this since no holy book has spelled it out? ... Women in villages in both Upper and Lower Egypt help their men till the land and plant crops. Some women do the fertilising, haul crops, lead animals, draw water for irrigation, and other chores. You may have observed that women in the villages work as hard as the strongest men and we see that their children are strong and healthy.

Specialised work for each sex is a matter of convention. It is not mandatory. We women are now unable to do hard work because we have not been accustomed to it. After long centuries of enslavement by men, our minds rusted and our bodies weakened. Is it right that they accuse us of being created weaker than them in mind and body?...

Men criticise the way we dress in the street. They have a point because we have exceeded the bounds of custom and propriety. We claim we are veiling but we are neither properly covered nor unveiled. I do not advocate a return to the veils of our grandmothers because it can rightly be called being buried alive, not *hijab*,[1] correct covering. The woman used to spend her whole life within the walls of her house not going out into the street except when she was carried to her grave. I do not, on the other hand, advocate unveiling, like Europeans, and mixing with men, because they are harmful to us.

If we had been raised from childhood to go unveiled and if our men were ready for it I would approve of unveiling for those who want it. But the nation is not ready for it now. Some of our prudent women do not fear to mix with men, but we have to place limits on those who are less prudent because we are quick to imitate and seldom find our authenticity in the veil.

I think the most appropriate way to dress outside is to cover the head and wear a coat with long sleeves which touches the ground the way the European women do. I am told this is the way women in Istanbul dress when they go out shopping.

The imprisonment in the home of the Egyptian woman of the past is detrimental while the current freedom of the Europeans is excessive. I cannot find a better model [than] today's Turkish woman. She falls between the two extremes and does not violate what Islam prescribes. She is a good example of decorum and modesty.

I have heard that some of our high officials are teaching their girls European dancing and acting. I consider both despicable—a detestable crossing of boundaries and a blind imitation of Europeans. Customs should not be abandoned except when they are harmful. European customs should not be taken up by Egyptians except when they are appropriate and practical. What good is there for us in women and men holding each other's waists dancing or daughters appearing on stage before audiences acting with bare bosoms in love scenes? This is contrary to Islam and a moral threat we must fight as much as we can. We must show our disdain for the few Muslim women who do these things, who otherwise would be encouraged by our silence to contaminate others. . . .

If we pursue everything western we shall destroy our own civilisation and a nation that has lost its civilisation grows weak and vanishes. . . .

Our beliefs and actions have been a great cause of the lesser respect that men accord us. How can a sensible man respect a woman who believes in magic, superstition, and the blessing of the dead and who allows women peddlars and washerwomen, or even devils, to have authority over her? Can he respect a woman who speaks only about the clothes of her neighbour and the jewellery of her friend and the furniture of a bride? . . . Good upbringing and sound education would elevate us in the eyes of men. We should get a sound education, not merely acquire the trappings of a foreign language and rudiments of music. Our education should also include home management, healthcare, and childcare. If we eliminate immodest behaviour on the street and prove to our husbands through good behaviour and fulfillment of duties that we are human beings with feelings, no less human [than] they are, and we do not allow them under any condition to hurt our feelings or fail to respect us, if we do all this, how can a just man despise us? As for the unjust man, it would have been better for us not to accept marriage to him.

Now I shall turn to the path we should follow. If I had the right to legislate I would decree:

1. Teaching girls the Quran and the correct Sunna.[2]
2. Primary and secondary school education for girls, and compulsory preparatory school education for all.

---

[1] *Hijab* in Arabic literally means "veil" or "partition"; it also means adherence to certain standards of modest dress for women.

[2] *Sunna* refers to the customs and traditions of the Islamic community.

3. Instruction for girls on the theory and practice of home economics, health, first aid, and childcare.
4. Setting a quota for females in medicine and education so they can serve the women of Egypt.
5. Allowing women to study any other advanced subjects they wish without restriction.
6. Upbringing for girls from infancy stressing patience, honesty, work and other virtues.

7. Adhering to the *Sharia*[3] concerning betrothal and marriage, and not permitting any woman and man to marry without first meeting each other in the presence of the father or male relative of the bride.
8. Adopting the veil and outdoor dress of the Turkish women of Istanbul.
9. Maintaining the best interests of the country and dispensing with foreign goods and people as much as possible.
10. Make it encumbent upon our brothers, the men of Egypt, to implement this programme.

---

[3]Literally, the "right path," or Islamic law.

South and Southeast Asia under Colonial Rule

Between 1906 and 1908, the Dutch added territories to their empire in the East Indian archipelago after fighting and defeating tribal peoples on Borneo, Celebes, and Bali. These were the very last acquisitions in a long series of Western conquests and territorial claims in South and Southeast Asia that date back to the sixteenth century, when Portugal established a string of fortified trading posts from India's west coast to the East Indies and Spain took control of the Philippines. After 1908, Western conquests in this vast region came to an end, but not before virtually all of its three hundred million inhabitants were under colonial rule.

The early 1900s brought other changes to the region. In 1901, the Dutch government rejected the long-standing imperialist assumption that colonies existed mainly to maximize profits for European businesses and generate income for European governments. Admitting that centuries of Dutch rule in the East Indies had brought misery to the region, the Dutch adopted a new Ethical Policy, in which the well-being of their colonial subjects was the primary focus. The policy laid out steps to protect the natives from abuse by officials, plantation owners, and lenders, and it allocated funds for a public health service, the opening of new farm lands, large-scale irrigation projects to increase rice production, an agricultural extension service, loans for native farmers, and most importantly, an expanded system of schools and colleges that were open to native peoples.

Important developments also took place in the Philippines and India. In the Philippines, nationalist revolutionaries rebelled against Spanish rule in 1896 and briefly declared an independent republic in 1898 after the U.S. Navy destroyed the Spanish fleet in Manila Bay in the opening days of the Spanish-American War. The United States saved the revolution, but then destroyed it when in a burst of imperialist fervor the Senate voted to annex the Philippines in 1899. In response, the Filipinos fought a bloody, no-holds-barred war against their new colonial master that lasted until 1902 at the cost to the Filipinos of twenty thousand military and two hundred thousand civilian deaths. Independence for the Philippines was delayed until 1946.

No anticolonial insurrection took place in India in the early 1900s, but here too there was growing opposition to colonial rule. By then most Indians had abandoned the view that British rule was a blessing that would bring to India the benefits of Western science, constitutional government, and prosperity. Many Indians were angered by Britain's one-sided economic policies, which they now believed drained off India's resources, stifled development, and damaged traditional industries. Others were offended by the British refusal to seriously consider their demands for a greater role in the colonial administration. Still others resented the British assumption that Western ways were superior to centuries-old Indian beliefs and practices. Against a backdrop of a severe economic recession in the early 1890s and no fewer than three major famines and a plague epidemic between 1896 and 1905, protests erupted in the wake of the unilateral British decision in 1905 to divide the populous province of Bengal into a Hindu-dominated west and a Muslim east. Viewed as another example of British high-handedness, the partition led to a decade of intense anti-British activity, including petition drives, protests, and a boycott of British imports.

Indian protests led to additional British repression and a few token reforms; the Filipino rebellion replaced one colonial master with another; the Dutch Ethical Policy fell short of achieving its lofty goals. Nonetheless, all three were important turning points in the history of imperialism. In adopting the Ethical Policy, the Dutch admitted that the moral underpinnings of traditional imperialism were flawed and should be abandoned. Protest in India and revolution in the Philippines both revealed the new power of nationalism among colonized peoples. Cracks in the foundations of imperialism had begun to appear.

"Freedom Is My Birthright"

11 ◆ Bal Gangadhar Tilak, *"TENETS OF THE NEW PARTY"*

Many histories of Indian nationalism begin with the founding of the Indian National Congress in 1885. In its early years, Congress was dominated by middle and upper-class Hindus, who gathered annually to hear speeches and pass resolutions on matters of interest to India's educated elite: access to higher positions in the Indian Civil Service and the army; a greater voice in provincial legislative councils; the expansion of educational opportunities; and the lowering of certain taxes. They did not seek independence. In 1906, however, the annual meeting of the organization was rocked by a bitter dispute between Moderates, who favored cooperation with the British and gradual reform, and Extremists, who formed a new

Source: Tilak: Bal Gangadhar Tilak, His Writings and Speeches, 3rd edition (Madras: Ganesh, 1922), 55–57, 61, 63–67.

faction within the Congress, known as the New Party, and sought immediate independence.

The leading spokesman for the New Party was Bal Gangadhar Tilak (1856–1920), a scholar and religious philosopher who, as the editor of a widely read Marathi-language newspaper, thundered against the evils of British rule and defended Hindu traditions. His mottos—"Militancy not Mendicancy" and "Freedom Is My Birthright, and I Shall Have It"—spread throughout India. Viewing him as a dangerous rabble-rouser, the British imprisoned him in 1897 and 1908 for sedition. In the following excerpt from a speech delivered in January 1907, Tilak sets forth his views on Indian independence in the wake of a contentious meeting of the Indian National Congress at which a schism within the organization had been narrowly avoided.

QUESTIONS FOR ANALYSIS

1. According to Tilak, what are the major differences between Moderates and Extremists?
2. In Tilak's view, why were many Indians at first convinced that British rule was a good thing?
3. Why, according to Tilak, have most Indians become disillusioned with British rule?
4. What does Tilak mean by "boycott"? Does it mean an economic boycott only?
5. What is Tilak's ultimate goal for India?

...One thing is granted, namely, that this government does not suit us. As has been said by an eminent statesman—the government of one country by another can never be a successful, and therefore, a permanent government. There is no difference of opinion about this fundamental proposition between the old and new schools. One fact is that this alien government has ruined the country. In the beginning, all of us were taken by surprise. We were almost dazed. We thought that everything that the rulers did was for our good and that this English government has descended from the clouds to save us from the invasions of Tamerlane and Genghis Khan,[1] and, as they say, not only from foreign invasions but from internecine warfare,

or the internal or external invasions, as they call it. We felt happy for a time, but it soon came to light that the peace which was established in this country did this ...—that we were prevented from going at each other's throats, so that a foreigner might go at the throat of us all. *Pax Britannica* [British peace] has been established in this country in order that a foreign government may exploit the country. That this is the effect of this *Pax Britannica* is being gradually realized in these days. It was an unhappy circumstance that it was not realized sooner. We believed in the benevolent intentions of the government, but in politics there is no benevolence. Benevolence is used to sugar-coat the declarations of self-interest and we were in

---

[1]Genghis (also Chingis or Jenghis) Khan (c. 1167–1277) was the Mongol conqueror who founded history's largest land empire, one that stretched from the Pacific to the Black Sea and from Siberia to Southeast Asia. Tamerlane, or Timur the Lame (1336–1405), of Turco-Mongol descent, was another famous conqueror; in 1398, he invaded India and took Delhi.

those days deceived by the apparent benevolent intentions under which rampant self-interest was concealed. That was our state then. But soon a change came over us. English education, growing poverty, and better familiarity with our rulers opened our eyes and our leaders'; especially, the venerable leader[2] who presided over the recent Congress was the first to tell us that the drain from the country was ruining it, and if the drain was to continue, there was some great disaster awaiting us. So terribly convinced was he of this that he went over from here to England and spent twenty-five years of his life in trying to convince the English people of the injustice that is being done to us. He worked very hard. He had conversations and inter-views with secretaries of state, with members of Parliament—and with what result?

He has come here at the age of eighty-two to tell us that he is bitterly disappointed....

You can now understand the difference be-tween the old and the new parties. Appeals to the bureaucracy are hopeless. On this point both the new and old parties are agreed. The old party believes in appealing to the British nation and we do not. That being our position, it logi-cally follows we must have some other method. There is another alternative. We are not going to sit down quiet. We shall have some other method by which to achieve what we want. We are not disappointed, we are not pessimists. It is the hope of achieving the goal by our own efforts that has brought into existence this new party....

We have come forward with a scheme which if you accept [it], shall better enable you to remedy this state of things than the scheme of the old school. Your industries are ruined ut-terly, ruined by foreign rule; your wealth is go-ing out of the country and you are reduced to the lowest level which no human being can oc-cupy. In this state of things, is there any other remedy by which you can help yourself? The remedy is not petitioning but boycott. We say prepare your forces, organize your power, and then go to work so that they cannot refuse you what you demand.... We are not armed, and there is no necessity for arms either. We have a stronger weapon, a political weapon, in boycott. We have perceived one fact, that the whole of this administration, which is carried on by a handful of Englishmen, is carried on with our assistance. We are all in subordinate service. This whole government is carried on with our assistance and they try to keep us in ignorance of our power of cooperation between ourselves by which that which is in our own hands at present can be claimed by us and ad-ministrated by us. The point is to have the en-tire control in our hands. I want to have the key of my house, and not merely one stranger turned out of it. Self-government is our goal; we want a control over our administrative ma-chinery. We don't want to become clerks and remain clerks. At present, we are clerks and willing instruments of our own oppression in the hands of an alien government, and that government is ruling over us not by its in-nate strength but by keeping us in ignorance and blindness to the perception of this fact.... What the new party wants you to do is to re-alize the fact that your future rests entirely in your own hands. If you mean to be free, you can be free; if you do not mean to be free, you will fall and be forever fallen. So many of you need not like arms; but if you have not the power of active resistance, have you not the power of self-denial and self-abstinence in such a way as not to assist this foreign government to rule over you? This is boycott and this is what is meant when we say, boycott is a politi-cal weapon. We shall not give them assistance to collect revenue and keep peace. We shall not assist them in fighting beyond the frontiers or

---

[2]A reference to Dadabhai Naoroji (1825–1917), one of the founders of the Indian National Congress and at the time of Tilak's speech the organization's president. Born into a prom-inent Mumbai family, Naoroji abandoned a career as a math-ematician and took up residence in England, where he ran a profitable trading company and did what he could to con-vince the government to improve conditions in India. He was elected to Parliament in 1892. Naoroji formulated the the-ory of the "drain," by which he meant the process by which Britain systematically exploited Indian wealth and resources.

outside India with Indian blood and money. We shall not assist them in carrying on the administration of justice. We shall have our own courts, and when time comes we shall not pay taxes. Can you do that by your united efforts? If you can, you are free from tomorrow.... This is a lesson of progress, a lesson of helping yourself as much as possible, and if you really perceive the force of it, if you are convinced by these arguments, then and then only is it possible for you to effect your salvation from the alien rule under which you labor at this moment.

There are many other points but it is impossible to exhaust them all in an hour's speech. If you carry any wrong impression come and get your doubts solved. We are prepared to answer every objection, solve every doubt, and prove every statement. We want your cooperation; without your help we cannot do anything singlehanded. We beg of you, we appeal to you, to think over the question, to see the situation, and realize it, and after realizing it to come to our assistance, and by our joint assistance to help in the salvation of the country.

"Our Obligations in the Indies"

❖

12 ◆ Pieter Brooshooft, *"THE ETHICAL DIRECTION OF COLONIAL POLICY"*

Following the bankruptcy and dissolution of the Dutch East India Company in 1799 and a brief period of British rule during the Napoleonic Wars, the East Indies came under the direct control of the Dutch government in 1816. Facing huge debts from a slump in coffee prices and the costs of fighting a four-year rebellion on the island of Java, in 1830 the government adopted the Culture (or Cultivation) System, a set of policies designed to generate funds to repair the sorry state of the home government's treasury. Lands in certain regions of Java were taken over by the government and devoted to coffee growing, and elsewhere peasants were required to devote one fifth of their land and sixty-six working days a year to growing cash crops such as sugar, tobacco, indigo, and spices. With quotas enforced by village chieftains, peasants were forced to sell these items to the Netherlands Trading Company, which had a monopoly on buying, transporting, and selling of East Indian goods in Europe.

When in the 1840s evidence of widespread abuses of the system and deepening poverty among the Javanese was revealed, the Culture System was modified to break the monopoly of the Netherlands Trading Company and give the Javanese greater control over their land. Although the government retained control of its coffee plantations, Dutch and Chinese investors were given the right to own or lease land on Java, and Javanese peasants were free to grow whatever crops they wished or lease part or all of their land to foreigners. Although the new system worked well at first, beginning in the 1880s, several factors—falling prices for exports, continuing high taxes, and population pressures—increased poverty among the native peoples.

Source: From Christian L. M. Penders, ed. and trans., *Indonesia: Selected Documents on Colonialism and Nationalism* (St. Lucia, Queensland: University of Queensland Press, 1977), 65–75. Used by kind permission of Dr. Christian L. M. Penders.

Against this backdrop, many journalists, left-leaning politicians, religious leaders, and former officials rejected past policies. Conrad Théodoor van Deventer, a former colonial official, introduced the concept of "a debt of honor," arguing that the Netherlands had a moral responsibility to use past profits from the sale of cash crops to underwrite policies that would benefit natives. Pieter Brooshooft (1845–1921), a journalist who had lived in the East Indies, wrote extensively about the abuses of Dutch colonialism and called for the adoption of a new "ethical policy." He summarized his ideas in a widely read pamphlet published in early 1901, "The Ethical Direction in Colonial Policy." Just months later, following elections that installed a sympathetic parliament, Queen Wilhelmina, under advice from her prime minister, announced the adoption of the Ethical Policy, aimed at bringing progress and prosperity to the peoples of the Indies.

QUESTIONS FOR ANALYSIS

1. How does Brooshooft characterize the overall effects of colonial rule on the people of Java?
2. What specific measures does he recommend to improve the lot of the Javanese?
3. According to Brooshooft, why are so many Javanese attracted to the idea of leasing their land to foreigners? Why, in his view, is this a potentially disastrous strategy for most Javanese?
4. Based on his analysis of the dangers of leasing their land, what can be concluded about Brooshooft's views of the qualities and characteristics of the Javanese?
5. What can be inferred about Brooshooft's views of the Javanese people's future once the Ethical Policy is put in place?

What should motivate us to carry out our obligations in the Indies is the best of human inclinations: the feeling for justice, the feeling that we should give the best we have got to the Javanese who have been subjugated by us against their will, the noble-minded impulse of the stronger one to treat the weaker one justly. And I find it pleasing to be able to point to growing signs here and there of this sense of justice. This is true of political parties as well as of individuals. . . . The Radical, Liberal-Democratic, and Socialist parties have subscribed far more strongly to the ethical principle in their colonial programmes. Only the Catholic Party, although wishing to see the Javanese prosperous, still would like the Netherlands to profit from them. . . .

It is extremely shameful for our government that as long as we have ruled Java, the Javanese have hardly drawn any income worth mentioning from their own fertile soil. The greatest profits regularly ended up in the hands of foreigners. The natives had to yield the largest and best part of their crop to the ruler, first as compulsive [forced] deliveries during the time of the [Dutch East India] Company, and later through forced labor under the Culture System. Until 1870 the State held on unscrupulously to this monopoly of easy profits, and the European private entrepreneur was not allowed to compete in the agricultural field. Then a change occurred. But unfortunately it was not the Ethical faction, with its desire to do justice to the Javanese, that turned the scales in the decision to abandon the exploitation by the

State, but it was the arrogant demand of Western capital, which sought new employment for the riches it had already gathered [in the colony]....

One section of the coffee plantations that still provided a nice profit were retained by the government and the Javanese continued to work under almost the same unfavourable conditions. And with respect to the less fertile lands ... good coffee lands were leased on a long-term basis to private European entrepreneurs and land-lease ordinances were issued in order to lure the lands of the Javanese into the hands of European sugar, indigo, and tobacco planters....

In any case the final result was that the agricultural land of the Indies, with the exception of what was absolutely necessary for the growing of food for the natives, was as legally as possible given into the hands of European and Chinese planters, while the natives could be hired by the foreigners to work on these lands for daily wages. But among these numerous and often-revised government regulations there were none that ensured the Javanese reasonable wages for the work performed. This, it was argued, would have been improper interference in private labor agreement.

But while helping to alienate [transfer] the agricultural land, [the government] did little if anything at all in the way of introducing measures to improve the ancient Javanese cultivation of rice ... and make it more profitable. So little has been done in extending irrigation that, according to the calculations of the irrigation expert Homan van der Heide, out of the 2,700,000 *bouws*[1] that are suitable for irrigation, only 300,000 *bouws* are fully irrigated, while 2,400,000 *bouws* are still waiting to be irrigated or improved ... And for whatever irrigation works that have been constructed, the Javanese have been made to pay more than enough because of the labor services demanded

during the construction and the increase in land tax during or after completion.

The government has also done nothing to improve rice production in other ways, such as the granting of premiums or loans to introduce better ploughs or hoes (the hand hoe is still the main tool), to improve preparation of the rice (this is still done by hand with a pounder on a block), or to introduce better fertilizers ... Now the government is to experiment with ... "demonstration fields", where the Javanese will be taught to work along more scientific lines. But as long as the government fails to give temporary financial help, the poor Javanese will not be able to pay for the tools and fertilizers needed for more intensive cultivation. It must also be mentioned here ... that in addition to lack of money and the stubborn attachment to tradition, the land tax is an important reason why the Javanese cannot improve their productivity. They know that every increase in production will be followed by an increase in this tax, which is already pressing so heavily on them....

The government has also done nothing to improve the cattle stocks of the natives, and it has not even got decent statistics...

In short, there is nothing to be seen of the "benefits" which Minister Cremer [a Liberal politician] ... has said repeatedly will make the Javanese love our rule. This is so at least with respect to ... rice cultivation. And one *bouw* of *sawah* [rice paddies] still produces only 25 to 30 *piculs*[2] of rice (there are some of 50 or 60 *piculs*, but also of 10 *piculs* and less), which—taking the average high price of two guilders—will fetch fifty to sixty guilders. The average land-holding (communal or individual) is 1 to 1½ *bouws* and this will steadily decrease because of the steep rise in population. The income from second crops per *bouw* can be put on the average at twenty-five guilders.[3] So one can calculate the income earned from Java's fertile soil by five-eighths of the people who have the most ancient rights to

---

[1]One bouw equals 1.75 acres.
[2]One picul equals 133.3 pounds.

[3]The guilder was the basic unit of the Dutch currency. At the time, 85 guilders would have been worth approximately $100 U.S.

the land and whose profession is agriculture. Not counting bad harvests or other misfortunes, the average yearly income of the Javanese farmer can at the highest be put at one hundred guilders.

[The Javanese] are also unable to earn more from their land by renting it to private European industry or by working on the plantations. Rents paid by the factory-owners for land are based on the productivity of this land when it is cultivated by the Javanese themselves.... So [land rents] are about the same as the income earned when the land is cultivated by the farmers themselves. But even if this [rent] was much higher, it would not be to the advantage of the village. This is because the private European plantation industry that has developed so strongly since 1870 is especially pernicious in that it takes away the land from the small man and gives him money in its place.

A good rice harvest provides the Javanese with food for almost the whole year. If there is a shortage in the last few months, they can fall back on the second crops, and so these families ... can look after themselves fairly well during the whole year. The rice is carefully stored in a *loemboeng* [little shed], but money on the other hand slips through the fingers of the Javanese like water and it seduces him because of a primitive and childlike love of pleasure. So if a representative of a sugar mill or indigo factory comes and asks to rent his land, the tinkling sound of the guilders is too attractive for him to refuse the offer. But the small amount of money is soon dissipated on small feasts such as weddings, births, and deaths, at which he likes to be extravagant; or it is spent on sweets or debauchery (gambling, opium, dancing girls), things he would otherwise not have indulged in. But he has lost his land for sixteen months. And the month of May, during which bushels of ripened rice flood the village and warm the hearts of old and young, brings him neither joy nor food. If there is a little money left, he will be able to buy some rice, but soon food will be lacking ... If he falls sick, there is no money or food at all. If he has a weak character, he becomes wanton and debauched ... He now has worries, debts, and bad habits ... And when the capitalist again knocks on his door in order to lease his land again for two years, ... pressed as he is from all sides he will snap up the chance. And the end comes when they have to sell their cattle, their house and land. The *gogol* [landed villager] then becomes an *orang menoempang* [laborer without land rights]. Village life has been demoralized and the villagers have been made unhappy....

My conclusion is that our policy with respect to native *agriculture* pushes the villagers slowly but surely into the same swamp of moral and physical misery into which the disinherited masses of Western society have sunk. These are at present struggling against the heartless suppressors and attempt to push themselves out of their misery. Once they are out, a bloody struggle will come about which will end an era of great misery. In the Indies this is only just beginning. And only later centuries will judge the period when a people was robbed of its land and was made the slave of insatiable fortune-hunters.

Reform and Revolution in East Asia

For centuries, China dominated East Asia. No other state in the region came close to matching its size, wealth, population, technology, trade, and military might. The Chinese called their country the Central Kingdom—the hub of the world—and viewed all other peoples as their inferiors. In the early 1900s, however, Chinese dominance in the region ended, at least for a time. Europeans, whom the Chinese dismissively called "western barbarians" or "long-nosed barbarians," now controlled extensive areas of the Central Kingdom as spheres of influence; American and European missionaries ran schools and sought converts throughout the land; Western businessmen controlled China's banks, railroads, and industries. After centuries of dismissing their neighbors as backward and decades of believing that Westerners were skilled at making weapons but little else, the Chinese were forced to recognize the need to reform their schools, laws, and government institutions by borrowing from Europe, the United States, and even Japan, where in the early 1900s thousands of Chinese students were attending schools and universities to find ways to revive their country's fortunes.

That earnest young Chinese should go to the land of the Japanese "dwarf people" to find enlightenment and inspiration is just one indication of how different the experiences of China and Japan had been in the nineteenth century. Beginning in the early 1800s, Tokugawa rulers of Japan and Manchu emperors of China faced similar challenges: how to deal with a host of domestic problems while simultaneously responding to threats from the West. In China's case, the Western threat became apparent with the Opium War (1839–1842), in which Great Britain defeated China and forced the emperor to accept the first of a series of "unequal treaties" that would require China to pay large amounts of reparations, open ports for trade, cede or lease territories to European states, accept foreign missionaries, and make other concessions to the Western powers in foreign-controlled "spheres of influence." In Japan's case, the crisis came in the 1850s, when in the wake of the "opening of Japan" by the U.S. Navy in 1853–1854, the Tokugawa also were forced to accept humiliating treaties that required Japan to open the country to foreign trade, maintain low tariff levels on Western imports, and permit Western missionary activity.

So strong was the confidence of the Chinese in the soundness and superiority of their institutions that they failed to grasp the gravity of their problems. Only after the massive Taiping Rebellion, a massive peasant revolt that lasted from 1850 to 1864 and cost an estimated twenty million lives, and another loss to the French and British in the Second Opium War (1856–1860) did officials adopt a policy of "self-strengthening," which entailed military modernization and bureaucratic reform along Western lines but otherwise was committed to preserving China's traditional Confucian society. The "self-strengtheners" achieved some impressive results, but in the face of conservative opposition and inconsistent support from the imperial court they were unable to prevent further military defeats and humiliations, one of which came at the hands of the Japanese in the Sino-Japanese War in 1894–1895.

The Japanese, like the Chinese, debated how to respond to their foreign and domestic crises. The debate, however, ended abruptly in 1867–1868, when a faction of rebellious aristocrats overthrew the shogun and took control of the government in the name of the emperor. In the wake of these events, known as the Meiji Restoration (because it was carried out in the name of an emperor whose reign name was Meiji—"enlightened rule"), Japan's new leaders dismantled much of the country's traditional society and embarked on a crash program of Western-inspired military modernization, industrial development, and educational reform. Japan stunned China with its victory in the Sino-Japanese War and then stunned the world with its victory over Russia in the Russo-Japanese War of 1904–1905.

By the early 1900s, Japan had not only staved off the imperialist threat from the West but also had become an imperialist power itself, with control over Taiwan, Korea, the Ryukyu Islands, and the southern part of Sakhalin Island; it also became the dominant influence in much of Manchuria. China's leaders, shaken by China's loss to Japan and the failure of the anti-Western Boxer Rebellion in 1901, finally committed themselves to a program of reform no less urgent and ambitious than that of Japan's Meiji leadership thirty years earlier. It was, however, too little and too late. In 1911–1912, with barely a push from any organized revolutionary group, the Qing dynasty fell and was not replaced by a new imperial line. China became a republic, and for the first time in over one thousand years faced a future without the authority of an emperor, the rule of scholar-officials, and the guidance of Confucian philosophy. Such was the extraordinary state of affairs in East Asia at the beginning of the new century.

A Revolutionary Formula for China's Revival

❖

13 ◆ Hu Hanmin, *THE SIX PRINCIPLES OF THE PEOPLE'S REPORT*

By 1901 the prognosis for China's imperial regime had deteriorated from poor to critical. Plagued throughout the nineteenth century by peasant revolts, military defeats, foreign exploitation, and failed reforms, China in the 1890s and early 1900s reached a low point. Its humiliating defeat in 1895 by Japan in the Sino-Japanese War set off a struggle between conservatives and reformers, with conservatives ascendant after the suppression of the One Hundred Days reform movement by Empress Dowager Cixi in 1898. Reformers regained the upper hand after the failure of the antiwestern Boxer Rebellion in 1901. Their New Policy Reforms encouraged Chinese youths to study abroad; envisioned broad educational reforms; established military academies; sought to support Chinese-owned businesses; and changed the system of recruiting government officials when the ancient civil service examinations were abolished in 1905. The reforms failed to save the regime. They burdened the peasantry with higher taxes, alienated large landowners, and failed to satisfy the generals, business people, and intellectuals who were convinced that China's only hope lay in ousting the Qing Dynasty and rebuilding the country from its foundations.

China's leading revolutionary was Sun Yat-sen (1866–1925), a man far different from previous Chinese reformers. Born to a poor rural family from the Guangzhou region and educated in Hawaii and missionary schools in China, he developed a

Source: From *Sources of Chinese Tradition*, by William Theodore de Bary. Copyright © 1960 by Columbia University Press. Reprinted with the permission of the publisher via Copyright Clearance Center.

worldview more Western than Confucian. Galled by China's military impotence and Qing ineptitude, in 1894 he founded the secret Revive China Society, which in 1895 made plans to capture Guangzhou and make it its base. The plot was uncovered, and Sun and his associates were forced into exile. In 1905 Sun joined his Revive China Society with secret societies from China, overseas Chinese groups, and Chinese student organizations in Japan to form the Revolutionary Alliance (also known as the Chinese United League, Chinese Alliance and United Allegiance Society). After sixteen years of traveling, planning, writing, and organizing, his and other revolutionaries' hopes were realized when Sun became provisional president of China in 1912 after the Revolution of 1911 had ended the Qing Era.

The following excerpts are taken from a manifesto prepared by Hu Hanmin (1879–1936), a close associate of Sun Yat-sen, and published with Sun's endorsement in the Revolutionary Alliance's party organ, the *People's Journal*, in April 1906. Drawing on strands of Western political thought and practice, it sought to undercut those Chinese reformers who remained loyal to the dynasty and favored constitutional monarchy. In the excerpt below, we have included only the first three of the "six principles" discussed by Hu Hanmin. The final three principles discuss China's potential role in achieving world peace and the reasons why Japan and the Western powers should support their cause. The first three principles (nationalism democracy, socialism) later served as the platform for the Guomindang, or Nationalist Party, founded in 1912 from a merger of the Revolutionary Alliance with five smaller pro-revolution groups.

QUESTIONS FOR ANALYSIS

1. How does the manifesto characterize the Manchu as a people?
2. Why, according to the manifesto, will the cause of reform inevitably fail if the Manchu Dynasty remains in power?
3. How does the document define "constitutional democracy," and why is this form of government the only acceptable form of government for post-Manchu China?
4. The document suggests that China will easily make the transition from absolutism to democracy. Why?
5. What are the most important features of Chinese socialism as outlined in this document?
6. According to the manifesto, why have landlords and the "landlord system" had such negative consequences for China?

1. OVERTHROW OF THE PRESENT EVIL GOVERNMENT

This is our first task. That a fine nation should be controlled by an evil one and that, instead of adopting our culture, the Manchus should force us to adopt theirs, is contrary to reason and cannot last for long. For the sake of our independence and salvation, we must overthrow the Manchu dynasty. The Manchus have hurt the Chinese people so much that there has arisen an inseparable barrier between them.

Some have argued that the Manchus can be assimilated to Chinese culture. . . . Those who advocate assimilation of the Manchus without having them overthrown merely serve as tools of the tyrannical dynasty and are therefore shameless to the utmost. . . . As an inferior minority, the Manchus rule the majority by means of political power. If their regime is overthrown, they will have nothing to maintain their existence. Whether they will flee to their old den [in the North] as did the defeated Mongols,[1] or whether they will be assimilated to the Chinese as were the conquered Di, Xiang, Xianli[2] tribes, we do not know. But unless their political power is overthrown, the Chinese nation will forever remain the conquered people without independence, and, being controlled by a backward nation, will finally perish with it in the struggle with the advanced foreign powers. . . .

The Manchu government is evil because it is the evil race which usurped our government, and their evils are not confined to a few political measures but are rooted in the nature of the race and can neither be eliminated nor reformed. Therefore, even if there are a few ostensible reforms, the evils will remain just the same. . . .

2. ESTABLISHMENT OF A REPUBLIC

That absolute monarchy is unsuitable to the present age requires no argument. Political observers determine the level of a country's civilization by inquiring whether its political system is despotic or not. It is but natural therefore that those who propose new forms of government in the twentieth century should aim at rooting out the elements of absolutism. Revolutions broke out in China one after another in the past, but because the political system was not reformed, no good results ensured. Thus the Mongol dynasty was overthrown by the Ming, but within three hundred years the Chinese nation was again on the decline.[3] For although the foreign rule was overthrown and a Chinese regime was installed in its place, the autocratic form of government remained unchanged, to the disappointment of the people.

According to the general theory of government, the opposite of autocracy is republican government, which, broadly speaking, may be divided into three kinds: first, aristocracy; second, democracy; and third, constitutional democracy. The latter is not only different from aristocracy but also from absolute democracy. People . . . all argue that the Chinese nation lacks the tradition of democracy in its history, thus undermining the morale of our patriots. Alas! they are not only ignorant of political science but unqualified to discuss history. . . . The constitutional government was established without difficulty in America because after its independence there was no class other than the common people. One of the great fetures of Chinese politics is that . . . there has existed no noble class (except for the Mongol and Manchu dynasties when a noble class was maintained according to then alien systems)[4]. After the overthrow of the Manchus, therefore, there will be no distinction between classes in China. . . . The establishment of constitutional

---

[1]The Yuan Dynasty, founded by the Mongol leader Kublai Khan in 1271, collapsed in 1368 and was succeeded by the Ming (1368–1644).

[2]Tribal peoples who at various times established their political authority in regions of northern and western China, but ultimately were defeated by the Chinese and adopted Chinese customs.

[3]After a period of rapid decline, Ming China was invaded by the northern Manchus, who established China's last imperial dynasty, the Qing, in 1644.

[4]Hu Hanmin is making the point that China, for most of its history, lacked a hereditary aristocratic ruling class such as the samurai in Japan or the feudal nobility in Europe. Politicial authority was exercised by scholar-officials, who were named to office on the basis of the results they achieved on China's civil service examinations.

government will be easier in China than in other countries. . . .

Since constitutional democracy can be established only after a revolution, it is imperative that following our revolution, only the best and the most public-spirited form of government should be adopted so that no defects will remain. Absolute government, be it monarchical or democratic, is government of injustice and inequality. . . . Constitutional democracy will have none of these defects, and equality will prevail. We can overthrow the Manchus and establish our state because Chinese nationalism and democratic thought are well developed. When we are able to do this, it is inconceivable that, knowing the general psychology of the people, we should abandon the government of equality and retain the distinction between ruler and ruled.

3. LAND NATIONALIZATION

The affliction of civilized countries in the modern age is not political classes but economic classes. Hence the rise of socialism. There are many socialist theories, but they all aim at leveling economic classes. Generally speaking, socialism may be divided into communism and collectivism, and nationalization of land is part of collectivism. Only constitutional democracies can adopt collectivism, for there the ruling authority resides in the state and the state machinery is controlled by a representative legislature. Thus there is no inequality involved if a democratic state, in reflecting social psychology, should adopt collectivism in order to promote the welfare of the people. Such, of course, cannot be said of a regime which allows of any political classes.

Not all collectivist theories can be applied to China at her present stage of development. But in the case of land nationalization we already

have a model for it in the well-field system[5] of the Three Dynasties, and it should not be difficult to introduce land nationalization as an adaptation of a past system to the present age of political reform. Nationalization of land is opposed to private ownership. It is based on the theory that since land is the essential element in production and is not man-made, any more than sunshine or air, it should not be privately owned.

The landlord system arises from many causes. At first land may be obtained as capital through accumulation of labor and used for productive purposes. Subsequently, as feudal domains develop, land is monopolized, and both capitalists and laborers become dependents of the feudal lords who are the first to receive the crops. . . .

The evil consequences of this system are that the landlord can acquire absolute power in society and thereby absorb and annex more land, that the farmers can be driven out of work, that people may be short of food and thus have to depend on outside supply, and that the entire country may be made poorer while capital and wealth all go to the landlords.

There are various measures for carrying out land nationalization, but the main purpose is to deprive the people of the right of landownership while permitting them to retain other rights over land. And these rights must be obtained by permission of the state. In this way the power of the landlord will be wiped out from the Chinese continent. Profit from land will be high, but only self-cultivating farmers can obtain land from the state. In this way people will increasingly devote themselves to farming and no land will be wasted. Landlords who in the past have been nonproductive profiteers will now be just like the common people. They will turn to productive enterprises and this will produce striking results for the good of the whole national economy.

---

[5] The communal land system in China during the Zhou Dynasty (c. 1046–256 BCE), in which each unit of land was divided into nine parts: eight fields were allocated to peasant families for their own use; the ninth field, centrally located, was farmed in common, with its produce turned over to the peasants' lord.

An Attack on Foot-binding
in China

◆

14 ◆ Qiu Jin,
AN ADDRESS TO TWO HUNDRED MILLION
FELLOW COUNTRYWOMEN

Beginning in the late ninth and tenth centuries C.E., millions of Chinese girls between the ages of five and nine had their feet tightly wrapped and gradually bent until the arch was broken and all the toes except the big toe were turned under. With feet growing to only half their normal size, these girls were condemned to lives as semicripples. Originally, foot-binding was limited to wealthy families who wanted to demonstrate that their women did not have to work. Gradually, however, the practice spread to all levels of society, and small feet began to have a strong erotic attraction for Chinese males. Girls with "big feet" were considered unmarriageable.

Although foot-binding always had its opponents (and was not practiced by Manchu women), only at the end of the nineteenth century did the practice come under widespread criticism. Many reformers and intellectuals considered foot-binding, along with opium smoking, one of the social customs that underlay the country's backwardness. Protestant missionaries, many of them women, also denounced the practice, and one of them, Mrs. Archibald Little, founded the Natural Foot Society in 1895. Also in the 1890s, anti-foot-binding societies, whose members agreed to arrange marriages for their daughters with unbound feet, were founded in major cities. In 1902, Empress Dowager Cixi outlawed foot-binding, but with little effect.

Among the Chinese women who attacked foot-binding, the most outspoken was Qiu Jin (1875–1907), who devoted her life to women's liberation and the overthrow of the Qing dynasty. Raised in a moderately wealthy family and well educated, Qiu was married to an older man at age twenty-one, but she left him in 1903 to study in Japan. On her return in 1906 she founded a women's magazine and became principal of a girls' school. It was in 1906 that she made the following speech. In 1907, she and her cousin were arrested and beheaded for revolutionary activity.

QUESTIONS FOR ANALYSIS

1. As described by Qiu, what kind of relationship did most Chinese girls have with their parents?
2. What can be learned from the source concerning Chinese marriage customs and the relationship between husbands and wives?

Source: Reprinted with the permission of Free Press, a Division of Simon & Schuster, Inc., from *Chinese Civilization: A Source Book*, Second Edition, Revised & Expanded by Patricia Buckley Ebrey. Copyright © 1993 by Patricia Buckley Ebrey. All rights reserved.

3. What were the motives, according to Qiu, for subjecting women to foot-binding and preventing them from learning how to read?
4. In Qiu's view, what share of the blame for their oppression must women themselves assume?
5. What are Qiu's solutions for China's problems?
6. What similarities do you see between the views of Qiu Jin and those of al-Badiya (Source 10)?

Alas! The greatest injustice in this world must be the injustice suffered by our female population of two hundred million. If a girl is lucky enough to have a good father, then her childhood is at least tolerable. But if by chance her father is an ill-tempered and unreasonable man, he may curse her birth: "What rotten luck: another useless thing." Some men go as far as killing baby girls while most hold the opinion that "girls are eventually someone else's property" and treat them with coldness and disdain. In a few years, without thinking about whether it is right or wrong, he[1] forcibly binds his daughter's soft, white feet with white cloth so that even in her sleep she cannot find comfort and relief until the flesh becomes rotten and the bones broken. What is all this misery for? Is it just so that on the girl's wedding day friends and neighbors will compliment him, saying, "Your daughter's feet are really small"? Is that what the pain is for?

But that is not the worst of it. When the time for marriage comes, a girl's future life is placed in the hands of a couple of shameless matchmakers and a family seeking rich and powerful in-laws. A match can be made without anyone ever inquiring whether the prospective bridegroom is honest, kind, or educated. On the day of the marriage the girl is forced into a red and green bridal sedan chair, and all this time she is not allowed to breathe one word about her future. After her marriage, if the man doesn't do her any harm, she is told that she should thank Heaven for her good fortune. But if the man is bad or he ill-treats her, she is told that her marriage is retribution for some sin committed in her previous existence. If she complains at all or tries to reason with her husband, he may get angry and beat her. When other people find out they will criticize her, saying, "That woman is bad; she doesn't know how to behave like a wife." What can she do? When a man dies, his wife must mourn him for three years and never remarry. But if the woman dies, her husband only needs to tie his queue[2] with blue thread. Some men consider this to be ugly and don't even do it. In some cases, three days after his wife's death, a man will go out for some "entertainment." Sometimes, before seven weeks have passed, a new bride has already arrived at the door.... Why is there no justice for women? We constantly hear men say, "The human mind is just and we must treat people with fairness and equality." Then why do they greet women like black slaves from Africa? How did inequality and injustice reach this state?

Dear sisters, you must know that you'll get nothing if you rely upon others. You must go out and get things for yourselves. In ancient times when decadent scholars came out with such nonsense as "men are exalted, women are lowly," "a virtuous woman is one

---

[1]Despite Qiu's use of the male pronoun, the actual work of binding feet was performed by female members of the girls' families, usually mothers.

[2]The braid of hair worn at the back of the head by Chinese men.

without talent," and "the husband guides the wife," ambitious and spirited women should have organized and opposed them.... Men feared that if women were educated they would become superior to men, so they did not allow us to be educated. Couldn't the women have challenged the men and refused to submit? It seems clear now that it was we women who abandoned our responsibilities to ourselves and felt content to let men do everything for us. As long as we could live in comfort and leisure, we let men make all the decisions for us. When men said we were useless, we became useless; when they said we were incapable, we stopped questioning them even when our entire female sex had reached slave status. At the same time we were insecure in our good fortune and our physical comfort, so we did everything to please men. When we heard that men liked small feet, we immediately bound them just to please them, just to keep our free meal tickets. As for their forbidding us to read and write, well, that was only too good to be true. We readily agreed.... It was only natural that men, with their knowledge, wisdom, and hard work, received the right to freedom while we became their slaves. And as slaves,

how can we escape repression? Whom can we blame but ourselves since we have brought this on ourselves? ...

...Let us all put aside our former selves and be resurrected as complete human beings. Those of you who are old, do not call yourselves old and useless. If your husbands want to open schools, don't stop them; if your good sons want to study abroad, don't hold them back. Those among us who are middle-aged, don't hold back your husbands lest they lose their ambition and spirit and fail in their work. After your sons are born, send them to schools. You must do the same for your daughters and, whatever you do, don't bind their feet. As for you young girls among us, go to school if you can. If not, read and study at home. Those of you who are rich, persuade your husbands to open schools, build factories, and contribute to charitable organizations. Those of you who are poor, work hard and help your husbands.... You must know that when a country is near destruction, women cannot rely on the men anymore because they aren't even able to protect themselves. If we don't take heart now and shape up, it will be too late when China is destroyed.

Sisters, we must follow through on these ideas!

The Reasons for Japanese Success

◈

15 ◆ Sakutaro Fujioka, *"SOCIAL CHANGE IN MEIJI JAPAN"*

By the early 1900s, it was clear that the Japanese had accomplished something of a miracle. In the four decades following the overthrow of the Tokugawa shogunate in 1867–1868, Japan had transformed itself from a secluded, preindustrial society, vulnerable to foreign exploitation, into a nation with a large

Source: Fujioka: Sakutaro Fujioka, "Social Change in Meiji Japan," in *Fifty Years of a New Japan*, ed. Shigenobu Okuma; trans Marcus Huish (London, Smith, Elder and Co., 1910), 443–458.

conscript army, a modern navy, parliamentary government, a developing industrial sector, research universities, railroads, a telegraph system, a mail service, and a system of near universal primary education. The Japanese defeat of a major European power, Russia, in the Russo-Japanese War of 1904–1905 was the culmination of series of military and diplomatic triumphs that included renegotiation of the unequal treaties with Western powers in 1894, victory over China in the Sino-Japanese War of 1894–1895, and the signing of an alliance treaty with Great Britain in 1902. Unique among other non-Western nations, Japan had successfully withstood the great challenge presented by the West.

Basking in the glow of their accomplishments, many Japanese statesmen, journalists, and academics in the early 1900s sought to explain the reasons for Japan's astounding success. A prominent example of such an effort is the two-volume collection of essays *Kaikoku gojunen shi* (Fifty Years of New Japan) edited by the distinguished statesman, Okuma Shigenobu, and published in 1909. Okuma, who at the time was serving as president of Waseda University in Tokyo, enlisted close to sixty distinguished authors to write articles on the changes experienced by Japan since the Meiji Restoration. Topics included religion, the arts, education, local government, the military, science, and much else. The following excerpt is from an essay "Social Change in the New Japan" by Fujioka Sakutaro (1870–1910), a professor at Tokyo University who wrote important books on the history of Japanese art and literature.

QUESTIONS FOR ANALYSIS

1. How does Fujioka define "Occidentalism" and "Nationalism"? How did they operate "hand in hand" to bring about the transformation of Japanese society?

2. How would you characterize Fujioka's assessment of the "state of Japan" at the time he wrote his essay? Of what is he most proud? What challenges does he see in Japan's future?

3. What concrete examples does Fujioka provide of ways "Occidentalism" has changed Japan?

4. How in Fujioka's view did ideas of social rank affect Japan's development before the Meiji Restoration? How did it make people "content?" How did the elimination of such ideas changes things in the Meiji period?

5. Compare Fujioka's view of nationalism with those of Hu Hanmin (Source 13) and von Treitschke (Source 3).

The scientific progress of the nineteenth century has brought about general improvement, and produced a great metamorphosis in all European countries, but this metamorphosis, remarkable as it is, is as nothing when compared with that which Japan has undergone in the past fifty years.

What is the cause of this miraculous change? ... The two chief reforming powers, among many minor ones, of modern Japan have been **Nationalism and Occidentalism.** To the casual observer it would seem that Nationalism, which insists on the rejection of foreign civilization and on the retention of national features, and Occidentalism, which admires all things Western and advocates the adoption and imitation of Western enlightenment are from their very nature incompatible. Yet, strange as it may sound, these two apparently conflicting principles acted hand in hand in fighting the old system and old usages in Japan, and finally succeeded in completely overthrowing the influence which had so long controlled the mind of the nation.

The Nationalism of those days was indeed nothing but Restoration. Its adherents believed that the political, social, and other numerous evils, which had arisen since the Middle Ages, were the result of partaking of foreign civilization to excess. They argued that Confucianism, which had come from China, had given them delicate rules of ethics, but at the same time had left many evil influences, and that Buddhism, likewise, imported from the same land, had had the effect of leading the people into negativism, pessimism, and morbid sentimentalism.... To wipe out these evils of alien civilization, people must return to their own ways ... when they were free from all foreign influences. They must retrace their steps to those of their ancestors. So they began to study ancient history and ancient literature, and some of the results soon became clearly visible.

That Occidentalism was the main cause of the recent changes we need hardly say. Up to half a century ago, the nation, avoiding all intercourse with foreigners, indulged in the happy dream that the Japanese were the mightiest nation under the sun. What was their surprise, then, when they were

brought face to face with the civilization of the West?... Western civilization ... seemed a marvel of marvels to them. But soon wonder gave place to admiration, which, in its turn, became a desire to import this civilization into their own country. As a reaction from their former pride, they now passed to the other extreme, namely, a sense of humiliation, and they became keenly anxious to take in everything Western. Thus politics, economics, natural science, and art—everything was taken from the West with insatiable avidity, and the customs and usages of the people underwent a complete change, so complete that those alone who witnessed it can believe it....

To cite some instances of the change: European clothes were at first used by officials as ceremonial costumes; then they were found very convenient to work in, and consequently came into popular use. Formerly holidays were limited to the five *sékku* festivals[1] and a few other occasions, but now Sunday has been made a day of universal rest. To-day even private people, who can afford it, live in large European houses, and many in the middle class furnish one or more rooms of their Japanese houses in European style and use them as studies or drawing-rooms. Foreign restaurants are met with almost everywhere, and often the tourist finds European dishes served in a Japanese hotel. Indeed, there is no Japanese homestead wherein one does not find some marks of Western influence ...

Until fifty years ago people did not know that the flesh of pigs and cows was eatable, or that coal was combustible; they had no petroleum lamps and no carriages drawn by horses. They had only black-and-white drawings and paintings in light colors, and they pleased their ears with the *koto* [harp] and *samisén* [three-stringed guitar]. But to-day foreign oil paintings and

[1]Originally, seasonal festivals in which offerings of food were made to the gods to mark the change in seasons. In the Tokugawa period, five of these festivals were made national holidays.

water colors have many admirers, and the piano and the violin are more fashionable than the native instruments.... It should be clearly understood that, wonderful and complete as the outward transformation has been, not one jot or one tittle of the nation's innate character has been allowed to change. Consequently we rest perfectly content with our altered aspect, and even pride ourselves on the successful introduction of a new civilization....

The first of the series of social changes in modern Japan was the destruction of social rank. Before the [Meiji] Restoration it was necessary, for the maintenance of peace and order, to attach great importance to classes and ranks. Roughly speaking, people were graded into four classes: *samurai*, farmers, artisans, and merchants, or more roughly into the two main classes of aristocrats and commoners. These ranks were strictly defined, and every individual had to rest contentedly in his own sphere. The *daimyo* were placed at the head of the aristocrats, and such was their authority that, if a merchant or a farmer met a *daimyo's* procession, he was bound to take off his shoes and prostrate himself on the road. Should a commoner offend a *samurai*, the latter was at liberty to slay him with his sword.

When the class system was preserved with so much strictness, people naturally pursued the avocations of the house [family] rather than their own choice. For instance, the carpenter's son became himself a carpenter, and a farmer's children were all brought up to follow the plough. A son who departed from his father's business was despised, and it was taken for granted that he would fail....

In the days when avocations were handed down from father to son and when social ranks were observed strictly, things were bound to be in the negative, and consequently men had to live in contentment and frugality. In such a time a trader, however clever and able, stood no chance of ever becoming a *daimyo*, and if a son should lose his family's property by reason of inordinate ambition, he would be called an unnatural son and be despised by all men. Every man naturally chose to live, under these circumstances, in his ancestral homestead, to engage in his hereditary occupation, and to lead a peaceful life, rather than to run so much risk....

This hermit people, which led such a peaceful and simple life, were happy and contented in spite of the low grade of their material progress, yet the mighty whirlwind of the Restoration, ...could not but crush this policy also. Thus, when old bigoted restrictions were removed and a new world dawned on the principle that where there is genius, there also are position and wealth, how could young people, full of energy and ambition, remain contented in the old homes of their fathers? Everyone, therefore, formed new schemes and attempted new enterprises, and out of the struggle poor people came out millionaires, while many of noble family sank to the rank of a beggar. Peer or commoner, one is now free to do anything and to indulge in any luxury. If one is rich enough, nothing prevents one from living like a king. In a word, the extremely negative age has given place to an extremely positive age.

However, some of our conservative scholars, who take it to heart that the customs and things of Old Japan are daily giving place to Western innovations, cry out that our ancient form must be preserved. Some foreign critics have even been known to say that Japan is losing her peculiar charm year by year, and that the beautiful Eastern paradise is transforming itself into a comical admixture of East and West....

The Japan of the present day gives one the impression that time and space are mixed up in this country, for we see in it a revival of ancient customs and at the same time Western civilization rapidly flowing over the land—in fact, the progress of many centuries and many countries seems to be crammed into one period and one place. Chaos is the avenue to assimilation; unity must needs be preceded by temporary confusion. What Japan has to do is to hammer and weld the civilizations of the two hemispheres and shape them into one harmonious whole. Things may be in disorder for a time, but this cannot be avoided, and after a while magnificent results will be reaped.

Neocolonialism and Revolution in Latin America

A popular slogan among Latin America's politicians, business leaders, and landowners in the late nineteenth century was "order and progress," and to an extent exceptional in the region's history, they achieved both. Around 1870, Latin America's economy entered a period of export-driven expansion that lasted until the 1920s. The region became a major supplier of foodstuffs, coffee, raw rubber, nitrates, copper, tin, and a host of other primary products to Europe and the United States and a major market for European and U.S. manufactured goods. Land prices soared, and English and U.S. capital flowed into Latin America as investments and loans.

Latin America's boom took place in a climate of relative political stability. In Argentina, Chile, and Brazil, this meant republican governments controlled by oligarchies of wealthy ranchers, planters, mine owners, and army officers, sometimes in alliance with businessmen in the import-export trade; in Mexico, Peru, Ecuador, and Venezuela, it meant rule by a dictator *(caudillo)* who also represented the interests of landowners and businessmen. Oligarchs and dictators alike sought economic growth by maintaining law and order, approving land confiscations from the Church and peasantry, and catering to the interests and needs of foreign businesses. They showed little interest in narrowing the gap between the rich and the poor or adhering to constitutional restraints when dealing with political dissent.

In the early twentieth century, Latin America was undergoing significant changes. The United States was replacing Great Britain as the region's leading trading partner. The arrival of millions of immigrants from Asia and Europe, urbanization, and nascent industrialization were reshaping many Latin American societies and increasing dissatisfaction with the political and economic status quo. New voices were raised against the economic and political influence of foreign powers, especially the United States, whose banks were investing many millions of dollars in Latin American enterprises and whose government in the 1890s and early 1900s sent in troops or threatened military force to protect its interests in Chile, Brazil, Nicaragua, Mexico, the Dominican Republic, Haiti, Venezuela, Honduras, and Guatemala. Political tensions throughout the region increased, and in one instance, Mexico, led to revolution.

Economic Dependency
and Its Dangers

◈

16 ◆ Francisco García Calderón,
LATIN AMERICA: ITS RISE AND PROGRESS

For most of the nineteenth century, the United States had relatively little involvement in Latin America. U.S. interests in the region focused almost exclusively on Mexico, whose territories in present-day Texas, California, Arizona and New Mexico became part of the United States after the U.S. victory in the Mexican War of 1846–1848. Other U.S. schemes to annex Cuba, Nicaragua, and the Mexican provinces of Yucatán and Lower California proved impractical or failed to generate support.

U.S.-Latin American relations began to change in the 1880s, however. As the United States became an industrial power, it gradually replaced Great Britain as the region's main purchaser of exports and supplier of manufactured goods. By 1910, U.S. investments in the region had increased to $1.6 billion, almost all of it "new money" invested since the end of the Civil War in 1865. As U.S. businesses expanded their operations in Latin America, successive administrations in Washington pledged to protect their interests. In 1905, President Theodore Roosevelt announced that the United States reserved the right to intervene in the internal affairs of any state in the Western Hemisphere that was guilty of "chronic wrongdoing," a euphemism for a failure to pay its debts or maintain law and order. Roosevelt's successor, William Howard Taft, was even more explicit. He stated that his foreign policy would include "active intervention to secure our merchandise and our capitalists' opportunity for profitable investment." These were not idle words. Between 1898 and 1934, the United States annexed Puerto Rico and intervened militarily in Cuba, Mexico, Guatemala, Honduras, Nicaragua, Panama, Colombia, and the Dominican Republic.

Condemnation of Latin America's economic dependence on foreigners and denunciations of "Yankee imperialism" became commonplace with the onset of the Great Depression, but such criticisms began earlier. One of the first such critics was the Peruvian diplomat and author Francisco García Calderón. Born into a wealthy and politically prominent family in Lima in 1883, García Calderón entered the Peruvian foreign service soon after graduating from the University of San Marcos. A career diplomat with postings to London, Paris, Brussels, and Lisbon, he wrote numerous essays and books on Latin America. His most widely read book was *Latin America: Its Rise and Progress*, which ranged over the region's history and discussed a number of contemporary issues, including immigration, the state of the economy, and Latin America's foreign relations. First published in 1912, it remained in print until the 1920s, having gone through numerous editions in several languages.

Source: Francisco García Calderón, *Latin America: Its Rise and Progress*, trans. Bernard Miall. New York: Charles Scribner's Sons (also London: T. Fisher Unwin, Ltd., 1913), pp. 298, 301–303, 306, 311, 378–382.

QUESTIONS FOR ANALYSIS

1. According to García Calderón, how has U.S. foreign policy toward Latin America evolved since the time of the Monroe Doctrine?
2. How does he explain these changes?
3. According to García Calderón, what benefits have accrued to Latin America as a result of foreign investments? How has Latin America been hurt by such investments?
4. How does García Calderón characterize Latin Americans, and how do they differ from the "Anglo-Saxons" of the United States?
5. How have the Latin American states contributed to their own economic problems?
6. If one accepts the premises of García Calderón's arguments, what would the Latin American states have had to do to overcome the problems connected with foreign economic dependency?

The nation [the United States] which was peopled by nine millions of men in 1820 now numbers eighty millions—an immense demographic power; in the space of ten years, from 1890 to 1900, this population increased by one-fifth. By virtue of its iron, wheat, oil, and cotton, and its victorious industrialism, the democracy aspires to a world-wide significance.... Yankee pride increases with the endless multiplication of wealth and population, and the patriotic sentiment has reached such intensity that it has become transformed into imperialism....

Interventions have become more frequent with the expansion of frontiers. The United States have recently intervened in the territory of Acre [in western Brazil], there to found a republic of rubber gatherers; at Panama, there to develop a province and construct a canal; in Cuba, to maintain order in the interior; in San Domingo, to support the civilizing revolution and overthrow the tyrants; in Venezuela, and in Central America, to enforce upon these nations ...

the political and financial tutelage of imperial democracy. In Guatemala and Honduras the loans concluded with the monarchs of North American finance have reduced the people to a new slavery. Supervision of the customs and the dispatch of pacificatory [peace-keeping] squadrons to defend the interests of the Anglo-Saxon[1] have enforced peace and tranquility: such are the means employed.... Mr. Pierpont Morgan[2] proposes to encompass the finances of Latin America by a vast network of Yankee banks. Chicago merchants and Wall Street financiers created the Meat Trust in the Argentine.... It has even been announced ... that a North American syndicate wished to buy enormous belts of land in Guatemala.... The fortification of the Panama Canal and the possible acquisition of the Galapagos Islands in the Pacific, are fresh manifestations of imperialistic progress.

Unexploited wealth abounds in [Latin] America. A forest of rubber ..., mines of gold

---

[1] A loosely used term, Anglo-Saxon usually refers to people of English descent.

[2] John Pierpont Morgan (1837–1913), founder of the investment bank J. P. Morgan and Company, was one of the wealthiest and most powerful financiers in the United States.

and diamonds; rivers which flow over beds of auriferous [gold-bearing] sand, ... coffee, cocoa, and wheat, whose abundance is such that these products are enough to glut the markets of the world. But there is no national capital [for investment]. This contrast between the wealth of the soil and the poverty of the States gives rise to serious economic problems....

Since the very beginnings of independence the Latin democracies, lacking financial reserves, have had need of European gold.... The necessities of the war [of independence] with Spain and the always difficult task of building up a new society demanded the assistance of foreign gold; loans accumulated.... The lamentable history of these bankrupt democracies dates from this period.

For geographical reasons, and on account of its very inferiority, South America cannot dispense with the influence of the Anglo-Saxon North, with its exuberant wealth and its industries. South America has need of capital, of enterprising men, of bold explorers, and these the United States supply in abundance. The defense of the South should consist in avoiding the establishment of privileges or monopolies, whether in favor of North Americans or Europeans.

The descendants of the Spanish conquerors, who knew nothing of labor or thrift, have incessantly resorted to fresh loans in order to fill the gaps in their budgets. Politicians knew of only one solution of the economic disorder—to borrow, so that little by little the Latin-American countries became actually the financial colonies of Europe.

Economic dependence has a necessary corollary—political servitude. French intervention in Mexico[3] was originally caused by the mass of unsatisfied financial claims; foreigners, the creditors of the State, were in favor of intervention. England and France, who began by seeking to ensure the recovery of certain debts, finally forced a monarch upon the debtor nation. The United States entertained the ambition of becoming the sole creditor of the [Latin] American peoples: this remarkable privilege would have assured them of an incontestable hegemony over the whole continent.

The budgets of various States complicate still further an already difficult situation. They increase beyond all measure, without the slightest relation to the progress made by the nation. They are based upon taxes which are one of the causes of the national impoverishment, or upon a protectionist tariff which adds greatly to the cost of life. The politicians, thinking chiefly of appearances, neglect the development of the national resources for the immediate augmentation of the fiscal revenues; thanks to fresh taxes, the budgets increase. These resources are not employed in furthering profitable undertakings, such as building railroads or highways, or increasing the navigability of the rivers. The bureaucracy is increased in a like proportion, and the budgets, swelled in order to dupe the outside world, serve only to support a nest of parasites. In the economic life of these countries the State is a kind of beneficent providence which ... increases the common poverty by taxation, display, useless enterprises, the upkeep of military and civil officials, and the waste of money borrowed abroad....

---

[3]In 1861, Spain, Great Britain, and France sent troops to Mexico to force the government to pay its debts. After gaining assurances of future payments, Spain and Great Britain withdrew their troops, but Emperor Napoleon III of France went forward with a plan to establish a new Mexican government under French protection. The French-sponsored candidate for emperor of Mexico was Archduke Ferdinand Maximilian of Hapsburg, brother of Austrian emperor Franz Josef. He served as emperor from 1863 to 1865, when the threat of U.S. intervention convinced Napoleon III to abandon his Mexican project.

To sum up, the new continent, politically free, is economically a vassal. This dependence is inevitable; without European capital there would have been no railways, no ports, and no stable government in [Latin] America. But the disorder which prevails in the finances of the country changes into a real servitude what might otherwise have been a beneficial relation.

A Call for Revolution
in Mexico

◈

17 ◆ *Program of the Liberal Party*

When Porfirio Díaz was elected president in 1876, Mexico had no railroads, factories, or significant foreign investment. It had a capital, Mexico City, notorious for floods and epidemics; an outdated silver industry; farms without modern equipment or fertilizers; and a desperately poor population that was 85 percent illiterate. When Díaz left office in 1911, Mexico had an oil industry; fifteen thousand miles of railroads; improved harbors; factories making cement, textiles, furniture, brick, and glass; a modernized silver industry; and a capital, Mexico City, that had a drainage system, electric trams, a new municipal palace, and a splendid national theater. The country still had a desperately poor population that was 85 percent illiterate.

Díaz's almost total disregard for the Mexican people's poverty was one reason why a small but articulate group of Mexicans turned against him in the early 1900s. Another reason was his disregard for the nation's liberal constitution, which he undermined through censorship, manipulation of elections, and the packing of the judiciary and provincial administration with favorites. Around 1900, his opponents began to demand an end to the dictatorship. His boldest critics were the three Flores Magón brothers, Jésus, Ricardo, and Enrique, who attacked the excesses of *Porifismo* in their weekly newspaper, *Regeneración*. After having been arrested three times, they fled across the border to San Antonio and then to St. Louis, where they continued to publish *Regeneración* and have copies smuggled into Mexico. Now dedicated to overthrowing Díaz through revolution, the three brothers and their followers formed the Liberal Party and published its program in 1906. It condemned Díaz for political abuses and outlined a new program of social and economic reform. Widely distributed in Mexico, the program, along with other writings of the Flores Magón brothers, contributed to the growth of the anti-Díaz movement leading up to the outbreak of the Mexican Revolution of 1910.

QUESTIONS FOR ANALYSIS

1. How would you characterize the tone, style, and use of language of the manifesto? What do these aspects of the document tell us about the authors' purposes in composing and distributing it?

Source: Bufe, Chaz and Mitchell Cowen Verter, eds., *Dreams of Freedom: A Ricardo Flores Magon Reader*. Oakland, California: © 2005 AK Press. pp. 125–129, passim. Used by permission of AK Press.

2. What individuals, organizations, and social groups are, according to the manifesto, responsible for the ills of Mexican society?
3. How does the document describe the plight of Mexico's rural and urban workers? How will their situation change after the revolution?
4. What kind of political future for Mexico is envisioned by the manifesto?
5. How does the document respond to the claim that the Liberal Party's goals are "utopian?"

MANIFESTO TO THE NATION: THE PLAN OF THE PARTIDO LIBERAL MEXICANO

Think, Mexicans, of what it would mean for the country if the program of the Partido Liberal Mexicano, today raised like a shining banner, were put into effect—a program calling you to a holy struggle for liberty and justice, to guide your steps along the way of redemption, to show you the luminous goal that you can reach only if you decide to unite your forces in order to stop being slaves. . . .

Everything will change in the future.

Public offices won't be for sycophants and schemers, but for those who, by their merits, make themselves worthy of the public trust; public functionaries won't be these depraved, vicious sultans who are today protected by the dictatorship and authorized to dispose of the homes, lives, and honor of the citizens; on the contrary, they will be men elected by the public to watch over the public's interests, and who, if they don't do so, will have to answer before the same people who had favored them; this disgusting venality that today characterizes the tribunals of justice will disappear, because there will be no dictatorship bestowing judicial robes upon its lackeys, but rather the people will designate with their votes those who administer justice, and because the responsibility of functionaries will not be a myth in the democratic future; the Mexican worker will stop being what he is today—an outcast in his own land; instead he'll be master of his own rights, dignified, free to defend himself from this vile exploitation which today is imposed upon him by

force; he will not have to work more than eight hours per day; he will not receive less than one peso per day; he will have time to rest, to have a good time, to educate himself, and to enjoy various comforts which he could never afford with his present salary of 50, or even 25, centavos per day; there won't be a dictatorship to counsel the capitalists who rob the worker and to protect the foreign forces who answer with a rain of bullets the peaceful petitions of Mexican workers; in contrast we'll have a government that, elected by the people will serve the people and which will watch over its compatriots, without attack from foreign interests, but also without permitting the excesses and abuses so common at present; the vast holdings that the big landowners hold empty and uncultivated will cease being silent and desolate testimony to the sterile power of a man and, collected by the state, will be distributed among those who want to work them; they will be converted into fertile and happy fields which give sustenance to many noble families; there will be lands for all who want to cultivate them, and the wealth they produce will not be for the enjoyment of a boss who puts in not the least effort in producing it, but it will be for the active worker who . . . will bring in the harvest that is his through his sweat and effort; with the throwing from power of the insatiable vampires who today exploit him, and who because of their greed crush him with debts and government loans; taxes will be reduced considerably; now, the fortunes of the government take their leave of the public treasury—when this doesn't happen, there will be a giant savings, and the taxes will have to come down . . . there will be no obligautory military service, this pretext under which the current honchos yank men from their homes because they dislike their prideful attitudes or because they're obstacles to the desires of the corrupt little tyrants to their abusing helpless women; education will be widespread, which is the basis of the betterment of all peoples; the clergy, this unrepentant traitor, this subject of Rome, this irreconcilable enemy of native liberties, in place of finding tyrants to serve and from whom to receive protection, will find instead inflexible laws which will put a limit on their excesses and which will confine them to the religious sphere; the expression of ideas will find no unjustifiable restrictions which impede the free judgment of civic men . . . and public peace will stop being a pretext under which governments persecute their enemies; all liberties will be restored to the people and not only will the citizens have won their political rights, but also a great economic improvement; not only will there be a triumph over tyranny, but also a triumph over misery. Liberty, prosperity: here is the synthesis of the program. . . .

Utopia! A dream! shout those who, hiding their terror through abject rationalizations, intend to stop the popular reclamations so as not to lose a lucrative post or a less-than-clean business. It's the old refrain of all of those who resist the great advances of the peoples; it's the eternal defense of infamy. They call "utopian" what is redemptory in order that it be attacked or destroyed; all those who have attacked our wise constitution[1] have wanted to excuse themselves by saying that it's unrealizable; today the lackeys of Porfirio Díaz repeat this thing necessary to hiding the crimes of the tyrant, and these miserable persons do not remember that

this constitution, which they call so utopian, so inadequate for our people, so impossible to put into practice, was perfectly realizable under noble rulers like Juárez and Lerdo de Tejada.[2] For evildoers, good must be unrealizable; for the cunning, honor must be unrealizable. The mouthpieces of despotism judge that the program of the Partido Liberal is impractical and even absurd; but you, Mexicans who aren't blinded by convenience nor by fear; you, noble men who desire the good of the country, will come to the simple realization of how much rudimentary justice this program contains.

Mexicans:

Upon the proclamation of its program by the Partido Liberal, with the inflexible purpose of putting it into practice, you are invited to take part in this great and redemptory work which must be in order to have forever a free, respectable happy country.

The decision is irrevocable. The Partido Liberal will fight without rest to fillfill the solemn promise that it makes today to the people, and there will be no obstacle that it will not overcome, nor any sacrifice that it will not accept to achieve its end. Today we call you to follow its banners, to fill its ranks, to augment its strength, and to make less difficult and less painful the victory. If you listen to the call and come to the post that befits your duty as Mexicans, you'll have a lot to thank the party for, since you'll be working for your own redemption; if you see with indifference the holy struggle to which we invite you, if you refuse to aid those who fight for right and justice, if through egotism or timidness you make

---

[1]A reference to the Constitution of 1857, a liberal constitution that gave birth to the Second Federal Republic of Mexico. It established individual rights such as freedoms of speech, conscience, the press, and assembly. It limited the powers of the Roman Catholic Church, reaffirmed the abolition of slavery, eliminated debtor prisons, and eliminated all forms of cruel and unusual punishment, including the death penalty. It established a republic with an elected general assembly. The constitution was suspended on several

occasions and ignored during much of the presidency of Porfirio Díaz.

[2]Benito Juárez (1806–1872), a Zapotec Indian, was president of Mexico for five terms between 1858 and 1872. He led liberal forces in the Reform War (1858–1861) and fought against the Austrian-born Emperor Maximilian, who had been placed on the Mexican throne by the French in 1864. Lerdo de Tejada (1823–1889), also a liberal, succeeded Sebastián Juárez as president, serving from 1872 to 1876.

yourselves accomplices of those who oppress us, the country owes you nothing other than contempt, and your rebellious conscience will never stop shaming you with the memory of your failure. Those who refuse to support the cause of liberty deserve to be slaves.

Mexicans:

Between that which despotism offers you and that which the program of the Partido Liberal offers you, choose! If you want shackles, misery, humiliation before foreigners, the grey life of the debased outcast, support the dictatorship which gives you all of this; if you prefer liberty, economic improvement, the raising up of the Mexican citizenry, the noble life of the man who is master of himself, come to the Partido Liberal that fraternizes with the noble and the virile, and join your efforts with those of all of us who fight for justice, to hurry the arrival of the radiant day on which tyranny will fall forever and the awaited democracy will surge forth with all the splendor of a star which never ceases shining brilliantly on the clear horizon of our country.

Reform, Liberty, and Justice.

PART TWO

Decades of War, Economic Upheaval, and Revolution, 1914–1939

When war came to Europe in the summer of 1914, many welcomed the conflict. Politicians hoped it would provide a respite from strikes, class antagonisms, socialist agitation, and suffragist demands. Generals looked forward to implementing their plans for rapid mobilization and quick victory; nationalists dreamed of settling old scores. Young men with dull jobs in shops or offices envisioned excitement, heroism, and being part of a great cause. Not a few philosophers and poets were sure that the war would rouse men from apathy, ennoble them, and inspire them to acts of self-sacrifice and courage; it would weed out the unfit, ensure a place for the strong, and thus contribute to human progress.

Those who were hoping for war got their wish, but as they soon learned, it was not the war they wanted. The short war promised by leaders became an unendurable four-year struggle in which the cheers, rousing marches, resplendent uniforms, and gleaming weapons of the first few weeks gave way to a reality of rat-infested trenches, land mines, shell shock, poison gas, barbed wire, suicide charges against machine-gun nests, massive battles that changed nothing, and unbearably long casualty lists. By the end of 1914, German and French forces had combined casualties of 300,000 dead and 600,000 wounded, and this was only a foretaste of the war's final toll: 65 to 75 million men mobilized; close to 10 million killed; 22 million wounded, of whom 7 million were permanently disabled. Costs were immense. In 1920, the Carnegie Endowment for International Peace put the war's direct and indirect costs at $338 billion (close to $3.6 trillion in 2011 dollars), a figure so high that errors of plus or minus several billions of dollars are insignificant. Such sacrifice might have been bearable if the war had settled anything, if it had "made the world safe for democracy," or at least had enabled the belligerents to return to prewar "normalcy" once it was over. Instead, it was the first in a series of events that ended with an even more terrible catastrophe, World War II.

The post–World War I treaties, dictated by the winners at the Paris Peace Conference, were soon censured for being too harsh or too lenient, too idealistic or too hard-headed. In any case, they failed. They fed old grievances, created new problems, and within fifteen years were being ignored. Economic disaster struck winners and losers alike. War debts and reparations entangled international finance; inflation ruined the middle class in Germany and Austria; sagging prices plagued farmers; and unemployment remained high, even during the "Roaring Twenties." Then the Great Depression struck in the 1930s, and with international trade halved and unemployment at all-time highs, capitalism's demise seemed imminent. The future of liberal democracy looked no brighter. Dictators replaced parliaments in much of Europe, and surviving democracies seemed flabby and weak compared to the dynamic new fascist and totalitarian regimes. Such was the sorry record of a civilization that only a few years earlier had regarded its institutions and values as the pinnacle of human achievement.

While the industrialized nations lurched from one crisis to another, Asia, Africa, and Latin America continued to struggle with problems of colonialism, economic dependency, and political instability. The war itself had a wide-ranging impact. It spurred industrialization in Japan, India, and Latin America when European factories could no longer supply overseas markets. Its senseless slaughter weakened colonialism by undermining the West's claims to moral superiority. The postwar treaties redrew the map of the Middle East by demolishing the Ottoman Empire, and they had provisions that angered Africans, Arabs, Chinese, and Indians by ignoring their interests despite contributions to the Allied cause.

The Great Depression also was a calamity for the nonindustrialized world. As factories closed in Europe and the United States, demand for raw materials plummeted. By 1932, cotton was selling at one-third, and raw rubber at one-fourth, their pre-1929 prices. Prices for Malayan tin, Chilean copper, and South African diamonds all plunged. Agricultural prices also were hard hit. The price of basic grains sank to historic lows, with rice growers and wheat farmers especially hard hit. Everywhere, unemployment grew, poverty deepened, and demand for European- and U.S.-manufactured goods slumped, accelerating the downward cycle of an imploding world economy.

Reaction to the Great Depression varied in the non-Western world. In Japan, economic hardship strengthened hard-line nationalists who trumpeted the benefits of imperialist expansion. In Latin America, it elicited a variety of political responses, mostly authoritarian, and inspired efforts to end the region's dependency on foreign manufactures. Throughout colonial Africa and Asia, it unified educated elites, peasants, and factory workers in opposition to colonial regimes that had created the system of export dependency and did nothing to fix it when it collapsed. From the East Indies to Africa, strikes, mass demonstrations, and the emergence of popular nationalist leaders were signs of increasingly restive colonial populations.

Many nationalist leaders, especially in Asia, became communists. This link between anticolonialism and Marxism is another example of how events in Europe—in this case the Russian Revolution of 1917—influenced non-Western politics. Impressed by a revolution that had taken place in a backward agrarian society and by the apparent success of Soviet economic planning in the 1930s, increasing numbers of Africans, Asians, and Latin Americans saw Marxism/Leninism as a weapon to end capitalism and colonialism alike. The strongest communist movement was in China, where in the 1930s the Communist Party under Mao Zedong battled Chiang Kai-shek's Nationalists in a prolonged civil war.

The communists ultimately won the civil war in China, and nationalists throughout Asia and Africa won the struggle for freedom and independence. In each case, World War II played a key role. But without World War I and the tumultuous events of the 1920s and 1930s, neither victory would have been possible.

CHAPTER 3

World War I and Its Global Significance

What if the Serb nationalist Gavrilo Princip had failed to assassinate Archduke Franz Ferdinand of Austria-Hungary in Sarajevo? What if German diplomats had discouraged their ally Austria-Hungary from its plan to invade Serbia for its government's alleged part in the crime? What if the Austro-Hungarians had abandoned their war plans when the Serbs accepted almost all the terms of the Austro-Hungarian ultimatum on July 25? What if Great Britain had made its proposal for a Great Power conference to mediate the crisis early in July, and not on July 26, when chances of success were minimal? What if European statesman had better understood what modern war was like and had worked harder to preserve the peace?

What if World War I had never happened?

Answers to such questions are impossible, but one thing is certain. Without World War I, twentieth-century history would have been different—profoundly so. World War I has been described as a turning point, a watershed, and a great divide between two eras. All of these descriptions are accurate. Between 1914 and 1918, the war killed or wounded almost thirty million human beings. After the killing stopped, it continued to put its stamp on all that followed.

In Europe, World War I was a prelude to political disaster. In the short run, it triggered the Russian Revolution of 1917, which in turn raised the specter of communism in the rest of Europe and played into the hands of right-wing dictators who promised to smash the "red menace." In the longer run, the war raised doubts about the wisdom of elected officials, eroded support for parliamentary governments, and thus contributed to the demise of liberalism and democracy in much of Europe in the 1920s and 1930s. The war fostered regimentation, encouraged the use of propaganda, made demands for total obedience and total commitment for soldiers and civilians alike, and transformed politics into a moral crusade. It created new grievances and resentments, and stirred unresolved hatreds that played into the hands of demagogues who offered seductive and simplistic solutions to complex problems. In all these ways it prepared the way for fascism and totalitarianism.

World War I also contributed to the economic catastrophes of the 1920s and 1930s. Without the massive borrowing to pay for the war, the inflation of the early 1920s might not have occurred. Without reparations and war debts, international financial markets might have avoided their unhealthy dependence on U.S. loans and capital in the 1920s, a situation that spelled disaster after the U.S. stock market crash of 1929. Without the expansion of agricultural production outside of Europe during the war, the surpluses of the 1920s might have been avoided along with the slump in farm incomes.

The war's impact stretched well beyond Europe. It encouraged colonized peoples to question the superiority and invulnerability of their European masters. It aroused nationalism by drafting colonial subjects from Africa and Asia into the fighting and then by dashing their hopes for greater self-rule once the war was over. It also planted seeds of doubt among Europeans about their capacity to rule.

But Gavrilo Princip did assassinate Archduke Franz Ferdinand; Germany offered Austria-Hungary a "blank check," not words of restraint; Austria-Hungary disregarded Serbia's response to its ultimatum; Great Britain's proposal for a Great Powers conference came too late. Statesmen could not prevent the Sarajevo crisis from becoming a war.

◆

The Trauma of the Trenches

Wars by their very nature are unpredictable, but rarely was the gap between expectations and reality greater than in World War I. Generals and politicians alike promised a short war. A few quick campaigns and a few decisive victories would "bring the boys home by Christmas," perhaps even by the fall. These victories would be won by tactics still inspired by the French commander Napoleon Bonaparte (1769–1821), who had taught that rapid troop movement, surprise, massive artillery fire, and huge infantry and cavalry charges were the keys to battlefield success. Élan and spirit would conquer all obstacles.

This was the war that soldiers anticipated as they marched off to what they imagined would be glorious adventure—an opportunity to fight for the flag or, Kaiser or queen, to wear colorful uniforms, and to win glory on the battlefield. The war they fought was nothing like the war they envisioned. After the Germans had almost taken Paris early in the fighting, the western front became the scene of a stalemate that lasted until the armistice on November 11, 1918. Along a four-hundred-mile line stretching from the English Channel through Belgium and France to the Swiss border, defense—a combination of trenches, barbed wire, land mines, poison gas, and machine guns—proved superior to offense—massive artillery barrages followed by charges of troops across no man's land to overrun enemy lines. Such attacks resulted in numbingly long casualty lists, but gains of territory that were measured in yards not miles.

There are many reasons why Europeans found World War I so demoralizing, so unsettling, and so devoid of any aspect or outcome that might have justified its costs. The disparity between expectations and reality—the theme of the sources in this section—is one of them.

The Romance of War

❖

18 ◆ *POPULAR ART AND POSTER ART FROM GERMANY, ENGLAND, AUSTRALIA, AND FRANCE*

By December 1914, the muddy reality of stalemate had replaced bright dreams of quick victory, and as casualties mounted, shock replaced enthusiasm. Governments no longer could rely on that early burst of patriotic fervor to ensure that men would volunteer, soldiers would reenlist, and citizens would buy war bonds and stoically endure food and fuel shortages. All sides therefore tried to prop up morale through censorship and propaganda. Press reports distorted casualty statistics, misrepresented troop morale, downplayed the hardships of trench warfare, and even described nonexistent victories in which troops overran enemy lines while brandishing swords. Ministries of propaganda churned out broadsheets and circulars describing the enemy's unreasonable war aims and atrocities. They also covered walls with thousands of posters that with their bright colors, catchy designs, and positive messages encouraged citizens to enlist, buy bonds, save fuel, start vegetable plots, and donate money to care for wounded veterans. Casualty lists and stories from soldiers on leave belied the messages of the broadsheets and posters, and as people came to recognize them for what they were—government-sponsored distortions—cynicism about the war deepened.

The four illustrations in this section portray the positive attitudes toward the war that all belligerents shared at the outset and which governments sought to perpetuate as the war dragged on. The first, *The Departure*, shows a German troop train departing for the front in the late summer or fall of 1914. Printed originally in the German periodical *Simplicissimus* in March 1915, it is the work of Bruno Wennerberg, a Swedish-born artist who moved permanently to Germany in 1898 and died there in 1950. That *Simplicissimus* published such an illustration shows the strength of nationalism at the war's start. Noted before the war for its irreverent satire and criticism of German militarism, *Simplicissimus*, on a decision by its editors, abandoned its antiestablishment stance and lent full support to the war effort.

The second illustration is from a series of cards an English firm, the Mitchell Tobacco Company, included in its packs of Golden Dawn cigarettes early in the war. It shows a sergeant offering smokes to his soldiers before battle. Tobacco advertising with military themes reached a saturation point in England during the war.

The third illustration is an Australian recruitment poster issued from 1915. Although Australia controlled its domestic affairs, Great Britain still managed its foreign policy, and hence when Great Britain went to war in 1914, so did Australia. The Australian parliament refused to approve conscription, however, so the government had to work hard to encourage volunteers. This poster appeared in 1915, when Australian troops were heavily involved in the Gallipoli campaign, the Allied effort to knock Ottoman Turkey out of the war. Appealing to members of sports clubs, it promised young men the opportunity to enlist in a battalion made up entirely of fellow sportsmen.

The fourth illustration, a poster from France, was designed to encourage the purchase of war bonds, which were sold by all major belligerents to finance the war. It appeared in 1916 during the German offensive at Verdun, which lasted from February to November and resulted in more than five hundred thousand French casualties. The French soldier shouts, "On les aura!" ("We'll get them!")— words ascribed to General Henri-Philippe Pétain, who was in charge of the Verdun defense until he was given command of all French armies in the field in the summer of 1916.

QUESTIONS FOR ANALYSIS

1. What messages about the war does each of the four illustrations communicate?
2. In what specific ways does each of them romanticize war and the life of a soldier?
3. What impressions of combat do the English tobacco card and the French war bond poster communicate?
4. What does Wennerberg's painting suggest about women's anticipated role in the war?

B. Wennerberg, The Departure

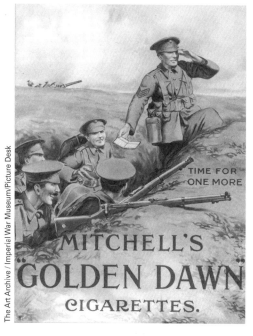

Advertisement card from Golden Dawn cigarettes

Australian recruitment poster (1915)

French poster encouraging purchase of war bonds (1916)

The Reality of War in Verse

❖

19 ◆ Wilfred Owen, *DULCE ET DECORUM EST and DISABLED*

So great was the carnage of World War I that no historian has captured its horror as vividly as have the poets and novelists who experienced it. Every major belligerent nation had writers who evoked the desolation and inhumanity of trench warfare. Among the most powerful was the British poet Wilfred Owen (1893–1918), who enlisted in the British army in 1915 at the age of 22. Wounded in 1917, he was hospitalized, released, and sent back to the trenches, where he was killed on November 4, 1918, one week before the armistice. His poem, "Dulce et Decorum Est," written in 1915, takes its title from a line by the ancient Roman poet Horace: "It is sweet and fitting to die for one's country." Its subject is a poison gas attack. The Germans launched the first large-scale gas attack in April 1915 when they released chlorine gas from cylinders and let the wind carry it toward French and Canadian troops in the vicinity of Ypres. Subsequently, both sides used poison gas, with phosgene and mustard gas being delivered by artillery shells by 1918. "Disabled," also written in 1915, describes a badly mutilated Scottish soldier who enlisted before he was eighteen, and now sits in a wheelchair in an institution where he survives, but barely.

QUESTIONS FOR ANALYSIS

1. How in "Dulce et Decorum Est" does Owen describe the mental and physical condition of the foot soldiers?
2. What imagery does he apply to the body of the gas victim?
3. Why does Owen find the plight of the young Scottish soldier so compelling?
4. In what specific ways do Owen's poems attempt to dispel the illusions about war represented in the art in the previous section?

DULCE ET DECORUM EST

Bent double, like old beggars under sacks,
Knock-kneed, coughing like hags, we cursed
    through sludge,
Till on the haunting flares we turned our backs
And towards our distant rest began the trudge.
Men marched asleep. Many had lost their boots
But limped on, blood-shod. All went lame;
    all blind;

Drunk with fatigue; deaf even to the hoots
Of tired, outstripped Five-Nines[1] that dropped
    behind.

Gas! GAS! Quick, boys! — An ecstasy of
    fumbling,
Fitting the clumsy helmets just in time;
But someone still was yelling out and
    stumbling,
And flound'ring like a man in fire or lime . . .

---

[1]Slang for artillery shells used by the Germans.

Dim, through the misty panes and thick green
    light,
As under a green sea, I saw him drowning.
In all my dreams, before my helpless sight,
He plunges at me, guttering, choking, drowning.

If in some smothering dreams you too
    could pace
Behind the wagon that we flung him in,
And watch the white eyes writhing in his face,
His hanging face, like a devil's sick of sin;
If you could hear, at every jolt, the blood
Come gargling from the froth-corrupted lungs,
Obscene as cancer, bitter as the cud
Of vile, incurable sores on innocent tongues, —
My friend, you would not tell with such
    high zest,
To children ardent for some desperate glory,
The old Lie: Dulce et decorum est
Pro patria mori.

DISABLED

He sat in a wheeled chair, waiting for dark,
And shivered in his ghastly suit of grey,
Legless, sewn short at elbow. Through the park
Voices of boys rang saddening like a hymn,
Voices of play and pleasure after day,
Till gathering sleep had mothered them
    from him.

About this time Town used to swing so gay
When glow-lamps budded in the light
    blue trees,
And girls glanced lovelier as the air grew
    dim, —
In the old times, before he threw away
    his knees.
Now he will never feel again how slim
Girls' waists are, or how warm their subtle
    hands.
All of them touch him like some queer disease.

There was an artist silly for his face,
For it was younger than his youth, last year.
Now, he is old; his back will never brace;
He's lost his colour very far from here,
Poured it down shell-holes till the veins
    ran dry,
And half his lifetime lapsed in the hot race
And leap of purple spurted from his thigh.

One time he liked a bloodsmear down his leg,
After the matches, carried shoulder-high.
It was after football, when he'd drunk a peg,
He thought he'd better join. — He wonders
    why.
Someone had said he'd look a god in kilts.
That's why; and maybe, too, to please his Meg,
Aye, that was it, to please the giddy jilts[2]
He asked to join. He didn't have to beg;
Smiling they wrote his lie; aged nineteen
    years.
Germans he scarcely thought of; all their guilt
And Austria's, did not move him. And no fears
Of Fear came yet. He thought of jewelled hilts
For daggers in plaid socks; of smart salutes;
And care of arms; and leave, and pay arrears;
Esprit de corps; and hints for young recruits.
And soon, he was drafted out with drums
    and cheers.

Some cheered him home, but not as crowds
    cheer Goal.
Only a solemn man who brought him fruits
Thanked him; and then inquired about his soul.

Now, he will spend a few sick years in institutes,
And do what things the rules consider wise,
And take whatever pity they may dole.
Tonight he noticed how the women's eyes
Passed from him to the strong men that were
    whole.
How cold and late it is! Why don't they come
And put him to bed? Why don't they come?

---

[2]Scottish slang for young girls.

Genocide in Eastern Turkey

"A coordinated plan of different actions aiming at the destruction of the essential foundations of the life of national groups, with the aim of annihilating the groups themselves." This was the chilling definition of a new word "genocide," coined in 1944 by the Polish lawyer and author Raphael Lemkin in his book *Axis Rule in Occupied Europe.* Lemkin used the word to describe the Nazis' extermination of Gypsies, Poles, Russians, and Jews during World War II, but his interest in the phenomenon of planned mass killings of ethnic or religious groups goes back to 1933, when he led a campaign to convince the Legal Council of the League of Nations to define what he called "crimes of barbarity" as a violation of international law. The crimes he had in mind had occurred in eastern Turkey during World War I and had resulted in the deaths of anywhere from six hundred thousand to more than a million Armenians.

The Ottoman government's campaign against its Armenian subjects was not the twentieth century's first genocide. That distinction belongs to the German campaign against the rebellious Herero people of German South-West Africa between 1904 and 1907, when General Lothar von Trotha sought to annihilate the Herero by executing all males and driving women and children into the desert, where they were expected to die of starvation or thirst. The massacre of Armenians, however, was the first such "crime of barbarity" to draw worldwide attention.

Armenians, who since the seventh century B.C.E. had lived in the region south of the Caucasus Mountains and between the Black and Caspian seas, became Christians around 300, and over time developed a distinctive Armenian Apostolic Church. The Armenian heartland was captured by the Ottoman Turks in the sixteenth century and, except for a portion taken over by Russia in 1828, remained under Ottoman rule until the empire's demise. Numbering slightly more than two million, Armenians, like other non-Muslim groups in the Ottoman Empire, were allowed to practice their religion and maintain their distinctive culture. However, they paid special taxes and were excluded from government posts.

During the nineteenth century, tensions worsened between Armenians and the empire's Muslims, many of whom resented that the Armenian community was experiencing a cultural and economic renaissance while the Ottoman Empire itself was falling apart. Many Armenians took advantage of the education offered by schools founded by U.S. and European missionaries, and increasing numbers of Armenians went abroad to study at Russian or European universities to prepare for careers in trade, industry, and banking. Muslim-Armenian relations deteriorated further when moderate Armenian leaders began to call for greater political autonomy and radical nationalists campaigned for independence.

Against this background, attacks on Armenians increased in the late 1800s, culminating in the massacre of as many as one hundred thousand Armenians by Ottoman troops between 1894 and 1896. Sultan Abdulhamid II, who ordered these massacres (or, according to some interpretations, stood by idly while they occurred), was overthrown in 1909, an event that brought to power the Young Turks, or the Committee of Union and Progress. To jealousy, religious antagonism, and political fears, the Young Turks added another ingredient to the anti-Armenian mix—nationalism. Rejecting the ethnic and religious pluralism of the Ottoman Empire, they favored an exclusively Turkish state in which Armenians would have no place.

Events in World War I, in which Turkey was allied with Germany, led directly to the Armenian genocide. By early 1915, a Turkish offensive against Russia in the Caucasus, in which some Armenians had aided the Russians by providing intelligence and attacking Muslims, had failed. With the Allies poised to launch a campaign to take the Dardanelles in the spring of 1915, Minister of Internal Affairs Talaat Pasha and Minister of War Enver Pasha sought to make the Armenians scapegoats for military defeats. On the night of April 23–24, 1915, scores of Armenian churchmen, intellectuals, educators, and business owners were arrested in Istanbul, sent to the countryside, and executed. Then in June Turkish leaders sought to stabilize the military situation in eastern Anatolia by deporting the Armenians who lived there. The Armenian genocide had begun.

Caravans of Death

❖

20 ◆ Mary L. Graffam,
LETTER FROM TURKEY, SUMMER 1915

Like the Nazi effort to exterminate Europe's Jews, the Turkish attempt to obliterate the Armenians took place under the cover of a world war, thus minimizing the chance of outside intervention. In the case of the Nazis, the outside world was unable to grasp the enormity of their crimes until the closing stages of the war. This was not the case in Turkey. With the United States still neutral in 1915, thousands of American missionaries, diplomats, and businesspeople resided in Turkey, and as a result, newspaper accounts, reports to U.S. Ambassador Henry Morgenthau, and hundreds of personal letters detailed the massacres. Germans and visitors from other neutral nations also provided testimony.

Witnesses described how in the wake of the arrests of April 23–24, Armenian soldiers in the Turkish army were disarmed, placed in labor battalions, or simply shot. Men were executed by Turkish troops, police, or local Turks and Kurds, while women, children, and old men were driven from their homes and preyed upon by bandits and local people as they marched for weeks over mountains and deserts toward the Syrian Desert or the swampy regions of the upper Euphrates

Source: Graffam Letter: "Letter Written by Miss Mary L. Graffam," in Arnold Toynbee, ed., *The Treatment of Armenians in the Ottoman Empire, 1915–1916* (London: Joseph Causten and Sons, 1916), 305–309.

River. When they reached their destinations, more perished from heat, starvation, and disease.

The following is typical of the many letters written by foreign eyewitnesses and later published in newspapers, missionary journals, or Armenian-language publications outside of Turkey. The author is Mary L. Graffam, a Protestant missionary from Massachusetts who was principal of a girls' school in Sivas, a city in north-central Turkey. It reveals the confusion and disbelief that attended the early deportations. Although the letter is undated, the events it describes took place in July 1915.

QUESTIONS FOR ANALYSIS

1. What can be learned from Graffam's letter about the motives of those who attacked the Armenians?
2. What evidence does the letter provide about the ways different groups of Armenians were treated?
3. The author is uncertain about the government's responsibility for ordering the massacres. What experiences did she have that help explain her uncertainty?
4. What do you make of the efforts of government officials to separate Graffam from the Armenian deportees? How does your answer relate to the issue raised in Question 3?

When we were ready to leave Sivas, the Government gave forty-five ox-carts for the Protestant townspeople and eighty horses, but none at all for our pupils and teachers; so we bought ten ox-carts, two horse arabas [wagons], and five or six donkeys, and started out. In the company were all our teachers in the college, about twenty boys from the college and about thirty of the girls'-school. It was as a special favour to the Sivas people, who had not done anything revolutionary, that the Vali [provincial governor] allowed the men who were not yet in prison to go with their families.

The first night we were so tired that we just ate a piece of bread and slept on the ground wherever we could find a place to spread a yorgan [blanket]. It was after dark when we stopped, anyway. We were so near Sivas that the gendarmes [armed rural police] protected us, and no special harm was done; but the second night we began to see what was before us. The gendarmes would go ahead and have long conversations with the villagers, and then stand back and let them rob and trouble the people until we all began to scream, and then they would come and

drive them away. Yorgans and rugs, and all such things, disappeared by the dozen, and donkeys were sure to be lost. Many had brought cows; but from the first day those were carried off, one by one, until not a single one remained.

We got accustomed to being robbed, but the third day a new fear took possession of us, and that was that the men were to be separated from us at Kangal. . . . Our teacher from Mandjaluk was there, with his mother and sisters. They had left the village with the rest of the women and children, and when they saw that the men were being taken off to be killed the teacher fled to another village, four hours away, where he was found by the police and brought safely with his family to Kangal, because the tchaoush [officer] who had taken them from Mandjaluk wanted his sister. I found them confined in one room. I went to the Kaimakam [district official] and got an order for them all to come with us.

At Kangal some Armenians had become Mohammedans, and had not left the village, but the others were all gone. . . . ? They said that a valley near there was full of corpses. At Kangal we also began to see exiles from Tokat. The sight was one to strike horror to any heart; they were a company of old women, who had been robbed of absolutely everything. At Tokat the Government had first imprisoned the men, and from the prison had taken them on the road.... After the men had gone, they arrested the old women and the older brides, perhaps about thirty or thirty-five years old. There were very few young women or children. All the younger women and children were left in Tokat...

When we looked at them we could not imagine that even the sprinkling of men that were with us would be allowed to remain. We did not long remain in doubt; the next day we had come to Hassan Tehelebi, and it was with terror in our hearts that we passed through that village about noon. But we encamped and ate our supper in peace, and even began to think that perhaps it was not so, when the Mudir [the official in charge] came round with gendarmes and began to collect the men.... The night passed, and only one man came back to tell the story of how every man was compelled to give up all his money, and all were taken to prison. The next morning they collected the men who had escaped the night before and extorted forty-five liras from our company, on the promise that they would give us gendarmes to protect us. One "company" is supposed to be from 1,000 to 3,000 persons. Ours was perhaps 2,000, and the greatest number of gendarmes would be five or six....

Broken-hearted, the women continued their journey....

As soon as the men left us, the Turkish drivers began to rob the women, saying: "You are all going to be thrown into the Tokma Su, [a local river] so you might as well give your things to us, and then we will stay by you and try to protect you." Every Turkish woman that we met said the same thing. The worst were the gendarmes, who really did more or less bad things. One of our schoolgirls was carried off by the Kurds twice, but her companions made so much fuss that she was brought back....

As we approached the bridge over the Tokma Su, it was certainly a fearful sight. As far as the eye could see over the plain was this slow-moving line of ox-carts. For hours there was not a drop of water on the road, and the sun poured down its very hottest. As we went on we began to see the dead from yesterday's company, and the weak began to fall by the way. The Kurds working in the fields made attacks continually, and we were half-distracted. I piled as many as I could on our wagons, and our pupils, both boys and girls, worked like heroes. One girl took a baby from its dead mother and carried it until evening. Another carried a dying woman until she died.... I counted forty-nine deaths, but there must have been many more. One naked body of a woman was covered with bruises. I saw the Kurds robbing the bodies of those not yet entirely dead....

The hills on each side were white with Kurds, who were throwing stones on the Armenians, who were slowly wending their way to the bridge. I ran ahead and stood on the bridge in the midst of a crowd of Kurds, until I was used up [exhausted]. I did not see anyone thrown into the water, but they said, and I believe it, that a certain Elmas, who has done handwork for me for years, was thrown over the bridge by a Kurd. Our badvelli's [pastor's] wife was riding on a horse with a baby in her arms, and a Kurd took hold of her to throw her over, when another Kurd said: "She has a baby in her arms," and they let her go....

The police for the first time began to interfere with me here, and it was evident that something was decided about me. The next morning after we arrived at this bridge, they wanted me to go to Malatia; but I insisted that I had permission to stay with the Armenians. During the day, however, they said that [I had been ordered] to come to Malatia, and that the others were going to Kiakhta. In Malatia I went at once to the commandant, a captain who they say has made a fortune out of these exiles. I told him how I had gone to Erzeroum last winter and how we pitied these women and children and wished to help them, and finally he sent me to the Mutessarif [district official]. The latter is a Kurd, apparently anxious to do the right thing; but he has been sick most of the time since he came, and the "beys" [Kurdish chiefs] here have had things more or less their own way, and certainly horrors have been committed....

My friends here are very glad to have me with them, for they have a very difficult problem on their hands and are nearly crazy with the horrors they have been through here. The Mutessarif and other officials here and at Sivas have read me orders from Constantinople [Istanbul] again and again to the effect that the lives of these exiles are to be protected, and from their actions I should judge that they must have received such orders; but they certainly have murdered a great many in every city. Here there were great trenches dug by the soldiers for drilling purposes. Now these trenches are all filled up, and our friends saw carts going back from the city by night. A man I know told me that when he was out to inspect some work he was having done, he saw a dead body which had evidently been pulled out of one of these trenches, probably by dogs.... The Beledia Reis [village chief] here says that every male over ten years old is being murdered, that not one is to live, and no woman over fifteen.

An Official Version of the Deportations

❖

21 ◆ Talaat Pasha, *POSTHUMOUS MEMOIRS*

At the conclusion of the war, officials of the Ottoman government and Great Britain declared their intention to punish the perpetrators of the Armenian genocide. Ottoman courts ordered the execution of two minor officials and one police officer, but other guilty parties were given prison sentences or convicted in absentia. Judicial proceedings were halted and all prisoners released when the Ottoman government was replaced by a new Turkish government under Mustafa Kemal in 1921. Also in 1921, British efforts to try Turkish officials in British military courts, already bogged down by legal and political difficulties, were abandoned. Throughout the process, efforts to punish those responsible were weakened by the fact that in November 1918 Turkey's wartime leaders fled the country and hence could not be tried in person.

Among those who fled was Talaat Pasha (1874–1921), the Ottoman minister of the interior during the war. Although the precise lines of authority in the Ottoman government are murky, there is little question that Talaat Pasha, along with Enver Pasha (minister of war) and Kemal Pasha (navy minister and military governor of Syria), were the key figures in the wartime administration. There is also little doubt that Talaat and Enver were mainly responsible for the government's Armenian policy. After he fled Turkey in 1918, Talaat lived in Europe until he was assassinated by an Armenian student in a Berlin suburb in 1921. The assassin was acquitted when a German court ruled that his act was justifiable homicide in view of Talaat's role in the 1915 massacres.

Before his death, Talaat had written a memoir that was unpublished at the time of his assassination. After his assassin's acquittal, Talaat's wife released the memoir to a Turkish newspaper. It was published in 1921 with the enigmatic opening words, "I do not tell all the truth, but all I tell is truth." In the following section, he gives his perspective on the Armenian question.

Source: Talaat Pasha: Talaat Pasha, "Posthumous Memoirs," *Current History,* Vol. 15, No. 1, pp. 294–295.

QUESTIONS FOR ANALYSIS

1. In what ways were the Armenians responsible for their own deportation, according to Talaat Pasha?
2. How credible do you find Talaat's arguments about the Armenians' responsibility for their fate?
3. How would you characterize Talaat's portrayal of his role in the massacres? Does he admit personal responsibility for the massacres?
4. Why, in Talaat's view, have the numbers of victims been exaggerated?
5. How and in what ways are Talaat's assertions confirmed or refuted by evidence provided in Graffam's letter?

The deportation of the Armenians, in some localities of the Greeks, and in Syria of some of the Arabs, was used inside and outside the empire as a source of attack on the Turkish Government. First of all, I wish to inform the public that the rumors of deportation and assassination were exceedingly exaggerated. The Greeks and the Armenians, taking advantage of the ignorance of the American and European public of the Near Eastern situation and of the character of the Turks, used the deportation as a means for propaganda, and painted it as best suited their aim. In saying this, I do not mean to deny the facts. I desire only to eliminate the exaggerations and to relate the facts as they occurred.

I admit that we deported many Armenians from our eastern provinces, but we never acted in this matter upon a previously prepared scheme. The responsibility for these acts falls first of all upon the deported people themselves. Russia, in order to lay hand on our eastern provinces, had armed and equipped the Armenian inhabitants of this district, and had organized strong Armenian bandit forces in the said area. When we entered the great war, these bandits began their destructive activities in the rear of the Turkish Army on the Caucasus front, blowing up the bridges, setting fire to the Turkish towns and

villages and killing the innocent Mohammedan [Muslim] inhabitants, regardless of age and sex. They spread death and terror all over the eastern provinces, and endangered the Turkish Army's line of retreat. All these Armenian bandits were helped by the native Armenians. When they were pursued by the Turkish gendarmes, the Armenian villages were a refuge for them. When they needed help, the Armenian peasants around them, taking their arms hidden in their churches, ran to their aid. Every Armenian church, it was later discovered, was a depot of ammunition. In this disloyal way they killed more than 300,000 Mohammedans, and destroyed the communication of the Turkish Army with its bases.[1]

The information that we were receiving from the administrators of these provinces and from the commander of the Caucasian Army gave us details of the most revolting and barbarous activities of the Armenian bandits. It was impossible to shut our eyes to the treacherous acts of the Armenians, at a time when we were engaged in a war which would determine the fate of our country. Even if these atrocities had occurred in a time of peace, our Government would have been obliged to quell such outbreaks. The Porte,[2] acting under the same obligation, and wishing to secure the safety of its army and its

---

[1]That Armenians served in the Russian army is hardly remarkable since many Armenians were Russian subjects. Although it is true some Armenians sympathized with the Allies and hoped for Turkey's defeat, many thousands of Armenians fought in the Ottoman army. It is also true that many Armenians were armed, but this was not solely the work of Russia. Many Armenians armed themselves

before the war for self-defense. The assertions "every Armenian church" was an arms depot and that Armenians had killed three hundred thousand Turks are certainly exaggerations.

[2]The Porte, or Sublime Porte, was a term for the Ottoman government. It refers to the building that housed the high officials of the Ottoman state.

citizens, took energetic measures to check these uprisings. The deportation of the Armenians was one of these preventive measures.

I admit also that the deportation was not carried out lawfully everywhere. In some places unlawful acts were committed. The already existing hatred among the Armenians and Mohammedans, intensified by the barbarous activities of the former, had created many tragic consequences. Some of the officials abused their authority, and in many places people took preventive measures into their own hands and innocent people were molested. I confess it. I confess, also, that the duty of the Government was to prevent these abuses and atrocities, or at least to hunt down and punish their perpetrators severely. In many places, where the property and goods of the deported people were looted, and the Armenians molested, we did arrest those who were responsible and punished them according to the law. I confess, however, that we ought to have acted more sternly, opened up a general investigation for the purpose of finding out all the promoters and looters and punished them severely....

But we could not do that. Although we punished many of the guilty, most of them were untouched. These people, whom we might call outlaws, because of their unlawful attitude in disregarding the order of the Central Government, were divided into two classes. Some of them were acting under personal hatred, or for individual profit. Those who looted the goods of the deported Armenians were easily punishable and we punished them. But there was another group, who sincerely believed that the general interest of the community necessitated the punishment alike of those Armenians who massacred the guiltless Mohammedans and those who helped the Armenian bandits to endanger our national life. The Turkish elements here referred to were short-sighted, fanatic, and yet sincere in their belief. The public encouraged them, and they had the general approval behind them. They were numerous and strong. Their open and immediate punishment would have aroused great discontent among the people, who favored their acts. An endeavor to arrest and to punish all these promoters would have created anarchy in Anatolia at a time when we greatly needed unity. It would have been dangerous to divide the nation into two camps, when we needed strength to fight outside enemies. We did all that we could, but we preferred to post-pone the solution of our internal difficulties until after the defeat of our external enemies....

These preventive measures were taken in every country during the war, but, while the regrettable results were passed over in silence in the other countries, the echo of our acts was heard the world over, because everybody's eyes were upon us.

The Russian Revolution and the Beginnings of the Soviet State

Among the results of World War I, the downfall of Russia's tsarist regime and its replacement by a Marxist-inspired Bolshevik dictatorship is one of the most important. Tsar Nicholas II (r. 1894–1917), facing military defeat, army desertions, widespread peasant violence, and rioting in Petrograd, abdicated in March 1917, and the tsarist autocracy was replaced by the Provisional Government, which was to govern Russia until a constituent assembly could meet and write a new constitution. Seven months later, the Bolsheviks wrested power from the Provisional Government and, after three years of civil war, established the world's first communist state.

Discontent had plagued Nicholas II's reign from the start, but it intensified in 1905 when Russia's sorry performance in the Russo-Japanese War and the government's bloody overreaction to a peaceful workers' demonstration in St. Petersburg in January sparked nationwide strikes, rural violence, and demands for constitutional reform. The tsar responded with his October Manifesto, in which he promised a democratically elected parliament, or duma, and freedom of the press. Russians soon realized, however, that the tsar had no intention of abandoning control of such crucial areas as finance, defense, and ministerial appointment. Nor did he have any interest in working with uncooperative parliaments. He dissolved the first two dumas and then changed the election rules in 1907 to disenfranchise workers, peasants, and his non-Russian subjects. His chief minister Peter Stolypin tried to hold things together by cracking down on dissidents and implementing modest reforms. Meanwhile, Constitutional Democrats, Socialist Revolutionaries, Mensheviks, and Bolsheviks, although deeply divided on tactics and goals, plotted to achieve their one common purpose—the overthrow of the tsar's government.

It was a weak and tottering tsarist Russia that entered World War I in August 1914. Less than three years later, it became the war's most significant political casualty.

Anarchy and Revolution in Russia, 1917

◆

22 ◆ *ARMY INTELLIGENCE REPORTS,* and *REPORTS OF THE PETROGRAD TELEGRAPH AGENCY, SEPTEMBER–OCTOBER 1917*

After Nicholas II's abdication on March 2, 1917,[1] an awkward political situation developed in which power was divided between the Provisional Government, which was to rule until a constitution could be written, and the Petrograd (formerly St. Petersburg) Soviet of Workers' Deputies, an elected council representing peasants, workers, and soldiers. The Petrograd Soviet, which gradually came under the control of radical Bolsheviks, exercised no political authority as such, but its broad support among workers, peasants, and soldiers meant that the Provisional Government could take no significant action without its support. The result was a "dual power" arrangement in which effective government was impossible.

---

[1]Throughout this section, we have used the dates of the old-style Julian calendar, which then was used in Russia. It was two weeks behind the Gregorian calendar used in the West. After taking power, the Bolsheviks ordered the adoption of the Gregorian calendar starting on January 31, 1918.

This was just the type of situation in which an intense, persuasive, ruthless, and single-minded revolutionary like Lenin (see Source 4) might be able to take control of events and achieve his goals. Having spent the war in exile in Switzerland, Lenin returned to Russia on April 3, 1917, with the help of the German army. He immediately sought to convince his fellow Bolsheviks to reject compromise with the Provisional Government and press forward toward a true socialist revolution. The Bolsheviks gained support among city-dwellers, peasants, and soldiers after the failure of the army's Galician offensive in late June, General Kornilov's failed right-wing coup in August, and the continued support of the war effort by the Bolsheviks' main rivals, the Socialist Revolutionaries and Mensheviks.

As politicians and revolutionaries in Petrograd anxiously debated their next moves in the late summer and fall, Russia descended into anarchy, and Bolshevik party membership increased from 250,000 to 350,000. On October 10, Bolshevik leaders agreed in principle to seizing power through an insurrection. Two weeks later, on the evening of October 24, Bolsheviks occupied key government offices, took over telegraph offices and railroad stations, and set up roadblocks around the city. On October 25, they seized the Winter Palace, the seat of the Provisional Government. In a nearly bloodless coup, Russia's most radical socialist party had seized control of the world's largest nation.

The following excerpts shed light on the state of Russia in the weeks preceding the Bolshevik coup. The first section draws on material from army intelligence reports submitted to the Provisional Government; the second and third sections contain excerpts from reports of the Petrograd Telegraph Agency, a news service founded in 1904.

QUESTIONS FOR ANALYSIS

1. What are the soldiers' main grievances according to the intelligence reports?
2. What are the concrete signs of the breakdown of discipline in the Russian army?
3. What difference and similarities do you see in the nature and causes of the violence in rural and urban areas?
4. According to the wire service and army intelligence reports, what are the signs that the soldiers and Russian people whose actions are described were motivated by political ideologies?
5. What evidence do the documents provide about the Provisional Government's response to the rioting and breakdown of discipline among the soldiers?

THE DISINTEGRATION OF THE ARMY

Northern front.—The situation in the army has not changed and may be described as a complete lack of confidence in the officers and the higher commanding personnel. The belief is growing among the soldiers that they cannot be punished for what they do.... The influence of Bolshevik ideas is spreading very rapidly. To this must be added a general weariness, an irritability, and a desire for peace at any price.

Any attempt on the part of the officers to regulate the life of the army ... is looked upon by the soldiers as counter-revolution ... and stigmatized as a "Kornilov"[1] move.... Considerable numbers of soldiers ... feigning sickness are leaving the front for the hospital....

12th Army.—... Again and again one hears the orders of the Provisional Government severely criticized. The committee of the 95th Regiment ... declared Kerensky[2] a traitor....

Apart from the Bolsheviks not a single [political] movement has any popularity. Those who read moderate newspapers are looked upon as "bourgeoisie" and "counter-revolutionists." An intensive agitation is being conducted in favor of an immediate cessation of military operations on all fronts. Whenever a whole regiment or battalion refuses to carry out a military order, the fact is immediately made known to other parts of the army through special agitators....

Western front.—... Because of general war weariness, bad nourishment, mistrust of officers, etc., there has developed an intense defeatist agitation accompanied by refusals to carry out orders, threats to the commanding personnel, and attempts to fraternize with Germans. Everywhere one hears voices calling for immediate peace, because, they say, no one will stay in the trenches during the winter....

The attitude of the soldiers is very definitely expressed in the press.... The moderate newspapers ... try to warn their readers against entertaining false hopes, since the coalition of the Central Powers is not at all inclined to stretch a fraternal hand to the Russian proletariat....

In direct opposition to this are the newspapers *Izvestiia* (of the Minsk Soviet of Workers' and Soldiers' Deputies) and *Molot*[3].... Their method of argument is quite simple and comprehensible to the masses. It runs as follows: All the ministers of the Provisional Government are subservient to the bourgeoisie and are counter-revolutionists; they continue to wage war to please the Allied and the Russian capitalists; the government introduced the death penalty with the view of exterminating the soldiers, workers, and peasants....

Among the phenomena indicative of tendencies in the life in the rear of the Western front are the recent disturbances at the replacement depot in Gomel. On October 1 over eight thousand soldiers who were to be transferred to the front demanded to be sent home instead.... Incited by agitators they stormed the armory, took ... winter equipment, and assaulted the Assistant Commissar... Similar events.... have taken place in Smolensk....

Southwestern front.—... Defeatist agitation is increasing and the disintegration of the army is in full swing. The Bolshevik wave is growing steadily, owing to general disintegration in the rear, the absence of strong power, and the lack of supplies and equipment. The dominant theme of conversation is peace at any price and under any condition. Every order, no matter what its source, is met with hostility....

The guard-cavalry corps of the 2d Army passed a resolution of no confidence in the majority of officers. The soldiers are engaging in organized armed invasions of the surrounding country estates, plundering provisions ... of which there is a scarcity in the army. Not a thing can be done to counteract this restlessness....

The following general conclusions may be drawn: ... The approaching winter campaign has accelerated the disintegration of the army and increased the longing for peace. It is necessary to leave nothing undone which might supply the soldiers with food, shoes, and winter clothing; ... [and] to improve the discipline in the reserve regiments. Otherwise the ranks will be filled with such material as will lead to the complete demoralization and destruction of the army....

---

[1] A reference to the so-called Kornilov Affair, a failed coup led by General Lavr Kornilov, commander in chief of the Russian army, to overthrow the Provisional Government in September 1917.

[2] Alexander Kerensky (1881–1970) was a Socialist Revolutionary who served as minister of war and later prime minister of the Provisional Government.

[3] *Izvetsiia* (literally "delivered messages") and *Molot* ("the hammer") were names adopted by newspapers published by soviets in several Russian cities.

RURAL VIOLENCE

Kishinev, September 26. Local reports testify to the growth of agrarian disturbances in all uezds.[4] Fear is expressed that the sowing will not be done in time or properly.

Tambov, September 27. Accurate information about the disorders in Kozlov Uezd has not been received up to the present time. It is definitely known that one estate has been pillaged and twenty-five have been burned....

Saratov, October 10. The agrarian disturbances in Serdobsky Uezd embrace a large district. Peasants are stealing cattle, dividing the land and forests, and carrying off the grain. The uezd officials appealed for the aid of troops. It is feared that a great store of government liquor will be pillaged.

Kishinev, October 10. Peasants of Megura village, Beletsky Uezd, influenced by propaganda, began to divide among themselves the land and pastures of the neighboring estates of Borchel and Slobodzei.

Zhitomir, October 12. A number of despatches have been received by the gubernia[5] commissar about disturbances in the gubernia. Forests and crops are being destroyed. Troops have been sent to quell the disorders....

Voronezh, October 20. In Zadonsky Uezd in the district of the village of Zhivotinsky, the estates of Chertkov and other landowners have been partially destroyed by the peasants. More than 60,000 puds of wheat and other grain have been burned.[6] Valuable old furniture has been destroyed....

Zhitomir, October 23. After returning from a journey to Volhynia the assistant commissar gave a report on the situation. According to him, Volhynia is in a state of complete anarchy. In many uezds there is general destruction of the forests and seizure of privately owned land. In Staro-Konstantinovsky Uezd the Bolsheviks have seized power.

Spassk, October 27. A wave of destruction swept over the whole uezd. Felling and stealing of trees is

going on. The estate of Shreder has been pillaged and set on fire. The estate of Count Grabbe has been destroyed, including his valuable library.

Nizhni-Novgorod, November 1. According to the latest information the uprising has spread over six uezds, in which many estates have been pillaged and burned.

TOWNS AND CITIES

Kharkov, September 24. Information has been received about disorders in Bakhmut. On the evening of September 22 a wine storehouse was broken into and a large amount of liquor seized. The drunken crowds who took part in the destruction of the wine storehouse started to march through the streets singing and creating a disturbance. The population of the city is alarmed. The Jews have left the city. All stores are closed and the residents do not venture on the streets. Soldiers from the local garrison took part in the disturbance....

Astrakhan, September 25. As a result of the reduction of the bread ration, a large crowd went to the opposite bank of the Volga where the gubernia food committee is located, and demanded an explanation from the chairman of the committee. They then broke into the commissariat, fell upon Sklabinsky, the gubernia commissar, and threw him into the street....

Kazan, September 27. As a result of the agitation against the grain monopoly, in the village of Bolshoi Sundur, Zapolsky, the chairman of the volost food administration, was tortured and then killed....

Tashkent, September 27. In connection with the aggravation of the provisions question, a number of soldiers decided to arrest the food manager ... and his two assistants. It was decided to transfer the business of provisions into the hands of the workers and soldiers and not to permit the shipment of manufactured goods to Bokhara. For this purpose a special

---

[4]An administrative district below the provincial level, often translated as "county."
[5]A major administrative subdivision, often translated as "province."

[6]A pud, or pood, is a measurement of weight equal to approximately 36 pounds.

guard was sent to the station. At the same time it was decided to conduct a general search through the entire city. On September 25, at a meeting attended by thousands of soldiers and workers, the resignation of the executive committee of the Soviet of Deputies was demanded. Speakers proclaimed Bolshevik slogans. A provisional revolutionary committee of fourteen was elected....

Rostov-on-Don, October 10. In Azov, as a result of the dissatisfaction of the population with the rise in the price of bread and flour, disorder broke out. A crowd of residents marched to the city hall, broke into the food department, and attacked the government employees, who fled. When a member of the municipal government, Makarovsky, attempted to quiet the crowd, he was thrown down the stairs from the second floor, after which books, orders, and papers which were found in the department were flung about....

Kharkov, October 11. During the past few days pillaging has been going on in the city. As a result of the shortage of staple goods and manufactured articles, rumors are abroad concerning the hiding of goods, and unauthorized searches are being conducted. Brigands plunder the goods and handle proprietors roughly. It is in this way that ... an innocent artisan, the Jew, Morein, was killed....

Tiflis, October 17. According to information from Kutais, disorder began on October 15 with the destruction of one of the wine cellars, where eight barrels of wine were broken open and emptied. The drunken rioters, joined by ever increasing crowds, began to break into grocery and other shops and also into private quarters; in many places they started fires; the local chemical plant was burned and the freight station was robbed.

Saratov, October 18. In Petrovsk, prisoners in jails and detention houses were released by the crowds....

Forging the Soviet State

❖

23 ◆ *COMMUNIST DECREES AND LEGISLATION, 1917–1918*

On October 25, 1917, with the Bolsheviks in control of public buildings and other key points in Petrograd, Lenin confidently opened the Second Congress of Soviets with the words, "We shall now proceed to construct the Socialist order." As Lenin soon found out, building that new socialist order proved difficult. Although the Bolsheviks had a broad set of revolutionary aspirations for Russia, they had no blueprint for governing the country or restructuring Russian society. Furthermore, the Bolsheviks were a minority party, as shown by the results of the elections for the Constituent Assembly in November 1917, which gave the Bolsheviks only 29 percent of the vote, as opposed to 58 percent for the Socialist Revolutionaries. Finally, they faced formidable problems—a ruined economy, continuing involvement in World War I until March 1918, and civil war from 1918 to 1921.

Despite these challenges, the Bolsheviks had no choice but to plunge ahead. In their first year in power, they issued hundreds of decrees that touched every aspect of Russian life and government, and initiated programs and policies that in some cases lasted until the Soviet Union's demise in 1991.

The following is a sample of the decrees the Bolsheviks issued in 1917 and 1918. The Decree on Land, issued on October 26 by the Second Congress of Soviets only hours after the Bolsheviks seized power, recognized land seizures that peasants had already carried out.

The Decree on Suppression of Hostile Newspapers and the Decree Dissolving the Constituent Assembly were two important steps toward one-party dictatorship. The Bolsheviks, both before and after seizing power, had supported convening a popularly elected Constituent Assembly. But the election of November 1917 gave the Socialist Revolutionaries a strong majority. The assembly convened on January 5, 1918, only to be dissolved by the Bolsheviks on January 7.

The Edict on Child Welfare, issued in January 1918, was the brainchild of Alexandra Kollontai (1873–1952), a leading Social Democrat who fled Russia in 1908 to escape arrest and, like Lenin, returned to Petrograd after the tsar abdicated. She became a member of the executive committee of the Petrograd Soviet and played a leading role in the Bolshevik coup. As commissioner of social welfare under the Bolsheviks, she was responsible for laws that legalized abortion, liberalized marriage and divorce, and granted women legal equality with men.

The Decree on Nationalization of Large-Scale Industries was issued in June 1918 after the beginning of the civil war. Until then, industry had remained under private ownership, supposedly subject to "workers' control." Now it was nationalized without compensation to the owners.

QUESTIONS FOR ANALYSIS

1. What rationale is provided in these documents for the "undemocratic" steps taken by the Bolsheviks to dissolve the Constituent Assembly and close down hostile newspapers?
2. What are the economic ramifications of the decrees on land use and nationalization of industry? Who benefits and who is hurt?
3. How will these decrees change essential features of Russian society and social relationships?
4. In what specific ways do these decrees increase the role of the state? What implications might this have for the Soviet Union's future?

DECREE ON LAND, OCTOBER 26, 1917[1]

1) *Private ownership of land shall be abolished forever ...*
   All land ... *shall be alienated without compensation* and become the property of the whole people, and pass into the use of all those who cultivate it....
2) All mineral wealth, e.g., ore, oil, coal, salt, etc., as well as all forests and waters of state importance, shall pass into the exclusive use of the state. All the small streams, lakes, woods, etc., shall pass into the use of the communities, to be administered by the local self-government bodies.

3) Lands on which *high-level scientific* farming is practiced, e.g., orchards, plantations, seed plots, nurseries, hot-houses, etc. *shall not be divided up, but shall be converted into model farms,* to be turned over for exclusive use *to the state or to the communities,* depending on the size and importance of such lands.

6) The right to use the land shall be accorded to all citizens of the Russian state (without distinction of sex) desiring to cultivate it by their own labor, with the help of their

[1]*Source:* V. I. Lenin, *Selected Works, Vol. II, Book I* (Moscow: Progress Publishers, 1964) pp. 382–384.

families, or in partnership, but only as long as they are able to cultivate it....

DECREE ON SUPPRESSION OF HOSTILE NEWSPAPERS, OCTOBER 27, 1917[2]

Everyone knows that the bourgeois press is one of the most powerful weapons of the bourgeoisie. Especially in this critical moment when the new authority, that of the workers and peasants, is in process of consolidation, it was impossible to leave this weapon in the hands of the enemy at a time when it is not less dangerous than bombs and machine guns. This is why temporary and extraordinary measures have been adopted for the purpose of cutting off the stream of mire and calumny in which the ... press would be glad to drown the young victory of the people.

As soon as the new order will be consolidated, all administrative measures against the press will be suspended; full liberty will be given it within the limits of responsibility before the laws, in accordance with the broadest and most progressive regulations in this respect....

DECREE DISSOLVING THE CONSTITUENT ASSEMBLY, JANUARY 7, 1918[3]

The October Revolution, by giving the power to the Soviets, and through the Soviets to the toiling and exploited classes, aroused the desperate resistance of the exploiters, and in the crushing of this resistance it fully revealed itself as the beginning of the socialist revolution. The toiling classes learnt by experience that the old bourgeois parliamentarism had outlived its purpose and was absolutely incompatible with the aim of achieving Socialism, and that not national institutions, but only class institutions (such as the soviets), were capable of overcoming the resistance of the propertied classes and of laying the foundations of a socialist society. To relinquish the sovereign power of the soviets, to relinquish the Soviet republic won by the people, for the sake of bourgeois parliamentarism and the Constituent Assembly, would now be a retrograde step and cause the collapse of the October workers' and peasants' revolution....

The Right Socialist Revolutionary and Menshevik parties are in fact waging outside the walls of the Constituent Assembly a most desperate struggle against the Soviet power, calling openly in their press for its overthrow and characterizing as arbitrary and unlawful the crushing by force of the resistance of the exploiters by the toiling classes, which is essential in the interests of emancipation from exploitation. They are defending the saboteurs, the servitors of capital, and are going to the length of undisguised calls to terrorism, which certain "unidentified groups" have already begun to practice. It is obvious that under such circumstances the remaining part of the Constituent Assembly could only serve as a screen for the struggle of the counterrevolutionaries to overthrow the Soviet power.

Accordingly, the Central Executive Committee resolves: The Constituent Assembly is hereby dissolved.

EDICT ON CHILD WELFARE, JANUARY 1918[4]

After a search that has lasted centuries, human thought has at last discovered the radiant epoch where the working class, with its own hands, can freely construct that form of maternity protection which will preserve the child for the mother and the mother for the child....

The new Soviet Russia calls all you working women, you working mothers with your sensitive hearts, you bold builders of a new social life, you teachers of the new attitudes, you children's doctors and midwives, to devote your minds and emotions to building the great edifice that will

[2]*Source:* From *Hearings before a Subcommittee of the Judiciary Committee*, U.S. Senate, 65th Congress, 3rd Session, February 11, 1919 to March 10, 1919, Washington D.C., Government Printing Office, 1243.
[3]*Source:* V. I. Lenin, Selected Works, Vol. II, Book I (Moscow: Progress Publishers, 1964) pp. 382–384.
[4]*Source: Selected Writings of Alexandra Kollontai*, © 1978. Reproduced by permission of Lawrence Hill Books, Chicago Review Press.

provide social protection for future generations. From the date of publication of this decree, all large and small institutions under the commissariat of social welfare that serve the child, from the children's home in the capital to the modest village crèche [day nursery] shall be merged into one government organization and placed under the department for the protection of maternity and childhood. As an integral part of the total number of institutions connected with pregnancy and maternity, they shall continue to fulfill the single common task of creating citizens who are strong both mentally and physically....

For the rapid elaboration and introduction of the reforms necessary for the protection of childhood in Russia, commissions are being organized under the auspices of the departments of maternity and childhood.... The commissions must base their work on the following main principles:

1. The preservation of the mother for the child: milk from the mother's breast is invaluable for the child.
2. The child must be brought up in the enlightened and understanding atmosphere provided by the socialist family.
3. Conditions must be created which permit the development of the child's physical and mental powers and the child's keen comprehension of life.

DECREE ON NATIONALIZATION OF LARGE-SCALE INDUSTRIES, JUNE 28, 1918[5]

For the purpose of combating decisively the economic disorganization and the breakdown of

the food supply, and of establishing more firmly the dictatorship of the working class and the village poor, the Soviet of People's Commissars has resolved:

1. To declare all of the following industrial and commercial enterprises which are located in the Soviet Republic, with all their capital and property, whatever they may consist of, the property of the Russian Socialist Federated Soviet Republic. [A long list of mines, mills, and factories follows.]
2. The administration of the nationalized industries shall be organized ... by the different departments of the Supreme Council of National Economy.
4. Beginning with the promulgation of this decree, the members of the administration, the directors, and other responsible officers of the nationalized industries will be held responsible to the Soviet Republic both for the intactness and upkeep of the business and for its proper functioning....
5. The entire personnel of every enterprise—technicians, workers, members of the board of directors, and foremen—shall be considered employees of the Russian Socialist Federated Soviet Republic; their wages shall be fixed in accordance with the scales existing at the time of nationalization and shall be paid out of the funds of the respective enterprises....
6. All private capital belonging to members of the boards of directors, stockholders, and owners of the nationalized enterprises will be attached pending the determination of the relation of such capital to the turnover capital and resources of the enterprises in question....

[5]*Source:* Decree on Nationalization of Large-Scale Industry: from James Bunyan, Civil War, Intervention and Communism in Russia, 397–398. Baltimore: Johns Hopkins Press, (1936).

◆

The Peace That Failed

On January 19, 1919, thousands of diplomats, ministers, journalists, and observers gathered in Paris for the first session of the peace conference that was to reorder the world after World War I. Participants included delegates from the nations that had been on the winning side, observers from the defeated Central

Powers, and spokespersons of numerous religious and ethnic groups—Arabs, Egyptians, Kurds, Irish, Zionists, Persians, Indians, Vietnamese, Africans, African-Americans, and Armenians. Women's organizations and even supporters of the tsarist cause in Russia were also represented.

The postwar treaties were largely the work of just three leaders: Prime Minister Georges Clemenceau of France, Prime Minister David Lloyd George of Great Britain, and President Woodrow Wilson of the United States. A year earlier, in January 1918, Wilson had issued his famous Fourteen Points, a document that many assumed would be the basis of the postwar treaties. Wilson called for open diplomacy, free trade, reduced armies, and national self-determination in Europe. Although Germany would be required to return Alsace-Lorraine to France and abandon conquered territories in Russia and Belgium, there was no talk of harshly punishing Germany. Colonial claims were to be "readjusted" in a process in which "the interests of the populations concerned must have equal weight with the equitable claims of the government whose title is being determined." Finally, Wilson called for the founding of a "general association of nations" whose purpose was to preserve peace and guarantee the political integrity of great and small nations alike.

Lloyd George and Clemenceau had different agendas. Clemenceau wanted to protect French security by weakening and punishing Germany. Lloyd George was more flexible, but whatever moderate inclinations he might have had were outweighed by his recent election promises to "hang the emperor" and "squeeze the German lemon until the pips squeak." Neither leader was interested in considering the opinions of Africans and Asians in "readjusting colonial claims."

Divided by personal and philosophical conflicts, saddled by conflicting claims and promises, and subject to intense political pressures, the peacemakers faced issues of daunting complexity. In just a few months they were expected to solve political problems around the globe—problems that still would have taxed their wisdom and foresight if they had been addressed one by one without undue pressure. By May they completed the treaty dealing with Germany, the Treaty of Versailles, which the Germans grudgingly signed on June 28, 1919. They also produced broad outlines of treaties to be completed later for Austria, Hungary, Bulgaria, and Ottoman Turkey. Mistakes and blunders were made, and it is easy to understand why. Understanding them makes them no less tragic.

The Allies' "Last Horrible Triumph"

❖

24 ❖ *COMMENTS OF THE GERMAN DELEGATION TO THE PARIS PEACE CONFERENCE ON THE CONDITIONS OF PEACE, OCTOBER 1919*

The Germans had expected to win the Great War but had lost. In defeat they had expected to be treated with justice and moderation, and again they were bitterly disappointed. The new democratic German government had no voice

Source: "Comments of the German Delegation to the Paris Peace Conference on the Conditions of Peace". Reprinted by permission of the publisher from International Conciliation, No.143 (Washington, DC; Carnegie Endowment for International Peace, 1919), pp. 1208, 1210–1213, 1215–1222. www.carnegieendowment.org

in writing the Treaty of Versailles, and when it received a draft of the treaty in late April 1919, it responded with a list of complaints and counterproposals. All but a few of them were rejected. Germany's chancellor Philipp Scheidemann resigned, saying, "What hand would not wither when it signed such a treaty?" The German National Assembly voted in June to accept the treaty but with two reservations: it rejected the claim that Germany was solely responsible for the war and the provision that the kaiser and other high officials were to be tried as war criminals. The Allies dismissed their complaints and demanded a positive reply in twenty-four hours. Threatened with invasion, the assembly accepted the treaty as written. It was signed on June 28, 1919, and German humiliation was complete.

Germany lost all of its colonies, 13 percent of its land, and 10 percent of its population. Alsace and Lorraine, won from France in 1871, were returned to France. Northern Schleswig went to Denmark, parts of Posen and West Prussia went to Poland, while smaller bits of territory went to Belgium and Czechoslovakia. The coal mines of the Saar Basin were given to France for fifteen years, at which time the German government could buy them back; the Saar region itself was to be administered by the League of Nations, the international organization founded as part of the Paris Peace Settlement. East Prussia was cut off from the rest of Germany by territory ceded to Poland, and the largely German port of Danzig on the Baltic Sea came under Polish economic control. The Germans were permitted to have no air force, a navy of approximately two dozen ships, and a volunteer army of no more than one hundred thousand officers and men. Article 231, the "war-guilt" clause, held Germany and its allies responsible for causing the war. On the basis of this claim, Germany was held accountable for all Allied losses and damages and would be required to pay reparations. In 1921, the sum was set at $33 billion (approximately $415 billion in 2011 dollars).

On the day the treaty was signed, the nationalist newspaper *Deutsche Zeitung* published the following statement on its front page:

> Vengeance! German nation! Today in the Hall of Mirrors the
> disgraceful treaty is being signed. Do not forget it! . . . The German
> people will with unceasing labor, press forward to reconquer the place
> among nations to which it is entitled. Then vengeance will come for
> the shame of 1919!

Few Germans did not harbor such sentiments somewhere in their hearts during the 1920s. Nationalist and antidemocratic politicians learned how to play on these resentments, and in so doing undermined the democratic government that had signed the treaty. Of those politicians, the most successful was Adolf Hitler, whose Nazis took power in 1933 and immediately set out to destroy the Versailles settlement.

The reasons for German resentment are spelled out in the following comments and observations. They were submitted in October 1919 by the German delegation to the Paris Peace Conference, which continued to meet after the signing of the Versailles Treaty until January 21, 1920.

QUESTIONS FOR ANALYSIS

1. In Germany's view, how would the country have been treated differently if the principles they attribute to President Wilson had been applied?
2. What does the document reveal about the difficulty of applying the principle of ethnic self-determination in Europe?
3. To what higher "fundamental" laws does the document appeal to in order to strengthen German assertions?
4. What view of colonialism is expressed in the document? Why do the authors claim that Germany has a right to its colonies?
5. According to the authors of the German complaint, how will various provisions of the treaty hurt Germany's economy?
6. Do you agree with the authors of the document that Germany was being poorly treated? What response to their complaints might defenders of the treaty have made?

Although President Wilson, in his speech of October 20th, 1916, has acknowledged that "no single fact caused the war, but that in the last analysis the whole European system is in a deeper sense responsible for the war, with its combination of alliances and understandings, a complicated texture of intrigues and espionage that unfailingly caught the whole family of nations in its meshes" ... Germany is to acknowledge that Germany and her allies are responsible for all damages which the enemy Governments or their subjects have incurred by her and her allies' aggression.... Apart from the consideration that there is no incontestable legal foundation for the obligation for reparation imposed upon Germany, the amount of such compensation is to be determined by a commission nominated solely by Germany's enemies, Germany taking no part.... The commission is plainly to have power to administer Germany like the estate of a bankrupt.[1]

As there are innate rights of man, so there are innate rights of nations. The inalienable fundamental right of every state is the right of self-preservation and self-determination. With this fundamental right the demand here made upon Germany is incompatible. Germany must promise to pay an indemnity, the amount of which at present is not even stated. The German rivers are to be placed under the control of an international body upon which Germany's delegates are always to be but the smallest minority. Canals and railroads are to be built on German territory at the discretion of foreign authorities.

These few instances show that that is not the just peace we were promised, not the peace "the very principle of which," according to a word of President Wilson, "is equality and the common participation in a common benefit...."

In such a peace the solidarity of human interests, which was to find its expression in a League of Nations, would have been respected. How often Germany has been given the promise that this League of Nations would unite the belligerents, conquerors as well as conquered, in a permanent system of common rights! ...

... But in contradiction to them, the Covenant of the League of Nations has been framed without the cooperation of Germany. Nay, still more. Germany does not even stand on the list of those States that have been invited to join the League of Nations. What the treaty of peace proposes to establish, is rather a continuance of the present hostile coalition which does not deserve the name of "League of Nations." ... The old political system based on force and with its tricks and rivalries will thus continue to thrive!

---

[1] A Reparations Commission appointed by the Peace Conference set the final sum at $33 billion in 1921. In the meantime, Germany was required to make an interim payment of $5 billion.

Again and again the enemies of Germany have assured the whole world that they did not aim at the destruction of Germany. In contradiction to this, the peace document shows that Germany's position as a world power is to be utterly destroyed. The Germans abroad are deprived of the possibility of keeping up their old relations in foreign countries and of regaining for Germany a share in world commerce, while their property, which has up to the present been confiscated and liquidated, is being used for reparation instead of being restored to them....

In this war, a new fundamental law has arisen which the statesmen of all belligerent peoples have again and again acknowledged to be their aim: the right of self-determination. To make it possible for all nations to put this privilege into practice was intended to be one achievement of the war.... Neither the treatment described above of the inhabitants of the Saar[2] region as accessories to the [coal] pits nor the public form of consulting the population in the districts of Eupen, Malmédy and Prussian Moresnet[3] ··· comply in the least with such a solemn recognition of the right of self-determination. The same is also true with regard to Alsace-Lorraine. If Germany has pledged herself "to right the wrong of 1871,"[4] this does not mean any renunciation of the right of self-determination of the inhabitants of Alsace-Lorraine. A cession of the country without consulting the population would be a new wrong, if for no other reason, because it would be inconsistent with a recognized principle of peace.

On the other hand, it is incompatible with the idea of national self-determination for two and one-half million Germans to be torn away from their native land against their own will. By the proposed demarcation of the boundary, unmistakably German territories are disposed of in favor of their Polish neighbors. Thus, from the Central Silesian districts of Guhrau and Militsch certain portions are to be wrenched away, in which, beside 44,900 Germans, reside at the utmost 3,700 Poles....

This disrespect of the right of self-determination is shown most grossly in the fact that Danzig[5] is to be separated from the German Empire and made a free state. Neither historical rights nor the present ethnographical conditions of ownership of the Polish people can have any weight as compared with the German past and the German character of that city.... Likewise the cession of the commercial town of Memel[6], which is to be exacted from Germany, is in no way consistent with the right of self-determination. The same may be said with reference to the fact that millions of Germans in German-Austria are to be denied the union with Germany which they desire and that, further, millions of Germans dwelling along our frontiers are to be forced to remain part of the newly created Czecho-Slovakian State.

Even as regards that part of the national territory that is to be left to Germany, the promised right of self-determination is not observed. A Commission for the execution of the indemnity shall be the highest instance for the whole State[7]. Our enemies claim to have

---

[2]After fifteen years, the people of the Saar would have a plebiscite to decide if they would remain under the administration of a League of Nations commission or become part of France or Germany. In 1935, they voted to become part of Germany.

[3]Moresnet, an area of some fourteen hundred acres and the site of a valuable zinc mine, was annexed outright by Belgium. In Eupen and Malmédy, those who objected to the transfer of the areas to Belgium could sign their names in a public registry. On the basis of this "plebiscite," both areas became Belgian.

[4]Following the Prussian victory over France in the Franco-Prussian War, the Treaty of Frankfurt ceded to Germany the previously French province of Alsace and much of the province of Lorraine.

[5]Danzig was administered by the League of Nations, but its economy would be controlled by Poland.

[6]Memel, the German name for the Lithuanian city of Klaipéda, was detached from Germany and made into a protectorate administered of France and Great Britain. In 1924, it became part of Lithuania.

[7]This concern was well founded. After the Germans fell behind in their payments in 1923, the French-controlled Reparations Commission ordered French and Belgian troops into Germany's Ruhr region to collect coal and transport it to the border under military protection.

fought for the great aim of the democratization of Germany. To be sure, the outcome of the war has delivered us from our former authorities, but instead of them we shall have in exchange a foreign, dictatorial power whose aim can and must be only to exploit the working power of the German people for the benefit of the creditor states....

The fact that this is an age in which economic relations are on a world scale, requires the political organization of the civilized world. The German Government agrees with the Governments of the Allied and Associated Powers in the conviction that the horrible devastation caused by this war requires the establishment of a new world order, an order which shall insure the "effective authority of the principles of international law," and "just and honorable relations between the nations." ...

There is no evidence of these principles in the peace document which has been laid before us. Expiring world theories, emanating from imperialistic and capitalistic tendencies, celebrate in it their last horrible triumph. As opposed to these views, which have brought unspeakable disaster upon the world, we appeal to the innate sense of right of men and nations, under whose token the English State developed, the Dutch People freed itself, the North American nation established its independence, France shook off absolutism. The bearers of such hallowed traditions cannot deny this right to the German people, that now for the first time has acquired in its internal polities the possibility of living in harmony with its free will based on law.

The Betrayal of Arab Nationalism

❖

25 ◆ *GENERAL SYRIAN CONGRESS OF DAMASCUS, RESOLUTION OF JULY 2, 1919*

Lured by Great Britain's promises of an independent Arab state, Arabs under Sharif Husayn (1856–1931), the ruler of the western lands of the Arabian Peninsula, revolted against Ottoman rule in 1916. In 1918, with the end of the war, the Arabs looked forward to self-rule.

At the Paris Peace Conference, however, it became apparent that the British and French had no interest in honoring their wartime promises to the Arabs. Instead, they planned to divide the Arab Middle East between them, just as they had agreed to do during the war. This troubled Woodrow Wilson, who proposed in March 1919 that a commission of inquiry composed of U.S., British, French, and Italian representatives visit the Middle East to gather information so that a settlement could be achieved on the "most scientific basis." The French, British, and Italians refused to cooperate, however, so the commission became a U.S. undertaking, led by educator Henry C. King and industrialist and diplomat Charles R. Crane.

By the time the commission began its inquiry in the summer of 1919, the fate of the region had been sealed by Article 22 of the League of Nations Covenant, which was part of the Versailles Treaty. Article 22 decreed that the Arab regions of the defunct Ottoman Empire, along with Germany's former colonies, were to become League of Nations mandates administered by Great Britain, France, Japan, Australia, or South Africa because they were not ready for self-rule. The system was correctly viewed as a thinly disguised version of old-style colonialism.

Source: Damascus Congress: *Foreign Relations of the United States: Paris Peace Conference, 1919* Vol. 12, pp. 789–781.

Faced with the prospect of French or British control and in anticipation of the King-Crane Commission's visit, Syrian nationalists called a congress, also attended by Palestinian and Lebanese delegates, that adopted the following resolution on July 2, 1919. The King-Crane Commission included the resolution in its report, but Britain and France ignored it and went on with their plans to establish mandates. In March 1920, a second Syrian congress proclaimed Syrian independence, but the new state, which included Palestine and Lebanon, lasted only four months. In July 1920, the French easily crushed the Syrian army, whose ammunition ran out after only a few hours of fighting. On July 25, 1920, the French entered Damascus, ushering in two decades of turbulent French control.

QUESTIONS FOR ANALYSIS

1. In what ways and for what reasons does the resolution reject the premises of Article 22 of the League of Nations Covenant?
2. How do the delegates envision the mandate system, if forced to accept it?
3. How does the resolution distinguish between Zionists and Jews already residing in Palestine?
4. Why did the delegates prefer the United States as the nation to offer Syria economic and technical aid?
5. All of the resolutions except resolution 5 were accepted unanimously at the congress. Why do you think it was the exception?

We the undersigned members of the General Syrian Congress, meeting in Damascus on Wednesday, July 2nd, 1919 … provided with credentials and authorizations by the inhabitants of our various districts, Muslims, Christians, and Jews, have agreed upon the following statement …

1. We asked absolutely complete political independence for Syria within these boundaries. The Taurus System on the North; Rafah and a line running from Al Jauf to the south of the Syrian and the Hejazian line to Akaba on the south; the Euphrates and Khabur Rivers and a line extending east of Abu Kamal to the east of Al Jauf on the east; and the Mediterranean of the west.[1]

2. We ask that the Government of this Syrian country should be a democratic civil constitutional Monarchy on broad decentralization principles, safeguarding the rights of minorities, and that the King be the Emir Feisal,[2] who carried on a glorious struggle in the cause of our liberation and merited our full confidence and entire reliance.

3. Considering the fact that the Arabs inhabiting the Syrian area are not naturally less [capable] than other more advanced races and that they are by no means less developed than the Bulgarians, Serbians, Greeks, and Romanians at the beginning of their independence, we protest against Article 22 of the Covenant of the League of Nations, placing us among the nations in their middle stage of development which stand in need of a mandatory power.

[1] The territory described includes the region presently administered by the Palestinian National Authority and the states of Syria, Lebanon, Israel, and Jordan.
[2] Prince Feisal (also spelled *Feysel* and *Faysal*), the son of Sharif Husayn, was an Arab military hero in the Anglo-Arab struggle against the Turks. After the French drove him from Syria in 1920, the British installed him as king of Iraq.

4. In the event of the rejection by the Peace Conference of this just protest for certain considerations that we may not understand, we, relying on the declarations of President Wilson that his object in waging war was to put an end to the ambition of conquest and colonization, can only regard the mandate mentioned in the Covenant of the League of Nations as equivalent to the rendering of economic and technical assistance that does not prejudice our complete independence. And desiring that our country should not fall a prey to colonization and believing that the American Nation is farthest from any thought of colonization and has no political ambition in our country, we will seek the technical and economic assistance from the United States of America, provided that such assistance does not exceed 20 years.

5. In the event of America not finding herself in a position to accept our desire for assistance, we will seek this assistance from Great Britain, also provided that such assistance does not infringe the complete independence and unity of our country and that the duration of such assistance does not exceed that mentioned in the previous article.

6. We do not acknowledge any right claimed by the French Government in any part whatever of our Syrian country and refuse that she should assist us or have a hand in our country under any circumstances and in any place.

7. We oppose the pretensions of the Zionists to create a Jewish commonwealth in the southern part of Syria, known as Palestine, and oppose Zionist migration to any part of our country; for we do not acknowledge their title but consider them a grave peril to our people from the national, economical, and political points of view. Our Jewish compatriots shall enjoy our common rights and assume the common responsibilities.

8. We ask that there should be no separation of the southern part of Syria, known as Palestine, nor of the littoral western zone, which includes Lebanon, from the Syrian country. We desire that the unity of the country should be guaranteed against partition under whatever circumstances.

9. We ask complete independence for emancipated Mesopotamia[3] and that there should be no economic barriers between the two countries.

10. The fundamental principles laid down by President Wilson in condemnation of secret treaties impel us to protest most emphatically against any treaty that stipulates the partition of our Syrian country and against any private engagement aiming at the establishment of Zionism in the southern part of Syria; therefore we ask the complete annulment of these conventions and agreements.[4]

The noble principles enunciated by President Wilson[5] strengthen our confidence that our desires emanating from the depths of our hearts, shall be the decisive factor in determining our future; and that President Wilson and the free American people will be our supporters for the realization of our hopes, thereby proving their sincerity and noble sympathy with the aspiration of the weaker nations in general and our Arab people in particular.

We also have the fullest confidence that the Peace Conference will realize that we would not have risen against the Turks, with whom we had participated in all civil, political, and representative privileges, but for their violation of our national rights, and so will grant us our desires in full in order that our political rights may not be less after the war than they were before, since we have shed so much blood in the cause of our liberty and independence.

---

[3]The region of present-day Iraq.
[4]The passage refers to the Balfour Declaration of 1916, in which Great Britain pledged its support for a Jewish homeland in Palestine, and the Sykes-Picot Agreement of 1916, in which Great Britain and France agreed to divide former Ottoman territories between them.
[5]Wilson's Fourteen Points.

The Chinese May Fourth Movement

◆

26 ◆ Deng Yingchao, *MEMOIRS*

By the mid-1910s, the dreams of Chinese revolutionaries who had overthrown the Qing dynasty and founded a republic in 1911 had turned to dust. Sun Yat-sen, the intellectual father of the revolution, resigned his presidency in 1912 after serving only one month. His successor, General Yuan Shikai, undermined the deliberations of the parliament elected to write a constitution; outlawed Sun Yat-sen's political party, the Guomindang; and by late 1915 was preparing to have himself elevated to the position of emperor. With the central government bankrupt and the country falling under the control of local warlords, the Japanese seized German concessions in Shandong province at the beginning of World War I and in 1915 presented China with Twenty-One Demands. They required that China recognize their political and economic ascendancy in Shandong, Manchuria, and Inner Mongolia; grant Japan a number of economic concessions; and accept Japanese advisors in its ministries of police, the military, and finance. Militarily impotent and dependent on Japanese loans, the government successfully resisted Japanese demands to place advisors in its ministries, but otherwise acquiesced.

Although it had no army or navy capable of fighting, China entered World War I in August 1917 on the Allied side, mainly to gain an advantage in postwar peace negotiations. In the following months, some one hundred thousand Chinese arrived in Europe after crossing the Pacific, traveling across Canada by train, and finally shipping across the Atlantic. In France and Belgium they built roads and docks, dug trenches, and worked in factories and munitions dumps. Two thousand Chinese perished in Europe, and another 543 died when their ship was sunk in transit.

When the Chinese delegation left for the Paris Peace Conference, the Chinese had hopes that China would regain control of Shandong province and perhaps win other concessions. But the treaty writers rejected every Chinese claim and plea. When the news reached China, it sparked the May Fourth Movement, an outburst of public anger, nationalism, and reforming zeal that opened new possibilities for Chinese culture and politics in the 1920s and 1930s.

The following memoir describes the events of May 4, 1919, their background, and their influence on subsequent political and cultural movements. It was written by Deng Yingchao (1904–1992), who at the time was a student in Tianjin, a city in Hebei province some seventy-five miles east of Beijing. She soon joined the Communist Party, married Zhou Enlai (later foreign minister of the Peoples' Republic of China), and remained active in Party affairs until her death in 1992.

Source: Reprinted with the permission of Free Press, a division of Simon & Schuster, Inc., from *Chinese Civilization: A Source Book*, Second Edition, Revised and Expanded by Patricia Buckley Ebrey. Copyright © 1993 by Patricia Buckley Ebrey. All rights reserved.

QUESTIONS FOR ANALYSIS

1. The students originally demonstrated over the Versailles Treaty but quickly moved on to other issues. What were these other issues and how were they connected with the treaty?
2. What attitude did the participants in the May Fourth Movement have toward the West?
3. What methods did the students utilize to spread their ideas among the people? How effective were they?
4. How, according to Deng Yingchow, did the May Fourth Movement affect Chinese feminism?

On May 4, 1919, the students in Beijing staged a massive demonstration, demanding the punishment of traitors and the rejection of the Versailles Peace Treaty. In a moment of extreme anger, they burned down [a residential building] and beat up many traitors. The news of this demonstration reached Tianjin the next day, shaking the façade of complacency to its very foundation. Students gathered in groups to discuss the Beijing demonstration, and it was decided that we should not hesitate for a moment in rallying behind our Beijing compatriots in this patriotic movement. On May 7 the Tianjin students staged a demonstration of their own, and shortly afterwards such organizations as the Association of Tianjin Students and the Association of Patriotic Women in Tianjin came into existence. Most members of the latter organization were actually women students.... Simple and uncomplicated, we relied heavily on our selfless patriotism for our strength. Besides the two slogans previously mentioned, we also called for the abolition of the Twenty-One Demands, the return of Qingdao,[1] the boycott of Japanese goods, the use of Chinese goods only, and, most important of all, "We are determined that we shall not be slaves to any foreigners in our own country."

At that time the government was in the hands of the Peiyang warlords who responded to the students' patriotic movement with suppression and employed such methods as secret informers, bayonets, bullets, high-pressured water hoses, clubs, and massive arrests to carry out their policy of oppression. Like a piece of steel, we were tempered with fire during this period of struggle and gradually raised our own level of political consciousness. Keep in mind that the May Fourth Movement occurred at the end of World War I when new cultures and new ideas rushed into old China like a roaring torrent. These new cultures and new ideas, plus the knowledge of the successful October Revolution in Russia made a deep impression on every youth of China. Not surprisingly, young people played a most important and most progressive role in the May Fourth Movement; it was they who pushed the movement ahead and enabled it to continue to advance....

... Nevertheless, our own intuition told us that a patriotic movement, to be effective, had to be more than just a students' movement and that we had to awaken all of our brethren for the attainment of a common goal. We therefore stressed the importance of propaganda work. Many oratorical teams were organized, and I was elected captain of speakers for the Association of Patriotic Women as well as head of the oratorical division for the Association of Tianjin Students. My duty was to provide speakers in different areas on a regular basis.

---

[1]A port city in the German concession in Shandong province occupied by the Japanese early in World War I.

At the beginning we, as female students, did not enjoy the same freedom of movement as our male counterparts, insofar as our speaking tours were concerned. According to the feudal custom of China, women were not supposed to make speeches in the street; we, therefore, had to do our work indoors. We gave speeches in such places as libraries and participated in scheduled debates, all inside a hall or room. The audience was large and responsive in each of these meeting, as we emphasized the duty of everyone to save our country and the necessity of punishing those who sold out our country to the enemy. Many speakers broke down when they spoke of the sufferings of the Koreans under the Japanese rule, the beatings of the Beijing students by the secret police, and our inherent right to assembly for patriotic purposes. Needless to say, the audience was greatly moved by speakers of this kind.

Besides making speeches, we also conducted house-to-house visits which often took us to more remote areas of the city and also to the slums. Some of the families we visited received us warmly, while others slammed their doors in our faces before we could utter a single word. In the latter case we simply moved on to the next house instead of being discouraged.... [We] also paid great attention to the use of written words.... The Association of Tianjin Students published a journal which started as a half-weekly but became a daily shortly afterwards....

On October 10, 1919, the various patriotic organizations in Tianjin sponsored an all-citizen congress, in which the participants would demand the punishment of officials who were traitors, the boycott of Japanese goods, and the exercise of such inalienable rights as those of free speech and demonstrations. Before the congress was called into session, we received information that Yang Yide (nicknamed Gangster Yang), the police commissioner of Tianjin, was ready to use force to dissolve the congress if it were held and to

disperse any crowd gathered for the purpose of staging a demonstration....

As had been expected, the police, with fixed bayonets, quickly moved in to surround us as soon as the meeting began.... Not until the meeting was over and the march began did they clash with us. Steadily they closed in, as our vanguards proceeded to march forward....

We shouted loudly, trying desperately to convert brutal police into compassionate patriots. But the police refused to be converted as they hit us with rifle butts and systematically broke the eyeglasses of many students. In retaliation we hit them with bamboo placards and knocked hats from their heads. When they bent down to pick up their hats, we pushed forward so as to continue our march.

... We marched through the city streets until we finally arrived at police headquarters. We demanded to see commissioner Yang and protested against his brutality toward the students. Not until dawn the next day did we finally disperse and proceed home.

Angered by the October Tenth Incident as described above, we female students in Tianjin decided that no longer did we wish to honor the feudal custom of China and that we, female students in Tianjin, had as much right to speak in the street as our male counterparts. The very next day we began to make speeches in the street. From street to street and before one audience after another, we condemned commissioner Yang for having committed brutality against the students.

In the wake of the May Fourth Movement came the feminist movement which was in fact one of its democratic extensions. Among the demands we raised at that time were sexual equality, abolition of arranged marriage, social activities open to women students, freedom of romantic love and marriage, universities open to women students, and employment of women in government institutions. The first step we took toward sexual equality was to merge the associations of male and female students in Tianjin to form a new organization which students of both sexes could join. . . .

As pioneers in the feminist movement who had had the rare opportunity to work side by side with men, we female students in the merged association were conscious of the example we had to set so that no man in the future could deny women the opportunity to work on the ground of alleged incompetence. In short, we worked doubly hard. Fortunately for us, the male students in the association, having been imbued with the new thought of the West, were ready to accept us as equals and judged us according to our performance rather than our sex.

CHAPTER 4

Decades of Crisis in the Western World and the Soviet Union

In May 1920, Warren G. Harding, an Ohio senator and soon to be twenty-ninth president of the United States, told an audience in Boston, "America's present need is not heroics, but healing; not nostrums, but normalcy; not revolution, but restoration,... not surgery, but serenity." The term *normalcy* caught the public's attention, and "return to normalcy" became a phrase that expressed the aspirations of millions on both sides of the Atlantic in the postwar era. Normalcy lacked a precise definition, but to most it conjured up vague and not very accurate images of the way things were before 1914—a time of moral certitudes and political calm, when men and women could lead lives free of turmoil and conflict.

Dreams of normalcy never came close to being realized. The war's wounds were too deep, its political and economic consequences too profound, and its psychological impact too devastating. There would be no going back to "normal times"; there would only be a stumbling forward into a world whose contours were being continually redrawn by political conflict, economic catastrophe, new trends in mass culture, and the transformation of daily life by urbanization, the automobile, and radio. Crisis and conflict were "normal" in the 1920s and 1930s, not the tranquility for which Harding and so many others had yearned.

For the Western world, the interwar years fall into three distinct periods. Between 1918 and 1923, postwar political and economic problems dominated. The Bolshevik Revolution of 1917 spawned civil war in Russia, inspired communist revolts in Germany and Hungary, and raised fears of revolution throughout Europe and the United States. Border disputes and ethnic conflicts embroiled the newly created states of eastern and central Europe. Demobilization, the closing of wartime industries, and inflation caused economic hardship and sparked major strikes in Western Europe and the United States. In 1923, Germany defaulted on its reparations payments, and in response, Belgium and France dispatched soldiers to the Ruhr region to make sure that they would continue to receive their promised allocations of German coal. German miners responded with slowdown strikes and sabotage, further contributing to the collapse of the German mark, which sunk in value to 4.2 billion marks to the dollar by the end of 1923.

By 1924, however, the Ruhr crisis had ended, and the West entered a brief period of economic revival and political calm that lasted until 1929. Street fighting and insurrections gave way to political stability, albeit at the expense of democratic institutions in several states. The Locarno Treaties of 1925, signed by Germany, France, Belgium, the United Kingdom, and Italy, were hailed as the first step toward international cooperation and harmony. In them, Germany renounced claims to Alsace-Lorraine and its right to remilitarize unilaterally in return for League of Nations membership and French promises to accelerate troop withdrawals from the Rhineland. In 1928, almost every country in the world signed the Kellogg-Briand Pact, in which war was renounced as an instrument of national policy. After 1923, Western economies leaped forward, and as "good times" returned, many hoped that the Roaring Twenties would be the start of a better era.

Such hopes came crashing to the ground with the collapse of the U.S. stock market in October 1929. The ensuing financial crisis laid bare the weaknesses of the economic recovery, and soon the world was engulfed in an economic slump of unprecedented severity. Bank failures, boarded-up factories, and unemployment rates as high as 40 percent spelled misery for millions of people and accelerated the collapse of European liberal democracy. Authoritarian regimes replaced six parliamentary governments in the 1920s, and nine more did so in the 1930s. The most significant democratic failure was Germany's Weimar Republic, which gave way to the totalitarian regime of Hitler and the Nazis in 1933. As Hitler rearmed Germany and embarked on his plan to overturn the Versailles settlement, one diplomatic crisis followed another until the fall of 1939, when Europe again was at war.

Underlying the ebb and flow of economic shifts and political events were broad changes in Western life and culture. Politics no longer was the exclusive domain of aristocrats and wealthy bourgeoisie. More than ever before, mass politics was the order of the day, not only in democracies, but also in Nazi Germany, Fascist Italy, and Stalin's Soviet Union, where propaganda campaigns and political spectacles were carefully orchestrated to ensure popular support. This was also an era of mass culture. Radio programming, tabloid newspapers, and the cinema all were geared to mass audiences, as were advertising campaigns to encourage the purchase of automobiles, household appliances, golf clubs, phonographs, canned goods, beauty aids, and a long list of other products. Some intellectuals and social commentators welcomed these changes as positive and liberating; others deplored the debasement of taste and the erosion of standards. All could agree, however, that the "normalcy" of the prewar era was gone.

Modernism and Mass Culture Between the Wars

The term *modernism* is used to describe the art, music, and literature that emerged in the 1920s and continued to set the tone for Western culture until the 1950s and beyond. It is difficult to define. If one examines modern literature, modern painting, modern architecture, modern sculpture, modern music, and modern dance to see what characteristics they share, modernism is reduced to something broad and general: a rejection of tradition; an abandonment of inherited rules, forms, and themes; and a commitment to experimentation.

The triumph of modernism after World War I owes something to simple demographics. The prewar avant-garde consisted mainly of iconoclastic young men who, if they survived the war, reached maturity and gained followers in the 1920s and 1930s. Composer Igor Stravinsky gained international fame with his ballet scores written between 1910 and 1913 and lived until 1971; painter Pablo Picasso founded the cubist movement around 1907 and lived until 1973; poet T. S. Eliot wrote his first important poems between 1909 and 1911 and lived until 1967. But it was the war itself that consigned the old order to oblivion and affirmed modernism's triumph. It confirmed the bankruptcy of traditional values and the need to create a new culture in keeping with the modern age.

Along with modernism, mass culture was another feature of the 1920s and 1930s. It too had prewar roots. Before 1914, the appearance of mass circulation newspapers, increasing sales of pulp fiction and inexpensive magazines, the popularity of music hall entertainment, and the large crowds flocking to baseball parks and soccer stadiums all indicated that the "masses"—factory workers, shopkeepers, clerks, stenographers, servants, and laborers—were becoming an important cultural force. They became an even greater force in the 1920s and 1930s. By then the eight-hour workday, paid vacations, and workless weekends had become standard, and incomes had risen to the point at which people below the ranks of the bourgeoisie could afford their own entertainment and recreation.

The emergence of mass culture also had much to do with three prewar inventions that were refined, commercialized, and made affordable to the general public: the radio, the phonograph, and the cinema. The radio, developed in the 1890s and used on a limited basis by armies during World War I, became fully commercialized in the 1920s. By the end of the decade, millions of listeners could gather around their home radios and hear music, news, dramas, and sporting events. The phonograph, invented in 1878, reached a level of quality and affordability in the 1920s that made it a major part of evolving mass culture. In the United States alone, manufacturers turned out more than two million phonographs and one hundred million records annually. The film industry moved into an era of better quality full-length films with sound that were shown in sumptuously decorated movie palaces seating as many as five thousand patrons. By the 1930s, trips to the "movies" became routine on both sides of the Atlantic, and Hollywood became synonymous with glamour, adventure, and escape from the drabness of the Great Depression. The age of the masses had arrived, and for better or worse, soap operas, matinee idols, Hollywood epics, tabloid newspapers, sports heroes, and short-lived "dance crazes" were now part of Western culture.

The Look of Modernity

◆

27 ◆ Walter Gropius, *DESSAU BAUHAUS—PRINCIPLES OF BAUHAUS PRODUCTION* and *EXAMPLES OF BAUHAUS DESIGN*

Much of modern art, music, and literature has been geared toward a small, sophisticated audience of individuals who can appreciate and understand its complexities, obscurities, and frequently disturbing messages. Even in the heyday of modernism, only a tiny minority could say honestly that their lives had been touched by dadaist painting, atonal music, or stream-of-consciousness literature. This is not the case, however, with modern architecture and design. In these two areas, modernism has given a distinctive twentieth-century look to human-constructed objects that are part of people's daily lives: the buildings where they work, live, and study; the furniture in their homes; the clothes and jewelry they wear; the utensils, plates, and appliances they use in their kitchens; and much else. For this, a German school of art and design that lasted only fourteen years, the Bauhaus, can be given much of the credit.

The Bauhaus (German for House of Construction or Building School) was the creation of architect Walter Gropius. Born in 1883 in Berlin and trained in Berlin and Munich, Gropius achieved continent-wide prominence for the factories and office buildings he designed before World War I. After the war, he became director of two state-supported schools—one for art and one for crafts—in Weimar. He merged these in 1919 to form the Bauhaus. With some of Europe's most brilliant architects, painters, and sculptors on its faculty, the Bauhaus integrated crafts and aesthetic training. Its objective was to develop every area of design (architecture, painting, sculpture, furniture, fabrics, jewelry, ceramics, stagecraft, and costume) in ways appropriate to modern industrial society. Forced to move to Dessau in 1925 after the German state of Thuringia cut off funds, and then to Berlin when Nazis took over the Dessau city council, the school was shut

Source: Walter Gropius, "Dessau Bauhaus—Principles of Bauhaus Production," from *Bauhaus* by Frank Whitford. pp. 205–207. © 1984 Thames and Hudson Ltd, London. Reprinted by kind permission of Thames & Hudson.

down for good after Hitler took power in 1933. The Bauhaus, claimed the Nazis, represented Jewish-Marxist art. Gropius, who had resigned as director of the school in 1927, moved to the United States, where as head of Harvard's architecture department, he trained a generation of U.S. architects. He died in 1969.

This section illustrates some of the basic principles of Bauhaus and, by extension, modern design. It begins with a statement by Gropius from a pamphlet published in 1927, "Dessau Bauhaus—Principles of Bauhaus Construction." Four examples of Bauhaus design follow: the main Bauhaus building in Dessau, designed by Gropius; a master's (faculty member's) house from the Dessau complex, also designed by Gropius; a chair designed in 1927 by Marcel Breuer (a Bauhaus alumnus who fled Germany and later joined Gropius at Harvard) made of steel tubing and steel thread; and a brass and ebony teapot made in 1924 from a design by Marianne Brandt (a member of the Bauhaus faculty).

QUESTIONS FOR ANALYSIS

1. Why, in Gropius's view, have recent developments created the need for a new approach to housing and furnishings design?
2. According to Gropius, what characteristics must a modern dwelling and its furnishings have to put them "in harmony" with the modern world?
3. What views of the modern world does Gropius imply or state?
4. What have been the differences between craft production and industrial production in the view of Gropius? What changes in their relationship does he anticipate?
5. What characteristics do Gropius's Dessau buildings, Breuer's tubular chair, and Brandt's teapot have in common?
6. In what ways do these buildings and objects exemplify Gropius's ideals?

The Bauhaus intends to contribute to the development of housing—from the simplest appliance to the complete dwelling—in a way which is in harmony with the spirit of the age....

Convinced that household appliances and furnishings must relate to each other rationally, the Bauhaus seeks—by means of systematic theoretical and practical research into formal, technical and economic fields—to derive the form of an object from its natural functions and limitations.

Modern man, who wears modern not historical dress, also requires a modern dwelling which is in harmony with himself and with the times in which he lives, and is equipped with all the modern objects in daily use.

The nature of an object is determined by what it does. Before a container, a chair or a house can function properly its nature must first be studied, for it must perfectly serve its purpose; in other words it must function practically, must be cheap, durable and "beautiful." Research into the nature of objects leads one to conclude that forms emerge from a determined consideration of all the modern methods of production and construction and of modern materials. These forms diverge from existing models and often seem unfamiliar and surprising....

Only by constant contact with advanced technology, with the diversity of new materials and with new methods of construction, is the creative individual able to bring objects into a vital relationship with the past, and to develop from that a new attitude to design, namely:

Determined acceptance of the living environment of machines and vehicles.

Organic design of objects in terms of their own laws and determined by their contemporaneity, without Romantic beautification and whimsy.

Exclusive use of primary forms and colors comprehensible to everyone.

Simplicity in multiplicity, economical use of space, material, time and money.

The creation of standard types for all objects in daily use is a social necessity.

For most people the necessities of life are the same. The home, its furnishings and equipment are required by everybody, and their design is more a matter of reason than of passion. The machine, which creates standard types, is an effective means of liberating the individual from physical labor through mechanical aids—steam and electricity—and giving him mass-produced products cheaper and better than those made by hand....

The Bauhaus workshops are essentially laboratories in which prototypes suitable for mass production and typical of their time are developed with care and constantly improved....

The Bauhaus believes that the difference between industry and the crafts consists less in the tools each uses than in the division of labor in industry and the unity of labor in the crafts. But the crafts and industry are constantly moving closer. Traditional crafts have changed: the crafts of the future will have a unity of labor in which they will be the medium of experimental work for industrial production....

Bauhaus production is therefore not in competition with industry and craftsmen; it rather provides them with new opportunities for growth....

Bauhaus-Archiv Berlin

Dessau Bauhaus Building (1925–1926), Walter Gropius, architect

Bauhaus-Archiv Berlin / Art Resource, NY

Master's (faculty member's) House (1926) from the Dessau complex, Walter Gropius, architect

DeA Picture Library / Art Resource, NY

Marcel Breuer, Tubular Steel Chair (1925)

Neue Galerie New York / Art Resource, NY

Marianne Brandt, Small Tea-Essence Pot (1924)

Perils of Mass Culture: The Threat to Morality

❖

28 ◆ Senator Henry L. Myers,
U.S. SENATE SPEECH, JUNE 29, 1922

Is mass culture dangerous to morals? So it would seem from the persistent outcries directed toward many of its modern manifestations: jazz music, rock and roll, pulp fiction, rap lyrics, television violence, video games, dance styles too numerous to count, and, more than anything else, films. Early filmmakers knew that sex, violence, and sensationalism sold tickets, hence they produced more than their share of films featuring bawdy comedy, lurid murder scenes, and, by the standards of the day, torrid romance. In 1908, citing moral dangers, the mayor of New York City, George B. McClellan, threatened to close the city's cinemas, and in the 1910s state and local censorship boards proliferated. In response, filmmakers in 1909 founded their own self-regulating body, the National Board of Censorship (later named the National Board of Review), which they hoped would head off censorship by the federal government.

The industry's censorship problems peaked in the early 1920s. In their efforts to fill seats in the new theaters built after the war, producers released a spate of films with titles such as *The Blushing Bride, Forbidden Fruit, The Plaything of Broadway, Luring Lips, The Restless Sex,* and *Passion's Playground.* In 1920, scandals rocked Hollywood when one of its biggest stars, Roscoe "Fatty" Arbuckle, was accused (and later acquitted) of raping and murdering a young actress at a wild San Francisco party; a Hollywood producer, William Desmond Taylor, was found dead in a drug-related murder; and a number of prominent actors and actresses, including Rudolph Valentino, became involved in highly publicized divorces.

Against this background, several members of Congress reintroduced legislation to set up a national board of film censorship. One of its supporters was Senator Henry Myers (1861–1929) of Montana, who presented his views of the film industry in a Senate speech in June 1922.

The efforts of Myers and like-minded members of Congress failed. Bills calling for federal regulation of films were voted down, in no small part because of the lobbying efforts of Will Hays, recently hired by the film industry to serve as a spokesman for a new organization, the Motion Picture Producers and Distributors of America. However, Hays did ban Arbuckle, a convenient scapegoat for the industry's problems, from the screen, thereby showing his seriousness of purpose.

QUESTIONS FOR ANALYSIS

1. What is Myers's rationale for involving the federal government in censoring the film industry?
2. What signs of moral deterioration does Myers detect in the United States? To what degree does he believe the film industry is to blame for this deterioration?

Source: Congressman Meyer's speech on cinema: from *Congressional Record*, June 29, 1922, pp. 9655–9657.

3. Why does Myers believe that industry efforts to regulate itself will fail?
4. What type of regulation of the film industry does he foresee?

The motion picture is a great invention, and it has become a powerful factor for good or bad in our civilization....

Through motion pictures the young and the old may see depicted every good motive, laudable ambition, commendable characteristic, ennobling trait of humanity. They may be taught that honesty is the best policy; that virtue and worth are rewarded; that industry leads to success....

However, from all accounts, the business has been conducted, generally speaking, upon a low plane and in a decidedly sordid manner. Those who own and control the industry seem to have been of the opinion that the sensual, the sordid, the prurient, the phases of fast life, the ways of extravagance, the risqué, the paths of shady life, drew the greatest attendance and coined for them the most money, and apparently they have been out to get the coin, no matter what the effect upon the public, young or old; and when thoughtful people have suggested or advocated official censorship, in the interest of good citizenship and wholesome morals, the owners of the industry have resented it and, in effect, declared that it was nobody's business other than theirs and concerned nobody other than them what kind of shows they produced; that if people did not like their shows they could stay away from them; that it was their business, and they would conduct it as they might please....

In that they are mistaken. The State has an interest in citizenship and a concern in the education of the young. The State has an interest in good morals. It regulates in many ways all of those things. The motion-picture industry vitally concerns all of those things—citizenship, education, morals—and is therefore subject to regulation by the State. It has become a public utility, and is therefore the legitimate subject of State regulation....

The industry has gone so far in defying public sentiment, and has been so flagrant in its abuse of its privileges that a public sentiment for censorship has been aroused which will not

be brooked. It may be temporarily checked; it may be temporarily lulled by fair promises, but it is bound to grow, because censorship is needed and would be a good thing....

I believe that a great deal of the extravagance of the day, a great deal of the disposition to live beyond one's means, yea, a great deal of the crime of the day comes from moving pictures. Through them young people gain ideas of fast life, shady ways, laxity of living, loose morals. Crime is freely depicted in alluring colors. Lax morals are held up lightly before them. The sensual is strongly appealed to. Many of the pictures are certainly not elevating; some, at least, are not fit to be seen.

About 18 months ago, in this city, there occurred a foul and most shocking murder.... Four youths of this city, in age from 15 to 20 years, as I recollect, stole an automobile, and in it followed an honest, peaceable, industrious barber as he was going to his loving family and quiet home after a day's work, and overtaking him, one of the youths jumped out of the automobile, in a residential section of the city, and murdered him by firing a pistol at him at close range. The victim dropped dead. The youths became panic-stricken on account of close-at-hand pedestrians and fled in the stolen machine....

I have no doubt those young criminals got their ideas of the romance of crime from moving pictures. I believe moving pictures are doing as much harm to-day as saloons did in the days of the open saloon—especially to the young. They are running day and night, Sunday and every other day, the year round, and in most jurisdictions without any regulation by censorship. I would not abolish them.... I would close them on Sunday and regulate them week days by judicious censorship....

When we look to the source of the moving pictures, the material for them, the personnel of those who pose for them, we need not wonder that many of the pictures are pernicious....

At Hollywood, Calif., is a colony of these people, where debauchery, riotous living, drunkenness, ribaldry, dissipation, free love, seem to be conspicuous. Many of these "stars," it is reported, were formerly bartenders, butcher boys, sopers, swampers,[1] variety actors and actresses, who may have earned $10 or $20 a week, and some of whom are now paid, it is said, salaries of something like $5,000 a month or more, and they do not know what to do with their wealth, extracted from poor people, in large part, in 25 or 50 cent admission fees, except to spend it in riotous living, dissipation, and "high rolling."

There are some of the characters from whom the young people of to-day are deriving a large part of their education, views of life, and

character-forming habits. From these sources our young people gain much of their views of life, inspirations, and education. Rather a poor source, is it not? Looks like there is some need for censorship, does it not? ...

There was recently some reference in Washington papers to a suggested effort by the Washington Chamber of Commerce or Board of Trade, one or the other, I do not recall which, to induce the Hollywood motion-picture colony to move to this community and establish itself at Great Falls, near this city. I hope it may not be done. From all accounts the Washington Chamber of Commerce or Board of Trade would better invite here a colony of lepers or an institution for the propagation and dissemination of smallpox....

---

[1]In American slang, *butcher boys* were thugs; *sopers* were drug addicts; *swampers* were unskilled laborers.

The Impact of the Great Depression

For a few glorious years from 1924 to 1929, people in the industrialized world could believe that postwar economic problems had been solved. Fueled by investments and loans from a booming United States, Europe's economy revived. Inflation was under control. Industrialized nations experienced higher employment, increased output, and expanded foreign trade. Despite lagging agricultural prices and pockets of high unemployment, optimism reigned, and stock prices, especially on the New York Stock Exchange, skyrocketed. In the summer of 1929, an article in a U.S. magazine touted stock market investing as a sure way to wealth. It was entitled "Everyone Ought to be Rich."

Optimism evaporated in October 1929, when prices on the exchange began a decline that soon laid bare all the underlying weaknesses of the international economy. As personal fortunes disappeared, banks began to fail by the thousands, investments plummeted, prices and wages fell, and unemployment lines and soup kitchens became features of the urban landscape. The stock market crash caused U.S. bankers to call in short-term loans from European creditors, and in the spring of 1931, major banks in Austria and Germany failed. Worse, the crash stopped the flow of investment dollars to Europe, where the number of boarded-up factories, unemployed workers, and ruined farmers soon reached frightening levels.

More than anything else, the Great Depression was a tragedy for millions of men and women who lost jobs, farms, investments, homes, savings, personal possessions, health, dignity, and hope. But it also had important political ramifications. It undermined parliamentary governments in Germany, Austria, and other Central and Eastern European states, and came close to doing so in Belgium and France. It heightened social tensions and encouraged many of its victims to believe that economic hardship was the fault of Jews, communists, capitalists, or some other convenient scapegoat. International cooperation declined as politicians immersed themselves in domestic issues, raised tariffs, and convinced themselves and their compatriots that their economic problems could be blamed on foreigners or perhaps solved by rearmament or foreign conquests.

The Great Depression also prompted new thinking about the role and purposes of government. It soon became apparent that time-honored governmental responses to recessions—encouraging private charity, slashing government spending, raising tariffs, or just waiting passively for the business cycle to turn upward—were inadequate and perhaps counterproductive. A new vision of governmental activism, exemplified by Franklin D. Roosevelt's "New Deal" in the United States, emerged. It viewed the state as responsible for society's economic well-being and its citizens' social welfare. It utilized economic planning, regulation, and deficit spending to stimulate demand and maintain high employment. It viewed tax policy as a means of redistributing wealth from the rich to the poor. It also created a host of new programs and entitlements to protect people from poverty and ensure decent housing, adequate health care, and "social security" in old age. The trend toward big government and the welfare state was of necessity strengthened and accelerated as a result of the economic catastrophe of the 1930s.

The Victims of the Depression in Germany

29 ◆ H. Hessell Tiltman, *SLUMP! A STUDY OF STRICKEN EUROPE TODAY*

H. Hessell Tiltman (1897–1977) was a British author-journalist best known for his coverage of East Asia in the 1930s and 1940s. During the late summer and autumn of 1932, as European correspondent for the *Manchester Guardian,* he traveled across Europe to observe the effects of the Great Depression. On his return he recorded his impressions in a widely read book, *Slump! A Study of Stricken Europe Today.* In the following selection, he describes the effects of the Great Depression on the people of Germany's two largest cities, Hamburg and Berlin. He visited Germany at a time of high political tension. After two rounds of voting, in March and April, the aging war hero Paul von Hindenburg was elected to a term as president, but Adolf Hitler won close to 40 percent of the votes. In late July, shortly before Tiltman's visit, Reichstag elections gave the Nazis 37.8 percent of the vote, making them the largest party in parliament. Among the Nazis' competitors, the Social Democrats, a moderate socialist party and the main supporter of Germany's democratic government, received 21.9 percent of the votes; the Communist Party and the Center Party received 14.6 and 12.3 percent respectively.

Source: From H. Hessel Tiltman, *Slump! A Study of Stricken Europe Today,* © 1932, pp. 24–25, 32–35, 39–41.

QUESTIONS FOR ANALYSIS

1. What economic data does Tiltman provide to back up his assertion that of all the countries of Europe, Germany has suffered most from the "slump"?
2. How has the Great Depression affected the economic situations of the German families mentioned by Tiltman?
3. What does Tiltman's account have to say about the emotional and psychological damage of unemployment?
4. What connection does Tiltman make between Germany's economic woes and Germany's political situation?

HAMBURG

With over 200,000 of Greater Hamburg's 758,000 workers totally unemployed, and most of the remainder working twenty-four hours a week, the number of families which can afford 14/– a week[1] rent is rapidly declining. In the case of the shipyard workers, such a rent would, in many cases, absorb nearly the whole of their earnings for a 24-hour week, leaving them less than 5/– a week for food, clothing and all other expenses. Incomes, even for the lucky ones still at work, are to-day so low in Hamburg that [decent apartments] are quite beyond the means of the mass of the population. They could not pay the rents—and in Germany the tenant who owes rent can, under a new decree enforced by the present government, be evicted at twelve hours' notice.

Hence the fact that thousands of families cannot aspire to more than one room for four or five people, with another family of the same size crowded into the adjoining room. Those who have had to leave former homes owing to rent debts are forced in many cases, both at Hamburg and elsewhere in Germany, to live in sheds on allotments outside the city—without cooking facilities, water or sanitation....

The general standard of living of Hamburg's one-and-a-half million population has declined by over 25 percent since the beginning of the trade slump. That is a general figure—what it

means to the city and to the individual families was explained to me by the Director of Unemployment for the city....

"In June, 1931, we had only 132,000 unemployed," he said, "and of that number 55,000 were still in receipt of the first category dole (the highest rate of unemployment benefit, originally paid for the first 20 weeks but now paid for only 6 weeks), and 33,000 on the second category dole (paid for 52 weeks), leaving only about 40,000 who had exhausted both grades of unemployment insurance benefits and were provided for by welfare relief.

"That was a year ago. Now, with unemployment swollen to 208,000, there are only 32,143 on the first category dole, and 62,456 on the second category dole. The balance not eligible for payments in either of these classes now numbers over 100,000 families."...

Official figures show that the amount spent in relieving unemployment during the six years to 1930 was £600,000,000. Since that date the scale of all payments, including municipal relief, has been reduced on three occasions, the last a cut of approximately 23 per cent in June, 1932, so that to-day the majority of the workless in Germany are receiving weekly sums upon which it is impossible to starve and equally impossible to banish hunger....

---

[1]Tiltman expresses income and expenditures in units of British money. The number left of the slash represents shillings, twenty of which make up a pound; the number on the right of the slash represents pence, twelve of which make up a shilling. The symbol of pence is "d." Tiltman assumed that one German shilling had the purchasing power of one German mark, just over four of which equaled one U.S. dollar.

Food is the great topic of conversation in Germany, to-day. Since Lausanne[2] it has replaced even reparations as the burning question of the hour. Where two Englishmen will, in nine cases out of ten, begin discussing sport, two Germans will ask each other why they and their families should go hungry in a world stuffed with food. Why German children should be suffering from rickets for the first time since the Allied blockade?[3] And especially why Germany should be drinking a coffee substitute made from rye while in Brazil they are using unsaleable coffee as fuel for locomotives?

These problems worry other people besides the financiers and economists. Which explains the avid interest which all classes in Germany are taking in politics. In no country I know, not even excepting Soviet Russia, are there so many people listening to political speeches every night of the week.

When men and women, in their tens of thousands, will sit for four hours listening to impassioned oratory from National Socialists, Centre Party men, Socialists, Communists—or anyone else with anything to say—and cheerfully fight in defence of their opinions on the way home, it means that politics have ceased to be a subject for academic debate, and have become a matter of bread and butter....

BERLIN

IN June, 1929, eight and a half out of every hundred German trade unionists were unemployed. In June, 1932 ... forty-four out of every hundred were workless. Spread over all Germany, that figure means, in the words of a famous Trade Union leader with whom I talked in Berlin, that there are to-day 6,000,000 families, totalling at least 18,000,000 men, women, and children, existing on unemployment "insurance payments or municipal relief...."

Production of iron and steel ... is down to only 20 percent of the 1928 figure and still falling. The value of German exports in 1931 was £275,000,000 less than in 1929. Imports were cut in half in the same two years. Germany's savings fell from £375,000,000 in 1929 to a minus quantity, invested capital having been spent, in 1931. Her national income dropped by 5/- in every pound during 1931—a 25 percent decline in the course of a single year.

Is it altogether surprising, in the face of these figures revealing the effects of the international trade crisis upon the fortunes of German industries, that the city of Berlin, with its bourgeois appearance and palaces, provided the German Communist Party with 382,317 votes at the Reichstag elections held on July 31, 1932? ...

The inhabitants of Berlin in 1932 are like the inhabitants of Petrograd in 1917, conscious of living over a powder-magazine....

Beneath the surface of Berlin life I saw overcrowding, because those living on relief can rarely afford more than one room, however large the family.

I saw hunger, because, as I have said, these victims cannot escape that horror. I saw rags, because the welfare centres can no longer supply anyone with even second-hand shoes until *both* the soles of the existing pair have been worn to nothing....

But more painful than any of these things, I saw utter despair. Some of the wives could still hold up their heads and be interested in the life about them, but most of the men were shattered in spirit and breaking in health. They had fought despair for one year, two years, maybe even three years. But it got them in the end....

I went to another home—two rooms occupied by a builders' labourer, unemployed for over two years....

---

[2]A reference to the Lausanne Conference, held in late June and early July 1932, at which Great Britain, France, and Germany agreed to suspend Germany's reparation payments imposed by the Versailles Treaty.
[3]The Allies (mainly the British Royal Navy) imposed a blockade on Germany throughout World War I. It contributed to severe food shortages in Germany and, according to German delegates at Paris Peace Conference, resulted in the deaths of approximately 760,000 civilians.

The husband had just drawn 32/–, two weeks' relief payment, and I went out with the wife to spend it.

The first 9/– went to pay a debt at the grocer's, A cwt. of coal cost another 1/6½; 12/– went to pay the fortnight's rent; 2/6 liquidated a debt for potatoes eaten during the previous week. Seven shillings were left, and the wife spent this on eggs, dripping, bread, potatoes and cabbage—which may be described as the universal diet of the German workless. On that menu, they had to exist for another week at least.

When we returned, the husband was sitting on a box, his head in his hands—gazing fixedly into space.... As a trade unionist, he had been a member of the Social Democratic Party, the bulwark of the German Republic. Now he was nothing—too broken in spirit to care....

A moment later two young men, clad in leather jackets, burst into that cellar-room with a stamp of feet, to provide another glimpse of the curses which afflict Germany to-day, This time the curse, not of poverty, but of Hitlerism....

Compared with the Socialist worker, wearied by waiting for the turn of the tide, these two members of the Nazi "S.A."[4] represented another world—a Germany which has lost its patience and demands the impossible under threat of instant reprisals.

The sight of a foreigner in no way cooled their truculence. On the contrary, upon learning that I had been asking questions concerning the lives of the workless, they began to shout their opinions of what should be done to whatever "is the German equivalent of 'nosey parkers' [snoops]."

It was the wife who ended the incident, womanlike, by the simple expedient of pushing the two embryo Hitlers into the inner room and, after closing the door upon them, standing before it while she explained that they were friends of her husband, who were enthusiastic followers of the Nazi chief. I do not doubt their enthusiasm. Those two young workless men were walking evidence ... of the fact that whatever else Adolf Hitler has, or has not, done, he has enabled a large number of Germans to keep up their spirits ... at a time when Germany's spirits were in danger of sinking to zero.

---

[4]Abbreviation for *Sturmabteilung*, a Nazi paramilitary organization noted for its violence and antisemitism; also known in English as the "Brown Shirts" or "Storm Troopers."

Government Promises a "New Deal"

❖

30 ◆ Franklin D. Roosevelt, *ANNUAL ADDRESS TO CONGRESS, JANUARY 4, 1935*

Herbert Hoover, who was just finishing his first year as president when the stock market crashed, was deeply concerned about the human costs of the Depression, but his commitment to volunteerism and a balanced budget doomed his efforts to mitigate its effects. His refusal to commit the federal government to relief or recovery programs infuriated Americans, who came to believe he was indifferent to their suffering and interested mainly in protecting business. In 1932, the voters overwhelmingly supported the Democrat Franklin D. Roosevelt, who in the campaign had promised them a new deal.

Source: Record, 74th Congress, 1st Session, pp. 94–97.

Franklin D. Roosevelt was born into a wealthy upstate New York family in 1882. A Harvard graduate and a lawyer, he had served as a New York state legislator, assistant secretary of the navy under Wilson, the Democratic vice-presidential candidate in 1920, and governor of New York between 1928 and 1932. Taking office when the Depression was at its worst and promising "bold and persistent experimentation," the president pushed forward a program to resolve the crises of a collapsing banking system, crippling unemployment, and agricultural and industrial breakdown. Two years later, in 1935, with the Depression far from over, Roosevelt shifted his priorities in what is sometimes called the "Second New Deal," from relief and recovery to basic social and economic reforms.

In the following message to Congress, delivered in January 1935, Roosevelt outlines some of his ideas about the role of government and the nation's economic well-being.

QUESTIONS FOR ANALYSIS

1. How does Roosevelt perceive the "state of the nation" in 1935? What has been accomplished and what does his administration still need to do?
2. What evidence does Roosevelt's speech provide that his administration's interests were shifting from relief and recovery to more basic reforms? What groups and regions in U.S. society were most likely to benefit from his proposals?
3. How would you describe Roosevelt's long-term goals for American society?
4. Taken as a whole, how would his proposals result in an expansion of the federal government?

Throughout the world change is the order of the day. In every nation economic problems, long in the making, have brought crises of many kinds for which the masters of old practice and theory were unprepared. In most nations, social justice, no longer a distant ideal, has become a definite goal, and ancient governments are beginning to heed the call....

We find our population suffering from old inequalities, little changed by past sporadic remedies. In spite of our efforts and in spite of our talk, we have not weeded out the overprivileged and we have not effectively lifted up the underprivileged. Both of these manifestations of injustice have retarded happiness. No wise man has any intention of destroying what is known as the "profit motive," because by the profit motive we mean the right by work to earn a decent livelihood for ourselves and for our families.

We have, however, a clear mandate from the people, that Americans must forswear that conception of the acquisition of wealth which,

through excessive profits, creates undue private power over private affairs and, to our misfortune, over public affairs as well. In building toward this end we do not destroy ambition, nor do we seek to divide our wealth into equal shares on stated occasions.... But we do assert that the ambition of the individual to obtain for him and his a proper security, a reasonable leisure, and a decent living throughout life is an ambition to be preferred to the appetite for great wealth and great power....

In defining immediate factors which enter into our quest, I have spoken to the Congress and the people of three great divisions: first, the security of a livelihood through the better use of the national resources of the land in which we live; second, the security against the major hazards and vicissitudes of life; third, the security of decent homes....

A study of our national resources ... shows the vast amount of necessary and practicable work which needs to be done for the development and preservation of our national wealth for the enjoyment and advantage of our people in generations to come. The sound use of land and water is far more comprehensive than the mere planting of trees, building of dams, distributing of electricity, or retirement of submarginal land. It recognizes that stranded populations, either in the country or the city, cannot have security under the conditions that now surround them.

To this end we are ready to begin to meet this problem—the intelligent care of population throughout our nation in accordance with an intelligent distribution of the means of livelihood for that population. A definite program for putting people to work, of which I shall speak in a moment, is a component part of this greater program of security of livelihood through the better use of our national resources.

Closely related to the broad problem of livelihood is that of security against the major hazards of life.... I shall send to you, in a few days, definite recommendations ... These recommendations will cover the broad subjects of unemployment insurance and old-age insurance, of benefits for children, for mothers, for the handicapped, for maternity care, and for other aspects of dependency and illness where a beginning can now be made.

The third factor—better homes for our people—has also been the subject of experimentation and study. Here, too, the first practical steps can be made through the proposals which I shall suggest in relation to giving work to the unemployed....

The first objectives of emergency legislation of 1933 were to relieve destitution, to make it possible for industry to operate in a more rational and orderly fashion, and to put behind industrial recovery the impulse of large expenditures in government undertakings. The purpose of the National Industrial Recovery Act[1] to provide work for more people succeeded in a substantial manner within the first few months of its life, and the act has continued to maintain

employment gains and greatly improved working conditions in industry....

But the stark fact before us is that great numbers still remain unemployed. A large proportion of these unemployed and their dependents have been forced on the relief rolls.... The lessons of history, confirmed by the evidence immediately before me, show conclusively that continued dependence upon relief induces a spiritual and moral disintegration fundamentally destructive to the national fiber. To dole out relief in this way is to administer a narcotic, a subtle destroyer of the human spirit.... Work must be found for able-bodied but destitute workers....

I am not willing that the vitality of our people be further sapped by the giving of cash, of market baskets, of a few hours of weekly work cutting grass, raking leaves, or picking up papers in the public parks. We must preserve not only the bodies of the unemployed from destitution but also their self-respect, their self-reliance, and courage and determination. This decision brings me to the problem of what the government should do with approximately 5 million unemployed now on the relief rolls.

About 1.5 million of these belong to the group which in the past was dependent upon local welfare efforts. Most of them are unable, for one reason or another, to maintain themselves independently—for the most part, through no fault of their own. Such people, in the days before the great depression, were cared for by local efforts—by states, by counties, by towns, by cities, by churches, and by private welfare agencies....

There are, however, an additional 3.5 million employable people who are on relief. With them the problem is different and the responsibility is different. This group was the victim of a nation-wide depression caused by conditions which were not local but national. The federal government is the only governmental agency with sufficient power and credit to meet this situation.... It is a duty dictated by every intelligent consideration of national policy to ask you to make it possible

---

[1]The National Industrial Recovery Act established the National Recovery Administration (NRA), which sought to revive U.S. industry by allowing industrial and trade associations to draft codes setting production levels, wages, price policies, and working conditions.

for the United States to give employment to all of these 3.5 million employable people now on relief, pending their absorption in a rising tide of private employment....

It is my thought that ... all emergency public works shall be united in a single new and greatly enlarged plan. With the establishment of this new system, we can supersede the Federal Emergency Relief Administration[2] with a coordinated authority which will be charged with the orderly liquidation of our present relief activities and the substitution of a national chart for the giving of work....

The work itself will cover a wide field, including clearance of slums, which for adequate reasons cannot be undertaken by private capital; in rural housing of several kinds, where, again, private capital is unable to function; in rural electrification; in the reforestation of the great watersheds of the nation; in an intensified program to prevent soil erosion and to reclaim blighted areas; in improving existing road systems and in constructing national highways designed to handle modern traffic; in the elimination of grade crossings; in the extension and enlargement of the successful work of the Civilian Conservation Corps;[3] in nonfederal work, mostly self-liquidating and highly useful to local divisions of government; and on many other projects which the nation needs and cannot afford to neglect....

The ledger of the past year shows many more gains than losses. Let us not forget that, in addition to saving millions from utter destitution, child labor has been for the moment outlawed, thousands of homes saved to their owners, and, most important of all, the morale of the nation has been restored. Viewing the year 1934 as a whole, you and I can agree that we have a generous measure of reasons for giving thanks.

---

[2]The Federal Emergency Relief Administration (FERA) furnished funds to state and local agencies for relief. It spent close to $3 billion before it was replaced in 1935 by programs that provided work rather than cash payments.

[3]The Civil Conservation Corps (CCC) employed 2.5 million young men to work on reforestation and flood control projects.

◆

Liberalism and Democracy Under Siege

On April 2, 1917, U.S. President Woodrow Wilson went before a joint session of Congress to seek a declaration of war against Germany so that the world could "be made safe for democracy." As late as 1921, it appeared that such a goal had been realized, at least in Europe. Except for Bolshevik Russia, all twenty-seven European states, including the six new states created by postwar treaties, were democracies with parliamentary governments, constitutions, and guarantees of basic freedoms. In 1922, however, when Benito Mussolini established a dictatorship in Italy, this was the beginning of an authoritarian tide that swept across Europe, leaving only ten parliamentary democracies when World War II started in 1939. They included the four Scandinavian states of Finland, Sweden, Norway, and Denmark; Czechoslovakia in Eastern Europe; the three small states of Belgium, the Netherlands, and Switzerland; and only two major powers, Britain and France.

No single cause can explain the failure of liberal democracy throughout much of Europe. General factors include the shallowness or absence of a parliamentary tradition; inexperienced leadership; fears of communism; low levels of education and literacy; the continued hostility to democracy on the part of powerful elites; ethnic conflict; and the difficulty of reintegrating millions of veterans into civilian life. The single most important factor, however, was the devastating human cost of the Great Depression. In the face of this calamity, dispirited Europeans turned to antidemocratic leaders and movements that offered simple explanations and miraculous solutions for their nations' problems.

Most of the new authoritarian regimes exemplified traditional conservatism in that they represented the interests of landowners, large businesses, the army, and certain elements within organized churches—whose opposition to democracy predated World War I. Such governments shut down parliaments, abolished opposing political parties, ended free speech, and promised order, if necessary, through force. But they offered no new ideologies, no blueprints for social change, and no grandiose plans for territorial expansion. The antidemocratic movement known as fascism was far different. Applied mainly to Mussolini's Italy and Hitler's Germany, but also to its supporters in other European states, fascism rejected liberalism, socialism, and democracy. It also glorified violence and war, saw life in terms of struggle, promoted service to the nation as the supreme calling, and required absolute obedience to a single infallible ruler. Fascist regimes turned schools, theaters, newspapers, churches, museums, and radio broadcasts into instruments of propaganda. They also brought catastrophe to the people they ruled, the groups they hated, and the nations they attacked.

The State as a Spiritual and Moral Fact

❖

31 ◆ Benito Mussolini, *THE POLITICAL AND SOCIAL DOCTRINE OF FASCISM*

Benito Mussolini (1883–1945), Europe's first fascist dictator, was the son of a blacksmith and a schoolteacher who, as a youth, participated in socialist and revolutionary political movements. He discarded radicalism for nationalism during World War I, when as a journalist he called for Italy's entry into World War I and served as a soldier until he was wounded in 1917. After the war, he founded his own private army of some forty unemployed veterans, which he called the *Fasci italiani di Combattimento.* The ultranationalist fascists portrayed themselves as Italy's only protection from socialists, communists, labor unions, and anarchists, whom they battled in the streets. Many Italians, dismayed by inflation, high taxes, widespread unemployment, strikes, rural violence, corruption, and ineffectual leadership, looked to the Fascists for Italy's salvation. In 1921, Mussolini was elected to the Italian Chamber of Deputies as leader of the newly formed Italian Fascist Party, which now had three hundred thousand members. In 1922, even though the Fascists and their supporters

Source: Mussolini, "Fascism." Reprinted by permission of the publisher from *International Conciliation*, No.306 (Washington, DC; Carnegie Endowment for International Peace, 1935), pp. 35–37. www.carnegieendowment.org

controlled less than 10 percent of the seats in the Italian parliament, Mussolini demanded that King Victor Emmanuel III name him premier. When the king hesitated, Mussolini organized a march on Rome, in which thousands of Fascists converged on the capital, prompting the resignation of the cabinet and causing the king to name Mussolini premier. The Fascists quickly suppressed opposition and undermined the Italian parliamentary system. By 1924, a Fascist dictatorship under *Il Duce,* "The Leader," was secure.

Claiming that fascism was based on "action," not ideology, Mussolini at first declined to explain its doctrines. In 1932, however, he wrote (or had written for him) the following statement in *Enciclopedia Italiana.*

QUESTIONS FOR ANALYSIS

1. What is Mussolini's rationale for opposing pacifism and glorifying war?
2. To Mussolini, what are the flaws of Marxism?
3. What is the rationale for the fascist rejection of democracy?
4. What is the relationship between the individual and the state according to Mussolini?
5. What does Mussolini mean when he says, "the State is spiritual and moral fact"?
6. Most of what Mussolini wrote describes what fascism opposes. Are there positive features in its ideology?

The Fascist State organizes the nation, but leaves a sufficient margin of liberty to the individual; the latter is deprived of all useless and possibly harmful freedoms, but retains what is essential; the deciding power in this question cannot be the individual, but the State alone. . . .

Fascism is the doctrine best adapted to represent the tendencies and the aspirations of a people, like the people of Italy, who are rising again after many centuries of abasement and foreign servitude. But empire demands discipline, the co-ordination of all forces and a deeply felt sense of duty and sacrifice: this fact explains many aspects of the practical working of the regime, the character of many forces in the State, and the necessarily severe measures which must be taken against those who would oppose this spontaneous and inevitable movement of Italy in the twentieth century, and would oppose it by recalling the outworn ideology of the nineteenth century—repudiated wheresoever there has been the courage to

undertake great experiments of social and political transformation: for never before has the nation stood more in need of authority, of direction, and of order. If every age has its own characteristic doctrine, there are a thousand signs which point to Fascism as the characteristic doctrine of our time. For if a doctrine must be a living thing, this is proved by the fact that Fascism has created a living faith; and that this faith is very powerful in the minds of men, is demonstrated by those who have suffered and died for it.

Fascism, the more it considers and observes the future and the development of humanity quite apart from political considerations of the moment, believes neither in the possibility nor the utility of perpetual peace. It thus repudiates the doctrine of Pacifism—born of a renunciation of the struggle and an act of cowardice in the face of sacrifice. War alone brings up to its highest tension all human energy and puts the stamp of nobility upon the peoples who have the courage to meet it. All other trials are substitutes, which never really put men into the position where they have to make the great decision—the alternative of life or death. Thus a doctrine which is founded upon this harmful postulate of peace is hostile to Fascism. And thus hostile to the spirit of Fascism, though accepted for what use they can be in dealing with particular political situations, are all the international leagues and societies which, as history will show, can be scattered to the winds when once strong national feeling is aroused by any motive—sentimental, ideal, or practical. This anti-pacifist spirit is carried by Fascism even into the life of the individual; the proud motto of the Squadrista,[1] "*Me ne frego*" (I don't give a damn), written on the bandage of the wound, is an act of philosophy not only stoic, the summary of an education not only political it is the education to combat, the acceptance of the risks which combat implies, and a new way of life for Italy....

Such a conception of life makes Fascism the complete opposite of that doctrine, the base of the so-called scientific and Marxian Socialism, the materialist conception of history; according to which the history of human civilization can be explained simply through the conflict of interests among the various social groups and by the change and development in the means and instruments of production. That the changes in the economic field—new discoveries of raw materials, new methods of working them, and the inventions of science—have their importance no one can deny; but that these factors are sufficient to explain the history of humanity excluding all others is an absurd delusion. Fascism, now and always, believes in holiness and in heroism; that is to say, in actions influenced by no economic motive, direct or indirect.... And above all Fascism denies that class war can be the preponderant force in the transformation of society. These two fundamental concepts of Socialism being thus refuted, nothing is left of it but the sentimental aspiration—as old as

humanity itself—towards a social convention in which the sorrows and sufferings of the humblest shall be alleviated. But here again Fascism repudiates the conception of "economic" happiness, to be realized by Socialism and, as it were, at a given moment in economic evolution to assure to everyone the maximum of well-being. Fascism denies the materialist conception of happiness as a possibility, and abandons it to its inventors, the economists of the first half of the nineteenth century: that is to say, Fascism denies the validity of the equation, well-being = happiness, which would reduce men to the level of animals, caring for one thing only—to be fat and well-fed—and would thus degrade humanity to a purely physical existence.

After Socialism, Fascism combats the whole complex system of democratic ideology, and repudiates it.... Fascism denies that the majority, by the simple fact that it is a majority, can direct human society; it denies that numbers alone can govern by means of a periodic consultation, and it affirms the immutable, beneficial, and fruitful inequality of mankind, which can never be permanently leveled through the mere operation of a mechanical process such as universal suffrage.... Democracy is a regime nominally without a king, but it is ruled by many kings—more absolute, tyrannical, and ruinous than one sole king, even though a tyrant....

The foundation of Fascism is the conception of the State, its character, its duty, and its aim. Fascism conceives of the State as an absolute, in comparison with which all individuals or groups are relative, only to be conceived of in their relation to the State.... In 1929, at the first five-yearly assembly of the Fascist regime, I said:

"For us Fascists, the State is not merely a guardian, preoccupied solely with the duty of assuring the personal safety of the citizens; nor is it an organization with purely material

---

[1]Party members who did much of the street fighting against socialists and communists during the early struggle for power.

aims, such as to guarantee a certain level of well-being and peaceful conditions of life; for a mere council of administration would be sufficient to realize such objects. . . . The State, as conceived of and as created by Fascism, is a spiritual and moral fact in itself . . . and such an organization must be in its origins and development a manifestation of the spirit. The State is the guarantor of security both internal and external, but it is also the custodian and transmitter of the spirit of the people, as it has grown up through the centuries in language, in customs, and in faith. And the State is not only a living reality of the present, it is also linked with the past and above all with the future, and thus transcending the brief limits of individual life, it represents the immanent spirit of the nation. . . The individual in the Fascist State is not annulled but rather multiplied, just in the same way that a soldier in a regiment is not diminished but rather increased by the number of his comrades.

The Dreams of the Führer

❖

32 ◆ Adolf Hitler, *MEIN KAMPF*

The Nazi movement was born on January 5, 1919, when seven men gathered in a Munich tavern to form the German Workers' Party, renamed a year later the National Socialist German Workers' Party. It died on April 30, 1945, in a bunker beneath the streets of a ravaged and burning Berlin when Adolf Hitler put a gun to his head and committed suicide. The Nazi movement existed for slightly more than twenty-six years, and its leader, Hitler, was Germany's dictator for only thirteen of them, from 1933 to 1945. Yet in this brief time, so heinous were the Nazis' deeds, and so great their transgressions, that as long as the slightest moral sense remains among human beings, Nazism will be remembered as an archsymbol of human depravity and viciousness.

During the 1920s, the National Socialists espoused a program of nationalism, anticommunism, opposition to the Weimar Republic, antisemitism, repudiation of the Versailles Treaty, remilitarization, and a return to the old German values of home, hearth, family, and land. Despite the appeal of such ideas to many Germans and Hitler's unquestioned skill as an agitator, the party made little progress in the 1920s. In 1928, it had fewer than one hundred thousand members and won only 2.8 percent of the vote in the national elections. The Nazis' fortunes improved dramatically in 1929 and 1930 as the economy slowed and then crashed, and the Weimar government limped from one crisis to another. In the elections of September 1930, the Nazis won 107 seats in the Reichstag, making them the second largest party after the Social Democrats. They became the largest party in November 1932 when they won 196 seats and approximately one third of the popular vote. With coalition governments dissolving almost as soon as they were formed and Germany close to political collapse, in January 1933 President von Hindenburg offered Hitler the chancellorship in the hope that as the leader of Germany's largest party, Hitler could end the parliamentary crisis. In a way, he did just that.

Source: Excerpts from *Mein Kampf*, by Adolph Hitler, translated by Ralph Manheim. © 1943, renewed 1971 by Houghton Mifflin Harcourt Publishing Company. Reprinted in the United States of America by permission of Houghton Mifflin Harcourt Publishing Company. All rights reserved. Published by Hutchinson and reprinted by permission of Random House Group Ltd. in North America.

On March 23, 1933, with nearly one hundred communist and socialist deputies in jail or in hiding from the secret police, and with Hitler's supporters surrounding the Reichstag and screaming threats against anyone who voted against Hitler, Germany's postwar experiment with democracy ended. Two thirds of the deputies to the Reichstag voted for the Enabling Act, which gave Hitler dictatorial powers and an opportunity to implement his cruel, fantastic dreams.

Born to an Austrian customs official and his German wife in 1889, Adolf Hitler moved to Vienna at the age of nineteen to seek a career as an artist or architect. His efforts failed, however, and he lived at the bottom of Viennese society, drifting from one low-paying job to another. In 1912, he moved to Munich where his life fell into the same purposeless pattern. Enlistment in the German army in World War I rescued Hitler, giving him comradeship and a sense of direction he had lacked. After the war, a shattered Hitler returned to Munich where in 1919 he joined the small German Workers' Party, which in 1920 changed its name to the National Socialist German Workers' Party, or Nazis.

After becoming the leader of the National Socialists, Hitler staged an abortive coup d'état against the government of the German state of Bavaria in 1923. For this, he was sentenced to a five-year prison term (serving only nine months), during which time he wrote the first volume of *Mein Kampf* (My Struggle). To a remarkable degree, this work, which he completed in 1925, provided the ideas that inspired his millions of followers and guided the National Socialists until their destruction in 1945.

QUESTIONS FOR ANALYSIS

1. What broad purpose does Hitler see in human existence?
2. How, in Hitler's view, are the Aryans and Jews dissimilar?
3. What is Hitler's view of political leadership?
4. What role do parliaments play in a "folkish" state, according to Hitler?
5. How does Hitler plan to reorient German foreign policy? What goals does he set for Germany, and how are they to be achieved?
6. Based on these excerpts, what can you infer about his objections to the ideologies of democracy, liberalism, and socialism?
7. How do Hitler's views of race compare to those of von Treitschke (Source 3)?

NATION AND RACE

There are some truths that are so plain and obvious that for this very reason the everyday world does not see them or at least does not apprehend them....

So humans invariably wander about the garden of nature, convinced that they know and understand everything, yet with few exceptions are blind to one of the fundamental principles Nature uses in her work: the intrinsic segregation of the species of every living thing on the earth.... Each beast mates with only one of its own species: the titmouse with titmouse, finch with finch, stork with stork, field mouse with field mouse, house mouse with house mouse, wolf with wolf.... This is only natural.

Any cross-breeding between two not completely equal beings will result in a product that is in between the level of the two parents. That means that the offspring will be superior to the parent who is at a biologically lower level of being but inferior to the parent at a higher level. This means the offspring will be over-come in the struggle for existence against those at the higher level. Such matings go against the will of Nature for the higher breeding of life.

A precondition for this lies not in the blend-ing of beings of a higher and lower order, but rather the absolute victory of the stronger. The stronger must dominate and must not blend with the weaker orders and sacrifice their powers. Only born weaklings can find this cruel, but after all, they are only weaker and more narrow-minded types of men; unless this law dominated, then any conceivable higher evolution of living organisms would be unthinkable....

Nature looks on this calmly and approv-ingly. The struggle for daily bread allows all those who are weak, sick, and indecisive to be defeated, while the struggle of the males for females gives to the strongest alone the right or at least the possibility to reproduce. Always this struggle is a means of advancing the health and power of resistance of the species, and thus a means to its higher evolution.

As little as nature approves the mating of higher and lower individuals, she approves even less the blending of higher races with lower ones; for indeed otherwise her previous work toward higher development perhaps over hun-dreds of thousands of years might be rendered useless with one blow. If this were not the case, progressive development would stop and even deterioration might set in....

All the great civilizations of the past died out because contamination of their blood caused them to become decadent.... In other words, in order to protect a certain culture, the type of human who created the culture must be preserved. But such preservation is tied to the inalterable law of the necessity and the right of victory of the best and the strongest.

Whoever would live must fight. Who-ever will not fight in this world of endless competition does not deserve to live.... He interferes with the victory path of the best race and with it, the precondition for all human progress....

It is an idle undertaking to argue about which race or races were the original standard-bearers of human culture and were therefore the true founders of everything we conceive by the word humanity. It is much simpler to deal with the question as it pertains to the present, and here the answer is simple and clear. What we see before us today as human culture, all the yields of art, science, and technology, are almost exclusively the creative product of the Aryans.[1] Indeed this fact alone leads to the not unfounded conclusion that the Aryan alone is the founder of the higher type of humanity, and further that he represents the prototype of what we understand by the word: MAN. He is the Prometheus[2] from whose brow the bright spark of genius has forever burst forth, time and again rekindling the fire, which as knowledge has illuminated the night full of silent mysteries, and has permitted humans to ascend the path of mastery over the other beings of the earth. Eliminate him—and deep darkness will again descend on the earth after a few thousand years; human civilization will die out and the earth will become a desert....

The Jew provides the greatest contrast to the Aryan. With no other people of the world has the instinct for self-preservation been so developed as by the so-called chosen race.[3] The best proof

---

[1]Aryan, strictly speaking, is a linguistic term referring to a branch of the Indo-European family of languages known as Indo-Iranian. It also is used to refer to a people who as early as 4000 B.C.E. began to migrate from their homeland in the steppes of western Asia to Iran, India, Mesopotamia, Asia Minor, and Europe. In the nineteenth century, Aryan was used to refer to the racial group that spoke Indo-European

languages. According to Hitler and the Nazis, the Aryans provided Europe's original racial stock and stood in contrast to other peoples such as the Jews, who spoke Semitic languages.
[2]In Greek mythology, Prometheus was the titan (titans were offspring of Uranus, Heaven, and Gaea, Earth) who stole fire from the gods and gave it to humans, along with all other arts and civilization.

of this statement rests in the fact that this race still exists. Where can another people be found in the past 2,000 years that has undergone so few changes in its inner qualities, character, etc. as the Jews? What people has undergone upheavals as great as this one—and nonetheless has emerged unchanged from the greatest catastrophes of humanity? What an infinitely tenacious will to live and to preserve one's kind is revealed in this fact....

Since the Jew ... never had a civilization of his own, others have always provided the foundations of his intellectual labors. His intellect has always developed by the use of those cultural achievements he has found ready at hand around him. Never has it happened the other way around.

For though their drive for self-preservation is not smaller, but larger than that of other people, and though their mental capabilities may easily give the impression that their intellectual powers are equal to those of other races, the Jews lack the most basic characteristic of a truly cultured people, namely an idealistic spirit.

It is a remarkable fact that the herd instinct brings people together for mutual protection only so long as there is a common danger that makes mutual assistance necessary or unavoidable. The same pack of wolves that an instant ago combined to overcome their prey will soon after satisfying their hunger again become individual beasts.... It goes the same way with the Jews. His sense of self sacrifice is only apparent. It lasts only so long as it is strictly necessary.... Jews act together only when a common danger threatens them or a common prey attracts them. When these two things are lacking, then their characteristic of the crassest egoism returns as a force, and out of this once unified people emerges in a flash a swarm of rats fighting bloodily against one another....

That is why the Jewish state—which should be the living organism for the maintenance and improvement of the race—has absolutely no borders. For the territorial definition of a state always demands a certain idealism of spirit on the part of the race which forms the state and especially an acceptance of the idea of work.... If this attitude is lacking then the prerequisite for civilization is lacking.

[Hitler describes the process by which Jews in concert with communists have come close to subverting and controlling the peoples and nations of Europe.]

Here he stops at nothing, and his vileness becomes so monstrous that no one should be surprised if among our people the hateful figure of the Jew is taken as the personification of the devil and the symbol of evil....

How close they see their approaching victory can be seen in the frightful way that their dealings with members of other races develop.

The black-haired Jewish youth, with satanic joy on his face, lurks in wait for hours for the innocent girls he plans to defile with his blood, and steal the young girl from her people. With every means at hand he seeks to undermine the racial foundations of the people they would subjugate....

Around those nations which have offered sturdy resistance to their internal attacks, they surround them with a web of enemies; thanks to their international influence, they incite them to war, and when necessary, will plant the flag of revolution, even on the battlefield.

In economics he shakes the foundations of the state long enough so that unprofitable business enterprises are shut down and come under his financial control. In politics he denies the state its means of self-preservation, destroys its means of self-maintenance and defense, annihilates faith in state leadership, insults its history and traditions, and drags everything that is truly great into the gutter.

---

[3]A reference to the Jewish belief that God had chosen the Jews to enter into a special covenantal relationship in

which God promised to be the God of the Hebrews and favor them in return for true worship and obedience.

Culturally, he pollutes art, literature and theater, makes a mockery of natural sensibilities, destroys every concept of beauty and nobility, the worthy and the good, and instead drags other men down to the sphere of its own lowly type of existence.

Religion is made an object of mockery, morality and ethics are described as old-fashioned, until finally the last props of a people for maintaining their existence in this world are destroyed.

PERSONALITY AND THE IDEAL OF THE FOLKISH[4] STATE

... The folkish state must care for the wellbeing of its citizens by recognizing in everything the worth of the person, and by doing so direct it to the highest level of its productive capability, thus guaranteeing for each the highest level of participation.

Accordingly, the folkish state must free the entire leadership, especially those in political leadership, from the parliamentary principle of majority rule by the multitude, so that the right of personality is guaranteed without any limitation. From this is derived the following realization. *The best state constitution and form is that which with unquestioned certainty raises the best minds from the national community to positions of leading authority and influence....*

There are no majority decisions, rather only responsible individuals, and the word "advice" will once again have its original meaning. Each man will have advisers at his side, *but the decision will be made by one man.*

The principle that made the Prussian army in its time the most splendid instrument of the German people will have to become someday the foundation for the construction of our completed state: *authority of every leader downward and responsibility upward....*

This principle of binding absolute responsibility with absolute authority will gradually bring forth an elite group of leaders which

today in an era of irresponsible parliamentarianism is hardly thinkable.

THE DIRECTION AND POLITICS OF EASTERN EUROPE

The foreign policy of the folkish state has as its purpose to guarantee the existence on this planet of the race that it gathers within its borders. With this in mind it must create a natural and healthy ratio between the number and growth of the population and the extent and quality of the land and soil.... Only a sufficiently large space on the earth can assure the independent existence of a people....

The National Socialist movement must seek to eliminate the disproportion between our people's population and our territory—viewing this as a source of food as well as a basis for national power—and between our historical past and our present hopeless impotence. While doing so it must remain conscious of the fact that we as protectors of the highest humanity on earth are bound also by the highest duty that will be fulfilled only if we inspire the German people with the racial ideal, so that they will occupy themselves not just with the breeding of good dogs, horses, and cats but also show concern about the purity of *their own* blood....

State boundaries are made by man and can be changed by man.

... And only in force lies the right of possession. If today the German people are imprisoned within an impossible territorial area and for that reason are face to face with a miserable future, this is not the commandment of fate, any more than a revolt against such a situation would be a violation of the laws of fate; ... the soil on which we now live was not bestowed upon our ancestors by Heaven; rather, they had to conquer it by risking their lives. So with us, in the future we will win soil and with it the means of existence of the people ... only through the power of the triumphant sword.

But we National Socialists must go further: *The right to land and soil will become an obligation*

---

[4]The word Hitler uses, *völkisch*, is an adjective derived from *Volk*, meaning "people" or "nation," which Hitler defined in a racial sense; thus a "folkish" state is one that expresses

the characteristics of and furthers the interests of a particular race, in this case, the Aryans.

if without further territorial expansion a great people is threatened with its destruction. And that is particularly true when the people in question is not some little nigger people, but the German mother of life, which has given cultural shape to the modern world. *Germany will either become a world power or will no longer exist. . . .*

And so we National Socialists consciously draw a line below the direction of our foreign policy before the *war. We take up where we broke off six hundred years ago. We put a stop to the eternal pull of the Germans toward the south and western Europe and turn our gaze to the lands of the east. We put an end to the colonial and commercial policy of the prewar period and shift to the land-oriented policy of the future.*

When today we speak of new territory and soil in Europe, we think primarily of *Russia* and her subservient border states.

◆

The Stalin Revolution in the Soviet Union

After Lenin suffered a debilitating stroke in 1922 and died in January 1924, the Communist Party of the Soviet Union was racked by controversy over its leadership and direction. Factions led by Leon Trotsky, Lev Kamenev, Gregory Zinoviev, and Nikolai Bukharin fought for party offices and engaged in highly intellectualized debates about industrial policy, the peasant question, the meaning of socialism, international communism, and party governance. The winner in the power struggle, however, was Joseph Stalin, a man noted more for his political and organizational skills than his intellect. As general secretary of the party, through his control of patronage and his ability to dispense favors to local officials he was able to steadily increase the number of his supporters in party congresses and ultimately the politburo, the Party's central executive committee. One by one, his opponents were voted down, removed from office, expelled from the party, and often exiled to Siberia. When the Fifteenth Party Congress in December 1927 condemned "all deviations from the party line" (then largely decided by Stalin himself), Stalin's control was complete. The stage was set for a new round of earthshaking economic and political changes for the Soviet people.

Joseph Stalin (1879–1953), born Joseph Dzhugashvili, was the son of a shoemaker from the province of Georgia. He was a candidate for the priesthood before he abandoned Christianity for Marxism and joined the Bolshevik wing of the Social Democratic Party in 1903. His position in the party rose steadily, and between periods of exile he attended party congresses in Stockholm and London. Exiled to Siberia, he returned to Petrograd in 1917 after the fall of the tsar and sat on the twelve-member Central Committee that organized the overthrow of the Provisional Government. In 1922, he was named general secretary of the Bolshevik Party and, a few years later, commissar of nationalities. Having crushed his opponents in the struggles following Lenin's death, Stalin launched a bold restructuring of the Soviet economy in 1928, setting the Soviet Union on a path it would follow until the mid-1980s.

The Soviet Model of Economic Planning

❖

33 ◆ Joseph Stalin,
THE RESULTS OF THE FIRST FIVE-YEAR PLAN

In 1928, the New Economic Policy (NEP), which Lenin had adopted in 1921, still guided Soviet economic life. Through the NEP, Lenin had sought to restore agriculture and industry after seven years of war, revolution, and civil strife. Although the state maintained control of banks, foreign trade, and heavy industry, peasants could sell their goods on the open market, and small business owners could hire laborers, operate small factories, and keep their profits. The NEP saved the USSR from economic collapse, but its acceptance of private profit and economic competition troubled Marxist purists and did little to foster large-scale industrialization. Thus in 1928, Stalin abandoned the NEP and replaced it with the first Five-Year Plan, which established a centralized planned economy in which Moscow bureaucrats regulated agriculture, manufacturing, finance, and transportation. In agriculture, the plan abolished individual peasant holdings and combined them into large collective and state farms. This meant the obliteration of the class of prosperous and successful peasant farmers known as kulaks. In manufacturing, the plan concentrated on heavy industry and the production of goods such as tractors, trucks, and machinery. Second and third Five-Year Plans were launched in 1933 and 1938.

   In the following report, delivered to the Central Committee of the Communist Party of the Soviet Union in January 1933, Stalin outlines the goals and achievements of the first Five-Year Plan.

QUESTIONS FOR ANALYSIS

1. According to Stalin, was socialist theory or the defense of the Soviet Union the more important reason for launching the Five-Year Plans?
2. Why, according to Stalin, did heavy industry play such an important role in the Five-Year Plans?
3. Why, in Stalin's view, was the collectivization of agriculture such a key component of the Five-Year Plan?
4. What did Stalin see as the main obstacles to the success of the Five-Year Plan?
5. In Stalin's view, how have the people of the Soviet Union benefited from the Five-Year Plan? What sacrifices have they been asked to make?
6. How, according to Stalin, does the success of the Five-Year Plan prove communism's superiority to capitalism?

The fundamental task of the Five-Year Plan was to convert the U.S.S.R. from an agrarian and weak country, dependent upon the caprices of the capitalist countries, into an industrial and powerful country, fully self-reliant and independent of the caprices of world capitalism.

   The fundamental task of the Five-Year Plan was, in converting the U.S.S.R. into an

Source: Stalin, *Leninism Selected Writings* (NY: 1942), "The Results of the Five-Year Plan," pp. 242, 244, 246, 248, 252–254 passim, 258–262, passim. Used by permission of International Publishers.

industrial country, fully to eliminate the capitalist elements, to widen the front of the socialist forms of economy, and to create the economic base for the abolition of classes in the U.S.S.R., for the construction of socialist society.

The fundamental task of the Five-Year Plan was to create such an industry in our country as would be able to re-equip and reorganize, not only the whole of industry, but also transport and agriculture—on the basis of socialism.

The fundamental task of the Five-Year Plan was to transfer small and scattered agriculture onto the lines of large-scale collective farming, so as the ensure the economic base for socialism in the rural districts and thus to eliminate the possibility of the restoration of capitalism in the U.S.S.R.

Finally, the task of the Five-Year Plan was to create in the country all the necessary technical and economic prerequisites for increasing to the utmost the defensive capacity of the country, to enable it to organize determined resistance to any and every attempt at military intervention from outside....

The main link in the Five-Year Plan was heavy industry, with machine building at its core. For only heavy industry is capable of reconstructing industry as a whole, as well as the transport system and agriculture, and of putting them on their feet.... Hence, the restoration of heavy industry had to be made on the basis of the fulfillment of the Five-Year Plan....

But the restoration and development of heavy industry, particularly in such a backward and poor country as our country was at the beginning of the Five-Year Plan period, is an extremely difficult task; for, as is well known, heavy industry calls for enormous financial expenditures and the availability of a certain minimum of experienced technical forces, without which, speaking generally, the restoration of heavy industry is impossible. Did the party know this, and did it take this into consideration? Yes, it did.... The party declared frankly that this would call for serious sacrifices, and that we must openly and consciously make these sacrifices if we wanted to achieve our goal....

◆ ◆

What are the results of the Five-Year Plan in four years in the sphere of *industry*? ...

We did not have an iron and steel industry, the foundation for the industrialization of the country. Now we have this industry.

We did not have a tractor industry. Now we have one.

We did not have an automobile industry. Now we have one.

We did not have a machine-tool industry. Now we have one.

We did not have a big and up-to-date chemical industry. Now we have one.

We did not have a real and big industry for the production of modern agricultural machinery. Now we have one.

We did not have an aircraft industry. Now we have one.

In output of electric power we were last on the list. Now we rank among the first.

In the output of oil products and coal we were last on the list. Now we rank among the first....

And as a result of all this the capitalist elements have been completely and [irrevocably] eliminated from industry, and socialist industry has become the sole form of industry in the U.S.S.R.

And as a result of all this our country has been converted from an agrarian into an industrial country; for the proportion of industrial output, as compared with agricultural output, has risen from 48 per cent of the total in the beginning of the Five-Year Plan period (1928) to 70 per cent at the end of the fourth year of the Five-Year Plan period (1932)....

Finally, as a result of all this the Soviet Union has been converted from a weak country, unprepared for defense, into a country mighty in defense, a country prepared for every contingency, a country capable of producing on a mass scale all modern weapons of defense and of equipping its army with them in the event of an attack from without....

We are told: This is all very well; but it would have been far better to have abandoned the policy of industrialization, and to have produced more cotton, cloth, shoes, clothing, and other articles of general use....

... Of course, out of the 1,500,000,000 rubles in foreign currency that we spent on purchasing equipment for our heavy industries, we could have set apart a half for the purpose of importing raw cotton, hides, wool, rubber, etc. Then we would now have more cotton cloth, shoes and clothing. But we would not have a tractor industry or an automobile industry; we would not have anything like a big iron and steel industry; we would not have metal for the manufacture of machinery—and we would be unarmed, while we are surrounded by capitalist countries which are armed with modern technique.... Our position would be more or less analogous to the present position of China, which has no heavy industry and no war industry of her own and which is pecked at by everybody who cares to do so....

The Five-Year Plan in the sphere of agriculture was a Five-Year Plan of collectivization. What did the party proceed from in carrying out collectivization?

The party proceeded from the fact that in order to consolidate the dictatorship of the proletariat and to build up socialist society it was necessary, in addition to industrialization, to pass from small, individual peasant farming to large-scale collective agriculture equipped with tractors and modern agricultural machinery, as the only firm basis for the Soviet power in the rural districts.

The party proceeded from the fact that without collectivization it would be impossible to lead our country onto the highroad of building the economic foundations of socialism, impossible to free the vast masses of the laboring peasantry from poverty and ignorance....

The party has succeeded, in a matter of three years, in organizing more than 200,000 collective farms and about 5,000 state farms specializing mainly in grain growing and livestock raising, and at the same time it has succeeded, in the course of four years, in enlarging the crop area by 21,000,000 hectares.[1]

The party has succeeded in getting more than 60 percent of the peasant farms, which account for more than 70 percent of the land cultivated by peasants to unite into collective farms, which means that we have *fulfilled* the Five-Year Plan *threefold*.

The party has succeeded in creating the possibility of obtaining, not 500,000,000 to 600,000,000 poods[2] of marketable grain, which was the amount purchased in the period when individual peasant farming predominated, but 1,200,000,000 to 1,400,000,000 poods of grain annually.

The party has succeeded in routing the kulaks as a class, although they have not yet been dealt the final blow; the laboring peasants have been emancipated from kulak bondage and exploitation, and a firm economic basis for the Soviet government, the basis of collective farming, has been established in the countryside.

The party has succeeded in converting the U.S.S.R. from a land of small peasant farming into a land where agriculture is run on the largest scale in the world....

Do not all these facts testify to the superiority of the Soviet system of agriculture over the capitalist system? Do not these facts go to show that the collective farms are a more virile form of farming than individual capitalist farms?...

... Was the party right in pursuing the policy of an accelerated tempo of collectivization? Yes, it was absolutely right, even though certain excesses were committed in the process.[3] In pursuing the policy of eliminating the kulaks as a class, and in destroying the kulak nests, the party could not stop half way. It was necessary to carry this work to completion....

---

[1] In the metric system, a hectare is slightly less than 2.5 acres.

[2] A Russian measure of weight equal to about thirty-six pounds.

[3] Stalin is understating the case more than a little. It is estimated that as many as fifteen million people died as a result of the forced collectivization campaign and the ensuing famine.

What are the results of these successes as regards the improvement of the material conditions of the workers and peasants? . . .

In our country, in the U.S.S.R., the workers have long forgotten unemployment. Some three years ago we had about one and a half million unemployed. It is already two years now since unemployment has been completely abolished. . . . Look at the capitalist countries: what horrors are taking place there as a result of unemployment! There are now no less than thirty to forty million unemployed in those countries. . . .

Every day they try to get work, seek work, are prepared to accept almost any conditions of work but they are not given work, because they are "superfluous." And this is taking place at a time when vast quantities of goods and products are wasted to satisfy the caprices of the darlings of fate, the scions of capitalists and landlords. The unemployed are refused food because they have no money to pay for the food; they are refused shelter because they have no money to pay rent. How and where do they live? They live on the miserable crumbs from the rich man's table; by raking [searching through] refuse cans, where they find decayed scraps of food; they live in the slums of big cities, and more often in hovels outside of the towns, hastily put up by the unemployed out of packing cases and the bark of trees. . . .

One of the principal achievements of the Five-Year Plan in four years is that we have abolished unemployment and have relieved the workers of the U.S.S.R. of its horrors.

The same thing must be said in regard to the peasants. They, too, have forgotten about the differentiation of the peasants into kulaks and poor peasants, about the exploitation of the poor peasants by the kulaks, about the ruin which, every year, caused hundreds of thousands and millions of poor peasants to go begging. . . .

[The Five-Year Plan] has undermined and smashed the kulaks as a class, thus liberating the poor peasants and a good half of the middle peasants from bondage to the kulaks. . . . It has thus eliminated the possibility of the differentiation of the peasantry into exploiters—kulaks—and exploited—poor peasants. It has raised the poor peasants and the lower stratum of the middle peasants to a position of security in the collective farms, and has thereby put a stop to the process of ruination and impoverishment of the peasantry. . . .

Now there are no more cases of hundreds of thousands and millions of peasants being ruined and forced to hang around the gates of factories and mills. That is what used to happen; but that was long ago. Now the peasant is in a position of security; he is a member of a collective farm which has at its disposal tractors, agricultural machinery, a seed fund, a reserve fund, etc., etc.

Such are the main results of the realization of the Five-Year Plan in industry and agriculture; in the improvement of the conditions of life of the working people and the development of the exchange of goods; in the consolidation of the Soviet power and the development of the class struggle against the remnants and survival of the dying classes.

The Great Terror

❖

34 ❖ *OPERATIONAL ORDER 00447 "CONCERNING THE PUNISHMENT OF FORMER KULAKS, CRIMINALS AND OTHER ANTI-SOVIET ELEMENTS"*

Cruel mass campaigns to obliterate real or imagined enemies were common features of Soviet political life in the 1920s and 1930s. Nothing, however, matched the horrific purges, arrests, and killings that took place on Stalin's orders between 1936 and 1938. In just thirty months, security forces arrested over two million people, 90 percent of whom either confessed their guilt or were found guilty after a perfunctory trial. Blood smears on many of the victims' signed confessions are chilling indicators of the routine use of torture by interrogators. Slightly more than half of the guilty were shot, and the rest were sent to prison or one of the notorious Soviet work camps, or Gulags. The Great Terror resulted directly in the deaths of between 950,000 and 1,200,000 people, a figure that includes those who were shot and those who died from abuse or disease while incarcerated.

The victims included dozens of high-ranking officials, many thousands of party members, scientists, engineers, writers, and judges who were accused of harboring Trotskyite sympathies, plotting to assassinate Stalin, or committing any number of other "counterrevolutionary" or "anti-Soviet" crimes. Particularly hard hit was the Soviet military. In June 1937, eight senior officers were arrested for spying for Japan or Germany and were shot after brutal interrogations. This was the beginning of a purge that resulted in the execution of 30,000 to 40,000 officers, including 3 of 5 marshals (the highest rank in the Red Army); 13 of 15 army commanders; 8 of 9 admirals; 50 of 57 army corps commanders; 154 of 186 division commanders; 16 of 16 army commissars; and 25 of 28 army corps commissars. Other targets were foreigners and Soviet citizens of foreign extraction, including Poles, Balts, Finns, Germans, Central Asians, Koreans, and Chinese. Overall, most of the victims were peasants, workers, and various marginal people such as repeat criminals, "slackers," the homeless, the unemployed, and others who deviated from Soviet norms and expectations.

What Stalin and his associates hoped to achieve through the purges is unclear. Stalin's lust for power and vengefulness undoubtedly played a role. But so too did his sense that despite the widely trumpeted government claims of success, industrialization and rural collectivization were both being held back by "slackers," saboteurs, and others who resented the new economic order launched by the Five-Year Plans. Perceived foreign threats also played a role. German rearmament under Hitler, the outbreak of the Spanish Civil War in 1936, the rise of militarism in Japan, the signing of the Anti-Comintern Pact (ostensibly against the Communist International but actually directed against the Soviet Union) by Germany and Japan in 1936, and the Japanese invasion of China in 1937 all sent

Source: From J. Arch Getty and Oleg V. Naumov, *The Road to Terror: Stalin and the Self-Destruction of the Bolsheviks, 1932–1939* (New Haven: Yale University Press, 1999), 473–479. Used by permission of Yale University Press.

Stalin and his entourage into a panic over the prospect of having to fight a two-front war that would threaten the very existence of the Soviet state. Seen in this light, the Great Terror was an effort to suppress suspect political, social, and ethnic groups to bolster state security and gird the nation for a fight for its life.

Among the countless government documents generated during the Great Terror, the following directive is among the most disturbing. Drawn up on Stalin's orders, Operational Order Number 00447 was approved by the Politburo and sent out to local party, police, and judicial officials in the summer of 1937. The first part of the directive requires local officials to meet quotas for the arrest and sentencing of individuals guilty of various vaguely defined crimes. Of these, 75,900 people were to be shot and 193,000 sent to Gulags. The second part outlines the logistical and financial details of the operation. The order remained in effect until November 1938, and during that time the Politburo routinely approved requests of local officials to increase their quotas. As a result, between 767,000 and 800,000 people were arrested and convicted, three times more than what had been originally demanded.

QUESTIONS FOR ANALYSIS

1. What social, religious, and political groups are the targets for the purge outlined in this document?
2. Of what specific crimes are they guilty? In what way do their actions threaten the Soviet state?
3. How are families of the accused "traitors" to be treated?
4. Aside from the police and judicial officials, what other groups are expected to play an active role in the purge? Be sure to consider those who are mentioned in the document and those who are not.
5. We know that the actual number of arrests and executions far exceeded the quotas spelled out in the document. What explains this fact?

TOP SECRET: OPERARTIONAL ORDER

It has been established by investigative materials relative to the cases of anti-Soviet formations that a significant number of former kulaks[1] who had earlier been subjected to punitive measures and who had evaded them, who had escaped from camps, exile, and labor settlements, have settled in the countryside. This also includes many church officials and sectarians[2] who had been formerly put down, former active participants of anti-Soviet armed campaigns. Significant cadres of anti-Soviet political parties (SRs, Georgian Mensheviks, Dashnaks, Musavatists, Ittihadists, etc.[3]), as well as cadres of former active members of bandit uprisings, Whites,[4] repatriates, and so on remain nearly untouched in the countryside. Some of the above-mentioned elements, leaving the countryside for the cities, have

---

[1]The term kulak refers to a class of relatively well-off peasants who were opposed to Stalin's policy of collectivization and liquidated en masse in the late 1920s/early 1930s

[2]"Church officials" refers to clergy of the Russian Orthodox Church, which was never officially banned under Stalin but was subject to continuous persecution; "sectarians" was a term applied to any number of dissenting Christian groups that had broken away from Orrhodox Christianity.

[3]The term "SRs" refers to the Socialist Revolutionary party, a major rival to the Bolsheviks leading up to and during the revolution; it ceased to exist in 1918. The term Menshevik refers to the faction within the Social Democratic party that broke with Lenin's Bolsheviks in 1904; although outlawed by the Soviet government in 1921, it continued to have a strong following in Georgia. Dashnaks were Armenian socialists; Musavatists were members of a liberal-nationalist party in Azerbaijan; Ittiihadists were members of an Azerbaijani Islamist party.

[4]"Whites" refers to any anti-Bolshevik group during the Russian Civil War (1918–1921).

infiltrated enterprises of industry, transport, and construction. Besides, significant cadres of criminals are still entrenched in both countryside and city. These include horse and cattle thieves, recidivist thieves, robbers, and others who had been serving their sentences and who had escaped and are now in hiding. Inadequate efforts to combat these criminal bands have created a state of impunity promoting their criminal activities. As has been established, all of these anti-Soviet elements constitute the chief instigators of every kind of anti-Soviet crimes and sabotage in the kolkhozy [collective farms] and sovkhnozy [state farms] as well as in the field of transport and in certain spheres of industry. The organs of state security are faced with the task of mercilessly crushing this entire gang of anti-Soviet elements, of defending the working Soviet people from their counterrevolutionary machinations, and, finally, of putting an end, once and for all, to their base undermining of the foundations of the Soviet state. Accordingly, I therefore ORDER THAT AS OF 5 AUGUST 1937, ALL REPUBLICS AND REGIONS LAUNCH A CAMPAIGN OF PUNITIVE MEASURES AGAINST FORMER KULAKS, ACTIVE ANTI-SOVIET ELEMENTS, AND CRIMINALS....

The organization and execution of this campaign should be guided by the following:

I. GROUPS SUBJECT TO PUNITIVE MEASURES

1. Former kulaks who have returned home after having served their sentences and who continue to carry out active, anti-Soviet sabotage.
2. Former kulaks who have escaped from camps or from labor settlements, as well as kulaks who have been in hiding ... who carry out anti-Soviet activities.

3. Former kulaks and socially dangerous elements who were members of insurrectionary, fascist, terroristic, and bandit formations, who have served their sentences, who have been in hiding from punishment, or who have escaped from places of confinement and renewed their anti-Soviet, criminal activities.
4. Members of anti-Soviet parties, former Whites, gendarmes, [Tsarist security police], bureaucrats, bandits, gang abettors, ... re-émigrés, who are in hiding from punishment, who have escaped from places of confinement, and who continue to carry out active anti-Soviet activities.
5. Persons unmasked by investigators and who are the most hostile and active members of Cossack–White Guard[5] insurrectionary organizations slated for liquidation and fascist, terroristic, and espionage-saboteur counterrevolutionary formations.... and others, who are presently held in prisons, camps, labor settlements, and colonies and who continue to carry out in those places their active anti-Soviet sabotage.
7. Criminals (bandits, robbers, recidivist thieves, professional contraband smugglers, recidivist swindlers, cattle and horse thieves) who are carrying out criminal activities and who are associated with the criminal underworld.

II. CONCERNING THE PUNISHMENT TO BE IMPOSED ON THOSE SUBJECT TO PUNITIVE MEASURES AND THE NUMBER OF PERSONS SUBJECT TO PUNITIVE MEASURES

1. All kulaks, criminals, and other anti-Soviet elements subject to punitive measures are broken down into two categories:

---

[5]The term "Cossack" refers to a historic people from southern Russia and the Ukraine with a strong military tradition; many fought against the Bolsheviks in the civil war. "White Guard" is a term for the military arm of the White movement.

a) To the first category belong all the most active of the above-mentioned elements. They are subject to immediate arrest and, after consideration of their case by the troikas [3-man judicial panels], to be shot.

b) To the second category belong all the remaining less active but nonetheless hostile elements. They are subject to arrest and to confinement in concentration camps for a term ranging from 8 to 10 years, while the most vicious and socially dangerous among them are subject to confinement for similar terms in prisons....

2. In accordance with the registration data presented by the people's commissars of the republic NKVD[6] and by the heads of territorial and regional boards of the NKVD, the following number of persons subject to punitive measures is hereby established:

	First Category	Second Category	Total
Azerbaijan SSR	1,500	3,750	5,250
Armenian SSR	500	1,000	1,500
Belorussian SSR	2,000	10,000	12,000
Georgian SSR	2,000	3,000	5,000
Kirghiz SSR	250	500	750
Tadzhik SSR	500	1,300	1,800
Turkmen SSR	500	1,500	2,000

[The document continues, listing quotas for 41 more districts; the Moscow region has the highest quota, with 5,000 to be executed and 30,000 to be imprisoned.]

4. The families of those sentenced in accordance with the first or second category are not as a rule subject to punitive measures. Exceptions to this include: Families,

members of which are capable of active anti-Soviet actions. Pursuant to the special decree by the three-man commission, members of such families are subject to being transferred to camps or labor settlements....

5. All families of persons punished in accordance with the first and second categories are to be registered and placed under systematic observation....

IV. ORDER FOR CONDUCTING THE INVESTIGATION

1. Investigation shall be conducted into the case of each person or group of persons arrested. The investigation shall be carried out in a swift and simplified manner. During the course of the trial, all criminal connections of persons arrested are to be disclosed.

2. At the conclusion of the investigation, the case is to be submitted for consideration to the troika....

GENERAL COMMISSAR FOR INTERNAL SECURITY

N. YEZHOV

Strictly secret. . . .

Protocol #51 of the Politburo [Central Committee]
DECISION of 31 July 1937.
Re: THE NKVD

5. To issue to the NKVD 75 million rubles from the reserve fund of the Council of People's Commissars to cover operational expenses associated with the implementation of the operation, of which 25 million rubles is to be earmarked for payment of rail transport fees.

---

[6] The People's Commissariat for Internal Affairs was the public and secret police organization of the Soviet Union; it replaced the GPU, the Government Political Organization, in 1934.

6. To require the People's Commissariat for Transport and Communications to grant the NKVD rolling stock in accordance with its demand for the purpose of transporting the condemned within the regions and to the camps.

7. To utilize as follows all the kulaks, criminals, and other anti-Soviet elements condemned under the second category to confinement in camps for periods of time:

    a) on construction projects currently under way. . . . ;

    b) on constructing new camps in the remote areas of Kazakhstan;

    c) on the construction of new camps especially organized for timber works undertaken by convict labor.

8. To propose to the People's Commissariat for Forestry that it forthwith transfer to the GULAG[7] of the NKVD the following forest tracts for the purpose of organizing camps for forest works. [List follows] . . .

12. To propose to the regional and territorial committees of the VKP [All Union Communist Party] and of the All-Union Leninist Communist Union of Youth in regions where camps are being organized, to assign to the NKVD the necessary number of . . . members in order to bring the administrative and camp security apparat to full strength. . . .

13. To require the People's Commissariat for Defense to summon from the Workers' and Peasants' Red Army reserves 240 commanding officers and political workers in order to bring the cadres of the supervisory personnel of the military security forces of newly organized camps to full strength. . . .

14. To require the People's Commissariat for Health to issue to the GULAG of the NKVD 150 physicians and 400 medical attendants for service in the newly organized camps.

15. To require the People's Commissariat for Forestry to issue to the GULAG 10 eminent specialists in forestry and to transfer 50 graduates of the Leningrad Academy of Forest Technology of Forest Technology to the GULAG.

---

[7] GULAG refers to the Soviet government agency in charge of administering the system of forced labor camps.

CHAPTER 5

Latin America in an Era of Economic Challenge and Political Change

For much of the world, the great catalyst for change in the early twentieth century was World War I. The turning point for Latin America, however, came not with the Great War, but with the Great Depression. The worldwide economic slump of the 1930s fully exposed the dangers of the region's reliance on agricultural and mineral exports as engines of economic growth. As factories closed and unemployment lines lengthened in Europe and the United States, demand for Latin America's food products and raw materials collapsed. The unit price and quantity of the region's exports both declined, with the result that their total value between 1930 and 1934 was half of what it had been between 1925 and 1929. This catastrophic drop deprived the region of the foreign exchange needed to buy manufactured goods at a time when plunging stock prices and bank failures in the industrialized world shut off the flow of foreign loans and investments. Insolvent governments faced capital shortages which impeded plans to end the economic slump through industrialization. Latin Americans came to resent European and especially U.S. ownership of the region's assets. Once welcomed as a way of attracting capital and encouraging growth, foreign ownership in the 1930s was more frequently condemned as imperialist plunder.

Economic catastrophe accelerated the demise of the old political order. Oligarchic rule by wealthy landowners had already begun to disintegrate in the early 1900s. By then, urbanization, immigration, and modest industrialization had made society more complex and diversified. In Mexico City, Rio de Janeiro, Buenos Aires, and other cities, a factory-based working class emerged, and a middle class made up of professionals, office workers, teachers, writers, and small business owners grew steadily. These groups rejected the oligarchies' economic priorities, and their growing assertiveness challenged the political monopoly of the great landowners. Their strength was revealed in Mexico in 1910 when middle-class reformers in alliance with rural rebels overthrew the dictatorship of Porfirio Diáz, and in Argentina in 1912 when the government extended the right to vote to all adult males.

In 1919, the urban working class emerged as an important force when it mounted massive strikes and demonstrations in Mexico City, Santiago, Lima, Buenos Aires, and elsewhere. A number of oligarchical regimes were able to ride out the 1920s (in some cases by making minor concessions to the middle class), but none survived the economic storm of the 1930s.

Political and social conflict in the 1920s and 1930s was accompanied by the disintegration of many longstanding intellectual and cultural assumptions. These assumptions included faith in science and liberalism, a belief in white racial superiority, and a conviction that all things European equaled progress, whereas all things American (meaning Indian) represented backwardness. The liberalism of the white ruling class faced opposition not only from conservative Catholics but also from nationalists, communists, anarchists, trade unionists, and fascists who in various contexts and at different times spoke on behalf of the middle class, the proletariat, the military, and Indians, blacks, and mixed bloods. Modernist artists and writers, like their counterparts in Europe, rejected liberalism, questioned reason and science, and sought to articulate the components of a new cultural identity and of a new society. By the 1920s, this quest for self-definition led many intellectuals to discover popular traditions and ethnic, especially Indian, lore, which they regarded as touchstones of cultural identity.

Out of this ideological and cultural ferment, no new consensus emerged. In Chile, Uruguay, and Venezuela, oligarchic rule gave way to dominance by new middle-class groups that frequently disagreed about fundamental issues. Mexico became a one-party state controlled by the National Revolutionary Party, which, despite its name, until the mid-1930s was more interested in capitalist development than social reform. A new kind of populist, quasi-fascist leader emerged in the persons of Getúlio Vargas in Brazil and Juan Perón in Argentina. Strong-arm dictators, essentially old-style *caudillos,* held sway in Cuba, the Dominican Republic, El Salvador, Haiti, Honduras, Nicaragua, Paraguay, and Guatemala.

As a result of all these factors, Latin America in the 1920s and 1930s faced deepening fragmentation, instability, and conflict. Old views and institutions were discredited, but no one could agree on what should replace them. A democratic government might come to power briefly, only to be overthrown by the army; populist politicians might institute reforms, only to see them canceled by a conservative government that replaced them. A few countries—Mexico, Chile, Uruguay for a time, Costa Rica, Venezuela, and perhaps Colombia—had some success dealing with these competing cross-currents, but in the rest, the conflicts were so deep and the gaps between regions and classes were so vast that few governments could govern effectively or even hope to survive for long.

New Social and Political Currents:
Feminism and *Indigenismo*

The drive for women's rights in Latin America began in the 1870s in the region's most urbanized and economically advanced states—Argentina, Chile, Uruguay, and Brazil. In all four, liberal governments in the late 1800s established secular schools for girls as part of an effort to end the Roman Catholic Church's control of education. This led to the founding of teacher-training schools for women and the emergence of teaching as an important female profession.

Schoolteachers, along with small numbers of professional women, recent arrivals from Europe, and socialists, provided leadership for Latin American feminism in the early 1900s. They edited journals, organized conferences, and formed societies for the purposes of self-improvement and publicity. Most feminists supported better education for women, access to the professions, improved health care, and greater equality between husbands and wives. There were disagreements, however, over issues of divorce and women's suffrage. Moderates feared liberalized divorce laws would weaken marriage, whereas socialists and liberals feared that if devout Catholic women were given the vote, they overwhelmingly would support conservative parties that defended Church privilege.

Feminists made gains in the 1920s and 1930s. In 1929, Ecuador became the first Latin American state to grant women the vote. In the 1930s, women also won the right to vote in national elections in Brazil, Uruguay, and Cuba, and in provincial and municipal elections in Mexico, Peru, and Argentina. Progress also was made in education. In several states, increasing numbers of women were admitted to universities. In Chile in the 1920s, women received 25 percent of all degrees. Fewer gains were made in the area of married women's rights; by the late 1930s, only Mexico, Argentina, Chile, and Uruguay had revised their civil codes to limit husbands' authority over their wives and children.

Along with *feminismo*, *indigenismo* was another word added to Latin America's vocabulary in the early twentieth century. Sometimes translated into English as "Indianism," *indigenismo* became an important movement in states with large Indian populations such as Mexico, Bolivia, Peru, Guatemala, and Ecuador. A term with cultural and political connotations, *indigenismo* meant both an affirmation of the value of the Indians' culture and also a commitment to improving their economic and social condition. It was part of the general reaction against the assumptions and policies of the late-nineteenth- and early-twentieth-century oligarchies, whose leaders had disdained the Indians' culture and condoned the landowning elite's exploitation of the native population. It also resulted from the greater awareness of Indian problems that grew out of Indian revolts in Peru and the demands for land reform during the Mexican Revolution.

In the 1920s and 1930s, increasing numbers of writers explored the theme of Indian exploitation, and many intellectuals asserted that Indian culture and values could become a source of national regeneration. Politicians also showed greater interest in Indian problems. The Mexican Constitution of 1917 committed the government to land reform, and during the 1920s and 1930s, millions of acres of land were returned to peasant communities. No one solved the "Indian problem," however, and in Mexico and the Andean states, Indians remained at the bottom of the economic and social order.

Costs and Benefits of Latin American Feminism

35 ◆ Amanda Labarca, *WHERE IS WOMAN GOING?*

Amanda Labarca was born in 1886 into the family of a successful merchant in Santiago, Chile. Educated in private girls' schools, she attended the University of Chile, where she received a degree in education. After her marriage to Guillermo Hubertson, the couple pursued graduate studies at Columbia University and the Sorbonne in Paris, and traveled extensively in the United States and Europe. By the time Labarca returned to Chile in 1918, she was a feminist. As director of a girls' school in Santiago, in 1919 she helped found the National Council of Women of Chile, an organization dedicated to improving women's legal, civil, and educational status. In 1922, she became a professor of education at the University of Chile, and in 1931 was appointed director of secondary education for the nation. A well-known figure in international feminist circles, she traveled extensively and published more than twenty books of fiction and social commentary.

The following excerpt is taken from an article, "¿Adónde va la mujer?" (Where is Woman Going?), which first appeared in the 1920s and was republished in an anthology by the same name in 1934. In it Labarca discusses the positive and negative effects of feminism on the region's middle-class women.

QUESTIONS FOR ANALYSIS

1. On the basis of Labarca's essay, how can one characterize views of women and the status of women in Latin American societies before the rise of feminism?
2. In Labarca's view, how have twentieth-century developments eroded traditional views? What were the underlying causes of these developments?
3. According to Labarca, what "losses" have middle-class women experienced as a result of women's changing social role? Who is largely to blame for these losses?
4. How does Labarca view the fundamental characteristics of men and women?
5. Is Labarca optimistic about women's future in Latin America? Why or why not?

Source: From Benjamin Keen, *Latin American Civilization*, © 1974 Benjamin Keen, pp. 427–429. Used by kind permission of Gail Keen.

Has feminism brought gains or losses to the Latin-American middle-class girl of today?

Gains. First of all, the consciousness of her own worth in the totality of human progress. Today's girl knows that there are no insurmountable obstacles to the flight of her intelligence; that the question of whether her entire sex is intelligent will not be raised before she is permitted to engage in any intellectual activity; that in the eyes of the majority her womanhood does not mark her with the stigma of irremediable inferiority, and that if she has talent she will be allowed to display it.

The law codes have returned to her, in large part, control over her life and property. She has well-founded hopes of seeing abolished within her lifetime the laws that still relegate her, in certain aspects, to the position of a second-class citizen, and that accord her unequal legal treatment.

She has made progress in economic liberty, [the] basis of all independence, whether it be a question of a simple individual or one of nations. Today she is gaining admission into fields of labor forbidden to her mother.

Before her extends an unbounded horizon of opportunities. Hopes! She can live her years of illusions imagining—like every adolescent male—that the whole world awaits her, and that only her own limitations can prevent her from ascending the highest peaks of this world.

She has won liberty, including—it may seem ridiculous to mention it—the liberty of going about without papa or the classic brother at her side. . . .

She has lost, in the first place, the respect of the male majority. One might say that formerly consideration for women formed part of good breeding, and it was denied only to one who by her conduct showed that she did not merit it. Today it is the other way around. In general, woman receives no tribute, and she must prove convincingly that she is a distinguished personage before receiving the homage that once was common.

Which has diminished—the respect or the quality of respectability? . . .

Men used to expect of woman a stainless virtue, perfect submission—after God, thy husband, orders the epistle of St. Paul[1]—and a life-long devotion to the orbit in which her man revolved. A saint in the vaulted niche of her home, saint to the world, mistress of her four walls, and slave to her man. In exchange for this—respect and devotion. True, the father or husband sometimes played the role of sacristan[2] to the saint. They allowed no one to fail to reverence her, but they themselves took liberties and even mistreated her—conduct that the saint had to bear with resignation . . . she had no recourse. . . .

It is unnecessary to refer again to the upheavals that the invention of machinery brought to the world, the sharp rise in the cost of living, and the pauperization of the household, which from producer was reduced to being a simple consumer. It became impossible for a man of average means to satisfy the needs of all his womenfolk, and women had to enter offices, the professions, and other remunerative employment that had been men's traditional source of income. Woman has gone out into the world, and although this fact in itself is an economic imperative and does not essentially imply the abandonment of any virtue, the ordinary man has denied her his respect. . . .

. . . For the ordinary man, woman's freedom is license; her equality, the right to treat her without courtesy.

She has lost in opportunities for marriage, for establishing a household, and for satisfying that yearning for maternity that is her fundamental instinct. The more cultured a woman, the more difficult for her to find a husband, because it is normal for her to seek refuge, understanding, and guidance in a person superior to herself. And the latter do not always prefer cultured women. They imagine that knowledge makes

---

[1]The apostle Paul in I Corinthians 7:39 and other places in his epistles speaks of the need for wives to be obedient to their husbands.

[2]A church official in charge of caring for the vestments and sacred utensils used in religious services, and, in some cases, the entire church building.

them unfeeling—an absurd notion—that it makes them domineering—which concerns not acquired knowledge but character—or that it makes them insufferably pedantic.... For their wives men prefer the "old-fashioned" girl.

That is the pathos of the tragedy of middle-class women in the Latin countries. Evolution has taken place in opposition to the fundamental convictions of men, who only tolerate it—in the case of their daughters, for example—because imperious necessity dictates it, and only with profound chagrin. Men—I repeat that I speak of the majority—continue to judge women from the viewpoint of fifty years ago, and if they retain some respect and esteem in their inner beings, they tender it to the woman who remained faithful to the classic type—the woman who has progressed they place very close to those for whom they have no respect.

Men cannot understand that external conditions—culture, profession, liberty—have not radically transformed the classic femininity, the maternal instincts, the impulses of the sweet Samaritan,[3] the yearnings of a noble spirituality. The cases of this kind that he knows about do not convince him; he imagines that they constitute exceptions.

Nor are men of more advanced ideas free from this attitude. And it would be amusing—if it did not have tragic implications—to observe what a socialist, a radical, a communist, proclaims on the public platform and what he praises in the intimacy of his home.

Man and woman. Feared and beloved master; slave, sweetly, or tyrannically subjugated; wall and ivy. Today divergent and almost hostile, but not comrades. Woman and man cannot yet be comrades, save in an infinitely small number of cases. The relationship of comrades implies equality, confidence, and the same criteria for judging each other.

"But if she acknowledges her bitter lot, why not turn back?" ... Impossible. Time does not turn back. New social theories will solve these problems and create new ones on the way to an inscrutable future that human faith ... imagines must be a better one.

Meanwhile, sisters, let us not preach feminism to women; let us win over the men, in the hope that our daughters may pay less dearly for their cup of happiness.

---

[3]In the parable of the Good Samaritan (Luke 10:30–37), Jesus tells the story of the Samaritan woman who helped an injured man who had been ignored by others. A Samaritan thus came to mean a compassionate person, one willing to help the distressed.

The Indian in Peru: A Marxist Perspective

❖

36 ◆ José Carlos Mariátegui, *THE PROBLEM OF THE INDIAN* and *THE PROBLEM OF LAND*

Beginning in the 1870s, the economic situation of Peru's Indians, already one of extreme poverty, deteriorated even further. With worldwide demand for Peru's agricultural products increasing and land prices soaring, wealthy landowners (*hacendados*), with the help of lawyers, local officials, and favorable laws, acquired increasing amounts of Indian communal lands. As a result, by the early

---

Source: From *Seven Interpretive Essays on Peruvian Reality* by Jose Carlos Mariategui, translated by Marjory Urquidi, Copyright © 1971. By permission of the University of Texas Press.

1900s, Peru's Indians, more than 50 percent of the population, overwhelmingly were landless peasants providing cheap labor for white hacienda owners and bound to the land either through long-term labor contracts or because of indebtedness to the landowner.

The deterioration of Peruvian Indian life was accompanied by increasing concern for their welfare on the part of some Peruvians. Intellectuals at the University of San Marcos in Lima sought to dispel the notion that Indians were inherently inferior to whites. Some went further to suggest that Indian culture and values could serve as a source of national revival. Educators and clergy recommended programs of education and moral instruction to teach Indians sobriety and good work habits. The radical writer Manuel Gonzalez Prada (1848–1918) went further; he urged the Indians to arm themselves and rebel.

José Carlos Maríategui (1895–1930) was not, therefore, the first Peruvian to speak out on Indian issues. Nor was he Peru's first Marxist. In 1924, the Peruvian exile Raúl Haya de la Torre founded the American Popular Revolutionary Alliance, a party with a strong Marxist component, and the author Luís E. Valcarel hailed peasant revolts in the highlands as the first rumblings of a revolution that would usher in true egalitarianism. Maríategui's accomplishment was to provide an analysis of Peruvian society by bringing together a passionate concern for the Indians' welfare and the scientific socialism of Marx.

Maríategui, born in 1895 and raised in poverty by his mother, a seamstress, had only a few years of schooling. At age fourteen he became a printer's apprentice for a newspaper in Lima, Peru's largest city, and continued his self-education. By the age of twenty-one he was writing news stories, poetry, and reviews for his newspaper and other Lima periodicals, and had written a full-length drama performed in a Lima theater. A harsh critic of Peru's politicians for their neglect of the poor, especially the Indians, Maríategui was exiled to Europe in 1919. Returning to Peru in 1923 as a Marxist, he worked to strengthen the labor movement, wrote hundreds of articles, and helped found the Socialist Party of Peru in 1928. His *Seven Interpretative Essays on Peruvian Reality*, his major work, appeared in 1928. Before he died at age thirty-five, he participated in discussions leading to the formation of the Peruvian Communist Party, formally organized a month after his death in 1930.

The following selection consists of excerpts from two essays in *Seven Interpretive Essays on Peruvian Reality*, "The Problem of the Indian," and "The Problem of Land."

QUESTIONS FOR ANALYSIS

1. According to Maríategui, what is at the root of the problems of Indian poverty in Peru?
2. Maríategui rejects previous "solutions" to the problem of Indian poverty. What were they, and why, in his opinion, did they fail?
3. What in Maríategui's view is the only viable solution to the "problem of the Indian"?
4. Does Maríategui indicate how he hopes to accomplish his goals?

THE PROBLEM OF THE INDIAN

The problem of the Indian is rooted in the land tenure system of our economy. Any attempt to solve it with administrative ... measures, through education or by a road building program, is superficial and secondary as long as the feudalism of the *gamonales* [great landowners] continues to exist.

Gamonalismo[1] necessarily invalidates any law or regulation for the protection of the Indian. The hacienda owner, the *latifundista*[2] is a feudal lord. The written law is powerless against his authority, which is supported by custom and habit. Unpaid labor is illegal, yet unpaid and even forced labor survive in the latifundium. The judge, the subprefect, the commissary, the teacher, the tax collector, all are in bondage to the landed estate. The law cannot prevail against the *gamonales*. Any official who insisted on applying it would be abandoned and sacrificed by the central government....

The oldest and most obvious mistake is, unquestionably, that of reducing the protection of the Indian to an ordinary administrative matter. From the days of Spanish colonial legislation, wise and detailed ordinances, worked out after conscientious study, have been quite useless. The republic, since independence,[3] has been prodigal in its decrees, laws, and provisions intended to protect the Indian against exaction and abuse. The *gamonal* of today ... however, has little to fear from administrative theory; he knows that its practice is altogether different.

The individualistic character of the republic's legislation has favored the absorption of Indian property by the latifundium system.... The appropriation of most communal and individual Indian property is an accomplished fact....

The assumption that the Indian problem is ethnic is sustained by the most outmoded repertory of imperialist ideas. The concept of inferior races was useful to the white man's West for purposes of expansion and conquest. To expect that the Indian will be emancipated through a steady crossing of the aboriginal race with white immigrants is an anti-sociological naiveté that could only occur to the primitive mentality of an importer of merino sheep. The people of Asia, who are in no way superior to the Indians, have not needed any transfusion of European blood in order to assimilate the most dynamic and creative aspects of Western culture. The degeneration of the Peruvian Indian is a cheap invention of sophists who serve feudal interests....

The tendency to consider the Indian problem as a moral one embodies a liberal, humanitarian, enlightened nineteenth-century attitude.... Humanitarian teachings have not halted or hampered European imperialism, nor have they reformed its methods. The struggle against imperialism now relies only on the solidarity and strength of the liberation movement of the colonial masses....

On a moral and intellectual plane, the church took a more energetic or at least a more authoritative stand centuries ago. This crusade, however, achieved only very wise laws and provisions. The lot of the Indian remained substantially the same.... To wipe out abuses, it would have been necessary to abolish land appropriation and forced labor, in brief, to change the entire colonial regime. Without the toil of the American Indian, the coffers of the Spanish treasury would have been emptied.

But today a religious solution is unquestionably the most outdated and antihistoric of all.... If the church could not accomplish its task in a medieval era, when its spiritual and intellectual capacity could be measured by friars like Las Casas,[4] how can it succeed with the elements in commands today?...

---

[1]A term for the social and political domination of rural Peru by wealthy landowners; sometimes translated as "feudalism."

[2]The owner of a *latifundio*, a large landed estate worked by farm laborers in a state of partial serfdom.

[3]Peruvian independence was achieved in 1824.

[4]Bartolomé de Las Casas (1474–1566) was a Spanish friar who denounced the Spaniards' exploitation of the Indians.

The belief that the Indian problem is one of education does not seem to be supported by even a strictly and independently pedagogical criterion.... School and teacher are doomed to be debased under the pressure of the feudal regime, which cannot be reconciled with the most elementary concept of progress and evolution. When this truth becomes partially understood, the saving formula is thought to be discovered in boarding schools for Indians. But the glaring inadequacy of this formula is self-evident in view of the tiny percentage of the indigenous school population that can be boarded in these schools.

THE PROBLEM OF LAND

Those of us who approach and define the Indian problem from a Socialist point of view must start out by declaring the complete obsolescence of the humanitarian and philanthropic points of view.... We shall try to establish the basically economic character of the problem. First, we protest against the instinctive attempt of the criollo or mestizo[5] to reduce it to an exclusively administrative, pedagogical, ethnic, or moral problem in order to avoid at all cost recognizing its economic aspect.... We are not satisfied to assert the Indian's right to education, culture, progress, love, and heaven. We begin by categorically asserting his right to land....

The agrarian problem is first and foremost the problem of eliminating feudalism in Peru, which should have been done by the democratic-bourgeois regime that followed the War of Independence. But in its one hundred years as a republic, Peru has not had a genuine bourgeois class, a true capitalist class. The old feudal class—camouflaged or disguised as a republican bourgeoisie—has kept its position.... During a century of Republican rule, great agricultural property actually has grown stronger

and expanded, despite the theoretical liberalism of our constitution and the practical necessities of the development of our capitalist economy. There are two expressions of feudalism that survive: the latifundium and servitude. Inseparable and of the same substance, their analysis leads us to the conclusion that the servitude oppressing the indigenous race cannot be abolished unless the latifundium is abolished....

Everyone knows that the liberal solution for this problem, in conformity with individualist ideology, would be to break up the latifundio in order to create small landed properties....

In conformity with my ideological position, I think that in Peru the hour for trying the liberal method, the individualist formula, has already passed. Leaving doctrinal reasons aside, I regard as fundamental an indisputable and concrete factor that gives a peculiar stamp to our agrarian problem: the survival of the Indian community and of elements of practical socialism in Indian life and agriculture.

In Peru, communal property does not represent a primitive economy that has gradually been replaced by a progressive economy founded on individual property. No; the "communities" have been despoiled of their land for the benefit of the feudal or semi-feudal latifundium, which is constitutionally incapable of technical progress.

The latifundium compares unfavorably with the "community" as an enterprise for agricultural production.... Large property seems to be justified by the interests of production, which are identified, at least in theory, with the interests of society. But this is not the case of the latifundium and, therefore, it does not meet an economic need. Except for sugar-cane plantations—which produce *aguardiente* [liquor] to intoxicate and stupefy the Indian peasant—the latifundium of the sierra generally grows the same crops as the "community," and it produces no more....

------

[5] A criollo (creole) is a Peruvian of European descent; a mestizo is a person of European-Indian descent.

The "community," on the one hand, is a system of production that keeps alive in the Indian the moral incentives that stimulate him to do his best work....

By dissolving or abandoning the "community," the system of the feudal latifundium has attacked not only an economic institution but also, and more important, a social institution, one that defends the indigenous tradition [and] maintains the function of the rural family....

Political Responses to the Great Depression

As the Great Depression spread economic misery across Latin America, one government after another fell in an epidemic of election swings, revolts, coups, and countercoups. The military seized power in Argentina and Peru in 1930, and Uruguay's constitutional government collapsed in 1933 when the elected president, Gabriel Terra, established a dictatorship. Dictators also took power in El Salvador, Guatemala, and Honduras, and, with the help of the U.S. government, in Nicaragua and the Dominican Republic. In Chile, however, the onset of the Depression led to the fall of a dictator, Carlos Ibáñez, in 1931. This was followed by a brief constitutional interlude and more military coups before the establishment of a center-right government under Arturo Alessandri. In Cuba, the dictator Gerardo Machado was forced into exile in 1933, but another dictator, Fulgencio Batista, took his place in 1934. Ecuador had no fewer than fourteen presidents between 1931 and 1940, and Paraguay had four different dictators. Only a few states such as Colombia managed to maintain a measure of political stability.

Whereas most of these regimes had little effect on their countries' long-term development, political changes in Mexico and Brazil had lasting consequences. In Mexico, these changes took place during the presidency of Lázaro Cárdenas, who between 1934 and 1940 revitalized Mexico's revolutionary tradition through educational reform, land redistribution, and nationalization of foreign-owned businesses. In Brazil, they were connected with the career of Getúlio Vargas, who seized power in 1930 and dominated Brazilian politics until 1945 and again from 1951 to 1954. By the end of the 1930s his *Estado Novo* (New State), a mixture of dictatorship, repression, anticolonialism, economic planning, nationalism, industrialization, and government-sponsored programs for housing, improved wages, and medical care provided Latin America with an authoritarian model for entry into the era of mass politics.

Economic Nationalism in Mexico

◆

37 ◆ Lázaro Cárdenas, *SPEECH TO THE NATION*

During the 1920s and early 1930s, Mexico's revolution stalled. Its 1917 constitution called for land reform, granted extensive rights to labor, and proclaimed the state's right to control foreign-owned businesses. But the two dominant politicians of the 1920s and early 1930s, Alvaro Obregón and Plutarco Elías Calles, had little enthusiasm for social reform despite their revolutionary rhetoric. Their rule mainly benefited generals, business interests, and landowners, and their gestures in the direction of land redistribution were modest. When in 1929 Calles organized Mexico's only national political party, the National Revolutionary Party (PNR), out of dozens of local political machines, his and his henchmen's political domination appeared secure.

Six years later, however, Calles was in exile in the United States, and progressives had taken control of the PNR. The reasons were twofold: the Great Depression and the emergence of a new leader, Lázaro Cárdenas. Born in 1895 to a poor family and with little formal education, Cárdenas achieved prominence in the 1910s as an officer in the revolutionary armies fighting the dictator Victoriano Huerta. In 1920, he was named governor of the state of Michoacán in west-central Mexico, where he earned a reputation as a progressive and honest administrator; between 1931 and 1934 he served terms as Mexico's minister of the interior and of war. In December 1933, Cárdenas, the candidate of the PNR's progressive wing, was nominated for president, and in 1934 he was elected. Immediately embarking on a program of land and labor reform, Cárdenas introduced sweeping reforms. The government confiscated millions of acres of land from large estates for redistribution to peasants, introduced free and compulsory primary education, and approved legislation to provide medical and unemployment insurance. His most audacious step, however, was the nationalization of Mexico's oil industry. In 1936, a labor dispute erupted into a strike against U.S.- and British-owned petroleum companies, and in the ensuing legal battle, seventeen oil companies rejected both the prounion ruling of an arbitration board appointed by Cárdenas and the decision of the Mexican Supreme Court, which upheld the board's ruling. In response, in 1938 Cárdenas expropriated the property of the oil companies.

Cárdenas announced this decision in a radio address to the Mexican people on March 18, 1938. In the following excerpt, Cárdenas, after recounting the events of the labor dispute, comments on the oil companies' role in Mexico's economic and social development.

QUESTIONS FOR ANALYSIS

1. In Cárdenas's account, which actions by the foreign oil companies forced him to nationalize their property?
2. According to Cárdenas, what truth is there in the oil companies' claims that their presence has been beneficial to Mexico?

Source: From Benjamin Keen, *Latin American Civilization*, © 1974 Benjamin Keen, pp. 362–364. Used by kind permission of Gail Keen.

3   Who, according to Cárdenas, is ultimately responsible for the actions of the oil companies?

4. Which political activities of the oil companies does Cárdenas condemn?

5. What hardship does Cárdenas foresee for the Mexican people as a result of nationalization?

6. In what ways does Cárdenas appeal to Mexican nationalism in his speech?

In each and every one of the various attempts of the Executive to arrive at a final solution of the conflict within conciliatory limits … the intransigence of the companies was clearly demonstrated.

Their attitude was therefore premeditated and their position deliberately taken, so that the Government, in defense of its own dignity, had to resort to application of the Expropriation Act, as there were no means less drastic or decision less severe that might bring about a solution of the problem.

For additional justification of the measure herein announced, let us trace briefly the history of the oil companies' growth in Mexico and of the resources with which they have developed their activities.

It has been repeated *ad nauseam* that the oil industry has brought additional capital for the development and progress of the country. This assertion is an exaggeration. For many years throughout the major period of their existence, the oil companies have enjoyed great privileges for development and expansion, including customs and tax exemptions and innumerable prerogatives; it is these factors of special privilege, together with the prodigious productivity of the oil deposits granted them by the Nation often against public will and law, that represent almost the total amount of this so-called capital.

Potential wealth of the Nation; miserably underpaid native labor; tax exemptions; economic privileges; governmental tolerance— these are the factors of the boom of the Mexican oil industry.

Let us now examine the social contributions of the companies. In how many of the villages bordering on the oil fields is there a hospital, or school or social center, or a sanitary water supply, or an athletic field, or even an electric plant fed by the millions of cubic meters of natural gas allowed to go to waste?

What center of oil production, on the other hand, does not have its company police force for the protection of private, selfish, and often illegal interests? These organizations, whether authorized by the Government or not, are charged with innumerable outrages, abuses, and murders, always on behalf of the companies that employ them.

Who is not aware of the irritating discrimination governing construction of the company camps? Comfort for the foreign personnel; misery, drabness, and insalubrity for the Mexicans. Refrigeration and protection against tropical insects for the former; indifference and neglect, medical service and supplies always grudgingly provided, for the latter; lower wages and harder more exhausting labor for our people.

The tolerance which the companies have abused was born, it is true, in the shadow of the ignorance, betrayals, and weakness of the country's rulers; but the mechanism was set in motion by investors lacking in the necessary moral resources to give something in exchange for the wealth they have been exploiting.

Another inevitable consequence of the presence of the oil companies, strongly characterized by their anti-social tendencies, and even more harmful than all those already mentioned, has been their persistent and improper intervention in national affairs.

The oil companies' support to strong rebel factions against the constituted government in the Huasteca region of Veracruz and in the

Isthmus of Tehuantepec during the years 1917 to 1920 is no longer a matter for discussion by anyone. Nor is anyone ignorant of the fact that in later periods and even at the present time, the oil companies have almost openly encouraged the ambitions of elements discontented with the country's government, every time their interests were affected either by taxation or by the modification of their privileges or the withdrawal of the customary tolerance. They have had money, arms, and munitions for rebellion, money for the anti-patriotic press which defends them, money with which to enrich their unconditional defenders. But for the progress of the country, for establishing an economic equilibrium with their workers through a just compensation of labor, for maintaining hygienic conditions in the districts where they themselves operate, or for conserving the vast riches of the natural petroleum gases from destruction, they have neither money, nor financial possibilities, nor the desire to subtract the necessary funds from the volume of their profits.

Nor is there money with which to meet a responsibility imposed upon them by judicial verdict, for they rely on their pride and their economic power to shield them from the dignity and sovereignty of a Nation which has generously placed in their hands its vast natural resources and now finds itself unable to obtain the satisfaction of the most elementary obligations by ordinary legal means.

As a logical consequence of this brief analysis, it was therefore necessary to adopt a definite and legal measure to end this permanent state of affairs in which the country sees its industrial progress held back by those who hold in their hands the power to erect obstacles as well as the motive power of all activity and who, instead of using it to high and worthy purposes, abuse their economic strength to the point of jeopardizing the very life of a Nation endeavoring to bring about the elevation of its people through

its own laws, its own resources, and the free management of its own destinies.

With the only solution to this problem thus placed before it, I ask the entire Nation for moral and material support sufficient to carry out so justified, important, and indispensable a decision.

The Government has already taken suitable steps to maintain the constructive activities now going forward throughout the Republic, and for that purpose it asks the people only for its full confidence and backing in whatever dispositions the Government may be obliged to adopt.

Nevertheless, we shall, if necessary, sacrifice all the constructive projects on which the Nation has embarked during the term of this Administration in order to cope with the financial obligations imposed upon us by the application of the Expropriation Act to such vast interests; and although the subsoil of the country will give us considerable economic resources with which to meet the obligation of indemnization which we have contracted, we must be prepared for the possibility of our individual economy also suffering the indispensable readjustments, even to the point, should the Bank of Mexico deem it necessary, or modifying the present exchange rate of our currency, so that the whole country may be able to count on sufficient currency and resources with which to consolidate this act of profound and essential economic liberation of Mexico.

It is necessary that all groups of the population be imbued with a full optimism and that each citizen, whether in agricultural, industrial, commercial, transportation, or other pursuits, develop a greater activity from this moment on, in order to create new resources which will reveal that the spirit of our people is capable of saving the nation's economy by the efforts of its own citizens.

And, finally, as the fear may arise among the interests now in bitter conflict in the field of international affairs[1] that a deviation of raw materials fundamentally necessary to the struggle in which the most powerful nations are engaged

---

[1]World War II in Europe was still more than a year away, but the Japanese invasion of China was in full swing, Spain was in the midst of its civil war, and Nazi Germany had just annexed Austria.

might result from the consummation of this act of national sovereignty and dignity, we wish to state that our petroleum operations will not depart a single inch from the moral solidarity maintained by Mexico with the democratic nations, whom we wish to assure that the expropriation now decreed has as its only purpose the elimination of obstacles erected by groups who do not understand the evolutionary needs of all peoples and who would themselves have no compunction in selling Mexican oil to the highest bidder, without taking into account the consequences of such action to the popular masses and the nations in conflict.

Brazilian Mass Politics and the *Estado Novo*

38 ◆ Getúlio Vargas, *EXCERPTS FROM SPEECHES AND INTERVIEWS, 1937–1940*

Not without growing opposition from the middle class and the military, wealthy coffee growers from the states of São Paulo and Minas Gerais maintained their grip on Brazilian politics during the "Old Republic" from 1889 to 1930. In 1930, however, with coffee prices in free fall, a disputed election led to a military coup and the installation as president of Getúlio Vargas. The era of the coffee oligarchy was over, and Brazilian politics embarked on a new path.

Born in 1883 into a politically active family of landowners from the state of Rio Grande do Sol, Vargas served in the army, studied law, and was elected as Rio Grande do Sol's congressman and governor before joining the national government as finance minister in 1926 and 1927. In 1930, he ran for president as the candidate of the Liberal Alliance, a coalition of the urban bourgeoisie, intellectuals, some landowners, and reform-minded army officers. He lost the fraud-filled election, and in its wake, his opponents barred his supporters from taking their seats in congress; in all probability his opponents also were behind the murder of his vice-presidential running mate. At this point, Vargas's supporters in the army deposed the president and named Vargas as head of a provisional government.

Having come to power in 1930 with the support of a diverse coalition, Vargas proceeded cautiously at first. He raised tariffs, encouraged industrialization, and sought to prop up the price of coffee. In 1932, he reduced the voting age to eighteen and granted working women the right to vote. In 1934, a new constitution strengthened the executive, gave the government greater control of the economy, and called for the gradual nationalization of foreign-owned businesses.

In 1935, Vargas began to move toward one-man rule. First the communist and fascist Integralist parties were banned, and then in 1937 he canceled elections, promulgated a new constitution, and assumed dictatorial powers. Brazil, he announced, had entered the era of the *Estado Novo*, the New State.

Source: E. Bradford Burns, *A Documentary History of Brazil*, pp. 347–353. (NY: Knopf, 1966). Reprinted by kind permission of Trinity Episcopal Church (Muscatine, Iowa) on behalf of the author.

In the following excerpts from interviews and speeches given between 1937 and 1940, Vargas outlines the general philosophy and goals of his New State.

QUESTIONS FOR ANALYSIS

1. According to Vargas, what were the major flaws of Brazilian politics before he took power?
2. What steps did Vargas take or does he plan to take to rid Brazil of these flaws?
3. Vargas claims his New State is democratic. Do his comments in his various speeches and interviews support such a claim?
4. Some commentators have discerned elements of fascism in Vargas's political philosophy and policies. Do you agree with such an assessment?
5. What specific policies does Vargas propose in order to appeal to the urban bourgeoisie and working class?

[INTERVIEW, MARCH 1938]

Among the profound changes brought about by the new regime are: the limitation of direct, universal suffrage, applicable only to specific questions that pertain to all citizens[1] ... ; the municipality as the base of the political system[2]; the substitution of the principle of the independence of powers[3] by the supremacy of the Executive; the strengthening of the power of the Union [as opposed to the states]; the effective and efficient participation of economic groupings, through their own organizations, in the constructive and organizational work of the government.[4]

The new system consecrates a government of authority by instituting as law the legislative decree, by giving to the President of the Republic powers to expedite law-decrees when congress is not in session, by attributing to him the prerogative to dissolve it in special cases, and by taking from the Judiciary the privilege of supreme interpretation of the constitutionality or unconstitutionality of the laws which involve public interests of great importance. These new powers, placed under the guard of the government, always overcome private interests.

Profoundly nationalistic, the regime insures and consolidates national unity and formally restricts the autonomy of the states[5] by suppressing regional symbols, extending intervention, establishing the supremacy of federal over local laws in the case of concurrent legislation by attributing to the central government the power to requisition at any time the state militias, etc.

The professions are represented in their own and independent chamber with consultative functions in all the projects concerning the national economy, and eventually it will have legislative functions.

---

[1]Such plebiscites were provided for in the 1937 constitution, but no such plebiscites were held during Vargas's dictatorship.

[2]Mayors were chosen by provincial governors, who in turn were chosen by the president.

[3]The separation of the executive, legislative, and judicial powers within government.

[4]This is a statement of the ideal of "corporatism," in which a society is organized into industrial and professional corporations serving as organs of political representation and exercising control over persons and activities within their jurisdiction. It is an ideology mainly identified with fascist Italy.

[5]In the Old Republic, states had exercised extensive political powers, and politicians from two states, São Paulo and Minas Gerais, dominated the federal government.

Truly we have instituted an essentially democratic regime because it does not base its representation on a system of indications and artificialities but rather on the direct collaboration of the people through their economic forces and their organizations of production and labor. Only thus can our present political structure make known the effective representation of Brazil....

[INTERVIEW, APRIL 1938]

The movement of November 10th[6] was, without doubt, brought about by the national will. We had need of order and security in order to carry on; conspiring against that was the critical state of political disintegration to which we had arrived. Gradually our public life had been transformed into an arena of sterile struggles where plots, clashing interests of the oligarchy, personal competition, and differences in personal interests were decided. Men of character drew away from it nauseated, leaving the field open to political professionals and to demagogic adventurers. It was thus that communism succeeded in infiltrating [the government] and came to be at one time a national danger.[7] Defeated in its violent attempt to seize power, it continued, nevertheless, its work of undermining authority by utilizing as its weapons the other evils that make the situation of the nation so unstable and chaotic: the weakness of political parties, regional jealousies, and dictatorial flights of fancy. Those three evils are in the final analysis simply the result of a single general cause ... the sterility and depletion of the sources from which the agents of stimulus and renovation of public life ought to come.... Foresight of the danger in which we found ourselves ... caused us decisively to favor the political unification of the nation; this is precisely why the regime was established on November 10th.

The Estado Novo embodies, therefore, the will and ideas which ... work against all the factors tending to weaken and dissolve the fatherland—extremism, sabotage, and compromise. It is ready to fight against those evils. It will mobilize all the best that we possess in order to make our nation strong, dignified, and happy.

[SPEECH, JULY 1938]

As Chief of Government, I systematically seek to listen to those who are informed, to appreciate the word of experts, to study and to boldly face the reality of facts. It was thus that, feeling the profound sentiment of the Brazilian people, I did all that was possible to save them from the dangers of extremism, both from the right as well as from the left....

I can affirm to you with certainty that the hours of greatest fear now have passed....

Through the spirit of good sense and through the persistent effort to reconcile the peace of the people with national dignity, we have given a notable example to the world. Thus we proceed ... trying to assure to all and to each a greater share of well-being and tranquility within the just equilibrium between the duties and prerogatives of the citizen.

[SPEECH, JULY 1938]

If you would ask me what is the program of the Estado Novo, I would tell you that its program is to crisscross the nation with railroads, highways, and airlines; to increase production; to provide for the laborer and to encourage agricultural credit; to expand exports; to prepare the armed forces so that they are always ready to face any eventuality; to organize public opinion so that there is, body and soul, one Brazilian thought.

---

[6] On November 10, 1937, Vargas announced to the nation that he had canceled the upcoming presidential elections, dissolved the legislature, and assumed dictatorial powers under a new constitution.

[7] In 1937, a wing of the Communist Party took part in an anti-Vargas revolt that was crushed by the government. Later in the year, the government circulated a forged document that supposedly outlined a communist plan to seize power.

[SPEECH, JANUARY, 1939]

By examining the government's activities, anyone can verify with his own eyes that the basic problems of Brazilian life were resolutely attacked: the increase and expansion of industrial and agrarian centers; the creation of new sources of wealth and the improvement of the processes of exportation ... ; the measures taken to raise the standard of living of the masses; financial support to the producing classes; economic assistance to the worker by means of social security ... a just salary, a good home, and the guarantee of his rights; the increase in the number of centers of technical, physical, and intellectual training; care for public hygiene and rural sanitation by making possible the profitable utilization of land abandoned or sacrificed because of climactic disturbances; the systematic repudiation of extremist ideologies and their ... followers; the combating of all agents of dissolution or weakening of the national energies by the reinforcement of Brazilian traditions and sentiments and the prohibition from functioning in this country of any organization with anti-national activities or linked to foreign political interests; finally the preparation of internal and external defense by the rearmament of our brave armed forces and the simultaneous education of the new generations inculcating in them the spirit and love of the fatherland, faith in its destinies and the desire to make it strong and respected.

CHAPTER 6

Colonial Africa Between the Wars

By 1920, the preliminaries of European colonialism in Africa had ended. Disputes among the colonial powers had been settled, African resistance crushed, and the deck of colonial powers reshuffled after World War I, when Germany had its colonies taken over as League of Nations mandates by France, Britain, Belgium, and South Africa. Europeans could now focus on creating an Africa in which they could exploit the continent's mineral wealth and agricultural products in efficiently run colonies populated by submissive, taxpaying natives. Europeans would, so they promised, educate some Africans, teach them moral principles, and prepare them for the day when they could rule themselves. No one had a timetable for independence, but all agreed it would take place far in the future. Some Europeans believed colonialism in Africa would last for centuries.

Although Africa's European masters had somewhat different philosophies about their roles in Africa, colonial administrations were all basically similar. Authority was exercised by a governor, who took orders from London, Paris, Brussels, or Lisbon but also decided many matters on his own. Serving under the governor were regional, provincial, and district officers, in addition to officials responsible for education, public works, and public health. The number of European administrators was small. In Nigeria in 1938, approximately forty million Nigerians were governed by fewer than fifteen hundred British officials, whose policies were implemented by African chiefs, clerks, policemen, and soldiers under the command of British officers. Africans held no positions of responsibility and had no meaningful voice in shaping policy.

The economic policies of the colonial powers were also similar: to extract maximum wealth from Africa at minimum cost. How this was to be achieved in any given colony depended on climate, mineral deposits, agricultural potential, access to the coast, and the size of the European population. In colonies with good farmland and valuable minerals, white rule meant large-scale land confiscations. In Kenya, Rhodesia, Mozambique, Angola, Uganda, French Equatorial Africa, and the Congo, millions of acres were appropriated and sold cheaply or given to Europeans. In 1913, the government of South Africa, a self-governing member of the British Commonwealth, allocated 90 percent of the country's land to whites, who made up slightly less than 20 percent of the population. In Kenya in the 1920s, approximately one thousand English settlers controlled almost five million acres of the best farmland. In contrast, in French West Africa, the Gold Coast, and parts of Nigeria, where few whites settled, African farmers held on to their land and grew crops for export. When marketing their coffee and cacao, however, their sole option was to sell to European exporters, who offered prices well below those of the world market.

To make their economic plans work, Europeans needed African labor. Few Africans, however, were interested in the Europeans' job offers. Most craftsmen and farmers had no use for European money and could provide for their families by working on their own. One European solution to this problem was force. Relying on loyal chiefs and colonial police to enforce their orders, Europeans coerced men to work building roads and offices, clearing fields, constructing railroads, carrying goods from place to place, and harvesting crops. Such systems of forced labor continued in the French colonies until 1946 and in Portuguese colonies until the 1960s. Another less blatantly coercive way to pressure Africans to accept wage-paying work was to impose taxes that had to be paid in cash only. This forced Africans to take wage-paying jobs to earn what they needed to pay the government.

The European assumption that Africans would endure the injustices of colonial rule for decades or even centuries was an enormous miscalculation. Some Africans—chiefs, petty traders, farmers who grew export crops, and small numbers of Africans who had opportunities to study in Europe—accepted, and perhaps even welcomed, European rule. Most, however, found colonialism oppressive and repugnant. For some, opposition took the form of joining African Christian churches that were run by blacks and preached that God did not want white people to rule over Africans. For some educated city-dwellers, it meant supporting the Pan-African movement, which demanded fairness for black people and urged recognition of Africa's achievements and potential. For still others, it meant joining organizations such as the African National Congress, which sought to hold back the racist tide in South Africa, or the National Congress of British West Africa, which sought a greater African voice in colonial administrations. In the 1930s, economic hardship and outrage over the Italian conquest of Ethiopia in 1935 and 1936 deepened African alienation. African nationalism was growing, and after World War II, its dreams of freedom and independence would be realized.

African Society and Identity Under Colonial Rule

Colonialism in Africa involved more than authoritarian rule and economic exploitation. Despite its relative brevity, it profoundly affected African life. It fostered population growth, encouraged urbanization, undermined African religions, altered gender relationships, introduced new sports and pastimes, changed how people dressed and what languages they spoke, and created new African perspectives on their place in the world. In the process, much of old Africa was lost. Whether such changes benefited Africa in the long run is till being debated. Unquestionably, however, for most Africans who lived through them in the 1920s and 1930s, these changes were unsettling, dispiriting, and demeaning.

The Africans' experiences were dispiriting and demeaning because so much of what took place under colonialism was predicated on the assumption of black inferiority. Colonialism's message was that Africans were incapable of governing themselves effectively; nor were they capable of managing a modern economy or of creating a viable culture and social order. For all these tasks they needed Europeans, who justified their authority by claiming their moral and intellectual superiority. Furthermore, Africans were told that to improve themselves as individuals—to become clerks or civil servants in the colonial administration or to become "assimilated" they would have to shed their Africanness and adopt the ideas, views, work habits, dress, and customs of Europeans. This was the price they needed to pay to overcome their backwardness.

Some Africans came to accept their supposed inferiority, causing them to discard their traditions in the pursuit of "civilization." As the following sources show, however, others rejected colonialism's message. They sought ways to preserve Africa's traditions and strengthen the African's self-respect.

Eagles into Chickens

◈

39 ◆ James Aggrey, *PARABLE OF THE EAGLE*

James Aggrey, an educator and clergyman who was among the most prominent Africans of his day, was born in 1875 in the Gold Coast, a British colony. Educated in a Protestant mission school and a convert to Christianity, at age twenty-three he traveled to the United States to study for the ministry. He remained in the United States for twenty years, studying economics and agriculture, speaking out against racial prejudice, and working among the poor blacks of South Carolina. He returned to Africa in 1918 and died in 1927. His "Parable of the Eagle" was written in the early 1920s.

Source: "Parable of the Eagle," from *Aggrey of Africa* by Edward W. Smith. Copyright © 1929 by SCM Press.

QUESTIONS FOR ANALYSIS

1. According to the lesson of Aggrey's parable, what psychological damage results from colonialism?
2. What possible implications does the parable have for colonial policies?

A certain man went through a forest seeking any bird of interest he might find. He caught a young eagle, brought it home and put it among his fowls and ducks and turkey, and gave it chickens' food to eat even though it was an eagle, the king of birds.

Five years later a naturalist came to see him and, after passing through his garden, said: "That bird is an eagle, not a chicken."

"Yes," said its owner, "but I have trained it to be a chicken. It is no longer an eagle, it is a chicken, even though it measures fifteen feet from tip to tip of its wings."

"No," said the naturalist, "it is an eagle still; it has the heart of an eagle, and I will make it soar high up to the heavens."

"No," said the owner, "it is a chicken, and it will never fly."

They agreed to test it. The naturalist picked up the eagle, held it up, and said with great intensity: "Eagle, thou art an eagle; thou dost belong to the sky and not to this earth; stretch forth thy wings and fly."

The eagle turned this way and that, and then, looking down, saw the chickens eating their food, and down he jumped.

The owner said: "I told you it was a chicken."

"No," said the naturalist, "it is an eagle. Give it another chance tomorrow."

So the next day he took it to the top of the house and said: "Eagle, thou art an eagle; stretch forth thy wings and fly." But again the eagle, seeing the chickens feeding, jumped down and fed with them.

Then the owner said: "I told you it was a chicken."

"No," asserted the naturalist, "it is an eagle, and it still has the heart of an eagle; only give it one more chance, and I will make it fly tomorrow."

The next morning he rose early and took the eagle outside the city, away from the houses, to the foot of a high mountain. The sun was just rising, gilding the top of the mountain with gold, and every crag was glistening in the joy of that beautiful morning.

He picked up the eagle and said to it: "Eagle, thou art an eagle; thou dost belong to the sky and not to this earth; stretch thy wings and fly!"

The eagle looked around and trembled as if new life were coming to it; but did not fly.

The naturalist then made it look straight at the sun. Suddenly it stretched out its wings and, with the screech of an eagle, it mounted higher and higher and never returned. It was an eagle, though it had been kept and tamed as a chicken!

My people of Africa, we were created in the image of God, but men have made us think that we are chickens, and we still think we are; but we are eagles. Stretch forth your wings and fly! Don't be content with the food of chickens!

The Value of African Religion

◈

40 ◆ Kabaka Daudi Chwa,
EDUCATION, CIVILIZATION, AND
"FOREIGNIZATION" IN BUGANDA

The Great Lakes region of east central Africa, dominated by the kingdom of Buganda, was an area of European missionary activity in the nineteenth century. British Protestant missionaries arrived in the region in 1877 and were followed by French Catholic missionaries in 1879. With traditional African religions already weakened by conversions to Islam, missionaries made many converts, especially among young courtiers in the entourage of Buganda's hereditary ruler, the kabaka. In the 1880s, Protestant-Catholic rivalries among the chiefs led to civil war, the weakening of the kabaka's power, and the establishment in 1894 of the British protectorate of Uganda, of which Buganda was the largest part.

Daudi Chwa (1897–1939) as a two-year-old was named kabaka after his father was deposed and exiled for leading a campaign against the British. A convert to Christianity, Chwa was a figurehead, because the British had given his chiefs a free hand to administer the colony. He did play a successful role in opposing a plan to consolidate Uganda, Kenya, and Tanganyika in the 1930s. Toward the end of his life, he developed reservations about the effects of colonial rule, especially on African culture. In 1935, he published his views in a pamphlet, "Education, Civilization, and 'Foreignization' in Buganda."

QUESTIONS FOR ANALYSIS

1. How would you characterize the traditional system of justice of the people of Buganda (the Baganda)? By what means did it try to deter behavior that ran counter to the people's rules and customs?
2. According to the kabaka, how and in what ways do traditional Baganda moral values resemble those of Christianity?
3. What have the Baganda gained and lost as a result of European colonialism, according to Chwa?
4. What sort of thinking about the "backwardness" of the Baganda does the kabaka try to counter in his letter?
5. In Daudi Chwa's view, what should be the proper balance between traditional African and European beliefs and practices?

Source: Mind of Buganda: Documents of the Modern History of an African Kingdom, by Donald Anthony Low, pp. 104–108. © 1971 by D. A. Low. Published by the University of California Press. Reprinted by permission of the University of California Press.

Every one knows that education and civilization were started simultaneously in this country in their respective rudimentary forms by the kind efforts of the members of the various Missionary Societies and have now been enhanced largely due to the assistance rendered by the Protectorate Government.

Naturally education and civilization gained tremendous favour among the Baganda,[1] and as a consequence there are numerous Schools in remote villages in Buganda Kingdom for the education of the young generation; while every facility and luxury which are the outcome of civilization are today being extended to all the Baganda, who can afford to avail themselves of the same, throughout the country.

Now my fears are that instead of the Baganda acquiring proper and legitimate education and civilization there is a possible danger that they may be drifting to "foreignisation." ... To be more explicit, what I mean by the word "foreignisation" is that instead of the Baganda acquiring proper education at the various Schools and of availing themselves of the legitimate amenities of civilization, I am very much afraid the young generation of this country is merely drifting wholesale towards "foreignization" of their natural instincts and is discarding its native and traditional customs, habits and good breeding. What is at present popularly termed as education and civilization of a Muganda[2] may be nothing more nor less than mere affectation of the foreign customs and habits of the Western Countries which in some instances are only injurious to our own inherent morals and ideals of native life.

I am well aware that it has been said more than once that the Baganda have neither morals nor public opinion, but I ... have always been very strongly opposed to this ... false accusation brought against the Baganda as a nation. I do not wish to be considered in this article to uphold the Baganda as a Nation of Angels—But what I do maintain is that prior to the advent of the Europeans the Baganda had a very strict moral code of their own which was always enforced by a constant and genuine fear of some evil or incurable or even fatal disease being suffered invariably by the breaker of this moral code. In fact I maintain the Baganda observed most strictly the doctrine of the Ten Commandments in spite of the fact that Christianity and the so-called Christian morals were absolutely unknown to the Baganda. For instance there was a very strong public opinion against the following offenses, which are the fundamental principles of the doctrine of the Ten Commandments:

(a) Theft was always punished very severely, invariably by the loss of the right hand of the offender, so as to render him incapable of committing the same offence again.

(b) Adultery was almost unknown among the Baganda and any man found guilty of such offence was always ostracised from Society.

(c) Murder was invariably followed by a very severe vendetta between the members of the family or clan of the victim and those of the offender.

(d) Filial obedience was most honoured among the Baganda and disobedience or disrespect of one's parents was always supposed to be punished by some higher power by the infliction of some horrible or incurable disease upon the offender.

(e) False evidence was looked upon with contempt. The person who bore false evidence and the person against whom it was given were both subjected to a very severe test by forcing them to drink a certain kind of strong drug known as "Madudu," which was supposed to result in making one of the parties who was in the wrong unconscious.

In this connection I should like to point out that although polygamy was universally recognized among the Baganda and was never considered as

---

[1]The Baganda are the people of the kingdom of Buganda.
[2]Muganda is the word (singular) for an individual living in the kingdom of Buganda.

immoral yet prostitution was absolutely unheard of. Civilization, education and freedom are the direct causes of the appalling state of affairs as regards prostitution and promiscuous relationships between the Baganda men and women.... As [an] illustration of the strictness of the old moral code of the Baganda I should like to point out here one of the most important native custom[s] of looking after the daughters in a Muganda's home. It was one of the worst filial offence[s] for a daughter to become pregnant while living with her parents. As soon as she was discovered in that condition she was at once expelled from her parents' house, and was absolutely cut off from them. She could not eat with them nor would her parents touch her until the child was born and some rites had been gone through which necessitated a great deal of hardship and shame on the part of the girl and her seducer. This custom was intended to stimulate morality among the Baganda girls, since any girl who went astray before she was given in marriage suffered this indignity and was always looked upon with contempt by all her relatives and friends. Furthermore any girl who was given in marriage and was found not to be virgin merited unspeakable disfavour in the eyes of her parents, relations and friends. All this, however, is of course, no longer the case. The present so-called education and civilization prevailing in this country has completely destroyed this moral code by removing the constant fear just referred to above from the minds of the young generation of the Baganda by the freedom and liberty which are the natural consequences of the present World civilization.

I think it would not be out of place to state here definitely that it is my firm belief that prior to the introduction of Christianity in this country the Baganda could not be classified as the worst type of a heathen tribe of Africa since they never indulged in any of the worst heathen customs or rites such as human sacrifice or torture which are found in other parts of Africa. Whilst on the other hand apart from their ignorance of Christianity and their practice of polygamy I am strongly of [the] opinion that most of the traditional customs and etiquette of the Baganda ... were quite [consistent] with the principles of Christianity. In support of this argument it is only necessary to mention a few customs of the Baganda to show that they unconsciously possessed a sense of modern Christian morality:

(a) It was one of the most important [behaviors] among the Baganda for one's neighbour to be considered as his own relative and to share with him in his happiness or unhappiness. For instance a Muganda would always invite his neighbour if he killed a chicken or goat to share it with him, whilst in case of any danger or misfortune it was always the duty of the nearest neighbour to render every assistance to the party in danger or distress.

(b) It was the recognized etiquette for a Muganda to salute every one that he met on the road, whether he knew him or not.

(c) When a Muganda was taking his meal and any one passed by, it was always the custom to invite him to share it with him.

(d) It was always the duty of every one who hears an alarm at any time of day or night or a cry for help to go at once and render assistance to the party in distress or danger....

(e) It was the duty of every Muganda, when requested, to assist any traveller in directing him to his destination, or to give him food or water, and even to give him shelter from rain or for the night....

My intention therefore in this article is to emphasize the fact that while boasting of having acquired Western education and civilization in an amazingly short period, we have entirely and completely ignored our native traditional customs. In other words we have "foreignised" our native existence by acquiring the worst foreign habits and customs of the Western people. I am only too well aware that this is inevitable in all countries where Western civilization has reached, so I have considered it my duty...to warn very strongly all members of the young generation of the Baganda that while they are legitimately entitled to strive to acquire education and civilization they should also take a very great care that acquisition of Western education and civilization does not automatically destroy their best inherent traditions and customs which, in my own opinion, are quite as good as those found among the Western Civilized countries.

White Rule, African Families

◈

41 ◆ Charlotte Maxeke,
SOCIAL CONDITIONS AMONG BANTU WOMEN AND GIRLS

Few groups in Africa were affected by colonialism as much as women. In traditional African villages, a division of labor between men and women had existed in which women were responsible for planting, weeding, harvesting, food preparation, and child care, whereas men cleared the land, built homes, herded cattle, and helped with fieldwork. Such arrangements broke down in West Africa when cash-crop agriculture was introduced. Men took over the farming of cotton or cocoa, leaving the responsibility of growing food for domestic consumption exclusively to women. Worse disruption took place in southern and eastern Africa, where men left their villages for wage-paying jobs in mines or cities. This meant long absences of husbands from their families, greater work and domestic responsibilities for women, and breakdowns of family life.

All these issues concerned the South African woman Charlotte Maxeke, the founder of the African National Congress Women's League and a social worker, teacher, and leader in the African Methodist Episcopal Church. Born Charlotte Makgomo in 1874, she received her primary and secondary education in South Africa. While in her early twenties, she toured England, Canada, and the United States with an African choir. She remained in the United States to study at Wilberforce College in Ohio, where she received her Bachelor of Science degree and met and married another South African, Reverend Marshall Maxeke. On her return to South Africa, she cofounded a secondary school with her husband and remained active in the African National Congress and church affairs until her death in 1939.

In 1930, she presented her views on the plight of black South African women and families in a speech delivered to a rally attended by white and black Christian youth.

QUESTIONS FOR ANALYSIS

1. What, according to Maxeke, are the reasons for the Bantu exodus from the countryside to cities?
2. What special challenges and difficulties confront newly arrived blacks in urban areas?
3. How do problems of men and women in such circumstances differ?

Source: Charlotte Maxeke, "Social Conditions Among Bantu Women and Girls," *Christian Students and Modern South Africa* (Fort Hare, Cape Province, Student Christian Association, 1931), pp. 111–118.

4. What seems to have been the effect of the changes Maxeke describes on children and young people?
5. What solutions to the problems confronting African women and their families does Maxeke propose? If implemented, would her suggestions likely be successful?

There are many problems pressing in upon us Bantu,[1] to disturb the peaceful working of our homes. One of the chief is perhaps the stream of Native life into the towns. Men leave their homes, and go into big towns like Johannesburg, where they get a glimpse of a life such as they had never dreamed existed. At the end of their term of employment they receive the wages for which they have worked hard, and which should be used for the sustenance of their families, but the attractive luxuries of civilisation are in many instances too much for them, they waste their hard earned wages, and seem to forget completely the crying need of their family out in the veld.[2]

The wife finds that her husband has apparently forgotten her existence, and she therefore makes her hard and weary way to the town in search of him. When she gets there, and starts looking round for a house of some sort in which to accommodate herself and her children, she meets with the first rebuff. The Location Superintendent[3] informs her that she cannot rent accommodation unless she has a husband. Thus she is driven to the first step on the downward path, for if she would have a roof to cover her children's heads a husband must be found, and so we get these poor women forced by circumstances to consort with men in order to provide shelter for their families. Thus we see that the authorities in enforcing the restrictions in regard to accommodation are often doing Bantu society a grievous harm, for they are forcing its womanhood, its wedded womanhood, to

the first step on the downward path of sin and crime.

Many Bantu women live in the cities at a great price, the price of their children; for these women, even when they live with their husbands, are forced in most cases to go out and work, to bring sufficient [food] into the homes and to keep their children alive. The children of these unfortunate people therefore run wild, and as there are not sufficient schools to house them, it is easy for them to live an aimless existence, learning crime of all sorts....

If these circumstances obtain when husband and wife live together in the towns, imagine the case of the woman whose husband has gone to town and left her, forgetting apparently all his responsibilities. Here we get young women, the flower of the youth of the Bantu, going up to towns in search of their husbands, and as I have already stated, living as the reputed wives of other men, because of the location requirements, or becoming housekeepers to men in the locations and towns, and eventually their nominal wives.

... Thus we see that the European is by his treatment of the Native in these ways which I have mentioned, only pushing him further and further down in the social scale, forgetting that it was he and his kind who brought these conditions about in South Africa, forgetting his responsibilities to those who labour for him and to whom he introduced the benefits, and evils, of civilisation....

Then we come to the *Land Question*. This is very acute in South Africa, especially from the Bantu

---

[1]In this context, blacks of South Africa who spoke languages in the Bantu family and who traditionally had been farmers and herders.
[2]The word for the grasslands of southern and eastern Africa in Afrikaans, the Dutch-based language spoken by South Africans of Dutch descent.

[3]A white official in charge of a black township. These townships, adjacent to white towns or cities, were areas where blacks by law were compelled to live.

point of view. South Africa in terms of available land is shrinking daily owing to increased population, and to many other economic and climatic causes. Cattle diseases have crept into the country, ruining many a stock farmer, and thus Bantu wealth is gradually decaying. As a result there are more and more workers making their way to the towns and cities such as Johannesburg to earn a living. And what a living! The majority earn about £3 10s. per month, out of which they must pay 25s. for rent, and 10s. for tram fares, so I leave you to imagine what sort of existence they lead on the remainder.

Here again we come back to the same old problem ... that of the woman of the home being obliged to find work in order to supplement her husband's wages, with the children growing up undisciplined and uncared for, and the natural following rapid decay of morality among the people. We find that in this state of affairs, the woman in despair very often decides that she cannot leave her children thus uncared for, and she therefore throws up her employment in order to care for them, but is naturally forced into some form of home industry, which, as there is very little choice for her in this direction, more often than not takes the form of the brewing and selling of Skokiaan.[4] Thus the woman starts on a career of crime for herself and her children, a career which often takes her and her children right down the depths of immorality and misery. The woman, poor unfortunate victim of circumstances, goes to prison, and the children are left even more desolate than when their mother left them to earn her living.... The children thus become decadent, never having had a chance in life. About ten years ago, there was talk of Industrial schools being started for such unfortunate children, but it was only talk, and we are to-day in the same position, aggravated by the increased numbers

steadily streaming in from the rural areas, all undergoing very similar experiences to those I have just outlined....

Many of the Bantu feel and rightly too that the laws of the land are not made for Black and White alike. Take the question of permits for the right to look for work.[5] To look for work, mark you! The poor unfortunate Native, fresh from the country does not know of these rules and regulations, naturally breaks them and is thrown into prison; or if he does happen to know the regulations and obtains a pass for six days, and is obliged to renew it several times, as is of course very often the case, he will find that when he turns up for the third or fourth time for the renewal of his permit, he is put into prison, because he has been unsuccessful in obtaining work. And not only do the Bantu feel that the law for the White and the Black is not similar, but we even find some of them convinced that there are two Gods, one for the White and one for the Black. I had an instance of this in an old Native woman who had suffered much, and could not be convinced that the same God watched over and cared for us all, but felt that the God who gave the Europeans their life of comparative comfort and ease, could not possibly be the same God who allowed his poor Bantu to suffer so. As another instance of the inequalities existing in our social scheme, we have the fact of Natives not being allowed to travel on buses and trams in many towns, except those specially designed for them.

In connection with the difficulty experienced through men being employed almost exclusively in domestic work in the cities, I would mention that this is of course one of the chief reasons for young women, who should rightly be doing that work, going rapidly down in the social life of the community; and it is here that joint service councils of Bantu and White women would be able to do so much for the

---

[4]Skokiaan is Afrikaans for Bantu beer, an alcoholic beverage brewed from sorghum.

[5]Introduced in 1923 and confirmed by legislation adopted in 1952, pass laws were designed to regulate movement of blacks in white urban areas. Outside designated "homelands," blacks were required to carry a pass that showed how long

and for what reason the bearer was permitted to be in a white area; it also included the bearer's photograph, fingerprints, employment status, and address. Without a valid pass, blacks could be fined, arrested, deported to a rural reserve, or forced to accept a low-paying job for a white employer.

good of the community. The solution to the problem seems to me to be to get women into service, and to give them proper accommodation, where they know they are safe. Provide hostels, and club-rooms, and rest rooms for these domestic servants, where they may spend their leisure hours, and I think you will find the problem of the employment of female domestic servants will solve itself, and that a better and happier condition of life will come into being for the Bantu.

... What we want is more co-operation and friendship between the two races, and more definite display of real Christianity to help us in the solving of these riddles. Let us try to make our Christianity practical.

Nationalism, Pan-Africanism, and Anticolonialism

Although it was clear by the 1920s and 1930s that efforts to block the European takeover of their continent had failed, Africans did not abandon the fight against colonial rule. Not a year passed in which a colonial government somewhere did not use police or troops to quell a tax rebellion, halt demonstrations against forced labor, or forcibly remove individuals from land confiscated by the government. Africans also found legal, nonviolent ways to demand fair treatment and defend their traditions. They organized political associations, edited journals, wrote books and newspaper editorials, joined independent African Christian churches, attended international meetings, and sent representatives to European capitals to state their grievances.

The short- and long-term goals of African opponents to colonialism varied widely. The Pan-African movement sponsored international meetings to publicize the abuses of colonialism and draw attention to black people's accomplishments; in the 1930s, some Pan-Africans concluded that Africans should seek immediate independence from colonial rule. Africans also joined political organizations to protect their rights and advance their interests. These organizations included the African National Congress, founded in South Africa in 1912; the National Congress of British West Africa, founded in 1920 by representatives from Nigeria, the Gold Coast, the Gambia, and Sierra Leone; and the East African Association, founded in Kenya in 1921. African workers joined labor unions and went on strike to improve wages and working conditions. Others joined sports and literary associations, singing groups, youth organizations, dance clubs, and African Christian churches that had broken away from mainline European dominations. Although not overtly political, such organizations gave Africans opportunities to express dissatisfaction with European rule in ways not likely to attract the attention of colonial officials. They also enabled Africans to preserve elements of their culture that otherwise might have been lost.

Anticolonial movements in Africa faced many obstacles in the 1920s and 1930s: the indifference of chiefs, farmers, and petty traders who benefited from European rule; the paucity of Africans with advanced education and political experience; the gap between educated city dwellers and illiterate villagers; and rivalries among different ethnic groups. They also were hindered by censorship and various other repressive measures enforced by colonial governments. Despite these barriers, new leaders emerged, political movements multiplied, and critics of colonialism gained followers. After World War II, Africans were ready to demand their independence.

A Plea to the World for Racial Equality

❖

42 ❖ 1921 PAN-AFRICAN CONGRESS, LONDON MANIFESTO

Pan-Africanism, which played a key role in African liberation and postcolonial politics, was originally inspired by black leaders from the United States and the West Indies in the early 1900s. With the partition of Africa in full swing, color barriers increasing in the West Indies, and lynching and racial violence growing in the United States, a West Indian lawyer, Henry Sylvester Williams, organized a Pan-African conference in London in 1900. Although most of the thirty-two delegates came from the United States and the West Indies, it caught the attention of Africans. A Nigerian newspaper, *The Lagos Standard*, called the meeting "an event in the history of race movements which for its importance and probable results is perhaps without parallel."

Pan-Africanism was revived in 1919 when the prominent American black W. E. B. Du Bois (1868–1963) organized the First Pan-African Congress (Williams's meeting had been a "conference," not a congress) in Paris to coincide with the Paris Peace Conference. He hoped to demonstrate the solidarity of black people and publicize their needs to the gathered statesmen and diplomats. In 1921, Du Bois organized a second conference that met sequentially in London, Brussels, and Paris. At the beginning of the 1921 meeting, the 113 delegates from Africa, the United States, England, and the West Indies adopted the London Manifesto. Its demands for racial justice and fair treatment of blacks were widely publicized in Africa, especially in the British colonies of West Africa.

Two more Pan-African congresses were held in the 1920s, but the meeting scheduled for late 1929 had to be canceled because of the U.S. stock market crash. Riddled by internal disagreements, the Pan-African movement weakened in the 1930s, but at the Fifth Pan-African Congress at Manchester, England, in 1945, it came alive with a new sense of purpose. With its call for African unity and the end of colonialism, it was one of the first steps in the post–World War II era toward the realization of African independence.

QUESTIONS FOR ANALYSIS

1. On what grounds does the London Manifesto reject the idea of inequality among the world's races?
2. According to the manifesto, what is the main obstacle to African advancement in the modern world?
3. What attitude is expressed in the manifesto toward whites?

Source: London Manifesto: "To the World," *The Crisis*, Vol. 23, November, 1921, pp. 5–10.

4. According to the manifesto, why should "advanced" people aid Africans?
5. Do the authors of the manifesto believe Africa is ready for independence? Why or why not?

The absolute equality of races, physical, political and social, is the founding stone of World Peace and human advancement. No one denies great differences of gift, capacity and attainment among individuals of all races, but the voice of Science, Religion and practical Politics is one in denying the God-appointed existence of super races or of races naturally and inevitably and eternally inferior.

That in the vast range of time, one group should in its industrial technique or social organisation or spiritual vision lag a few hundred years behind another or forge fitfully ahead or come to differ decidedly in thought, deed and ideal is proof of the essential richness and variety of human nature, rather than proof of the co-existence of demi-gods and apes in human form....

And of all the various criteria by which masses of men have in the past been judged and classified that of the color of the skin and texture of the hair is surely the most idiotic....

The insidious and dishonourable propaganda which for selfish ends so distorts and denies facts as to represent the advancement and development of certain races as impossible and undesirable should be met with wide-spread dissemination of the truth; the experiment of making the Negro slave a free citizen in the United States is not a failure; the attempts at autonomous government in Haiti and Liberia are not proofs of the impossibility of self-government among black men; the experience of Spanish America does not prove that mulatto democracy will not eventually succeed there; the aspirations of Egypt and India are not successfully to be met by sneers at the capacity of darker races....

If it be proven that absolute world segregation by group, colour or historic affinity is the best thing for the future world, let the white race leave the dark world and the dark races will gladly leave the white. But the proposition is absurd. This is a world of men—of men whose likenesses far outweigh their differences; who mutually need each other in labour and thought

and dream, but who can successfully have each other only on terms of equality, justice and mutual respect. They are the real and only peace-makers who work sincerely and peacefully to this end.

The beginning of Wisdom in inter-racial contact is the establishment of political institutions among suppressed Peoples. The habit of democracy must be made to encircle the earth. Despite the attempt to prove that its practice is the secret and divine Gift of the Few, no habit is more natural and more widely spread among primitive peoples or more easily capable of development among wide masses. Local self-government with a minimum of help and oversight can be established tomorrow in Asia, Africa, America and the Isles of the Sea [the Pacific Islands]. It will in many instances need general control and guidance but it will fail only when that guidance seeks ignorantly and consciously its own selfish ends and not the people's liberty and good.

Surely in the 20th century of the Prince of Peace [Jesus], in the millennium of Buddha and Mahmoud [Muhammad], and in the mightiest era of Human Reason there can be found in the civilised world enough human altruism, learning and benevolence to develop native institutions for the native's good rather than continuing to allow the majority of mankind to be brutalised and enslaved by ignorant and selfish agents of commercial institutions whose one aim is profit and power for the few.

And this brings us to the crux of the matter; it is to the shame of the world that today the relations between the main groups of mankind and their mutual [appraisal] and respect is determined chiefly by the degree in which one can subject the other to its service—enslaving labour, making ignorance compulsory, uprooting ruthlessly religion and custom and destroying government so that the favoured few may luxuriate in the toil of the tortured many....

The day of such world organisation is past and whatever excuse may be made for it in other ages, the 20th century must come to judge men as men and not as merely material and labour.... If we are coming to recognise that the great modern problem is to correct maladjustment in the distribution of wealth, it must be remembered that the basic maladjustment is in the outrageously unjust distribution of the world income between the dominant and suppressed peoples,—in the rape of land and raw material, the monopoly of technique and culture....

What, then, do those demand who see these evils of the colour line and racial discrimination, and who believe in the divine right of Suppressed and Backward Peoples to learn and aspire and be free?

The Suppressed Races through their thinking leaders are demanding:

1. The recognition of civilised men as civilised despite their race and colour.

2. Local self-government for backward groups, deliberately rising as experience and knowledge grow to complete self-government under the limitations of a self-governed world.

3. Education in self-knowledge, in scientific truth and in industrial technique, undivorced from the art of beauty.

4. Freedom in their own religion and customs and with the right to be non-conformist and different.

5. Co-operation with the rest of the world in government, industry and art on the basis of Justice, Freedom and Peace.

6. The ancient common ownership of the Land and its natural fruits and defence against the unrestrained greed of invested capital.

The world must face two eventualities; either the complete assimilation of Africa with two or three of the great world states, with political, civil and social power and privileges absolutely equal for its black and white citizens, or the rise of a great black African State, founded in Peace and Good Will, based on popular education, natural art and industry and freedom of trade, autonomous and sovereign in its internal policy, but from its beginning a part of a great society of peoples in which it takes its place with others as co-rulers of the world....

New Voices of African Radicalism

❖

43 ◆ Lamine Senghor,
THE NEGRO'S FIGHT FOR FREEDOM

Early African nationalists tended to be modest in their demands. Founders of the National Congress of British West Africa made polite requests for greater access to positions in the colonial administration but were eager to include a statement in their founding charter affirming "the attachment of the peoples of British West Africa to the British connection and unfeigned loyalty and devotion to the person of His Majesty." Leaders of the Pan African Movement were committed to African self-rule, but not any time soon. The statement on the subject in their 1920 manifesto—support for "local self-government for backward groups, deliberately rising as experience and judgment grow to complete self-government"—could

Source: From Dr. J. Ayo Langley, *Ideologies of Liberation in Black Africa* (London: Rex Collings, 1979), pp. 255–260, passim. Used by kind permission of Mrs. Mary Langley.

have been written by any number of European colonial officials. In French West Africa in the 1910s and 1920s, the leading advocate of equal rights for African blacks, Blaise Diagne (1872-1934), favored adoption of French cultural and social norms (assimilation) and closer ties with France (association), leading ultimately to the time when Africans would become full French citizens, with rights and legal status no different from those of white French people living in Paris or Lyons.

During the 1920s, however, more radical voices began to be heard. Among them was the voice of Lamine Senghor, a Senegalese who while living in Paris became a leader of a group of African students, war veterans, and expatriates who advocated immediate independence for Africa's colonies. Born in 1899, Senghor attended school and learned enough French to land a job in the office of a French merchant in Dakar. In 1915, he was recruited into the French army, and at some point in the long and bloody Battle of Verdun (February-December 1916) was wounded and gassed. He returned to France in 1922, where he worked as a postal clerk and took classes at the Sorbonne. He also became a member of the newly founded French Communist Party and of the Universal League for the Defense of the Negro Race, an organization that in opposition to Blaise Diagne sought immediate independence for France's African colonies. After becoming president of the League, he renamed it the Negro Defense Committee and edited the organization's newsletter. He also represented the organization in February 1927 at the organizing conference in Brussels of the League against Imperialism. This organization was the brainchild of the German communist Willi Münzenberg, who was supported in his efforts by the Communist International (Comintern), an organization founded in Russia in 1919 to encourage worldwide revolution. Viewed as a dangerous agitator, Senghor was arrested on his return to France and was released shortly before his death from tuberculosis in November 1927.

The following excerpt is from the speech Senghor delivered at the Brussels conference.

QUESTIONS FOR ANALYSIS

1. How does Senghor characterize the true goals French imperialism?
2. What specific features of French colonialism does he especially abhor?
3. How does Senghor justify his argument that Africans are still enslaved?
4. According to Senghor, how does the African struggle for independence relate to worldwide anticolonial movements? How does it relate to communism?

I have to convey to you the fraternal greetings of the Comité de Defense de la Race Négre. This committee for the liberation of the Negro race is a comprehensive organization of young Negroes resolved to take steps to bring about the liberation of their race. You are perhaps aware that ours is the most oppressed race in the world. This is the race which is oppressed by all the imperialists on earth, and whose life and death lie in the hands of its enemies. Therefore, we wish to fight for equality with other races which regard themselves as better than us, and before the whole world we ask them whether they are superior to us because their skin is white or their brain more cultured than ours. These races came to us under the pretext of bringing us civilization. Today we see a tragic picture in our country.

COLONIZATION

At this point I want briefly to say something controversial about the word 'colonization.' I want to reply to the speech made by our chairman, Hafiz Ramadan Bey,[1] who has asserted that Egypt is not a colony, and that she is free and independent. As representative of the Negro Defence Committee, I am bound to declare here that the Egyptian workers who support our committee are not of that opinion. They have come here to protest against British paternalism in Egypt and against the occupation of the Suez Canal by Britain. They wish to protest against British imperialism and they demand Egyptian independence. . . . What is colonization? To colonize is to rob a people of the right to manage its own affairs as best it can and as it sees fit. The Egyptians were deprived by Britain of that right. . . . [Egypt] is a colony like all other colonies which are under the yoke of international imperialism.

CIVILIZATION

I said to you a moment ago that when the French arrived they told us they were bringing us civilization. But instead of teaching us the French language and enlightening us about what they call civilization, they said that the Negroes must not receive any education, otherwise they would become civilized and one would not be able to do with them as one liked.

That is what French imperialism understands by 'civilizing' the Negro.

I shall quote you an example from the report of a former colonial administrator . . . published in several French newspapers. . . .

'I accuse the former Colonel Hutin, now General Hutin, Commander of the Legion of Honor, of ordering the looting of the Molanda trading post and of taking part in the looting.' . . .

'I accuse the officer and manager of the depot at Quesso of having committed a crime in February 1915, in order to extort a confession to a theft of 500 francs. He accused his orderly of pilfering the sum of money. In order to find out where the money was hidden, he had him undressed and his testicles placed on a table, and he crushed one of his testicles with a hammer. The private lost consciousness. He was revived, then they threatened to crush the other testicle as well if he did not confess where the money was.'

'I accuse the chief adjutant of the post at Bania of bringing before him a chieftain of the Gana tribe who refused to disclose the whereabouts of Mausers [German-made firearms] which his people had taken from German deserters. And I accuse the adjutant of crushing one of the Gana chieftain's hands between the two plates of a copying-press and of "tormenting" him (flaying him with knife-blades). He had the wounds filled with honey, and exposed him to the sun and the stings of the bees.'

Who can help shuddering at the thought that in the twentieth century Frenchmen commit atrocities such as these, worthy of the darkest Middle Ages?

FORCED LABOR

A recent decree of the general government of French West Africa placed the population at the disposal of the administration work that was in the so-called 'common interest.'[2]

In order to implement this decree the lieutenant governor of Mauritania [a French West African colony] lays down the conditions of work. In Art 3, he says: 'The length of the working day is fixed at ten hours with two hours' rest from work during the day.' In Art 9, he stipulates that 'The minimum daily wage of each labour shall be as follows: women and children, 1 franc 50; men, 2 francs per day.' You cannot refuse to work for

---

[1]An Egyptian exile living in Paris. He is correct that England declared Egyptian independence in 1922. But Senghor is also correct that it was independence with certain reservations. England continued to control the Suez Canal Zone and Anglo-Egyptian Sudan; it also retained responsibility for Egypt's defense and the protection of "foreign interests."

[2]Blaise Diagne's defense of the system of forced labor was a major reason why he came to be despised by Senghor and other radicals.

this wage. So you are forced to work ten hours a day in the African sun, and can only earn 2 francs. The women and children work just as long as the men, and despite all this they tell us that slavery is abolished, that the Negroes are free, that all men are equal, etc. I regard those who tell us this not idiots but as people who are poking fun at us.

SLAVERY

This also, we are told, has been abolished, and one might almost grant that the sale of slaves is forbidden, and that one can no longer sell Negroes to a white, to a Chinese, or even another Negro. But we see that the imperialists very democratically reserve the right to sell an entire Negro people to another imperialist.

What did France do with the Congo in 1912?[3] She simply handed it over to Germany. Did she ask the Negroes of the Congo whether they wanted to be exploited by the Germans?

Certain French politicians have even gone the length of writing in the French gutter press that the Negroes of the Antilles [French West Indies] are starting to demand too many rights, and that one would do better to sell them to the Americans; then one would at least make a profit out of it.

It is not true—slavery is not abolished. On the contrary it has been modernized.

INJUSTICE IS STILL MORE STRIKING IN FRANCE

We have seen that during the war as many Negroes as possible were recruited, to be used as

cannon-fodder. They recruited so many that the French governors refused to go on recruiting because they were afraid the people would revolt.

They let our comrades be slaughtered in the first Morocco war before the Great War of 1914.[4] They are still being butchered today in Morocco, in the Rif and in Syria,[5] Negroes are being sent to Madagascar; Negroes are sent to Indochina because it is near China which is setting them a splendid revolutionary example.[6]

To the Chinese I say: 'I would dearly embrace you, Comrades, because you set a good revolutionary example to all the peoples under the yoke of the colonizers, and I would that all of them would let themselves be influenced by your revolutionary spirit.' The French imperialists have sent Negroes to Indochina and ordered them to fire on the Indochinese in case they should rise up against the French colonies. They tell them that they are not of their race and that they should kill them. . . .

The Negroes have slept for too long. But beware! The man who has slept too well, and then awakes, will not fall asleep again.

I should like to give you two examples of how the 'mother-country' recognizes the services of those who were wounded in the war in order to save her, who were hit by bullets from the so-called 'enemy' and today are no longer able to work. A distinction is drawn between them and the French wounded who fought with them on the same battlefield and who, it seems, were defending the same mother-country. Just two examples: The French government gives a French soldier second-class, 90%, war-disabled, father of one child, an annual pension

[3] Senghor is referring to the provisions of the Treaty of Fez, adopted in March 1912, under which Germany accepted France's position in Morocco in return for territory in the French Equatorial African colony of Middle Congo. The territory became part of the German colony of Cameroon.
[4] Black African troops were used against rebellious Moroccan army units after the imposition of French rule in 1912.
[5] The Rif is a region of northern Morocco which had declared its independence from Spain in 1921. In the Rif

War of 1926, French troops, mostly recruited from Africa, came to the aid of Spain in its successful effort to return the territory to Spanish control. Syria became a French mandate after World War I.
[6] Senghor is expressing his identification with the Chinese Communist Party (founded in 1921), which in alliance with the Nationalists had launched the Northern Expedition against the warlords of northern China in 1926. The split between the Communist and Nationalist parties came just weeks after Senghor delivered his speech.

of 6,882 francs, while a Negro soldier second-class, likewise 90% war-disabled in the same French army, father of one child, receives 1,620 francs annually.

In accordance with Articles 10 and 12, a man 100% war- disabled (that is, a man who is no longer able to move and has to be carried everywhere) gets 15,390 francs if he is a white Frenchman; if he is a Negro he receives only 1,800 francs.

We have assembled to defend ourselves against these injustices, these horrors I have mentioned. Young Negroes are beginning to see things clearly. We know and ascertain that we are French when they need us to let us be killed or make us labour. But when it comes to giving us rights we are no longer Frenchmen but Negroes.

The congress gathered here has, I believe, realized the wish of many who, like me, would like to devote themselves completely to the task of world liberation. Those who have come here are the very people who are pursuing a revolutionary ideal and a human ideal and who sacrifice themselves and all their energies to eradicating this monstrous imperialist oppression the world over. The imperialist oppression which we call colonization at home and which here you term imperialism is one and the same thing. It all stems from capitalism. It is capitalism which breeds imperialism in the peoples of the leading countries. Therefore those who suffer under colonial oppression must join hands and stand side by side with those who suffer under the imperialism of the leading countries. Fight with the same weapons and destroy the scourge of the earth, world imperialism!

It must be destroyed and replaced by an alliance of the free peoples. Then there will be no more slavery.

CHAPTER 7

Asia in an Era of Nationalism and Revolution

Throughout most of history, Asia was the world's most important continent. River valleys in the Middle East, China, and India gave rise to humankind's first writing systems, cities, and organized states. Asian sages, prophets, and teachers inspired Confucianism, Hinduism, Buddhism, Judaism, Islam, and Christianity. Asians created large and successful empires; invented gunpowder, the compass, metallurgy, and produced the first book; made important discoveries in mathematics and astronomy; and for centuries had the world's largest and most sophisticated economies.

Yet by the 1920s and 1930s, virtually all of Asia consisted of Western colonies or territories such as Siberia, Central Asia, and Transcaucasia, which were parts of a European-based state, the Soviet Union. European penetration of Asia dates back to the sixteenth century, when the Portuguese forcibly entered Indian Ocean trade networks and the Russians made their first conquests in Western Siberia. The process accelerated in the nineteenth and early twentieth centuries, when the Dutch tightened their grip on the East Indies, the British extended their authority in India, Russia gained control of much of Central Asia, and France and Britain turned most of Southeast Asia into colonies. In addition, Western powers established spheres of influence up and down the coast of China, forced Japan to end its seclusion policy, and took over government finances and important sectors of the economy of Ottoman Turkey and Persia. Finally, after World War I, Lebanon, Syria, Palestine, Iraq, and Jordan became Western colonies in all but name when the French and British took them over as League of Nations mandates.

The high point of Western imperialism in Asia, reached after World War I, was followed by its rapid demise after World War II. Of the factors that contributed to this sudden turnabout, nationalism was the most important. Nationalism in the region first took root in the early 1900s, when Asians increasingly came to resent the exploitation and oppression that accompanied colonialism. It gathered strength from the example of Japan, whose remarkable transformation demonstrated that Asians, not just Europeans, were capable of industrialization and military modernization. It also was encouraged by events in China, whose 1911 revolution inspired hope that major political changes could occur elsewhere in the region.

Developments outside Asia also strengthened anticolonial movements. The slaughter of World War I, the failure of the Allies to honor wartime promises to Arabs and Indians, and the perceived hypocrisy of the League of Nations mandate system undermined the Europeans' claims of moral superiority and further embittered Asians against their colonial masters. The Russian Revolution also encouraged nationalism, especially in Southeast Asia and China. Soviet leaders denounced colonialism in all its forms and pledged support for political movements working to end the capitalist West's domination of Asia.

Asian nationalism also had social, economic, and cultural implications. Aware of their own societies' shortcomings, nationalist leaders understood that political independence would be meaningless if poverty, illiteracy, and economic underdevelopment continued. Thus, most nationalists were committed to programs of economic and political modernization, and some, such as Mao Zedong in China and Ho Chi Minh in Vietnam, sought social change through revolution. As a result, many nationalists found themselves in a dual struggle—not only against foreign rule, but also against the social and political conservatism of their compatriots.

Despite nationalism's growing strength, only a few colonies became independent between the wars. Although the British granted Egypt independence in 1922, they continued to maintain thousands of troops on Egyptian soil and kept control of Egypt's defense, communications systems, and foreign policy. In a somewhat similar arrangement, Britain granted Iraq independence in 1932 but maintained a strong military presence. Elsewhere, the Western powers held on to their colonies, and attempted to reassert or maintain their control during and after World War II. This proved beyond their will and capacity, however, and beginning with the independence of Lebanon (1943), Syria (1945), Jordan and the Philippines (1946), and India and Pakistan (1947), colonialism in Asia quickly unraveled.

Political Currents in the Middle East

The aftermath of World War I spelled disaster for the people of the Middle East. The Turks, a defeated ally of Germany, were forced in 1920 to accept the humiliating Treaty of Sèvres, which stripped Turkey of its Arab territories; limited the Turkish army to fifty thousand men; gave France, Britain, and Italy control of its finances; and proposed to cede parts of Turkey to Italy, Greece, Kurdistan, and Armenia. The Arabs, who in 1916 had rebelled against their Turkish overlords in the expectation that in return France and Great Britain would recognize an independent Arab state, soon learned that the British and French had other plans. Article 22 of the League of Nations Covenant, adopted in 1919, turned Iraq, Syria, Palestine, Lebanon, and Jordan into mandates administered by Britain or France until the region was ready for independence. Farther east, Persia, under the decrepit rule of the Qajar dynasty, was threatened by British plans to turn it into a protectorate.

Efforts to reverse the region's bleak postwar prospects had mixed results. Under the leadership of Mustafa Kemal, the Turks rallied to drive out Italian and Greek invaders and smash the nascent Armenian state. As a result, in 1923 the European powers agreed to replace the Treaty of Sèvres with the Treaty of Lausanne, which recognized Turkey's integrity and independence. In Iran (formerly Persia), after another strong military leader, Reza Khan (1878–1944), took power in 1921, he reorganized the army and established a government strong enough to discourage the British from pursuing their plan to establish a protectorate.

Arab efforts to attain independence and limit Jewish immigration to Palestine were less successful. Of the twenty Arab states that stretched from Morocco in the west to Iraq in the east, only Saudi Arabia and Yemen were independent in the interwar years. Egypt and Iraq attained a measure of self-rule, but it was compromised by Britain's continued military presence and its influence over foreign policy. The drive for independence was even more frustrating in Lebanon and Syria, where the French maintained control until 1943 and 1945 respectively. Arabs also were angered by the British tolerance of Jewish migration to Palestine, which rose dramatically in the 1930s as a result of the Nazi takeover in Germany.

While confronting these postwar problems, the people and leaders of the region faced many other difficult issues. Was the goal of Arab nationalism the expulsion of the British and French and the stifling of Jewish immigration to Palestine? Or was it the attainment of a single united Arab state? What was the best solution to the problems of poverty and illiteracy? How could the teachings of Islam be reconciled with the realities and demands of modernization? Was modernization itself desirable, and if so, how was it to be achieved? Questions such as these were not new. But in the face of the rapid changes that swept through the region in the first half of the twentieth century, finding answers to them became more urgent and difficult.

Secularism and Nationalism in Republican Turkey

❖

44 ❖ Mustafa Kemal, *SPEECH TO THE CONGRESS OF THE PEOPLE'S REPUBLICAN PARTY*

The archsymbol of aggressive secularism and nationalism in the Muslim world in the interwar years was Mustafa Kemal (1881–1938), a Turkish military hero during World War I who went on to serve as first president of the Republic of Turkey. Disgusted by the Ottoman sultan's acquiescence to the punitive Treaty of Sèvres and the Greek occupation of the Turkish port of Smyrna in 1919, Kemal assumed leadership of a resistance movement against both the sultan's government and the Allies. He led his supporters to victory over the Greeks and forced the annulment of the Sèvres Treaty in 1923.

In 1922, Kemal convened a National Assembly, which deposed the sultan and set the stage for a decade and a half of revolutionary change. Exercising broad powers as president, he sought to transform Turkey into a modern secular nation-state. To accomplish this, he stripped Islam of its control of education and the legal system, encouraged industrialization, accorded women full legal rights, mandated the use of a new Turkish alphabet, and ordered Turks to assume Western-style dress. Directing all Turks to adopt hereditary family names, he took the name Ataturk, or "Great Turk."

Having consolidated his authority, in 1927 Kemal decided to review his accomplishments and impress upon his subjects the need for continued support. He chose as the occasion the meeting of the People's Republican Party, founded by Ataturk and Turkey's only legal political party. Here he delivered an extraordinary speech. Having worked on it for three months (in the process exhausting dozens of secretaries), he delivered it over a period of six days.

In these excerpts, Kemal discusses Turkey's past and future; explains his reasons for abolishing the caliphate, the ancient office by virtue of which Ottoman sultans were viewed as rulers of all Muslims; and justifies his suppression of the Progressive Republican Party, which despite its name was a party of conservatives who opposed Kemal's plans to modernize Turkey.

QUESTIONS FOR ANALYSIS

1. What, according to Kemal, were the "erroneous ideas" that had guided the Ottoman state in the past?
2. Why does Kemal argue that nation-states, not empires, are the most desirable form of political organization?
3. What is Kemal's view of the West?
4. What are his views of Islam?
5. What arguments does Kemal offer against the continuation of the caliphate?
6. How does Kemal justify his suppression of the Progressive Republicans? What, in his view, were the positive results of this step?

Source: Mustafa Kemal, *Speech Delivered by Ghazi Mustapha Kemal* (Leipzig: K. F. Koehler, 1929), 376–379, 589–594, 717, 721–722.

[NATIONALISM AND EMPIRE]

We turn our minds to the times when the Ottoman state in Istanbul ... was master of the crown and the throne of the East-Roman [Byzantine] Empire. Among the Ottoman rulers there were some who endeavored to form a gigantic empire by seizing Germany and West-Rome [Western Europe]. One of these rulers hoped to unite the whole Islamic world in one body, to lead it and govern it. For this purpose he obtained control of Syria and Egypt and assumed the title of Caliph.[1] Another Sultan pursued the twofold aim, on the one hand of gaining the mastery over Europe, and on the other of subjecting the Islamic world to his authority and government.

The continuous counterattacks from the West, the discontent and insurrections in the Muslim world, as well as the dissensions between the various elements which this policy had artificially brought together had the ultimate result of burying the Ottoman Empire, in the same way as many others, under the pall of history. . . .

To unite different nations under one common name, to give these different elements equal rights, subject them to the same conditions and thus to found a mighty State is a brilliant and attractive political ideal; but it is a misleading one. It is an unrealizable aim to attempt to unite in one tribe the various races existing on the earth, thereby abolishing all boundaries.

Herein lies a truth which the centuries that have gone by and the men who have lived during these centuries have clearly shown in dark and sanguinary events.

There is nothing in history to show how the policy of Panislamism[2] could have succeeded or how it could have found a basis for its realization on this earth. As regards the result of the ambition to organize a State which should be governed by the idea of world-supremacy and include the whole of humanity without distinction of race, history does not afford examples of this. For us, there can be no question of the lust of conquest. . . .

The political system which we regard as clear and fully realizable is national policy. . . . This is borne out in history and is the expression of science, reason, and common sense.

In order that our nation should be able [to] live a happy, strenuous, and permanent life, it is necessary that the State should pursue an exclusively national policy and that this policy should be in perfect agreement with our internal organization and be based on it. When I speak of national policy, I mean it in this sense: To work within our national boundaries for the real happiness and welfare of the nation and the country by, above all, relying on our own strength in order to retain our existence. But not to lead the people to follow fictitious aims, of whatever nature, which could only bring them misfortune, and expect from the civilized world civilized human treatment, [and] friendship based on mutuality. . . .

[THE ISSUE OF THE CALIPHATE]

I must call attention to the fact that Hodja Shukri, as well as the politicians who pushed forward his person and signature, had intended to substitute the sovereign bearing the title of Sultan or Padishah by a monarch with the title of Caliph.[3] The only difference was that, instead of speaking of a monarch of this or that country

---

[1]A reference to Selim I, who conquered Egypt and Syria in 1515 and 1516; it is doubtful that he actually considered himself caliph.

[2]The program of uniting all Muslims under one government or ruler.

[3]The events took place in January 1923. After Sultan Mehmed V was deposed as sultan on November 1, 1922, his cousin, Abdulmejid, was designated caliph. Shukri was a *hodja* (or *hojja*), a Turkish religious leader; he hoped that Turkey would continue to support the caliphate even after the sultanate was abolished. In 1924, however, Kemal abolished the caliphate.

or nation, they now spoke of a monarch whose authority extended over a population of three hundred million souls belonging to manifold nations and dwelling in different continents of the world. Into the hands of this great monarch, whose authority was to extend over the whole of Islam, they placed as the only power that of the Turkish people, that is to say, only from 10 to 15 millions of these three hundred million subjects. The monarch designated under the title of Caliph was to guide the affairs of these Muslim peoples and to secure the execution of the religious prescriptions which would best correspond to their worldly interests. He was to defend the rights of all Muslims and concentrate all the affairs of the Muslim world in his hands with effective authority....

If the Caliph and Caliphate, as they maintained, were to be invested with a dignity embracing the whole of Islam, ought they not to have realized that a crushing burden would be imposed on Turkey, on her existence; her entire resources and all her forces would be placed at the disposal of the Caliph? ... I gave the people to understand that neither Turkey nor the handful of men she possesses could be placed at the disposal of the Caliph so that he might fulfill the mission attributed to him, namely, to found a State comprising the whole of Islam. The Turkish nation is incapable of undertaking such an irrational mission.

For centuries our nation was guided under the influence of these erroneous ideas. But what has been the result of it? Everywhere they have lost millions of men. "Do you know," I asked, "how many sons of Anatolia have perished in the scorching deserts of the Yemen? Do you know the losses we have suffered in holding Syria and Iraq and Egypt and in maintaining our position in Africa? And do you see what has come out of it? Do you know? New Turkey, the people of New Turkey, have no reason to think of anything else but their own existence and their own welfare. She has nothing more to give away to others."...

[THE SUPPRESSION OF OPPOSITION]

... As you know, it was at the time that the members of the opposition had founded a party under the name of "Republican Progressive Party" and published its program....

Could seriousness and sincerity be attributed to the deeds and attitude of people who avoided pronouncing even the word Republic and who tried to suppress the Republic from the very beginning, but who called the party Republican and even Republican Progressive? ...

Did those who appeared under the same flag, but who wanted to be regarded as progressive Republicans, not follow the deep design of provoking the religious fanaticism of the nation, putting them thus completely against the Republic, progress and reform?

Under the mask of respect for religious ideas and dogmas the new Party addressed itself to the people in the following words: "We want the re-establishment of the Caliphate; we do not want new laws; we are satisfied with the ... religious laws ... we shall protect the Medressas, the Tekkes, the pious institutions, the Softahs, the Sheikhs, and their disciples.[4] Be on our side; the party of Mustapha Kemal, having abolished the Caliphate, is breaking Islam into ruins; they will make you into unbelievers...."

Read these sentences, Gentlemen, from a letter written by one of the adherents of this program: "They are attacking the very principles which perpetuate the existence of the Mohamedan [Muslim] world.... The assimilation with the Occident means the destruction of our history, our civilization...."

Gentlemen, facts and events have proved that the program of the Republican Progressive Party has been the work emanating from the brain of traitors.... The Government and the Committee found themselves forced to take extraordinary measures.... For a considerable time they kept eight or nine divisions of the army

---

[4]A *medressa* is an advanced school of Islamic learning. A *tekke* is a small teaching mosque usually built over the tomb of a saint. A *softah* is a student in an Islamic school.

A sheikh, or *shaykh*, is a master of a religious order of Sufis, Muslims who adopt a mystical approach to their religion.

at war strength for the suppression of disorders, and put an end to the injurious organization which bore the name "Republican Progressive Party." The result was, of course, the success of the Republic....

Gentlemen, it was necessary to abolish the fez,[5] which sat on our heads as a sign of ignorance, of fanaticism, of hatred to progress and civilization, and to adopt in its place that hat, the customary headdress of the whole civilized world, thus showing, among other things, that no difference existed in the manner of thought between the Turkish nation and the whole family of civilized mankind. We did that while the law for the Restoration of Order[6] was still in force. If it had not been in force we should have done so all the same; but one can say with complete truth that the existence of this law made the thing much easier for us. As a matter of fact the application of the law for the Restoration of Order prevented the morale of the nation being poisoned to a great extent by reactionaries....

Gentlemen, while the law regarding the Restoration of Order was in force there took place also the closing of the Tekkes, of the convents, and of the mausoleums, as well as the abolition of all sects[7]

and all kinds of titles such as Sheikh, Dervish..., Occultist, Magician, Mausoleum Guard, etc.[8]

One will be able to imagine how necessary the carrying through of these measures was, in order to prove that our nation as a whole was no primitive nation, filled with superstitions and prejudices.... Ought one to conserve in the Turkish State, in the Turkish Republic, elements and institutions such as those which had for centuries given the nation the appearance of being other than it really was? Would one not therewith have committed the greatest, most irreparable error to the cause of progress and reawakening? ...

Gentlemen, at the same time the new laws were worked out and decreed which promise the most fruitful results for the nation on the social and economic plane, and in general in all the forms of the expression of human activity...the Citizens' Legal Code which ensures the liberty of women and stabilizes the existence of the family.

Accordingly we made use of all circumstances only from one point of view, which consisted therein: to raise the nation on to that step on which it is justified in standing in the civilized world, to stabilize the Turkish Republic more and more on steadfast foundations...and in addition to destroy the spirit of despotism forever.

---

[5]The fez was a brimless hat popular among Turkish men during the nineteenth century. It allowed the wearer to touch his forehead to the ground while kneeling during prayer without removing the hat.
[6]Adopted in 1925 in response to a Kurdish rebellion in eastern Anatolia, the Law for the Restoration of Order gave the government broad powers to suppress by administrative order any organization or publication that was deemed a threat to the law and order.

[7]Islamic religious orders.
[8]A dervish, or *darvish*, was a member of an Islamic sect famous for its whirling dances that symbolized the movement of the heavenly spheres. An Occultist was a Sufi who achieved a state of withdrawal from the world. A mausoleum guard guarded the tomb of a saint or holy person.

Impasse in Palestine

◆

45 ◆ *THE PEEL COMMISSION REPORT, JULY 1937*

Despite five wars, dozens of minor conflicts, frequent negotiations, and countless proposals and counterproposals, the Arab-Israeli conflict over Palestine remains a source of ongoing tension in the Middle East. Its immediate cause was the founding of the state of Israel in 1947 and the displacement of approximately

---

Source: Peel Commission Report, Report of the Palestine Royal Commission, June 22, 1937: Her Majesty's Printing Office.

750,000 Palestinian Arabs during and after the 1948 Arab-Israeli War. But the origins of the conflict go back much further.

Its beginnings can be traced back to 70 C.E., when the Jews were exiled from their Palestinian homeland by the Romans, forcing them to resettle in other parts of the Middle East, North Africa, Europe, and, much later, the Americas. Wherever they went, Jews were a small, frequently persecuted minority in predominantly Muslim or Christian societies. In their years of exile they maintained a strong attachment to the "Land of Canaan," which, according to Hebrew scriptures, God had given them as their promised land after becoming His chosen people. Only in the nineteenth century, however, did a number of Jewish leaders conclude that Jews could escape persecution and preserve their traditions only if they had their own homeland in Palestine. This movement came to be known as Zionism, a word coined in 1890 and derived from Mount Zion, one of two major hills overlooking Jerusalem, the ancient Jewish capital.

The first advocates of Jewish resettlement in Palestine were Russian Jews reacting to the anti-Jewish pogroms in Russia in the 1880s and 1890s. Political Zionism, which advocates the foundation of a Jewish state, dates from the late 1890s, when the Vienna-based journalist Theodor Herzl published *Der Judenstaat* (The Jewish State) in 1896 and one year later convened the first international Zionist conference in Basel, Switzerland. Despite the indifference and outright opposition of many assimilated European Jews, and despite many disagreements among the Zionists themselves, on the eve of World War I, approximately 60,000 Jews, about half of whom were recent immigrants, lived in Palestine compared to 620,000 Muslims and 70,000 Christians.

The situation in Palestine became more volatile after World War I. Palestinian Arabs, who identified themselves politically with Syria, were bitterly disappointed when Great Britain and France turned the former Arab provinces of the Ottoman Empire into mandates. Their disappointment deepened when the British, who held the Palestinian mandate, honored their wartime pledge to facilitate Jewish immigration to Palestine and make it a "national home" for Jews. Between 1919 and 1939, the number of Jews in Palestine grew from slightly under 10 percent to 30 percent of the population. They purchased land, established industries, founded schools and universities, and supported by the Zionist Organization, laid the groundwork for a Jewish state. Meanwhile, Arabs pressured British authorities to halt Jewish immigration and limit land transfers from Arabs to Jews. With Arab frustration growing, in 1936 Palestine experienced sporadic violence, which soon escalated into Arab general strikes, tax boycotts, bombings, and property destruction directed against Jews and British officials.

In response, the British government sent the former secretary of state for India, Lord William Peel, to Palestine to head a commission charged with investigating the causes of violence and recommending solutions. The commission published its report in mid-1937. Concluding that cooperation and compromise were impossible, it recommended partitioning Palestine into three parts: Jewish territory in the northwest; Arab territory in the east and south; and continued British control of Nazareth, Jerusalem, and a corridor between Jerusalem and the coast (see map on page 192). The proposals bitterly divided the Jews and were rejected totally by the Arabs. The political future of Palestine was not settled until 1948, when the British mandate ended and the independent state of Israel was born.

QUESTIONS FOR ANALYSIS

1. What do the Arab and Jewish lists of grievances reveal about the economic and social status of the two communities?
2. Given the two sides' lists of grievances, what reasonable chance did the British have of satisfying each side?
3. Why, according to the report's authors, are the Arab and Jewish communities inherently and permanently incompatible?
4. On what basis do the report's authors predict that the Arab-Jewish conflict will worsen?
5. Why, according to the report, does the use of force provide no long-term solution to the problems of the region?
6. How, according to the report, will continuation of the status-quo damage Great Britain's standing in the world?
7. Overall, does the tone and content of the report seem more sympathetic to the Arabs or Jews?
8. Arabs resolutely rejected the commission's plan for partition. Among Jews, the plan had supporters and opponents. What arguments might these groups have offered to defend their point of view?

CONCLUSIONS AND RECOMMENDATIONS

Arab Grievances

(1) The failure to develop self-governing institutions.
(2) The acquisition of land by the Jews.
(3) Jewish immigration.
(4) The use of Hebrew and English as official languages.
(5) The employment of British and Jewish officers, and exclusion of Arabs from the higher posts.
(6) The creation of a large class of landless Arabs, and the refusal of Jews to employ Arab labourers.
(7) Inadequate funds for Arab education.

Whilst we believe that these grievances are sincerely felt, we are of opinion that most of them cannot be regarded as legitimate under the terms of the Mandate and we are therefore not called upon to make recommendations on them. It is only in regard to the last that we are able to suggest any remedy. We would welcome increased expenditure on Arab education, especially in the direction of village agricultural schools.

Jewish Grievances

(1) Obstruction in the establishment of the National Home owing to dilatory action in dealing with proposals demanding executive action.
(2) The display of "pro-Arab" proclivities by officials and their failure to carry out the Mandate....
(3) Great delay in the decision of civil suits; inefficiency in criminal procedure, as instanced by the fact that 80 Jews were

murdered during 1936, and no capital sentence was carried out.

(4) Toleration by the Government of subversive activities, more especially those of the Mufti of Jerusalem.[1]

(5) As regards the land, failure to introduce a land system appropriate to the needs of the country, the continuance of the system of *Masha'a*;[2] no arrangement for the consolidation of holdings, great delay in the ascertainment of rights during land settlement, difficulty in obtaining a satisfactory title to land when purchased; ... insufficient encouragement of irrigation and drainage schemes.

(6) Reluctance really to facilitate [Jewish] immigration, ... and uncontrolled illegal Arab immigration.

(7) Trans-Jordan should be opened to Jewish immigration.[3]

(8) The necessary steps have not been taken to secure the removal or alleviation of restrictions on the importation of Palestine citrus fruits into foreign countries.

(9) Progressive Jewish Municipalities are unduly restricted by Government rules and regulations.

(10) Failure to ensure public security.

[While the authors of the report rejected most Arab grievances as "illegitimate" under terms of the mandate, they proposed numerous administrative and policy changes in response to the grievances of the Jewish community. They concluded the report as follows.]

These are the recommendations which we submit ... They are the best palliatives we can devise for the disease from which Palestine is suffering, but they are only palliatives. They might reduce the inflammation and bring down the temperature, but they cannot cure the trouble. The disease is so deep-rooted that, in our firm conviction, the only hope of a cure lies in a surgical operation.

THE POSSIBILITY OF A LASTING SETTLEMENT

The Forces of Circumstances

Before submitting the proposals we have to offer for its drastic treatment we will briefly re-state the problem of Palestine....

An irrepressible conflict has arisen between two national communities within the narrow bounds of one small country. About 1,000,000 Arabs are in strife, open or latent, with some 400,000 Jews. There is no common ground between them. The Arab community is predominantly Asiatic in character, the Jewish community predominantly European. They differ in religion and in language. Their cultural and social life, their ways of thought and conduct, are as incompatible as their national aspirations.... The War and its sequel have inspired all Arabs with the hope of reviving in a free and united Arab world the traditions of the Arab golden age. The Jews similarly are inspired by their historic past. They mean to show what the Jewish nation can achieve when restored to the land of its birth. National assimilation between Arabs

---

[1]A reference to Hajj Amin al-Husayni (1895[?]–1974), who as Mufti of Jerusalem (the Sunni cleric who oversaw Islamic holy places in Jerusalem) helped organize attacks on Jews and British officials in 1937–1938. He also helped found the Arab Higher Committee, which called for nonpayment of taxes, organized an Arab general strike, and demanded an end to Jewish immigration. The committee was banned by the British in September 1937. Al-Husayni fled to Lebanon and then Iraq to escape arrest. During World War II, he lived in Rome and Berlin and made pro-Axis radio broadcasts

for Arab audiences. His knowledge of and support for the Holocaust is the subject of ongoing debate among historians.

[2]The collective ownership of land by a village community.

[3]The emirate of Transjordan, to the east of the Jordan River, was created in 1921 to provide a kingdom for Abdullah I bin al-Hussein, a leader of the Arab revolt against Ottoman rule during World War I. The original mandate exempted Britain from the responsibility of encouraging Jewish immigration to Transjordan, so this grievance was rejected in the commission's report.

and Jews is thus ruled out.... Neither Arab nor Jew has any sense of service to a single State.

The conflict has grown steadily more bitter. It has been marked by a series of five Arab outbreaks, culminating in the rebellion of last year....

This intensification of the conflict will continue.... The educational systems, Arab and Jewish, are schools of nationalism, and they have only existed for a short time. Their full effect on the rising generation has yet to be felt. And patriotic "youth-movements," so familiar a feature of present-day politics in other countries of Europe or Asia, are afoot in Palestine. As each community grows, moreover, the rivalry between them deepens. The more numerous and prosperous and better-educated the Arabs become, the more insistent will be their demand for national independence and the more bitter their hatred of the obstacle that bars the way to it. As the Jewish National Home grows older and more firmly rooted, so will grow its self-confidence and political ambition....

Meantime the "external factors" will continue to play the part they have played with steadily increasing force from the beginning. On the one hand, Saudi Arabia, the Yemen, Iraq and Egypt are already recognized as sovereign states, and Trans-Jordan as an "independent government." In less than three years' time Syria and the Lebanon will attain their national sovereignty.[4] The claim of the Palestinian Arabs to share in the freedom of all Asiatic Arabia will thus be reinforced.... That they are as well qualified for self-government as the Arabs of neighbouring countries has been admitted.

On the other hand, the hardships and anxieties of the Jews in Europe are not likely to grow less in the near future.... The appeal to the good faith and humanity of the British people will lose none of its force. The Mandatory [Great Britain] will be urged unceasingly to admit as many Jews into Palestine as the National Home can provide with a livelihood and to protect them when admitted from Arab attacks....

In these circumstances, we are convinced that peace, order and good government can only be maintained in Palestine for any length of time by a rigorous system of repression.... If "disturbances," moreover, should recur on a similar scale to that of last year's rebellion, the cost of military operations must soon exhaust the revenues of Palestine and ultimately involve the British Treasury to an incalculable extent. The moral objections to maintaining a system of government by constant repression are self-evident. Nor is there any need to emphasize the undesirable reactions of such a course of policy on opinion outside Palestine.

And the worst of it is that such a policy leads nowhere. However vigorously and consistently maintained, it will not solve the problem. It will not allay, it will exacerbate the quarrel between the Arabs and the Jews. The establishment of a single self-governing Palestine will remain just as impracticable as it is now. It is not easy to pursue the dark path of repression without seeing daylight at the end of it....

In these last considerations lies a final argument for seeking a way out, at almost any cost, from the existing deadlock in Palestine. For a continuance or rather an aggravation—for that is what continuance will be—of the present situation cannot be contemplated without the gravest misgivings. It will mean constant unrest and disturbance in peace and potential danger in the event of war. It will mean a steady decline in our prestige. It will mean the gradual alienation of two peoples who are traditionally our friends: for already the Arabs of Palestine have been antagonized and the patience of their kinsmen throughout the Arab world is being strained; and already the Jews, particularly, we understand, in the United States, are questioning the sincerity with which we are fulfilling

---

[4]Saudi Arabia was recognized as an independent state in 1927; Iraq became independent in 1932, although Britain maintained military bases and continued to exercise influence over Iraqi foreign policy. The report exaggerates the progress toward independence in Egypt, Yemen, Syria, and Lebanon.

the promises we made and suggesting that negligence or weakness on our part is the real cause of all the trouble....

Manifestly the problem cannot be solved by giving either the Arabs or the Jews all they want.... But, while neither race can justly rule all Palestine, we see no reason why, if it were practicable, each race should not rule part of it.

No doubt the idea of Partition as a solution of the problem has often occurred to students of it, only to be discarded. There are many who would have felt an instinctive dislike to cutting up the Holy Land.... Others may have felt

that Partition would be a confession of failure. ... Others, again, if they thought of Partition, dismissed it, no doubt, as impossible. The practical difficulties seemed too great. And great they unquestionably are.... We do not underestimate them. They cannot be brushed aside. Nevertheless ... those difficulties do not seem so insuperable as the difficulties inherent in the continuance of the Mandate or in any other alternative arrangement which has been proposed to us or which we ourselves could devise. Partition seems to offer at least a chance of ultimate peace. We can see none in any other plan.

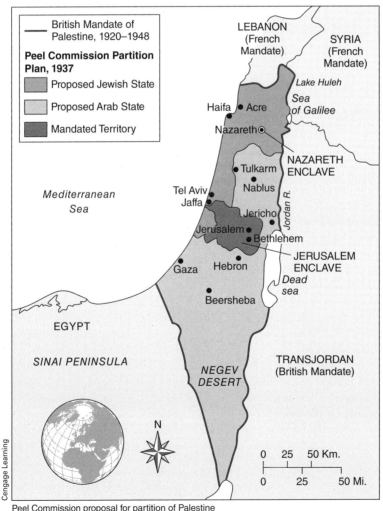

Peel Commission proposal for partition of Palestine

Anticolonialism in India and Southeast Asia

During the late nineteenth century, when Indians were already debating their colonial relationship with Great Britain and some were demanding independence, most Southeast Asians were just beginning to experience the full effects of direct European rule. Nevertheless, developments in both areas showed some marked similarities between the two world wars. In India and Southeast Asia alike, nationalism became a potent force, shaking the foundations of colonial rule.

Indian nationalism under the leadership of Mohandas Gandhi was transformed from an ideology of the educated elite into a mass movement. Despite differences in religion, wealth, education, and caste status, millions of Indians marched, demonstrated, boycotted British goods, and refused to obey British-imposed laws in an effort to achieve Indian self-rule by forcing the British to "quit India." The British responded with minor concessions but mostly with delaying tactics and repression.

Nationalist movements also intensified in Southeast Asia between the wars, but their strength, priorities, and tactics varied widely across a region marked by ethnic and cultural diversity and dissimilar styles of Western rule. Nationalism was weakest in areas such as the British-controlled Malay States and the French protectorates in Laos and Cambodia, where traditional rulers were retained and little economic modernization or urbanization occurred. Nationalism was strongest in the Dutch East Indies, Burma (present-day Myanmar), and Vietnam, where Western economic penetration and direct rule disrupted traditional economic, political, and social relationships.

Drawing strength and inspiration from both Western ideologies and their own religious and cultural traditions, nationalist leaders formed political parties and attempted to broaden nationalism's appeal by using newspapers, magazines, and the radio. Without exception, however, armed rebellions failed. Communist-inspired uprisings in Indonesia in 1926–1927 were crushed by the Dutch; so too was the anti-French rebellion led by the Vietnamese Nationalist Party in 1930.

These failures resulted partly from the colonial powers' superior military strength and partly from divisions within the nationalist movements. Western-educated intellectuals and politicians argued among themselves over political doctrine and founded a plethora of competing political parties and organizations. Conflicting regional loyalties and disagreements between secularized, Europeanized leaders and those with traditional religious views also weakened nationalist movements. Even Gandhi was unable to prevent the splintering of Indian nationalism into antagonistic Muslim and Hindu camps on the eve of World War II.

Interwar nationalist movements in India and Southeast Asia prepared the groundwork for independence after World War II. They also foretold the conflicts and divisions that would plague new states once independence had been achieved.

Gandhi's Hopes for India

❖

46 ◆ Mohandas Gandhi, *INDIAN HOME RULE*

Mohandas Gandhi, the outstanding figure in modern Indian history, was born in 1869 in a village north of Mumbai on the Arabian Sea. His father was a prominent government official who presided over an extended family devoted to strict Hindu practices. Gandhi studied law in England and, after failing to establish a law practice in India, moved to South Africa in 1893 to serve the Indian population.

In South Africa, he became incensed over discriminatory laws against Indian immigrants, most of whom were indentured servants, laborers, or small merchants. In his efforts to improve the lot of South Africa's Indians, Gandhi developed his doctrine of *satyagraha,* usually translated as "soul force." *Satyagraha* sought social justice not through violence but through love, noncompliance to unjust laws, a willingness to suffer, and conversion of the oppressor. Central to its strategy was nonviolent resistance: Gandhi's followers disobeyed unjust laws and accepted the consequences—even beatings and imprisonment—to reach the hearts of the British and change their thinking.

In 1915, Gandhi at the age of forty-five returned to India. By 1920, he was the dominant figure in the Congress Party, which under his leadership launched a noncooperation campaign against British rule between 1920 and 1922. When in 1922 villagers attacked and killed twenty-one policemen and rural watchmen, Gandhi called off the noncooperation campaign, but he continued the tactic of civil disobedience, organizing boycotts of British goods and leading protest marches against British measures such as the salt tax in 1930. Living a life of self-imposed chastity and poverty, he wrote letters, pamphlets, and books and delivered speeches in every corner of India denouncing British rule and urging Indians to address their society's ills. During the 1930s and the war years, his attacks on British rule intensified, and along with other Congress leaders he spent months in jail. As independence approached, he struggled to preserve Hindu-Muslim cooperation and prevent the partition of the nation into a predominantly Muslim Pakistan and a predominantly Hindu India. On January 30, 1948, just over four months after Indian and Pakistani independence, Gandhi was shot and killed by a Hindu zealot who resented Gandhi's commitment to Hindu-Muslim harmony.

The following selection is taken from *Hind Swaraj* (Indian Home Rule), a 100-page pamphlet Gandhi wrote in 1909 after meeting with a group of Indian nationalists in England who urged the use of force against British rule. Although written early in his political career and well before he emerged as India's inspirational leader, it contains core principles that guided Gandhi throughout his life. In the preface to the 1938 edition of the work, he wrote, "I have seen nothing to make me alter the views expounded in it." Composed

Source: Mohandas Gandhi, *Indian Home Rule* (Madras, India: Ganesh & Co., 1922), pp. 30–35, 47–50, 63–64, 85–86, 90–91. Copyright © 1922.

in the form of a dialogue between a reader and an editor (Gandhi), *Indian Home Rule* was originally published in 1909 in Gujarati. Banned in India, the book was published in English in South Africa in 1910 and in the United States in 1924. The first Indian edition appeared only in 1938, after the British ban was lifted.

QUESTIONS FOR ANALYSIS

1. What does Gandhi see as the major deficiencies of modern civilization?
2. How, according to Gandhi, has modern civilization affected women?
3. What is the basis for Gandhi's faith that Hindus and Muslims will be able to live together in peace in India?
4. What, according to Gandhi, is true civilization, and what is India's role in preserving it?
5. What leads Gandhi to conclude that love is stronger than force?
6. In your view, why did Gandhi's attack on civilization win him support among India's masses?

CIVILIZATION

READER: Now you will have to explain what you mean by civilization....

EDITOR: Let us first consider what state of things is described by the word "civilization." Its true test lies in the fact that people living in it make bodily welfare the object of life. We will take some examples: The people of Europe today live in better-built houses than they did a hundred years ago. This is considered an emblem of civilization, and this is also a matter to promote bodily happiness. Formerly, they wore skins, and used as their weapons spears. Now, they wear long trousers, and for embellishing their bodies they wear a variety of clothing, and, instead of spears, they carry with them revolvers containing five or more chambers. If people of a certain country, who have hitherto not been in the habit of wearing much clothing, boots, etc., adopt European clothing, they are supposed to have become civilized out of savagery. Formerly, in Europe, people plowed their lands mainly by manual labor. Now, one man can plow a vast tract by means of steam-engines, and can thus amass great wealth. This is called a sign of civilization. Formerly, the fewest men wrote books, that were most valuable. Now, anybody writes and prints anything he likes and poisons people's minds. Formerly, men traveled in wagons; now they fly through the air, in trains at the rate of four hundred and more miles per day. This is considered the height of civilization. It has been stated that, as men progress, they shall be able to travel in airships and reach any part of the world in a few hours. Men will not need the use of their hands and feet. They will press a button, and they will have their clothing by their side. They will press another button, and they will have their newspaper. A third, and a motor-car will be in waiting for them. They will have a variety of delicately dished up food. Everything will be done by machinery. Formerly, when people wanted to fight with one another, they measured between them their bodily strength; now it is possible to take away thousands of lives by one man working behind a gun from a hill. This is civilization. Formerly, men worked in the open air only so much as they liked. Now, thousands of workmen meet together and for the sake of maintenance work in factories or mines. Their condition is worse than that of beasts. They are obliged to work, at the risk of their lives, at most dangerous occupations, for the sake of millionaires. Formerly, men were made slaves under physical compulsion, now they are enslaved by temptation of money and of the luxuries that money can buy. There are now diseases of which people never dreamed before, and an army of doctors is engaged in finding out their cures, and so hospitals have increased. This is a test of civilization. Formerly, special messengers were required and much expense was incurred in order to send letters; today, anyone can abuse his fellow by means of a letter for one penny. True, at the same cost, one can send one's thanks also. Formerly, people had two or three meals consisting of homemade bread and vegetables; now, they require something to eat every two hours, so that they have hardly leisure for anything else. What more need I say? . . .

This civilization is irreligion, and it has taken such a hold on the people in Europe that those who are in it appear to be half mad. They lack real physical strength or courage. They keep up their energy by intoxication. They can hardly be happy in solitude. Women, who should be the queens of households, wander in the streets, or they slave away in factories. For the sake of a pittance, half a million women in England alone are laboring under trying circumstances in factories or similar institutions. This awful fact is one of the causes of the daily growing suffragette movement.

This civilization is such that one has only to be patient and it will be destroyed.

THE HINDUS AND MUSLIMS

READER: But I am impatient to hear your answer to my question. Has the introduction of Islam not unmade the nation?

EDITOR: India cannot cease to be one nation because people belonging to different religions live in it. The introduction of foreigners does not necessarily destroy the nation, they merge in it. A country is one nation only when such a condition obtains in it. That country must have a faculty for assimilation. India has ever been such a country. In reality, there are as many religions as there are individuals, but those who are conscious of the spirit of nationality do not interfere with one another's religion. If they do, they are not fit to be considered a nation. If the Hindus believe that India should be peopled only by Hindus, they are living in dreamland. The Hindus, the Muslims, the Parsees[1] and the Christians who have made India their country are fellow-countrymen, and they will have to live in unity if only for their own interest. In no part of the world are one nationality and one religion synonymous terms; nor has it ever been so in India.

READER: But what about the inborn enmity between Hindus and Muslims?

EDITOR: That phrase has been invented by our mutual enemy [the British]. When the Hindus and Muslims fought against one another, they certainly spoke in that strain. They have long since ceased to fight. How, then, can there be any inborn enmity? Pray remember this too, that we did not cease to fight only after British occupation. The Hindus flourished under Muslim sovereigns and Muslims under the Hindu. Each party recognized that mutual fighting was suicidal, and that neither party would abandon its religion by force of arms. Both parties, therefore, decided to live in peace. With the English advent the quarrels recommenced. . . .

Hindus and Muslims own the same ancestors, and the same blood runs through their veins. Do people become enemies because they change their religion? Is the God of the Muslim different from the God of the Hindu? Religions are different roads converging to the same point. What does it matter that we take different roads, so long as we reach the same goal? . . .

---

[1] Disciples of the Zoroastrian religion which was introduced to India by Persian refugees in the seventh and eighth centuries.

WHAT IS TRUE CIVILIZATION?

READER: You have denounced railways, lawyers and doctors. I can see that you will discard all machinery. What, then, is civilization?

EDITOR: The answer to that question is not difficult. I believe that the civilization India has evolved is not to be beaten in the world. Nothing can equal the seeds sown by our ancestors. Rome went, Greece shared the same fate, the might of the Pharaohs was broken, Japan has become westernized, of China nothing can be said, but India is still, somehow or other, sound at the foundation.... India remains immovable, and that is her glory. It is a charge against India that her people are so uncivilized, ignorant, and stolid, that it is not possible to induce them to adopt any changes. It is a charge really against our merit. What we have tested and found true on the anvil of experience, we dare not change....

Civilization is that mode of conduct which points out to man the path of duty. Performance of duty and observance of morality are convertible terms. To observe morality is to attain mastery over our mind and our passions. So doing, we know ourselves. The Gujarati[2] equivalent for civilization means "good conduct."

If this definition be correct, then India, as so many writers have shown, has nothing to learn from anybody else, and this is as it should be.

PASSIVE RESISTANCE

READER: Is there any historical evidence as to the success of what you have called soul-force or truth-force? No instance seems to have happened of any nation having risen through soul-force. I still think that the evil-doers will not cease doing evil without physical punishment.

EDITOR: ... The force of love is the same as the force of the soul or truth. We have evidence of its working at every step. The universe would disappear without the existence of that force....

Thousands, indeed, tens of thousands, depend for their existence on a very active working of this force. Little quarrels of millions of families in their daily lives disappear before the exercise of this force. Hundreds of nations live in peace. History does not and cannot take note of this fact. History is really a record of every interruption of the even working of the force of love or of the soul.... Soul-force, being natural, is not noted in history.

READER: According to what you say, it is plain that instances of the kind of passive resistance are not to be found in history. It is necessary to understand this passive resistance more fully. It will be better, therefore, if you enlarge upon it.

EDITOR: Passive resistance is a method of securing rights by personal suffering; it is the reverse of resistance by arms. When I refuse to do a thing that is repugnant to my conscience, I use soul-force. For instance, the government of the day has passed a law which is applicable to me: I do not like it; if, by using violence, I force the government to repeal the law, I am employing what may be termed body-force. If I do not obey the law and accept the penalty for its breach, I use soul-force. It involves sacrifice of self.

Everybody admits that sacrifice of self is infinitely superior to sacrifice of others. Moreover, if this kind of force is used in a cause that is unjust, only the person using it suffers. He does not make others suffer for his mistakes....

READER: From what you say, I deduce that passive resistance is a splendid weapon of the weak but that, when they are strong, they may take up arms.

EDITOR: This is gross ignorance. Passive resistance, that is, soul-force, is matchless. It is superior to the force of arms. How, then, can it be considered only a weapon of the weak? Physical-force men are strangers to the courage that is requisite in a passive resister....

What do you think? Wherein is courage required—in blowing others to pieces from behind a cannon or with a smiling face to approach a cannon and to be blown to pieces? Who is the true warrior—he who keeps death always as a bosom-friend or he who controls the death of others? Believe me that a man devoid of courage and manhood can never be a passive resister.

---

[2]An Indian dialect spoken in Gujarat, in northwest India.

This, however, I will admit: that even a man, weak in body, is capable of offering this resistance. One man can offer it just as well as millions. Both men and women can indulge in it. It does not require the training of an army; it needs no Jiu-jitsu. Control over the mind is alone necessary, and, when that is attained, man is free like the king of the forest, and his very glance withers the enemy.

Passive resistance is an all-sided sword; it can be used anyhow; it blesses him who uses it and him against whom it is used. Without drawing a drop of blood, it produces far-reaching results.

A Muslim's View of India's Future

❖

47 ◆ Muhammad Ali Jinnah,
SPEECH TO THE MUSLIM LEAGUE, 1940

Muhammad Ali Jinnah (1876–1948), the leader of India's Muslims between the wars, was raised in Lahore in present-day Pakistan, where his father was a successful businessman. A brilliant and prosperous lawyer who had studied in London and dressed like an English gentleman, Jinnah joined the Indian National Congress in 1906 and the Muslim League in 1913. After having been elected president of the League in 1916, he helped negotiate the Lucknow Pact (1916), by which the Congress and the League agreed to work together to bring about Indian independence. In 1920, however, he resigned from the Congress because of his opposition to Gandhi's civil disobedience campaign and Gandhi's refusal to support the concept of weighted voting rights for India's Muslims. Nonetheless, during the 1920s and early 1930s Jinnah continued to work for cooperation between Hindus and Muslims to further the cause of Indian independence.

In the late 1930s, however, chronic disagreements between Hindus and Muslims and mounting Hindu–Muslim violence convinced Jinnah that Muslims had no future in an independent India. He lent his support to the founding of an independent Muslim state, Pakistan, meaning "land of the pure." In 1947, his efforts were rewarded when the end of British rule resulted in the independence of not one new state, but two, India and Pakistan. Jinnah served as Pakistan's first governor-general, a post he held for only a year before his death in 1948.

The following selection is from a speech delivered to a meeting of the Muslim League in Lahore in 1940. In it, Jinnah expresses his support for the establishment of independent states in the northwestern and eastern parts of India where Muslims were in the majority.

QUESTIONS FOR ANALYSIS

1. What is the basis of Jinnah's objection to the statement he quotes from the London *Times?*
2. Why does Jinnah have so little hope that Hindus and Muslims will ever be able to live together peacefully in a united India?

Source: Allan, Gullum, ed., *Pakistan Movement Historic Documents* (Karachi: Published by Paradise Subscription Agency for the Dept. of International Relations, University of Karachi, 1967), pp. 174–189, passim. Used by permission of Paradise Subscription Agency.

3. What is the basis of Jinnah's assertion that Islam and Hinduism are "not religions in the strict sense of the word"?
4. How do Jinnah's views of Hindu–Muslim relations differ from those of Gandhi?
5. What is the basis of Jinnah's assertion that Muslims in India are "a nation according to any definition of a nation"?

A leading journal like the London *Times,* commenting on the Government of India Act of 1935,[1] wrote: "Undoubtedly the differences between the Hindus and Muslims are not of religion in the strict sense of the word but also of law and culture, that they may be said, indeed, to represent two entirely distinct and separate civilizations. However, in the course of time, the superstition will die out and India will be molded into a single nation." So, according to the London *Times,* the only difficulties are superstitions.... But surely it is a flagrant disregard of the past history of the subcontinent of India as well as the fundamental Islamic conception of society vis-a-vis that of Hinduism to characterize them as mere "superstitions." Notwithstanding a thousand years of close contact, nationalities, which are as divergent today as ever, cannot...be expected to transform themselves into one nation merely by means of subjecting them to a democratic constitution and holding them forcibly together by unnatural and artificial methods of British parliamentary statute. What the unitary government of India for one hundred fifty years had failed to achieve cannot be realized by the imposition of a central federal government....

...If the British government are really in earnest and sincere to secure [the] peace and happiness of the people of this subcontinent, the only course open to us all is to allow the major nations separate homelands by dividing India into "autonomous national states." There is no reason why these states should be antagonistic to each other. On the other hand, the rivalry and the natural desire and efforts on the part of

one to dominate the social order and establish political supremacy over the other in the government of the country will disappear....

It is extremely difficult to appreciate why our Hindu friends fail to understand the real nature of Islam and Hinduism. They are not religions in the strict sense of the word, but are, in fact, different and distinct social orders, and it is a dream that the Hindus and Muslims can ever evolve a common nationality, and this misconception...is the cause of most of our troubles and will lead India to destruction if we fail to revise our notions in time. The Hindus and Muslims belong to two different religious philosophies, social customs, and literatures. They neither intermarry nor interdine together and, indeed, they belong to two different civilizations which are based mainly on conflicting ideas and conceptions.... To yoke together two such nations under a single state, one as a numerical minority and the other as a majority, must lead to growing discontent and final destruction of any fabric that may be so built up for the government of such a state.

...History has also shown us many geographical tracts, much smaller than the subcontinent of India, which otherwise might have been called one country, but which have been divided into as many states as there are nations inhabiting them. The Balkan Peninsula comprises as many as seven or eight sovereign states. Likewise, the Portuguese and the Spanish stand divided in the Iberian Peninsula.... The present artificial unity of India dates back only to the British conquest and is maintained by the

---

[1]The act ended the system of "dyarchy" established by the 1919 Government of India Act. According to this system, Indians were given responsibility for organizing certain activities such as education while British officials would control finance and public order. Although the 1935 act gave

greater autonomy to the provinces to regulate their own affairs, it also included a number of "safeguards," which would allow British intervention if their interests were threatened. It also separated Burma and Aden from India and made them separate colonies.

British bayonet, but termination of the British regime, which is implicit in the recent declaration of His Majesty's government, will be the herald of the entire break-up with worse disaster than has ever taken place during the last one thousand years under Muslims....

Muslim India cannot accept any constitution which must necessarily result in a Hindu majority government. Hindus and Muslims brought together under a democratic system forced upon the minorities can only mean Hindu raj [rule]. Democracy of the kind with which the Congress High Command is enamored would mean the complete destruction of what is most precious in Islam....

Mussalmans [Muslims] are a nation according to any definition of a nation, and they must have their homelands, their territory, and their state. We wish to live in peace and harmony with our neighbors as a free and independent people. We wish our people to develop to the fullest our spiritual, cultural, economic, social, and political life in a way that we think best and in consonance with our own ideals and according to the genius of our people. Honesty demands and the vital interests of millions of our people impose a sacred duty upon us to find an honorable and peaceful solution, which would be just and fair to all. But at the same time we cannot be moved or diverted from our purpose and objective by threats or intimidations. We must be prepared to face all difficulties and consequences, make all the sacrifices that may be required of us to achieve the goal we have set in front of us.

Revolution and Oppression in Vietnam

❖

48 ◆ Nguyen Thai Hoc, *LETTER TO THE FRENCH CHAMBER OF DEPUTIES, 1930*

Having taken control of Vietnam's southern region, known as Cochin China, in the 1860s, the French extended their authority over Tongkin (northern Vietnam) and Annam (central Vietnam) in the 1880s. Convinced of their civilizing mission, they sought to undermine Vietnam's Confucian culture by creating a French-trained Vietnamese elite willing to cooperate with the colonial regime. Although some members of Vietnam's upper class resisted French rule (including the young emperor Duy Tân, whose plot to overthrow the French was uncovered in 1916), most at first sought some sort of compromise between Western culture and Confucianism and accepted French rule.

Accommodation and compromise gave way to revolutionary nationalism in the 1920s as Vietnamese anger grew over continuing exploitation and repression, even though ninety thousand Vietnamese troops and laborers had served in Europe during World War I. The leading nationalist organization was the Viet Nam Quoc Dan Dang (Vietnamese Nationalist Party, or VNQDD), founded in 1927 by Nguyen Thai Hoc, a teacher from Hanoi. As a young man, he had sought to improve conditions in Vietnam through moderate reforms, but he soon became disillusioned with the French and turned to revolution. The VNQDD

Source: Reprinted by permission of the author from Harry Benda and John Larkin, *The World of Southeast Asia*. Copyright © 1967.

was modeled on Sun Yat-sen's Chinese Nationalist Party, or Guomindang, and was dedicated to achieving an independent and democratic-socialist Vietnam. In 1929, with about fifteen hundred members and its leaders convinced that the general populace was ready for revolution, the VNQDD plotted an insurrection. Known as the Yen Bai uprising, it was crushed by the French in 1930, and VNQDD leaders were arrested and consigned to prison or executed.

While awaiting execution, Nguyen Thai Hoc wrote the following letter to France's parliament, the Chamber of Deputies. A defense of his actions and a denunciation of French colonialism, the letter was also released to the Vietnamese public.

QUESTIONS FOR ANALYSIS

1. In Nguyen Thai Hoc's view, what are French intentions in Vietnam and what has been the effect of French occupation?
2. How and why did Nguyen Thai Hoc evolve from a moderate reformer to a revolutionary?
3. If they had been implemented, how would his suggestions to Governor General Varenne have improved the lot of the Vietnamese people?
4. What does the French response to the Yen Bai uprising reveal about the nature of French colonial rule?
5. What do you suppose Nguyen Thai Hoc hoped to accomplish by writing this letter?

Gentlemen:

According to the tenets of justice, everyone has the right to defend his own country when it is invaded by foreigners, and according to the principles of humanity, everyone has the duty to save his compatriots when they are in difficulty or in danger. As for myself, I have assessed the fact that my country has been annexed by you French for more than sixty years. I realize that under your dictatorial yoke, my compatriots have experienced a very hard life, and my people will without doubt be completely annihilated, by the naked principle of natural selection. Therefore, my right and my duty have compelled me to seek every way to defend my country which has been invaded and occupied, and to save my people who are in great danger.

At the beginning, I had thought to cooperate with the French in Indochina[1] in order to serve my compatriots, my country and my people, particularly in the areas of cultural and economic development. As regards economic development, in 1925 I sent a memorandum to Governor General Varenne,[2] describing to him all our aspirations concerning the protection of local industry and commerce in Indochina. I urged strongly in the same letter the creation of a Superior School of Industrial Development in Tongkin. In 1926 I again addressed another letter to the then Governor General of Indochina in which I included some explicit suggestions to relieve the hardships of our poor people. In 1927, for a third time, I sent a letter to the Résident Supérieur[3] in Tongkin, requesting permission to publish a weekly magazine with the aim of safeguarding

---

[1]The French colonies in Laos, Cambodia, and Vietnam.
[2]Alexandre Varenne was governor-general of Indochina from 1925 to 1929.

[3]The chief administrator of northern Vietnam.

and encouraging local industry and commerce. With regard to the cultural domain, I sent a letter to the Governor General in 1927, requesting (1) the privilege of opening tuition-free schools for the children of the lower classes, particularly children of workers and peasants; (2) freedom to open popular publishing houses and libraries in industrial centers.

It is absolutely ridiculous that every suggestion has been rejected. My letters were without answer; my plans have not been considered; my requests have been ignored; even the articles that I sent to newspapers have been censored and rejected. From the experience of these rejections, I have come to the conclusion that the French have no sincere intention of helping my country or my people. I also concluded that we have to expel France. For this reason, in 1927, I began to organize a revolutionary party, which I named the Vietnamese Nationalist Party, with the aim of overthrowing the dictatorial and oppressive administration in our country. We aspire to create a Republic of Vietnam, composed of persons sincerely concerned with the happiness of the people. My party is a clandestine organization, and in February 1929, it was uncovered by the security police. Among the members of my party, a great number have been arrested. Fifty-two persons have been condemned to forced labor ranging from two to twenty years. Although many have been detained and many others unjustly condemned, my party has not ceased its activity. Under my guidance, the Party continues to operate and progress towards its aim.

During the Yen Bai uprising someone succeeded in killing some French officers. The authorities accused my party of having organized and perpetrated this revolt. They have accused me of having given the orders for the massacre. In truth, I have never given such orders, and I have presented before the Penal Court of Yen Bai all the evidence showing the inanity of this accusation. Even so, some of the members of my party completely ignorant of that event have been accused of participating in it. The French Indochinese government burned and destroyed their houses. They sent French troops to occupy their villages and stole their rice to divide it among the soldiers. Not just members of my party have been suffering from this injustice—we should rather call this cruelty than injustice—but also many simple peasants, interested only in their daily work in the rice fields, living miserable lives like buffaloes and horses, have been compromised in this reprisal. At the present time, in various areas there are tens of thousands of men, women, and children, persons of all ages, who have been massacred.[4] They died either of hunger or exposure because the French Indochinese government burned their homes. I therefore beseech you in tears to redress this injustice which otherwise will annihilate my people, which will stain French honor, and which will belittle all human values.

I have the honor to inform you that I am responsible for all events happening in my country under the leadership of my party from 1927 until the present. You only need to execute me. I beg your indulgence for all the others who at the present time are imprisoned in various jails. I am the only culprit, all the others are innocent. They are innocent because most of them are indeed members of my party, and have joined it only because I have succeeded in convincing them of their duties as citizens of this country, and of the humiliations of a slave with a lost country. Some of them are not even party members.... I have the honor to repeat once again that you need execute only me. If you are not satisfied with killing one man, I advise you to kill also the members of my family, but I strongly beg your indulgence towards those who are innocent.

Finally, I would like to declare in conclusion: if France wants to stay in peace in Indochina, if France does not want to have increasing troubles with revolutionary movements, she should

---

[4]A substantial number of civilian deaths did occur as a result of French actions following the revolt, but Nguyen Thai Hoc's estimate of tens of thousands of deaths is an exaggeration.

immediately modify the cruel and inhuman policy now practiced in Indochina. The French should behave like friends to the Vietnamese, instead of being cruel and oppressive masters.

They should be attentive to the intellectual and material sufferings of the Vietnamese people, instead of being harsh and tough.

Please, Gentlemen, receive my gratitude.

◆

Intellectual Ferment and Political Change in East Asia

The overthrow of the Qing dynasty in 1912 resulted not in China's long-awaited national revival, but instead four decades of political disintegration, civil war, diplomatic setbacks, foreign invasion, and immense suffering for the Chinese people. Following the revolution, Sun Yat-sen and his dreams of a democratic China were pushed aside by General Yuan Shikai, who ruled as a dictator between 1912 and 1916, and had himself declared emperor before he died in 1916. After his death, China was carved up by dozens of generally unscrupulous and irresponsible warlords, whose authority was based on their private armies and whose goals were limited to self-enrichment and self-preservation. With an ineffectual national government, the Chinese endured continuing Western domination of their coastal cities, and they could offer only weak resistance when the Japanese occupied Manchuria in 1931 and invaded China itself in 1937.

In politics, Chinese who grieved over the state of their country had two options. The Nationalist Party, or Guomindang (GMD), which had been founded in 1912 by Sun Yat-sen, was theoretically dedicated to Sun's "three principles of the people"—democracy, nationalism, and livelihood—and came to be identified with the educated, Western-oriented bourgeoisie of China's coastal cities. The Chinese Communist Party (CCP), founded in 1921, was inspired by Marxism-Leninism, with leadership provided by intellectuals and its major support eventually coming from the peasants. Aided by agents of the Soviet Union, the GMD and the CCP formed a coalition in 1923 and launched the Northern Expedition against the warlords in 1926. The alliance broke apart in 1927, however, when Sun's successor, Chiang Kai-shek purged the Communists from the alliance and ordered his troops to kill Communist leaders who were gathered in Shanghai. Communist survivors under the leadership of Mao Zedong fled to the countryside, where they established a stronghold in south central China. This they held in until 1934, when an attack by the Guomindang army again forced them to flee, this time China's remote northwest.

After breaking with the Communists and attaining control of the lower Yangzi valley, Chiang Kai-shek and the Nationalists established a Nanjing-based regime that laid claim to be China's sole legitimate government despite the fact that warlords still controlled major parts of the country and his communist rivals stubbornly maintained their hold in the northwest. During the so-called Nanjing decade from 1928 to 1937, a central banking system was established, a national railway system was begun, and industrial growth occurred in coastal cities. But Chiang ruled as a dictator with little enthusiasm for social reform. His priority was expanding and modernizing the army and using it against his warlord and Communist rivals. This changed in 1937, when war broke out with Japan and China was plunged into a bloody eight-year struggle against a cruel and determined invader.

In contrast to the turmoil and conflict of China, the 1910s and 1920s were decades of growing prosperity and general confidence for Japan. During World War I, Japan expanded its holdings in Manchuria, acquired former German concessions in China's Shandong Province, and increased its industrial output. With the unequal treaties with the West distant memories, colonies in Taiwan and Korea, a dominant role in Manchuria, a growing economy, and a constitutional government, Japan had become a wealthy and powerful nation. The 1920s also saw a blossoming of parliamentary government and liberal reform. The political balance in Japan shifted from the armed forces and bureaucracy, both subject only to the emperor, to the political parties, whose power base was the elected Diet and whose leaders had close ties with big business. This shift translated into solid gains for democracy, liberalism, social reform, and a foreign policy of international cooperation. In the 1930s, however, the balance of power shifted again, this time away from the parties to the military.

During the late 1920s, unease about the country's future deepened. The Soviet Union continued to maintain large numbers of troops in Siberia and was embarking on a crash program of industrialization; Chiang Kai-shek was extending his authority over the warlords of northern China. The economy showed signs of slowing and then crashed when the Great Depression struck in 1930. Party government lost support, nationalism broadened its appeal, and the military was inspired to take bold steps. In 1931, army officers arranged an explosion on the tracks of a Japanese-controlled railroad in Manchuria and, without the approval of the civilian government, used this as an excuse to capture important cities in the region and establish the puppet state of Manchukuo. In Japan itself, right-wing extremists assassinated business and political leaders and plotted to overthrow the government. In February 1936, officers and troops of the First Division attacked and briefly occupied government offices in Tokyo. The government suppressed the rebellion and executed its leaders, but to many Japanese the rebels were heroes, not traitors. Constitutional government survived, but when Japanese and Chinese troops clashed outside Beijing in the summer of 1937, the ensuing war between China and Japan put political authority firmly in the hands of militarists and nationalists.

Nationalism continued to inspire the Japanese during World War II. Citizens accepted privation, soldiers fought with fanatical determination, and young pilots sacrificed their lives by crashing their planes into U.S. warships. But nationalism was not enough, and defeat came in August 1945.

The New Culture Movement and the West

◈

49 ◆ Hu Shi,
OUR ATTITUDE TOWARD MODERN CIVILIZATION OF THE WEST

The New Culture Movement, an outburst of literary activity and intellectual inquiry into China's past and future in the 1920s, is traditionally dated from May 4, 1919, when students from area colleges and universities met in Beijing and demonstrated against provisions of the Paris peace settlement that granted the former German concession in Shandong province to Japan. The events of May 4, however, only served to intensify and accelerate intellectual and literary developments that had begun several years earlier at Beijing University, where a number of young professors had begun to explore new intellectual and cultural paths for China.

All intellectuals connected with the New Culture Movement looked to the West for guidance and inspiration, but none more so than Hu Shi (1891–1962), a professor of philosophy at Beijing University. Born in Shanghai and raised by his mother in poverty after his father, a government official, died when he was four, Hu was educated in the Confucian classics, English, and Western science. At the age of nineteen, he received a scholarship to study at Cornell University, where he earned a bachelor's degree in philosophy, and later at Columbia University, where he worked toward his doctorate. On his return to China in 1917, he joined the Beijing University faculty. In his writings and speeches he promoted Western thought and urged intellectuals to use vernacular Chinese rather than classical Chinese as a written language. After serving as ambassador to the United States between 1938 and 1943, he returned to China in 1946 to serve as chancellor of Beijing University. He fled China after the Communist victory in 1949 and lived in semiretirement in New York City until his death in 1962.

The following excerpt is taken from an essay written in 1926. In it, Hu answers the argument that traditional Chinese values were more humane and less materialistic than those of the West, and hence more beneficial to humankind's spiritual development.

QUESTIONS FOR ANALYSIS

1. How does Hu explain the attraction of condemning Western civilization for its materialism while praising Eastern civilization for its "spirituality"?
2. On what basis does Hu reject this argument?
3. What does Hu see as the major accomplishments of Western civilization?
4. What does Hu mean when he refers to the "new religion" developing in Western civilization?
5. In what ways do Hu's attitudes toward the West differ from those of Gandhi (Source 46)? How might one explain these differences?

THE "MATERIALISM" OF WESTERN SOCIETIES

One of the most baseless, most harmful statements has to do with the condemnation of Western civilization as "materialistic" and the praise of Oriental civilization as "spiritual."... In the past it was used to provide some kind of psychological lift, or self-congratulatory consolation, when we, the Oriental people, were cruelly oppressed and badly humiliated by the Occidentals. During the past few years when the Westerners themselves, in reaction to the disastrous World War I, became increasingly disillusioned with a modern civilization based upon the advance of science and technology, we have often heard from their scholars the praise of the so-called spiritual civilization of the East. Though this praise results from [a] ... mentality of a temporary nature, it is more than welcome to the culturally chauvinistic Orientals. It strengthens the bias about the alleged superiority of Oriental civilization....

Throughout history the greatest tragedy has always been man's inability to ward off hunger and cold despite his hard labor. How can we in good conscience lecture a man about to be starved to death on the virtue of contentment, fate, and self-satisfaction? A man who condemns material comfort for no other reason than its unavailability to him can be compared to the fox in a Western fable who announces proudly that it does not like sour grapes when the grapes, ripe and sweet, are too high for it to reach. Poverty is not something to be proud of: those who state otherwise are either indulging in self-deception or too lazy to do something about it. More pathetic still are those who fast, mutilate their bodies, or commit suicide by fire, all in the name of "spiritual civilization." All these people ... are mentally ill, really, since their attitude toward life is that of a dying man....

Unlike its Oriental counterpart, the modern civilization of the West takes into full consideration the importance of material enjoyment. It has as its foundation two basic concepts. First, the purpose of life is the pursuit of happiness. Second, poverty is a sin; so is physical weakness or illness. The second concept, logically, is a derivative of the first. The goal of this civilization is, in short, the enrichment of life. As poverty is a sin, the Westerners devote their energy to the opening up of natural resources, the promotion of industry, the improvement of manufactured products, and the expansion of commerce. As physical weakness or illness is also a sin, they spare no effort in the study and improvement of medical care, the promotion of sanitation, hygiene, physical fitness and sports, the prevention of contagious disease, and the improvement of heredity. Since the pursuit of happiness is the purpose of life, they busy themselves with the enhancement of comfort in their living quarters, the improvement of transportation and communication, the beautification of their cities, the promotion of the arts, the assurance of safety in their streets, and finally, the security of incorruptibility in government and among government officials. To be sure, Western civilization contains in it certain elements that sometimes prompt its adherents to commit aggression, pillage, or even mass murder, which has to be condemned, of course. Neither can it be denied that it has brought benefit to those who embrace it.

THE NEW RELIGION

Though modern civilization of the West has not yet dissociated itself from the religion of the past [Christianity], one nevertheless senses that a new religion has been slowly developing.... Not surprisingly, the first characteristic of the new religion is its logic and rationality. As modern science enables man to discover new knowledge, to conquer nature for his own benefit, and to do ... things that historically have been regarded as unattainable or even inconceivable, man's confidence in himself has increased enormously, and he believes, for the first time, that he can shape the future in accordance with his own wishes. Not surprisingly, the second characteristic of the new religion is its humanism. The acquisition of more and more knowledge not only enhances man's ability to cope with his environment but also broadens his social perspective, thus increasing his empathy with his fellow men. Not surprisingly, the third characteristic of the new religion is its social ethics.

... All the old religions stress salvation on an individual basis, and all the old ethics centers on the cultivation of moral worth, again of a personal nature. The adherents of old religions do occasionally speak of the necessity of "saving" others, but they are more than satisfied if they can somehow save themselves. Forever looking inward and, as a result, becoming more and more involved with no one except themselves, they lose contact with the outside world. They do not understand worldly problems, let alone resolve them.... What is the use of this so-called self-cultivation of virtues if the net result is a mummy-like parasite, totally ignorant of practical matters and insensitive to the suffering of others? ...

OCCIDENTAL AND ORIENTAL CIVILIZATIONS COMPARED

As "discontent" characterizes the modern civilization of the West, "content" characterizes the traditional civilization of the East. Being content, we Orientals do not strive for the improvement of our living standard, do not pay much attention to new discoveries and new inventions, and do not, even remotely, contemplate upon such "strange" ideas as the conquest of nature. We relish our ignorance, find satisfaction with the status quo, however unpleasant, and speak resignedly about our "fate." We are not even reformers, let alone revolutionaries. We are, in fact, the obedient servants of our rulers, whomever they happen to be.

Basic Tenets of Chinese Communism

❖

50 ◆ Mao Zedong,
REPORT ON AN INVESTIGATION OF THE PEASANT MOVEMENT IN HUNAN and *STRATEGIC PROBLEMS OF CHINA'S REVOLUTIONARY WAR*

Mao Zedong was born into a well-to-do peasant family in Hunan province in 1893 and as a university student participated in the Revolution of 1911. During the next several years, while serving as an assistant librarian at Beijing University, he embraced Marxism and helped organize the Chinese Communist Party, which was officially founded in 1921. Originally given the task of working with urban labor unions, Mao gradually came to believe that peasants, whose capacity for class revolution was discounted by orthodox Marxist-Leninists, would lead China to socialism.

After the break with the Guomindang in 1927, the Communists took their small army to the remote and hilly region on the Hunan-Jiangxi border, where in 1931 they proclaimed the Chinese Soviet Republic. In 1934, Chiang Kai-shek's troops surrounded the Communists' forces, but as they moved in for the kill, more than one hundred thousand Communist troops

Source: From Mao Zedong, *Selected Works of Mao Tse-Tung*. pp. 89–90, 92–96, 103–105. (International Publishers, Inc.) Copyright © 1965. Reprinted by permission.

and officials escaped and embarked on what is known as the Long March. This legendary trek lasted more than a year and covered more that six thousand miles before the survivors found safety in the remote mountains around Yan'an in Shaanxi province. Mao, now the party's recognized leader, rebuilt his army and readied his followers for the struggle against the Guomindang and the Japanese.

The following excerpts are from two of Mao's most important writings. The first, his "Report on an Investigation of the Peasant Movement in Hunan," was written in 1927 after he visited Hunan province to study the region's peasant associations, groups of peasants who with the help of Communist organizers had seized land, humiliated and killed landlords, and taken control of their villages. The second excerpt is taken from his "Strategic Problems of China's Revolutionary War," which was based on a series of lectures presented to the Red Army College in late 1936, less than a year before the Japanese invasion.

QUESTIONS FOR ANALYSIS

1. What specific developments in Hunan reinforced Mao's convictions about the peasantry's potential as a revolutionary force?
2. What criticisms have been made of the Hunan peasant movement, and how does Mao attempt to counter these criticisms?
3. What can be learned from these two writings about Mao's view of the role of the Communist Party in China's revolutionary struggle?
4. According to Mao, what have been the sources of oppression for the Chinese people? Once these sources of oppression have been removed, what will China be like?
5. What, according to Mao, are the four unique characteristics of China's revolutionary war, and how do they affect his military strategy?
6. What are the characteristics of Mao's "active defense" as opposed to "passive defense"?

REPORT ON AN INVESTIGATION OF THE PEASANT MOVEMENT IN HUNAN

... All talk directed against the peasant movement must be speedily set right. All the wrong measures taken by the revolutionary authorities concerning the peasant movement must be speedily changed. Only thus can the future of the revolution be benefited. For the present upsurge of the peasant movement is a colossal event. In a very short time, in China's central, southern and northern provinces, several hundred million peasants will rise like a mighty storm, like a hurricane, a force so swift and violent that no power, however great, will be able to hold it back. They will smash all the trammels that bind them and rush forward along the road to liberation. They will sweep all the imperialists, warlords, corrupt officials, local tyrants and evil gentry into their graves. Every revolutionary party and every revolutionary comrade will be put to the test, to be accepted or rejected as they decide. There are three alternatives. To march at their head and lead them? To trail behind them, gesticulating and criticizing? Or to stand in their way and oppose them? Every Chinese is free to choose, but events will force you to make the choice quickly....

"Yes, peasant associations are necessary, but they are going rather too far." This is the opinion of the middle-of-the-roaders. But what is the actual situation? True, the peasants are in a sense "unruly" in the countryside. Supreme in authority, the peasant association allows the landlord no say and sweeps away his prestige. This amounts to striking the landlord down to the dust and keeping him there.... People swarm into the houses of local tyrants and evil gentry who are against the peasant association, slaughtering their pigs and consuming their grain. They even loll for a minute or two on the ivory-inlaid beds belonging to the young ladies in the households of the local tyrants and evil gentry. At the slightest provocation they make arrests, crown the arrested with tall paper-hats, and parade them through the villages, saying, "You dirty landlords, now you know who we are!" ... This is what some people call "going too far," or "exceeding the proper limits in righting a wrong," or "really too much." Such talk may seem plausible, but in fact it is wrong. First, the local tyrants, evil gentry and lawless landlords have themselves driven the peasants to this. For ages they have used their power to tyrannize over the peasants and trample them underfoot; that is why the peasants have reacted so strongly.... Secondly, a revolution is not a dinner party, or writing an essay, or painting a picture, or doing embroidery; it cannot be so refined, so leisurely and gentle, so temperate, kind, courteous, restrained and magnanimous. A revolution is an insurrection, an act of violence by which one class overthrows another. A rural revolution is a revolution by which the peasantry overthrows the power of the feudal landlord class. Without using the greatest force, the peasants cannot possibly overthrow the deep-rooted authority of the landlords which has lasted for thousands of years.... To put it bluntly, it is necessary to create terror for a while in every rural area, or otherwise it

would be impossible to suppress the activities of the counter-revolutionaries in the countryside or overthrow the authority of the gentry.

A man in China is usually subjected to the domination of three systems of authority: (1) the state system,... ranging from the national, provincial and county government down to that of the township; (2) the clan system, ... ranging from the central ancestral temple and its branch temples down to the head of the household; and (3) the supernatural system (religious authority), ranging from the King of Hell down to the town and village gods belonging to the nether world, and from the Emperor of Heaven down to all the various gods and spirits belonging to the celestial world. As for women, in addition to being dominated by these three systems of authority, they are also dominated by the men (the authority of the husband). These four authorities—political, clan, religious and masculine—are the embodiment of the whole feudal-patriarchal system and ideology, and are the four thick ropes binding the Chinese people, particularly the peasants....

The political authority of the landlords is the backbone of all the other systems of authority. With that overturned, the clan authority, the religious authority and the authority of the husband all begin to totter.... In many places the peasant associations have taken over the temples of the gods as their offices. Everywhere they advocate the appropriation of temple property in order to start peasant schools and to defray the expenses of the associations, calling it "public revenue from superstition." In Liling County, prohibiting superstitious practices and smashing idols have become quite the vogue....

In places where the power of the peasants is predominant, only the older peasants and the women still believe in the gods, the younger peasants no longer doing so. Since the latter control the associations, the overthrow of religious authority and the eradication of superstition are going on everywhere. As to the authority of the husband, this has always been weaker among the poor peasants because, out of economic necessity, their womenfolk have to do more manual labor than the women of the richer classes and therefore have more say and greater power of decision in family matters. With the increasing bankruptcy of the rural economy in recent years, the basis for men's domination over women has already been weakened. With the rise of the peasant movement, the women in many places have now begun to organize rural women's associations; the opportunity has come for them to lift up their heads, and the authority of the husband is getting shakier every day. In a word, the whole feudal-patriarchal system and ideology is tottering with the growth of the peasants' power.

STRATEGIC PROBLEMS OF CHINA'S REVOLUTIONARY WAR

What then are the characteristics of China's revolutionary war?

I think there are four.

The first is that China is a vast semi-colonial country which is unevenly developed both politically and economically....

The unevenness of political and economic development in China—the coexistence of a frail capitalist economy and a preponderant semi-feudal economy; the coexistence of a few modern industrial and commercial cities and the boundless expanses of stagnant rural districts; the coexistence of several millions of industrial workers on the one hand and, on the other, hundreds of millions of peasants and handicraftsmen under the old regime; the coexistence of big warlords controlling the Central government and small warlords controlling the provinces; the coexistence of two kinds of reactionary armies, i.e., the so-called Central army under Chiang Kai-shek and the troops of miscellaneous brands under the warlords in the provinces; and the coexistence of a few railway and steamship lines and motor roads on the one hand and, on the other, the vast number of wheelbarrow paths and trails for pedestrians only, many of which are even difficult for them to negotiate....

The second characteristic is the great strength of the enemy.

What is the situation of the Guomindang, the enemy of the Red Army? It is a party that has seized political power and has relatively stabilized it. It has gained the support of the principal counter-revolutionary countries in the world. It has remodeled its army, which has thus become different from any other army in Chinese history and on the whole similar to the armies of the modern states in the world; its army is supplied much more abundantly with arms and other equipment than the Red Army, and is greater in numerical strength than any army in Chinese history ...

The third characteristic is that the Red Army is weak and small....

Our political power is dispersed and isolated in mountainous or remote regions, and is deprived of any outside help. In economic and cultural conditions the revolutionary base areas are more backward than the Guomindang areas. The revolutionary bases embrace only rural districts and small towns....

The fourth characteristic is the Communist Party's leadership and the agrarian revolution.

This characteristic is the inevitable result of the first one. It gives rise to the following two features. On the one hand, China's revolutionary war, though taking place in a period of reaction in China and throughout the capitalist world, can yet be victorious because it is led by the Communist Party and supported by the peasantry. Because we have secured the support of the peasantry, our base areas, though small, possess great political power and stand firmly opposed to the political power of the Guomindang which encompasses a vast area; in a military sense this creates colossal difficulties for the attacking Guomindang troops. The Red Army, though small, has great fighting capacity, because its men under the leadership of the Communist Party have sprung from the agrarian revolution and are fighting for their own interests, and because officers and men are politically united.

On the other hand, our situation contrasts sharply with that of the Guomindang. Opposed to the agrarian revolution, the Guomindang is deprived of the support of the peasantry. Despite the great size of its army it cannot arouse the bulk of the soldiers or many of the lower-rank officers, who used to be small producers, to risk their lives voluntarily for its sake. Officers and men are politically disunited and this reduces its fighting capacity....

Military experts of new and rapidly developing imperialist countries like Germany and Japan positively boast of the advantages of strategic offensive and condemn strategic defensive. Such an idea is fundamentally unsuitable for China's revolutionary war. Such military experts point out that the great shortcoming of defense lies in the fact that, instead of gingering up [enlivening] the people, it demoralizes them.... Our case is different. Under the slogan of safeguarding the revolutionary base areas and safeguarding China, we can rally the greatest majority of the people to fight single-mindedly, because we are the victims of oppression and aggression....

In military terms, our warfare consists in the alternate adoption of the defensive and the offensive. It makes no difference to us whether our offensive is regarded as following the defensive or preceding it, because the turning-point comes when we smash the campaigns of "encirclement and annihilation." It remains a defensive until a campaign of "encirclement and annihilation" is smashed, and then it immediately begins as an offensive; they are but two phases of the same thing, as one campaign of "encirclement and annihilation" of the enemy is closely followed by another. Of the two phases, the defensive phase is more complicated and more important than the offensive phase. It involves numerous problems of how to smash the campaign of "encirclement and annihilation." The basic principle is for active defense and against passive defense.

In the civil war, when the Red Army surpasses the enemy in strength, there will no longer be any use for strategic defensive in general. Then our only directive will be strategic offensive. Such a change depends on an overall change in the relative strength of the enemy and ourselves.

The Agenda of Japanese Ultranationalism

◆

51 ◆ The Black Dragon Society, *ANNIVERSARY STATEMENT, 1930*

In 1881, a group of former samurai (warrior-aristocrats) founded the Genyosha, a secret society dedicated to Japanese expansion in Asia, the preservation of traditional Japanese culture, and absolute dedication to the emperor. In 1901, several of its members broke away to found the Black Dragon Society, which promoted war with Russia as a means of expanding Japan's influence on the mainland. In the early 1900s, the society continued to advocate an aggressive foreign policy to make Japan the dominant force in Asia. It also denounced democracy, capitalism, Americanization, socialism, party politics, and big business, all of which it viewed as threats to Japanese culture and further Japanese expansion. Although the membership of the Black Dragon Society and similar organizations was small, its self-promotion, assassinations, and strong-arm tactics kept alive its brand of extreme nationalism, allowing it to flourish in the troubled atmosphere of the 1930s.

Source: From *Sources of Japanese Tradition, Vol. II*, by Tsunada, de Bary, and Keene. © 1964 Columbia University Press.

In 1930, the Black Dragon Society published the two-volume *Secret History of the Annexation of Korea*, in which it claimed a key role in inspiring early Japanese expansionism. The second volume concluded with the following statement.

QUESTIONS FOR ANALYSIS

1. What is there in the Black Dragon Society's philosophy that explains its interventions in Korea, China, and the Philippines?
2. In what ways, according to the authors of the document, has Japanese foreign policy been thwarted in the years since World War I?
3. According to the society, how has Japan's domestic situation deteriorated?
4. According to the society, what is the root of Japan's problems, and what solutions does it offer?
5. What might explain the appeal of such ideas to the Japanese populace?

From the first, we members of the Amur [Black Dragon] Society have worked in accordance with the imperial mission for overseas expansion to solve our overpopulation problem; at the same time, we have sought to give support and encouragement to the peoples of East Asia. Thus we have sought the spread of humanity and righteousness throughout the world by having the imperial purpose extend to neighboring nations.

Earlier, in order to achieve these principles, we organized the Heavenly Blessing Heroes in Korea in 1894 and helped the Tong Hak rebellion there in order to speed the settlement of the dispute between Japan and China.[1] In 1899 we helped Aguinaldo in his struggle for independence for the Philippines.[2] In 1900 we worked with other comrades in helping Sun Yat-sen start the fires of revolution in South China. In 1901 we organized this Society and became exponents of the punishment of Russia, and thereafter we devoted ourselves

to the annexation of Korea while continuing to support the revolutionary movement of China....

During this period we have seen the fulfillment of our national power in the decisive victories in the two major wars against China and Russia,[3] in the annexation of Korea, the acquisition of Taiwan and Sakhalin, and the expulsion of Germany from the Shandong Peninsula.[4] Japan's status among the empires of the world has risen until today she ranks as one of the three great powers, and from this eminence she can support other Asiatic nations....

However, in viewing recent international affairs it would seem that the foundation established by the great Meiji emperor is undergoing rapid deterioration. The disposition of the gains of the war with Germany was left to foreign powers [a reference to the Paris Peace Conference], and the government, disregarding the needs of national defense, submitted to

---

[1] The Tonghak, or Eastern Learning, Movement drew on Daoist, Buddhist, Confucian, and Catholic traditions. In 1894, its followers rebelled against the China-oriented government of Korea because of its corruption and indifference to the plight of the poor. Japanese and Chinese troops intervened, leading to the Sino-Japanese War of 1894–1895. The result was China's recognition of Korea's independence.
[2] Emilio Aguinaldo (1869–1964) led an insurrection against the Spaniards in 1898 and established the

Philippine Republic in January 1899. Following the Spanish-American War, he resisted the U.S. takeover, but was defeated and retired from politics.
[3] Victory over China in the Sino-Japanese War (1894–1895) and over Russia in the Russo-Japanese War (1904–1905).
[4] Japan received Taiwan after the Sino-Japanese War. Its authority over Korea and its claim to the southern half of Sakhalin Island were recognized after the Russo-Japanese War. Japan was granted former German concessions in China's Shandong province after World War I.

unfair demands to limit our naval power.[5] Moreover, the failure of our China policy[6] made the Chinese more and more contemptuous of us, so much so that they have been brought to demand the surrender of our essential defense lines in Manchuria and Mongolia. Furthermore, in countries like the United States and Australia our immigrants have been deprived of rights which were acquired only after long years of struggle, and we now face a highhanded anti-Japanese expulsion movement which knows no bounds.[7] Men of purpose and of humanity who are at all concerned for their country cannot fail to be upset by the situation.

When we turn our attention to domestic affairs, we feel more than deep concern. There is a great slackening of discipline and order. Men's hearts are becoming corrupt. Look about you! Are not the various government measures and establishments a conglomeration of all sorts of evils and abuses? The laws are confusing, and evil grows apace. The people are overwhelmed by heavy taxes, the confusion in the business world complicates the livelihood of the people, the growth of dangerous thought threatens social order, and our national polity, which has endured for three thousand years, is in danger. This is a critical time for our national destiny; was there ever a more crucial day? What else can we call this time if it is not termed decisive?

And yet, in spite of this our government, instead of pursuing a farsighted policy, casts about for temporary measures. The opposition party simply struggles for political power without any notion of saving our country from this crisis. And even the press, which should devote itself to its duty of guiding and leading society, is the same. For the most part it swims with the current, bows to vulgar opinions, and is chiefly engrossed in money making. Alas! Our empire moves ever closer to rocks which lie before us....

Therefore we have determined to widen the scope of our activity. Hereafter, besides our interest in foreign affairs, we will give unselfish criticism of internal politics and of social problems, and we will seek to guide public opinion into proper channels.... We are resolved to reform the moral corruption of the people, restore social discipline, and ease the insecurity of the people's livelihood by relieving the crises in the financial world, restore national confidence, and increase the national strength, in order to carry out the imperial mission to awaken the countries of Asia. In order to clarify these principles, we here set forth our platform to all our fellow patriots:

PLATFORM

1. Developing the great plan of the founders of the country, we will widen the great Way of Eastern culture, work out a harmony of Eastern and Western cultures, and take the lead among Asian peoples.

2. We will bring to an end many evils, such as formalistic legalism; it restricts the freedom of the people, hampers common sense solutions, prevents efficiency in public and private affairs, and destroys the true meaning of constitutional government. Thereby we will show forth again the essence of the imperial principles.

3. We shall rebuild the present administrative systems. We will develop overseas expansion through the activation of our diplomacy, further the prosperity of the people by reforms in internal government, and solve problems of labor and management by the establishment of new social policies. Thereby we will strengthen the foundations of the empire.

---

[5]The Washington Conference of 1921 set Japan's naval strength at 60 percent of that of the United States and that of Great Britain.

[6]The Twenty-One Demands, submitted by Japan to China in 1915, would have established broad Japanese influence over the Chinese government. China successfully resisted these demands.

[7]Both Australia and the United States severely restricted Japanese immigration in the 1920s.

4. We shall carry out the spirit of the Imperial Rescript[8] to Soldiers and Sailors and stimulate a martial spirit by working toward the goal of a nation in arms. Thereby we look toward the perfection of national defense.

5. We plan a fundamental reform of the present educational system, which is copied from those of Europe and America; we shall set up a basic study of a national education originating in our national polity. Thereby we anticipate the further development and heightening of the wisdom and virtue of the Yamato race.[9]

---

[8]Issued by the emperor in 1882, the rescript stated that supreme command of the armed forces rested in the hands of the emperor alone, thus strengthening the military's independence from civilian control.

[9]Yamato is the name of the dominant native ethnic group of Japan. The term originated in the late 1800s to distinguish the people of mainland Japan from other minority ethnic groups who resided in the peripheral areas of Japan such as the Ainu, Ryukyuan, and Nivkh.

PART THREE

From World War II to the Early 1970s: Decolonization, and Economic Recovery

Decades of Conflict, Decolonization, and Economic Recovery

During the 1930s, the world's Great Powers marched and stumbled into the century's second global war, World War II. With no effective response from individual states or the League of Nations, authoritarian regimes in Italy, Germany, and Japan committed one act of aggression after another: Japan invaded Manchuria in 1931 and China in 1937; Italy conquered Ethiopia in 1935; Nazi Germany, having begun to rearm in 1935, reoccupied the Rhineland in 1936, annexed Austria in 1938, and occupied Czechoslovakia in March 1939. Then just before dawn on September 1, 1939, assured that its new ally, the Soviet Union, would do nothing, Germany unleashed its troops, tanks, and planes on Poland. Two days later, Great Britain and France declared war on Germany, and for the second time in just over two decades, Europe was at war.

In 1941, the European war and the Sino-Japanese War fused into a truly global struggle. In June, Germany invaded the Soviet Union and in December, Japan attacked the Philippines, the Dutch East Indies, the British colony of Malaya, and the U.S. naval base at Pearl Harbor in Hawaii. The attack on Pearl Harbor, which resulted in the death of 2,402 U.S. military personnel, brought the United States into the war. In the following three and a half years, humanity's costliest and deadliest war was fought at sea, on tiny South Pacific islands, in North Africa, and across Eurasia. Only in 1945, with the unconditional surrender of Germany in May and of Japan in August, did the fighting stop.

Unlike the mood following World War I, when victors and vanquished alike failed to comprehend how drastically the war had altered life and dreamed of a "return to normalcy," the atmosphere after World War II was pervaded by a sense that human affairs had changed irrevocably. Of the early twentieth century's Great Powers, Germany, Japan, and Italy had been crushed, Great Britain was economically exhausted, and France was haunted by its capitulation to the Germans in 1940 after only six weeks of fighting. World affairs were now dominated by the United States and the Soviet Union, whose ideological differences and mutual distrust made a third world war seem likely. Asia and Africa also seemed on the brink of momentous changes. Nationalists and Communists resumed their battle for the control of China, and leaders of anticolonial movements in dozens of colonies prepared to renew their struggles for independence.

Soviet-U.S. conflict, daunting economic problems, and potential upheavals in Africa and Asia all seemed to suggest that the century's second postwar era would be as unsettled and as difficult as its first had been. Such pessimism, however, proved to be unwarranted. West Germany and Japan made successful transitions to democracy. The Cold War remained cold. Confrontations over Berlin (1948 and 1958), Soviet intervention in Hungary (1956) and Czechoslovakia (1968), and the Cuban missile crisis (1962) were all resolved without warfare. The one hot war between communist and noncommunist forces, in Korea (1950–1953), resulted in several million military and civilian deaths but remained localized. Furthermore, colonialism ended in Asia and Africa without the long and bloody struggles many had anticipated. Of the approximately sixty colonies that achieved independence between 1947 and 1975, most did so peacefully. Exceptions were Algeria, Kenya, and Rhodesia, where relatively large European settler populations blocked or complicated independence movements; other exceptions were Vietnam and the East Indies, where the French and Dutch, respectively, unsuccessfully used force to prevent independence.

The postwar era's most impressive achievement was economic growth. World War I had been followed by currency devaluations, slumping agricultural prices, an international financial crisis, the U.S. stock market crash, and ultimately the Great Depression. World War II, in contrast, was followed by a few years of economic readjustment and then twenty-five years of expansion. The main beneficiaries of this economic growth were the capitalist countries of the West and Japan, where a surge in consumerism and increased rates of automobile and home ownership were signs of growing prosperity. Other parts of the world also benefited from the postwar boom. Economic growth in the Soviet Union and its eastern European satellites was even more rapid than that of the West, lending substance to Soviet Premier Nikita Khrushchev's boast in 1959 that the Soviet Union would economically "bury" the United States. Even Africans and Asians, who remained poor by Western standards, benefited from strong demand for their nations' minerals and agricultural exports.

By the late 1960s, however, signs of economic decline and political discontent were beginning to appear. Rebellions in Poland and Czechoslovakia challenged Soviet domination of Eastern Europe. In the United States, Western Europe, and Japan, radicalized students protested the Vietnam War, social injustice, and university policies through strikes and demonstrations; in the United States urban black ghettos erupted into violence. Against this backdrop of political turmoil, the revival of feminism and the emergence of an environmental movement added to the atmosphere of protest and disenchantment.

Conflict was not limited to the Western democracies and Eastern Europe. The mid to late 1960s saw civil war and a drift toward military rule in much of Africa, and clashes between right-wing military governments and radical leftist groups in Latin America. Chaos gripped China after Mao Zedong launched the Great Proletarian Cultural Revolution in 1965.

The economic boom also was slowing down. In the West, rates of industrial production began to fall, and inflation and labor-management conflict increased. The delicate balance of international finance was threatened by ballooning

U.S. government deficits. In the Soviet bloc, agricultural and industrial output also began to slump despite rosy government reports to the contrary. Then in the wake of the October War between Egypt and Israel in 1973, Arab oil-producing countries embargoed oil shipments to the United States, and in 1974 the Organization of Petroleum Exporting Countries quadrupled the price of oil. Decline and retrenchment struck oil-dependent industrialized states and commodity-producing economies alike. The twentieth century's closest approximation of a golden age was coming to an end.

CHAPTER 8

World War II and Its Aftermath

Whether World War II is dated from July 7, 1937, when Japan declared war on China, or from September 1, 1939, when Germany invaded Poland, by the time it ended in August 1945, it had become the most murderous and costly war in history. It involved no fewer than sixty belligerent states, which mobilized over ninety million men and women to fight in their armed forces. Government expenditures have been estimated at more than one trillion dollars (ten trillion in 2011 dollars); losses from property destruction and economic dislocation are incalculable. Battles were fought by armies of unprecedented size. Hitler attacked the Soviet Union in June 1941 with 10,000 to 15,000 tanks; 8,000 planes; and 2.9 million troops, 1.3 million of whom were dead or wounded within a year. Three years later, in June 1944, the Allies launched their cross-Channel invasion of Nazi-held northern Europe, the largest amphibian military operation in history. The Normandy invasion force consisted of more than 1.5 million ground and support troops, who were transported to the landing sites in more than 4,400 ships and were supported by 11,000 fighters, bombers, transport planes, and gliders.

Inevitably, casualties were enormous. An estimated 60 million people died, over half of them civilians. According to the doctrine of "total war" embraced by all belligerents, obliterating the enemies' industries and infrastructure and killing or crushing the spirit of civilians were as important as winning battles. Bombing raids by Japan on Shanghai in 1937 and by Germany on Warsaw in 1939 and on London, Coventry, and Rotterdam in 1940 were precedents for aerial attacks on enemy population centers throughout the war. In 1942, British and American bombing raids began targeting German cities. Among their deadliest attacks were the firebombing of Hamburg in July 1943, which killed 50,000 civilians, and the bombing of Dresden in February 1945, which killed 25,000 people, some of whom were cremated by flamethrowers because proper burials were impossible. Japan became the target of American bombing raids in 1944 and 1945. The firebombing of Tokyo in March 1945, which killed 125,000, was a prelude to the dropping of atomic bombs on Hiroshima and Nagasaki in August 1945, which killed 200,000 human beings but ended the war.

The brutalization of warfare took other grotesque and atrocious forms. Examples include the Japanese "rape of Nanjing" in October 1937, in which approximately one hundred thousand Chinese were massacred and thousands of Chinese women were raped; the Soviet murder of close to twenty thousand Poles were deemed to be "unfriendly" to the Soviet Union; German mistreatment of Russian prisoners of war, which led to the death of three million through famine and exposure; the use of slave labor in munitions plants and construction projects by the Japanese and Germans; and the German murder of hostages in response to assassinations and acts of sabotage. Most appalling was the Nazis' war against European Jews. On orders from the German government, six million Jews were gassed, shot, tortured, starved to death, worked to death, killed in medical experiments, or murdered in acts of individual cruelty. This was approximately half of the twelve million the Nazis had hoped to exterminate.

Such enormous suffering was not entirely in vain. The war's perpetrators (Italy, Germany, and Japan) were crushed, and the ideologies that had inspired them (radical nationalism, racism, and militarism) were discredited. The war came to symbolize the triumph of good over evil, and fueled hope that human beings might still be capable of creating and living in a just, peaceful, and humane society. It also created a host of new and intractable problems, not the least of which was the conflict between the world's two new superpowers, the United States and the Soviet Union. Tensions that first surfaced in the closing months of the war soon blossomed into a full-fledged ideological conflict, with the stakes nothing less than the world's political and economic future. The Cold War, a legacy of World War II, would dominate international politics for the next fifty years, until it, like every other war in human history, finally came to an end.

◆

Appeasement and the Origins of World War II in Europe

On taking power in January 1933, Hitler immediately set out to overturn the hated Treaty of Versailles. He took Germany out of the League of Nations, ordered German rearmament, reoccupied the Rhineland, and annexed Austria. Then in 1938, Hitler turned his attention to Czechoslovakia, a nation created twenty years earlier by the Treaty of Versailles. He demanded the annexation to Germany of the Sudetenland, territory in northern, southwestern, and western Czechoslovakia that contained some three million ethnic Germans and much of the nation's industry. The Czechs stood firm, and in mid-September Hitler announced that he would risk world war to unite the Sudeten Germans with the fatherland. Frantic efforts to preserve peace came to a climax in late September with the Munich Conference, attended by Hitler, the Italian dictator Benito Mussolini, the prime minister of France, Edouard Daladier, and the prime minister of Great Britain, Neville Chamberlain. Czechoslovakia was not represented.

Daladier and Chamberlain agreed to the immediate German occupation of the Sudetenland, Polish annexation of Czechoslovakia's coal-rich area of Teschen, and the transfer of parts of the eastern province of Slovakia to Hungary. Hitler agreed to "personally guarantee" the boundaries of the shrunken Czechoslovak state. War was avoided.

Chamberlain, the main architect of the Munich agreement, returned home to cheering crowds, and for a few months he was the hero who had ensured "peace in our time." History, however, has been unkind to Chamberlain and the Munich agreement. "Munich" is now remembered as a symbol of cowardice, betrayal, and capitulation to aggression. In March 1939, Hitler sent troops into Czechoslovakia and occupied Prague; in September 1939, he invaded Poland. War, as it turned out, had not been avoided for long.

The Munich agreement was the climax of a policy of appeasement pursued throughout the 1930s by Great Britain and, to a degree, France in their dealings with Germany, Italy, and Japan. To its advocates, it was a realistic and pragmatic policy that sought to avoid war over peripheral issues while seeking an overall settlement of larger diplomatic problems. This meant a willingness to jettison some aspects of the Versailles Treaty and to tolerate acts of aggression in Manchuria, China, Ethiopia, and Central Europe as long as vital Anglo-French interests were not threatened. The expectation was that once the aggressor nations had been "appeased," they would become respectable, cooperative members of the international community.

Was appeasement a reasonable and morally justifiable policy to prevent the great powers from stumbling into wars over nonvital issues? Or was it an admission of weakness and an invitation to further aggression? As the following documents show, the merits and limitations of appeasement were topics of intense debate in prewar Britain. They have continued to be so to the present day.

The Search for "Peace in Our Time"

❖

52 ◆ Neville Chamberlain, *EXCERPTS FROM CORRESPONDENCE, DIARY, AND SPEECHES*

Neville Chamberlain, the son of the prominent politician Joseph Chamberlain (See source 1), was born in 1869 in Birmingham, a city where he had a successful business and political career before entering national politics on being elected to Parliament as a Conservative in 1918. Having served as chancellor of the exchequer and minister of health in the 1920s, he again served as chancellor of the exchequer during the darkest days of the Great Depression between 1931 and 1937. In 1937 he became prime minister, an office he held until May 1940, when, in the wake of Britain's failed attempt to take back Norway from the Germans, he was forced to turn over the premiership to Winston Churchill. He served in Churchill's war cabinet until he resigned because of poor health in September 1940. He died of cancer two months later.

The following excerpts provide insights into his thinking about war and peace, British interests, and the best way to deal with Hitler. The first excerpt is from a letter to his sister, Ida, in March 1938. It was written directly after the *Anschluss* (political union) of Germany and Austria and at a time when the Spanish Civil War was turning in favor of Francisco Franco and the Nationalists, who, with the help of Germany and Italy, were overcoming the republican Loyalists. The second excerpt is from a speech to Parliament on July 26, 1938, when Hitler was pressing his demands for the Sudetenland. The third excerpt is from a diary entry of September 11, 1938, when war over the Sudetenland seemed imminent. Four days later, a week of intense diplomacy commenced when Chamberlain flew to Berchtesgaden to meet with Hitler. On September 22, he informed Hitler that the Sudetenland was his as long as he would guarantee Czechoslovakia's new borders. Believing the crisis had passed, Chamberlain was shocked to learn on September 27 that Hitler was threatening to occupy the Sudetenland immediately and demanding that Czechoslovakia give up other territories to Poland and Hungary. This new demand provided the background for the fourth excerpt, Chamberlain's radio address to the nation on September 28.

On September 29, Chamberlain flew to Munich, and there with Daladier gave in to Hitler's demands. For his part, Hitler promised to make no further territorial demands on Czechoslovakia.

QUESTIONS FOR ANALYSIS

1. What views does Chamberlain express about Hitler and the strength of Germany? Is he consistent in his views?
2. Why is Chamberlain convinced that Great Britain can do nothing militarily to help the Czechs in their conflict over the Sudetenland?
3. How would you characterize Chamberlain's attitude toward Czechoslovakia?
4. Were there any circumstances under which Chamberlain would have been willing to take Britain to war in 1938?
5. What role does public opinion seem to play in Chamberlain's foreign policy decisions?
6. Aside from his short-term goal of preventing war over the Sudetenland issue, what was Chamberlain's long-term diplomatic goal?

[LETTER TO HIS SISTER, MARCH 1938]

With Franco in Spain by the aid of German guns and Italian planes, with a French government in which one cannot have the slightest confidence and which I suspect to be in closish [close] touch with our Opposition,[1] with the Russians stealthily and cunningly pulling all the strings behind the scenes to get us involved in war with Germany ... and finally with a Germany flushed with triumph, and all too conscious of her power, the prospect looked bleak indeed. In face of such problems, to be badgered and pressed to come out and give a clear, decided, bold, and unmistakable lead, show "ordinary courage," and all the rest of the twaddle, is calculated to vex the man who has to take responsibility for the consequences. As a matter of fact, the plan of the "Grand Alliance," as Winston calls it, had occurred to me long before he mentioned it.[2] ... It is a very attractive idea; indeed, there is almost everything to be said for it until you come to examine its practicability. From that moment its attraction vanishes. You have only to look at the map to see that nothing that France or we could do could possibly save Czechoslovakia from being overrun by the Germans, if they wanted to do it. The Austrian frontier is practically open; the great Skoda[3] munitions works are within easy bombing distance of the German aerodromes, the railways all pass through German territory, Russia is 100 miles away. Therefore we could not help Czechoslovakia—she would simply be a pretext for going to war with Germany. That we could not think of unless we had a reasonable prospect of being able to beat her to her knees in a reasonable time, and of that I see no sign. I have therefore abandoned any idea of giving guarantees to Czechoslovakia, or the French in connection with her obligations to that country.

[1]The Labour Party, the main rival to Chamberlain's party, the Conservatives.
[2]Winston Churchill had been demanding a common front among Britain, the Soviet Union, and France against Hitler.

Source: Chamberlain, Letter to sister; diary entry: From Keith Fieling, *The Life of Neville Chamberlain* (London: Macmillan and Co. Ltd., 1946), 347–348, 360–361.

[SPEECH TO PARLIAMENT, JULY 26, 1938]

If only we could find some peaceful solution of this Czechoslovakian question, I should myself feel that the way was open again for a further effort for a general appeasement—an appeasement which cannot be obtained until we can be satisfied that no major cause of difference or dispute remains unsettled. We have already demonstrated the possibility of a complete agreement between a democratic and a totalitarian state, and I do not myself see why that experience should not be repeated. When Herr Hitler made his offer of a naval treaty[4] under which the German fleet was to be restricted to an agreed level bearing a fixed ratio to the size of the British fleet, he made a notable gesture of a most practical kind in the direction of peace, the value of which it seems to me has not ever been fully appreciated as tending toward this general appeasement.... Since agreement has already been reached on that point, I do not think that we ought to find it impossible continue our efforts at understanding, which, if they were successful, would do so much to bring back confidence....

Source: From Neville Chamberlain, *The Struggle for Peace.* Copyright © 1939 Hutchinson Publishing. Used with kind permission from Cadbury Research Library: Special Collections, University of Birmingham.

[DIARY ENTRY, SEPTEMBER 11, 1938]

I fully realise that, if eventually things go wrong and the aggression takes place, there will be many, including Winston, who will say that the British government must bear the responsibility, and that if only they had had the courage to tell Hitler now that, if he used force, we should at once declare war, that would have stopped him. By that time it will be impossible to prove the contrary, but I am

[3]Located in Pilzen, the Skoda works, founded by Emil von Skoda (1839–1900), were a major weapons producer.
[4]The Anglo-German Naval Agreement of 1935, by which Great Britain agreed to allow Germany to build a navy 35 percent as large as Britain's.

satisfied that we should be wrong to allow the most vital decision that any country could take, the decision as to peace or war, to pass out of our hands into those of the ruler of another country, and a lunatic at that. I have been fortified in this view by reading a very interesting book on the foreign policy of Canning.[5] ... Over and over again Canning lays it down that you should never menace unless you are in a position to carry out your threats, and although, if we have to fight I should hope we should be able to give a good account of ourselves, we are certainly not in a position in which our military advisers would feel happy in undertaking to begin hostilities if we were not forced to do so.

Source: Chamberlain, Letter to sister; diary entry: From Keith Fieling, *The Life of Neville Chamberlain* (London: Macmillan and Co. Ltd., 1946), 347–348, 360–361.

[RADIO SPEECH TO THE NATION, SEPTEMBER 28, 1938]

First of all I must say something to those who have written to my wife or myself in these last weeks to tell us of their gratitude for my efforts and to assure us of their prayers for my success. Most of these letters have come from women—mothers or sisters of our own countrymen. But there are countless others besides—from France, from Belgium, from Italy, even from Germany, and it has been heart-breaking to read of the growing anxiety they reveal and their intense relief when they thought, too soon, that the danger of war was past.

[5]George Canning (1770–1827) was foreign secretary between 1822 and 1827 and served briefly as prime minister in 1827. The book referred to is probably Harold Temperley, *The Foreign Policy of Canning, 1822–1827* (London, 1925).

If I felt my responsibility heavy before, to read such letters has made it seem almost overwhelming. How horrible, fantastic, incredible it is that we should be digging trenches and trying on gas-masks here because of a quarrel in a far-away country between people of whom we know nothing....

You know already that I have done all that one man can do to compose this quarrel. After my visits to Germany I have realized vividly how Herr Hitler feels that he must champion other Germans, and his indignation that grievances have not been met before this. He told me privately, and last night he repeated publicly, that after this Sudeten German question is settled, that is the end of Germany's territorial claims in Europe....

However much we may sympathize with a small nation confronted by a big and powerful neighbor, we cannot in all circumstances undertake to involve the whole British Empire in war simply on her account. If we have to fight it must be on larger issues than that. I am myself a man of peace to the depths of my soul. Armed conflict between nations is a nightmare to me; but if I were convinced that any nation had made up its mind to dominate the world by fear of its force, I should feel that it must be resisted. Under such a domination life for people who believe in liberty would not be worth living; but war is a fearful thing, and we must be very clear, before we embark on it, that it is really the great issues that are at stake, and that the call to risk everything in their defense, when all the consequences are weighed, is irresistible.

Source: From Neville Chamberlain, *The Struggle for Peace.* Copyright © 1939 Hutchinson Publishing. Used with kind permission from Cadbury Research Library: Special Collections, University of Birmingham.

"A Disaster of the First Magnitude"

53 ◆ Winston Churchill, *SPEECH TO PARLIAMENT, OCTOBER 5, 1938*

Winston Churchill was born in 1874 at Blenheim Palace, outside of Oxford, the son of Lord Randolph Churchill and his American wife, Jennie Jerome. An undistinguished student at Harlow School, he attended the Royal Military College

Source: Churchill speech: *Hansard's Parliamentary Debates,* 5th series, Vol. 339), Cols. 359–371, 373.

at Sandhurst and, after receiving his commission, served in Cuba, the Sudan, and India. While covering the Boer, or South African, War (1899–1902) as a correspondent for the *Morning Post*, his capture and daring escape from captivity made him a celebrity.

In 1900, he was elected to Parliament as a Conservative. He served in Parliament for the next fifty years, in which time he held almost all the high offices of state, including two terms as prime minister. Out of office from 1929 to 1939, he became a leading critic of Prime Minister Stanley Baldwin's India policy, which seemed to point to independence, and a strong proponent of British rearmament and a tough line against Hitler. When war was declared, Churchill was invited to become first lord of the admiralty by Chamberlain, whom he succeeded as prime minister in May 1940.

In the following speech—one of his most famous—Churchill denounced the Munich settlement on October 5, 1938. At a time when Chamberlain had overwhelming approval, Churchill's views were unpopular but uncannily prescient.

QUESTIONS FOR ANALYSIS

1. In what specific ways does Churchill view the Munich agreement as a "total and unmitigated defeat"?
2. What, according to Churchill, were the specific mistakes of British diplomacy in their dealings with Hitler?
3. How do Churchill's and Chamberlain's views of Germany differ? How do these views affect their ideas on foreign policy?
4. What, according to Churchill, will be the consequences of appeasement?
5. If given the opportunity, how might Chamberlain have responded to Churchill's speech?

If I do not begin this afternoon by paying the usual, and indeed almost invariable, tributes to the prime minister for his handling of this crisis, it is certainly not from lack of any personal regard. We have always, over a great many years, had very pleasant relations, and I have deeply understood from personal experiences of my own in a similar crisis the stress and strain he has had to bear; but I am sure it is much better to say exactly what we think about public affairs, and this is certainly not the time when it is worth anyone's while to court political popularity....

I will, therefore, begin by saying the most unpopular and most unwelcome thing. I will begin by saying what everybody would like to ignore or forget but which must nevertheless be stated, namely, that we have sustained a total and unmitigated defeat, and that France has suffered even more than we have....

... The utmost my right honourable Friend, the prime minister, has been able to secure by all his immense exertions, by all the great efforts and mobilization which took place in this country, and by all the anguish and strain through which we have passed in this country, the utmost he has been able to gain *{Hon. Members: "Is Peace"}*. I thought I might be allowed to make that point in its due place, and I propose to deal with it. The utmost he has been able to gain for Czechoslovakia and in the matters which were in dispute has been that the German dictator, instead of snatching his victuals from the table has been content to have them served to him course by course....

◆ ◆

All is over. Silent, mournful, abandoned, broken, Czechoslovakia recedes into the darkness. She has suffered in every respect by her association with the Western democracies and with the League of Nations, of which she has always been an obedient servant....

I venture to think that in the future the Czechoslovak state cannot be maintained as an independent entity. You will find that in a period of time which may be measured by years, but may be measured only by months, Czechoslovakia will be engulfed in the Nazi regime.... It is the most grievous consequence which we have yet experienced of what we have done and of what we have left undone in the last five years: five years of futile good intention, five years of eager search for the line of least resistance, five years of uninterrupted retreat of British power, five years of neglect of our air defenses....

When I think of the fair hopes of a long peace which still lay before Europe at the beginning of 1933 when Herr Hitler first obtained power, and of all the opportunities of arresting the growth of the Nazi power which have been thrown away, when I think of the immense combinations and resources which have been neglected or squandered, I cannot believe that a parallel exists in the whole course of history. So far as this country is concerned the responsibility must rest with those who have the undisputed control of our political affairs. They neither prevented Germany from rearming, nor did they rearm ourselves in time. They quarreled with Italy without saving Ethiopia. They exploited and discredited the vast institution of the League of Nations and they neglected to make alliances and combinations which might have repaired previous errors, and thus they left us in the hour of trial without adequate national defense or effective international security....

We are in the presence of a disaster of the first magnitude which has befallen Great Britain and France. Do not let us blind ourselves to that. It must now be accepted that all countries of Central and Eastern Europe will make the best terms they can with the triumphant Nazi power.... The road down the Danube Valley to the Black Sea, the resources of corn and oil, the road which leads as far as Turkey, has been opened. In fact, if not in form, it seems to me that all those countries of middle Europe, all those Danubian countries, will, one after another, be drawn into this vast system of power politics (not only power military politics but power economic politics) radiating from Berlin, and I believe this can be achieved quite smoothly and swiftly and will not necessarily entail the firing of a single shot.... We are talking about countries which are a long way off and of which, as the prime minister might say, we know nothing. *(Interruption)* ...

What will be the position, I want to know, of France and England this year and the year afterward? What will be the position of that Western Front of which we are in full authority the guarantors? ... Relieved from all anxiety in the East, and having secured resources which will greatly diminish, if not entirely remove, the deterrent of a naval blockade, the rulers of Nazi Germany will have a free choice open to them in what direction they will turn their eyes. If the Nazi dictator should choose to look westward, as he may, bitterly will France and England regret the loss of that fine army of ancient Bohemia[1] which was estimated last week to require not fewer than thirty German divisions for its destruction.... Many people, no doubt, honestly believe that they are only giving away the interests of Czechoslovakia, whereas I fear we shall find that we have deeply compromised, and perhaps fatally endangered, the safety and even the independence of Great Britain and France.... You have to consider the character of the Nazi movement and the rule which it implies. The prime minister desires to see cordial relations between this country and Germany.

---

[1]Bohemia was the major western province of Czechoslovakia.

There is no difficulty at all in having cordial relations with the German people. Our hearts go out to them. But they have no power. You must have diplomatic and correct relations, but there can never be friendship between the British democracy and the Nazi power, that power which spurns Christian ethics, which cheers its onward course by a barbarous paganism, which vaunts the spirit of aggression and conquest, which derives strength and perverted pleasure from persecution, and uses, as we have seen, with pitiless brutality, the threat of murderous force. That power cannot ever be the trusted friend of the British democracy....

We have passed an awful milestone in our history, when the whole equilibrium of Europe has been deranged, and that the terrible words have for the time being been pronounced against the Western democracies:

"Thou art weighed in the balance and found wanting."

And do not suppose that this is the end. This is only the beginning of the reckoning. This is only the first sip, the foretaste of a bitter cup which will be proffered to us year by year unless by a supreme recovery of moral health and martial vigor, we arise again and take our stand for freedom as in the olden times.

The Final Solution: Perpetrators and Victims

Antisemitism was not a Nazi invention. In Europe's Middle Ages, Jews were victims of mob violence, forced to live in restricted neighborhoods, or ghettos, subjected to special taxes, and excluded from most professions. By 1500, persecution and expulsions had driven most Jews out of Western and Central Europe to the east, where intolerance, ghettoization, and sporadic massacres continued. In the nineteenth century, anti-Jewish laws were abolished in much of Europe, and Jews were free to attend universities and participate more fully in their country's economic, political, and cultural life. But old prejudices persisted, and in an era of social change, nationalism, and new racial doctrines, antisemitism intensified. Jews fared worst in Russia and the Russian-governed areas of Poland, Ukraine, and Lithuania. In these areas, where millions of Jews lived, the tsar's government enforced and extended anti-Jewish laws and encouraged mob attacks (pogroms) on Jewish communities to deflect attention from its own failures.

As shown in *Mein Kampf* (Source 32), Hitler made virulent antisemitism a cornerstone of National Socialism. Millions of Germans were attracted to his racial theories and his claim that a Jewish-Communist conspiracy had caused Germany's defeat in World War I. Their votes helped carry the Nazis to power in January 1933.

Once in authority, the Nazis began to implement their anti-Jewish policies. Jewish shops were plundered while police looked the other way; Jewish physicians were excluded from hospitals; Jewish judges lost their posts; Jewish students were denied admission to universities; and Jewish veterans were stripped of their benefits. In 1935, the Nazis promulgated the Nuremberg Laws, which deprived Jews of citizenship and outlawed marriage between Jews and non-Jews. On the night of November 9 to 10, 1938, the Nazis organized nationwide violence against Jewish synagogues and shops in what came to be known as *Kristallnacht*, night of the broken glass.

After the war began, conquests in Eastern Europe provided the Nazis new opportunities to deal with the "Jewish problem." In early 1941, they began to deport Jews from Germany and conquered territories to Poland and Czechoslovakia, where they were used as slave laborers or placed in concentration camps. In June 1941, special units known as *Einsatzgruppen* (task forces) were organized to exterminate Jews in conquered territories on the eastern front. In eighteen months, they gunned down over one million Jews and smaller numbers of Roma (Gypsies) and Slavs. In January 1942, at the Wannsee Conference outside Berlin, Nazi leaders approved the Final Solution to the so-called Jewish problem. Their goal was the extermination of European Jewry, and to reach it they constructed special death camps where their murderous work could be carried out efficiently and quickly.

When World War II ended, the Nazis had not achieved their goal of annihilating all of Europe's Jews. They did, however, slaughter close to six million, thus earning themselves a permanent place in the long history of humankind's inhumanity.

"Führer, You Order, We Obey"

◈

54 ◆ Rudolf Höss, *MEMOIRS*

Born in 1900, Rudolf Höss abandoned plans to become a priest after serving in World War I and instead turned to politics. He became active in a number of right-wing organizations, including the Nazi Party, which he joined in 1922. After serving a jail sentence between 1924 and 1928 for participating in the murder of a teacher suspected of "treason," he resumed his work for the party. In 1934, he became a member of the Nazi SS, or *Schutzstaffel* (guard detachment), which under its director Heinrich Himmler, grew from a small security force into a powerful elite organization involved in police work, state security, intelligence gathering, administration of conquered territories, and management of the concentration camps.

After postings at the Dachau and Sachsenhausen camps, Höss was appointed commandant of Auschwitz, a huge, sprawling complex where over one million Jews were gassed or shot and tens of thousands of prisoners served as slave laborers in nearby factories. In 1943, Höss became overseer of all the Third Reich's concentration camps, but he returned to Auschwitz in 1944 to oversee the murder of four hundred thousand Hungarian Jews. After his capture in 1946, Höss was tried and convicted by the international military tribunal at Nuremberg for crimes against humanity. He was hanged on April 16, 1947. While awaiting trial, Höss was encouraged by prosecutors to compose his memoirs to sharpen his recollection of his experiences. In the following passage, he discusses his views of the Jews and his reaction to the mass killings he planned and witnessed.

Source: From Rudolph Höss, *Death Dealer: The Memoirs of the SS Kommandant at Auschwitz*, edited by Steven Paskuly, trans. Andrew Pollinger (Amherst, NY: Prometheus Books, 1992), pp. 141, 142, 156–59, 161–64. Copyright © 1992 by Steven Paskuly. All rights reserved. Used with permission of the publisher; www.prometheusbooks.com.

QUESTIONS FOR ANALYSIS

1. According to Höss, what was his attitude toward the Jews and the Final Solution?
2. How do his statements about the Jews fit in with his assertion that he was a "fanatic National Socialist"?
3. How does Höss characterize his role in the mass extermination of the Jews?
4. How did his involvement in the Holocaust affect him personally? How, according to Höss, did it affect other German participants?
5. What would you describe as the key components of Höss's personality? To what extent was his personality shaped by the Nazi philosophy to which he was dedicated?
6. How can one balance Höss's role as a commandant of a killing center and his comments about his family life?
7. What insights does this excerpt provide about the extent to which the German people knew of and participated in the Holocaust?

Since I was a fanatic National Socialist, I was firmly convinced that our idea would take hold in all countries, modified by the various local customs, and would gradually become dominant. This would then break the dominance of international Jewry. Anti-Semitism was nothing new throughout the whole world. It always made its strongest appearance when the Jews had pushed themselves into positions of power and when their evil actions became known to the general public.... I believed that because our ideas were better and stronger, we would prevail in the long run....

I want to emphasize here that I personally never hated the Jews. I considered them to be the enemy of our nation. However, that was precisely the reason to treat them the same way as the other prisoners. I never made a distinction concerning this. Besides, the feeling of hatred is not in me, but I know what hate is, and how it manifests itself. I have seen it and I have felt it.

This original order of 1941 to annihilate all the Jews stated, "All Jews without exception are to be destroyed." ...

When [Himmler] gave me the order personally in the summer of 1941 to prepare a place for mass killings and then carry it out, I could never have imagined the scale, or what the consequences would be. Of course, this order was something extraordinary, something monstrous. However, the reasoning behind the order of this mass annihilation seemed correct to me. At the time I wasted no thoughts about it. I had received an order; I had to carry it out. I could not allow myself to form an opinion as to whether this mass extermination of the Jews was necessary or not. At the time it was beyond my frame of mind. Since the Fuhrer himself had ordered "The Final Solution of the Jewish Question," there was no second guessing for an old National Socialist, much less an SS officer. "Fuhrer, you order. We obey" was not just a phrase or a slogan. It was meant to be taken seriously.[1]

Since my arrest I have been told repeatedly that I could have refused to obey this order, and even that I could have shot Himmler dead. I do not believe that among the thousands of SS officers there was even one who would have

---

[1]All SS members swore the following oath: "I swear to you Adolf Hitler, as Führer and Chancellor of the Reich, loyalty and bravery. I vow to you and to the authorities appointed by you obedience unto death, so help me God."

had even a glimmer of such a thought. . . . Of course, many SS officers moaned and groaned about the many harsh orders. Even then, they carried out every order. . . . As leaders of the SS, Himmler's person was sacred. His fundamental orders in the name of the Fuhrer were holy. There was no reflection, no interpretation, no explanation about these orders. They were carried out ruthlessly, regardless of the final consequences, even if it meant giving your life for them. Quite a few did that during the war.

It was not in vain that the leadership training of the SS officers held up the Japanese as shining examples of those willing to sacrifice their lives for the state and for the emperor, who was also their god. SS education was not just a series of useless high school lectures. It went far deeper, and Himmler knew very well what he could demand of his SS.

Outsiders cannot possibly understand that there was not a single SS officer who would refuse to obey orders from Himmler, or perhaps even try to kill him because of a severely harsh order. Whatever the Fuhrer or Himmler ordered was always right. Even democratic England has its saying, "My country, right or wrong," and every patriotic Englishman follows it.

◆ ◆

Before the mass destruction of the Jews began, all the Russian politruks[2] and political commissars were killed in almost every camp during 1941 and 1942. According to the secret order given by Hitler, the Einsatzgruppen searched for and picked up the Russian politruks and commissars from all the POW camps. They transferred all they found to the nearest concentration camp for liquidation. . . . The first small transports were shot by firing squads of SS soldiers.

While I was on an official trip, my second in command, Camp Commander Fritzsch, experimented with gas for killings. He used a gas called Cyclon B, prussic acid,[3] which was often used as an insecticide in the camp to exterminate lice and vermin. There was always a supply on hand. When I returned Fritzsch reported to me about how he had used the gas. We used it again to kill the next transport.

The gassing was carried out in the basement of Block 11. I viewed the killings wearing a gas mask for protection. Death occurred in the crammed-full cells immediately after the gas was thrown in. Only a brief choking outcry and it was all over. . . .

At the time I really didn't waste any thoughts about the killing of the Russian POWs. It was ordered; I had to carry it out. But I must admit openly that the gassings had a calming effect on me, since in the near future the mass annihilation of the Jews was to begin. Up to this point it was not clear to me . . . how the killing of the expected masses was to be done. Perhaps by gas? But how, and what kind of gas? Now we had discovered the gas and the procedure. I was always horrified of death by firing squads, especially when I thought of the huge numbers of women and children who would have to be killed. I had had enough of hostage executions, and the mass killings by firing squad order by Himmler and Heydrich.[4]

Now I was at ease. We were all saved from these bloodbaths, and the victims would be spared until the last moment. That is what I worried about the most when I thought of Eichmann's[5] accounts of

---

[2]Communist party members.

[3]Cyclon (or more commonly, Zyclon) B is the trade name for a blue crystalline substance whose active ingredient, hydrocyanic acid, was mainly used for pest control; it sublimates into a gas when exposed to air, causing death by combining with red blood cells and preventing them from carrying oxygen to the body.

[4]Reinhard Heydrich (1904–1942) was Himmler's chief lieutenant in the SS. He organized the execution of Jews in Eastern Europe in 1941.

[5]Adolf Eichmann (1906–1962) was a Nazi bureaucrat originally involved with Jewish emigration. After the Wannsee Conference he was given responsibility for organizing the deportation of approximately three million Jews to death camps. He fled to Argentina in 1946 but was captured by Israeli agents who took him to Israel, where he was tried and executed in 1962.

the mowing down of the Jews with machine guns and pistols by the Einsatzgruppe. Horrible scenes were supposed to have occurred: people running away even after being shot, the killing of those who were only wounded, especially the women and children. Another thing on my mind was the many suicides among the ranks of the SS Special Action Squads who could no longer mentally endure wading in the bloodbaths. Some of them went mad. Most of the members of the Special Action Squads drank a great deal to help get through this horrible work. According to [Captain] Hoffle's accounts, the men of Globocnik's[6] extermination section drank tremendous quantities of alcohol.

In the spring of 1942 the first transports of Jews arrived from Upper Silesia. All of them were to be exterminated. They were led from the ramp across the meadow, later named section B-II of Birkenau,[7] to the farmhouse called Bunker I. Aumeier, Palitzsch, and a few other block leaders led them and spoke to them as one would in casual conversation, asking them about their occupations and their schooling in order to fool them. After arriving at the farmhouse they were told to undress. At first they went very quietly into the rooms where they were supposed to be disinfected. At that point some of them became suspicious and started talking about suffocation and extermination. Immediately a panic started. Those still standing outside were quickly driven into the chambers, and the doors were bolted shut. In the next transport those who were nervous or upset were identified and watched closely at all times. As soon as unrest was noticed these troublemakers were inconspicuously led behind the farmhouse and killed with a small-caliber pistol, which could not be heard by the others....

I also watched how some women who suspected or knew what was happening, even with the fear of death all over their faces, still managed enough strength to play with their children and to talk to them lovingly. Once a woman with four children, all holding each other by the hand to help the smallest ones over the rough ground, passed by me very slowly. She stepped very close to me and whispered, pointing to her four children, "How can you murder these beautiful, darling children? Don't you have any heart?" ...

Occasionally some women would suddenly start screaming in a terrible way while undressing. They pulled out their hair and acted as if they had gone crazy. Quickly they were led behind the farmhouse and killed by a bullet in the back of the neck from a small-caliber pistol.... As the doors were being shut, I saw a woman trying to shove her children out the chamber, crying out, "Why don't you at least let my precious children live?" There were many heartbreaking scenes like this which affected all who were present....

The mass annihilation with all the accompanying circumstances did not fail to affect those who had to carry it out. They just did not watch what was happening. With very few exceptions all who performed this monstrous "work" had been ordered to this detail. All of us, including myself, were given enough to think about which left a deep impression. Many of the men often approached me during my inspection trips through the killing areas and poured out their depression and anxieties to me, hoping that I could give them some reassurance. During these conversations the question arose again and again, "Is what we have to do here necessary? Is it necessary that hundreds of thousands of women and children have to be annihilated?"

---

[6]Odilio Globocnik (1904–1945) was the officer responsible for organizing and training SS units in Poland for the purpose of carrying out the Final Solution. In 1943, he was transferred to Trieste, where he oversaw the campaign against Yugoslavian partisans and also played a role in the persecution of Italy's Jews. After he was captured by British troops at the end of the war, he committed suicide in May 1945.

[7]Birkenau was the German name for the town where a large addition to the Auschwitz complex was built in late 1941 and early 1942.

And I, who countless times deep inside myself had asked the same question, had to put them off by reminding them that it was Hitler's order. I had to tell them that it was necessary to destroy all the Jews in order to forever free Germany and the future generations from our toughest enemy.

It goes without saying that the Hitler order was a firm fact for all of us, and also that it was the duty of the SS to carry it out. However, secret doubts tormented all of us. Under no circumstances could I reveal my secret doubts to anyone. I had to convince myself to be like a rock when faced with the necessity of carrying out this horrible severe order, and I had to show this in every way, in order to force all those under me to hang on mentally and emotionally....

Hour upon hour I had to witness all that happened. I had to watch day and night, whether it was the dragging and burning of the bodies, the teeth being ripped out, the cutting of the hair,[8] I had to watch all this horror. For hours I had to stand in the horrible, haunting stench while the mass graves were dug open, and the bodies were dragged out and burned. I also had to watch the procession of death itself through the peephole of the gas chamber because the doctors called my attention to it. I had to do all this because I was the one to whom everyone looked, and because I had to show everybody that I was not only the one who gave the orders and issued the directives, but that I was also willing to be present at whatever task I ordered my men to perform....

And yet, everyone in Auschwitz believed the Kommandant really had a good life. Yes, my family had it good in Auschwitz, every

wish that my wife or my children had was fulfilled. The children could live free and easy. My wife had her flower paradise.... By the same token no former prisoner can say that he was treated poorly in any way in our house. My wife would have loved to give a present to every prisoner who performed a service for us. The children constantly begged me for cigarettes for the prisoners. The children especially loved the gardeners. In our entire family there was a deep love for farming and especially for animals. Every Sunday I had to drive with them across all the fields, walk them through the stables, and we could never skip visiting the dog kennels.

Their greatest love was for our two horses and our colt. The prisoners who worked in the household were always dragging in some animal the children kept in the garden. Turtles, martens, cats, or lizards; there was always something new and interesting in the garden. The children splashed around in the summertime in the small pool in the garden or the Sola River. Their greatest pleasure was when daddy went into the water with them. But he had only a little time to share all the joys of childhood.

Today I deeply regret that I didn't spend more time with my family. I always believed that I had to be constantly on duty. Through this exaggerated sense of duty I always had made my life more difficult than it actually was. My wife often urged me, "Don't always think of your duty, think of your family too." But what did my wife know about the things that depressed me? She never found out.[9]

---

[8]Teeth from the corpses were soaked in muriatic acid to remove muscle and bone before the gold fillings were extracted. Some of the gold was distributed to dentists who used it in fillings for SS men and their families; the rest was deposited in the Reichsbank. Hair was used to make felt and thread.

[9]In an interview with a court-appointed psychiatrist during the Nuremberg trials in 1946, Höss stated that his wife actually did learn of his involvement in the mass executions at the camp, and that afterward they became estranged and ceased having sexual relations.

Evil

◆

55 ◆ *"B.F.," RECOLLECTIONS*

The following is an excerpt from one of several thousand interviews of Holocaust survivors conducted immediately after the war by representatives of the YIVO Institute for Jewish Research, an organization founded in Vilna, Poland, in 1925, and relocated to New York City in 1940. It is one of the premier academic institutions devoted to the history of East European Jewry.

B. F. was a Jew born in Warsaw, Poland, in 1928. In 1935, he and his family moved to Lodz, also in Poland, where he resided at the time of the Nazi conquest in 1939. Sent to the Warsaw ghetto, he escaped, was recaptured, and was finally sent to Sobibór, a Nazi death camp at which approximately 250,000 Jews were executed in 1942 and 1943. In the fall of 1943, just before the camp closed, B.F. participated in a breakout in which several hundred Jewish prisoners turned on their captors and escaped. Having survived the war and now eighteen years old, he recounted his experiences in an interview recorded in 1945. Like many other interviewees, he requested that his full name be withheld.

QUESTIONS FOR ANALYSIS

Readers are encouraged to formulate their own questions about the events described in this source.

After our train moved in, the doors were thrown open and armed Germans and Ukrainians, cracking whips, drove us out of the wagons. We had bloody welts all over our bodies. The day we came to Sobibor was May fifth in the year '42. We were led through a second tower to an assembly point which was ringed by barbed-wire fences, with posts on the wire perimeters capped by some sort of metal hoods. They split us up here—men to one side and women and children to the other. Soon, SS squads came in and led the women with the children away. Where they were being taken to we didn't know, but off in the distance we heard screams of people being beaten and stripped and then we heard the rumblings of motors being started. It was the women and children being killed. We could sense in the air that, locked up like this between the wires, we'd be

slaughtered right here. Night fell and we fell into a panic. We'd been told that in Belzec [a death camp in southeast Poland], people were burned alive in pits. We wouldn't believe this while we were in the ghetto, but here, when we saw a fire in the distance, we were sure they were burning people. We were overcome with fear and started saying our *viduyim.*[1]

There were thirty men in our group. They divided us up right away. Some were used to sort our belongings.... I was taken into the second group and set to work digging a latrine. I never held a shovel in my life and a German who guarded us at work noticed my "skill" and let fly such a blow over my head that he nearly split my skull. That was when I learned how to work.

We worked from daybreak till nine, then they gave us breakfast. Bread and fingerbowls of fat was all we got and afterwards, they put

---

[1]A prayer of confession said by Jews before their death.

Source: Isaiah Trunk, *Jewish Responses to Nazi Persecution* (New York: Stein & Day, 1978), pp. 268–277, passim. Copyright © 1978 by Isaiah Trunk. Reprinted with permission of Scarborough House Publishers.

us to work till late evening. As night fell, we were all lined up and an SS man informed us nothing would happen to us if we behaved well. If we didn't—they'd "make us a gift" of a bullet to the head.... Then, simply because he had the urge, he picked two men out—one who had stomach pains and the other who just wasn't to his liking—and led them off into the woods where he shot them. Most of the time, the men returned from work beaten, bloodied, and injured all over the body....

This is what the system of going into the "bath" was like: As soon as a train with a transport of people arrived, everyone was either pulled off violently or made to jump. They were all forced to march into that sealed area. Later, the people were led off in groups of thousands, sometimes groups of hundreds. An SS man addressed them, saying since there was a war on, everyone had to work and they were about to be transported somewhere else for labor. They'd be well taken care of. Children and the old wouldn't have to work, but wouldn't lack food either. So great attention must be paid to cleanliness and we had to take a bath first. Those from the West would always applaud at this point. Later, when the Polish Jews arrived, they knew all this ended in death and screamed and made an uproar. So he said to them: "*Ruhe,*[2] I know you long for death already, but you won't be obliged so easily. First, you must work." And he kept punishing them and demoralizing them like this.

Inside the first barrack, they had their coats, jackets, and pants taken off and in the second barrack, had to strip down completely nude. They were told in that first speech that they wouldn't need any towel or soap—they'd find all that in the bath. All this led to them being brought naked into the third barrack near the bath. There was a special cell there where they were kept on arranged benches, guarded by Germans. Not a sound was permitted. Twenty barbers cut off the women's hair. When the women came in naked and saw the men there, they pulled back, but the Germans dragged them and beat them forward. They had

to sit naked. I was one of the barbers. To shave someone's head lasted half a minute. We held the long hair out from the head and snipped it off all along the scalp so that "stairs" were left—tufts of hair sticking out from the scalp. The foreign Jews[3] didn't suspect anything; they were just sorry about losing their hair. The Germans said it didn't matter—in half a year, the hair'd grow back. But on the other side, the Polish Jews screamed and wouldn't let us cut their hair, and they were beaten, and tortured. From there, they went straight through a corridor into a chamber....

I was in the camp eighteen months already. The next day, a transport of Czech Jews was brought to the camp. They came at three in the morning and we were chased out of the bunks in the dead of night. We hauled the bundles off the train, running between two rows of Ukrainians who did nothing but beat us savagely....

That evening, SS man Paul harangued us as usual. He says he has to have five men for the *Lazarett.* What's a *Lazarett?* Well, a *Lazarett* is a place you don't have to work, you can sleep without interruption and don't have to bear any more burdens. But the real *Lazarett,* which means field hospital, was a small structure with a cross and icon of Jesus inside—probably from before the war—and there was a pit there where he'd lower people down and shoot them. This was his own *Lazarett....* Every day, that monster had to have from three to five Jews in his *Lazarett* and he'd pick them out himself or just ask, "*Ja,* well, who's sick today? Who doesn't want to work anymore?" Or he just grabbed them at random. If he hated someone, he simply pointed his finger at them and said, "*Komm, komm* [Come, come] you look like you don't want to work anymore," and then led them away. There were times when some Jews had heard before what the *Lazarett* meant, and they came forward to die voluntarily, because this life had driven them mad with despair. Victims succumbed like this every day.... Death came

---

[2] German, meaning "Be calm."

[3] Jews from outside of Poland.

in many ways: sometimes by shooting, sometimes being bludgeoned to death with clubs. Some committed suicide. There were times we got up in the barrack in the morning, and before our eyes, saw several Jews hanging from the rafters.

The most cruel death was at the jaws of Paul's dog, "Bari." Paul would yell at him: "Bari! Be my deputy!" and the dog tore people into pieces and devoured them. As soon as he got his jaws on you, there was no way out. He snapped you around, whirling you and tearing at you so long, till there was nothing left for his jaw to clamp down on....

Paul the murderer fell bewitched of a Czech Jewish girl. She cleaned up in his barrack and his attitude to us now became less sadistic. The other Germans realized this. One time, they waited till he left for the day, then came and shot the girl. When he got back, they teased him: "Well, Paul, where's your Jewish girl now?" He was so enraged, he persecuted us even more than before. He'd stand by the barrack door through which we hauled the packs, with a hatchet in his hand, and whenever the urge took him, he just swung away till he hacked someone down in a pool of blood. When the new latrines were dug and he came upon some impurity, he threatened all of us with execution. Once, he walked into the latrine area and saw two Jews stooping over the ditch, but there was a pile nearby so he dragged the two Jews over and made them eat it. They fell into a swoon, begging to be shot instead. But he wouldn't

call back his order. They had to keep eating and then heaved up for the rest of the day....

Sometimes, naked women hid out under the garbage, under rags. One time, I was about to sort through the rags when I take a look and see a woman lying among them. What do I do? I can't pull the rags away because a German will spot her immediately, so I went off to another pile of rags, but it didn't work—she was found out. She was led off and clubbed to death.

Another time, after one of the disinfections,[4] we found a child, one and a half years old, among the rags. But a Ukrainian immediately ordered me to take the child to the garbage pit, where he said: "*Ach,* a waste of a bullet!" and took a garbage shovel and split open the baby into pieces. The child hardly let out a whimper....

They made no fuss over children. Finally, the women rebelled. While stripping, they would scream out and attack the Germans, clawing at them and yelling. "You've lost the war anyway! Your death will be a lot crueler than ours! We're defenseless, we have to go to our death— but your women and children will be burned alive!!!" And they screeched and wailed....

While we cut their hair, we stole some conversation with the women—as long as no German was watching, of course....

They asked us how we were still able to work for "them" while everyone else was dead. We answered, "You have it better. You're going to die soon—but we have to keep working, getting beaten all the time, till we're finally exterminated too."

---

[4]Disinfection of clothes.

◆

The Dawn of the Atomic Age

The chain of events and decisions that led to the dropping of atomic bombs on Hiroshima and Nagasaki on August 6 and August 9, 1945, began six years earlier with a letter sent to President Franklin D. Roosevelt on August 2, 1939. It was written by Léo Szilárd and Albert Einstein, both of whom were distinguished European-born physicists who had immigrated to the United States to escape the scourge of Nazi antisemitism. The letter, signed only by Einstein because of his worldwide fame and because Szilárd was considered a security risk, warned that German scientists were pursuing research on nuclear chain reactions with the goal of producing weapons of enormous power. The letter recommended that the U.S. government fund and coordinate similar research. Encouraged by his scientific advisors and by reports on the progress of nuclear research in England, in the early summer of 1941 the president appointed a committee to direct the research and provided modest funding. After Pearl Harbor it became an effort directed by the Army and code-named the Manhattan Project.

The Manhattan Project became a huge, desperate enterprise, costing approximately $2 billion and employing over one hundred thousand persons. They worked under the direction of the country's leading nuclear physicists and engineers at thirty-seven installations and a dozen university laboratories. Success came on July 16, 1945, when the first atomic bomb, two thousand times more powerful than the largest conventional bomb, was exploded in the New Mexico desert. In less than a month, atomic bombs reduced Hiroshima and Nagasaki to ashes, and World War II was over.

The Atomic Age had begun, accompanied by an intense debate over the decision to use the bomb. Had it been morally and militarily justified? Had there been ways to have demonstrated the power of the bomb without using it against Japan? Had the bombs been used to gain a diplomatic advantage over the Soviet Union in the anticipated postwar competition for power? Had racism played a role in the decision? Had the military use of atomic bombs made it more difficult to control the postwar development of nuclear weapons? These are just a few of the questions to consider as you read the following sources.

August 6, 1945

❖

56 ◆ Iwao Nakamura and Atsuko Tsujioka, *RECOLLECTIONS*

In 1951, Dr. Arata Osada, a professor of education at Hiroshima University, sponsored a project in which Japanese students from primary grades through the university level were asked to write down their memories of the August 6 bombing and its aftermath. Moved by their recollections, he arranged to have published a sample of their compositions in 1951. His stated purpose was to reveal the horrors of nuclear war and thereby encourage nuclear disarmament. An English translation appeared in 1980.

QUESTIONS FOR ANALYSIS

Readers are encouraged to formulate their own questions about the events and experiences described in these sources.

Source: From *Children of Hiroshima,* Arata Osada, © 1981 London: Taylor and Francis, pp. 173–177, 265–269; original published in 1980 by Publishing Committee for "Children of Hiroshima." Reproduced by permission of Taylor & Francis Books UK.

IWAO NAKAMURA

11th Grade Boy
(5th Grade at the Time)

Today, as I begin to write an account of my experiences after five years and several months have passed, the wretched scenes of that time float up before my eyes like phantoms. And as these phantoms appear, I can actually hear the pathetic groans, the screams.

In an instant it became dark as night, Hiroshima on that day. Flames shooting up from wrecked houses as if to illuminate this darkness. Amidst this, children aimlessly wandering about, groaning with pain, their burned faces twitching and bloated like balloons. An old man, skin flaking off like the skin of a potato, trying to get away on weak, unsteady legs, praying as he went. A man frantically calling out the names of his wife and children, both hands to his forehand from which blood trickled down. Just the memory of it makes my blood run cold. This is the real face of war....

I, who cannot forget, was in the fifth year of primary school when it happened. To escape the frequent air raids, I and my sisters had been evacuated to the home of our relatives in the country, but on August 2 returned to my home at Naka Kakomachi during the summer vacation, to recover from the effects of a summer illness that had left me very weak....

It was after eight on August 6 and the midsummer sun was beginning to scorch down on Hiroshima. An all-clear signal had sounded and with relief we sat down for breakfast a little later than usual. Usually by this time, my father had left the house for the office and I would be at the hospital for treatment.

I was just starting on my second bowl of rice. At that moment, a bluish-white ray of light like a magnesium flare hit me in the face, a terrific roar tore at my eardrums and it became so dark I could not see anything. I stood up, dropping my rice bowl and chopsticks. I do not know what happened next or how long I was unconscious. When I came to, I found myself trapped under what seemed like a heavy rock, but my head was free. It was still dark but I finally discovered that I was under a collapsed wall. It was all so sudden that I kept wondering if I was dreaming. I tried very hard to crawl free, but the heavy wall would not budge. A suffocating stench flooded the area and began to choke me. My breathing became short, my ears began to ring, and my heart was pounding as if it were about to burst. "I can't last much longer," I said to myself, and then a draft of cold air flowed past me and some light appeared. The taste of that fresh air is something I shall never forget. I breathed it in with all my might. This fresh air and the brighter surroundings gave me renewed vigor and I somehow managed to struggle out from under the wall....

Nothing was left of the Hiroshima of a few minutes ago. The houses and buildings had been destroyed and the streets transformed into a black desert, with only the flames from burning buildings giving a lurid illumination to the dark sky over Hiroshima. Flames were already shooting out of the wreckage of the house next door. We couldn't see my two brothers. My mother was in tears as she called their names. My father went frantic as he dug among the collapsed walls and scattered tiles. It must have been by the mercy of God that we were able to rescue my brothers from under the wreckage before the flames reached them. They were not hurt, either. The five of us left our burning home and hurried toward Koi. Around us was a sea of flames. The street was filled with flames and smoke from the burning wreckage of houses and burning power poles which had toppled down blocked our way time after time, almost sending us into the depths of despair. It seems that everyone in the area had already made their escape, for we saw no one but sometimes we heard moans, a sound like a wild beast.... As we passed Nakajima Primary School area and approached Sumiyoshi Bridge, I saw a damaged water tank in which a number of people had their heads down, drinking. I was so thirsty and attracted by the sight of people that I left my parents' side without thinking, and approached the tank. But when I got near and was able to see into the tank, I gave an involuntary cry and backed away. What I saw reflected in the blood-stained water were the faces of monsters. They had leaned over the side of the tank and died in that position. From the burned shreds of their sailor uniforms, I knew they were schoolgirls, but they had no hair left and their burned faces were crimson with blood; they no longer appeared human. After we came out on the main road and crossed Sumiyoshi Bridge, we finally came across some living human beings—but maybe it would be more correct to say that we met some people from Hell. They were naked and their skin, burned and bloody, was like red rust and their bodies were bloated up like balloons.... The houses on both sides of this street, which was several dozen yards wide, were in flames so that we could only move along a strip in the center about three or four yards wide. This narrow passage was covered with seriously burned and injured people, unable to walk, and with dead bodies, leaving hardly any space for us to get through. At places, we were forced to step over them callously, but we apologized in our hearts as we did this. Among them were old people pleading for water, tiny children seeking help, students unconsciously calling for their parents, brothers, and sisters, and there was a mother prostrate on the ground, moaning with pain but with one arm still tightly embracing her dead baby. But how could we help them when we ourselves did not know our own fate?

ATSUKO TSUJIOKA

Student, Hiroshima Women's Junior College

It happened instantaneously. I felt as if my back had been struck with a big hammer, and then as if I had been thrown into boiling oil. I was unconscious for a while. When I regained my senses, the whole area was covered with black smoke.... I lay on the ground with my arms pressed against my chest, and called for help, again and again: "Mother! Mother! Father!"

But, of course, neither Mother nor Father answered me.... I could hear the other girls shouting for their mothers in the hellish darkness, and I sensed that they were getting away. I got up and just ran after them desperately. Near Tsurumi Bridge, a red hot electric wire got wrapped around my ankles. I pulled free of it somehow, without thinking, and ran to the foot of the Tsurumi Bridge. By that time, there was white smoke everywhere. I had been working in a place called Tanaka-cho, about 600 yards from the blast center....

There was a large cistern at the foot of the bridge. In the tank were some mothers, one holding her naked, burned baby above her head, and another crying and trying to give her baby milk from her burned breast. Also in the tank were schoolchildren, with only their heads, and their hands clasped in prayer, above the surface of the water. They were sobbing for their parents, but everyone had been hurt, so there was no one to help them. People's hair was white with dust, and scorched; they did not look human. "Surely not me," I thought, and I looked down at my hands. They were bloody and what looked like rags hung from my arms, and inside was fresh-looking flesh, all red, white and black. I was shocked and reached for the handkerchief I carried in the pocket of my trousers, but there was no handkerchief or pocket. The lower part of the trousers had been burned away. I could feel my face swelling up, but there was nothing I could do about it....

We heard people calling for help inside wrecked buildings, and then saw the same buildings go up in flames. A boy of about six, covered in blood, was jumping up and down in front of one of the burning houses, holding a cooking pot in his hands and yelling something we could not understand.... I wonder what happened to those people? And the ones trapped in the buildings. In our rush to get home quickly, the four of us were proceeding toward the center of the atomic explosion, in the opposite direction from everyone else. However, when we reached Inarimachi, we could not go any further because the bridge had been destroyed, so we headed for Futaba Hill, instead. My legs gave out near Futaba, and I almost crawled the last part of the way to the foot of the hill, saying, "Wait for me! Please wait for me!"

Luckily for us, we met some kind soldiers in white coats there, who took us to a place we could lie down and rest, and treated our wounds. They dug around and told me that they had removed pieces of tile from the back of my head. They bandaged my head for me and tried to console us by saying, "Rest here now. Your teacher is bound to come and get you soon." ...

That first night ended. There were cries for water from early morning. I was terribly thirsty. ...

Mercurochrome had been painted on my burns once, and they got black and sticky. I tried to dry them out in the sun. My friends and the other people were no longer able to move. The skin had peeled off of their burned arms, legs and backs. I wanted to move them, but there was no place on their bodies that I could touch. Some people came around noon on the second day and gave us some rice balls. Our faces were burned and swollen so badly that we could hardly open our mouths, so we got very little of the rice into them. My eyes had swollen up by the third day, and I could not move around. ...

People who came to the barracks would call out the names and addresses of the people they were looking for. My father and four or five of our neighbors had been searching for me since the bombing. They found me in a corner of the barracks at the foot of Futaba Hill, on the evening of the third day. They were able to find me because the wooden name tag my father had written for me was on my chest. The writing on the tag had been burned all the way through it, as if it had been etched.

"Atsuko! This is your father!"

I was so happy I couldn't speak. I only nodded my head. My eyes were swollen closed. I could not see my father, but I was saved.

I still have the scars from that day; on my head, face, arms, legs and chest. There are reddish black scars on my arms and the face that I see in the mirror does not look as if it belongs to me. It always saddens me to think that I will never look the way I used to. I lost all hope at first. I was obsessed with the idea that I had become a freak and did not want to be seen by anyone. I cried constantly for my good friends and kind teachers who had died in such terrible way.

My way of thinking became warped and pessimistic. Even my beautiful voice, that my friends had envied, had turned weak and hoarse. When I think of the way it was then, I feel as if I were being strangled. But I have been able to take comfort in the thought that physical beauty is not everything, that a beautiful spirit can do away with physical ugliness. This has given me new hope for the future. I am going to study hard and develop my mind and body, to become someone with culture and inner beauty.

"The Face of War Is the Face of Death"

57 ◆ Henry L. Stimson, *THE DECISION TO USE THE ATOMIC BOMB*

President Truman, who did not even know about the Manhattan Project as a senator from Missouri and as vice president under Roosevelt, learned of the new weapon in a meeting with Secretary of War Henry L. Stimson on April 25, two weeks after President Roosevelt's death. Truman's first response was to appoint a small committee, known as the Interim Committee, to advise him on the use of atomic weapons during and after the war. Its members included Stimson and seven others: George Harrison, an insurance executive who was a special assistant to Stimson; James Byrnes, a presidential advisor and soon secretary of state;

Source: From *Harper's Magazine*, February 1947. © The Harper's Magazine Foundation. Reproduced here with the indirect permission of the Harper's editors: In view of the exceptional public importance of this article, permission is given to any newspaper or magazine to reprint it, in part or (preferably, since its effect is cumulative) in full, with credit to Harper's Magazine but without charge.

Ralph Bard, undersecretary of the navy; William Clayton, assistant secretary of state; Vannevar Bush, president of the Carnegie Institution in Washington; Karl Compton, president of the Massachusetts Institute of Technology; and James Conant, president of Harvard University. They were advised by the Scientific Panel, made up of four persons who had played leading roles in the Manhattan Project: Enrico Fermi, of Columbia University; Arthur H. Compton, of the University of Chicago; Ernest Lawrence, of the University of California at Berkeley; and Robert Oppenheimer, director of the atomic energy research project at Los Alamos, New Mexico.

The chair of the Interim Committee, and the author of the following excerpt, was Stimson. Born in 1867 in New York City and a graduate of Harvard University and Yale Law School, Stimson had a distinguished career as a lawyer and public servant. Having served as secretary of war under President Taft and secretary of state under President Hoover, he was named secretary of war by Roosevelt in 1940, even though he was a Republican. In 1947, after his retirement from public service and less than three years before his death in 1950, he published "The Decision to Use the Atomic Bomb" in *Harper's Magazine.* It focused on the work of the Interim Committee and the reasons why Stimson advised President Truman to drop atomic bombs on Japan without warning. Excerpts from the article follow.

QUESTIONS FOR ANALYSIS

1. How did the background and specific purposes of the Manhattan Project affect decision making in 1945?
2. For those who supported the immediate use of the bombs, what goals did they hope to achieve?
3. How was the choice of Hiroshima and Nagasaki as targets related to these goals?
4. What were Stimson's views of the nature of war? How did his views affect his decision to support the immediate use of atomic bombs?

GOALS OF THE MANHATTAN PROJECT

The original experimental achievement of atomic fission had occurred in Germany in 1938, and it was known that the Germans had continued their experiments. In 1941 and 1942 they were believed to be ahead of us, and it was vital that they should not be the first to bring atomic weapons into the field of battle. Furthermore, if we should be the first to develop the weapon, we should have a great new instru-ment for shortening the war and minimizing destruction. At no time, from 1941 to 1945, did I ever hear it suggested by the President, or by any other responsible member of the govern-ment, that atomic energy should not be used in the war. All of us of course understood the ter-rible responsibility involved in our attempt to unlock the doors to such a devastating weapon; President Roosevelt particularly spoke to me many times of his own awareness of the cata-strophic potentialities of our work. But we were at war, and the work must be done....

RECOMMENDATION OF THE INTERIM COMMITTEE AND THE SECRETARY OF WAR

The discussions of the committee ranged over the whole field of atomic energy, in its political, military, and scientific aspects.... The committee's work included the drafting of the statements which were published immediately after the first bombs were dropped, the drafting of a bill for the domestic control of atomic energy, and recommendations looking toward the international control of atomic energy....

On June 1, after its discussions with the Scientific Panel, the Interim Committee unanimously adopted the following recommendations:

(1) The bomb should be used against Japan as soon as possible.

(2) It should be used on a dual target—that is, a military installation or war plant surrounded by or adjacent to houses and other buildings most susceptible to damage, and

(3) It should be used without prior warning [of the nature of the weapon]. One member of the committee, Mr. Bard,[1] later changed his view and dissented from recommendation....

In reaching these conclusions the Interim Committee carefully considered such alternatives as a detailed advance warning or a demonstration in some uninhabited area. Both of these suggestions were discarded as impractical. They were not regarded as likely to be effective in compelling a surrender of Japan, and both of them involved serious risks. Even the New Mexico test would not give final proof that any given bomb was certain to explode when dropped from an airplane. Quite apart from the generally unfamiliar nature of atomic explosives, there was the whole problem of exploding a bomb at a predetermined height in the air by a complicated mechanism which could not be tested in the static test of New Mexico. Nothing would have been more damaging to our effort to obtain surrender than a warning or a demonstration followed by a dud—and this was a real possibility. Furthermore, we had no bombs to waste. It was vital that a sufficient effect be quickly obtained with the few we had....

... The committee's function was, of course, entirely advisory. The ultimate responsibility for the recommendation to the President rested upon me, and I have no desire to veil it. The conclusions of the committee were similar to my own, although I reached mine independently. I felt that to extract a genuine surrender from the Emperor and his military advisers, they must be administered a tremendous shock which would carry convincing proof of our power to destroy the Empire. Such an effective shock would save many times the number of lives, both American and Japanese, that it would cost.

The facts upon which my reasoning was based and steps taken to carry it out now follow.

The principal political, social, and military objective of the United States in the summer of 1945 was the prompt and complete surrender of Japan. Only the complete destruction of her military power could open the way to lasting peace....

As we understood it in July, there was a very strong possibility that the Japanese government might determine upon resistance to the end, in all the areas of the Far East under its control. In such an event the Allies would be faced with the enormous task of destroying an armed force of five million men and five thousand suicide aircraft, belonging to a race which had already amply demonstrated its ability to fight literally to the death.

The strategic plans of our armed forces for the defeat of Japan, as they stood in July, had

---

[1]Undersecretary of the navy and a member of the Interim Committee. He was the only member of the committee to oppose its recommendations. In protest, he resigned.

been prepared without reliance upon the atomic bomb, which had not yet been tested in New Mexico. We were planning an intensified sea and air blockade, and greatly intensified strategic air bombing, through the summer and early fall, to be followed on November 1 by an invasion of the southern island of Kyushu. This would be followed in turn by an invasion of the main island of Honshu in the spring of 1946. The total U.S. military and naval force involved in this grand design was of the order of 5,000,000 men; if all those indirectly concerned are included, it was larger still.

We estimated that if we should be forced to carry this plan to its conclusion, the major fighting would not end until the latter part of 1946, at the earliest. I was informed that such operations might be expected to cost over a million casualties to American forces alone. Additional large losses might be expected among our allies, and, of course, if our campaign were successful and if we could judge by previous experience, enemy casualties would be much larger than our own....

[On July 28, after Japan rejected the Potsdam ultimatum, giving their leaders the choice of immediate surrender or the "utter destruction of the Japanese homeland," plans went forward for using the atomic bombs.]

Because of the importance of the atomic mission against Japan, the detailed plans were brought to me by the military staff for approval. With President Truman's warm support I struck off the list of suggested targets the city of Kyoto. Although it was a target of considerable military importance, it had been the ancient capital of Japan and was a shrine of Japanese art and culture. We determined that it should be spared. I approved four other targets including the cities of Hiroshima and Nagasaki.

Hiroshima was bombed on August 6, and Nagasaki on August 9. These two cities were active working parts of the Japanese war effort. One was an army center; the other was naval and industrial. Hiroshima was the headquarters of the Japanese Army defending southern Japan and was a major military storage and assembly point. Nagasaki was a major seaport and it contained several large industrial plants of great wartime importance. We believed that our attacks had struck cities which must certainly be important to the Japanese military leaders, both Army and Navy, and we waited for a result. We waited one day.

FINAL REFLECTIONS

... As I look back over the five years of my service as Secretary of War, I see too many stern and heartrending decisions to be willing to pretend that war is anything else than what it is. The face of war is the face of death; death is an inevitable part of every order that a wartime leader gives. The decision to use the atomic bomb was a decision that brought death to over a hundred thousand Japanese. No explanation can change that fact and I do not wish to gloss it over. But this deliberate, premeditated destruction was our least abhorrent choice. The destruction of Hiroshima and Nagasaki put an end to the Japanese war. It stopped the fire raids and the strangling blockade; it ended the ghastly specter of a clash of great land armies.

◆

From World War II to the Cold War

In April 1945, the Allies, led by Great Britain, the United States, and the Soviet Union, defeated Hitler and were planning their campaign to defeat Japan. Less than a year later, however, in March 1946, the British wartime leader Winston Churchill warned in a famous speech delivered at Westminster College in Missouri that an "iron curtain" was descending across Soviet-dominated Eastern Europe, and called for an Anglo-American alliance to halt Soviet expansion. One year after that, in March 1947, President Harry Truman, in an address to Congress, denounced the Soviet Union as a menace to peace and committed the United States to support "free peoples who are resisting attempted subjugation by armed minorities or by outside pressures." Truman's aide, Clark Clifford, described the speech as "the opening gun in a campaign to bring the people up to the realization that the war isn't over by any means." In April 1947, another presidential aide, Bernard Baruch, gave the war a name. It was a "cold war," a war that would dominate international politics until the last decade of the twentieth century.

Historians have minutely explored the causes of the Cold War, and have written a great deal about which side—the Soviet Union or the United States—was to blame for bringing it about. One thing is certain, however: 1946 was a pivotal year in Soviet-U.S. relations. Until then, despite wartime disagreements and postwar conflicts over Iran and Turkey, there were still those on both sides who sought cooperation, not confrontation, between the two superpowers. In 1946, however, attitudes hardened, and moderates such as U.S. Secretary of Commerce Henry Wallace and the Soviet career diplomat Maxim Litvinov resigned or were removed from office. When negotiations over nuclear arms control failed in June and the Paris foreign ministers' conference over Eastern Europe ended acrimoniously in August, further Soviet-U.S. conflict seemed inevitable.

Two documents written in 1946 illustrate the chill in U.S.-Soviet relations, and in no small measure contributed to it. The first, composed in February 1946 by the Moscow-based career diplomat George Kennan and known as the Long Telegram, profoundly affected U.S. policy toward the Soviet Union. It analyzed the historical and ideological roots of Soviet foreign policy and recommended a policy of "containment" to prevent Soviet expansion. The second document, a telegram written in September 1946 by the Soviet ambassador to the United States, Nikolai Novikov, warned Soviet leaders that the U.S. government was bent on crippling the Soviet Union and achieving world dominance. It is a revealing example of Soviet perceptions during these early stages of the Cold War.

The Sources of Soviet Conduct

❖

58 ◆ George Kennan, *THE LONG TELEGRAM*

Born in Milwaukee in 1904, George Kennan entered the U.S. Foreign Service directly after his graduation from Princeton in 1925. Having mastered Russian through studies at the University of Berlin, he had postings in Moscow, Berlin, and Prague before returning to Moscow in 1944 as special advisor to the U.S. ambassador to the Soviet Union, Averell Harriman. In early February 1946, he received a directive from the State Department to analyze the implications of a recent Stalin speech that Washington viewed as confrontational and hostile. Kennan used the opportunity to write what is arguably the best-known such dispatch in the history of U.S. diplomacy. It was read by State Department officials, cabled to U.S. embassies

Source: From *Origins of the Cold War: The Novikov, Kennan, and Roberts 'Long' Telegrams of 1946*. Copyright © by the Endowment of the United States Institute of Peace, 1993. Used with permission by the United States Institute of Peace, Washington, D.C.

around the world, and made required reading for hundreds of military officers. In 1947, an edited version of the telegram was published as an article written by "X" in the journal *Foreign Affairs*. Kennan's telegram gave direction and purpose to U.S. foreign policy. Its recommendation to undertake long-term "containment" of Russia's expansionist tendencies through the application of counterforce became the foundation of U.S. Cold War strategy.

In 1947, Kennan was appointed head of the State Department's newly created policy planning staff. Convinced that a successful containment policy did not require a huge arms build-up, he opposed the formation of the North Atlantic Treaty Organization and increased military spending. Kennan resigned from the State Department in 1950 to join the Institute for Advanced Study at Princeton. His appointment as ambassador to the Soviet Union in 1952 ended a year later, after the Russians expelled him over remarks he made about Soviet mistreatment of Western diplomats. In 1956, he became permanent professor of historical studies at the institute in Princeton, a tenure broken only by a stint as U.S. ambassador to Yugoslavia (1961–1963). He died in Princeton in 2005 at age 101.

QUESTIONS FOR ANALYSIS

1. What views of capitalism and socialism are presented, according to Kennan, in official Soviet propaganda?
2. What does Kennan consider to be the outstanding characteristics of Russia's past?
3. How, according to Kennan, has this past affected the policies and views of the Soviet government since 1917?
4. In Kennan's view, what role does communist ideology play in shaping the policies of the Soviet government?
5. According to Kennan's analysis, what strengths and weaknesses does the Soviet Union bring to the anticipated conflict with the United States?
6. What, in Kennan's view, are the implications of his analysis for U.S. foreign and domestic policy? What must be done to counter the inevitable Soviet threat?

PART 1: BASIC FEATURES OF POSTWAR SOVIET OUTLOOK, AS PUT FORWARD BY OFFICIAL PROPAGANDA MACHINE, ARE AS FOLLOWS

(a) USSR still lives in antagonistic "capitalist encirclement" with which in the long run there can be no permanent peaceful coexistence....

(b) Capitalist world is beset with internal conflicts, inherent in nature of capitalist society.... Greatest of them is that between England and US.

(c) Internal conflicts of capitalism inevitably generate wars. Wars thus generated may be of two kinds: intra-capitalist wars between two capitalist states and wars of intervention against socialist world. Smart capitalists, vainly seeking escape from inner conflicts of capitalism, incline toward latter....

PART 2: BACKGROUND OF OUTLOOK

... At bottom of Kremlin's neurotic view of world affairs is traditional and instinctive Russian sense of insecurity. Originally, this was insecurity of a peaceful agricultural people trying to live on vast exposed plain in neighborhood of fierce nomadic peoples. To this was added, as Russia came into contact with economically advanced West, fear of more competent, more powerful, more highly organized societies in that area. But this latter type of insecurity was one which afflicted Russian rulers rather than Russian people; for Russian rulers have invariably sensed that their rule was relatively archaic in form, fragile and artificial in its psychological foundations, unable to stand comparison or contact with political systems of Western countries. For this reason they have always feared foreign penetration, feared direct contact between Western world and their own, feared what would happen if Russians learned truth about world without or if foreigners learned truth about world within. And they have learned to seek security only in patient but deadly struggle for total destruction of rival power, never in compacts and compromises with it.

It was no coincidence that Marxism, which had smoldered ineffectively for half a century in Western Europe, caught hold and blazed for the first time in Russia. Only in this land which had never known a friendly neighbor or indeed any tolerant equilibrium of separate powers, either internal or international, could a doctrine thrive which viewed economic conflicts of society as insoluble by peaceful means. After establishment of Bolshevist regime, Marxist dogma, rendered even more truculent and intolerant by Lenin's interpretation, became a perfect vehicle for sense of insecurity with which Bolsheviks, even more than previous Russian rulers, were afflicted. In this dogma, with its basic altruism of purpose, they found justification for their instinctive fear of outside world, for the dictatorship without which they did not know how to rule, for cruelties they did not dare to inflict, for sacrifices they felt bound to demand. In the name of Marxism they sacrificed every single ethical value in their methods and tactics. Today they cannot dispense with it. It is fig leaf of their moral and intellectual respectability. Without it they would stand before history, at best, as only the last of that long succession of cruel and wasteful Russian rulers who have relentlessly forced country on to ever new heights of military power in order to guarantee external security of their internally weak regimes. ... Thus Soviet leaders are driven [by] necessities of their own past and present position to put forward a dogma which [apparent omission] outside world as evil, hostile and menacing, but as bearing within itself germs of creeping disease and destined to be wracked with growing internal convulsions until it is given final coup de grace by rising power of socialism and yields to new and better world. ...

PART 3: PROJECTION OF SOVIET OUTLOOK IN PRACTICAL POLICY ON OFFICIAL LEVEL

We have now seen nature and background of Soviet program. What may we expect by way of its practical implementation? ...

On official plane we must look for following:

(a) Internal policy devoted to increasing in every way strength and prestige of Soviet state: intensive military-industrialization; maximum development of armed forces; great displays to impress outsiders; continued secretiveness about internal matters, designed to conceal weaknesses and to keep opponents in the dark.

(b) Wherever it is considered timely and promising, efforts will be made to advance official limits of Soviet power. ...

(c) Russians will participate officially in international organizations where they see opportunity of extending Soviet power or of inhibiting or diluting power of others....

(d) Toward colonial areas and backward or dependent peoples, Soviet policy ... will be directed toward weakening of power and influence and contacts of advanced Western nations, on theory that insofar as this policy is successful, there will be created a vacuum which will favor Communist-Soviet penetration....

(e) Russians will strive energetically to develop Soviet representation in, and official ties with, countries in which they sense strong possibilities of opposition to Western centers of power. This applies to such widely separated points as Germany, Argentina, Middle Eastern countries, etc.

(f) In international economic matters, Soviet policy will really be dominated by pursuit of autarchy[1] for Soviet Union and Soviet-dominated adjacent areas taken together....

PART 4: FOLLOWING MAY BE SAID AS TO WHAT WE MAY EXPECT BY WAY OF IMPLEMENTATION OF BASIC SOVIET POLICIES ON UNOFFICIAL, OR SUBTERRANEAN PLANE...

(a) To undermine general political and strategic potential of major Western Powers. Efforts will be made in such countries to disrupt national self-confidence, to hamstring measures of national defense, to increase social and industrial unrest, to stimulate all forms of disunity. All persons with grievances, whether economic or racial, will be urged to seek redress not in mediation and compromise, but in defiant, violent struggle for destruction of other elements of society. Here poor will be set against rich, black against white, young against old, newcomers against established residents, etc.

(b) In foreign countries Communists will, as a rule, work toward destruction of all forms of personal independence—economic, political or moral. Their system can handle only individuals who have been brought into complete dependence on higher power. Thus, persons who are financially independent—such as individual businessmen, estate owners, successful farmers, artisans—and all those who exercise local leadership or have local prestige—such as popular local clergymen or political figures—are anathema....

(c) Everything possible will be done to set major Western Powers against each other. Anti-British talk will be plugged among Americans, anti-American talk among British. Continentals, including Germans, will be taught to abhor both Anglo-Saxon powers.[2] ...

PART 5: PRACTICAL DEDUCTIONS FROM STANDPOINT OF US POLICY

In summary, we have here a political force committed fanatically to the belief that with US there can be no permanent modus vivendi,[3] that it is desirable and necessary that the internal harmony of our society be disrupted, our traditional way of life be destroyed, the international authority of our state be broken, if Soviet power is to be secure.... In addition, it has an elaborate and far-flung apparatus for exertion of its influence in other countries, an

---

[1]Economic self-sufficiency as a national policy; getting along without goods from other countries.
[2]England and the United States.

[3]Latin for manner of living; hence, a temporary agreement in a dispute pending final settlement.

apparatus of amazing flexibility and versatility, managed by people whose experience and skill in underground methods are presumably without parallel in history. Finally, it is seemingly inaccessible to considerations of reality in its basic reactions. . . . This is admittedly not a pleasant picture. Problem of how to cope with this force [is] undoubtedly greatest task our diplomacy has ever faced and probably greatest it will ever have to face. . . . But I would like to record my conviction that problem is within our power to solve—and that without recourse to any general military conflict. And in support of this conviction there are certain observations of a more encouraging nature I should like to make:

(1) Soviet power, unlike that of Hitlerite Germany, is neither schematic[4] nor adventuristic. It does not work by fixed plans. It does not take unnecessary risks. Impervious to logic of reason, and it is highly sensitive to logic of force. For this reason it can easily withdraw—and usually does—when strong resistance is encountered at any point. Thus, if the adversary has sufficient force and makes clear his readiness to use it, he rarely has to do so. . . .

(2) Gauged against Western world as a whole, Soviets are still by far the weaker force. Thus, their success will really depend on degree of cohesion, firmness and vigor which Western world can muster. . . .

(3) Success of Soviet system, as form of internal power, is not yet finally proven. . . .

(4) All Soviet propaganda beyond Soviet security sphere is basically negative and destructive. It should therefore be relatively easy to combat it by any intelligent and really constructive program.

For these reasons I think we may approach calmly and with good heart problem of how to deal with Russia. As to how this approach should be made, I only wish to advance, by way of conclusion, following comments:

(1) Our first step must be to apprehend, and recognize for what it is, the nature of the movement with which we are dealing. We must study it with same courage, detachment, objectivity, and same determination not to be emotionally provoked or unseated by it, with which doctor studies unruly and unreasonable individual.

(2) We must see that our public is educated to realities of Russian situation. . . .

(3) Much depends on health and vigor of our own society. World communism is like malignant parasite which feeds only on diseased tissue. This is point at which domestic and foreign policies meet. Every courageous and incisive measure to solve internal problems of our own society, to improve self-confidence, discipline, morale and community spirit of our own people, is a diplomatic victory over Moscow worth a thousand diplomatic notes and joint communiqués. . . .

(4) We must formulate and put forward for other nations a much more positive and constructive picture of sort of world we would like to see than we have put forward in past. . . .

(5) Finally we must have courage and self-confidence to cling to our own methods and conceptions of human society. After all, the greatest danger that can befall us in coping with this problem of Soviet communism is that we shall allow ourselves to become like those with whom we are coping.

---

[4]In this context, having a definite outline or plan to follow.

The U.S. Drive for World Supremacy

◈

59 ◆ Nikolai Novikov,
TELEGRAM, SEPTEMBER 27, 1946

U.S. diplomatic and military personnel were not the only readers of Kennan's Long Telegram. At some point after its appearance, excerpts or the full document fell into the hands of the Soviets, and a response was soon forthcoming. It took the form of a cable sent to Moscow from Washington in September 1946 by the recently appointed Soviet ambassador to the United States, Nikolai Novikov. Trained in the early 1930s at Leningrad University in Middle Eastern economics and languages, Novikov hoped to pursue an academic career, but instead was drafted into the foreign service. He was named ambassador to Egypt in 1941 and also served as liaison to the Yugoslav and Greek governments in exile, both of which were located in Cairo. Early in 1945, he was posted to Washington, DC, where he was named deputy chief of the Soviet mission; in April, he became Soviet ambassador to the United States. He resigned from the foreign service in 1947 and returned to the Soviet Union, where he lived in obscurity until his death in 1989.

We have little information about the background of Novikov's telegram, which was unknown to scholars until it was distributed by a Soviet official to a group of Soviet and U.S. historians attending a meeting on the origins of the Cold War in Washington in 1990. According to Novikov's memoir (which was made public in 1990), he was requested to write an analysis of U.S. foreign policy goals at the Paris foreign ministers' conference in late summer 1946 by the Soviet foreign minister Viacheslav Molotov (1890–1986). Also according to Novikov, Molotov examined an early outline of the document in Paris and made several suggestions on how it might be improved. This information lends credence to the theory that Molotov, who favored a hard line against the West, wanted Novikov's report to present a dark and perhaps exaggerated picture of U.S. foreign policy goals to strengthen his hand against moderates.

We know that Molotov read Novikov's completed cable. What happened next is unclear. Did Molotov show the telegram to Stalin and other high-ranking officials? Did the telegram contribute to the atmosphere of confrontation building in 1946? The answer to both questions is probably "yes," meaning that Novikov's cable did indeed play an important role in the Cold War's murky beginnings.

QUESTIONS FOR ANALYSIS

1. What specific evidence does Novikov cite to prove his assertion that the ultimate goal of U.S. foreign policy is world domination?
2. In Novikov's view, how is the goal to be achieved?
3. What is Novikov's evaluation of U.S. strengths and weaknesses?

Source: From *Origins of the Cold War: The Novikov, Kennan, and Roberts 'Long' Telegrams of 1946.* Copyright © by the Endowment of the United States Institute of Peace, 1993. Used with permission by the United States Institute of Peace, Washington, D.C.

4. What point of view does he express concerning Anglo-American cooperation? Is this something the Soviet Union should fear? Why or why not?
5. How does Novikov's analysis compare with Kennan's description in the Long Telegram of the "Basic Features of Postwar Soviet Outlook, as Put Forward by Official Propaganda Machine"? What do your conclusions reveal about the reasons why Novikov's memorandum was written?
6. How does Novikov's assessment of U.S. foreign policy compare with Kennan's assessment of Soviet foreign policy goals?

The foreign policy of the United States, which reflects the imperialist tendencies of American monopolistic capital, is characterized in the postwar period by a striving *for world supremacy*.... All the forces of American diplomacy—the army, the air force, the navy, industry, and science—are enlisted in the service of this foreign policy. For this purpose broad plans for expansion have been developed and are being implemented through diplomacy and the establishment of a system of naval and air bases stretching far beyond the boundaries of the United States, through the arms race, and through the creation of ever newer types of weapons.

... The foreign policy of the United States is conducted now *in a situation that differs greatly* from the one that existed in the prewar period. This situation does not fully conform to the calculations of those reactionary circles which hoped that during the Second World War they would succeed in avoiding, at least for a long time, the main battles in Europe and Asia....

In this regard, it was thought that the main competitors of the United States would be crushed or greatly weakened in the war, and the United States by virtue of this circumstance would assume *the role of the most powerful factor* in resolving the fundamental questions of the postwar world. These calculations were also based on the assumption ... that the Soviet Union, which had been subjected to the attack of German Fascism in June 1941, would also be exhausted or even completely destroyed as a result of the war.

Reality did not bear out the calculations of the American imperialists....

The enormous relative weight of the USSR in international affairs in general and in the European countries in particular, the independence of

its foreign policy, and the economic and political assistance that it provides to neighboring countries, both allies and former enemies, has led to the growth of the political influence of the Soviet Union in these countries and to the further strengthening of democratic tendencies in them.

Such a situation in Eastern and Southeastern Europe cannot help but be regarded by the American imperialists as an obstacle in the path of the expansionist policy of the United States....

One of the stages in the achievement of dominance over the world by the United States is its *understanding with England concerning the partial division of the world on the basis of mutual concessions.* The basic lines of the secret agreement between the United States and England regarding the division of the world consist, as shown by facts, in their agreement on the inclusion of Japan and China in the sphere of influence of the United States in the Far East, while the United States, for its part, has agreed not to hinder England either in resolving the Indian problem or in strengthening its influence in Siam[1] and Indonesia....

The American policy *in China* is striving for the complete economic and political submission of China to the control of American monopolistic capital. Following this policy, the American government does not shrink even from interference in the internal affairs of China. At the present time in China, there are more than 50,000 American soldiers....

China is gradually being transformed into a bridgehead for the American armed forces. American air bases are located all over its territory.... The measures carried out in northern

---

[1]Thailand.

China by the American army show that it intends to stay there for a long time.[2]

In Japan, despite the presence there of only a small contingent of American troops, control is in the hands of the Americans....

Measures taken by the American occupational authorities in the area of domestic policy and intended to support reactionary classes and groups, which the United States plans to use in the struggle against the Soviet Union, also meet with a sympathetic attitude on the part of England....

◆ ◆

Obvious indications of the U.S. effort to establish world dominance are also to be found in the increase in military potential in peacetime and in the establishment of a large number of naval and air bases both in the United States and beyond its borders.

In the summer of 1946, for the first time in the history of the country, Congress passed a law *on the establishment of a peacetime army, not on a volunteer basis but on the basis of universal military service.* The size of the army, which is supposed to amount to about one million persons as of July 1, 1947, was also increased significantly. The size of the navy at the conclusion of the war decreased quite insignificantly in comparison with wartime. At the present time, the American navy occupies first place in the world, leaving England's navy far behind, to say nothing of those of other countries.

Expenditures on the army and navy have risen colossally, amounting to 13 billion dollars according to the budget for 1946–47 (about 40 percent of the total budget of 36 billion dollars). This is more than ten times greater than corresponding expenditures in the budget for 1938, which did not amount to even one billion dollars....

The establishment of American bases on islands that are often 10,000 to 12,000 kilometers from the territory of the United States and are on the other side of the Atlantic and Pacific oceans clearly indicates *the offensive nature of the strategic concepts* of the commands of the U.S. army and navy. This interpretation is also confirmed by the fact that the American navy is intensively studying the naval approaches to the boundaries of Europe. For this purpose, American naval vessels in the course of 1946 visited the ports of Norway, Denmark, Sweden, Turke, and Greece....

All of these facts show clearly that a decisive role in the realization of plans for world dominance by the United States is played by its armed forces.

◆ ◆

... In recent years American capital has penetrated very intensively into the economy of the *Near Eastern* countries, in particular into the oil industry. At present there are American oil concessions in all of the Near Eastern countries that have oil deposits (Iraq, Bahrain, Kuwait, Egypt, and Saudi Arabia). American capital, which made its first appearance in the oil industry of the Near East only in 1927, now controls about 42 percent of all proven reserves in the Near East, excluding Iran....

... The strengthening of U.S. positions in the Near East and the establishment of conditions for basing the American navy at one or more points on the Mediterranean Sea ... will therefore signify the emergence of a new threat to the security of the southern regions of the Soviet Union.

... The ruling circles of the United States obviously have a sympathetic attitude toward *the idea of a military alliance with England,* but at the present time the matter has not yet culminated in an official alliance. Churchill's

---

[2]Beginning in late September 1945, 50,000 U.S. Marines were deployed to northern China to assist in disarming and repatriating the Japanese troops and civilians in China and in controlling ports, railroads, and airfields. This was in addition to approximately 60,000 U.S. soldiers remaining in China at the end of the war. Beginning in 1946 the number of U.S. troops steadily declined, and at no time were there U.S. air bases "all over" China.

speech in Fulton[3] calling for the conclusion of an Anglo-American military alliance for the purpose of establishing joint domination over the world was therefore not supported officially by Truman or Byrnes,[4] although Truman by his presence [during the "Iron Curtain" speech] did indirectly sanction Churchill's appeal.

Even if the United States does not go so far as to conclude a military alliance with England just now, in practice they still maintain very close contact on military questions. . . .

◆ ◆

. . . One of the most important elements in the general policy of the United States, which is directed toward limiting the international role of the USSR in the postwar world, is the *policy with regard to Germany.* In Germany, the United States is taking measures to strengthen reactionary forces for the purpose of opposing democratic reconstruction. Furthermore, it displays special insistence on accompanying this policy with completely inadequate measures for the demilitarization of Germany. . . .

. . . Instead, the United States is considering the possibility *of terminating the Allied occupation* of German territory before the main tasks of the occupation—the demilitarization and democratization of Germany—have been implemented. This would create the prerequisites for the revival of an imperialist Germany, which the United States plans to use in a future war on its side. One cannot help seeing that such a policy has a clearly outlined *anti-Soviet edge* and constitutes a serious danger to the cause of peace.

. . . The numerous and extremely hostile statements by American government, political, and military figures with regard to the Soviet Union and its foreign policy are very characteristic of the current relationship between the ruling circles of the United States and the USSR. These statements are echoed in an even more unrestrained tone by the overwhelming majority of the American press organs. *Talk about a "third war,"* meaning a war against the Soviet Union, and even a direct call for this war—with the threat of using the atomic bomb—such is the content of the statements on relations with the Soviet Union by reactionaries at public meetings and in the press. . . .

The basic goal of this anti-Soviet campaign of American "public opinion" is to exert political pressure on the Soviet Union and compel it to make concessions. Another, no less important goal of the campaign is the attempt *to create an atmosphere of war psychosis* among the masses, who are weary of war, thus making it easier for the U.S. government to carry out measures for the maintenance of high military potential. . . .

. . . Of course, all of these measures for maintaining a high military potential are not goals in themselves. They are only intended *to prepare the conditions for winning world supremacy* in a new war, the date for which, to be sure, cannot be determined now by anyone, but which is contemplated by the most bellicose circles of American imperialism.

Careful note should be taken of the fact that the preparation by the United States for a future war is being conducted with the prospect of *war against the Soviet Union,* which in the eyes of American imperialists is the main obstacle in the path of the United States to world domination.

---

[3]A reference to Churchill's Iron Curtain Speech, delivered at Westminster College in Fulton, Missouri, in March 1946.

[4]James Byrnes (1879–1972), secretary of state from 1945 to 1947.

CHAPTER 9

The Industrialized West in an Era
of Economic Growth and Social Change

In the three decades after World War II, the people and nations of the industrialized West experienced swift and profound changes. Ideologies that had attracted millions of passionate followers before the war either died, as did fascism, or lost support, as did communism. Except for Greece, Spain, and Portugal, where dictatorships persisted, democratic governments committed to guaranteeing their citizens' well-being through unemployment insurance, state-supported pension systems, public housing, and, in some cases, economic planning gave Western Europe and the United States political tranquility that lasted until the late 1960s.

Diplomatic relationships also were transformed. European states accepted a diminished role in world affairs, and the United States took its place alongside the Soviet Union as one of the world's two superpowers. Such role reversals were especially difficult for the French and the British, who for more than a century had considered it their God-given right to manage world affairs. It was also challenging for Americans, many of whom were still uncomfortable with political and military commitments outside the Western Hemisphere.

European states lost something else after World War II: their colonies. Between the late 1940s and the early 1970s, some seventy former colonies in Africa and Asia became sovereign states, and the era of European imperialism came to an end. For the former colonial powers, this was another sign of their dwindling importance in world affairs. For the United States and the Soviet Union, these newly independent nations provided a vast new arena in which their ideological and political struggles could be played out.

Western economies also changed significantly in the postwar era. The 1950s and 1960s were golden years of economic expansion—a time when economists, politicians, and journalists routinely used the word *miracle* to describe the transition from wartime devastation to postwar affluence.

Between 1950 and 1973, the economies of Great Britain and the United States expanded at an annual rate of 3 percent, while in Germany, the growth rate averaged 6 percent a year, and labor shortages required the hiring of more than a million and a half workers from Italy, Greece, Turkey, and elsewhere. The French gross national product tripled between 1950 and 1973, while in Italy industrial production rose 70 percent between 1958 and 1963. Europe's smaller nations also participated in the postwar boom. By the 1970s, the people of Switzerland and Scandinavia had the highest standards of living in the world.

Social change was the inevitable consequence of economic growth. Urbanization accelerated as millions of small farmers and farm workers, unable to survive economically in an era of mechanized, scientific agriculture, moved to cities. Before World War II, agriculture, fishing, and forestry still employed around 20 percent of the population in Great Britain and Belgium, 25 percent of the population in the United States, and between 35 and 40 percent in France, Austria, and the Scandinavian countries. In the 1950s and 1960s, these percentages decreased by half. Urbanization was accompanied by a surge in consumer spending, as Europeans, Americans, Canadians, and Australians filled their apartments and new suburban homes with refrigerators, televisions, stereos, electric toasters, washing machines, and telephones, products no longer viewed as luxuries but as necessities of modern life. The greatest symbol of postwar affluence was the automobile. In the United States, new car sales jumped from 69,500 in 1945 to 7.9 million in 1955. In Europe, where car ownership was rare before World War II, the number of cars on the road increased from 5 million in 1948 to 44 million in 1965.

In politics, liberal democracy triumphed throughout the West. After France granted voting rights to women in 1945 and Italy did so in 1946, all adult citizens in Western democracies could vote in national elections except the women of Switzerland, who did not receive full voting rights until 1971. These voters mainly supported parties of the moderate right or moderate left, resulting in centrist governments committed to capitalism but supportive of state economic planning and a range of state-supported social programs.

The postwar years were not without conflict. The United States was plagued with racial tensions. In the 1950s, France came close to civil war over the issue of Algerian independence. Politicians everywhere continued to argue over taxes, social legislation, and foreign policy. But the wrenching divisions of previous decades—democracy or dictatorship, capitalism or socialism—no longer stirred passionate debate.

This changed in the late 1960s, when a wave of protests, demonstrations, and radical movements, driven mainly by young people, swept across the West. The first such protests took place in the United States in the mid-1960s: militant blacks challenged moderates for leadership within the civil rights movement; student demonstrations connected with the "free-speech movement" convulsed the University of California at Berkeley; and sporadic protests against U.S. participation in the Vietnam War burgeoned into a full-blown antiwar movement. In 1968, university campuses across Europe and the United States experienced strikes, sit-ins, demonstrations, and riots in which students sought goals that ranged from changing examination policies to ending capitalism. The late 1960s also saw the emergence of movements for women's liberation, homosexual rights, justice for Chicanos and American Indians, and a wide spectrum of environmental causes. More broadly, the youth counterculture rejected old standards of decorum and behavior in the name of liberation and rebellion.

These were heady times, and some radicals excitedly talked of revolution. No revolutions occurred, however, and the political institutions of postwar Western societies remained intact. But the culture and values of the West were indelibly transformed by the ferment of ideas and movements that emerged in the late 1960s and early 1970s.

◆

The Beginnings of a New Europe

At the close of World War II, Western Europe was a region of flattened cities, crippled industries, and deeply indebted governments facing food shortages, widespread homelessness, and millions of refugees. Rebuilding commenced soon after the war ended, but conditions reached a low point in 1947, when a fiercely cold winter in the north was followed by an abnormally hot, dry summer that led to widespread crop failures. As food rations were slashed and coal supplies dwindled, the people suffered and politicians and economists worried about the sustainability of Europe's modest economic recovery.

Paradoxically, despite their postwar problems and their recent record of war and economic failure, Europeans still ruled vast empires in Africa, Asia, and Oceania. Furthermore, most Europeans still believed that the continued existence of these empires was both just and necessary. It was necessary, they were convinced, because their colonial subjects were still not ready for self-rule despite decades, and in some cases centuries, of tutelage under their colonial masters. It was also necessary for the colonial powers themselves. Their empires strengthened their claims to great power status despite their wartime suffering and the emergence of the two new superpowers, the United States and the Soviet Union. Colonies were also expected to contribute to Europe's economic recovery.

Over the next twenty-five years, Western Europe did have an impressive economic recovery, but colonies, most of which were independent by the early 1970s, had little to do with it. Instead, Europeans drew on other sources of economic strength and renewal. Much of their industrial plant and basic infrastructure survived the war. Europe also had a large supply of skilled workers, technicians, and engineers who were ready to be put to work building new homes and apartments and repairing merchant fleets, railroad lines, bridges, canals, and roads. Europe's economic recovery was also sustained and strengthened by a massive infusion of U.S. aid that began as soon as the war ended. As a result of the Marshall Plan, between 1948 and 1951 the U.S. government sent $13 billion (approximately $125 billion in 2011 currency values) to Western European nations. Used to pay debts, purchase imports, modernize factories, and build infrastructure, U.S. aid contributed to Europe's ongoing economic recovery, lessened the appeal of communism, and strengthened the European market for U.S. products.

The Marshall Plan also contributed to increased political cooperation among the European states. The Organization of European Economic Cooperation, founded in 1948, brought together representatives of eighteen European nations to identify projects, coordinate planning, and allocate U.S. funds. Its success encouraged those who believed that the relatively small states of Europe could achieve prosperity and a meaningful international role only if they created a union that would serve the political and economic interests of Europe as a whole, not just those of individual states. Although the European parliament, which first met in 1952, had no authority to make actual laws, and the plan to create an all-European military force was abandoned in 1954, the experiments in economic cooperation were remarkably successful. The European Coal and Steel Community (1951) coordinated the coal and steel industries of the Netherlands, Belgium, Luxemburg, Italy, Germany, and France, and the European Economic Community, or Common Market (1957), ended all tariffs and other trade barriers among the same six nations. Industry boomed, and trade increased among the six members by 50 percent between 1958 and 1960 alone. Even before Great Britain, Denmark, and Ireland joined the Community in 1973, Common Market nations were a powerful force in the world economy.

Europe's economic boom made possible another distinctive feature of Europe's postwar history: the broad acceptance of what came to be known as the "welfare state." Basic welfare provisions had been in place in most European states by the 1930s, with some programs, such as Germany's, dating back to the 1880s. What the political leaders of postwar Europe instituted was something much more generous and comprehensive. Citizens became eligible for state-sponsored and state-guaranteed services in the areas of education, medical care, housing, recreation, subsidized or state-owned public transportation, and publically funded artistic and cultural activities. They would also benefit from the security provided by state-sponsored insurance against accidents, illness, unemployment, and the hazards of old age. Funding mechanisms and eligibility criteria varied, but every western European nation in the postwar era at some level became a "welfare state." It was a distinctive feature of the "new Europe" that emerged in the quarter century after World War II.

Great Britain Lets Go of India

60 ◆ *DEBATE IN THE HOUSE OF COMMONS, MARCH 1947*

British and Indian leaders had debated the timing and framework of Indian independence for decades, but World War II brought the issue to a head. Many Indians, embittered by the meager benefits they had received for their sacrifices in World War I, showed little enthusiasm for the British cause in World War II. In 1942, after Japan's lightning conquest of Southeast Asia, the British government offered India full dominion status after the war in return for its support in the war. Negotiations broke down, however, leading Gandhi to launch his last nationwide passive resistance campaign against British rule. Anti-British feeling intensified in 1943, when a disastrous famine took between one million and three million lives and the pro-Japanese Indian National Army organized by Subhas Bose declared war on Great Britain.

A shift in postwar British politics also affected India's future. Elections in 1945 initiated six years of rule by the Labour Party, which was less committed than the Conservatives to maintaining the empire. In early 1946, Prime Minister C. Clement Attlee dispatched a three-person cabinet mission to India charged with preserving Indian unity in the face of Hindu-Muslim enmity and arranging for India's independence as soon as possible. Although Hindus and Muslims could not reconcile their differences, on February 20, 1947, the government went ahead and announced that British rule would end in India no later than June 1948.

This led to an emotional two-day debate in Parliament in which Conservatives and some Liberals argued against immediate independence. Labour had a strong majority, however, and in March 1947 Parliament approved its plan. At midnight on August 15, 1947, predominantly Hindu India and predominantly Muslim Pakistan became independent states.

The following excerpts are from debates in Parliament on March 4 and 5, 1947. All speakers are in opposition to a proposal of Sir John Anderson, a Liberal from

Source: Parliamentary debates on Indian independence: From *Parliamentary Debates*, 5th Series, Vol. 434 (London: His Majesty's Printing Office, 1947).

Scotland, that Great Britain should promise independence by June 1948, but withdraw the offer and require further negotiations if a suitable Hindu-Muslim agreement could not be achieved.

QUESTIONS FOR ANALYSIS

1. What disagreement is revealed among the speakers on the subject of the benefits and harm of British colonial rule in India?
2. Several speakers who believed that British rule had benefited India still supported independence. Why?
3. The critics of British rule in India also supported immediate independence. What was their line of argument?
4. What view of India and its leaders do the speakers express?
5. According to the speakers, what military and economic realities make it impractical to continue British rule in India?
6. How do the speakers view developments in India as part of broader historical trends?
7. Most of the speakers were members of the Labour Party and thus sympathetic to socialism. What examples of a socialist perspective can you find in their speeches?

MR. CLEMENT DAVIES[1] (MONTGOMERY)

It is an old adage now, that "the order changeth; yielding place to new," but there has been a more rapid change from the old to the new in our time than ever before. We have witnessed great changes in each one of the five Continents, and for many of those changes this country and its people have been directly or indirectly responsible.... In all the lands where the British flag flies, we have taught the peoples the rule of law and the value of justice impartially administered. We have extended knowledge, and tried to inculcate understanding and toleration.

Our declared objects were twofold—first, the betterment of the conditions of the people and the improvement of their standard of life; and, second, to teach them the ways of good administration and gradually train them to undertake responsibility so that one day we could hand over to them the full burden

of their own self-government. Our teachings and our methods have had widespread effect, and we should rejoice that so many peoples in the world today are awake, and aware of their own individualities, and have a desire to express their own personalities and their traditions, and to live their own mode of life.... Our association with India during two centuries has been, on the whole—with mistakes, as we will admit—an honorable one. So far as we were able we brought peace to this great subcontinent; we have introduced not only a system of law and order, but also a system of administration of justice, fair and impartial, which has won their respect.... We have tried to inculcate into them the feeling that although they are composed of different races, with different languages, customs, and religions, they are really part of one great people of India.

The standard of life, pathetically low as it is, has improved so that during the last 30 years there has been an increase in the population of 100 million and they now number 400 million

[1] A London lawyer (1884–1962) who was a Liberal Member of Parliament from 1929 until the time of his death.

people. We have brought to them schools, universities, and teachers, and we have not only introduced the Indians into the Civil Service but have gradually handed over to them, in the Provinces and even in the Central Government, the administration and government of their own land and their own people.... Then in 1946, there was the offer of complete independence, with the right again, if they so chose, of contracting in and coming back within the British Commonwealth of Nations.[2]

I agree that these offers were made subject to the condition that the Indian peoples themselves would co-operate to form a Central Government and draw up not only their own Constitution, but the method of framing it. Unfortunately, the leaders of the two main parties in India have failed to agree upon the formation of even a Constituent Assembly, and have failed, therefore, to agree upon a form of Constitution....

What are the possible courses that could be pursued? ... The first of the courses would be to restore power into our own hands so that we might not only have a responsibility but the full means of exercising that responsibility. I believe that that is not only impossible but unthinkable at this present stage.... Secondly, can we continue, as we do at present, to wait until an agreement is reached for the formation of a Central Government with a full Constitution, capable of acting on behalf of the whole of India? The present state of affairs there and the deterioration which has already set in—and which has worsened—have shown us that we cannot long continue on that course.

The third course is the step taken by His Majesty's Government—the declaration made by the Government that we cannot and do not intend in the slightest degree to go back upon our word, that we do not intend to damp

the hopes of the Indian peoples but rather to raise them, and that we cannot possibly go on indefinitely as we have been going on during these past months; that not only shall they have the power they now really possess but after June 1948, the full responsibility for government of their own peoples in India....

MR. SORENSEN[3] (LEYTON, WEST)

I have considerable sympathy with the hon. and gallant Member for Ayr Burghs (Sir T. Moore),[4] because, politically, he has been dead for some time and does not know it. His ideas were extraordinarily reminiscent of 50 years ago, and I do not propose, therefore, to deal with so unpleasant and decadent a subject. When he drew attention to the service we have rendered to India—and we have undoubtedly rendered service—he overlooked the fact that India has had an existence extending for some thousands of years before the British occupation, and that during that period she managed to run schools, establish a chain of rest houses, preserve an economy, and reach a high level of civilization, when the inhabitants of these islands were in a condition of barbarism and savagery. One has only to discuss such matters with a few representative Indians to realize that they can draw up a fairly powerful indictment of the evil we have taken to India as well as the good....

Whatever may have been the origin of the various problems in India, or the degree of culpability which may be attached to this or that party or person, a situation now confronts us which demands a decision.... That is why, in my estimation, the Government is perfectly right to fix a date for the transference of power.... Responsibility is ultimately an Indian matter. Acute problems have existed

---

[2]The British Commonwealth of Nations was founded by Parliament in 1931 through the Statute of Westminster. It is a free association of nations comprised of Great Britain and a number of its former dependencies that have chosen to maintain ties of friendship and practical cooperation and acknowledge the British monarch as symbolic head of their association. Since 1946 it has been known as the Commonwealth of Nations.

[3]Richard Sorensen (b. 1884–1971) was a clergyman who served in Parliament as a member of the Labour Party from 1929 to 1931 and from 1939 to 1954.
[4]Lieutenant-Colonel Thomas Moore (1888–1971) was a Conservative Member of Parliament from 1929 to 1962. He had just spoken against the government's plan.

in India for centuries, and they have not been solved under our domination. Untouchability, the appalling subjugation of women, the division of the castes, the incipient or actual conflict between Muslim and Hindu—all those and many others exist.

I do not forget what is to me the most terrible of all India's problems, the appalling poverty. It has not been solved by us, although we have had our opportunity. On the contrary, in some respects we have increased that problem, because, despite the contributions that we have made to India's welfare, we have taken a great deal of wealth from India in order that we ourselves might enjoy a relatively higher standard of life. Can it be denied that we have benefited in the past substantially by the ignorant, sweated labor of the Indian people? We have not solved those social problems. The Indians may not solve them either. There are many problems that the Western world cannot solve, but at least, those problems are India's responsibility. Indians are more likely, because they are intimate with their own problems, to know how to find their way through those labyrinths than we, who are, to the Indian but aliens and foreigners.

Here I submit a point which surely will receive the endorsement of most hon. Members of this House. It is that even a benevolent autocracy can be no substitute for democracy and liberty....

I would therefore put two points to the House tonight. Are we really asked by hon. Members on the other side to engage in a gamble, first by continuing as we are and trying to control India indefinitely, with the probability that we should not succeed and that all over India there would be rebellion, chaos, and breakdown? Secondly, are we to try to reconquer India and in doing so, to impose upon ourselves an economic burden which we could not possibly afford? How many men would be required to keep India quiet if the great majority of the Indians were determined to defy our power? I guarantee that the number would not be fewer than a million men, with all the necessary resources and munitions of war. Are we to do this at a time when we are crying out for manpower in this country, when in the mines, the textile industry, and elsewhere we want every man we can possibly secure? There are already 1,500,000 men under arms. To talk about facing the possibility of governing and policing India and keeping India under proper supervision out of our own resources is not only nonsense, but would provide the last straw that breaks the camel's back....

FLIGHT-LIEUTENANT CRAWLEY[5] (BUCKINGHAM)

Right hon. and hon. Members opposite, who envisage our staying in India, must have some idea of what type of rule we should maintain. A fact about the Indian Services which they seem to ignore is that they are largely Indianized. Can they really expect the Services, Indianized to the extent of 80 or 90 percent, to carry out their policy any longer? Is it not true that in any situation that is likely to arise in India now, if the British remain without a definite date being given for withdrawal, every single Indian member of the Services, will, in the mind of all politically conscious Indians become a political collaborator? We have seen that in Palestine where Arab hates Arab and Jew hates Jew if they think they are collaborating with the British.[6] How could we get the Indianized part of the Service to carry out a policy which, in the view of all political Indians, is anti-Indian? The only conceivable way in which we could stay even for seven years in India would be by instituting a type of rule which we in this country abhor more than any other—a purely dictatorial rule based upon all the things we

[5]Aidan Crawley (1908–1992) was an educator and journalist who served in the Royal Air Force during World War II. He was a Labor Member of Parliament from 1945 to 1951.

[6]The British were attempting to extricate themselves from Palestine, which they had received as a mandate after World War I. It was the scene of bitter Arab-Jewish rivalry.

detest most, such as an informative police, not for an emergency measure, but for a long period and imprisonment without trial....

MR. HAROLD DAVIES[7] (LEEK)

I believe that India is the pivot of the Pacific Ocean area. All the peoples of Asia are on the move. Can we in this House, by wishful thinking, sweep aside this natural desire for independence, freedom, and nationalism that has grown in Asia from Karachi to Peking,[8] from Karachi to Indonesia and Indo-China? That is all part of that movement, and we must recognize it. I am not a Utopian. I know that the changeover will not be easy. But there is no hon. Member opposite who has given any concrete, practical alternative to the decision, which has been made by my right hon. Friends. What alternative can we give?

This little old country is tottering and wounded as a result of the wars inherent in the capitalist system. Can we, today, carry out vast commitments from one end of the world to another? Is it not time that we said to those for whom we have spoken so long, "The time has come when you shall have your independence. That time has come; the moment is here"? I should like to recall what Macaulay[9] said:

> Many politicians of our times are in the habit of laying it down as a self-evident proposition that no people ought to be free until they are fit to use their freedom. This maxim is worthy of the fool in the old story who resolved not to go into the water until he had learned to swim.

India must learn now to build up democracy.

---

[7]Harold Davies (1904–1984) was an author and educator who served in Parliament as a member of the Labor Party from 1959 to 1964.

[8]Karachi, a port city on the Arabian Sea, was soon to become Pakistan's first capital city. *Peking* is a variant spelling of Beijing.

[9]Thomas B. Macaulay (1800–1859) was an English essayist, historian, and statesman.

Economic Cooperation and Recovery

❖

61 ◆ Robert Schuman, *THE SCHUMAN DECLARATION, MAY 9, 1950*

A major step toward European integration was taken in 1951, when France, Germany, Italy, Belgium, the Netherlands, and Luxemburg agreed to form the European Coal and Steel Community (ECSC). By doing so, they limited import duties and quotas on coal and steel and placed production under the authority of a nine-member High Authority with the power of making and enforcing policy.

The ECSC was the brainchild of Jean Monnet (1888–1979), a French businessman and statesman known as the "Father of Europe." Born into a family of cognac merchants, he left school at age sixteen to work in the family business; later in life he was involved in international finance, consulting, and government service. Impressed by the Allies' coordination of economic activities in the two world wars and convinced that Europe had no future as a collection of small, individual

---

Source: From Pascal Fontaine, *Europe—A Fresh Start: The Schuman Declaration, 1950–1990* Luxemburg: (Office for Official Publications of the European Communities, 1990). © ECSC-EEE-EAEC, 1990. Used with permission.

states, he became a leading advocate of forging a true European community. After War II, the French government gave him the task of devising a plan to modernize the nation's economy. In this capacity, in 1950 he proposed coordinating the coal and steel industries of France, Germany, and other interested countries under the control of a supranational Higher Authority. Such a plan, he argued, would address French economic needs (access to German coal), political and economic realities (pressures to fully integrate West Germany into the European economy), and idealism (his long-standing commitment to a united Europe).

Monnet had little trouble convincing the government of the plan's advantages, and on May 7, 1950, the French foreign minister Robert Schuman presented Monnet's proposal to the world in a speech mainly written by Monnet. The Schuman Plan, as it came to be known, was approved by France, West Germany, Italy, Belgium, the Netherlands, and Luxembourg and went into operation in mid-1951. It was the model for the European Common Market, which "the six" approved in 1957, and was the ancestor of the Treaty of Maastricht of 1992, by which twelve members of the European Community agreed to form the European Union, adopt a common currency, and accept a commitment to control inflation and limit government debt.

QUESTIONS FOR ANALYSIS

1. According to Schuman's declaration, how will the coal and steel industries of participating countries be affected by the new organization it describes?
2. How, in Schuman's view, will the new organization help prevent war, and how will it benefit Europe and other parts of the world?
3. What powers will the High Authority exercise?
4. How will the exercise of these powers infringe on powers that national governments traditionally exercised?
5. What is the declaration's view of Europe's future?

World peace cannot be safeguarded without making efforts proportionate to the dangers which threaten it.

The contribution which an organized and active Europe can bring to civilization is indispensable to the maintenance of peaceful relations. For more than twenty years, France has acted as the champion of a united Europe, and has always had the defence of peace as an essential goal. When Europe has not shared this goal, we have had war.

Europe will not be made all at once, or according to a single, general plan. It will be built through definite achievements, first creating a [de facto] solidarity. The coming together of European nations requires that the age-old hostility between France and Germany be eliminated. The essential project ought therefore to affect France and Germany above all.

With this as our plan, the French government proposes to take action immediately in a limited but decisive area.

The French government proposes to place the whole of the French and German output of coal and steel under a joint High Authority in an organization open to the participation of other European countries.

Combining coal and steel production will immediately assure the setting up of common foundations of economic development, the first step of a European federation, and will alter the destiny of regions so long devoted to the production of armaments, of which they have been the most constant victims.

The fusion of production formed in this way will mean that any war between France and Germany will become not only unthinkable but materially impossible. The founding of this powerful manufacturing association, open to all countries who will wish to join it, will establish the true foundations of economic unification, by furnishing to all those countries the basic materials of industrial production under the same conditions.

This production will be offered to the whole world without distinction or exclusion in order to contribute to the raising of the standard of living, and to the progress of peaceful enterprises. With ever growing wealth, Europe will be able to pursue the realization of one of its essential tasks: the development of the African Continent.

As the fusion of interests required for the establishment of an economic market will be easily and quickly achieved, it introduces the condition for a larger and broader community among nations long separated by bloody conflict.

By placing basic production under joint control and by the institution of a new High Authority, whose decisions will be binding for France, Germany and the countries who join it, this proposal will achieve the first definite stages of a European federation indispensable to the preservation of peace.

In order to reach the goals just defined, the French government is ready to begin negotiations on the following points:

The mission entrusted to the high economic authority will be to insure as quickly as possible the

- modernization of production and the improvement of quality,
- the provision of identical conditions of coal and steel in both the French and German markets, and in the markets of associated countries as well,
- the development of common export procedures to other countries, and
- the harmonization of living and working conditions in these countries.

To reach these goals from the very different conditions which actually exist in the production of the participating countries, certain arrangements will have to be made, including the adoption of a plan for production and investments, the institution of price mechanisms and adjustments, the creation of a redeployment fund facilitating the rationalization of production.

The movement of coal and steel supplies among the participating states will be immediately freed from all customs and will be unaffected by different transport tolls. Conditions spontaneously insuring the most rational distribution of high quality products will gradually prevail.

In contrast to an international cartel[1] committed to distribution and exploitation of national markets by restrictive practices and the expectation of high profits, the projected organization will insure the fusion of markets and the growth of production.

The essential principles and commitments defined above will be the object of a treaty signed by the states and submitted to their parliaments for ratification. The important negotiations to specify the implementation procedures will be conducted with the assistance of an arbiter chosen by general agreement. He will have the responsibility for seeing that the agreements conform to the principles and, in the event of some unresolvable difficulty, he will determine the solution which will be adopted.

The common High Authority responsible for the working of the whole system will be composed of independent persons designated by the governments, which equal representation for all parties. A president will be chosen by general agreement of the governments; his decisions will be enforceable in France and Germany, and in the other participating states. Suitable arrangements will allow for any necessary appeals against decisions of the High Authority.

---

[1]A cartel is an arrangement among competing firms that may involve some or all of the following: price fixing, agreement on industry output and market shares, allocation of territories, bid rigging, establishment of common sales agencies, and the division of profits. The aim of such collusion is to increase profits by reducing competition.

Goals and Priorities of the Welfare State

❧

62 ◆ 1945 Labour Party Manifesto: *"Let Us Face the Future: A Declaration of Labour Policy for the Consideration of the Nation"*

Unlike the experience of most Western European states, where the building blocks of the welfare state were put into place gradually in the postwar era, the British welfare system was instituted in just five years between 1945 and 1949. Its rapid implementation was made possible by the results of the 1945 parliamentary elections, in which the Labour Party won a resounding victory. Despite Churchill's heroic leadership in World War II, the Conservatives, who had dominated British interwar politics except for two brief periods, were roundly blamed for the diplomatic and economic failures of the 1930s. Labour ran on a platform that drew heavily on the Beveridge Report, a document produced in 1942 by a government panel under the direction of the economist and social reformer William Beveridge. It identified five Giant Evils in British society: squalor, ignorance, want, idleness, and disease. It then went on to propose widespread reform in the social welfare system to address them. This is exactly what Labour promised the electorate in its 1945 platform statement, "Let us Face the Future," which is excerpted here.

With a majority of almost one hundred seats over the Conservatives, in the five years it held power, Labour changed Britain more than any other government before or since. Major pieces of legislation included the Family Allowance Act of 1945 (which provided a monthly sum to families with children); the National Insurance Act of 1946 (which created a comprehensive system of unemployment, sickness, maternity, and pension benefits funded partly by the government); the National Health Services Act of 1946 (which provided free diagnosis and treatment of illnesses); and the Landlord and Tenant Act of 1949 (which implemented a system of rent control). Labour also made good on its promise to nationalize crucial or "underperforming" businesses, including the Bank of England, the coal industry, railways, utilities, and many hospitals. In Britain and elsewhere in Europe, state control of industries and government economic planning, in the Party's view, went hand in hand with the implementation of the new welfare state.

QUESTIONS FOR ANALYSIS

1. According to the party statement, in what sense did the British people "lose the peace" after World War I?
2. What is the main cause of "depression and unemployment" according to the Labour Party? What policies does it propose to deal with this problem?

Source: 1945 Labour Party Program: "Let Us Face The Future: A Declaration of Labour Policy for the Consideration of the Nation," (London: The Labour Party, 1945).

3. The Labour Party proposes nationalization of major British industries. What problems will nationalization address and solve?
4. What will be the role of the state in the areas of housing, education, recreation, health, and social insurance?
5. What arguments might Conservatives have made to counter the specifics and general thrust of the Labour platform?

Victory in War must be followed by a Prosperous Peace

Victory is assured for us and our allies in the European war. The war in the East goes the same way.... The people will have won both struggles. The gallant men and women in the Fighting Services, in the Merchant Navy, Home Guard and Civil Defence, in the factories and in the bombed areas—they deserve and must be assured a happier future than faced so many of them after the last war. Labour regards their welfare as a sacred trust....

The people made tremendous efforts to win the last war also. But when they had won it they lacked a lively interest in the social and economic problems of peace, and accepted the election promises of the leaders of the anti-Labour parties at their face value. So the "hard-faced men who had done well out of the war"[1] were able to get the kind of peace that suited themselves. The people lost that peace. And when we say "peace" we mean not only the [Versailles] Treaty, but the social and economic policy which followed the fighting.

In the years that followed, the "hard-faced men" and their political friends kept control of the Government. They controlled the banks, the mines, the big industries, largely the press and the cinema. They controlled the means by which the people got their living. They controlled the ways by which most of the people learned about the world outside. This happened in all the big industrialized countries.... Similar forces are at work today.

What the Election will be about

Britain's coming Election will be the greatest test in our history of the judgement and common sense of our people.

The nation wants food, work and homes. It wants more than that—it wants good food in plenty, useful work for all, and comfortable, labour—saving homes that take full advantage of the resources of modern science and productive industry. It wants a high and rising standard of living, security for all against a rainy day, an educational system that will give every boy and girl a chance to develop the best that is in them....

The nation needs a tremendous overhaul, a great programme of modernisation and re-equipment of its homes, its factories and machinery, its schools, its social services.

Jobs for All

What will the Labour Party do?

First, the whole of the national resources, in land, material and labour must be fully employed. Production must be raised to the highest level and related to purchasing power. Over-production is not the cause of depression and unemployment; it is under-consumption that is responsible....

Secondly, a high and constant purchasing power can be maintained through good wages, social services and insurance, and taxation which bears less heavily on the lower income groups....

Thirdly, planned investment in essential industries and on houses, schools, hospitals and civic centres will occupy a large field of capital expenditure. A National Investment

---

[1]These were the well-known words used by Conservative politician Stanley Baldwin to describe the new members of Parliament elected in December 1918.

Board will determine social priorities and promote better timing in private investment.... The location of new factories will be suitably controlled and where necessary the Government will itself build factories. There must be no depressed areas in the New Britain.

Fourthly, the Bank of England with its financial powers must be brought under public ownership, and the operations of the other banks harmonised with industrial needs.

Industry in Service of the Nation

The Labour Party is a Socialist Party, and proud of it....

But Socialism cannot come overnight, as the product of a week-end revolution. The members of the Labour Party, like the British people, are practical-minded men and women.

There are basic industries ripe and over-ripe for public ownership and management in the direct service of the nation. There are many smaller businesses rendering good service which can be left to go on with their useful work.

There are big industries not yet ripe for public ownership which must nevertheless be required by constructive supervision to further the nation's needs and not to prejudice national interests by restrictive anti-social monopoly or cartel agreements—caring for their own capital structures and profits at the cost of a lower standard of living for all.

In the light of these considerations, the Labour Party submits to the nation the following industrial programme:

1. Public ownership of the fuel and power industries. For a quarter of a century the coal industry, has been floundering chaotically under the ownership of many hundreds of independent companies. Amalgamation under public ownership will bring great economies in operation and make it possible to modernise production methods and to raise safety standards in every colliery in the country.

Public ownership of gas and electricity undertakings will lower charges, prevent competitive waste, open the way for co-ordinated research and development, and lead to the reforming of uneconomic areas of distribution....

2. Public ownership of inland transport. Co-ordination of transport services ... cannot be achieved without unification. And unification without public ownership means a steady struggle with sectional interests or the enthronement of a private monopoly, which would be a menace to the rest of industry.

3. Public ownership of iron and steel. Private monopoly has maintained high prices and kept inefficient high-cost plants in existence. Only if public ownership replaces private monopoly can the industry become efficient....

4. Public supervision of monopolies and cartels with the aim of advancing industrial efficiency in the service of the nation....

5. A firm and clear-cut programme for the export trade. We would give State help in any necessary form to get our export trade on its feet and enable it to pay for the food and raw materials without which Britain must decay and die. But State help on conditions—conditions that industry is efficient and go-ahead. Laggards and obstructionists must be led or directed into better ways.

6. The shaping of suitable economic and price controls to secure that first things shall come first in the transition from war to peace and that every citizen (including the demobilised Service men and women) shall get fair play. There must be priorities in the use of raw materials, food prices must be held, homes for the people for all before luxuries for the few....

Houses and the Building Programme

Housing will be one of the greatest and one of the earliest tests of a Government's real determination to put the nation first. Labour's pledge is firm and direct—it will proceed with a housing programme with the maximum practical speed until every family in this island has a good standard of accommodation. That may well mean centralising and pooling of building materials and components by the State, together with price control....

Education and Recreation

An important step forward has been taken by the passing of the recent Education Act.[2] Labour will put that Act not merely into legal force but into practical effect, including the raising of the school leaving age to 16 at the earliest possible moment, "further" or adult education, and free secondary education for all....

National and local authorities should co-operate to enable people to enjoy their leisure to the full, to have opportunities for healthy recreation. By the provision of concert halls, modern libraries, theatres and suitable civic centres, we desire to assure to our people full access to the great heritage of culture in this nation.

Health of the Nation and its Children

By good food and good homes, much avoidable ill-health can be prevented. In addition the best health services should be available free for all. Money must no longer be the passport to the best treatment.

In the new National Health Service there should be health centres where the people may get the best that modern science can offer, more and better hospitals, and proper conditions for our doctors and nurses. More research is required into the causes of disease and the ways to prevent and cure it.

Labour will work specially for the care of Britain's mothers and their children—children's allowances and school medical and feeding services, better maternity and child welfare services. A healthy family life must be fully ensured and parenthood must not be penalised if the population of Britain is to be prevented from dwindling.

Social Insurance against the Rainy Day

The Labour Party has played a leading part in the long campaign for proper social security for all—social provision against rainy days, coupled with economic policies calculated to reduce rainy days to a minimum. Labour led the fight against the mean and shabby treatment which was the lot of millions while Conservative Governments were in power over long years.[3] A Labour Government will press on rapidly with legislation extending social insurance over the necessary wide field to all.

But great national programmes of education, health and social services are costly things. Only an efficient and prosperous nation can afford them in full measure....

There is no good reason why Britain should not afford such programmes, but she will need full employment and the highest possible industrial efficiency in order to do so.

---

[2] The Education Act of 1944 made secondary school free to all pupils. It had the effect of opening secondary schools to girls and members of the working class.
[3] Legislation passed in 1931 required persons who applied for unemployment benefits to undergo a review by a government official to prove they had no hidden savings or other sources of support. The "means test" was widely resented as a demeaning experience.

◆

Discontent in the Midst of Prosperity: The United States in the 1950s and Early 1960s

For many Americans, the 1950s and the 1960s were the best years in the nation's history. The country had survived the Great Depression, won World War II, and made the transition from all-out war to peacetime. Confident of their power, secure in their values, and trusting of their leaders, Americans were content to enjoy their homes, automobiles, television sets, and other consumer goods. In 1954, General Electric launched an advertising campaign with the motto "Progress Is Our Most Important Product." The phrase captured the mood of an optimistic era before assassinations, urban riots, the Vietnam War, oil spills, energy shortages, youth rebellion, and "stagflation" generated conflict and self-doubt in the late 1960s and 1970s.

More than anything else, progress in the 1950s and 1960s meant economic progress. Buoyed by cheap energy, large-scale government spending, little foreign competition, and easy credit, the United States experienced employment growth, low inflation, and rising prosperity. Although Americans made up only 6 percent of the world's population, in the mid-1950s they produced almost half of the world's manufactured goods and owned 75 percent of the world's automobiles, 60 percent of its telephones, and 30 percent of its radios and televisions. By 1960, more cars were owned in Los Angeles County than in all of Asia. Between 1950 and 1963, the U.S. gross national product nearly doubled, and real wages rose better than 30 percent. Never, so it seemed, had so many Americans had it so good.

The postwar era was not, however, entirely a time of "happy days," as the popular television show of the same name in the 1970s saw it. Between 1950 and 1953, slightly less than thirty-seven thousand U.S. troops died in Korea. Although after Korea the Cold War remained cold, Americans practiced civil defense drills and built bomb shelters in their backyards to calm their fears of nuclear attack. Unemployment hovered between 5 and 6 percent even during the 1950s boom, and it reached 7.5 percent in 1958, a year of recession. With poverty defined as having an annual income of $3,000 for a family of four and $4,000 for a family of six, 20 to 25 percent of the population lived in poverty.

The largest single group within the poor was made up of African-Americans. Almost one century after the end of slavery, racism pervaded U.S. society. In the early 1950s, Southern segregation laws required separate, but rarely equal, facilities for blacks and whites in public transportation, schools, swimming pools, drinking fountains, parking lots, and even cemeteries. Fewer than 5 percent of eligible blacks in the South could vote. Conditions were only marginally better for many blacks who had moved north. Incomes were high in comparison to what they had earned in the South, but housing for blacks was in short supply, inner-city schools were underfunded, and many employment opportunities consisted of unskilled, dead-end jobs.

As the United States moved into the 1960s, however, change was in the air. For many, the 1960 election of young President John F. Kennedy held out the promise of political change and social justice. Civil rights groups and the courts had already launched a full-scale assault on racial segregation. Women were beginning to question their prescribed roles as wives and mothers. The American public was becoming aware of the dangers of environmental pollution. Businesses were beginning to lose markets to Japanese and German competitors. By 1963, sixteen thousand U.S. troops were in Vietnam to prop up the anticommunist regime of Ngo Dinh Diem. Then, on November 22, 1963, President Kennedy was assassinated in Dallas. His vice–president, Lyndon Baines Johnson, somberly assumed the presidency of a nation on the brink of a trying new era.

"The Problem That Has No Name"

❖

63 ◆ Betty Friedan, *THE FEMININE MYSTIQUE*

After women received the right to vote in most Western democracies in the 1920s, feminist movements lost momentum. In the 1930s and 1940s, women devoted their energies to surviving the Great Depression and contributing to their nations' efforts in World War II. During the war, millions of women took factory jobs vacated by men serving in the military. By 1944, some 19.4 million American women (37 percent of the adult female population) held paying jobs outside the home, including 350,000 women in the armed forces. After 1945, however, the family-centered ethos of the postwar era consigned women to a domestic role, in which their primary functions were cooking, cleaning, caring for husbands, and raising children. In the United States, popular television comedies of the 1950s and early 1960s such as *Leave It to Beaver*, *The Adventures of Ozzie and Harriet*, and *Father Knows Best* all centered on "ideal" American families made up of working fathers, stay-at-home mothers, and well-scrubbed children who lived in uncluttered homes in all-white suburbs.

That such a life was unrealistic for many U.S. women is confirmed by the large number of women who held paying jobs in the 1950s. That such a life was emotionally and intellectually unfulfilling for millions of middle-class women is confirmed by the enormous popularity of a book published in 1963: Betty Friedan's *The Feminine Mystique*.

In the mid-1950s, Betty Friedan, a 1942 graduate of Smith College, was a housewife in a New York City suburb, a mother, and a writer for popular women's magazines. By the standards of the day she was successful, yet she was troubled by a "nameless, aching dissatisfaction" and became convinced that "there was something very wrong about the way American women were trying to lead their lives." She was also influenced by her reading of the French writer

Source: From *The Feminine Mystique* by Betty Friedan. Copyright © 1983, 1974, 1973, 1963 by Betty Friedan. Used by permission of W.W. Norton & Company, Inc.

Simone de Beauvoir's *The Second Sex*, which in 1949 had argued that women were made to see themselves as deficient, dependent, and insignificant because of traditions of patriarchy deeply rooted in the Western past. In 1963, Friedan published *The Feminine Mystique*, in which she rejected the idea that women's lives should revolve around home, husband, and family. The book caused millions of men and women on both sides of the Atlantic to reconsider the place of women in society and was an inspiration for the revitalization of feminism. In 1966, Friedan was one of the founders of the National Organization for Women and served as its first president.

QUESTIONS FOR ANALYSIS

1. What is the social and educational background of the women whose lives Friedan discusses in *The Feminine Mystique*?
2. What is the problem facing these women, and why does it have no name?
3. Based on her description of the troubles facing women in American society, what solutions do you think Friedan would propose for solving them?

The problem lay buried, unspoken, for many years in the minds of American women. It was a strange stirring, a sense of dissatisfaction, a yearning that women suffered in the middle of the twentieth century in the United States. Each suburban wife struggled with it alone. As she made the beds, shopped for groceries, matched slipcover material, ate peanut butter sandwiches with her children, chauffeured Cub Scouts and Brownies, lay beside her husband at night—she was afraid to ask even of herself the silent question—"Is this all?"

For over fifteen years there was no word of this yearning in the millions of words written about women, for women, in all the columns, books and articles by experts telling women their role was to seek fulfillment as wives and mothers.... Experts told them how to catch a man and keep him, how to breast-feed children and handle their toilet training, how to cope with sibling rivalry and adolescent rebellion; how to buy a dishwasher, bake bread, cook gourmet snails, and build a swimming pool with their own hands; how to dress, look, and act more feminine and make marriage more exciting; how to keep their husbands from dying young and their sons from growing into delinquents. They were taught to pity the neurotic, unfeminine, unhappy women who wanted to be poets or physicists or presidents. They learned that truly feminine women do not want careers, higher education, political rights—the independence and the opportunities that the old-fashioned feminists fought for. Some women, in their forties and fifties, still remembered painfully giving up those dreams, but most of the younger women no longer even thought about them. A thousand expert voices applauded their femininity, their adjustment, their new maturity. All they had to do was devote their lives from earliest girlhood to finding a husband and bearing children....

In the fifteen years after World War II, this mystique of feminine fulfillment became the cherished and self-perpetuating core of contemporary American culture. Millions of women lived their lives in the image of those pretty pictures of the American suburban housewife, kissing their husbands goodbye in front of the picture window, depositing their station-wagonsful of children at school, and smiling as they ran the new electric waxer over the spotless kitchen floor.... They had no thought for the unfeminine problems of the world outside the home; they wanted the men to make the major decisions. They gloried in their role as women, and wrote proudly on the census blank: "Occu-pation: housewife." ...

If a woman had a problem in the 1950's and the 1960's, she knew that something must be wrong with her marriage, or with herself. Other women were satisfied with their lives, she thought. What kind of a woman was she if she did not feel this mysterious fulfillment waxing the kitchen floor? She was so ashamed to ad-mit her dissatisfaction that she never knew how many other women shared it.... For over fifteen years women in America found it harder to talk about this problem than about sex. Even the psy-choanalysts had no name for it. When a woman went to a psychiatrist for help, as many women did, she would say, "I'm so ashamed," or "I must be hopelessly neurotic." "I don't know what's wrong with women today," a suburban psychi-atrist said uneasily. "I only know something is wrong because most of my patients happen to be women. And their problem isn't sexual." ...

Gradually I came to realize that the prob-lem that has no name was shared by countless women in America.... I saw the same signs in suburban ranch houses and split-levels on Long Island and in New Jersey and Westchester County; in colonial houses in a small Massachu-setts town; on patios in Memphis; in suburban and city apartments; in living rooms in the Midwest. Sometimes I sensed the problem, not as a reporter, but as a suburban housewife, for during this time I was also bringing up my own three children in Rockland County, New York. I heard echoes of the problem in college dormitories and semi-private maternity wards, at PTA meetings and luncheons of the League of Women Voters, at suburban cocktail par-ties, in station wagons waiting for trains, and in snatches of conversation overheard at Schrafft's. The groping words I heard from other women, on quiet afternoons when children were at school or on quiet evenings when husbands worked late, I think I understood first as a woman long before I understood their larger so-cial and psychological implications.

Just what was this problem that has no name? ... Sometimes a woman would say "I feel empty somehow ... incomplete." Or she would say, "I feel as if I don't exist." Sometimes she blotted out the feeling with a tranquilizer. Sometimes she thought the problem was with her husband, or her children, or that what she really needed was to redecorate her house, or move to a better neigh-borhood, or have an affair, or another baby....

Most men, and some women, still did not know that this problem was real. But those who had faced it honestly knew that all the superficial remedies, the sympathetic advice, the scolding words and the cheering words were somehow drowning the problem in unreality. A bitter laugh was beginning to be heard from American women. They were admired, envied, pitied, theo-rized over until they were sick of it, offered drastic solutions or silly choices that no one could take seriously. They got all kinds of advice from the growing armies of marriage and child-guidance counselors, psychotherapists, and arm-chair psy-chologists, on how to adjust to their role as house-wives. No other road to fulfillment was offered to American women in the middle of the twen-tieth century. Most adjusted to their role and suf-fered or ignored the problem that has no name. It can be less painful for a woman, not to hear the strange, dissatisfied voice stirring within her.

It is no longer possible to ignore that voice, to dismiss the desperation of so many American women. This is not what being a woman means, no matter what experts say.... The women who suffer this problem have a hunger that food can-not fill. It persists in women whose husbands are struggling interns and law clerks, or prosperous doctors and lawyers; in wives of workers and ex-ecutives who make $5,000 a year or $50,000. It is not caused by lack of material advantages; it may not even be felt by women preoccupied with desperate problems of hunger, poverty or illness. And women who think it will be solved by more money, a bigger house, a second car, moving to a better suburb, often discover it gets worse....

If I am right, the problem that has no name stirring in the minds of so many American women today is not a matter of loss of femininity or too much education, or the demands of domesticity. It is far more important than anyone recognizes.

It is the key to these other new and old problems which have been torturing women and their husbands and children, and puzzling their doctors and educators for years. It may well be the key to our future as a nation and a culture. We can no longer ignore that voice within women that says: "I want something more than my husband and my children and my home."

A Cry for Racial Justice

❖

64 ❖ Martin Luther King, Jr., *LETTER FROM BIRMINGHAM JAIL*

On December 1, 1955, in Montgomery, Alabama, Mrs. Rosa Parks, a black seamstress who was sitting in the back of a bus in the "colored section," refused to give up her seat to a white man who had to stand. She was arrested and fined, and in response, a young Baptist pastor organized a citywide boycott by blacks of Montgomery's bus system. The U.S. civil rights movement had begun in earnest, and with it, the pastor, Martin Luther King, Jr., achieved national and international fame as its leader. Until his assassination in 1968, King's bravery, moral vision, and moving words inspired millions of followers and forced the nation to confront its long history of racial prejudice and suppression.

Martin Luther King, Jr. was born in Atlanta in 1929, the son of Reverend Martin Luther King and Mrs. Alberta Williams King. Educated at Morehouse College, Crozier Theological Seminary, and Boston University, King served as a pastor in Montgomery and then became co-pastor of the Ebenezer Baptist Church in Atlanta with his father. After the Montgomery bus boycott, he became president of the Southern Christian Leadership Council (SCLC) and organized voter registration drives in Georgia, Alabama, and Virginia. His "I Have a Dream" speech, given at the March on Washington in April 1963, provided the civil rights movement with one of its most memorable moments. In the mid-1960s, King extended his activities to northern cities and spoke out against the Vietnam War. In April 1968, he traveled to Memphis, Tennessee, to support a strike by sanitation workers. There, on April 4, he was assassinated, by James Earl Ray, a career criminal who had escaped from the Missouri Penitentiary in 1967.

King's "Letter from Birmingham Jail," was composed in 1963 while he was serving a jail sentence for participating in civil rights demonstrations in Birmingham, Alabama. It was a response to eight white Alabama clergymen who had criticized his leadership in the civil rights movement.

QUESTIONS FOR ANALYSIS

1. What specific criticisms have been leveled against King's campaign in Birmingham? What alternatives do King's critics recommend?
2. In what specific ways does King respond to these criticisms?

Source: "Letter from a Birmingham Jail," From *Martin Luther King, Jr., Why We Can't Wait* (New York: Harper and Row, 1963). Reprinted by arrangement with the Heirs to the Estate of Martin Luther King, Jr., c/o Writers House, Inc. as agent for the proprietor New York, NY. Copyright 1963 Dr. Martin Luther King, Jr., copyright renewed 1991 by Coretta Scott King.

3. King describes his method as "nonviolent direct action." What does he mean by this?
4. According to King, what are the main obstacles preventing blacks from achieving their goals in the civil rights movement?
5. King identifies the U.S. civil rights movement with the efforts of Asians and Africans to throw off the bonds of imperialism. Is his analogy valid? Why or why not?

My Dear Fellow Clergymen,

While confined here in the Birmingham city jail, I came across your recent statement calling our present activities "unwise and untimely." Seldom, if ever, do I pause to answer criticism of my work and ideas. If I sought to answer all of the criticisms that cross my desk, my secretaries would be engaged in little else in the course of the day, and I would have no time for constructive work. But since I feel that you are men of genuine good will and your criticisms are sincerely set forth, I would like to answer your statement in what I hope will be patient and reasonable terms....

You may well ask, "Why direct action? Why sit-ins, marches, etc.? Isn't negotiation a better path?" You are exactly right in your call for negotiation. Indeed this is the purpose of direct action. Nonviolent direct action seeks to create such a crisis and establish such creative tension that a community that has constantly refused to negotiate is forced to confront the issue. It seeks so to dramatize the issue that it can no longer be ignored.... Just as Socrates felt that it was necessary to create a tension in the mind so that individuals could rise from the bondage of myths and half-truths to the unfettered realm of creative analysis and objective appraisal, we must see the need of having nonviolent gadflies[1] to create the kind of tension in society that will help men to rise from the dark depths of prejudice and racism to the majestic heights of understanding and brotherhood.... Too long

has our beloved Southland been bogged down in the tragic attempt to live in monologue rather than dialogue....

We have waited for more than 340 years for our constitutional and God-given rights. The nations of Asia and Africa are moving with jet-like speed toward the goal of political independence, and we still creep at horse and buggy pace toward the gaining of a cup of coffee at a lunch counter. I guess it is easy for those who have never felt the stinging darts of segregation to say, "Wait." But when you have seen vicious mobs lynch your mothers and fathers at will and drown your sisters and brothers at whim; when you have seen hate-filled policemen curse, kick, brutalize and even kill your black brothers and sisters with impunity; when you see the vast majority of your twenty million Negro brothers smothering in an airtight cage of poverty in the midst of an affluent society; when you suddenly find your tongue twisted and your speech stammering as you seek to explain to your six-year-old daughter why she can't go to the public amusement park that has just been advertised on television, and see tears welling up in her little eyes when she is told that Funtown is closed to colored children, and see the depressing clouds of inferiority begin to form in her little mental sky, and see her begin to distort her little personality by unconsciously developing a bitterness toward white people; when you have to concoct an answer for a five-year-old son asking in agonizing pathos: "Daddy, why do white people treat colored

---

[1]A purposely annoying person who stimulates analysis and debate about ideas and behavior through persistent criticism.

people so mean?"; when you take a cross country drive and find it necessary to sleep night after night in the uncomfortable corners of your automobile because no motel will accept you; when you are humiliated day in and day out by nagging signs reading "white" and "colored"; when your first name becomes "nigger" and your middle name becomes "boy" (however old you are) and your last name becomes "John," and when your wife and mother are never given the respected title "Mrs."; when you are harried by day and haunted by night by the fact that you are a Negro, living constantly at tiptoe stance never quite knowing what to expect next, and plagued with inner fears and outer resentments; when you are forever fighting a degenerating sense of "nobodiness," then you will understand why we find it difficult to wait.... I hope, sirs, you can understand our legitimate and unavoidable impatience.

You express a great deal of anxiety over our willingness to break laws. This is certainly a legitimate concern. Since we so diligently urge people to obey the Supreme Court's decision of 1954[2] outlawing segregation in the public schools, it is rather strange and paradoxical to find us consciously breaking laws. One may well ask, "How can you advocate breaking some laws and obeying others?" The answer if found in the fact that there are two types of laws: there are *just* and there are *unjust* laws. I would agree with Saint Augustine[3] that "Any unjust law is no law at all."

Let me give an explanation. An unjust law is a code inflicted upon a minority which that minority had no part in enacting or creating because they did not have the unhampered right to vote. Who can say that the legislature of Alabama which set up the segregation laws was democratically elected? Throughout the state

of Alabama all types of conniving methods are used to prevent Negroes from becoming registered voters and there are some counties without a single Negro registered to vote despite the fact that the Negro constitutes a majority of the population. Can any law set up in such a state be considered democratically structured?

You spoke of our activity in Birmingham as extreme. At first I was rather disappointed that fellow clergymen would see my nonviolent efforts as those of the extremist. I started thinking about the fact that I stand in the middle of two opposing forces in the Negro community. One is a force of complacency made up of Negroes who, as a result of long years of oppression, have been so completely drained of self-respect and a sense of "somebodiness" that they have adjusted to segregation, and, of a few Negroes in the middle class who, because of a degree of academic and economic security, and because at points they profit by segregation, have unconsciously become insensitive to the problems of the masses. The other force is one of bitterness and hatred, and comes perilously close to advocating violence. It is expressed in the various black nationalist groups that are springing up over the nation, the largest and best known being Elijah Muhammad's Muslim movement.[4] This movement is nourished by the contemporary frustration over the continued existence of racial discrimination. It is made up of people who have lost faith in America, who have absolutely repudiated Christianity, and who have concluded that the white man is an incurable "devil." I have tried to stand between these two forces, saying that we need not follow the "do-nothingism" of the complacent or the hatred and despair of the black nationalist. There is the more excellent way of love and

---

[2]*Brown* v. *Board of Education* is the Supreme Court decision that grew out of a suit filed in Kansas by Oliver Brown against the Topeka Board of Education when his daughter was denied permission to attend an all-white school in her neighborhood. The court ruled that segregation at all levels of public schooling is illegal.

[3]St. Augustine of Hippo (354–430 C.E.), a North African bishop and theologian, was a seminal figure in the history of Christian thought.

[4]Founded in Detroit in the early 1930s, the Black Muslims in 1934 came under the leadership of Elijah Muhammad, a Georgian originally named Elijah Poole. He moved the organization's headquarters to Chicago, where he preached black self-reliance and separatism from white society. At the time of his death in 1975, Black Muslims numbered between one hundred fifty thousand and two hundred thousand followers.

nonviolent protest. I'm grateful to God that, through the Negro church, the dimension of nonviolence entered our struggle. If this philosophy had not emerged, I am convinced that by now many streets of the South would be flowing with floods of blood....

We will reach the goal of freedom in Birmingham and all over the nation, because the goal of America is freedom. Abused and scorned though we may be, our destiny is tied up with the destiny of America. Before the Pilgrims landed at Plymouth we were here. Before the pen of Jefferson etched across the pages of history the majestic words of the Declaration of Independence,

we were here. For more than two centuries our foreparents labored in this country without wages; they made cotton king; and they built the homes of their masters in the midst of brutal injustice and shameful humiliation—and yet out of a bottomless vitality they continued to thrive and develop. If the inexpressible cruelties of slavery could not stop us, the opposition we now face will surely fail. We will win our freedom because the sacred heritage of our nation and the eternal will of God are embodied in our echoing demands....

Yours for the cause of Peace and Brotherhood,

MARTIN LUTHER KING, JR.

Silent Spring and the New Environmentalism

❖

65 ◆ Rachel Carson, *Rachel Carson Answers Her Critics*

For most of the twentieth century, environmental issues in the United States truly mattered to only small numbers of government officials and private citizens. Most Americans remained convinced of nature's limitless resiliency or resisted environmental reforms because they were too expensive or flew in the face of individualism and economic opportunity. This changed in the 1960s, when millions became deeply apprehensive about environmental degradation and committed themselves to a wide spectrum of environmental causes. It was easy for Americans to sense that things had gone drastically wrong when they were barred from swimming in dying lakes and rivers, listened to daily smog reports on the radio, and worried about links between nuclear fallout from atomic weapons testing and higher rates of cancer. To a remarkable degree, however, this new environmental consciousness also resulted from a single book, *Silent Spring*, whose publication in 1962 can be said to mark the beginning of the modern environmental movement in the United States.

The author of *Silent Spring*, Rachel Carson (1907–1964), was a graduate of the Pennsylvania College for Women in Pittsburgh and received further education at the Woods Hole Marine Biology Laboratory in Massachusetts and The Johns Hopkins University. She combined careers as a writer and an official in the U.S. Fish and Wildlife Service until royalties from her bestseller *The Sea Around Us* (1951) allowed her to devote herself fully to research and writing. Another best-seller, *The Edge of the Sea*, followed in 1955. Then in 1962 she published *Silent Spring* on a topic suggested to her by a friend who was convinced that a spraying program to exterminate mosquitoes in her hometown of Duxbury, Massachusetts, was also killing birds. Carson's main target in *Silent Spring* was the growing use of synthetic herbicides and pesticides, especially the widely used insecticide DDT (dichlorodiphenyltrichloroethane). A beautifully written book (according one admirer, "a masterpiece of scientific accuracy couched in the language of the poet"), *Silent Spring* struck a responsive chord among its readers and remained on the New York *Times* bestseller list for a year. It also had its share of detractors and critics, mainly from the chemical industry and government agencies such as the U.S. Department of Agriculture. Already unnerved by the growing numbers of scientific studies that attributed harmful side effects to herbicide and pesticide use, they tried to convince the book's publisher to suppress the book, and after having failed to do so, subjected the book to a campaign of condemnation and ridicule. Slightly over a year after the book's publication, Carson, who had been warned by supporters to expect such an assault, defended her arguments in an article published in *Audubon Magazine* in November, 1963.

Even today, although Carson's importance in the rise of environmentalism is universally recognized, *Silent Spring* remains controversial. In 2007 Senator Tom Coburn of Oklahoma put a halt to a bill that would have honored Rachel Carson's legacy one hundred years after her birth. He blamed Carson for using "junk science" to turn public opinion against chemicals, including DDT, which, he asserted, could have prevented the spread of insect-borne diseases such as malaria. *Silent Spring,* he argued, had thus contributed to millions of preventable deaths.

QUESTIONS FOR ANALYSIS

1. In what sense does Carson believe that humankind in the mid-twentieth century is reaching a turning point in regard to its relationship to the environment?
2. How does Carson justify efforts to protect animals and plants, even "useless" ones, from the damaging effects of pesticides and herbicides?
3. According to Carson, what organizations and institutions are behind the effort to discredit *Silent Spring*? What methods are they using in their campaign? What are their motives?
4. According to Carson how can the efforts to discredit her conclusions best be resisted? Do you sense she optimistic or pessimistic about the outcome?

We live in a time of challenge, which is also a time of opportunity. We live in a time when it is easy to despair, but which is also a time of great hope. We live in a time when it is necessary to know for what we stand, and to take that stand with courage.

It is, then, a time when we must have a realistic sense of values. We must decide what is worth while. We must be able to separate the trivia of today from the enduring realities of the long tomorrow.

"A thing of beauty is a joy for ever," said the poet Keats.[1] In modern times that humane and perceptive jurist, Justice William O. Douglas[2], has said that the right to search out a rare wildflower is just as inalienable as the right of a stock man to search out grass or of a lumberman to claim a tree.

There are scientific reasons as well as those which are esthetic. The world is inhabited by living species that are not only beautiful but full of meaning and significance. The evolution of the plants of today took millions upon millions of years. Who are we to assume the right, in this 20th century—a mere instant in time—who are we to say that those who come after us may never see some of today's rare and endangered species?

What right do we have to destroy the scientific record contained in a living species? How do we know that we may not have great need of what it has to tell us—or of the function it performs? . . .

In this rather tough and materialistic world, then, how much room is there for concern about our wildflowers? About all of nature? Are we being impractical when we protest the substitution of the "brownout" for the color and beauty of flowers along our roads? Are we being sentimental when we care whether the robin returns to our dooryard and the veery sings in the twilight woods?

I am confident that the verdict of history will show that we—far from being the heedless sentimentalists—were indeed the tough-minded realists.

A world that is no longer fit for wild plants, that is no longer graced by the flight of birds, a world whose streams and forests are empty and lifeless is not likely to be fit habitat for man himself, for these things are symptoms of an ailing world. . . .

In SILENT SPRING I gave many examples of the destruction of wildlife following the use of insecticides. I am sure I do not need to tell you that a determined effort is now being made to discredit these reports. People are told that the incidents I reported happened years ago, that better methods, better controls now make this sort of thing impossible. We are told that destruction of wildlife occurs only when insecticides are improperly used—"follow the directions and no harm will result."

Even as these reassurances are anxiously being given out, the newspapers carry other reports. . . .

• A few weeks ago, Canadian newspapers carried a warning that woodcock being shot during the hunting season in New Brunswick were carrying residues of the insecticide heptachlor and might be dangerous if used as food. These birds had wintered in the Southern United States, where heptachlor was used in the fire ant program. . . .

• For a number of years the eagle populations have shown an alarming decline. The Fish and Wildlife Service recently made news by announcing its discovery of lethal quantities of DDT in eagles found dead in the wild. . . .

• In Southern Michigan, state agricultural officials are again using the very poisonous insecticide dieldrin in their campaign against the Japanese beetle. According to a report sent me by a biologist on the scene the destruction of rabbits, squirrels, pheasants, and many songbirds is again great. . . .

• And in the Boston area, as a legacy from years of insecticide spraying, fish in the Framingham, Mass. reservoir are carrying DDT in amounts 10 times the legally permissible level. . . .

I was amused recently to read a bit of wishful thinking in one of the trade magazines. Industry "can take heart," it said, "from the fact that the

---

[1] John Keats (1795-1821) was an English Romantic poet. The words quoted are the opening line of "Endymion" (1818).

[2] William O. Douglas (1898-1980) served as an associate justice of the Supreme Court from 1939 to 1975. He was an avid outdoorsman, whose decisions favored environmental causes. In a dissenting opinion written in *Sierra Club v. Morton* (1972), he argued that inanimate objects (rivers, lakes, beaches, groves of trees, etc.) should have legal standing to sue in court.

main impact of the book (i.e., SILENT SPRING) will occur in the late fall and winter—seasons when consumers are not normally active buyers of insecticides . . . it is fairly safe to hope that by March or April SILENT SPRING no longer will be an interesting conversational subject."

If the tone of my mail from readers is any guide, and if the movements that have already been launched gain the expected momentum, this is one prediction that will not come true.

As you know, the threat to wildflowers and other native plants along the highways of America has become a conservation crisis. Blanket spraying of chemical herbicides to control roadside vegetation is turning our roads into barren, unsightly wastes. The wildflowers, the ferns, the shrubs bright with flowers or berries are rapidly being replaced by nearly lifeless strips. . . .

I have seen it happen along the roads in Maine where I spend the summers. I have heard the bitter complaints of the tourists and "summer people"—who came expecting beauty and found, instead, desolation.

This is one instance in which the tourists are right. For there is even more than beauty involved. Natural vegetation has its place in the economy of nature. The many millions of acres of roadside borders and highway right-of-ways are—or could be—an excellent wildlife habitat. If maintained as a community of shrubs and wildflowers, they provide food and shelter for birds and many small mammals, and for the bees too—the wild pollinators so important in maintaining many crops and other plants.

Blanket spraying destroys these natural communities. It is expensive. It contains the feature of built-in obsolescence, and has to be repeated year after year. This presumably makes the manufacturers and salesmen of chemicals happy. But it is not good community economics, and it is not good conservation. . . .

It is not necessary to feel that all who take the opposite view do so out of unworthy motives.

There are entomologists who sincerely believe that the temporary advantage of an all-out assault on an insect population is great enough to justify the risk of side effects. There are, no doubt, chemical manufacturers who cannot see beyond the examples of beneficial use.

We take the long view. We do not ask that all chemicals be abandoned. We ask moderation.[3] We ask the use of other methods less harmful to our environment. But we would be naive and unworldly if we did not recognize the fact that this is a large industry, fighting with every device to preserve its profits.

Above all, we must not be deceived by the enormous stream of propaganda that is issuing from the pesticide manufacturers, and from industry-related—although ostensibly independent—organizations. . . .

There are other packets of material being issued by some of the state agricultural colleges, as well as by certain organizations whose industry connections are concealed behind a scientific front. This material, in enormous volume, is going to writers, editors, professional people, and other leaders of opinion.

It is characteristic of this material that it deals in generalities, unsupported by documentation. In its claims for safety to human beings, it ignores the fact that we are engaged in a grim experiment never before attempted. We are subjecting whole populations to exposure to chemicals which animal experiments have proved to be extremely poisonous and in many cases cumulative in their effect.

Those exposures now begin at or before birth and—unless we change our methods—will continue throughout the lifetime of those now living. No one knows what the result will be, because we have no previous experience to guide us.

Let us hope it will not take the equivalent of another thalidomide tragedy[4] to shock us into full awareness of the hazard.

---

[3] Several critics alleged that Carson had recommended banning insecticide and pesticide use.

[4] Thalidomide, a tranquilizer used to treat morning sickness during pregnancy, was withdrawn from the market in 1961-1962 after it was linked to birth defects that affected 10,000 to 20,000 babies worldwide.

The way is not made easy for those who would defend the public interest. In fact, a new obstacle has recently been created, and a new advantage has been given to those who seek to block remedial legislation. I refer to the income tax bill passed by the 87th Congress, a bill which becomes effective this year.

This bill contains a little known provision which permits certain lobbying expenses to be considered a business expense deduction. This means that the lobbyist may deduct expenses incurred in appearing before legislative committees or submitting statements on proposed legislation. It means, to cite a specific example, that the chemical industry may now work at bargain rates to thwart future attempts at regulation.

But what of the nonprofit organizations such as the garden clubs, the Audubon Societies, to be specific, and all other such tax-exempt groups? Their status is not changed. Under existing laws they stand to lose their tax-exempt status if they devote any "substantial" part of their activities to attempts to influence legislation. . . .

What happens, then, when the public interest is pitted against large commercial interests? Those organizations wishing to plead for protection of the public interest do so under the peril of losing the tax-exempt status so necessary to their existence. The industry wishing to pursue its course without the legal restraint is now actually subsidized in its efforts. . . .

There are other disturbing factors. One is the growing interrelations between professional organizations and industry, and between science and industry. For example, the American Medical Association, through its newspaper, has just referred physicians to a *pesticide trade association* for information to help them answer patients' questions about the effects of pesticides on man. . . .

I would like to see them referred to authoritative scientific or medical literature—not to a trade organization whose business it is to promote the sale of pesticides.

We see scientific societies acknowledging as "sustaining associates" [donors] a dozen or more giants of a related industry. When the scientific organization speaks, whose voice do we hear—that of science or of the sustaining industry? It might be a less serious situation if this voice were always clearly identified, but the public assumes it is hearing the voice of science.

Another cause of concern is the increasing size and number of industry grants to the universities. On first thought, such support of education seems desirable, but on reflection we see that this does not make for unbiased research—it does not promote a truly scientific spirit. . . .

These are large problems and there is no easy solution. But the problem must be faced. It must be clearly recognized by the public, for only then will it lose some of its power to stand in the way of public good.

As you listen to the present controversy about pesticides, I recommend that you ask yourself: Who speaks? And why?

The Late 1960s: Years of Protest and Polarization

In 1960, the Student League for Industrial Democracy had chapters on three campuses (Michigan, Columbia, and Yale) and fewer than one hundred members. In that same year, however, with a new name—Students for Democratic Society (SDS)—and an increasingly radical agenda, the organization began to grow. By 1962, it had one thousand members; by 1964, twenty-five hundred members;

and by 1968, more than one hundred thousand members on some three hundred campuses. In 1968 and 1969, the SDS played a key role in organizing demonstrations, sit-ins, teach-ins, student strikes, and building takeovers at Columbia, Harvard, Cornell, the University of California at Berkeley, as well as other campuses. With its radical critique of American higher education, its denunciations of corporate and bureaucratic power, and its opposition to the war in Vietnam, the SDS became a symbol of youthful political rebellion and a leading representative of the New Left.

The meteoric rise of the SDS is just one example of the swift and bewildering changes that took place in the United States and Europe in the late 1960s and the early 1970s. Large numbers of previously apathetic young people, galvanized by opposition to the war in Vietnam, rejected the values of consumerism, capitalism, imperialism, and the Cold War and sought to "change the system" by rebelling against the authority of parents, teachers, politicians, corporations, and university administrators. In 1968, student strikes and building takeovers, which militants viewed as the first steps toward the destruction of capitalism and bureaucratic oppression, took place at dozens of universities in Europe and the United States.

Feminism also underwent far-reaching changes. The moderate feminism represented by Simone de Beauvoir, Betty Friedan, and organizations such as National Organization for Women gave way to what came to be known as the women's liberation movement. Many feminists, especially younger ones, became radical and confrontational, with agendas that went beyond better pay, easier divorces, legalized abortions, and equal opportunities in jobs, schools, and athletics. Radical feminists questioned marriage, saw men as the enemy, and sought nothing less than the complete liberation of women from the weight of sexual taboos, archaic stereotypes, and male authority.

The struggle for civil rights in the United States also became more radical and confrontational. Beginning with the Watts riots in Los Angeles in 1965 and continuing for three more "long, hot summers," inner-city blacks expressed their rage through destructive riots. Leadership in the civil rights movement shifted from moderate organizations such as the National Association for the Advancement of Colored People (NAACP) to groups that rejected white members, appealed to black pride, and repudiated Martin Luther King, Jr.'s gospel of nonviolence. They included the Black Muslims, the Black Panthers, and the Student National Coordinating Committee (SNCC) during its radical phase in 1966–1967. The Black Panthers donned menacing paramilitary outfits and carried rifles, and H. Rap Brown, who became chair of SNCC in 1967, announced that "if America don't come around, we're going to burn it down."

The storm of youthful rebellion was intense but brief. In Europe, the university strikes of 1968 were never repeated. In the United States, campus demonstrations continued for a time, with the largest protests taking place in May 1970, after National Guard troops shot four Kent State University students who were protesting the U.S. invasion of Cambodia. Within two years after the Kent State protests, however, the SDS had broken apart; Haight-Ashbury had become a neighborhood of hard drugs, crime, and derelicts;

"Black Power" was a forgotten motto; and radical feminism had lost some of its appeal.

Despite the brevity of the youth rebellion, neither Europe nor the United States would be the same after the assault on hierarchy, privilege, and tradition. Black violence and militancy forced white Americans to appreciate the depth of black anger. Similarly, radical feminism alerted the European and American public to the full range of women's grievances, leading to expanded opportunities for women in schools, professions, marriage, and athletics. Campus protests helped end U.S. involvement in Vietnam, brought about changes in higher education, and created a culture of campus activism whose idealism and spirit were later redirected to causes such as environmentalism. Although no governments were toppled and no new utopias were achieved, the radical protests of the late 1960s had a permanent, perhaps even revolutionary impact on Western culture, values, and politics.

From Civil Rights to Black Power

❖

66 ◆ Student Nonviolent Coordinating Committee, *WE WANT BLACK POWER*

By the mid-1960s, the civil rights movement in the United States had made significant gains. Legal segregation in the South had been eliminated through Supreme Court decisions and laws such as the Civil Rights Act of 1964 and the Voting Rights Act of 1965. But legal and legislative victories did not translate into jobs, higher standards of living, or the end of de facto segregation and prejudice. Rising expectations frustrated by poverty and continued discrimination stoked anger among blacks, an anger that changed the civil rights movement and translated into riots in more than three hundred cities between 1964 and 1968.

The radicalization of the civil rights movement is epitomized by the history of the Student Nonviolent Coordinating Committee (SNCC), an organization mainly of college students founded in 1960 as a spinoff of Martin Luther King, Jr.'s Southern Christian Leadership Council. SNCC members led the fight for the integration of stores and restaurants in the South through sit-ins, and in 1964 organized a Freedom Summer in Mississippi to register black voters and teach literacy and black history in Freedom Schools. Nearly sixty thousand black Mississippians were registered to vote, but at great cost. Thirty buildings were bombed, hundreds of SNCC members were beaten and arrested, and seven members were murdered.

In 1966, a militant faction won control of the organization when it elected as chairman Stokely Carmichael, a recent graduate of Howard University in Washington, DC. In 1966, Carmichael first began the chant "Black Power! Black Power!" in a speech during a civil rights march from Memphis, Tennessee, to

Source: From *The Times Were a Changin': The Sixties Reader* by Irwin Unger and Debi Unger, copyright © 1998 by Irwin Unger. Used by permission of Three Rivers Press, a division of Random House, Inc.

Jackson, Mississippi. For many, "Black Power" replaced "We Shall Overcome" and "Freedom Now" as the slogan for the civil rights movement.

The Black Power movement had antecedents in Marcus Garvey's back-to-Africa crusade of the 1920s and in organizations such as the Nation of Islam, founded in the 1930s, which called for a separate black nation. In the late 1960s, "Black Power" was embraced by the Black Panthers, the Congress for Racial Equality (briefly), and SNCC. A nebulous term, "Black Power" could mean black pride, black control of black communities, or resistance to assimilation into a totally integrated society. To some, however, it also meant hatred of white society and an endorsement of violence, as is clear from the following pamphlet issued by SNCC national headquarters in Atlanta, in 1967, shortly after H. Rap Brown succeeded Carmichael as chair of the organization.

QUESTIONS FOR ANALYSIS

1. What goals are defined in this document for the Black Power movement?
2. Why do the authors of the pamphlet believe that creating a black culture is so important to their goals?
3. According to the leaflet, why are ghetto blacks most suited to leading the Black Power movement?
4. What views of whites are contained in the pamphlet?
5. In what specific ways do the ideas expressed in this leaflet differ from those of Martin Luther King, Jr., in his "Letter from Birmingham Jail" (source 64)?

The black man in America is in a perpetual state of slavery no matter what the white man's propaganda tells us.

The black man in America is exploited and oppressed the same as his black brothers are all over the face of the earth by the same white man. We will never be free until we are all free and that means all black oppressed people all over the earth.

We are not alone in this fight, we are a part of the struggle for self-determination of all black men everywhere. We here in America must unite ourselves to be ready to help our brothers elsewhere.

We must first gain BLACK POWER here in America. Living inside the camp of the leaders of the enemy forces, it is our duty to our Brothers to revolt against the system and create our own system so that we can live as MEN.

We must take over the political and economic systems where we are in the majority in the heart of every major city in this country as well as in the rural areas. We must create our own black culture to erase the lies the white man has fed our minds from the day we were born....

The black Brother in the ghetto will lead the Black Power Movement and make changes that are necessary for its success. The black man in the ghetto has one big advantage that the bourgeois Negro does not have despite his "superior" education. He is already living outside the value system white society imposes on all black Americans. He has to look at things from another direction in order to survive. He is ready. He received his training in the streets, in the jails, from the ADC[1] check his mother did not receive in time and

---

[1]ADC stands for Aid to Dependent Children, a form of welfare payment.

the head-beatings he got from the cop on the corner....

The bourgeois Negro has been force-fed the white man's propaganda and has lived too long in the half-world between white and phony black bourgeois society. He cannot think for himself because he is a shell of a man full of contradictions he cannot resolve. He is not to be trusted under any circumstances until he has proved himself to be "cured." There are a minute handful of these "cured" bourgeois Negroes in the Black Power Movement and they are most valuable but they must not be allowed to take control....

We have to all learn to become leaders for ourselves and remove all white values from our minds. When we see a Brother using a white value through error, it is our duty to the Movement to point it out to him. We must thank our Brothers who show us our own errors.... As a part of our education, we must travel to other cities and make contacts with the Brothers in all the ghettos in America so that when the time is right we can unite as one under the banner of BLACK POWER.

We have to learn that black is so much better than belonging to the white race with the blood of millions dripping from their hands that it goes far beyond any prejudice or resentment. We must fill ourselves with hate for all white things. This is not vengeance or trying to take the white oppressors' place to become new black oppressors but is a oneness with a worldwide black brotherhood.

We must infiltrate all government agencies. This will not be hard because black clerks work in all agencies in poor-paying jobs and have a natural resentment of the white men who run these jobs. People must be assigned to seek out these dissatisfied black men and women and put pressure on

them to give us the information we need. Any man in overalls, carrying a tool box, can enter a building if he looks like he knows what he is doing.

Modern America depends on many complex systems such as electricity, water, gas, sewerage, and transportation, and all are vulnerable. Much of the government is run by computers that must operate in air conditioning. Cut off the air conditioning and they cannot function. We must begin to investigate and learn all these things so that we can use them if it becomes necessary. We cannot train an army in the local park, but we can be ready for the final confrontation with the white man's system.

Remember your Brothers in South Africa and do not delude yourselves that it could not happen here....

We must stop fighting a "fair game." We must do whatever is necessary to win BLACK POWER. We must have to hate and disrupt and destroy and blackmail and lie and steal and become blood-brothers like the Mau-Mau.[2]

We must eliminate or render ineffective all traitors. We must make them fear to stand up like puppets for the white men, and we must make the world understand that these so-called men do not represent us or even belong to the same black race because they sold out their birthright for a mess of white society pottage.[3] Let them choke on it....

The political system, economic system, military system, educational system, religious system, and anything else you name is used to preserve the status quo of white America getting fatter and fatter while the black man gets more and more hungry.

We must spend our time telling our Brothers the truth.

---

[2]Mau-Mau refers to a militant nationalist movement directed against British rule that originated among the Kikuyu people of Kenya in the 1950s. In 1952, the British government launched a military operation against the Mau-Mau movement that lasted until 1956 and cost tens of thousands of lives.

[3]Genesis 25 and 27 tell the story of how Esau, the other son of the patriarch Isaac, sold his birthright to his younger brother, Jacob, for a "mess of pottage" in a moment of hunger.

We must tell them that any black woman who wears a diamond on her finger is wearing the blood of her Brothers and Sisters in slavery in South Africa, where one out of every three black babies dies before the age of one, from starvation, to make the white man rich. We must stop wearing the symbols of slavery on our fingers.

We must stop going to other countries to exterminate our Brothers and Sisters for the white man's greed. We must ask our Brothers which side they are on.

Once you know the truth for yourself, it is your duty to dedicate your life to recruiting your Brothers and to counteract the white man's propaganda.

We must disrupt the white man's system to create our own. We must publish newspapers and get radio stations. Black Unity is strength—let's use it now to get BLACK POWER.

The Emergence of Militant Feminism

◆

67 ◆ *"No More Miss America!"*

Feminism's revival in the United States began in the early 1960s with the appointment by President Kennedy of the Presidential Commission on the Status of Women in 1961, the publication of Betty Friedan's *The Feminine Mystique* in 1963, and the inclusion of gender as one of the categories protected by the Civil Rights Act of 1964. The National Organization for Women, after its founding in 1966, campaigned to redress gender-based vocational and educational inequalities, and seemed ready to assume leadership of a liberal and moderate feminist movement.

Within only a few years, however, calls for legal equality gave way to angry demands for women's liberation. Radical feminists of the late 1960s were young, and, like black militants, angry over the huge disparity between American rhetoric about equality and the reality of their lives. Beginning in 1967 and 1968, the first radical feminist groups formed in Chicago, New York, and San Francisco, and the first radical feminist journals began to appear. In 1967, the newly founded New York Radical Women pioneered the technique of consciousness-raising, in which women met to participate in open-ended discussions of how societal oppression affected their personal lives.

Then, in September 1968, an event took place that catapulted radical feminism into the headlines and made "women's liberation" a household phrase. On September 7, several hundred women, organized by the New York Radical Women, converged on Atlantic City, New Jersey, to protest the Miss America Pageant, which in the 1960s was network television's most widely watched show. Convinced that the pageant epitomized the evils of gender stereotyping, the women picketed, tossed symbols of female "enslavement and torture" (high heels, girdles, bras, and kitchen detergents) into a trash can, briefly interrupted the nationally televised closing ceremony, and crowned a

Source: From www.redstockings.org/. Used by permission. Further information about the 1968 Miss America Protest as well as materials from the 1960's rebirth years of feminism is available from the "Redstocking's Women's Liberation Archives for Action" at www.redstockings.org or PO Box 744 Stuyvesant Station, New York, NY 10009.

sheep as Miss America. While picketing, they handed out the ten-point manifesto included here.

Lavishly covered by the media, the Atlantic City demonstration brought the new feminist agenda into the limelight and was a catalyst for a half-decade of intense activity on behalf of women's liberation. Women demanded legalized abortion, denounced sexism in language and advertising, produced a huge quantity of feminist literature and scholarship, and founded hundreds of feminist organizations.

The manifesto of the New York Radical Women distributed in Atlantic City, was included in a press release composed by Robin Morgan, a founding member of New York Radical Women, and released on August 22, 1968. It offers an opportunity to compare the organization's views with those of Betty Friedan, whose *The Feminine Mystique* had appeared just five years earlier.

QUESTIONS FOR ANALYSIS

1. According to the Atlantic City protesters, what qualities are rewarded in the Miss America Pageant? How is this a disservice to American women in general?
2. What does the document reveal about links between the Miss America Pageant protest and other protest movements of the late 1960s?
3. According to the Atlantic City protesters, what flaws in American life other than sexism does the Miss America Pageant reveal?
4. How do the issues and tone of these two manifestoes differ from those of Friedan's *The Feminine Mystique* (Source 63)?

NO MORE MISS AMERICA

On September 7th in Atlantic City, the Annual Miss America Pageant will again crown "your ideal." But this year, reality will liberate the contest auction-block in the guise of "genyooine" de-plasticized, breathing women. Women's Liberation Groups, black women, high-school and college women, women's peace groups, women's welfare and social-work groups, women's job-equality groups, pro-birth control and pro-abortion groups—women of every political persuasion—all are invited to join us in a day-long boardwalk-theater event, starting at 1:00 P.M. on the Boardwalk in front of Atlantic City's Convention Hall. We will protest the image of Miss America, an image that oppresses women in every area in which it purports to represent us. There will be: Picket Lines; Guerrilla Theater,[1] Leafleting; Lobbying Visits to the contestants urging our sisters to reject the Pageant Farce and join us; a huge Freedom Trash Can (into which we will throw bras, girdles, curlers, false eyelashes, wigs, and representative issues of *Cosmopolitan, Ladies' Home Journal, Family Circle,* etc.—bring any such woman-garbage you have around the house); we will also announce a Boycott of all those commercial products related to the Pageant, and the day will end with a Women's Liberation rally at midnight when Miss America is crowned on live television. Lots of other surprises are being planned (come and add your own!) but we do

---

[1]A term for a form of street theater with a radical political message. First used to describe the performances of the San Francisco Mime Troupe in 1966.

not plan heavy disruptive tactics and so do not expect a bad police scene. It should be a groovy day on the Boardwalk in the sun with our sisters. In case of arrests, however, we plan to reject all male authority and demand to be busted by policewomen only. (In Atlantic City, women cops are not permitted to make arrests—dig that!)

Male chauvinist-reactionaries on this issue had best stay away, nor are male liberals welcome in the demonstrations. But sympathetic men can donate money as well as cars and drivers. *We need cars* to transport people to New Jersey and back.

Male reporters will be refused interviews. We reject patronizing reportage. *Only newswomen will be recognized....*

The Ten Points We Protest:

1. *The Degrading Mindless-Boob-Girlie Symbol.* The Pageant contestants epitomize the roles we are all forced to play as women. The parade down the runway blares the metaphor of the 4-H Club county fair, where the nervous animals are judged for teeth, fleece, etc., and where the best "Specimen" gets the blue ribbon. So are women in our society forced daily to compete for male approval, enslaved by ludicrous "beauty" standards we ourselves are conditioned to take seriously.

2. *Racism with Roses.* Since its inception in 1921, the Pageant has not had one Black finalist, and this has not been for a lack of test-case contestants.[2] There has never been a Puerto Rican, Alaskan, Hawaiian, or Mexican-American winner. Nor has there ever been a *true* Miss America—an American Indian.

3. *Miss America as Military Death Mascot.* The highlight of her reign each year is a cheerleader-tour of American troops

abroad—last year she went to Vietnam to pep-talk our husbands, fathers, sons and boyfriends into dying and killing with a better spirit. She personifies the "unstained patriotic American womanhood our boys are fighting for." The Living Bra and the Dead Soldier. We refuse to be used as Mascots for Murder.

4. *The Consumer Con-Game.* Miss America is a walking commercial for the Pageant's sponsors. Wind her up and she plugs your product on promotion tours and TV—all in an "honest, objective" endorsement. What a shill.

5. *Competition Rigged and Unrigged.* We deplore the encouragement of an American myth that oppresses men as well as women: the win-or-you're-worthless competitive disease. The "beauty contest" creates only one winner to be "used" and forty-nine losers who are "useless."

6. *The Woman as Pop Culture Obsolescent Theme.* Spindle, mutilate, and then discard tomorrow. What is so ignored as last year's Miss America? This only reflects the gospel of our Society, according to Saint Male: women must be young, juicy, malleable— hence age discrimination and the cult of youth. And we women are brainwashed into believing this ourselves!

7. *The Unbeatable Madonna[3]-Whore Combination.* Miss America and Playboy's centerfold are sisters over the skin. To win approval, we must be sexy and wholesome, delicate but able to cope, demure yet titillatingly bitchy. Deviation of any sort brings, we are told, disaster: "You won't get a man!!"

8. *The Irrelevant Crown on the Throne of Mediocrity.* Miss America represents what women are supposed to be: inoffensive, bland, apolitical. If you are tall, short, over or under what weight The Man

---

[2]Actually, black contestants were officially barred from competing. Rule 7 of the Miss America rule book stated that "contestants must be of good health and of the white race." In protest, in August 1968 the NAACP organized a Miss Black America Contest, held in Atlantic City as a direct protest of the pageant. In 1970, the rule barring

black contestants was lifted, and in 1984 Vanessa Williams became the first black woman to become Miss America. Six other black women have since won the title.
[3]A reference to the Virgin Mary, not Madonna the popular singer and entertainer who burst on the American scene in the 1980s.

prescribes you should be, forget it. Personality, articulateness, intelligence, and commitment—unwise. Conformity is the key to the crown—and, by extension, to success in our Society.

9. *Miss America as Dream Equivalent To-?* In this reputedly democratic society, where every little boy supposedly can grow up to be President, what can every little girl hope to grow to be? Miss America. That's where it's at. Real power to control our own lives is restricted to men, while women get patronizing pseudo-power, an ermine clock and a bunch of flowers; men are judged by their actions, women by appearance.

10. *Miss America as Big Sister Watching You.* The pageant exercises Thought Control, attempts to sear the Image onto our minds, to further make women oppressed and men oppressors; to enslave us all the more in high-heeled, low-status roles; to inculcate false values in young girls; women as beasts of buying; to seduce us to ourselves before our own oppression.

Campus Outrage and Revolution in France

❖

68 ◆ EDITORIAL FROM *ACTION,* *"WHY WE ARE FIGHTING," MAY 7, 1968*

By the late 1960s, the number of university students in Europe and the United States had never been higher. In prewar Germany, Great Britain, and France, with a combined population of 150,000,000, only 150,000—approximately one-tenth of one percent of the total population—attended universities. Between 1960 and 1970, however, the number of French university students increased from 211,000 to 651,000, while in Great Britain, West Germany, and Italy the student population doubled. In the United States, which had pioneered mass college education, the 1960s began with 3,789,000 university students and ended with 7,850,000. For the first time in the nation's history, there were more university students than farmers.

As the number of university students grew, so did their political activism. In 1964 the Berkeley campus of the University of California was disrupted by student strikes and demonstrations when supporters of the Free Speech Movement challenged the university's decision to ban political groups from using a strip of land at the edge of the campus. In 1965 the first teach-in protesting the Vietnam War took place at the University of Michigan, and by 1967 student-led campaigns against draft boards, officer-training programs, university research for the defense department, and campus recruitment by defense contractors made college campuses the core of the antiwar movement. In Europe in the

Source: The French Student Uprising, November 1967–June 1968 by Alain Schnapp and Pierre Vidal-Naquet. English translation by Maria Jones. English translation copyright © 1971 by Beacon Press. Copyright © 1969 Éditions du Seuil. Originally published in French as *Journal de la Commune Étudiante: Textes et Documents Novembre 1967–Juin 1968.* Reprinted by permission of Georges Borchardt, Inc., for Éditions du Seuil.

mid-1960s, the German Socialist Student Union organized demonstrations against the Vietnam War, imperialism, and right-wing politicians, and Italian students occupied buildings and clashed with police to show their disgust with university practices.

None of this prepared the world for the eruptions on European and American campuses in 1968, however. Hundreds of thousands of students violently challenged the established order in campus takeovers, riots, and street clashes. Although opposition to U.S. involvement in Vietnam was a common theme—indeed, the dominant theme in the United States—no single cause or issue was at stake in the youth rebellion. In Germany, student ire focused on the Springer Press, a publisher of right-wing newspapers that students blamed for inspiring the attempted assassination of the student radical Rudi Dutschke in 1968. In Italy, the issue was an authoritarian and impersonal university system characterized by decaying buildings and indifferent professors. At Columbia, it was the university's plan to build a gymnasium on land that included a neighborhood playground.

Although student rebellions shocked the public and unsettled authorities in the United States, Germany, and Italy, in France they came close to launching a revolution. Student demonstrations began at the Nanterre campus, a new branch of the University of Paris built in one of France's worst slums. Months of agitation over teaching issues, examinations, and the right of males to visit females in their dormitories caused the dean to suspend classes on May 2. Student leaders then joined forces with radicals at the University of Paris, where demonstrations over the state of France and its system of higher education involved tens of thousands of students and led to arrests and clashes with riot police. In mid-May, industrial workers, who were concerned with rising unemployment and stagnant wages, threw in their lot with the students and joined them in a march through Paris with close to seven hundred thousand participants. In the following days, students reoccupied the university district, the Sorbonne, and approximately ten million workers, about sixty percent of the work force, went on strike. Revolution seemed imminent.

In late May and early June, however, the movement lost momentum in the face of a tough speech by President Charles de Gaulle, a promised wage increase for workers, counterdemonstrations organized by the government, and ideological divisions among the students. After a final clash between police and students on June 12, students abandoned control of the Sorbonne, and workers ended their general strike. In parliamentary elections held in late June, President de Gaulle's party won a resounding victory. The French student revolution was over, leaving a legacy of modest reforms in the university system, raises for French workers, and the memory of idealistic young people who thought they could change the world.

Weeks of protest produced a mountain of pamphlets, manifestoes, editorials, speeches, and proclamations. The following selection is taken from the May 7 edition of the newspaper *Action*, which during its brief existence in May and June served as a voice of the student movement. The editorial appeared a day after demonstrations in Paris had led to the first major clashes with police.

QUESTIONS FOR ANALYSIS:

1. How does the editorial characterize the French government?
2. According to the editorial, what other issues are at stake other than the specific grievances of the students at Nanterre?
3. According to the editorial, what do the French demonstrators have in common with student movements in other parts of Europe and the United States?
4. The editorial characterizes the French students' struggle as one against capitalism and the "bourgeois" order of society. What examples are provided to support this claim?
5. Based on the editorial's description of student grievances, what can you infer about the specific changes students envision for university education and French society?

THE REASONS FOR THE REVOLT

It is not with pleasure that students are confronting the gardes-mobiles [riot police] helmeted and armed to the teeth. It is not with pleasure that, at the period of examinations, students are responding to police violence.

It is never out of pleasure that one fights someone stronger than oneself.

For years students have been protesting the authoritarian methods that the government wanted to force upon them. Calmly, they protested against the Fouchet Reform, then against the Peyrefitte measures.[1] For years, calmly, but also in an atmosphere of general indifference the government ignored their protests just as it ignored the workers' protests. For years these protests remained vain and without response.

Today, the students are resisting.

Their only crime is to reject a University the sole goal of which is to train future bosses and docile tools for the economy. Their only crime is to reject an authoritarian and hierarchical social system which rejects any radical opposition; this means refusing to be the servants of this system.

For this crime alone, they are being rewarded by blackjacks and prison sentences.

University and *lycée* [high school] students have rallied and faced repression, because they want to defend themselves against police repression and the bourgeois government; the students are in a state of legitimate defense.

What you are also being led to believe is that this is merely a matter of the released inhibitions of a handful of isolated agitators who, of course, come from Nanterre, the source of all evil. Recourse to "nanterrorism" explains nothing. The government is easily reassured: the Nanterre "trouble makers" are not and never have been isolated. If this were not true, how may we explain the fact that students all over Europe are demonstrating? Where there is general unrest there are general causes.

---

[1] Christian Fouchet (1911–1974) was minister of education from 1962 to 1967. In February 1967, he announced wide-ranging reforms to include more programs in science and technology and to raise admissions and graduation standards. It was left to Alain Payerfitte (1925–1999), who was education minister in 1967–1968, to carry out the reforms.

Students and faculty complained that the reforms did not address problems of overcrowding and underfunding. Some believed new admissions standards (which no longer guaranteed university admission to any student who passed the national baccalaureate examination) disadvantaged working class students.

ALL OVER EUROPE

To stop the student revolt, beheading Nanterre would not be enough: the revolt that has now started in Paris has no boundaries; in Berlin, thousands of students have checkmated a strong reactionary governmental authority. The SDS[2] too was only a small handful of agitators; today it represents the only large movement opposed to growing fascism in Western Germany. In Italy, thousands of students have enforced their right to question the social system. They have responded to violent repression through demonstrations that were even more violent than those of last Friday. In Spain, England, Brazil; in Louvain [Belgium], throughout Europe and the world, students have taken to the streets to confront the forces of bourgeois "order." Everywhere, even in Paris, the violence of the repression has shown that governments are afraid of these movements, apparently so weak, but which have nevertheless begun to upset the existing order. However, press campaigns have tried to isolate and discredit the movements: it is not thanks to any particular love on the part of journalists that student revolts have made the front page of the newspapers. On the contrary, their only aim is to proportion the hate campaign to the potential danger to the social order.

THE SAME COMBAT

In Paris and in Nanterre they are not fighting alone; they are not fighting only for themselves. In Germany, on May first, tens of thousands of students and workers were *together*, on the initiative of the SDS, in the first anti-capitalist demonstration that has taken place in Berlin since Nazism. The "handful of agitators" became a mass movement. Those who are combating the capitalist University stood shoulder to shoulder with those who are combating capitalist exploitation.

In France we also know that our fight has only begun; we know that youth is sensitive to the capitalist crisis and to the crisis of imperialism oppressing people in Vietnam, in Latin America, everywhere in the Third World. In Redon, in Caen,[3] young workers are revolting violently, more violently than we are. On that subject the press, which is attacking us today, has remained silent. In spite of the government, in spite of the silence and the manipulations of its servile press, our struggle and theirs will converge.

Today students are becoming aware of what they are being trained for: to be managers for the existing economic system, paid to make it function in the best possible way. Their fight concerns all workers because it is also the workers' fight: they refuse to become professors in the service of an educational system which chooses the sons of the bourgeoisie and eliminates the others; sociologists who manufacture slogans for governmental election campaigns; psychologists responsible for making "worker teams function" in the best interest of the employers; managers responsible for applying against the workers a system to which they themselves are subjected.

Young people in the high schools, universities, and from the working class reject the future offered them by today's society; they reject unemployment, which is becoming a growing threat; they reject today's University, which gives them only worthless, ultra-specialized training and which, under the pretext of "selection," reserves know-how for sons of the bourgeoisie, and is but a tool for repression of all non-conformist ideas in the interest of the ruling class.

When young people resort to violent revolt, they are conscious of making this rejection stand out more clearly; they are conscious that their fight can give results only if the workers understand its meaning and make it their own. This is why today we are continuing the fight; this is why we appeal to you.

---

[2]SDS stands for Sozialistischer Deutsher Studentenbund (German Socialist Student Union). Founded in 1946 as the student organization for the Social Democratic Party, it severed its ties with the party in 1961. It had a membership of approximately 2,500 in 1968.

[3]Beginning in the fall of 1967, strikes accompanied by violence occurred at auto and truck manufacturing plants in Le Mans, Caen, and Redon.

CHAPTER 10

Worlds Apart: The Soviet Union, the Soviet Bloc, and China

For three decades after the Russian Revolution of 1917, the Union of Soviet Socialist Republics was the world's only Marxist state. Then in the decade following World War II, it was joined by twelve others. In Europe, Albania, Yugoslavia, Poland, Hungary, Bulgaria, Romania, Czechoslovakia, and East Germany became communist between 1945 and 1948; in Asia, communist regimes were established in North Korea in 1945, China and Mongolia in 1949, and North Vietnam in 1954. A handful of other states, most notably Cuba in 1959, also became communist, but in large measure the era of communist expansion ended in the mid-1950s. By then, approximately one-third of the world's people lived under communist rule.

During the 1950s and 1960s, these states existed in a largely self-contained universe separated economically and culturally from the rest of the world. This separation began in the 1920s and 1930s when many nations were unwilling to grant the USSR full diplomatic recognition and Stalin made the decision to concentrate on building "socialism in one country." It widened after World War II when mutual fears and hostilities generated by the Cold War created new barriers to trade, tourism, and cultural exchange.

During the 1950s and 1960s, self-contained development, not foreign trade, was the goal of communist economic planners, and what foreign trade took place was largely among the communist states themselves. Currencies of communist countries were not traded on international markets, and communist states did not participate in international agreements on trade and tariffs. Tourism between communist and noncommunist states was discouraged, and when journalists or scholars from one bloc visited a nation in the other ideological camp, their activities were closely monitored by police and intelligence agencies. The most powerful symbol of the division between the communist and non-communist worlds was the Berlin Wall, a twenty-five-mile barrier through Berlin constructed in 1961 on orders of the East German government to stop the flight of its citizens to the West.

Communist states all shared a number of common characteristics. Most, out of choice or coercion, at first modeled their political systems and economies on those of the Soviet Union. This meant control of the government by the Communist Party, and control of the Party by a dictator or a small handful of officials. It also meant abolition of rival political parties; eradication of opponents; the suppression of civil liberties; censorship; state control of newspapers, radio, and television; and the lavish use of propaganda. Economic policies followed the Stalinist model of central planning, nationalization of major industries and businesses, and the collectivization of agriculture. The goal was rapid industrialization, with iron and steel, heavy machinery, and power generation taking precedence over consumer goods. Most communist regimes were aggressively secular and sought to undermine established religions.

Communist states did collaborate with one another. In 1949, after rejecting the U.S. offer of economic aid as part of the Marshall Plan, the Soviet Union and its European satellites formed the Council of Mutual Economic Assistance (Comecon) to facilitate and coordinate economic development. In 1955, the same group of nations ratified the Warsaw Pact, in which they pledged to come to one another's defense if attacked. This was a response to the acceptance of West Germany into the North Atlantic Treaty Organization (NATO), the anti-Soviet military alliance founded in 1949 and consisting originally of Canada, the United States and ten European states. The Soviet Union and China signed a pact of friendship and cooperation in 1950, and during the 1950s the Soviet Union provided China with financial and technical aid.

There were, however, fissures within the communist camp from the start. Yugoslavia's Marshal Tito gradually broke with Stalin in 1947 and 1948, and he held Yugoslavia out of Comecon and the Warsaw Pact. Albania at first aligned itself with the Soviet Union, then switched to China, and in the early 1970s embarked on an independent course. Ideological differences and border disputes turned China and the Soviet Union into bitter antagonists in the 1960s, and in the 1970s many world leaders anticipated a full-scale war between the two communist powers.

Furthermore, many communist states sought to develop their own distinct variety of socialism. China abandoned central planning during the Great Leap Forward (1958–1960), and Yugoslavia fashioned a mixed economy in the 1950s, as did Hungary in the 1960s. Poland resisted both agricultural collectivization and suppression of the Roman Catholic Church. Broad-based movements for democratization materialized in Poland and East Germany in 1953, Hungary in 1956, and Czechoslovakia in 1968, only to have them crushed by military force. Even the Soviet Union experimented with liberalization and economic reform after Stalin's death in 1953. The communist family of nations in the 1950s and 1960s was neither static nor lacking in conflict.

Destalinization and Dissent in the Soviet Union

Following their heroic and costly victory over Germany in World War II, the Soviet people looked forward to an era of greater freedom, less censorship, and better standards of living. Unfortunately, their aspirations did not match those of their leader, Joseph Stalin. In the face of staggering economic problems and threats from the West in the emerging Cold War, his priorities were rebuilding industry and maintaining a strong military, including the development of atomic weapons. His Fourth and Fifth Five-Year Plans, adopted in 1946 and 1951, stressed heavy industry rather than of agriculture and consumer needs, just as previous Five-Year Plans had done in prewar years. As a result, the Soviet Union remained the world's second greatest industrial state after the United States, but the Soviet people faced food rationing, housing shortages, and demands for ever-greater sacrifices. They also experienced renewed terror and repression. By 1952, more than 2.5 million individuals were being held in labor camps, one-third of whom had been accused of vaguely defined "crimes against the revolution." When in late 1952 nine prominent physicians were arrested and tried for attempting to undermine the state by poisoning high officials and intentionally misdiagnosing their medical problems, a new era of show trials and terror seemed imminent.

No such trials occurred, however. One month after Stalin died of a stroke on March 5, 1953, the Soviet Union's new collective leadership announced that a reexamination of the case had shown that the charges against the doctors were false and their confessions had been obtained by torture. The doctors were exonerated, and the seven who had survived their imprisonment were freed. The acknowledgment that the "Doctors' Plot" was a fraud was an early indication that the USSR was entering a decade of modest reform.

Although the Soviet Union's new leaders differed on many issues, they agreed that no single individual should be allowed to have the kind of dictatorial power exercised by Stalin. Instead, they favored collective rule by the roughly twenty-five men who were members of the Politburo (known as the Presidium between 1952 and 1966) and the Secretariat, the two chief executive bodies of the Soviet Communist Party and the Soviet state. From 1957 until his fall in 1964, Nikita Khrushchev was recognized as the undisputed leader of the Party and the government, but he was "first among equals," not an all-powerful dictator.

The Soviet Union's new leaders also restrained the activities of the secret police, presided over a "thaw" in the country's cultural and intellectual life, and reduced the use of terror as an instrument of government. Within a year of Stalin's death, they released almost one million prisoners from jails and labor camps. In economic matters, they retained the basic features of Stalin's centrally planned economy, but they accorded more decision-making powers to regional economic councils and gave greater autonomy and incentives to factory managers. They also sought to increase agricultural production by opening up millions of acres of "virgin land" to cultivation.

Many of these policies, especially in agriculture, were failures; others, such as greater freedom for artists and writers, were never popular with conservatives. In any case, this brief spurt of reformism did not survive the fall of Khrushchev in 1964. His successors repudiated his risky economic and political experiments, choosing instead to pursue cautious, uninspired policies that propped up the Soviet system but failed to address its flaws. The Soviet Union entered a period of stagnation that lasted twenty years and set the stage for its dissolution in 1991.

Stalin's Posthumous Fall

❖

69 ◆ Nikita Khrushchev, *SPEECH TO THE TWENTIETH PARTY CONGRESS, FEBRUARY 25, 1956*

"Destalinization"—the Soviet government's retreat from the policies and ruling style of its long-time dictator—began shortly after Stalin's death in 1953. Nonetheless, the slightly more than one thousand Communist officials who attended the Twentieth Party Congress in Moscow were uniformly shocked when on February 25, 1956, Nikita Khrushchev, the Party's first secretary and former Stalin confidant, presented a "secret speech" that required them to abandon deep-seated beliefs about Stalin and their country's recent past. As described by Khrushchev, Stalin was neither a hero nor a visionary. Instead, he was a suspicious, cruel, and selfish tyrant whose intentions, policies, judgment, and wartime leadership were uniformly flawed. Following the speech, Stalin's name was removed from cities, landmarks, and facilities that had been named after him, and in 1961 his remains were transferred from the Lenin Mausoleum, where his glass-covered coffin had rested next to Lenin's, to a gravesite under the Kremlin wall alongside those of minor Soviet generals and politicians. While alive, Stalin had held on to power for a quarter of a century; after his death, he held on to his reputation for just a few years.

Although destalinization was supported by a number of reform-minded Soviet politicians, Khrushchev was its main proponent. Born into poverty and with little formal education, Khrushchev joined the Communist Party after World War I and rapidly rose in its ranks after he abandoned his career as a mine overseer and devoted himself fully to Party work. In the 1930s, he became a protégé of Stalin, who appointed him to leadership positions in Moscow and Ukraine. He dutifully and efficiently carried out Stalin's directives during the Terror of 1936–1938, and as a result he was named to the Politburo in 1939. After the war, he took over his old job as Moscow Party chief while also serving as first secretary of the Central Committee of the Communist Party. For several years before Stalin's death, he was part of the inner circle that regularly joined Stalin for nights of eating, drinking, and watching American films at the Kremlin or in Stalin's country home.

Source: Khrushchev's "secret speech": *Congressional Record: Proceedings and Debates of the 84th Congress, 2nd session* (May 22, 1956–June 11, 1956), C11, Part 7 (June 4, 1956), pp. 9389–9403.

Despite his close ties with Stalin, after the dictator's death Khrushchev became the leading proponent of destalinization. His denunciation of Stalin at the Twentieth Party Congress was intended to solidify his support as leader of the proreform faction and discredit his conservative rivals. In the short term this strategy was successful, but the "secret" speech had unintended consequences once its contents became known. It raised doubts about a party that had allowed Stalin to gain and misuse such great power. It also helped inspire revolts in 1956 in Hungary and Poland, further weakening the Soviet Union's control over its satellites and temporarily strengthening the position of Khrushchev's opponents.

Khrushchev outmaneuvered his adversaries and in 1958 was elevated to the position of premier, giving him dominance over the party and state. Following a number of diplomatic missteps, however, in 1964 the Central Committee voted to remove him from office. He was provided with a pension and an apartment, and after overcoming a bout of severe depression managed to write his memoirs, which were published in 1970. Although harassed by the security police, he was not shot, as surely he would have been except for the destalinization campaign he himself had sponsored.

QUESTIONS FOR ANALYSIS

1. According to Khrushchev, did Stalin have any redeeming features, or is his assessment of the dictator totally negative?
2. In Khrushchev's view, in what ways did Stalin's approach to government differ from that of Lenin?
3. According to Khrushchev, what were the salient features of Stalin's personality?
4. What were Khrushchev's criticisms of Stalin's Great Purge of 1936–1938?
5. What, in Khrushchev's view, were Stalin's deficiencies as a wartime leader?
6. How does Khrushchev respond to the rhetorical question he poses for himself, "Where were the members of the Politburo?" Why did they not assert themselves against the cult of the individual? What is you evaluation of his responses?

After Stalin's death, the Central Committee began to implement a policy of explaining concisely and consistently that it is impermissible and foreign to the spirit of Marxism-Leninism to elevate one person, to transform him into a superman possessing supernatural characteristics, akin to those of a god. Such a man supposedly knows everything, sees everything, thinks for everyone, can do anything, is infallible in his behavior.

Such a belief about a man, and specifically about Stalin, was cultivated among us for many years....

At present, we are concerned with a question which has immense importance for the Party now and for the future—with how the cult of the person of Stalin has been gradually growing, the cult which became at a certain specific stage the source of a whole series of exceedingly serious and grave perversions of Party principles, of Party democracy, of revolutionary legality....

[STALIN'S GOVERNING STYLE]

While ascribing great importance to the role of the leaders and organizers of the masses, Lenin at the same time mercilessly stigmatized every manifestation of the cult of the individual...

Lenin taught that the Party's strength depends on its indissoluble unity with the masses, on the fact that behind the Party follows the people—workers, peasants, and the intelligentsia. Lenin said, "Only he who believes in the people, who submerges himself in the fountain of the living creativeness of the people, will win and retain power."

As later events have proven, Lenin's anxiety [about Stalin] was justified. In the first period after Lenin's death. Stalin still paid attention to his advice, but later he began to disregard the serious admonitions of Vladimir Ilyich [Lenin].... The negative characteristics of Stalin, which, in Lenin's time, were only incipient, transformed themselves during the last years into a grave abuse of power by Stalin, which caused untold harm to our Party....

There was no matter so important that Lenin himself decided it without asking for advice and approval of the majority of the Central Committee members or of the members of the Central Committee's Politburo. In the most difficult period for our Party and our country, Lenin considered it necessary regularly to convoke Congresses, Party Conferences and Plenary sessions of the Central Committee at which all the most important questions were discussed and where resolutions, carefully worked out by the collective of leaders, were approved.

Whereas, during the first few years after Lenin's death, Party Congresses and Central Committee Plenums took place more or less regularly, later, when Stalin began increasingly to abuse his power, these principles were brutally violated. This was especially evident during the last 15 years of his life.... It should be sufficient to mention that during all the years of the Patriotic War [World War II] not a single Central Committee Plenum took place....

In practice, Stalin ignored the norms of Party life and trampled on the Leninist principle of collective Party leadership.

[THE GREAT PURGE]

Stalin acted not through persuasion, explanation and patient cooperation with people, but by imposing his concepts and demanding absolute submission to his opinion. Whoever opposed these concepts or tried to prove his [own] viewpoint and the correctness of his [own] position was doomed to removal from the leadership collective and to subsequent moral and physical annihilation. This was especially true during the period following the 17th Party Congress [1934], when many prominent Party leaders and rank-and-file Party workers, honest and dedicated to the cause of Communism, fell victim to Stalin's despotism....

A fact worth noting is that extreme repressive measures were not used against the Trotskyites, the Zinovievites, the Bukharinites,[1] and others during the course of the furious ideological fight against them [in the 1920s]. The fight was on ideological grounds. But some years later, when socialism in our country was fundamentally constructed, when the exploiting classes were generally liquidated, when Soviet social structure had radically changed,... when the ideological opponents of the Party were long since defeated politically—then repression directed against them began. It was precisely during this period that the practice of mass repression through the Government apparatus was born, first against the enemies of Leninism, long since politically defeated by the Party—and subsequently also against many honest Communists, against those Party cadres who had borne the heavy load of the Civil War and the first and most difficult years of industrialization and collectivization, who had fought actively against

---

[1]Trotskyites were followers of Leon Trotsky, who had been Stalin's main rival for control of the Party after Lenin's death; Grigory Zinoviev was a one-time ally of Stalin who gravitated to the Trotsky camp after breaking with Stalin in 1925; Nikolai Bukharin was a "right deviationist" who opposed Stalin's plan to collectivize agriculture.

the Trotskyites and the rightists for the Leninist Party line.

Stalin originated the concept "enemy of the people." This term automatically made it unnecessary that the ideological errors of a man or men engaged in a controversy be proven. It made possible the use of the cruelest repression, violating all norms of revolutionary legality, against anyone who in any way disagreed with Stalin, against those who were only suspected of hostile intent, against those who had bad reputations. The concept "enemy of the people" actually eliminated the possibility of any kind of ideological fight or the making of one's views known on this or that issue, even [issues] of a practical nature. On the whole, the only proof of guilt ... was the "confession" of the accused himself. As subsequent probing has proven, "confessions" were acquired through physical pressures against the accused. This led to glaring violations of revolutionary legality and to the fact that many entirely innocent individuals—who in the past had defended the Party line—became victims....

Arbitrary behavior by one person encouraged and permitted arbitrariness in others. Mass arrests and deportations of many thousands of people, execution without trial and without normal investigation created conditions of insecurity, fear and even desperation....

Stalin was a very distrustful man, sickly suspicious.... He could look at a man and say: "Why are your eyes so shifty today?" or "Why are you turning so much today and avoiding to look me directly in the eyes?" The sickly suspicion created in him a general distrust even toward eminent Party workers whom he had known for years. Everywhere and in everything he saw "enemies," "two-facers" and "spies." Possessing unlimited power, he indulged in great willfulness and stifled people morally as well as physically. A situation was created where one could not express one's own volition.

[STALIN AS WARTIME LEADER]

"During ... and after the war ...", Stalin advanced the thesis that the tragedy our nation experienced in the first part of the war was the result of an "unexpected" attack by the Germans against the Soviet Union. But, comrades, this is completely untrue. As soon as Hitler came to power in Germany he assigned to himself the task of liquidating Communism. The fascists were saying this openly. They did not hide their plans.

In order to attain this aggressive end, all sorts of pacts and blocs were created, such as the famous Berlin-Rome-Tokyo Axis.[2] Many facts from the prewar period clearly showed that Hitler was going all out to begin a war against the Soviet state, and that he had concentrated large armies, together with armored units, near the Soviet borders.

Documents which have now been published show that [as early as] April 3, 1941 Churchill, through his ambassador to the USSR, ... personally warned Stalin that the Germans had begun regrouping their armed units with the intent of attacking the Soviet Union.

We must assert that information of this sort concerning the threat of German armed invasion of Soviet territory was coming in also from our own military and diplomatic sources. However, because the leadership was conditioned against such information, such data was dispatched with fear and assessed with reservation....

Very grievous consequences, especially with regard to the beginning of the war, followed Stalin's annihilation of many military commanders and political workers during 1937–1941 because of his suspiciousness and through slanderous accusations.... During this time, the cadre of leaders who had gained military experience.... was almost completely liquidated.

The policy of large-scale repression against military cadres led also to undermined military

---

[2]In 1936, Germany and Japan signed the Anti-Cominterm Pact, by which the two powers agreed to consult with one another and decide on "appropriate action" if either was

attacked by the Soviet Union. In 1937, Italy also signed the pact. The three nations came to be known as the Axis Powers during World War II.

discipline, because for several years officers of all ranks and even soldiers in Party and Komsomol cells were taught to "unmask" their superiors as hidden enemies.

However, we speak not only about the moment when the war began, which led to our Army's serious disorganization and brought us severe losses. Even after the war began, the nervousness and hysteria which Stalin demonstrated while interfering with actual military operations caused our Army serious damage.

Stalin was very far from understanding the real situation that was developing at the front. This was natural because, during the whole Patriotic War, he never visited any section of the front....

[THE ISSUE OF SHARED RESPONSIBILITY]

Some comrades may ask us: Where were the members of the Politburo? Why did they not assert themselves against the cult of the individual in time? And why is this being done only now? First of all, we have to consider the fact

that the members of the Politbiuro viewed these matters in a different way at different times. Initially, many of them backed Stalin actively because he was one of he strongest Marxists and his logic, his strength and his will greatly influenced [Party] cadres and Party work....

Later, however, Stalin, abusing his power more and more, began to fight eminent Party and Government leaders and to use terroristic methods against honest Soviet people....

It is clear that such conditions put every member of the Politburo in a very difficult situation. And, when we also consider the fact that in the last years Central Committee Plenary sessions were not convened and that sessions of the Politburo occurred only occasionally, from time to time, then we will understand how difficult it was for any member of the Politbiuro to take a stand against one or another unjust or improper procedure, against serious errors and shortcomings in leadership practices.

As we have already shown, many decisions were taken either by one person or in a roundabout way, without collective discussion....

Voices of Dissent

❧

70 ◆ Andrei Sakharov, Roy Medvedev, and Valentin Turchin, *LETTER TO COMRADES BREZHNEV, KOSYGIN, AND PODGORNY*

Following Stalin's death in 1953, the Soviet Union's new leaders tolerated a brief "thaw" in the country's cultural life in which artists, writers, and composers demanded greater freedom and in some of their works made sharp criticisms of Soviet society. This was followed by a "freeze" between 1956 and 1958 in the wake of the Hungarian revolt of 1956 and the foreign publication in 1957 of Boris Pasternak's *Doctor Zhivago*, the novel, in which the hero's deeply spiritual nature is crushed by the Russian Revolution and the civil war. Beginning in 1958, Khrushchev presided over another thaw, but he was leaning toward renewed repression when he fell from power in 1964.

Repression proved to be the policy of Khrushchev's cautious successors, Leonid Brezhnev (1906–1982) and Alexis Kosygin (1904–1980). Nonconforming writers continued to produce literary works, but with no publishing opportunities in the

Source: From *An End to Silence: Uncensored Opinion in the Soviet Union*, edited by Stephen F. Cohen, translated by George Saunders. Copyright © 1982 by W.W. Norton & Company, Inc. Used by permission of W.W. Norton & Company, Inc.

Soviet Union, they circulated them in handwritten, typed, or mimeographed versions or had them published abroad. In 1966, the government sought to intimidate writers by bringing to trial and sentencing to hard labor two authors, Andrei Siniavsky and Juli Daniel, who had arranged to have their works smuggled into the Soviet Union after publication in the West. When outraged intellectuals campaigned to overturn their sentences, the government arrested four of their defenders in 1967 and gave them harsher punishments than those imposed on Siniavsky and Daniel.

The government's crackdown galvanized many other writers to continue the fight for their freedoms. In 1970, the nuclear physicist Andrei Sakharov (1921–1989) organized the Human Rights Movement, intended to protest official policies that denied human rights; other dissidents produced the underground Russian journal *The Chronicle of Current Events*, which published reports of human rights abuses. The government responded by sending some of its critics into exile or to psychiatric hospitals to cure their "insanity." During this stand-off, Sakharov, with the help of Roy Medvedev, a historian, and Valentin Turchin, a physicist, sent an appeal for greater freedom to the country's three most powerful politicians, Leonid Brezhnev, the Party secretary; Alexis Kosygin, the premier; and Nikolai Podgorny, the first secretary of the Politburo.

Nothing came of the three authors' appeal. Five years later, in 1975, Sakharov was awarded the Nobel Peace Prize for his efforts on behalf of disarmament and Soviet democratization. The government refused him permission to leave the Soviet Union to receive the award, and in 1980 sent him into internal exile in the city of Gorky. Sakharov was released in 1986 and died three years later.

QUESTIONS FOR ANALYSIS

1. How would you characterize the three authors' attitude toward socialism and Marxism?
2. What, according to the authors, are the main problems facing the Soviet Union, and what has caused these problems?
3. How do the authors view the West?
4. What do the authors mean by the term democracy?
5. How, in the authors' opinion, will democratic reforms help solve the Soviet Union's economic and political problems?

Respected Comrades:

Over the past decade, menacing signs of breakdown and stagnation have begun to show themselves in the economy of our country, the roots of which go back to an earlier period and are very deep-seated.... A great mass of data is available showing mistakes in the determination of technical and economic policy in industry and agriculture and an intolerable procrastination about finding solutions to urgent problems. Defects in the system of planning, accounting, and incentives often cause contradictions between local and departmental interests and those of the state and nation. As a result, new means of developing production potential are not being discovered or properly put to use, and technical progress has slowed down abruptly. For these very reasons, the natural wealth of the country is often destroyed with impunity and without any supervision or controls: forests are leveled, reservoirs polluted, valuable agricultural land flooded, soil eroded or salinized, and so on. The chronically difficult situation in agriculture, particularly in regard to livestock, is well known. The population's real income in recent years has hardly grown at all; food supply and medical and consumer services are improving very slowly, and with unevenness between regions. The number of goods in short supply continues to grow. There are clear signs of inflation.

Of particular concern regarding our country's future is the lag in the development of education: our total expenditures for education in all forms are three times below what they are in the United States, and are rising at a slower rate. Alcoholism is growing in a tragic way, and drug addiction is beginning to surface. In many regions of the country, the crime rate is climbing systematically. Signs of corruption are becoming more and more noticeable in a number of places. In the work of scientific and scientific-technical organizations, bureaucratism, departmentalism . . . and lack of initiative are becoming more and more pronounced. . . .

In comparing our economy with that of the United States, we see that ours lags behind not only in quantitative but also—most regrettable of all—in qualitative terms. . . . We outstrip America in coal production, but we lag behind in the output of oil, gas, and electric power; we lag behind tenfold in the field of chemistry, and we are infinitely outstripped in computer technology. The latter is especially crucial, because the introduction of electronic computers into the economy is a phenomenon of decisive importance. . . . Nevertheless, our stock of computers is *1 percent* of that of the United States. . . . We simply live in another age. . . .

The source of our difficulties does not lie in the socialist system; on the contrary, it lies in those peculiarities and conditions of our life that run counter to socialism and are hostile to it. The source lies in the antidemocratic traditions and norms of public life established in the Stalin era, which have not been decisively eliminated to this day.

Noneconomic coercion, limitations on the exchange of information, restrictions on intellectual freedom, and other examples of the antidemocratic distortion of socialism that took place under Stalin were accepted in our country as an overhead expense of the industrialization process. . . . But there is no doubt that . . . these phenomena have become the main brake on the development of the productive forces in this country. As a consequence of the increased size and complexity of economic systems, the problems of management and organization have moved to the forefront. These problems demand the creative participation of millions of people on all levels of the economic system. They demand the broad exchange of information and ideas. . . .

However, we encounter certain insurmountable obstacles on the road toward the free exchange of ideas and information. Truthful information about our shortcomings is hushed up on the grounds that it "may be used by enemy propaganda." Exchange of information with foreign countries is restricted for fear of "penetration by an enemy ideology." Theoretical generalizations and practical proposals, if they seem too bold to some individuals, are nipped in the bud without any discussion, because of the fear that they might "undermine our foundations." . . . Under such circumstances, the conditions are created for the advancement up the rungs of the official ladder not of those who distinguish themselves by their professional qualities and commitment to principles but of those who verbally proclaim their devotion to the Party but in practice are only concerned with their own narrow personal interests or are passive timeservers. . . .

The overwhelming majority of the intelligentsia and the youth recognize the need for democratization, and the need for it to be cautious and gradual, but they cannot understand or condone measures of a patently antidemocratic nature. And, indeed, how can one justify the confinement in prisons, camps, and insane asylums of people who hold oppositionist views but whose opposition stands on legal ground, in the area of ideas and convictions? In many instances, no opposition was involved, but only a striving for information, or simply a courageous and unprejudiced discussion of important social questions....

... Democratization, with its fullness of information and clash of ideas, must restore to our ideological life its dynamism and creativity ... and eliminate the bureaucratic, ritualistic, dogmatic, openly hypocritical, and mediocre style that reigns today....

What is in store for our nation if it does not take the course toward democratization? The fate of lagging behind the capitalist countries and gradually becoming a second-rate provincial power ... ; the growth of economic difficulties; increasingly tense relations between the Party and government apparatus, on the one hand, and the intelligentsia, on the other; the danger of ill-considered moves to the left or right; exacerbation of national problems, because the movement for democratization emanating from below in the national republics inevitably assumes a nationalistic character....

Respected comrades! There is no way out of the difficulties now facing our country except a course toward democratization, carried out by the Soviet Communist Party in accordance with a carefully worked-out plan. A turn to the right—that is, a victory for the forces that advocate a stronger administration, a "tightening of the screws"—would not only fail to solve any of the problems but, on the contrary, aggravate them to an extreme point and lead our country into a tragic impasse. The tactic of waiting passively would ultimately have the same result. Today, we still have the chance to take the right road and to carry out the necessary reforms. In a few years, it may be too late.

Unrest in Eastern Europe and Soviet Response

Despite strict state controls, protest and rebellion marked the forty-year history of the Soviet Union's East European empire. Soviet troops had to intervene in East Germany in 1953, when after Stalin's death, strikes in Berlin sparked nationwide demonstrations for better pay and free elections. Peace was restored, but several thousand civilians were killed and twenty thousand were arrested.

Disturbances also took place in Poland in 1956, after expectations of change were heightened by Khrushchev's destalinization campaign and his efforts to patch up differences with Yugoslavia, a communist state that had pursued an independent, non-Soviet path toward socialism. Strikes and demonstrations calling for economic reform, protection of the Catholic Church, and the removal of Soviet troops ended in a compromise between Khrushchev and Poland's new leader, Wladyslaw Gomulka: Poland would remain a one-party communist state and a member of the Warsaw Pact, but its leaders would be accorded more control over the nation's domestic affairs.

In Hungary in 1956, protesters had more ambitious goals than those of the Poles: free elections, the return to power of reformist politician Imre Nagy, the reinstatement of banned political parties, and Hungary's withdrawal from the Warsaw Pact.

In November, with Nagy reinstated as prime minister, the security police disbanded, banned political parties reorganizing, and free elections planned, Soviet leaders sent in troops. They crushed the revolt at the cost of three thousand Hungarians killed and thirteen thousand injured. In the crackdown that followed, between two thousand and twenty-five hundred insurgents were executed, twenty thousand were imprisoned, and thousands more were sent to prison camps. No fewer than two hundred thousand Hungarians fled the country for new lives in the West.

History repeated itself in 1968 in Czechoslovakia, where moderate economic reforms in the mid-1960s raised hopes for political liberalization. The country's authoritarian premier, Antonín Novotný, resisted further change, however, and in the face of demonstrations in Prague and mounting criticism from intellectuals, he resigned in favor of Alexander Dubček in January 1968. Dubček presided over the so-called Prague Spring, in which censorship was loosened, restrictions on travel were lifted, and a reduction of party control over all aspects of society was promised. By summer, fearing that Czechoslovakia would become another Hungary, Soviet leaders ordered an invasion by Soviet and some Warsaw Pact troops that easily snuffed out the reform movement. Dubček was removed from office, and all Communists who had supported reform—about one-third of the party's membership—were expelled from the party or demoted. For the next twenty years, Czechoslovakia had one of the Soviet bloc's most oppressive regimes.

Although the suppression of the Czechoslovakian reform movement resulted in only a few casualties, its psychological and political impact on Eastern Europe was greater than that of the Soviet invasion of Hungary in 1956. Unlike the Hungarians, the Czechs had not sought the end of Communist rule or withdrawal from the Warsaw Pact. They had advocated a program of moderate reform that was broadly supported by party members. Its destruction crushed hopes for the liberalization of Eastern Europe's communist regimes, which now were revealed as lacking both political legitimacy and a capacity to change.

Socialism with a Human Face

◈

71 ◆ Ludvík Vaculík, *TWO THOUSAND WORDS TO WORKERS, FARMERS, SCIENTISTS, ARTISTS, AND EVERYONE*

The climax of the Prague Spring came in April 1968, when after months of debate, the Czechoslovakian Communist Party issued its Action Program. Envisioning a less oppressive form of socialism—"socialism with a human face"—it called for a reduction in state power, more freedom for farmers and factory managers, strengthening of the courts and parliament, and the recognition of civil liberties.

Source: From *Czechoslovakia: The Party and the People*, by Andrew Oxley, Andrew Ritchie and Alex Pravda, pp. 261–268. Allen Lane; First American Edition edition (January 29, 1973). Used by kind permission of Andrew Ritchie.

The Party would retain power, but it would be more responsive to the needs of farmers, consumers, students, workers, and other interest groups.

While party leaders debated how to implement their program, and progressives called for rapid and thoroughgoing reforms, pressure on Czechoslovakia from the Soviet Union and other Warsaw Pact countries intensified. State-controlled newspapers throughout the Soviet bloc denounced the reform movement. In May, the Soviet Union ordered twenty-five thousand troops to the Czech-Polish border to prepare for military exercises to be held in Czechoslovakia in June. Then on June 27, with special party elections about to begin, there appeared in four Prague newspapers an essay, "Two Thousand Words," written by Ludvík Vaculík, (pronounced Vaht-*soo*-leek), a prominent novelist and journalist. The essay, signed by many public figures, denounced the Communist Party and called on the people to maintain pressure on their leaders to push forward with reform. It warned that unless the democratic movement maintained its momentum, conservatives would reassert their authority.

Vaculík's essay elicited a strong positive response among its readers, who sent thousands of supporting letters, resolutions, and telegrams to members of the National Assembly and Party leaders. Vaculík's essay also elicited a response in Moscow and other Warsaw Pact capitals. By giving the impression that the Czech reform movement was about to spin out of control, it strengthened the hand of politicians who favored military intervention.

Intervention came on the night and early morning of August 20 to 21, when Warsaw Pact troops invaded Czechoslovakia and occupied its major cities. Within weeks, political conditions were "normalized," and strict Party rule was imposed. Vaculík lost his job with the Writers' Union and, as an unemployed author, remained under police scrutiny until the collapse of Czechoslovakian communism in 1989.

QUESTIONS FOR ANALYSIS

1. What are Vaculík's views of the failings of the Czechoslovakian Communist Party? What role, if any, should the Party play in the process of reforming Czechoslovakian society?
2. According to Vaculík, what have been the results of communist rule of Czechoslovakian politics and society?
3. What strategy does Vaculík envision for saving the Czechoslovakian reform movement and pushing it forward?
4. If the reform movement had succeeded as Vaculík had hoped, what would Czechoslovakian government and society have looked like?
5. How do Vaculík's views compare to those expressed two years later by Sakharov, Medvedev, and Turchin in their letter to the Soviet leadership (Source 70)?

The life of this nation was first of all threatened by the war [World War II]. Then still more bad times followed, together with events which threatened the spiritual health and character of the nation. Most of the people of Czechoslovakia optimistically accepted the socialist programme, but its direction got into the wrong people's hands. It would not have mattered so much that they did not possess enough experience as statesmen, have enough practical knowledge or intellectual training, if they had at least had more common sense and humanity, if they had been able to listen to other people's opinions, and if they had allowed themselves to be replaced as time passed by more capable people.

After the war people had great confidence in the Communist Party, but it gradually preferred to have official positions instead of the people's trust, until it had only official positions and nothing else. . . . The incorrect line of the leadership turned the Party from a political party and ideological grouping into a power organization which became very attractive to power-hungry egotists, reproachful cowards and people with bad consciences. When they came into the Party, its character and behaviour began to be affected. Its internal organization was such that good people, who might have maintained its development for it to have fitted into the modern world, could not wield any influence at all. . . . Many communists opposed this decline, but not in one single case did they have any success in preventing what happened.

The conditions in the Communist Party were the model for and the cause of an identical situation in the state. . . . There was no criticism of the activity of the state and economic organizations. Parliament forgot how to debate: the government forgot how to govern and the directors how to direct. Elections had no significance and the laws lost their weight. We could not trust representatives on any committee, and even if we did, we could not ask them to do anything, because they could accomplish nothing. What was still worse was that we could hardly trust each other any more. There was a decline of individual and communal honour. You didn't get anywhere by being honest and it was useless expecting ability to be appreciated. Most people, therefore, lost interest in public affairs; they worried only about themselves and about their money. . . . To sum up, the country reached a point where its spiritual health and character were both threatened.

We are all of us together responsible for the present state of affairs, and the communists among us are more responsible than others. But the main responsibility rests with those who were part of, or the agents of, uncontrolled power. . . .

These rulers' greatest guilt, and the worst deception they perpetrated, was to make out that their arbitrary rule was the will of the workers. If we were to continue to believe this deception, we would have now to blame the workers for the decline of our economy, for the crimes committed against innocent people, for the introduction of the censorship which made it impossible for all this to be written about. The workers would now have to be blamed for the wrong investments, for the losses in trade, for the shortage of flats [apartments]. Of course, no sensible person believes in such guilt on the part of the workers. We all know, and especially every worker knows, that in actual fact the workers made no decisions about anything. . . . While many workers had the impression that they were in control, a specially educated group of Party officials and officials of the state apparatus ruled. In fact, they took the place of the overthrown class and themselves became the new aristocracy.

◆   ◆

Since the beginning of the year, we have been taking part in the revival process of democratization. It began in the Communist Party. Even non-communists, who until recently expected no good to come from it, recognize this fact. We should add, however, that the process could not have begun anywhere else. After all, only the communists could for twenty years lead anything like a full political life, only the communists were in a position to know what was happening and where, only the opposition within the Communist Party were privileged enough to be in contact with the enemy. . . .

The revival process hasn't come up with anything very new. It is producing ideas and suggestions many of which are older than the errors of our socialism, and others which came up to the surface after being in existence underground for a long time. They should have come out into the open a long time ago, but they were suppressed. . . .

Let us not, therefore, underestimate the significance of criticism from the ranks of writers and students....

It took several months for many of us to believe that we really could speak out, and many people still do not believe it. But nevertheless, we have spoken out, and such a huge number of things have come out into the open that somehow we must complete our aim of humanizing this régime. If we don't, the revenge of the old forces would be cruel. So we are turning now mainly to those who have been waiting. This moment will be a decisive one for many years to come.

The summer is approaching, with its holidays, when, as is our habit, we shall want to drop everything and relax. We can be quite sure however that our dear adversaries will not indulge in any summer recreations, that they will mobilize all their people, and that even now they are trying to arrange for a calm Christmas! So let us be careful about what happens, let's try to understand it and respond to it. Let's give up this impossible demand that someone above us must always provide us with the only, possible interpretation of things, one simple conclusion....

Above all, we shall have to oppose the view, should it arise, that it is possible to conduct some sort of a democratic revival without the communists or possibly against them.... The communists have well-constructed organizations and we should support the progressive wing within them. They have experienced officials and, last but not least, they also have in their hands the decisive levers and buttons. Their Action Program has been presented to the public. It is a programme for the initial adjustment of the greatest inequalities, and no one else has any similarly concrete program. We must demand that local Action Programs be submitted to the public in each district and each community. By doing so, we shall have suddenly taken very ordinary and long-expected steps in the right direction....

◆ ◆

Fears have recently been expressed that the democratization process has come to a halt. This feeling is partly caused by the fatigue brought on by the worrying times, and partly because the times of surprising revelations, resignations from high places and intoxicating speeches of a quite unprecedented bravery, are now past. The conflict of forces, however, has merely become hidden to a certain extent. The fight is now being waged about the content and form of laws, over the kind of practical steps that can be taken. And we must also give the new people, the ministers, prosecutors, chairmen and secretaries, time to work. They have the right to this time so that they can either prove their worth or their worthlessness....

The practical quality of the future democracy depends on what becomes of the enterprises [factories], and what will happen in them....

We can demand more money—but although it can be printed, it will be worth less. We should instead demand that directors and chairman explain to us [the workers] the nature and extent of the capital they want for production, to whom they want to sell their products and for how much, what profit they can expect to make, and the percentage of this profit that is to be invested in the modernization of production and the percentage to be shared out.

Under quite superficially boring headlines, a very fierce struggle is going on in the press about democracy and who leads the country. Workers can intervene in this struggle by means of the people they elect to enterprise administrations and councils.[1] As employees, they can do what is best for themselves by electing as their representatives on trade union organs their natural leaders, capable and honest people, no matter what their party affiliation is.

If at the moment we cannot expect any more from the central political organs, we must

---

[1]In the late spring, workers at many factories had formed councils to protect their interests during the anticipated process of economic reform.

achieve more in the districts and smaller communities. We should demand the resignation of people who have misused their power, who have damaged public property, or who have acted in a dishonest or brutal way. We have to find ways and means to persuade them to resign, through public criticism, for instance, through resolutions, demonstrations, demonstration work brigades, collections for retirement gifts for them, strikes, and picketing their houses. We must however, reject improper or illegal methods... and let us set up special citizens' committees and commissions to deal with subjects that nobody is yet interested in. It's quite simple, a few people get together, elect a chairman, keep regular minutes, publish their findings, demand a solution and do not allow themselves to be intimidated.

We must turn the district and local press, which has degenerated into a mouthpiece for official views, into a platform for all the positive political forces....Let us establish committees for the defence of the freedom of the press. Let us organize our own monitoring services at meetings. If we hear strange news, let's check on it ourselves, and let's send delegations to the people concerned, and if need be publish their replies. Let us support the security organs when they prosecute real criminal activity. We do not mean to cause anarchy and a state of general instablity....

The recent apprehension is the result of the possibility that foreign forces may intervene in our internal development. Face to face with these superior forces, the only thing we can do is to hold our own and not indulge in any provocation. We can assure our government—with weapons if need be—as long as it does what we give it a mandate to do, and we must assure our allies that we will observe our alliance, friendship and trade agreements. But excited accusations and ungrounded suspicions will make our government's position much more difficult and cannot be of any help to us....

This spring, as after the war [World War II], we have been given a great chance. We have once again the opportunity to take a firm grip on a common cause, which has the working title of socialism, and to give it a form which will much better suit the once good reputation that we had and the relatively good opinion that we once had of ourselves. The spring has now come to an end and it will never return. By winter we will know everything.

The Brezhnev Doctrine

❖

72 ◆ Leonid Brezhnev,
SPEECH TO THE FIFTH CONGRESS OF THE POLISH UNITED WORKERS' PARTY

After the invasion of Czechoslovakia, Soviet leader Leonid Brezhnev sought to justify what many considered to have been an overreaction to a moderate reform movement that had sought neither the end of communism nor independence from the Soviet bloc. In what became known as the Brezhnev Doctrine, Brezhnev claimed that socialist states had the right to intervene in the domestic affairs of another socialist state if communism were threatened. Such is his theme in the following selection, taken from a speech delivered to a Polish Communist Party congress in November 1968.

Although Soviet leaders denied that a "Brezhnev Doctrine" ever was official Soviet policy, the Soviet reformer Mikhail Gorbachev saw reason to repudiate it

Source: Brezhnev, "Speech to the Fifth Congress of the Polish United Workers' Party," from *Current Digest of the Soviet Press*, 20 (46), 1968, pp. 3–5. Copyright East View Information Services, Inc. Used by permission.

formally in 1989. The Brezhnev Doctrine, he jokingly said, was to be replaced by the "Sinatra Doctrine." Just as the American singer proudly proclaimed in his popular song that "I did it my way," the European satellites would now be allowed to do things "their way" in ordering their affairs.

QUESTION FOR ANALYSIS

1. What, or whom, does Brezhnev blame for the increased activity of forces hostile to socialism in Czechoslovakia?
2. What, according to Brezhnev, are the "common natural laws of socialist construction" that justify outside intervention in the affairs of socialist states?
3. How, according to Brezhnev, do socialist and "imperialist" nations view the issue of nations' "sovereign rights" differently?
4. Reduced to its basics, what is the definition of the Brezhnev Doctrine as spelled out in this speech?

The might of the socialist camp today is such that the imperialists fear military defeat in the event of a direct clash with the chief forces of socialism.... However, it is a fact that in the new conditions the imperialists are making increasingly frequent use of different and more insidious tactics. They are seeking out the weak links in the socialist front, pursuing a course of subversive ideological work inside the socialist countries, trying to influence the economic development of these countries, attempting to sow dissension, drive wedges between them and encourage and inflame nationalist feelings and tendencies, and are seeking to isolate individual socialist states so that they can then seize them by the throat one by one. In short, imperialism is trying to undermine socialism's solidarity precisely as a world system....

Socialist states stand for strict respect for the sovereignty of all countries. We resolutely oppose interference in the affairs of any states and the violation of their sovereignty.

At the same time, affirmation and defense of the sovereignty of states that have taken the path of socialist construction are of special significance to us communists. The forces of imperialism and reaction are seeking to deprive the people first in one, then another socialist country of the sovereign right they have earned to ensure prosperity for their country and well-being

and happiness for the broad working masses by building a society free from all oppression and exploitation. And when encroachments on this right receive a joint rebuff from the socialist camp, the bourgeois propagandists raise the cry of "defense of sovereignty" and "noninterference." It is clear that this is the sheerest deceit and demagoguery on their part. In reality these loudmouths are concerned not about preserving socialist sovereignty but about destroying it.

It is common knowledge that the Soviet Union has really done a good deal to strengthen the sovereignty and autonomy of the socialist countries.... But it is well known, comrades, that there are common natural laws of socialist construction, deviation from which could lead to deviation from socialism as such. And when external and internal forces hostile to socialism try to turn the development of a given socialist country in the direction of restoration of the capitalist system, when a threat arises to the cause of socialism in that country—a threat to the security of the socialist commonwealth as a whole—this is no longer merely a problem for that country's people, but a common problem, the concern of all socialist countries.

It is quite clear that an action such as military assistance to a fraternal country to end a threat to the socialist system is an extraordinary measure, dictated by necessity; it can be called forth only by the overt actions of enemies of socialism within the country and beyond its boundaries, actions that create a threat to the common interests of the socialist camp.

Experience bears witness that in present conditions the triumph of the socialist system in a country can be regarded as final, but the restoration of capitalism can be considered ruled out only if the Communist party, as the leading force in society, steadfastly pursues a Marxist-Leninist policy in the development of all spheres of society's life; only if the party indefatigably strengthens the country's defense and the protection of its revolutionary gains, and if it itself is vigilant and instills in the people vigilance with respect to the class enemy and implacability toward bourgeois ideology; only if the principle of socialist internationalism is held sacred, and unity and fraternal solidarity with the other socialist countries are strengthened.

◆

Utopian Dreams in Mao's China

On October 1, 1949, with the armies of Chiang Kai-shek in full retreat, Mao Zedong, the leader of the Chinese Communist Party, stood above the Gate of Heavenly Peace in Beijing and proclaimed the People's Republic of China. China's civil war had ended, and the fate of 540 million Chinese lay in the hands of Mao and a small group of close associates who for twenty-five years had struggled to unify China under communist rule.

China's new leaders had ambitious, even grandiose, plans for their country. They envisioned a strong, independent China, no longer vulnerable to imperialism and its attendant humiliations. They envisioned a China in which poverty would be eradicated through agricultural modernization, industrialization, and a program of road-building, railroad construction, and energy development. They envisioned a China in which ancient inequalities—between men and women, landlords and peasants, the learned and the illiterate, bureaucrats and the people—would no longer exist.

But was it possible to achieve rapid economic development in a truly egalitarian society? Finding an answer to this question became the great challenge for China's policymakers. Mao, whose opinion mattered most, believed that both goals could be achieved simultaneously by tapping the potential of the Chinese people, who, under the guidance of the Party, would dedicate themselves to achieving a modernized, communist China, not self-enrichment. Their energy and willpower, not the planning of bureaucrats, the research of scientists, or the know-how of engineers, would create a prosperous and egalitarian China.

Mao never realized his dreams. His economic and political experiments proved disastrous, and after his death in 1976, his successors abandoned revolutionary egalitarianism for a development strategy based on a principle that Mao had despised—one in which the interests of society were best served when individuals were free to pursue their own personal gain.

Industrial Heroism in the Great Leap Forward

❖

73 ◆ Tan Manni, *LUSHAN'S PIG-IRON "SPUTNIK"*

In its first decade, Communist China experienced profound changes. Between 1949 and 1953, large-scale businesses were nationalized, and land was seized from rich landowners and redistributed to peasants. In 1953, in imitation of the Soviet Union, China instituted its first Five-Year Plan. Its key components were centralized economic planning, the collectivization of agriculture, and rapid industrialization, with emphasis on steel, industrial equipment, chemicals, and electric power.

Despite impressive economic growth in the 1950s, Mao was unhappy with the Soviet model of economic development. Farm output registered only minor gains, and what increases occurred came largely from private plots rather than common lands. The Soviet model, he believed, had other dangers. Central planning meant larger and more powerful bureaucracies, and rapid industrialization brought disproportionate wealth and status to elite managers and engineers. Thus in late 1957, Mao led China into a new stage of its socialist development—the Great Leap Forward.

The Great Leap Forward shifted the focus of China's economic development from cities to the countryside, where millions of peasants, in the selfless pursuit of socialism, would dedicate themselves to road construction, farming, stock-raising, iron-making, and other enterprises. Their efforts would transform China into a modern socialist society in just a few years. It began in late 1957, when millions of peasants were put to work on water control and irrigation projects that supposedly opened up many millions of acres to cultivation in a few months. It was thought that equally impressive gains could be achieved by consolidating China's 740,000 cooperative farms into giant communes. By the end of 1958, 120 million households, or 99 percent of the rural population, had joined 26,000 communes, which Party officials ran according to strict egalitarian principles: private plots were abolished; commune members all received the same pay and food ration irrespective of their work; and families were organized collectively, with meals and child care provided by the commune. Commune members did more than farm. They also joined militias, built and operated backyard iron foundries, worked on construction projects, and prospected for uranium. Those with talent were encouraged to write inspirational poetry and songs.

The Great Leap Forward was a disaster. People were worked to exhaustion; the backyard iron foundries produced millions of iron pots and tools, but most were unusable; worst of all, farm output failed to reach unrealistically high production targets, and as the communes' grain, vegetables, and meat were handed over to the state to feed city dwellers, famine swept through rural China. It claimed as many as forty-five million lives between 1958 and 1962.

Why did the Great Leap Forward fail? Some answers are provided by the following article, even though the author, Tan Manni, wrote it to impress his readers with its great achievements. The article appeared in 1959 in *China Reconstructs*, an English-language magazine published in Shanghai designed to

Source: Lushan's "Sputnik": Tan Man-ni, "Lushan's Pig-Iron Sputnik," *China Reconstructs*, vol. 8, no. 1 (January 1959), 6–9.

give a positive image of life in China. In the article, Tan describes how a commune in Lushan County, a region in Jianxi Province, reached a "sputnik" in iron production. *Sputnik* is the name of the first human-made satellite sent into orbit by the USSR in 1957, and in this instance was a metaphor for high achievement.

QUESTIONS FOR ANALYSIS

1. What does the selection reveal about the level of economic and technological development in Lushan County at the time of the Great Leap Forward?
2. According to the author, how do the workers view their labors? What methods have been used to motivate them?
3. What does the article reveal about the reason for the poor quality of pig iron produced in the Lushan county foundries?
4. How does the article help explain the reasons for the fall in agricultural production during the Great Leap Forward?
5. What changes in social and family relationships accompanied the Great Leap Forward? Why were they necessary?

Furnace fields are everywhere ... plots of hundreds of small earthen furnaces were "growing," in late autumn when I was there, alongside fields of sweet potatoes and tobacco....

Small red flags fly overhead indicating the sections belonging to the various companies and squads of farmer-steelworkers, who are organized like militia units....

At one of the ten-foot-high furnaces, a man climbs a wooden ladder to dump coke and firewood through the top. After a few minutes beside the 1,000-degree heat, he descends and another worker goes up to tamp the fuel down with his rake. A third man follows to pull the hot rake away from the blast of the fire. Beside the furnace another crew is pushing the handle of the huge homemade wooden bellows. With all his might one of them pulls the handle, half as tall as himself, and pushes it back with the weight of his body. Three other men standing by to take their turns jokingly cheer him on....

The river a few miles away from the county town is another scene of activity. Undaunted by cold north wind, 25,000 students, women, and local government workers are ankle-deep in the water, washing for the iron-bearing sand that has been carried down from the nearby mountains. On the banks, groups of students off their working shift hold classes, and a crew of older women minds the children for the mothers beside the temporary living quarters made for workers from distant parts of the county....

The office of the county Communist Party committee where I stayed in the county town of Lushan is like the headquarters of an army, for the party had undertaken direct leadership of the iron campaign. Any time of the day or night, one can hear someone shouting into the telephone, "Long distance ... urgent ... coal ... tons."

This is the verve which enabled Lushan, the small mountainous county which six months ago possessed neither a blast furnace nor an engineer, or even an automobile, to startle the entire country by proving it could turn out 1,000 tons of iron a day. That record on last August 28 opened a new page in the nation-wide campaign for iron and steel, for it did away with the belief that smelting by local methods does not add up to much.

Lushan's achievement was called a "sputnik," and within the next month it inspired seventy-three more counties to reach that level. Now the record has been surpassed hundreds of times, but the county's 430,000 people are still seized by the iron and steel fever. Each day 100,000 of them work directly in its production, and many thousands more "at the rear" help transport ore after a day's work in the fields.

The people of Lushan began making small amounts of iron early in the summer, in line with the country's policy of developing small local industry as well as large plants, and to meet their own needs in making labor-saving farm machinery.... In Lushan, local materials and simple homemade tools were used to cut down initial investment, and half of the funds were contributed by the people themselves. A dozen blacksmiths, who at the beginning did not know how to smelt ore, led by the party vice-secretary, studied and experimented until they found a suitable process, and then passed the technique on to 600 other farmer-steelworkers....

... The farming had to be done with as few people as possible so as to free as many workers as possible to build and operate more furnaces, and mine and transport ore and coal....

As the work could not go ahead without full mass support and understanding, the meetings to discuss the proposal [to set higher production goals] became hot debates—a struggle of ideas. It was through this that the farmers came to realize their real power to produce. Party leaders put the need for iron in terms of the county's own needs—it could bring hydroelectric power stations on every one of the 600 reservoirs the people had built in the spring, better farm tools and machines, multi-storied buildings. They also pointed out that more iron for national construction would mean more tractors, rail lines and other improvements for all.

The way [to proceed], most people agreed, was large-scale organization. Lushan's mountains had ore but few people to do the mining. On the plains, on the other hand, there was manpower to spare. So their co-ops[1] decided that only by merging could they better deploy the working force. This later formed the basis for the people's commune which now embraces all of Lushan County.

Suggestions for nurseries and canteens to release more women were also adopted. In one large village alone, these measures freed 2,100 women for productive work....

When the time came to sign up for iron work, 95 percent of the county's able-bodied persons applied, and 65,000 were soon actually making iron. Shock teams were organized to man the furnaces, mine the ore, mold crucibles, and repair roads to facilitate transport. They built 500 new furnaces, and methods were developed to make the older ones yield twenty times as much iron per heat.

In the fortnight which preceded the target date of August 28, few people got a full night's sleep. It was just in those weeks that news came of the aggressive military build-up by the United States in the Taiwan Straits area and of provocations against the mainland.[2] Determination became even greater. On August 27, just as the furnaces were being lit, word arrived about the nation-wide call to raise the 1958 national production of steel to 10.7 million tons, twice as much as the year before. On August 28, Lushan's furnaces yielded 1,068 tons of pig iron. The "sputnik" had succeeded and Lushan had set a new standard for local iron production.

Soon the daily average was far surpassing this one-time figure. In the autumn, 40,000 more workers came from neighboring counties. By early November early November 150,000 tons were being produced in one day—as much as had been planned for the whole year.

---

[1]Cooperative farms, typically consisting of approximately thirty households.
[2]In August 1958, China demanded the withdrawal of U.S. forces from Taiwan after the Chinese air force began bombing raids against Quemoy, an offshore island near the port of Amoy controlled by the Nationalist government of Taiwan. A standoff ensued. China continued the bombardments until December but made no attacks on the supply ships sent to Quemoy under U.S. Navy escort.

Creating a New China in the Great Proletarian Cultural Revolution

◈

74 ◆ *ONE HUNDRED ITEMS FOR DESTROYING THE OLD AND ESTABLISHING THE NEW*

By mid-1959, it was clear that the Great Leap Forward had failed. In response, the Central Committee of the Communist Party removed Mao from the day-to-day control of the Party and shifted power to Deng Xiaoping and Liu Shaoqi, who sought to revive China's economy by dismantling Mao's experiment. Communes were reduced in size, and hundreds of thousands of failed rural industrial enterprises were scrapped. Peasants once more were allowed to farm private plots and sell their products for profit. Central planning was reinstated, and incentives for successful managers and productive workers were revived. As a result, between 1960 and 1965 industrial production grew by 11 percent a year, and grain production grew from 195 million tons in 1961 to 240 million tons in 1965.

Despite China's recovery, its leaders remained bitterly divided. On one side were moderate supporters of Deng and Liu who believed that China's most pressing need—economic development—could best be achieved through central planning; reliance on the contributions of university-trained engineers, managers, and scientists; and acceptance of incentives as a means of boosting production. On the other side were Mao and his disciples, who wanted economic development, but not at the expense of social equality, ongoing revolution, and ideological purity.

During the early 1960s, Mao gained support within the army and from a small but influential group of radical intellectuals. By late spring of 1966, Mao felt strong enough to launch what came to be known as the Great Proletarian Cultural Revolution. He and his supporters purged opponents from the Ministry of Culture and encouraged demonstrations by high school and university students against administrators and moderate Party members. Given red arm bands and copies of the "little red book," *Quotations from Chairman Mao*, students were released from classes to crusade against the "four olds" of Chinese society—old customs, old habits, old culture, and old thinking. These vague guidelines, along with Mao's directive to "destroy the old and construct the new," gave the student Red Guards many potential targets, as the following document demonstrates.

This list of demands was drawn up by Red Guards between the ages of fifteen and eighteen who attended the Maoism School, formerly known as Beijing Middle School Number 26. The list, compiled in August 1966, offers insights into the goals, opinions, and motives of the Red Guards, who, along with radicalized workers, kept China in a state of extraordinary turmoil between 1966 and 1969.

___

Source: From *Chinese Sociology & Anthropology*, vol. 2, no. 3/4 (Spring/Summer 1970): 214–216. English-language translation copyright © 1970 by M.E. Sharpe, Inc. Reprinted with permission. All Rights Reserved. Not for Reproduction.

QUESTIONS FOR ANALYSIS

1. What view of Mao Zedong is presented in the students' list of proposals?
2. How do the authors of the manifesto characterize the bourgeoisie? What concrete steps are proposed to limit the wealth and status of the bourgeoisie?
3. What economic proposals are contained in the students' list? In what ways will their proposed changes benefit the peasants and workers?
4. According to the manifesto, what changes are necessary in Chinese family life and education to bring them into conformity with Mao Zedong thought?
5. The authors of the manifesto express an interest in ridding China of gambling, swearing, "decadent" music, drinking, smoking, and "weird" clothing. What may explain the students' strong views on these matters?

The onrushing tide of the Great Proletarian Cultural Revolution is just now crashing down on the remnant strength of the bourgeoisie with the might of a thunderbolt, washing the old ideology, the old culture, the old customs, and the old habits of the bourgeoisie down the stream. Chairman Mao tells us: "In the last analysis, all the truths of Marxism can be summed up in one sentence. 'To rebel is justified.'" The present Great Proletarian Cultural Revolution must overthrow the old ideology, the old culture, the old customs, and the old habits; to rebel all out against the bourgeoisie is to completely smash the bourgeoisie, to establish the proletariat on a grand scale, to make the radiance of great Mao Zedong Thought illuminate the entire capital, the entire nation, the entire world. Armed with great Mao Zedong Thought we are the most militant troops, the mortal enemy of the "four olds"; we are the destroyers of the old world; we are the creators of the new world.... We must thoroughly clear the books of the utterly illogical capitalist system....

◆　◆

... Under the charge of residential committees, every street must set up a quotation plaque; every household must have on its walls a picture of the Chairman plus quotations by Chairman Mao.

... More quotations by Chairman Mao must be put up in the parks. Ticket takers on buses and conductors on trains should make the propagation of Mao Zedong Thought and the reading of Chairman Mao's quotations their primary task....

... Printing companies must print quotations by the Chairman in large numbers; they must be sold in every bookstore until there is a copy of the *Quotations from Chairman Mao* in the hands of everyone in the whole country.

... With a copy of the *Quotations from Chairman Mao* in the hands of everyone, each must carry it with him, constantly study it, and do everything in accord with it....

... Neighborhood work must put Mao Zedong Thought in first place, must set up small groups for the study of Chairman Mao's works, and must revolutionize housewives....

... Broadcasting units must be set up in every park and at every major intersection, and, under the organizational responsibility of such organs as the Red Guards, propagate Mao Zedong Thought and current international and national events....

... Letters and stamps must never have bourgeois things printed on them (such as cats, dogs, or other artistic things). Politics must be predominant. A quotation by Chairman Mao or a militant utterance by a hero must be printed on every envelope....

... Shop windows cannot be dominated by displays of scents and perfumes. They must be decorated with simplicity and dignity and must put Mao Zedong Thought first.

... Theaters must have a strong political atmosphere. Before the movie starts, quotations from Chairman Mao must be shown. Don't let the bourgeoisie rule our stages. Cut the superfluous hooligan scenes, and reduce the price of tickets on behalf of the workers, peasants, and soldiers.

... Literary and art workers must energetically model in clay heroic images of workers, peasants and soldiers engaged in living study and living application of chairman Mao's works. Their works must be pervaded by the one red line of Mao Zedong Thought....

... In a proletarian society, private enterprise cannot be allowed to exist. We propose to take all firms using joint state and private management and change them to state management and change joint state and private management enterprises into state-owned enterprises.

... Our socialist society absolutely cannot allow any hoodlums or juvenile delinquents to exist. We order you right this minute to get rid of your blue jeans, shave off your slick hairdos, take off your rocket shoes, and quit your black[1] organizations. Beijing is the heart of world revolution.... We warn you: You are not allowed to go on recklessly doing your evil deeds—if you do, you will be responsible for the consequences.

... All who are in service trades are not permitted to serve the bourgeoisie. Clothing stores are firmly prohibited from making tight pants, Hong Kong-style suits, weird women's outfits, and grotesque men's suits....

... All daily necessities (perfume, snowflake cream,[2] etc.) that do not serve the broad worker, peasant, and soldier masses must be prohibited from sale right away....

... All the landlords, rich-peasants, counter-revolutionaries, hooligans, Rightists, and other members of the bourgeois class are not permitted to collect pornographic books and decadent records. Whoever violates this rule will, when discovered, be treated as guilty of attempting to restore the old order, and his collections will be destroyed.

... Children must sing revolutionary songs. Those rotten tunes of the cat and dog variety must never again waft in the air of our socialist state. In this great socialist state of ours, absolutely no one is allowed to play games of chance.

... The bastards of the bourgeoisie are not allowed to hire governesses. Whoever dares to violate or resist this rule and thus continues to ride on the heads of the laboring people will be severely punished....

... Every industrial enterprise must abolish the bourgeois bonus award system. In this great socialist nation of ours, the broad worker, peasant, soldier masses, armed with the great Mao Zedong Thought, have no need for material incentives.

... Heads of families are not allowed to educate their children with bourgeois ideology. The feudal family-head system[3] will be abolished.

... You old bastards of the bourgeoisie who receive high salaries, listen well: Before Liberation you rode on the heads of the people, sometimes severe, sometimes lenient. Now you still receive salaries many times more than ten times higher than those of the workers. You are thus drinking the blood of the people—you are guilty. Starting in September, you are ordered to lower your high salaries to the level of those of the workers....

... Landlords, rich-peasants, counterrevolutionaries, hooligans, Rightists, and capitalists, when they go out, must wear plaques as monsters and freaks under the supervision of the masses....

... All circus and theater programs must be changed. They must put on meaningful things. Actors are not allowed to dress up in strange fashions, because we don't need those filthy things....

... Nobody may address letters to "Sir" so and so. The whole range of feudal practices must be abolished and new customs advocated....

... All those athletic activities that don't correspond with practical significance will be

---

[1]Black was associated with reactionary politics.
[2]Facial cream.
[3]In the traditional Chinese family, the father was the center of authority. In theory, he controlled the family's property and arranged marriages for his children. In encouraging young people to reject the values of their parents and elders—indeed, to denounce them to authorities for erroneous thinking—the Cultural Revolution rejected the ancient doctrine of filial piety, according to which children owed their parents unquestioned reverence and obedience.

appropriately reduced. Physical education for national defense, such as swimming, mountain climbing, shooting, etc., will be greatly developed so that gradually every youth or adult over fifteen years of age will have a range of enemy-killing abilities. All the people are soldiers, always prepared to annihilate the invading enemy....

... We order those under thirty-five to quit drinking and smoking immediately. Bad habits of this sort absolutely may not be cultivated.

... Telling jokes, uttering profanities, and doing vulgar things are strictly forbidden....

... The responsible organizations must do their best to find ways to establish public toilets in the various alleys so as to reduce the heavy work of the sanitation workers....

... From now on, all universities, high schools, and vocational schools will be run as communist schools with part-time work and part-time study and part-time farming and part-time study.

... We students must respond to Chairman Mao's appeal. Students must also learn from the workers, the peasants, and the soldiers, and each year during their vacations they must go to factories, farms, and military camps to train themselves....

... Schools must use Mao's works as textbooks and educate the youth in Mao Zedong Thought....

... Schools must destroy the feudal teacher-student etiquette and establish an equal relationship between teacher and student.

CHAPTER 11

The Emergence of a Third World

In an article "Three Worlds, One Planet," published in 1952 in the magazine *L'Observateur*, French demographer Alfred Sauvy coined the phrase *Third World* to describe the regions of Asia and Africa that were just beginning to emerge from colonial rule. He sought to draw a distinction between the Third World and the *First World*, which consisted of Western or Westernized capitalist states (the nations of Western Europe, the United States, Japan, along with Canada, Australia, and New Zealand) and the *Second World*, which was made up of the communist bloc (the Soviet Union, its east European satellites, and China). Sauvy also sought to draw an analogy between the role of the Third World in the early 1950s and that of the *Third Estate* during French Revolution of the 1790s. In France, the oppressed Third Estate, made up of the middle class and peasants, had sought equality with the privileged first two estates, the clergy and nobility, just as the "ignored, exploited, and despised" people of the Third World were seeking equality and justice after World War II.

During the 1950s and 1960s, journalists, historians, politicians, and political commentators built on Sauvy's ideas and by the late 1960s had reached a consensus about what it meant to be part of the Third World. All Third World states, first of all, had been subjected to some form of Western imperialism. In Africa and Asia, this had meant the loss of political independence and the subordination of both regions' economic interests to those of the colonizers. In Latin America, which came to be viewed as part of the Third World, it had meant foreign intervention in the region's domestic politics and foreign control of much of its economic life, even after political independence from Spain and Portugal had been achieved in the early 1800s.

Another characteristic of the Third World was nonalignment in the Cold War, a policy that first gained attention during the African-Asian Conference held in the Indonesian city of Bandung in 1955. Hosted by Indonesia's Premier Sukarno and attended by representatives of twenty-nine African and Asian countries, delegates announced their intention to serve as a buffer between the United States and the Soviet Union and by doing so lessen the danger of war between them. The delegates also condemned runaway military spending by the superpowers, called for increased economic aid to poor nations, and denounced all manifestations of colonialism, not only in Asia and Africa, but also in Eastern Europe.

Widespread poverty also defined Third World societies. In the optimistic atmosphere of the 1950s and 1960s, it was believed that Third World poverty was the result of colonial exploitation and would disappear once Asia, Africa, and Latin America were free to follow their own paths of economic development and modernization. Development meant industrialization, accompanied ideally by the formation of stable, democratic governments, whereas modernization meant a transition from traditional customs and attitudes to the scientific and secular values of developed nations, primarily those in the West.

For a time, such optimism seemed well grounded. In the 1950s and 1960s, food production increased in Africa, Asia, and Latin America, and the economic boom ensured healthy prices for these regions' agricultural and mineral exports. Governments embarked on ambitious economic development plans, and in the 1960s, per capita income grew. Only in the 1970s, with its spiraling oil prices and worldwide economic downturn did Third World economic prospects darken.

Another characteristic of the Third World was its growing importance in world affairs. Third World nations were important sources of food, minerals, oil, and other commodities; they commanded key points on the world's sea lanes, including the Suez Canal, the Panama Canal, and the Straits of Hormuz in the Persian Gulf; they also were recipients of substantial foreign investment that needed protection. In politics, newly independent states played an increasingly important role in the United Nations, where by the early 1970s, the Third World was the largest single voting bloc in the General Assembly.

Most importantly, the Third World became a battleground in the Cold War. For many states in Africa and Asia, independence from a colonial power was followed by interference in their affairs by one or both of the world's new superpowers, the United States and the Soviet Union. These rivals, for a host of ideological, diplomatic, economic, and strategic reasons, provided arms to opposing sides in civil wars, arranged assassination plots, worked to destabilize unfriendly regimes, helped organize coups, and propped up sympathetic rulers through grants of military and foreign aid. Such interference prolonged civil wars, enabled corrupt autocrats to stay in power, and led to shooting wars in Korea and Vietnam.

◆

Sources of Conflict in the Middle East

In the years following World War II, Western imperialism in the Middle East ended, leaving behind a legacy of new states, new ideologies, and new aspirations. Not surprisingly, the region experienced its share of conflict and volatility. It included conservative monarchies in Saudi Arabia and Jordan; even more conservative sheikdoms in the Persian Gulf; modernizing dictatorships in Iran, Egypt, and Libya; and democracies in Turkey and Israel. Coups d'état took place in Egypt, Turkey, Iran, and Libya, and civil wars occurred in Yemen and Lebanon. The Middle East experienced wars in 1948, 1956, and 1967, and a cold war between Egypt and Saudi Arabia (over a civil war in Yemen) that lasted from 1962 to 1970. Between 1954 and 1962, Algeria became the site of a bloody conflict that was both a war of independence against French rule and also a civil war among competing Algerian factions.

Politics in the region were complicated by long-standing ethnic rivalries, religious divisions, and fundamental political disagreements. Maronite Christians, Sunni Muslims, and Shiite Muslims shared power in Lebanon; Kurds made up a large minority in Turkey, Iran, and Iraq; Shiite Muslims and smaller sects such as the Druze and the Alawi (whom the orthodox do not consider to be Muslim) lived in largely Sunni Syria; Shiites made up 20 percent of the population in Iraq. On political issues, nationalists, liberals, socialists, communists, and monarchists competed for power and public support, as did secularists, who admired the West, and Muslim fundamentalists, who considered the West satanic.

By far, the greatest destabilizing force in the region was the existence of Israel. The founding of Israel in 1948 was the culmination of events that go back to the 1890s, when European Zionists set out to achieve the goal of creating a Jewish state in Palestine. Jewish migration to the region was already a major source of conflict in the 1930s (see Source 45, "The Peel Report"). After World War II, Jews and Arabs both wanted an end to the British mandate, with the Arabs, however, demanding a unified state with an Arab majority, and the Jews demanding the partition of Palestine and their own Jewish state. With compromise impossible and violence mounting, the British handed over the Palestinian issue to the United Nations, which in November 1947 voted in favor of separate Jewish and Arab states. On May 14, 1948, Jewish leaders formally established the state of Israel, and on the same day Egypt, Iraq, Syria, and Jordan declared war on the new state, vowing its destruction.

Palestine as an Arab Homeland

❖

75 ❖ *THE PALESTINE NATIONAL CHARTER*

Arab armies were defeated in the Arab-Israeli War of 1948 to 1949, but the real losers were Palestinian Arabs. Approximately one hundred fifty thousand Palestinians remained in Israel during and after the war and became Israeli citizens. Although subject to restrictions, they had political rights, economic benefits, and educational opportunities. Some four hundred thousand Palestinians who lived in the West Bank, a region of Palestine not conquered by Israel, became subjects of the king of Jordan, who annexed the territory in 1949.

Anywhere from five hundred thousand to eight hundred thousand Palestinians fled their homes in Israel during the war; they became refugees in squalid camps on the borders of Israel in the Gaza region, the West Bank, Syria, and Lebanon. In 1967, after the third Arab-Israeli war (the Six-Day War) the number of Palestinian refugees swelled by another two hundred thousand when the West Bank was conquered by the Israelis and incorporated into Israel.

During the 1950s, numerous welfare agencies, social organizations, and paramilitary groups were founded to serve the needs of refugees and keep alive the goal of Palestinian statehood. At a summit meeting in 1964, Arab leaders approved the founding of the Palestine Liberation Organization (PLO), with responsibility for overseeing and coordinating all these Palestinian organizations. Later in the year, representatives of the organizations met in Jerusalem and formed a PLO executive board, laid plans for the formation of a Palestinian army, and began work on a national charter. The Palestine National Charter, after several revisions, was approved at a meeting of the Fourth Palestine National Council in 1968. Excerpts from the document follow.

QUESTIONS FOR ANALYSIS

1. How does the charter define a Palestinian?
2. Why does the charter equate Zionism with imperialism? Why does it equate Zionism with racism?
3. How valid are these comparisons in your view?
4. On what grounds does the charter reject the validity of the UN decision to partition Palestine in 1947?
5. How do the authors of the charter propose to achieve liberation from Israel?

1. Palestine, the homeland of the Palestinian Arab people, is an inseparable part of the greater Arab homeland, and the Palestinian people are a part of the Arab Nation.
2. Palestine, within the frontiers that existed under the British Mandate, is an indivisible territorial unit.

3. The Palestinian Arab people alone have legitimate rights to their homeland, and shall exercise the right of self-determination after the liberation of their homeland, in keeping with their wishes and entirely of their own accord.

Source: From Yeyoshafat Herkabi, *The Palestine Covenant and Its Meaning.* Copyright © 1979. Reproduced by permission from Vallentine Mitchell & Co. Ltd.

4. The Palestinian identity is an authentic, intrinsic and indissoluble quality that is transmitted from father to son. Neither the Zionist occupation nor the dispersal of the Palestinian Arab people as a result of the afflictions they have suffered can efface this Palestinian identity.

5. Palestinians are Arab citizens who were normally resident in Palestine until 1947. This includes both those who were forced to leave or who stayed in Palestine. Anyone born to a Palestinian father after that date, whether inside or outside Palestine, is a Palestinian.

6. Jews who were normally resident in Palestine up to the beginning of the Zionist invasion are Palestinians.

7. Palestinian identity, and material, spiritual and historical links with Palestine are immutable realities. It is a national obligation to provide every Palestinian with a revolutionary Arab upbringing, and to instill in him a profound spiritual and material familiarity with his homeland and a readiness for armed struggle and for the sacrifice of his material possessions and his life, for the recovery of his homeland....

8. The Palestinian people is at the stage of national struggle for the liberation of its homeland. For that reason, differences between Palestinian national forces must give way to the fundamental difference that exists between Zionism and imperialism on the one hand and the Palestinian Arab people on the other. On that basis, the Palestinian masses, both as organizations and as individuals, whether in the homeland or in such places as they now live as refugees, constitute a single national front working for the recovery and liberation of Palestine through armed struggle.

9. The Palestinian Arab people hereby affirm their unwavering determination to carry on the armed struggle and to press on towards popular revolution for the liberation of and return to their homeland. They also affirm their right to a normal life in their homeland, to the exercise of their right of self-determination therein and to sovereignty over it.

10. Commando action[1] constitutes the nucleus of the Palestinian popular war of liberation. This requires that commando action should be escalated, expanded and protected, and that all the resources of the Palestinian masses and all scientific potentials available to them should be mobilized and organized to play their part in the armed Palestinian revolution....

12. The Palestinian Arab people believe in Arab unity. To fulfill their role in the achievement of that objective, they must, at the present stage in their national struggle, retain their Palestinian identity and all that it involves, work for increased awareness of it and oppose all measures liable to weaken or dissolve it....

14. The destiny of the Arab nation, indeed the continued existence of the Arabs, depends on the fate of the Palestinian cause. This interrelationship is the point of departure of the Arab endeavor to liberate Palestine. The Palestinian people are the vanguard of the movement to achieve this sacred national objective.

15. The liberation of Palestine is a national obligation for the Arabs. It is their duty to repel the Zionist and imperialist invasion of the greater Arab homeland and to liquidate the Zionist presence in Palestine....

16. On the spiritual plane, the liberation of Palestine will establish in the Holy Land an atmosphere of peace and tranquility in which all religious institutions will be safeguarded and freedom of worship and the right of visit guaranteed to all without discrimination or distinction of race, color, language or creed. For this reason the people of Palestine look to all spiritual forces in the world for support.

---

[1]Commandos are highly trained soldiers who operate in small units usually inside enemy territory.

17. On the human plane, the liberation of Palestine will restore to the Palestinians their dignity, integrity and freedom. For this reason, the Palestinian Arab people look at all those who believe in the dignity and freedom of man for support....

19. The partition of Palestine, which took place in 1947, and the establishment of Israel, are fundamentally invalid, however long they last, for they contravene the will of the people of Palestine and their natural right to their homeland and contradict the principles of the United Nations Charter, foremost among which is the right of self-determination.

20. The Balfour Declaration, the Mandate Instrument, and all their consequences, are hereby declared null and void.[2] The claim of historical or spiritual links between the Jews and Palestine is neither in conformity with historical fact nor does it satisfy the requirements for statehood. Judaism is a revealed religion; it is not a separate nationality, nor are the Jews a single people with a separate identity; they are citizens of their respective countries....

22. Zionism is a political movement that is organically linked with world imperialism and is opposed to all liberation movements or movements for progress in the world. The Zionist movement is essentially fanatical and racialist; its objectives involve aggression, expansion and the establishment of colonial settlements, and its methods are those of the Fascists and the Nazis. Israel acts as cat's paw[3] for the Zionist movement, a geographic and manpower base for world imperialism and a springboard for its thrust into the Arab homeland to frustrate the aspirations of the Arab nation to liberation, unity and progress. Israel is a constant threat to peace in the Middle East and the whole world. Inasmuch as the liberation of Palestine will eliminate the Zionist and imperialist presence in that country and bring peace to the Middle East, the Palestinian people look for support to all liberals and to all forces of good, peace and progress in the world, and call on them, whatever their political convictions, for all possible aid and support in their just and legitimate struggle to liberate their homeland.

[2]The Balfour Declaration of 1917 pledged Great Britain to support the establishment of a "national home" for the Jewish people in Palestine.

[3]Someone or something used by another as a tool.

Palestine as a Jewish Homeland

◆

76 ◆ Chaim Herzog, *SPEECH TO THE UNITED NATIONS GENERAL ASSEMBLY, NOVEMBER 10, 1975*

In the mid-1970s, the Palestine Liberation Organization, with the support of most Arab states, began a campaign to discredit Israel in international forums. In the summer of 1975, at the urging of the PLO, the Organization of African Unity and the Conference of Non-Aligned Nations both condemned Zionism as racist and imperialist and grouped Israel with the white racist regimes of Rhodesia and

Source: From *Who Stands Accused?* by Chaim Herzog. Copyright © 1978 by the State of Israel. Used by permission of Random House, Inc.

South Africa. Several months later, a similar anti-Israel resolution was proposed in the General Assembly of the United Nations.

Chaim Herzog, Israeli ambassador to the UN, denounced the resolution in the following speech delivered on November 10, 1975. The Irish-born Herzog, who had emigrated to Palestine in 1935 and had served as a tank commander in the British army in World War II, was a successful lawyer with a distinguished career in public service before accepting the post at the UN. Just hours after delivering his speech, a coalition of Muslim, Third World, and Soviet-bloc nations approved the proposed resolution, which states that "Zionism is a form of racism and racial discrimination."

QUESTIONS FOR ANALYSIS

1. What does Herzog mean when he says, "Zionism is to the Jewish people what the liberation movements of Africa and Asia have been to their own people"?
2. How does Herzog's historical perspective on Palestine differ from that of the 1968 Palestine National Charter?
3. What is at stake in the debate on the resolution, other than the existence of Israel?

It is symbolic that this debate ... should take place on November 10. Tonight, thirty-seven years ago, has gone down in history as Kristallnacht, the Night of the Crystals. This was the night in 1938 when Hitler's Nazi storm-troopers launched a coordinated attack on the Jewish community in Germany, burned the synagogues in all its cities and made bonfires in the streets of the Holy Books and the Scrolls of the Holy Law and Bible. It was the night when Jewish homes were attacked and heads of families taken away, many of them never to return. It was the night when the windows of all Jewish businesses and stores were smashed, covering the streets in the cities of Germany with a film of broken glass which dissolved into the millions of crystals which gave the night its name. It was the night which led eventually to the crematoria and the gas chambers, Auschwitz, Birkenau, Dachau, Buchenwald, Theresienstadt and others. It was the night which led to the most terrifying holocaust in the history of man.

It is indeed befitting ... that this debate, conceived in the desire to deflect the Middle East from its moves towards peace and born of a deep pervading feeling of anti-Semitism, should take place on the anniversary of this day. It is indeed befitting ... that the United Nations, which began its life as an anti-Nazi alliance, should thirty years later find itself on its way to becoming the world center of anti-Semitism. Hitler would have felt at home on a number of occasions during the past year, listening to the proceedings in this forum, and above all to the proceedings during the debate on Zionism.

It is sobering to consider to what level this body has been dragged down if we are obliged today to contemplate an attack on Zionism. For this attack constitutes not only an anti-Israeli attack of the foulest type, but also an assault in the United Nations on Judaism—one of the oldest established religions in the world, a religion which has given the world the human values of the Bible, and from which two other great religions, Christianity and Islam, sprang. Is it not tragic to consider that we here at this meeting in the year 1975 are contemplating what is a scurrilous attack on a great and established religion which has given to the world the Bible with its Ten Commandments, the great prophets of old, Moses, Isaiah, Amos; the great thinkers of history, Maimonides, Spinoza, Marx, Einstein,[1] many of the masters of the arts

---

[1] Maimonides (1135–1204) and Baruch Spinoza (1632–1677) were prominent philosophers. Einstein (1879–1955) was of course a giant of modern physics. There is some irony in Herzog's mention of Karl Marx; every communist state in the UN voted for the anti-Zionist resolution.

and as high a percentage of Nobel Prize-winners in the world, in sciences, in the arts and in the humanities as has been achieved by any people on earth? ...

I do not come to this rostrum to defend the moral and historical values of the Jewish people. They do not need to be defended. They speak for themselves. They have given to mankind much of what is great and eternal. They have done for the spirit of man more than can readily be appreciated by a forum such as this one.

I come here to denounce the two great evils which menace society in general and a society of nations in particular. These two evils are hatred and ignorance. These two evils are the motivating force behind the proponents of this resolution and their supporters. These two evils characterize those who would drag this world organization, the ideals of which were first conceived by the prophets of Israel, to the depths to which it has been dragged today.

The key to understanding Zionism is in its name. The eastern-most of the two hills of ancient Jerusalem during the tenth century B.C. was called Zion. In fact, the name Zion, referring to Jerusalem, appears 152 times in the Old Testament. The name is overwhelmingly a poetic and prophetic designation. The religious and emotional qualities of the name arise from the importance of Jerusalem as the Royal City and the City of the Temple. "Mount Zion" is the place where God dwells. Jerusalem, or Zion, is a place where the Lord is King, and where He has installed His King, David.

King David made Jerusalem the capital of Israel almost three thousand years ago, and Jerusalem has remained the capital ever since. During the centuries the term "Zion" grew and expanded to mean the whole of Israel. The Israelites in exile could not forget Zion. The Hebrew Psalmist sat by the waters of Babylon and swore: "If I forget thee, O Jerusalem, let my right hand forget her cunning." This oath has been repeated for thousands of years by Jews throughout the world. It is an oath which was made over seven hundred years before the advent of Christianity and over twelve hundred years before the advent of Islam, and Zion came

to mean the Jewish homeland, symbolic of Judaism, of Jewish national aspirations.

While praying to his God every Jew, wherever he is in the world, faces towards Jerusalem. For over two thousand years of exile these prayers have expressed the yearning of the Jewish people to return to their ancient homeland, Israel. ...

Zionism is the name of the national movement of the Jewish people and is the modern expression of the ancient Jewish heritage. The Zionist ideal, as set out in the Bible, has been, and is, an integral part of the Jewish religion.

Zionism is to the Jewish people what the liberation movements of Africa and Asia have been to their own people. ...

In modern times, in the late nineteenth century, spurred by the twin forces of anti-Semitic persecution and of nationalism, the Jewish people organized the Zionist movement in order to transform their dream into reality. Zionism as a political movement was the revolt of an oppressed nation against the depredation and wicked discrimination and oppression of the countries in which anti-Semitism flourished. It is no coincidence that the co-sponsors and supporters of this resolution include countries who are guilty of the horrible crimes of anti-Semitism and discrimination to this very day.

Support for the aim of Zionism was written into the League of Nations Mandate for Palestine and was again endorsed by the United Nations in 1947, when the General Assembly voted by overwhelming majority for the restoration of Jewish independence in our ancient land.

The re-establishment of Jewish independence in Israel, after centuries of struggle to overcome foreign conquest and exile, is a vindication of the fundamental concepts of the equality of nations and of self-determination. To question the Jewish people's right to national existence and freedom is not only to deny to the Jewish people the right accorded to every other people on this globe, but it is also to deny the central precepts of the United Nations.

Racism and Ethnic Conflict in Independent Africa

Beginning in the late nineteenth century, it took the European powers only two and a half decades to impose their authority on the continent. After World War II, it took them even less time to leave. After the Gold Coast gained independence from Great Britain in 1957 and became Ghana, decolonization proceeded in a rush. Between 1957 and 1975, no less than forty-six former African colonies became sovereign states. After 1975, only Rhodesia (which became independent Zimbabwe in 1980) and South-West Africa (which became independent Namibia in 1990) remained under European rule.

At first, the new African states made progress toward reaching one of their primary goals, improving their people's standard of living. Through the 1960s, annual growth rates were between 3 percent and 4 percent, and inflation was kept to reasonable levels. Between 1960 and 1972, the number of African students attending schools and universities increased from 17.8 million to 37.6 million. Such accomplishments, however, were short-lived. In a catastrophe that no one anticipated, in the 1970s, a host of problems, including rapid population growth, drought, falling commodity prices, increased energy costs, mismanagement, civil wars, and government corruption soon sent Africa's economies into free fall.

Maintaining stable democratic governments proved even more difficult. Burdened by poor communications, low literacy levels, widespread poverty, arbitrarily drawn national boundaries, foreign interference, and the persistence of local and ethnic loyalties, democracy in Africa became a case of "one man, one vote, once," as one constitutional government after another fell victim to rebellion, civil war, and rule by corrupt and irresponsible autocrats. Ghana, which in 1957 became Africa's first new independent state, set a pattern. Kwame Nkrumah, the leader of the independence movement and Ghana's first prime minister, soon scuttled the constitution, had political opponents jailed without trial, and abolished all political parties except the Convention People's Party, which he had founded. While the economy suffered from plummeting cocoa prices, Nkrumah shifted from capitalism to socialism and sponsored massive public works projects, one of which was turning his ancestral hut into a national shrine.

Blacks in South Africa faced a different kind of challenge. Ever since South Africa had gained its independence from Great Britain in 1910, they along with Indians and coloreds (people of mixed blood), had steadily lost ground politically and economically as a result of discriminatory laws imposed by the white minority. In the 1950s and early 1960s, a barrage of legislation sponsored by the National Party turned South African discrimination policies into something much harsher—the apartheid system. Nonwhites lost their remaining political rights; mixed marriages and interracial sex were outlawed; and segregation was decreed for schools, technical colleges, universities, public transportation, restaurants, theaters, and sports facilities. Apartheid also demanded residential segregation, requiring blacks to live in urban townships or rural homelands known as bantustans. Unlike European colonialism, which melted away soon after the first sign of black nationalism, apartheid persisted despite black resistance and pressure from the international community. It ended only in 1994, when blacks received the right to vote for members of a parliament that would serve for five years and write a new constitution. The era of white rule in sub-Saharan Africa was finally over.

The Colonial Legacy: Ethnic Tensions in Nigeria

◆

77 ◆ C. Odumegwu Ojukwu, *SPEECHES AND WRITINGS*

When Nigeria became independent in 1960, its constitution was the product of protracted deliberations involving British administrators and representatives of the colony's major ethnic groups, the Hausa-Fulani, the Yoruba, and the Igbo. It established a central government with a prime minister and legislature, and three provinces with extensive powers: the Northern Region, which was dominated by the Hausa-Fulani and was overwhelmingly Muslim; the Western Region, which was dominated by the Yoruba and was Protestant; and the Eastern Region, which was dominated by the Igbo and was mainly Roman Catholic. Denouncing corruption and the government's failure to address mounting economic problems, army officers (mostly Igbo) led a coup d'état in 1966 and then created a strong centralized national government at the expense of the provinces. This angered the Hausa-Fulani and the Yoruba, who feared that the more highly educated and economically sophisticated Igbo would dominate the new regime. The result was another coup, led by Yakubu Gowon, an army officer from the Northern Region, and massacres of Igbo living outside the Eastern Region. The Eastern Region refused to recognize the new government and declared itself the independent Republic of Biafra in May 1967.

The leader of the Biafran independence movement was C. Odumegwu Ojukwu, who was born into a wealthy Igbo family and educated in England, where he received a master's degree in history from Oxford. He rose through the ranks of the Nigerian army and in 1967 became head of state and army commander-in-chief of newly independent Biafra. Immediately attacked by Nigerian forces, Biafra held out until 1970, when Ojukwu capitulated and fled to Guinea. Yakubu Gowon now ruled a reunited Nigeria, which he divided into twelve provinces rather than three to defuse ethnic conflict. Until 1999, when Nigeria became a democracy, the country was ruled by a series of military dictators, interrupted by one democratic interlude between 1979 and 1983.

Source: Excerpts from Part I: pp. 1, 11–12, 179; Part II: 2, 3–5, 58, 164–5, 172–3, 223–4 from *Biafra: Volume I Selected Speeches; Volume 2 Random Thoughts* by C. Odumegwu Ojukwu. Copyright © 1969, renewed 1997 by Chukwuemeka Odumegwu Ojukwu. Reprinted by permission of HarperCollins Publishers.

The following excerpts are from General Ojukwu's speeches and writings from 1966 to 1969. They reveal his views of Nigeria's history and politics and his thoughts on the meaning of Biafran independence.

QUESTIONS FOR ANALYSIS

1. In Ojukwu's opinion, how did the British and the Northern Nigerians contribute to the problems of the Nigerian state?
2. What characteristics define the people of Eastern Nigeria, in Ojukwu's view?
3. According to Ojukwu, what have been the major flaws of the Nigerian government since independence? How will the new state of Biafra avoid these shortcomings?
4. What specific reasons does Ojukwu provide for the decision of Eastern Nigerians to secede?
5. What does Ojukwu see as the broader significance of the Biafran independence movement?

THE BACKGROUND OF A CRISIS

The constitutional arrangements of Nigeria, as imposed upon the people by the erstwhile British rulers, were nothing but an implicit acceptance of the fact that there was no basis for Nigerian unity.

It was Britain, first, that amalgamated the country in 1914, unwilling as the people of the North were.[1] It was Britain that forced a federation of Nigeria, even when the people of the North objected to it very strongly. It was Britain, while keeping Nigeria together, that made it impossible for the people to know themselves and get close to each other, by maintaining an apartheid policy in Northern Nigeria which herded all Southerners into little reserves, barring them from Northern Nigerian schools, and maintaining different systems of justice in a country they claimed to be one.[2]

It was Britain, for her economic interest, that put the various nations in Nigeria side by side and called it a federation, so as to have a large market....

On October 1, 1960, independence was granted to the people of Nigeria in a form of "federation," based on artificially made units. The Nigerian Constitution installed the North in perpetual dominance over Nigeria.... Thus were sown, by design or by default, the seeds of factionalism and hate, of struggle for power at the center, and of the worst types of political chicanery and abuse of power. One of two situations was bound to result from that arrangement: either perpetual domination of the rest of the country by the North ... or dissolution of the federation bond....

Nigeria in the end came to be run by compromises made and broken between the Northerners and consenting Southern politicians. This led to interminable violent crises, to corruption and nepotism, and to the arbitrary use of power....

Key projects in the National Development Plan were not pursued with necessary vigor. Instead of these, palaces were constructed for the indulgence of ministers and other holders of public offices—men supposed to serve the interest of the common man. Expensive fleets of flamboyant and luxurious cars were purchased. Taxpayers' money was wasted on unnecessary foreign travel by ministers, each competing with the other only in their unbridled excesses.

---

[1] The provinces of Northern and Southern Nigeria were brought under a common administration by Sir Frederick Lugard, governor-general of Nigeria between 1912 and 1919.

[2] Many Eastern Nigerians had moved to other parts of the country, mainly to pursue business opportunities. Many believed they were treated as second-class citizens, especially in the Muslim north.

... Internal squabbles for parochial and clannish patronage took the place of purposeful coordinated service of the people. Land, the basic heritage of the people, was converted into the private estates of rapacious individuals who, thus trampling on the rights of the people, violated their sacred trust under this system.... Nepotism became rife. Tribalism became the order of the day. In appointments and promotions mere lip service was paid to honesty and hard work.

GRIEVANCES OF THE EASTERN NIGERIANS

In the old Federation some of you here will remember quite vividly what the contribution of the people from this area, now known as Biafra, was to the betterment of the areas in which we chose to reside and believed was our country. Socially we gave our best in Nigeria. Politically, we led the struggle for independence and sustained it. Economically, the hope of Nigeria was embedded deeply in this area and we contributed everything for the common good of Nigeria.

Our people moved from this area to all parts of the old Federation, and particularly to Northern Nigeria. Where there was darkness we gave them light! In Northern Nigeria, where they had no shelter we gave them houses. Where they were sick, as indeed most Northerners are, we brought them health. Where there was backwardness we brought progress. And where there was ignorance we brought them education. As a result of all this, we became people marked out in the various communities in which we lived.

Initially we were marked out as people who were progressive. Next, as people who were successful. Finally as people who should be the object of jealousy—people who were to be hated, and this hatred arose as a result of our success.... We were relegated to the position of second-class citizens and later to slavery—yes, slavery—because as we worked, our masters enjoyed the fruits of our labor.

We reached a stage where the people from this part were fast losing their identity. They hid away the fact that they came from this area....

The Northern attitude is the attitude of horse and rider.... We were carrying the North physically, economically, and in every other way. For all that we received no thanks. They only got furious if we did not travel fast enough. Then they would kick. But, for every mule there comes a time when it bucks and says, "No, I will carry no more." We have bucked. We will carry Northern Nigeria no more!

THE NEW BIAFRAN SOCIETY

Born out of the gruesome murders and vandalism of yesterday, Biafra has come to stay as a historical reality. We believe that the future we face and our battle for survival cannot be won by bullets alone, but by brainpower, modern skills, and the determination to live and succeed....

Nepotism and tribalism are twin evils. I believe that these can be avoided if we set about making sure that every appointment in our society is based on one and only one criterion—merit. We should ensure that this term "merit" is no mumbo-jumbo. It should be something that is obvious for everyone to see: that is, when you have given somebody a job, the reason for giving that job to that person in preference to others must be generally clear....

Tribalism is, perhaps, more deeply rooted.... When I first came to this area as the military governor, one of the first things I did was to erase tribe from all public documents. We are all Biafrans. "Where do you come from?" you are asked, and the answer is simple: "I come from Biafra." The government must not emphasize tribal origin if it is trying to stamp out tribalism....

Every effort should be made by future governments to educate our people away from tribalism. I would like to see movement of people across tribal frontiers. The government should encourage people to move from their own areas to be educated elsewhere. Yes, I would even go further to support government measures to encourage intertribal marriages.... It is only a gesture, but if the government really believes that tribalism could be wiped out, something like a bounty should be given to that young man who marries across tribe, to show that the government appreciates what he has done....

I see a new breed of men and women, with new moral and spiritual values, building a new society—a renascent and strong Biafra.

I see the realization of all our cherished dreams and aspirations in a revolution which will not only guarantee our basic freedoms but usher in an era of equal opportunity and prosperity for all.

I see the evolution of a new democracy in Biafra as we advance as partners in our country's onward march to her destiny.

When I look into the future, I see Biafra transformed into a fully industrialized nation, wastelands and slums giving way to throbbing industrial centers and cities....

I see agriculture mechanized by science and technology....

I see a Republic knit with arteries of roads and highways; a nation of free men and women dedicated to the noble attributes of justice and liberty for which our youth have shed their blood; a people with an art and literature rich and unrivaled.

I am sure all Biafrans share these hopes for our country's future and destiny.... We are building a society which will destroy the myth that the black man cannot organize his own society.

... We are taking our rightful place in the world as human beings.... The black man cannot progress until he can point at a progressive black society. Until a society, a virile society entirely black, is established, the black man, whether he is in America, whether he is in Africa, will never be able to take his place side by side with the white man. We have the unique opportunity today of breaking our chains.

... We owe it, therefore, to Africa not to fail. Africa needs a Biafra. Biafra is the breaking of the chains....

Apartheid's Bitter Fruits

◈

78 ◆ Nelson Mandela,
THE RIVONIA TRIAL SPEECH TO THE COURT

In 1912, two years after South Africa had been granted independence from Great Britain, blacks formed the African National Congress (ANC) to foster black unity and win political rights. At first, the ANC sought to reach its goals through petitions and appeals to white politicians, but following the implementation of apartheid after World War II, it sponsored campaigns of passive resistance and supported strikes by black labor unions. The result was more government repression.

Predictably, some blacks turned to sabotage and terrorism. Among them was Nelson Mandela (b.1918), the son of a tribal chieftain, who became a lawyer and an ANC activist in the 1940s. After the ANC was outlawed in 1960, and after he organized a three-day general strike in 1961, Mandela went into hiding. While avoiding a nationwide manhunt, he helped found *Umkhonto we Sizwe* (Spear of the Nation), a branch of the ANC that carried out bombings in several cities. Arrested in 1962, probably as a result of a tip from U.S. CIA agents, he was convicted for helping organize the nationwide strike in 1961 and sentenced to five years in prison. While serving this sentence, he and nine others (including five South

Source: Nelson Mandela, *No Easy Walk to Freedom*, ed. Ruth First (New York: Basic Books, 1965), pp. 163–168. Copyright © 1965. Used by permission of Pearson Education.

African whites) were accused of acts of sabotage and other crimes that were equivalent of treason. On his conviction in 1964, he was given a life sentence and sent to the notorious prison on Robben Island, some seven miles off South Africa's southwestern coast near Cape Town. He remained there until 1990, when he was released by President F. W. de Klerk as one of the first steps toward the abolition of the apartheid system. On May 10, 1994, after South Africa's first democratic election, he became the country's first black president.

The following excerpt comes from a speech Mandela delivered on April 20, 1964, in which he opened his defense against charges of treason before Judge Quartus de Wet, who decided the case and passed sentences once he decided on the defendants' guilt.

QUESTIONS FOR ANALYSIS

1. Why did Mandela decide that the ANC must resort to violence to achieve its goals?
2. What distinction does Mandela draw between sabotage and terrorism?
3. What attractions did Mandela and other ANC leaders see in communism?
4. What aspects of apartheid does Mandela find most degrading?
5. According to Mandela, how does apartheid affect the daily lives of the blacks?
6. How does Mandela's description of life in the black townships compare with Charlotte Maxeke's description of South African urban life in the 1930s (see Source 41)?

In my youth ... I listened to the elders of my tribe telling stories of the old days. Amongst the tales they related to me were those of wars fought by our ancestors in defense of the fatherland.... I hoped then that life might offer me the opportunity to serve my people and make my own humble contribution to their freedom struggle. This is what has motivated me in all that I have done in relation to the charges made against me in this case....

I have already mentioned that I was one of the persons who helped to form Umkhonto. I, and the others who started the organization, did so for two reasons. Firstly, we believed that as a result of Government policy, violence by the African people had become inevitable, and that unless responsible leadership was given to canalize and control the feelings of our people, there would be outbreaks of terrorism which would produce an intensity of bitterness and hostility between the various races of this country which

is not produced even by war. Secondly, we felt that without violence there would be no way open to the African people to succeed in their struggle against the principle of White supremacy. All lawful modes of expressing opposition to this principle had been closed by legislation, and we were placed in a position in which we had either to accept a permanent state of inferiority, or to defy the Government....

But the violence which we chose to adopt was not terrorism. We who formed Umkonto were all members of the African National Congress, and had behind us the ANC tradition of non-violence and negotiation as a means of solving political disputes. We believed that South Africa belonged to all the people who lived in it, and not to one group, be it Black or White. We did not want an interracial war, and tried to avoid it to the last minute....

The African National Congress was formed in 1912 to defend the rights of the African people.... For thirty-seven years—that is until 1949—it adhered strictly to a constitutional struggle. It put forward demands and resolutions; it sent delegations to the Government in the belief that African grievances could be settled through peaceful discussion and that Africans could advance gradually to full political rights. But White Governments remained unmoved, and the rights of Africans became less instead of becoming greater....

Even after 1949, the ANC remained determined to avoid violence. At this time, however, there was a change from the strictly constitutional means of protest which had been employed in the past. The change was embodied in a decision which was taken to protest against apartheid legislation by peaceful, but unlawful, demonstrations against certain laws. Pursuant to this policy the ANC launched the Defiance Campaign, in which I was placed in charge of volunteers. This campaign was based on the principles of passive resistance. More than 8,500 people defied apartheid laws and went to jail. Yet there was not a single instance of violence in the course of this campaign....

In 1960 there was the shooting at Sharpeville,[1] which resulted in the proclamation of a state of emergency and the declaration of the ANC as an unlawful organization. My colleagues and I, after careful consideration, decided that we would not obey this decree. The African people were not part of the Government and did not make the laws by which they were governed. We believed in the words of the Universal Declaration of Human Rights,[2] that "the will of the people shall be the basis of authority of the Government," and for us to accept the banning was equivalent to accepting the silencing of the Africans for all time. The ANC refused to dissolve, but instead went underground....

... Each disturbance pointed clearly to the inevitable growth among Africans of the belief that violence was the only way out—it showed that a Government which uses force to maintain its rule teaches the oppressed to use force to oppose it....

Four forms of violence were possible. There is sabotage, there is guerrilla warfare, there is terrorism, and there is open revolution. We chose to adopt the first method and to exhaust it before taking any other decision.

In the light of our political background the choice was a logical one. Sabotage did not involve loss of life, and it offered the best hope for future race relations. Bitterness would be kept to a minimum and, if the policy bore fruit, democratic government could become a reality....

Attacks on the economic life lines of the country were to be linked with sabotage on Government buildings and other symbols of apartheid. These attacks would serve as a source of inspiration to our people. In addition, they would provide an outlet for those people who were urging the adoption of violent methods and would enable us to give concrete proof to our followers that we had adopted a stronger line and were fighting back against Government violence....

◆ ◆

Another of the allegations made by the State is that the aims and objects of the ANC and the Communist Party are the same....

It is true that there has often been close cooperation between the ANC and the Communist Party. But cooperation is merely proof of a common goal—in this case the removal of White supremacy—and is not proof of a complete community of interests....

It is perhaps difficult for White South Africans, with an ingrained prejudice against

---

[1]The Sharpeville Massacre took place in 1960 when police killed 69 and wounded 178 anti-apartheid demonstrators.

[2]The Universal Declaration of Human Rights was adopted by the United Nations on December 10, 1948.

communism, to understand why experienced African politicians so readily accept communists as their friends. But to us the reason is obvious. Theoretical differences amongst those fighting against oppression is a luxury we cannot afford at this stage. What is more, for many decades communists were the only political group in South Africa who were prepared to treat Africans as human beings and their equals; who were prepared to eat with us, talk with us, live with us, and work with us. They were the only political group which was prepared to work with the Africans for the attainment of political rights and a stake in society. Because of this, there are many Africans who, today, tend to equate freedom with communism....

South Africa is the richest country in Africa, and could be one of the richest countries in the world. But it is a land of extremes and remarkable contrasts. The Whites enjoy what may well be the highest standard of living in the world, whilst Africans live in poverty and misery. Forty percent of the Africans live in hopelessly overcrowded and, in some cases, drought-stricken Reserves, where soil erosion and the overworking of the soil make it impossible for them to live properly off the land. Thirty percent are laborers, labor tenants, and squatters on White farms and work and live under conditions similar to those of the serfs of the Middle Ages. The other 30 percent live in towns where they have developed economic and social habits which bring them closer in many respects to White standards. Yet most Africans, even in this group, are impoverished by low incomes and [the] high cost of living....

The lack of human dignity experienced by Africans is the direct result of the policy of White supremacy. White supremacy implies Black inferiority. Legislation designed to preserve White supremacy entrenches this notion. Menial tasks in South Africa are invariably performed by Africans. When anything has to be carried or cleaned the White man will look around for an African to do it for him, whether the African is employed by him or not. Because of this sort of attitude, Whites tend to regard Africans as a separate breed. They do not look upon them as people with families of their own; they do not realize that they have emotions—that they fall in love like White people do; that they want to be with their wives and children like White people want to be with theirs; that they want to earn enough money to support their families properly, to feed and clothe them and send them to school. And what "house-boy" or "garden-boy" or laborer can ever hope to do this? ...

Poverty and the breakdown of family life have secondary effects. Children wander about the streets of the townships because they have no schools to go to, or no money to enable them to go to school, or no parents at home to see that they go to school, because both parents (if there be two) have to work to keep the family alive. This leads to a breakdown in moral standards, to an alarming rise in illegitimacy, and to growing violence which erupts, not only politically, but everywhere. Life in the townships is dangerous. There is not a day that goes by without somebody being stabbed or assaulted....

During my lifetime I have dedicated myself to this struggle of the African people. I have fought against White domination, and I have fought against Black domination. I have cherished the ideal of a democratic and free society in which all persons live together in harmony and with equal opportunities. It is an ideal which I hope to live for and to achieve. But if needs be, it is an ideal for which I am prepared to die.

South and Southeast Asia After Colonialism

In the two decades after World War II, the peoples of South and Southeast Asia achieved independence from foreign rule, though how they achieved it varied widely. In the Philippines, it was the culmination of a long-standing U.S. plan to prepare the Filipinos for self-government. In India, it was the result of a protracted struggle on the part of the Indian people against British rule. In the Dutch East Indies, French Indochina, and British-controlled Burma, Singapore, and Malaya, Western imperialism effectively ended with the Japanese conquests of 1942, but in the case of Indochina and the East Indies, it took several years of fighting after World War II before the Dutch and French realized this and relinquished control of their colonies.

After achieving independence, the new nations of South and Southeast Asia faced similar problems. All had high levels of poverty, widespread illiteracy, and little industry. All but a few had populations divided by race, language, and ethnic background. India was predominantly Hindu, but had large Sikh and Muslim minorities; so great was its linguistic diversity that its parliament approved no less than fourteen official languages in the 1950s. Burma had a population in which approximately one-third of its people practiced religions and spoke languages different from those of the Buddhist majority. In Malaysia, the Malays, mainly farmers, and the Chinese, mainly businesspeople, viewed each other with distrust, as did Tamils and Sinhalese in Ceylon (Sri Lanka) and Muslims and Catholics in the Philippines. Pakistan was divided into two sections, two thousand miles apart, in which the people of West Pakistan spoke Urdu, grew wheat, and worried about drought, while those in East Pakistan spoke Hindi, grew rice, and worried about floods. Indonesia was a nation of seventy-six million people who spoke two hundred fifty different languages and lived on thousands of islands that stretched across a distance equal to that between Boston and Ireland.

The region's new states all faced formidable political challenges. Although most started out as parliamentary democracies, democracy soon gave way to authoritarian regimes installed by the military in Burma, Pakistan, Thailand, and Indonesia. Vietnam, which was divided into a communist north and a noncommunist south after the French departed in 1954, became the scene of major U.S. military intervention to prevent the unification of the country under communist rule. The number of U.S. troops fighting in Vietnam grew slowly under Presidents Eisenhower and Kennedy, peaked at over five hundred thousand under President Johnson, and then declined under President Nixon, whose policy of Vietnamization resulted in U.S. troop withdrawals but continued support for the army of South Vietnam. Laos and Cambodia were also drawn into the struggle. The Ho Chi Minh Trail, by which North Vietnam sent troops and supplies to the south, ran through both countries, and this led to U.S. bombings, intervention to prop up anticommunist rulers, and the invasion of Cambodia by U.S. and South Vietnamese troops in 1970.

The U.S. mission in Southeast Asia failed on all fronts. Although the United States lost fifty-eight thousand troops, dropped more bombs on North Vietnam than it had dropped in all of World War II, and spent billions of dollars, in April 1975 South Vietnamese resistance collapsed, and Vietnam was united under communist rule. Later in the year communist regimes also gained control of Cambodia and Laos.

For Cambodians, the horror was not quite over. During the rule of the communist dictator Pol Pot, forced labor, starvation, systematic torture, and massacres of intellectuals, political opponents, and resident Vietnamese resulted in an estimated 1.7 million deaths. Only the invasion and occupation of Cambodia by North Vietnam in 1979 brought this chapter in the history of Southeast Asia to a close.

Nehru's Blueprint for India

❖

79 ◆ Jawaharlal Nehru,
SPEECHES AND WRITINGS, 1954–1957

Born into a prestigious upper-class family in 1889, Jawaharlal Nehru was educated in England at Harrow School and Cambridge University before studying law in London. On his return to India in 1912, he became a member of the Indian National Congress, which since 1885 had worked for increased Indian participation in the colonial administration and ultimately Indian independence. In 1919, Nehru decided to devote himself completely to the independence movement after troops, on orders from a British officer, fired into a crowd of demonstrators in Amritsar, killing several hundred. He was elected president of the Congress in 1929. Repeatedly arrested by the British for acts of civil disobedience and other political actions, he spent a total of nine years in prison. After World War II, he took part in the negotiations that led to the creation of the separate states of India and Pakistan.

After independence in 1947, he helped craft India's constitution and served as head of the Congress Party and prime minister until his death in 1964. In the following excerpts from speeches and writings of the 1950s, he discusses his ideas about India's future.

QUESTIONS FOR ANALYSIS

1. According to Nehru, what are the major problems and challenges facing his new country?
2. In his view, who or what is to blame for these problems?
3. What does Nehru mean by the term "planning," and why, in his view, is it so important for India's future?

4. Similarly, what does he mean by "secularism," and why is it important for India's future?
5. Gandhi and Nehru are viewed as India's two greatest leaders in the twentieth century. In what ways do their views of India and its future resemble and differ from each other?

[PLANNING AND THE WELFARE STATE]

An Address to the Indian National Congress, Avadi, January 22, 1955

Planning[1] is essential, and without it there would be anarchy in our economic development. About five years ago, planning was not acceptable to many people in high places but today it has come to be recognized as essential even by the man in the street. . . .

. . . We cannot have a welfare state in India with all the socialism or even communism in the world unless our national income goes up greatly. Socialism or communism might help you to divide your existing wealth . . . but in India, there is no existing wealth for you to divide; there is only poverty to divide. It is not a question of distributing the wealth of the few rich men here and there. That is not going to make any difference. . . . We must produce wealth, and then divide it equitably. How can we have a welfare state without wealth? Wealth need not mean gold and silver but wealth in goods and services. Our economic policy must therefore aim at plenty. . . .

. . . The conception of planning today is not to think of the money we have and then to divide it up in the various schemes but to measure the physical needs, that is to say, how much of food the people want, how much of clothes they want, how much of housing they want, how much of education they want, how much of health services they want, how much of work and employment they want, and so on. We calculate all these and then decide what everyone in India should have of these things. Once we do that, we can set about increasing production and fulfilling these needs. It is not a simple matter because in calculating the needs of the people, we have to calculate on the basis not only of an increasing population but of increasing needs. . . . Therefore, we have to keep in mind that the extra money that goes into circulation because of the higher salaries and wages, affects consumption. So we find out what in five years' time will be the needs of our people, including even items needed by our Defence Services. Then we decide how to produce those things in India. In order to meet a particular variety of needs we have now to put up a factory which will produce the goods that we need five years hence. Thus, planning is a much more complicated process than merely drawing up some schemes and fixing a system of priorities. . . .

But production is not all. . . . Mass production inevitably involves mass consumption, which in turn involves many other factors, chiefly the purchasing power of the consumer. Therefore planning must take note of the need to provide more purchasing power by way of wages, salaries and so on. Enough money should be thrown in to provide this purchasing power and to complete the circle of production and consumption. You will then produce more and consume more, and as a result your standard of living will go up. . . .

Source: Saravapelli Gopal, ed., *Jawaharlal Nehru An Anthology* (Delhi: Jawaharlal Nehru Memorial Fund, 1980): 311, 312.

---

[1]"Planning" in the sense of economic planning by the central government. Since his first visit to the Soviet Union in the 1920s, Nehru was a great admirer of the Soviet Union's state-controlled economy as means of achieving rapid industrialization and economic growth. India's "five year plans" were modeled on those of the Soviet Union.

[CAPITALISM, SOCIALISM, AND DEMOCRACY]

Speech to All-India Congress Committee, January 4, 1957

The whole of the capitalist structure is based on some kind of an acquisitive society. It may be that, to some extent, the tendency to acquisitiveness is inherent in us. A socialist society must try to get rid of this tendency to acquisitiveness and replace it by co-operation. You cannot bring about this change by a sudden law. There have to be long processes of training the people; without this you cannot wholly succeed. Even from the very limited point of view of changing your economic structure, apart from your minds and hearts, it takes time to build a socialist society. The countries that have gone fastest have also taken time. I would like you to consider that the Soviet Union, which has gone fast in industrialization, has taken thirty-five years or more over it. Chairman Mao of the People's Republic of China—which is more or less a communist state—said, about three or four years ago, that it would take China twenty years to achieve some kind of socialism. Mind you, this [is] in spite of the fact that theirs is an authoritarian state, and the people are exceedingly disciplined and industrious. Chairman Mao was speaking as a practical idealist. We must realize that the process of bringing socialism to India, especially in the way we are doing it, that is, the democratic way, will inevitably take time.

We have definitely accepted the democratic process. Why have we accepted it? . . . Because we think in the final analysis it promotes the growth of human beings and of society; because we have said in our Constitution, we attach great value to human freedom; because we want the creative and adventurous spirit of man to grow. It is not enough for us merely to produce the material goods of the world. We do not want high standards of living, but not at the cost of man's creative spirit, his creative energy, his spirit of adventure; not at the cost of all those fine things of life which have ennobled man throughout the ages.

Source: Jawaharlal Nehru's Speeches, Vol. 3 (Kolkata: Government of India Ministry of Information and Broadcasting, 1958): 52, 53.

[INDIA AS A SECULAR STATE]

A circular to the Pradesh Congress Committees, August 5, 1954

We call our state a secular one. The word 'secular' perhaps is not a very happy one. And yet, for want of a better word, we have used it. What exactly does it mean? It does not obviously mean a state where religion as such is discouraged. It means freedom of religion and conscience, including freedom for those who may have no religion. It means free play for all religions, subject only to their not interfering with each other or with the basic conceptions of our state. It means that the minority communities, from the religious point of view, should accept this position. It means, even more, that the majority community, from this point of view, should fully realize it. For, by virtue of numbers as well as in other ways, it is the dominant community and it is its responsibility not to use its position in any way which might prejudice our secular ideal.

The word 'secular,' however, conveys something much more to me, although that might not be its dictionary meaning. It conveys the idea of social and political equality. Thus, a caste-ridden society[2] is not properly secular. I have no desire to interfere with any person's belief, but when those beliefs become petrified in caste divisions, undoubtedly they affect the social structure of the state. They prevent us from realizing the idea of equality which we

---

[2]The Indian caste system, which dates from 1000–800 B.C.E., is a rigid form of social differentiation in which groups, traditionally linked to occupational specialties, are ranked on a hierarchical scale. Each caste has its own code of appropriate behavior, and marriage and such activities as dining are generally restricted to members of the same caste. At the bottom of the social order are Dalits, or "untouchables," individuals who are considered impure by caste Hindus. Throughout much of Indian history they were barred from schools and places of worship and associated with "unclean" professions such as leatherwork, butchering, and removal of rubbish, animal carcasses, and waste. India's constitution barred untouchability, and since the 1950s, the government has enacted many laws to protect and improve the socio-economic conditions of its Dalit population.

claim to place before ourselves. . . . We have opposed communalism[3] and continue to be stoutly opposed to it. It is, in fact, a negation of nationalism and of the nation-state. . . . Casteism is as dangerous as communalism, and both are effective barriers, if they are strong enough, to the development of true democracy and equality.

We are apt to take pride in our tradition of tolerance. It is always dangerous to have this complacent attitude about oneself because it hides the truth from us. Few people see their own weaknesses and failings although they are wide awake to the failings in others.

Source: Selected Works of Jawaharlal Nehru, Second Series, Volume 26 (New Delhi: Jawaharlal Nehru Memorial Fund, 1984): 200, 201.

[THE ROLE OF WOMEN]
Speech at Shailabala Women's College, Cuttack, February 13, 1957

There is a strange condition in India. On the one hand, throughout history and in modern times as well, there have been women who have earned a name for themselves by their work and spirit of service. There is no doubt about it that in the last three decades women have played a major role in our freedom struggle. When Gandhiji's call came, women came out in large numbers to participate in national tasks[4]. . . . It was a difficult time and thousands of people were in jail. It was at such a time that he asked the women to join in and women who had never stepped foot outside their homes, came out in large numbers to join the freedom struggle . . .

But once the movement was over, the women somehow slipped back into their old traditional roles. However, even now you will find that women are leading in many fields in India . . . There are many women in the forefront of national tasks and at the same time, it is equally true that the majority of our women are backward and suppressed.

There are many factors which create obstacles in their path and suppress them . . . We must hold on to the good cultural traditions of our country, there is no doubt about that. But India is a very ancient country. The older a country grows, many good as well as bad accretions cling on and the bad things shackle growth. . . . India has had a wealth of high principles and ideals and a rich cultural heritage. But there are outmoded customs too which have shackled Indian society and weakened it. This weakness led to India's downfall and we fell to foreign invaders. Now other shackles remain and we must rid ourselves of some of our evil customs and habits and outmoded traditions. As a matter of fact, the worst shackle is poverty. We must get rid of it. . . .

There are community development schemes for rural uplift. It is not possible for the central or state governments to do these things unless the people in the villages themselves do it. . . . It is the people in the villages who must strive to improve their condition by building roads, schools, hospitals—and by increasing agricultural production . . . Women must be a part of that otherwise the country will go down further. Therefore it becomes very essential that women must be educated so that they can participate in national tasks in whichever way they can . . .

We have passed some laws in parliament last year pertaining to the status of women.[5] Some people are opposed to these reforms saying they were against our ancient traditions. They were wrong . . . They have helped to improve the condition of women in India somewhat.

We must try to understand these things well. The days of blind superstition are over. The superstitious cannot progress . . .

Source: Selected Works of Jawaharlal Nehru, Second Series, Volume 36 (New Delhi: Jawaharlal Nehru Memorial Fund, 2005): 121, 122.

[3]In South Asia this refers to an attitude in which one's primary allegiance is to an ethnic or religious group rather than to the nation at large.

[4]Gandhi enlisted many thousands of women to participate in his campaign against British rule, especially boycotts of British goods and the nationwide marches, demonstrations, and acts of civil disobedience in 1930 to protest the British monopoly on salt production.

[5]In May 1956, the Indian parliament passed a bill that for the first time provided for a share of the father's property to a daughter on his death granted women absolute right to self-acquired property.

[CONSEQUENCES OF THE CASTE SYSTEM]

Speech at a public meeting in Seurat, October 30, 1955

Casteism is yet another dangerous feeling which exists in India, especially among the Hindus. It has been responsible for dividing the country and the great discrimination that exists. We have high castes and low castes and untouchability and what not which have weakened Hindu society tremendously in the past. How can there be strength in a society which is divided into innumerable groups? We want that there should be complete unity and harmony among the people of India whether they are Hindus, Muslims, Sikhs, Christians or Parsees, instead of all our time being wasted in meaningless taboos. How can Hindus hope to progress if they are constantly preoccupied with such petty matters? It is indeed strange that there are innumerable countries and peoples and races and religions in the world but there is no country in the world except India in which untouchability or taboos regarding commensality [the act of dining at the same table] exist. People who come from outside are often surprised, for they simply cannot understand these things . . .

If you read the ancient history of India, you will find that there was no untouchability then. People were very adventurous and would cross the seas and visit foreign lands. You will find ample evidence of the spread of Indian culture and art and civilization all over South-East Asia, in Java, and Sumatra and elsewhere, and the impact of India was great. Then later, some of the religious leaders began to introduce all sorts of narrow-minded injunctions and taboos against travel, saying that crossing the seas would destroy one's religion. The result was that we began to live like frogs in a well while the world advanced, we remained backward . . . So, though our country is a large one, in a sense it became a sort of cage in which our thinking was imprisoned.

Source: Selected Works of Jawaharlal Nehru, Second Series, Volume 30 (New Delhi: Jawaharlal Nehru Memorial Fund, 2002): 111.

Two Perspectives on the War in Vietnam

❖

80 ◆ *HO CHI MINH-JOHNSON CORRESPONDENCE, FEBRUARY 1967*

By early 1967, it was clear that there would be no quick American victory in Vietnam. Despite the commitment of approximately four hundred thousand U.S. troops and devastating bombing attacks on North Vietnam, the war had become a deadly stalemate that bitterly divided the American people. Faced with these realities, President Johnson and his advisors renewed their efforts to end the war through negotiation. In February 1967, Johnson wrote directly to the North Vietnamese leader, Ho Chi Minh, spelling out the U.S. negotiating stance. Ho rejected Johnson's proposal, and formal negotiations between the two sides did not begin until May 1968. By then, another one hundred thousand U.S. troops had been committed to Vietnam.

It is not surprising that Ho Chi Minh was reluctant to negotiate an agreement that fell short of his goal of a united, communist Vietnam. Born in 1890, Ho, then known as Nguyen Sinh Cung, left French Indochina at the age of twenty-one to

Source: From President Ho Chi Minh Answers President L.B. Johnson. Copyright © 1967, pp. 9–12, 27–29.

work on a French oceangoing ship and then at a hotel in London. Toward the end of World War I he moved to France, where he became a socialist and tried to convince negotiators at the Paris Peace Conference to accept a plan for Vietnamese independence. In 1920, he was one of the founders of the French Communist Party and became a student of Lenin's writings. In 1923, he went to the Soviet Union, and after a year of training returned to Indochina, where he organized the Indochinese Communist Party in 1930. Forced to flee during the 1930s, he returned to Vietnam in 1943 and founded the communist-controlled League for the Independence of Vietnam, or Viet Minh, which campaigned against the occupying Japanese while building a base for a postwar independence movement. With Japan's defeat in 1945, Ho proclaimed the independent Democratic Republic of Vietnam and became its first president. Until his death in 1969, he led his country during eight years of warfare against the French and fifteen years of warfare against the anticommunist South Vietnamese regime established in 1954 at the Geneva Conference.

The following selection includes an excerpt from President Johnson's letter to Ho Chi Minh sent on February 8, 1967, and the entire text of Ho's response dated February 15. The exchange reveals the broad differences in the thinking of the two statesmen.

QUESTIONS FOR ANALYSIS

1. According to Johnson's letter, what had the Vietnamese proposed as conditions for beginning "direct bilateral talks"?
2. Why does Johnson reject the Vietnamese proposal, and what does he propose instead?
3. In the last paragraph of his letter, Ho Chi Minh states, "Our cause is absolutely just." What is the basis of his assertion?
4. Why does Ho reject President Johnson's proposal for negotiations? What counterproposal does he make?

His Excellency Ho Chi Minh
President, Democratic Republic of Vietnam

Dear Mr. President,

I am writing to you in the hope that the conflict in Vietnam can be brought to an end. The conflict has already taken a heavy toll—in lives lost, in wounds inflicted, in property destroyed, and in simple human misery. If we fail to find a just and peaceful solution, history will judge us harshly....

In the past two weeks, I have noted public statements by representatives of your government suggesting that you would be prepared to enter into direct bilateral talks with representatives of the U.S. Government, provided that we ceased "unconditionally" and permanently our bombing operations against your country and all military actions against it. In the last days, serious and responsible parties have assured us indirectly that this is in fact your proposal.

Let me frankly state that I see two great difficulties with this proposal. In view of your public position, such action on our part would inevitably produce worldwide speculation that discussions were under way and would impair the privacy and secrecy of those discussions. Secondly, there would inevitably be grave concern on our part whether your government would make use of such action by us to improve its military position.

With these problems in mind, I am prepared to move even further toward an ending of the hostilities than your government has proposed in either public statements or through private diplomatic channels. I am prepared to order a cessation of bombing against your country and the stopping of further augmentation of U.S. forces in South Vietnam as soon as I am assured that infiltration into South Vietnam by land and by sea has stopped. These acts of restraint on both sides would, I believe, make it possible for us to conduct serious and private discussions leading toward an early peace. . . .

As to the site of the bilateral discussions I propose, there are several possibilities. We could, for example, have our representatives meet in Moscow where contacts have already occurred. They could meet in some other country such as Burma. You may have other arrangements or sites in mind, and I would try to meet your suggestions. . . .

Sincerely,

LYNDON B. JOHNSON

To His Excellency Mr. Lyndon B. Johnson
President
United States of America

Your Excellency,

On February 10, 1967, I received your message. This is my reply.

Vietnam is thousands of miles away from the United States. The Vietnamese people have never done any harm to the United States. But contrary to the pledges made by its representative at the 1954 Geneva Conference, the U.S. Government has ceaselessly intervened in Vietnam, it has unleashed and intensified the war of aggression in South Vietnam with a view to prolonging the partition of Vietnam and turning South Vietnam into a neo-colony and a military base of the United States. For over two years now, the U.S. Government has, with its air and naval forces, carried the war to the Democratic Republic of Vietnam, an independent and sovereign country.

The U.S. Government has committed war crimes, crimes against peace and against mankind. In South Vietnam, half a million U.S. and satellite troops have resorted to the most inhuman weapons and the most barbarous methods of warfare, such as napalm,[1] toxic chemicals and gases, to massacre our compatriots, destroy crops, and raze villages to the ground. In North Vietnam, thousands of U.S. aircraft have dropped hundreds of thousands of tons of bombs, destroying towns, villages, factories, roads, bridges, dikes, dams, and even churches, pagodas, hospitals, schools. In your message, you apparently deplored the sufferings and destructions in Vietnam. May I ask you: Who has perpetrated these monstrous crimes? It is the U.S. and satellite troops. The U.S. Government is entirely responsible for the extremely serious situation in Vietnam.

The U.S. war of aggression against the Vietnamese people constitutes a challenge to the countries of the socialist camp, a threat to the national independence movement, and a serious danger to peace in Asia and the world.

The Vietnamese people deeply love independence, freedom and peace. But in the face of the U.S. aggression, they have risen up, united as one man, fearless of sacrifices and hardships; they are determined to carry on their Resistance

---

[1]Napalm is a military incendiary substance made up of gasoline, other fuels, and a gelling agent (made up of naphthenic and palmitic acids from which is derived the acronym *napalm*). A napalm-armed bomb or flamethrower broadcasts the substance over a wide area where it burns with intense heat. Its use to destroy villages and defoliate jungles to reveal enemy camps was bitterly protested by antiwar activists.

until they have won genuine independence and freedom and true peace. Our just cause enjoys strong sympathy and support from the peoples of the whole world including broad sections of the American people.

The U.S. Government has unleashed the war of aggression in Vietnam. It must cease this aggression. This is the only way to the restoration of peace. The U.S. Government must stop definitively and unconditionally its bombing raids and all other acts of war against the Democratic Republic of Vietnam, withdraw from South Vietnam all U.S. and satellite troops, recognize the South Vietnam National Front for Liberation,[2] and let the Vietnamese people settle themselves their own affairs. Such is the basic content of the four-point stand of the Government of the Democratic Republic of Vietnam, which embodies the essential principles and provisions of the 1954 Geneva Agreements on Vietnam. It is the basis of a correct political solution to the Vietnam problem.

In your message, you suggested direct talks between the Democratic Republic of Vietnam and the United States. If the U.S. Government really wants these talks, it must first of all stop unconditionally its bombing raids and all other acts of war against the Democratic Republic of Vietnam. It is only after the unconditional cessation of the U.S. bombing raids and all other acts of war against the Democratic Republic of Vietnam that the Democratic Republic of Vietnam and the United States could enter into talks and discuss questions concerning the two sides.

The Vietnamese people will never submit to force; they will never accept talks under the threat of bombs.

Our cause is absolutely just. It is to be hoped that the U.S. Government will act in accordance with reason.

Sincerely,

HO CHI MINH

---

[2]The National Liberation Front, was founded in 1960 by supporters of Ho Chi Minh in South Vietnam. It became the umbrella organization under which guerrilla warfare was waged against the South Vietnamese government.

Revolution and Reaction in Latin America

In August 1961, delegates to a meeting of the Organization of American States in Uruguay approved a set of goals for the Alliance for Progress, a program proposed by U.S. President John F. Kennedy to foster Latin American democracy, economic development, and social reform with the help of billions of U.S. dollars. The list of goals, known as the Charter of Punta del Este, was ambitious. Over the next ten years participants were to achieve economic growth of 2.5 percent per year, more equitable distribution of national income, greater industrialization, agrarian reform, elimination of adult illiteracy, price stability, improved health care, reduced infant mortality, increased life expectancy by at least five years, and much more. The result would be "maximum levels of well-being, with equal opportunities for all, in democratic societies adapted to their own needs and desires."

The Alliance for Progress achieved few of these goals. By the early 1970s, Latin America was experiencing widening trade deficits, weakened commodity prices, and double- and even triple-digit inflation. Governments were making little headway against the problem of mass poverty, which worsened as a result of population growth and depressed wages. Programs for social reform, adopted by Guatemala and Bolivia in the early 1950s, Peru in 1968, and Chile in the early 1970s, either languished or were quashed by right-wing governments on seizing power.

One state that experienced major reforms was Fidel Castro's Cuba. After the overthrow of the dictator Fulgencio Batista in 1959, Castro's government carried out land reform, nationalized industries, provided universal health care and education, and in the short term raised Cubans' standards of living. Paradoxically, Castro's Cuba also dimmed the prospects for social reform elsewhere in the region. The Cuban model frightened Latin America's elites, who rallied behind military dictatorships that promised to halt the spread of communism.

Many of these military regimes were supported by the U.S. government, whose political involvement in Latin America reached new heights during the Cold War. Even before the Cuban Revolution, the Eisenhower administration sought to limit social and economic reform in Bolivia after a revolution in 1952, cooperated with Great Britain to overthrow a left-leaning administration in British Guiana, and trained and outfitted rebels who ousted Guatemala's democratically elected government in 1954 after its plans for land reform threatened the U.S. banana conglomerate, the United Fruit Company.

Efforts to overthrow Castro failed, however. Assassination plots came to nothing, and the CIA-planned invasion of Cuba in April 1961 by anti-Castro exiles was crushed. The United States also attempted to counter communism with the Alliance for Progress, the economic development program that failed, and support for right-wing governments, a program that in the short run succeeded. During the 1970s, repressive authoritarian regimes proliferated in Central and South America. They used death squads, assassins, torturers, and U.S.-equipped armies against leftist politicians, social reformers, and revolutionaries. Communism was contained, but poverty, inflation, and foreign debt became worse than ever.

"Create Two, Three, or Many Vietnams"

❖

81 ◆ Ernesto "Che" Guevara, *MESSAGE TO THE TRICONTINENTAL*

Ernesto Guevara (nicknamed "Che," the colloquial Argentinean term for "mate") was born into a well-to-do Argentinean family in 1928 and was trained as a doctor. After traveling through much of Latin America, including Guatemala, where he fought against the CIA-sponsored invasion of 1954, he was introduced to Fidel Castro, a young Cuban, in Mexico City in 1955. Castro, who had been fighting to overthrow Cuban dictator Fulgencio Batista since 1953, convinced Guevara to join the band of fighters he was organizing to land in Cuba and renew the struggle. After the expeditionary force reached Cuba in 1956, Guevara proved his mastery of guerrilla warfare and became Castro's second in command. He led the troops that took Havana in January 1959.

Source: Bonachea, Rolando & Nelson Valdes, *Che: Selected Works of Ernesto Guevara,* pp.170–183, © 1969 Massachusetts Institute of Technology, by permission of The MIT Press.

Once Castro was in power, Guevara served as head of the national bank and minister of industry. Especially after 1964, however, he dedicated most of his efforts to the cause of Third World revolution, something he believed could be achieved in Asia, Africa, and Latin America of rural insurrection and guerrilla warfare. He expressed these ideas in his widely read article "Message to the Tricontinental," published in April, 1967 in the *Tricontinental*, a journal of the Organization of Solidarity of Asian, African, and Latin American Peoples, founded under Cuban auspices at an international conference held in Havana in January, 1966.

By the time the article appeared, Guevara had left Cuba for Bolivia, where he worked to organize guerrillas fighting against the right-wing generals who had seized power in 1964. Hunted down and captured by government troops, he was executed by a firing squad in October 1967. Che lived on, however, as a revolutionary hero for student radicals around the world, who chanted "Che lives!" and carried posters with his image as they marched and demonstrated in the late 1960s.

QUESTIONS FOR ANALYSIS

1. According to Guevara, how is U.S. imperialism manifested in Latin America?
2. What factors, according to Guevara, make Latin America a promising area for revolutionary activity?
3. How does Guevara view the future of the revolutionary movement in Latin America?
4. What does Guevara specifically mean when he envisions "two, three, or many Vietnams"?
5. What are Guevara's hopes for the future of Latin America and the world?

The solidarity of all progressive forces of the world with the people of Vietnam is today similar to the bitter agony of the plebeians urging on the gladiators in the Roman arena. It is not a matter of wishing success to the victim of aggression, but of sharing his fate; one must accompany him to his death or to victory.

When we analyze the lonely situation of the Vietnamese people, we are overcome by anguish at this illogical fix in which humanity finds itself.

U.S. imperialism is guilty of aggression—its crimes are enormous and cover the whole world. But imperialism is bogging down in Vietnam, is unable to find a way out, and desperately seeks one that will overcome with dignity this dangerous situation in which it now finds itself. . . .

What role shall we, the exploited people of the world, play? The peoples of the three continents focus their attention on Vietnam and learn their lesson. Because imperialists blackmail humanity by threatening it with war, the wise reaction is

not to fear war. The general tactics of the people should be to launch a constant and firm attack on all fronts where the confrontation is taking place.

In those places where the meager peace we have has been violated, what is our duty? To liberate ourselves at any price. . . .

The fundamental field of imperialist exploitation comprises the three underdeveloped continents: America, Asia, and Africa. Every country has also its own characteristics, but each continent as a whole also represents a certain unity. Our America is integrated by a group of more or less homogeneous countries and in most parts of its territory U.S. monopoly capital maintains an absolute supremacy. Puppet governments, or, in the best of cases, weak and fearful local rulers, are incapable of contradicting orders from their Yankee master.

The line of action, at the present time, is limited to the brutal use of force with the purpose of thwarting the liberation movements, no matter of what type they might happen to be.

Under the slogan "We shall not allow another Cuba" hides the possibility of perpetrating aggression without fear of reprisal (such as the one carried out against the Dominican Republic or before that the massacre in Panama)[1] and the clear warning stating that the Yankee troops are ready to intervene anywhere in America where the established order may be altered, thus endangering their interests. This policy enjoys almost absolute impunity: the Organization of American States[2] is a suitable mask, in spite of its unpopularity; the inefficiency of the United Nations is ridiculous as well as tragic; the armies of all American countries are ready to intervene in order to smash their peoples. . . . There are no other alternatives; either a socialist revolution or a make-believe revolution. . . .

In Latin America armed struggle is underway in Guatemala, Colombia, Venezuela, and Bolivia, and the first uprisings are appearing in Brazil. Other foci of resistance appear and are then extinguished. But almost every country of this continent is ripe for a type of struggle that, in order to achieve victory, cannot be content with anything less than establishing a government of a socialist nature.

On this continent for all practical purposes only one tongue is spoken (with the exception of Brazil, with whose people those who speak Spanish can easily make themselves understood, owing to the great similarities of our languages). There is also such a great similarity among the classes of the different countries that an identification exists among them of an "international American" type, much more complete than that of other continents. Language, customs, religion, a common foreign master unite them. The degree and forms of exploitation are similar for both the exploiters and the exploited in many of the countries of our America. And rebellion is ripening swiftly.

We may ask ourselves: How will this rebellion come to fruition? What type will it be? We have maintained for quite some time now that, owing to the similarity of national characteristics, the struggle of our America will achieve continental proportions. It will be the scene of many great battles fought for the liberation of humanity.

Many will perish, victims of their errors; others will fall in the hard battle ahead; new fighters and new leaders will appear in the heat of the revolutionary struggle. The people will produce their fighters and leaders in the selective process of the war itself—and Yankee agents of repression will increase. Today there are military "advisers" in all the countries where armed struggle exists, and the Peruvian army, trained and advised by the Yankees, apparently carried out a successful action against the revolutionaries in that country. But if the foci of war grow with sufficient political and military wisdom, they will become practically invincible, obliging the Yankees to send reinforcements. In Peru itself many new figures, practically unknown, are now tenaciously and firmly reorganizing the guerrilla movement. Little by little the obsolete weapons which are sufficient for the repression of small armed bands will be exchanged for modern armaments and the United States military "advisers" will be substituted by United States soldiers until at a given moment they will be forced to draft increasingly greater numbers of regular troops to ensure the relative stability of a government whose national puppet army is disintegrating before the attacks of the guerrillas. It is the road of Vietnam; it is the road that will be followed in our America, with the special characteristic that the armed groups may create something like coordinating councils to frustrate the repressive efforts of Yankee imperialism and contribute to the revolutionary cause.

America, a forgotten continent in the world's more recent liberation struggles, which is now beginning to make itself heard through the Tricontinental in the voice of the vanguard of its

---

[1]In 1965, President Lyndon Johnson dispatched Marines to the Dominican Republic to suppress a rebellion against the military dictatorship that had taken power by a coup d'état two years earlier. In 1959, one hundred would-be revolutionaries who landed in Panama were trapped and annihilated by Panamanian and U.S. troops.

[2]At the time of its founding in 1948, the Organization of American States consisted of 21 American countries that pledged "to achieve an order of peace and justice, to promote their solidarity, to strengthen their collaboration, and to defend their sovereignty, their territorial integrity, and their independence." Communist Cuba was expelled from the organization in 1962.

peoples, the Cuban Revolution, has before it a task of much greater relevance: to create a second or a third Vietnam, or the second and third Vietnam of the world. . . .

The beginnings will not be easy; . . . . All of the oligarchies' power of repression, all of their brutality and demagoguery will be placed at the service of their cause. Our mission, in the first hours, will be to survive; later, we shall follow the perennial example of the guerrilla carrying out armed propaganda (in the Vietnamese sense, that is, the propaganda of bullets, of battles won or lost—but fought—against the enemy). The great lesson of the invincibility of the guerrillas will take root in the dispossessed masses: the galvanizing national spirit, preparation for harder tasks, for resisting even more violent repression; hatred as an element of struggle, relentless hatred of the enemy that impels us over and beyond the natural limitations of man and transforms us into effective, violent, selective, and cold killing machines. Our soldiers must be thus; a people without hatred cannot vanquish a brutal enemy. . . .

And let us develop a true proletarian internationalism, with international proletarian armies; let the flag under which we fight be the sacred cause of redeeming humanity so that to die under the flag of Vietnam, of Venezuela, of Guatemala, of Laos, of Guinea, of Colombia, of Bolivia, of Brazil—to name only a few scenes of today's armed struggle—will be equally glorious and desirable for an American, an Asian, an African, or even a European.

What a luminous, near future would be visible to us if two, three, or many Vietnams appeared throughout the world with their share of death and immense tragedies, their everyday heroism and repeated blows against imperialism, obliging it to disperse its forces under the attack and the increasing hatred of all the peoples of the earth!

And if we were all capable of uniting to make our blows more solid and infallible so that the effectiveness of every kind of support given to the struggling peoples were increased—how great and how near that future would be!

The Fall of Allende and the CIA

82 ◆ *CHURCH COMMITTEE REPORT ON COVERT ACTIONS IN CHILE, 1963–1973*

Established by the National Security Act of 1947, the Central Intelligence Agency (CIA) was in the vanguard of the U.S. campaign against international communism during the Cold War. CIA experts, researchers, and agents advised U.S. presidents on international developments; provided information on political and economic conditions in other countries; monitored foreign broadcasts, newspapers, and government communiqués; and engaged in more direct forms of espionage. As the following selection reveals, the goals of espionage included weakening, or removing from power, politicians perceived as threats to U.S. interests.

Chile, a country with a long democratic tradition and rich copper deposits, was the scene of intense CIA activity in the 1960s and early 1970s. In the 1964 presidential elections, the CIA helped undermine the candidacy of Salvador Allende, a

Source: Church Committee U.S. Congress. *Senate. Select Committee to Study Governmental Operations With Respect to Intelligence Activities, Covert Action in Chile 1963–1973: Staff Report* (Washington D.C.: U.S. Government Printing Office, 1975), 6–7, 9, 11, 14, 22, 23, 26, 27, 33, 39, 40.

physician-turned-politician who led a socialist-communist coalition on a platform of anti-imperialism, anticapitalism, land reform, and the nationalization of industry. Allende received 39 percent of the vote but was handily defeated by Eduardo Frei, a centrist Christian Democrat. By the next presidential election in 1970, the political situation had changed. Frei's Christian Democrats had run out of ideas, inflation was surging, and, most importantly, right-wing parties were running their own candidate rather than backing the Christian Democrats. Allende received 36 percent of the vote—less than in 1964, but enough to win a plurality. In October 1970, after a military coup failed to overturn the election, Allende became president.

Despite his narrow victory, Allende boldly proceeded with his socialist program. The government froze prices and raised wages, nationalized the copper industry and dozens of other sectors of the economy, and liquidated large estates as part of its land reform program. But Allende faced formidable obstacles. Radicals in his coalition demanded faster change, whereas conservatives and moderates remained inalterably opposed to his policies. Furthermore, the cessation of U.S. aid and foreign investments crippled a Chilean economy already weakened by the transition from private to government ownership. In September 1973, Allende's opponents within the military ended Chile's socialist experiment when they mounted a coup d'état that resulted in the death of Allende and five thousand other Chileans. It also resulted in the beginning of military rule under General Augusto Pinochet, who remained Chile's dictator until 1990.

Historians still debate the reasons for Allende's fall, but all agree his chances of survival were weakened by the destabilization campaign carried on by the CIA and other U.S. government agencies. The extent of this campaign was revealed in a report issued in 1975 by the U.S. Senate's Select Committee to Study Governmental Operations in Respect to Intelligence Activities. Better known as the "Church Committee" after its chair, Senator Frank Church of Idaho, its task was to investigate "illegal, improper, or unethical" CIA operations in Chile. The committee's findings, along with those of a House of Representatives committee, led to executive orders under President Ford and President Carter to increase presidential control of the CIA's covert operations and the passing by Congress of the Intelligence Oversight Act in 1980.

QUESTIONS FOR ANALYSIS

1. What does the Church Committee report reveal about U.S. Cold War attitudes and goals?
2. How much did the CIA destabilization efforts described in this document depend on the cooperation of Chileans?
3. What does the document reveal about the control and oversight of CIA operations by the executive branch?
4. The Church Committee was charged with judging whether CIA activities in Chile were "improper and immoral." What is your own judgment on this issue?

[THE 1964 ELECTION]

The United States was involved on a massive scale in the 1964 presidential election in Chile.... A total of nearly four million dollars was spent on some fifteen covert action projects, ranging from organizing slum dwellers to passing funds to political parties.

The goal, broadly, was to prevent or minimize the influence of Chilean Communists or Marxists in the government that would emerge from the 1964 election. Consequently, the U.S. sought the most effective way of opposing FRAP[1] (Popular Action Front), an alliance of Chilean Socialists, Communists, and several miniscule non-Marxist parties of the left which backed the candidacy of Salvador Allende. Specifically, the policy called for support of the Christian Democratic Party, the Democratic Front (a coalition of rightist parties), and a variety of anti-communist propaganda and organizing activities....

Covert action during the 1964 campaign was composed of two major elements. One was direct financial support of the Christian Democratic campaign. The CIA underwrote slightly more than half of the total cost of that campaign....

In addition to support for political parties, the CIA mounted a massive anti-communist propaganda campaign. Extensive use was made of the press, radio, films, pamphlets, posters, leaflets, direct mailings, paper streamers, and wall painting. It was a "scare campaign," which relied heavily on images of Soviet tanks and Cuban firing squads and was directed especially to women. Hundreds of thousands of copies of the anti-communist pastoral letter

of Pope Pius XI[2] were distributed by Christian Democratic organizations. They carried the designation, "printed privately by citizens without political affiliation, in order more broadly to disseminate its content." "Disinformation" and—"black propaganda"—material which purported to originate from another source, such as the Chilean Communist Party—were used as well.

The propaganda campaign was enormous. During the first week of intensive propaganda activity ..., a CIA-funded propaganda group produced twenty radio spots per day in Santiago and on 44 provincial stations; twelve-minute news broadcasts five times daily on three Santiago stations and 24 provincial outlets; thousands of cartoons, and much paid press advertising. By the end of June, the group produced 24 daily newscasts in Santiago and the provinces, 26 weekly "commentary" programs, and distributed 3,000 posters daily....

[THE 1970 ELECTION]

... In March 1970, the 40 Committee[3] decided that the United States should not support any single candidate in the election but should instead wage "spoiling" operations against the Popular Unity[4] coalition which supported the Marxist candidate, Salvador Allende. In all, the CIA spent from $800,000 to $1,000,000 on convert action to affect the outcome of the 1970 Presidential election....

There was a wide variety of propaganda products: a newsletter mailed to approximately two thousand journalists, academicians, politicians, and other opinion makers; a booklet

---

[1]FRAP stands for *Frente de Acción Popular* (Popular Action Front), a coalition of leftist parties that competed in elections in the 1950s and 1960s.
[2]Pius XI was pope from 1922 until 1939. A staunch anti-Marxist, in 1931 he issued the encyclical *Quadragesimo anno* (In the Fortieth Year), in which he stressed the need for Christian social action to deal with poverty.
[3]The 40 Committee was a subcabinet-level body of the executive branch with a mandate to review and approve major

covert actions by the CIA. It was chaired by the president's assistant for national security affairs, and included the undersecretary of state for political affairs, the deputy secretary of defense, the chairman of the Joint Chiefs of Staff, and the CIA director.
[4]Popular Unity (*Unidad Popular*) replaced FRAP as the main coalition of the left in the 1970 election.

showing what life would be like if Allende won the presidential election; translation and distribution of chronicles of opposition to the Soviet regime; poster distribution and sign-painting teams. The sign-painting teams had instructions to paint the slogan *"su paredón"* (your wall) on 2,000 walls, evoking an image of communist firing squads. The "scare campaign" ... exploited the violence of the invasion of Czecholovakia[5] with large photographs of Prague and of tanks in downtown Santiago. Other posters, resembling those used in 1964, portrayed Cuban political prisoners before the firing squad, and warned that an Allende victory would mean the end of religion and family life in Chile....

[BETWEEN SEPTEMBER 4 AND OCTOBER 24, 1970]

On September 4, 1970, Allende won a plurality in Chile's presidential election. Since no candidate had received a majority of the popular vote, the Chilean Constitution required that a joint session of its Congress decide between the first- and second-place finishers. The date set for the congressional session was October 24, 1970.

The reaction in Washington to Allende's plurality victory was immediate. The 40 Committee met on September 8 and 14 to discuss what action should be taken prior to the October 24 congressional vote. On September 15, President Nixon informed CIA Director Richard Helms[6] that an Allende regime in Chile would not be acceptable to the United States and instructed the CIA to play a direct role in organizing a military *coup d'etat* in Chile to prevent Allende's accession to the Presidency....

... U.S. Government efforts to prevent Allende from assuming office proceeded on two tracks. Track I comprised all covert activities approved by the 40 Committee, including political, economic and propaganda activities.... Track II activities in Chile were undertaken in response to President Nixon's September 15 order and were directed toward actively promoting and encouraging the Chilean military to move against Allende....

On October 24, 1970, Salvador Allende was confirmed as President by Chilean Congress. On November 3, he was inaugurated. U.S. efforts, both overt and covert, to prevent his assumption of office had failed.

[COVERT ACTION DURING THE ALLENDE YEARS, 1970–1973]

United States foreign economic policy toward Allende's government was articulated at the highest levels of the U.S. government, and coordinated by interagency task forces.... Richard Helms' notes from his September 15, 1970, meeting with President Nixon, ... contain the indication: "Make the economy scream." A week later Ambassador Korry[7] reported telling Frei, through his Defense Minister, that "not a nut or bolt would be allowed to reach Chile under Allende." ...

The policy of economic pressure ... was to be implemented through several means. All new bilateral foreign assistance was to be stopped.... The U.S. would use its predominant position in international financial institutions to dry up the flow of new multilateral credit or other financial assistance. To the extent possible, financial assistance or guarantees to U.S. private investment in Chile would be ended, and U.S. businesses would be made aware of the government's concern and its restrictive policies....

After the failure of Track II, the CIA rebuilt its network of contacts and remained close to Chilean military officers in order to monitor de-

---

[5]A reference to the Soviet invasion of Czechoslovakia in 1968 to halt the reform movement in the Czechoslovakian Communist Party.

[6]Director of the CIA from 1965 to 1973.
[7]Edward Korry, U.S. ambassador to Chile.

velopments within the armed forces. For their part, Chilean officers who were aware that the United States once had sought a coup to prevent Allende from becoming president must have been sensitive to indications of continuing U.S. support for a coup.

By September 1971 a new network of agents was in place and the Station was receiving almost daily reports of new coup plotting. The Station and Headquarters[8] began to explore ways to use this network. At the same time, and in parallel, the Station and Headquarters discussed a "deception operation" designed to alert Chilean officers to real or purported Cuban involvement in the Chilean army....

The CIA's information-gathering efforts with regard to the Chilean military included activity which went beyond the mere collection of information. More generally, those efforts must be viewed in the context of United States opposition, overt and covert, to the Allende government. They put the United States Government in contact with those Chileans who sought a military alternative to the Allende presidency....

[AFTER THE COUP D'ETAT]

Following the September 11, 1973, coup, the military Junta, led by General Augusto Pinochet, moved quickly to consolidate its newly acquired power. Political parties were banned, Congress was put in indefinite recess, press censorship was instituted, supporters of Allende and others deemed opponents of the new regime were jailed, and elections were put off indefinitely....

In addition, charges concerning the violation of human rights in Chile continue to be directed to the Junta. Most recently, a United Nations report on Chile charged that "torture centers" are being operated in Santiago and other parts of the country. The lengthy document, issued October 14, 1975, listed 11 centers where it says prisoners are being questioned "by methods amounting to torture." ...

The goal of covert action immediately following the coup was to assist the Junta in gaining a more positive image, both at home and abroad, and to maintain access to the command levels of the Chilean government. Another goal, achieved in part through work done at the opposition research organization before the coup, was to help the new government organize and implement new policies. Project files record that CIA collaborators were involved in preparing an initial overall economic plan which has served as the basis for the Junta's most important economic decisions.

---

[8]*Station* refers to the headquarters of agents in place in Chile; *Headquarters* refers to CIA headquarters in Langley, Virginia.

PART FOUR

The Recent Past: 1970s to the Present

Writing the history of the recent past presents unique difficulties. The historian's most basic task—getting the facts right and determining "what happened"—is relatively easy. Historians of the recent past have lived through the events they are describing, can interview eyewitnesses and participants, and have access not only to information contained in books, newspapers, and government documents, but also to visual evidence from films, video recordings, and photographs. Many historical documents have been digitized, making it possible to do historical research while sitting before one's computer rather than in distant archives and libraries.

Writing history, however, requires more than accurately telling "what happened." It also involves making interpretations, judging what's important and what's trivial, and determining how events fit into long-term patterns and trends. For these tasks, historians need a perspective that includes knowledge of what preceded and what followed the events they are describing. Historians of the recent past, not knowing the future, will always lack this perspective, and can make only educated guesses about the meaning and significance of events that have just taken place.

During the 1990s, for example, many historians, perhaps recalling the easy transition to democracy in post–World War II Italy, West Germany, and Japan, confidently predicted that the sudden disintegration of the Soviet Union in 1991 would have similar results in Russia and the newly independent states that had been part of the Soviet empire. So far their predictions have been wrong. With the exception of the three Baltic states, Lithuania, Estonia, and Latvia, early experiments with democracy in the 1990s brought widespread chaos, and the response was a quick revival of autocracy throughout much of the region. Promising stability and somewhat greater economic freedom, iron-fisted rulers seized power and have not let go.

In Russia, under the presidency of Vladimir V. Putin, who took power as president in 2000, the government took control of the media, stifled unfriendly journalists, and used the courts to harass and persecute its critics. Having established a system of "managed democracy," in which it is said that millions can vote, but only one vote (Putin's) matters, Putin was reelected in 2004 with 71 percent of the votes. His handpicked successor, Dmitry Medvedev, who was elected president in 2008, promptly named Putin as his prime minister. Then after Putin announced his intention to run for president in 2012, commentators predicted twelve more years of authoritarian rule. Some spoke of Putin as the "new Stalin." Such predictions need to be revised when after December 2011's parliamentary elections, support for Putin's United Russia party fell from 64% to under 50% in official counts and, according to independent monitors, was probably closer to 40%. More surprisingly, in the weeks following the election, many thousands of antigovernment demonstrators in Moscow and elsewhere poured into the streets to denounce vote rigging, corruption, and Putin himself. Putin's autocracy no longer appeared so formidable, and discussions of Russia's "new Stalin" gave way to speculation that recent events meant the "beginning of the end for Putin."

The twists and turns of Russian politics over the past twenty-five years provide just one example of how difficult it is for historians (and others) to assess the significance of events that have just occurred. Many other examples could be cited. Is the intensification of Islamic radicalism the first stage of a "battle of civilizations" between the West and Islam or a passing phase in Islam's history? What will be the long-term results of the wave of protests and rebellions that swept across the Arab world and toppled dictators in 2011? What are we to make of the bursting of the dot.com bubble between 2000 and 2002 and the worldwide economic collapse following the crash of the U.S. housing market in 2008? Are these signs of capitalism's fatal flaws or simply bumps in the road toward greater prosperity? The stunning reemergence of China as an economic powerhouse raises many questions, the most basic of which is whether its distinctive form of authoritarian capitalism provides a viable alternative to the democratic capitalism of the West.

The list goes on. Will late-twentieth-century environmentalism be hailed as a triumph of human foresight or mourned as a movement that came too late and accomplished too little? Are recent gains by Western women in education, job opportunities, and legal status the first step toward greater gender equality worldwide or will they remain a uniquely Western phenomenon? Will Africa lift itself from the curse of economic underdevelopment? No one will be able to answer these and countless other questions for another fifty years or more, and until then it is wise to keep in mind the response of the Chinese foreign minister Zhou Enlai when asked in the early 1970s about his views of the long-term significance of the French Revolution of the late eighteenth century: "It is too soon to tell."

CHAPTER 12

The 1970s and 1980s:
Years of Challenge and Change

In contrast to the 1950s and 1960s, decades of optimism and high hopes in much of the world, the 1970s and 1980s were years of lowered expectations and disillusionment with once promising political and economic formulas. Several factors contributed to this change, but the most important was the halt of postwar economic expansion. In the early 1970s, the world entered a period in which stagnation was accompanied by inflation, periods of sluggish growth were interrupted by three major recessions, some areas of the world flourished while others languished, and an oil shortage in the 1970s was followed by an oil glut in the 1980s.

Many factors contributed to the world economy's erratic performance, but the most important cause was the steep increase in energy costs. In October 1973, a barrel of oil sold by members of the Organization of Petroleum Exporting Countries (OPEC) cost $2.59, but by late 1980 the same amount of oil cost just over $30 (approximately $82 in 2011 dollars). Prices fell to under $20 a barrel by the mid-1980s, but by then higher energy costs had done their damage: inflation, shrunken corporate profits, trade deficits for oil-importing nations, and the erosion of consumer spending. Oil costs, however, were not the only culprit. Currency fluctuations, inflationary wage settlements in the late 1960s and early 1970s, decreased state spending in the face of rising deficits, declining productivity and investments, and a failure of oil-producing states to recycle their immense profits through loans and investments all played a role.

The effects of the "Great Slowdown" varied enormously. Oil producers at first enjoyed a windfall, but they faced a crisis in the mid-1980s when oil prices plummeted by 30 to 40 percent. Japan, Hong Kong, South Korea, Taiwan, and Singapore continued to find new markets for their cars, electronic goods, financial services, and textiles, and each experienced only slight increases in unemployment and inflation. In the United States, however, the average unemployment rate between 1973 and 1989 was 7.1 percent, compared to 4.8 percent between 1960 and 1973; in Europe unemployment grew from less than

3 percent in 1970 to more than 10 percent in 1986. Inflation was also a problem. The inflation rate in Europe and the United States rose to 13 percent in 1974, fell back to 8 percent by 1976, and returned to 13 percent in 1979 before gradually falling in the 1980s.

For sub-Saharan Africa, Latin America, and much of Asia, the 1970s and 1980s were catastrophic. Rising energy costs and declining growth rates among industrialized countries reduced demand and undercut prices for their agricultural and mineral exports, while their own energy bills went up like everyone else's. Economic growth virtually stopped and in a few cases ran into negative territory. Governments borrowed extravagantly, inflation soared, and poverty worsened.

Political volatility accompanied economic uncertainty. China, having survived the Great Leap Forward and the Cultural Revolution, abandoned Mao's efforts to combine economic development and egalitarianism when new leaders made economic growth rather than ideological purity their priority. Events in Iran revealed the power of religious fundamentalism when Iranians overthrew the shah in 1979 and instituted a government led by clerics determined to rule according to Islamic law. Conservative governments, in Great Britain under Margaret Thatcher and in the United States under Ronald Reagan, cut taxes, fought union demands for higher wages, and sought to eliminate or at least slow the growth of government entitlement programs. Throughout much of Latin America and Africa, dozens of democratic governments gave way to dictatorships.

Meanwhile, the Cold War continued. Despite U.S. involvement in Vietnam, Soviet-U.S. relations improved during the 1970s, the classic era of détente (French for "relaxation"). By the early 1980s, however, détente was in shambles, the victim of Soviet meddling in Africa, the Soviet invasion of Afghanistan in 1979, the U.S.-led boycott of the 1980 Moscow Olympics, and the policies and rhetoric of President Reagan, who, after taking office in 1981, boosted military spending, funded research for the "Star Wars" antimissile system, and denounced the Soviet Union with a vehemence not heard since the 1950s.

Then in 1985, the new premier of the Soviet Union, Mikhail Gorbachev, announced plans to rejuvenate Soviet communism by introducing policies based on *glasnost*, or openness, and *perestroika*, or restructuring. To the world's shock, this step led not to communism's revival but its demise. By 1991, communist regimes had disappeared throughout Eastern Europe, the Soviet Union had collapsed, and the Cold War, which had dominated international diplomacy for over four decades, had ended.

New Forces in the World Economy

Two developments in the 1970s and 1980s provide evidence of fundamental changes in the world economy. The first was the emergence of the Organization of Petroleum Exporting Countries (OPEC) as a major economic force. During the 1970s, OPEC's twelve Asian, African, and Latin American members shocked the world when they orchestrated a quadrupling of the price of oil in 1973–1974 and another quadrupling in 1979–1980. The second was the "economic miracle" that took place in Japan and somewhat later in South Korea, Taiwan, Hong Kong, and Singapore. As these "Asian Tigers" emerged as centers of international finance and leading exporters of steel, automobiles, electronic goods, and consumer items, the Pacific Rim became a major force in the world economy.

The emergence of OPEC took place against a background of soaring demand for oil during the postwar boom. World oil consumption grew from approximately 3.9 billion barrels in 1953 to 20.4 billion barrels in 1973. Nonetheless, prices stayed low, mainly because they were set by huge oil companies committed to keeping demand high and paying oil producers as little as possible. Oil-rich nations sought higher prices, and in 1960 five of them (Iran, Iraq, Saudi Arabia, Venezuela, and Kuwait) founded OPEC to achieve this goal. Despite their efforts and an expansion of OPEC membership in 1973, the price of oil adjusted for inflation was only half of what it had been in the early 1950s.

This changed in late 1973 and 1974, when four Arab oil producers (Saudi Arabia, Iraq, Kuwait, and the United Arab Emirates) decided to use oil as a political weapon after the outbreak of the Arab-Israeli war in October 1973, known as the Yom Kippur War in Israel and the Ramadan War in Muslim countries. To support Egypt and Syria, these states stopped oil deliveries to the United States, which was sending Israel weapons, and to the Netherlands, which had made available its airfields to Israel-bound U.S. supply planes. This step, combined with cuts in production, drove up the price of oil to $10 a barrel, a level that OPEC nations were able to maintain throughout the 1970s and push even higher after the outbreak of the Iran-Iraq War in 1979.

As gasoline prices soared in the United States during the 1970s, many Americans traded in their gas-guzzling Detroit-made Fords, Chevrolets, and Chryslers for fuel-efficient Japanese Toyotas, Datsuns, and Hondas. The fact that twenty years earlier the Japanese auto industry had hardly existed underscores the rapid transformation of Japan's economy. After their nation's defeat in World War II, business and government leaders concluded that Japan's economic recovery depended on producing manufactured goods, not just for domestic and Asian markets but also for the whole world. With a probusiness government, an industrious, well-educated work force, high rates of savings, a talented entrepreneurial class, and an intense competitive spirit, the Japanese succeeded spectacularly. They moved from steel and shipbuilding in the 1950s to electronics, computers, consumer goods, and automobiles in the 1960s and

1970s. By the mid-1980s, Japan had trade surpluses of more than $80 billion a year and one of the world's highest standards of living. By then, South Korea, Taiwan, Singapore, and Hong Kong had also emerged as financial and industrial powers, and many commentators began to speak of the late twentieth century as the dawn of the Pacific Era in the world's economy.

Middle Eastern Poltics and the Price of Oil

◆

83 ◆ Organization of Arab Petroleum Exporting Countries, *ADVERTISEMENT IN THE GUARDIAN, NOVEMBER 15, 1973*

In September 1973, representitives from the world's major oil companies were summoned to Vienna by the Organziation of Peroleum Exporting Countries (OPEC) to open negotiations in early October over oil prices and profits. OPEC leaders, representing the interests of eleven nations, had made no secret of their intent: they wanted significantly higher prices for oil and a greater share of the profits. As they prepared for the meeting, the oil companies knew they had a weak hand. Demand for oil showed no signs of abating; supplies were tight; American oil production was at full capacity; tensions in the Middle East were growing; Nigeria, recovering from a civil war, had just nationalized its petroleum industry; Libya and Iran had recently negotiated contracts that boosted their share of oil profits from fifty to fifty five percent, and included price increases that in Libya's case amounted to ninety cents a barrel. Then, just two days before the meeting began, Egypt and Syria, hoping to force Israel to relinquish the Arab territories it had won in the Six-Day War of 1967, launched a surprise attack on Israel, starting a war that would last three weeks.

While the war raged on, negotiators in Vienna were unable to bridge the gap between the oil companies' offer of a fifteen-cent price rise per barrel and OPEC's demand for doubling the price from three to six dollars. On October 14, the Vienna meeting broke up, and nine oil ministers, including those of Iran and the Arab oil states, convened two days later in Kuwait City to consider their position, which had been considerably changed by the Arab-Israeli war and by the revelation that on October 13, the United States had begun a massive effort to supply Israel with weapons and ammunition. On October 16, they announced their unilateral decision to raise the price of oil by seventy percent, to $5.11 a barrel. One day later, Arab oil producers (Qatar, Abu Dhabi, Iraq, Libya, the United Arab Emirates, and Saudi Arabia) announced a plan to immediately cut production by five percent and to continue to cut by another five percent per month

---

Source: "Arab Oil Policy in the Middle East Conflict," from *The Guardian,* 15 November, 1973. Copyright Guardian News & Media Ltd. 1973. Used with permission.

until Israel withdrew from the occupied territories. Then, on October 20, after it became known that the United States had proposed a $2.2 billion aid package for Israel, Saudi Arabia (followed by other Arab oil producers, but not Iraq) announced that they would cut off all shipments of oil—every drop—to the United States. The following week the embargo was extended to the Netherlands, the home country of the oil giant Royal Dutch Shell, and the one European government that had stated its strong support for Israel at the start of the war.

The unleashing of the Arab Oil Weapon created panic among world statesmen and business leaders, a state of affairs the oil producers hoped to use to their political advantage, even after fighting in the Middle East ceased at the end of October. Countries supporting Israel (the United States, the Netherlands, and Canada) would be embargoed; those deemed friendly to the Arab cause would be placed on a list of "exempt" countries and would receive all of their prewar oil allocations; countries considered neutral would be subject to the monthly five percent cutbacks. Such incentives proved effective in the case of Japan, which received almost half its oil from the Middle East. After appearing on the list of "neutral states," it was elevated to "exempt status" after the government issued a statement endorsing various Arab positions.

The Arabs' diplomatic initiative was accompanied by a campaign to win public opinion to their side. In mid-November, the Organization of Arab Petroleum Exporting Countries took out full-page advertisements in major Western newspapers to explain their actions and spell out what governments had to do to keep the oil flowing. The text of the advertisement that follows appeared in the November 15 edition of *The Guardian*, a London-based newspaper with distribution throughout the United Kingdom.

By early 1974, a majority of Arab oil producers had concluded that the cutoffs were losing their economic effectiveness and that no further progress could be made on the diplomatic front until they ended. On March 18, with Syria and Libya dissenting, they voted to end the embargo and the monthly production reductions. But their use of the oil weapon had succeeded beyond their expectations. It altered the diplomacy and geopolitics of the Middle East and the entire globe, recast the relationship between oil users and oil producers, and transformed the world economy. It was a true turning point in twentieth-century history.

QUESTIONS FOR ANALYSIS

1. The advertisement claims that the Arab oil producing nations have made a "liberal and vital" contribution to the world economy. What is the basis of this claim?

2. According to the advertisement, why are Israel and its supporters among the major industrial powers to blame for the actions taken by the Arab oil producers?

3. According to the advertisement why have the Netherlands and the United States been singled out for a total embargo? What alleged actions by the United States further justifies the embargo?

4. What general and specific goals do the Arab oil producing nations hope to achieve by using the oil weapon?

ARAB OIL POLICY IN THE MIDDLE EAST CONFLICT

It is an irrefutable fact that the Arab Petroleum Exporting Countries have made over the past decades, and are continuing to make, a liberal and vital contribution to the enhancement of the World economy, and consequently to the well-being and prosperity of all nations, through exporting their gradually depleted, and irreplaceable, natural resource: OIL. Equally irrefutable is the fact that in many Arab countries production has long surpassed the limit required by their own local economy and the needs of future generations for continued sources of income and energy. Nevertheless, they willingly decided to give first consideration to the mounting world-wide demand for their oil necessitated by the increasing requirements of energy as a key factor in maintaining the growth of production in all spheres. Thus, demonstrating their unequivocal desire to play their role in promoting international cooperation and the well-being of mankind, they continued to increase their oil production and exports while being fully aware of the fact that by doing so they were indeed sacrificing their own interests.

On the other hand, for six years, the Arab Oil Exporting countries saw vast areas of the territories of three Arab countries[1] being perpetually occupied and ravished by the Israeli aggressors who acquired these Arab lands by force during the June War in 1967. During all these years, in spite of the innumerable peace offers and endeavours on the part of the Arab States and the peace-loving nations, and indeed by the United Nations Security Council and General Assembly, Israel remained intransigent and lent a deaf ear to all the efforts that have been made to induce her to respect and implement the U.N. resolution[2] calling upon her to withdraw from the Arab occupied territories on the basis of the U.N. Charter's provision, asserted in its resolution, concerning the inadmissibility of the acquisition of lands by force.

It is, needless to say, that the responsibility for the implementation of the U.N. resolutions, representing the consensus of the world community's will, lies squarely on the shoulders of all member-states of the World Organisation, and particularly on the permanent members of the Security Council.[3] However, most of the major industrial powers failed to show any intention of taking meaningful and effective action indicating their willingness to discharge their responsibility as they should. On the contrary, some powers acted in such a manner as to encourage the Israeli aggressors to maintain their intransigence, and even consolidate their occupation of the Arab lands by the creation of the so-called "new facts," blatantly defying the World Organization and breaking the principles of International law, as well as making mockery of the legitimate rights of the Arab people.

The 1967 Israeli aggression caused the closure of the Suez Canal,[4] thus disrupting world trade and inflicting immeasurable damage to the interests of the world community. During the present war, Israel did not hesitate in raiding, bombarding and destroying the oil

---

[1]After the Six-Day War of 1967 Israel seized the Sinai Peninsula and Palestine's Gaza Strip from Egypt, the Palestinian West Bank and East Jerusalem from Jordan, and the Golan Heights from Syria.

[2]United Nations Security Council Resolution 242, adopted on November 22, 1967 in the aftermath of the Six-Day War, called for 1) the withdrawal of Israeli armed forces from territories occupied in the recent conflict and 2) the recognition by every state in the area of Israel's right to exist.

[3]Permanent members of the Security Council at the time were the Republic of China (Taiwan), the Soviet Union, the United States, the United Kingdom, and France.

[4]Israeli aggression "caused" the closing of the canal in the sense that its surprise attack on Syria and Egypt in June 1967 at the beginning of the Six-Day War led to the Egyptian decision to close the canal to all traffic. The Egyptian blockade remained in effect until 1975.

export terminals in the East Mediterranean, thus aggravating the shortage of oil supplies to Europe.[5] Now, seeing for the third time that Israel, encouraged and abetted by the United States, is persisting in its aggressive policy and defying Arab rights, the Arab Petroleum Exporting Countries have found themselves constrained to end their self-imposed economic sacrifices; namely producing quantities of their depleting oil resources far exceeding the requirements of their own economic needs. They will continue to pursue this course of action until such time as the international community decides to act and take decisive and effective measures to remedy the situation and induce Israel to withdraw from Arab lands and impress upon the United States how costly the latter's policy of unlimited and unequivocal support for Israel has proved to be to the major industrial countries.

Consequently, the Arab Petroleum Ministers, meeting in Kuwait on the 17th October, 1973, have resolved that all Arab Oil Exporting Countries shall forthwith cut their production respectively by no less than 5% of the September production, and maintain the same rate of reduction each month thereafter until the Israeli forces are fully withdrawn from all Arab territories occupied during the June 1967 War, and the legitimate rights of the Palestinian people are restored.

However, the Arab countries represented in this conference wish to assure friendly countries, especially those who helped or are helping the Arabs in their just cause effectively, that they shall not be made to suffer from the Arab oil cut. Such countries will continue to receive the same quantities supplied to them from the Arab countries before the cut. On the other hand, countries which demonstrate

moral and material support to the Israeli enemy will be subjected to severe and progressive reduction in Arab oil supplies, leading to a complete halt.

THE U.S.A. & HOLLAND

Acting upon the above resolutions . . . the Arab Oil Exporting Countries found it necessary to impose a total embargo on oil exports to the U.S.A. and Holland in view of the active support given to the Israelis during this war, in terms of massive arms supplies and facilities to help transporting the U.S. supply of deadly and sophisticated war material to Israel by air and sea.

The Arabs wish to make it plainly and explicitly known, however, that this embargo is not intended in any way to castigate the peoples of the countries concerned, with whom the Arabs wish to maintain the closest and warmest friendly relations; but this embargo is indeed directed against the Governments, or those responsible in the Governments, for the anti-Arab policy which the Arabs could only reply to in kind.

Evidently, the Arabs' embargo on the export of strategic products to hostile and unfriendly countries—especially in time of war—is entirely in line with similar policies pursued by other countries at war, and even by the U.S.A. which went so far with this policy as to place an embargo on wheat and food supplies *to countries which have no special relations nor share common interests with the United States.*[6]

It is with deep regret that the Arab countries found it necessary to take this decision which is bound to bring suffering to the peoples of the countries concerned: but until such time as the

---

[5]The two previous wars referred to here are the Six-Day War (1967) and the Suez War (1956). In the latter, Israel was allied with France and the United Kingdom in an effort to evict Egypt from the Suez Canal, which had been nationalized by the Egypt in July, 1956.

[6]The United States used trade sanctions as part of its foreign policy throughout the twentieth century. In the postwar

era, the Export Control Act of 1949 gave the president the power to limit the export of weapons and military technology to the Soviet Union and its east European satellites. In 1973 the only two countries subject to a total embargo, including food, were North Korea and Cuba.

Governments of the U.S.A. and Holland or any other country that takes a stand of active support to the Israeli aggressors reverse their positions and add their weight behind the World Community's concensus to end the Israeli occupation of Arab Lands and bring about the full restoration of the Legitimate rights of the Palestinian people, the Arab Oil Exporting Countries will not rescind their decision to impose a total embargo on oil exports to such countries.

Japan's Economic Miracle

◈

84 ◆ Akio Morita, *MADE IN JAPAN*

After World War II, a former Japanese naval lieutenant, Akio Morita, and a defense contractor, Masaru Ibuka, borrowed $500 to form the Tokyo Telecommunications Engineering Corporation. With plans to produce consumer goods for the domestic market, they built a small factory in Tokyo and began to manufacture electric rice cookers. In their first year, they had sales of $7,500 and a profit of $300. With an infusion of capital from Morita's father, who owned a sake brewery, the firm moved into consumer electronics with the marketing of a tape recorder in the early 1950s. Later in the decade, the firm burst into the international market with a miniaturized radio that used transistors, tiny new capacitors developed by Bell Laboratories in the United States, rather than electronic tubes. Named "Sony" from *sonus*, the Latin word for sound, the radio became so popular that Morita and Ibuka changed their company's name to the Sony Corporation in 1958. Beginning in the 1960s, the corporation branched out into chemicals, insurance, the recording industry, and real estate while introducing a stream of successful products, including transistorized tape recorders, videotape cameras and recorders, and color televisions. Although growth slowed in the 1970s, Sony rebounded in the 1980s and 1990s with the introduction of new electronic products and acquisitions such as of Columbia Films in 1989 for $3.4 billion.

During the 1980s, Morita, having presided over one of Japan's most spectacular economic success stories, relinquished some of his duties. This gave him time to write his memoirs, which were published in English in 1986 with the title *Made in Japan*. In the book, Morita discusses the unique features of Japanese business philosophy, underscoring the differences between Japanese and American attitudes and practices. It became required reading in many U.S. business schools before the Japanese economy entered a prolonged slump in the early 1990s. Morita died of pneumonia in 1999 at the age of seventy-eight.

Source: From *Made in Japan* by Akio Morita and Edwin M. Reingold, and Mitsuko Shimomura, copyright © 1986 by E.P. Dutton. Used by permission of Dutton, a division of Penguin Group (USA) Inc.

QUESTIONS FOR ANALYSIS

1. According to Morita, what were some of the obstacles Japan had to overcome to build its economy in the postwar years?
2. Why does Morita believe that good employee-employer relations are the key to business success?
3. What are some of the steps taken by the Sony Corporation to ensure good employee relations?
4. According to Morita, what are some of the differences between business executives in Japan and in the United States?
5. Why does Morita believe that Japanese business methods and philosophy are superior to those of Americans?

SELLING TO THE WORLD

Although our company was still small and we saw Japan as quite a large and potentially active market, it was the consensus among Japanese industrialists that a Japanese company must export goods in order to survive. With no natural resources except our people's energy, Japan had no alternative. And so it was natural for us to look to foreign markets. Besides, as business prospered, it became obvious to me that if we did not set our sights on marketing abroad, we would not grow to be the kind of company Ibuka and I had envisioned. We wanted to change the image of Japanese goods as poor in quality, and, we reasoned, if you are going to sell a high-quality, expensive product, you need an affluent market, and that means a rich, sophisticated country. Today, over 99 percent of all Japanese homes have color TV; more than 98 percent have electric refrigerators and washing machines; and the penetration rate for tape recorders and stereo systems is between 60 and 70 percent. But in 1958, the year after we produced our "pocketable" transistorized radio, only 1 percent of Japanese homes had a TV set, only 5 percent had a washing machine, and only two-tenths of 1 percent had an electric refrigerator. Fortunately, the Japanese economy began to grow vigorously from the mid-fifties onward.

Double-digit increases in the gross national product and low inflation gave a great boost to consumer spending. Many people say Japan's true postwar era really began in 1955, the year we introduced the first transistorized radio in Japan. The country's GNP grew, amazingly, by 10.8 percent. Japanese households needed everything, and because of the high savings rate, which in those days was over 20 percent, the people could afford to buy. So with good and growing markets at home and potential markets abroad, the world was beginning to look bright to us....

We were doing well, although we still had tough competition getting our name known in Japan, where brand consciousness and brand loyalty are very high. Overseas we were all on an even footing. And perhaps we were in a better position abroad than anybody. Quality Japanese consumer goods were virtually unknown before the war. The image of anything marked "Made in Japan" that had been shipped abroad before the war was very low. Most people in the United States and Europe, I learned, associated Japan with paper umbrellas, kimonos, toys, and cheap trinkets. In choosing our name we did not purposely try to hide our national identity— after all, international rules require you to state the country of origin on your product— but we certainly did not want to emphasize it and run the risk of being rejected before we could demonstrate the quality of our products. But I must confess that in the early days we printed the line "Made in Japan" as small as possible ...

ON MANAGEMENT

There is no secret ingredient or hidden formula responsible for the success of the best Japanese companies. No theory or plan or government policy will make a business a success; that can only be done by people. The most important mission for a Japanese manager is to develop a healthy relationship with his employees, to create a familylike feeling within the corporation, a feeling that employees and managers share the same fate. Those companies that are most successful in Japan are those that have managed to create a shared sense of fate among all employees, what Americans call labor and management, and the shareholders.

I have not found this simple management system applied anywhere else in the world, and yet we have demonstrated convincingly, I believe, that it works. For others to adopt the Japanese system may not be possible because they may be too tradition-bound, or too timid. The emphasis on people must be genuine and sometimes very bold and daring, and it can even be quite risky. But in the long run—and I emphasize this—no matter how good or successful you are or how clever or crafty, your business and its future are in the hands of the people you hire....

That is why I make it a point personally to address all of our incoming college graduates each year.... I always gather these new recruits together at headquarters in Tokyo, where we have an introductory or orientation ceremony. This year I looked out at more than seven hundred young, eager faces and gave them a lecture, as I have been doing for almost forty years.... The new employees are getting their first direct and sobering view of what it will be like in the business world. I tell them what I think is important for them to know about

the company and about themselves. I put it this way to the last class of entering employees:

"We did not draft you. This is not the army, so that means you have voluntarily chosen Sony. This is your responsibility, and normally if you join this company we expect that you will stay for the next twenty or thirty years.

"Nobody can live twice, and the next twenty or thirty years is the brightest period of your life. You only get it once.

"When you leave the company thirty years from now or when your life is finished, I do not want you to regret that you spent all those years here. That would be a tragedy. I cannot stress the point too much that this is your responsibility to yourself. So I say to you, the most important thing in the next few months is for you to decide whether you will be happy or unhappy here...."

The concept of lifetime employment arose when Japanese managers and employees both realized that they had much in common and that they had to make some long-range plans. The laws made it difficult legally, and expensive, to fire anybody, but that didn't seem like such a bad idea, since workers were badly in need of work, and struggling businesses needed employees who would remain loyal. Without class disputes, despite the Communist and Socialist party propaganda, the Japanese, who are a homogeneous people, were able to cooperate to provide for their common welfare. I have often said that the Japanese company has become very much a social security organization.

In the postwar era, the tax laws make it useless for a company to pay an executive a lot of money, because the graduated tax rises sharply very quickly, and you are very soon in the highest bracket. Company-paid amenities such as worker dormitories and allowances for commuting, for example, help workers make up for the tax system. Tax shelters and tax avoidance are virtually unknown in Japan. Today, the salary for a top management official is rarely more than seven or eight times that of an entry-level junior executive trainee. This means Japan has no multimillion-dollar brass, and companies give no huge executive bonuses, no stock options, no deferred income, no golden parachutes, and therefore the psychological, as well as the real, gap between employees is narrower than in other countries. There may be some exceptions to the general rule, but I am sure they are few.

What we in industry learned in dealing with people is that people do not work just for money and that if you are trying to motivate, money is not the most effective tool. To motivate people, you must bring them into the family and treat them like respected members of it. Granted, in our one-race nation this might be easier to do than elsewhere, but it is still possible if you have an educated population....

AMERICAN AND JAPANESE STYLES OF MANAGEMENT

But the differences between U.S. and Japanese companies go beyond the cultural. If you ask a Japanese executive, "What is your most important responsibility?" he will invariably say that continued employment and improving the livelihood of the workers is at or near the top of the list.... Making a profit will never be at the top of the list. Most of the American business executives I know put the highest priority on return to the investors or this year's profit. They have the responsibility because the investors gave it to them, and to stay in their jobs they have to continue to keep the investors happy. The board of directors represents the investors, and if top management fails to give the return the investors feel they need, he will be fired. For that reason he is entitled to use the factory and the machinery of the company, and also the workers, as tools to accomplish his aim. This can be detrimental.

Visiting an American television plant in the Midwest a few years ago, I commented to the manager that I thought he really needed to buy some more modern equipment in order to improve the company's productivity. He shocked me when he told me that his compensation was based on the company's financial performance and that he was not going to do anything, like making long-range investments, that might cut his compensation for the sake of the next manager who would be along in a year or so....

Generally, in the United States, management's attitude toward the labor force and even the lower-level executives is very hierarchical, much more so than in Japan, an Oriental country where Westerners always expect to see such hierarchies. When I visited the Illinois television assembly plant of Motorola, one of the first things I noticed was that the offices were air-conditioned, but out on the shop floor it was stifling, people were dripping with sweat, and big noisy fans were blowing the hot air around. The workers were plainly uncomfortable, and I thought, "How can you get quality work from people laboring under such conditions? And what kind of loyalty can they be expected to show to the big bosses in their cool offices!" In Japan people often used to say that the shop floor where the goods were made was always more comfortable than the workers' homes....

Amenities are not of great concern to management in Japan. The struggle for an office with a carpet, a water carafe, and an original oil painting on the wall is not common. Just recently a U.S. company, the maker of highly complex computerized graphics equipment, formed a joint venture with a Japanese company and the Japanese partner said to his foreign associate: "We would like you to design the showroom, but please allow us to design the office space upstairs." It seemed reasonable enough. The showroom was beautifully appointed, with soft lighting and comfortable chairs for visitors and clients. The equipment was highlighted using modern display techniques, and there were video demonstrations and elegant four-color brochures on the company and its equipment. Upstairs, the entire office staff was housed in one big open room without partitions, just a grid of desks with telephones, filing cabinets and other necessary furniture in a simple, very Spartan arrangement. The U.S. partner raised his eyebrows, and his Japanese colleague explained, "If Japanese clients come into the office of a new and struggling company and see plush carpet and private offices and too much comfort, they become suspicious that this company is not serious, that it is devoting too much thought and company resources to management's comfort, and perhaps not enough to the product or to potential customers. If we are successful after one year, we might put up low partitions. After two or three years, we might give the top executive a closed office. But for now we have to all be reminded that we are struggling together to make this company a success."

The Conservative Tilt in Western Societies

Skyrocketing oil prices, competition from the Pacific Rim, disruptions in the international monetary system, surplus industrial capacity, inflationary wage settlements made during the postwar boom, and growing government deficits all contributed to the economic malaise that affected Western industrial societies beginning in the early 1970s. The result was a decade and a half of "stagflation," in which slackening growth and high unemployment unexpectedly were accompanied not by falling prices, but by steady inflation. With economists at a loss to explain the causes of the slump or provide solutions to end it, politicians implemented temporary wage freezes, increased tariffs, provided subsidies for businesses, cut government spending, and devised new energy polices. But nothing worked.

These new economic realities bred pessimism and disillusionment. In Great Britain, disgust with the Labor government of Prime Minister James Callaghan peaked in the frigid winter of 1978 and 1979, when Callaghan refused to acknowledge there was a crisis in Britain even though the country was experiencing gas shortages, debilitating strikes, and protests by hospital and municipal employees over wage freezes and budget cuts. An editorial in the London *Sun* captured the national mood when under the headline, "Crisis? What Crisis?" it began by quoting the opening line from Shakespeare's *Richard III*, "Now is the winter of our discontent." Later in 1979, U.S. President Jimmy Carter discerned a similar level of discouragement among Americans, admitting in a televised speech that the country was experiencing a "crisis of confidence." "It is a crisis," he said, "that strikes at the very heart and soul and spirit of our national will."

Such feelings paved the way for a decade of political change in the 1980s. In May 1979, British voters returned the Conservatives to office under the leadership of Margaret Thatcher. The "Iron Lady," as she came to be known, privatized state-controlled businesses, declared war on labor unions, and cut welfare programs, assuring the British people that private enterprise and lower taxes, especially for the well-to-do, would reawaken the nation's entrepreneurial energies. When Ronald Reagan became U.S. president in 1981, he took a page from Thatcher's playbook, telling voters that "government is the problem, not the solution." His embrace of "trickle down" economic theory promised that lower taxes and other policies benefiting businesses and the wealthy would spur investment and ultimately benefit the lower and middle classes.

"Thatcherism" and "Reaganomics" were the prime examples of the conservative tilt of the 1980s, but it was not limited to Britain and the United States. With the exceptions of Sweden, which maintained its broad array of social programs, and France, which elected socialist governments in the early 1980s, retrenchment of social programs and shrinking government were the dominant trends. The welfare state survived, but in modified and diminished form.

The conservatism of the 1980s expressed itself in other ways as well. Individual politicians and new political movements denounced multiculturalism and demanded new policies to curtail immigration to Europe from Asia and Africa and to the United States from Mexico. Additionally, in the United States many individuals who were troubled by the erosion of "traditional values" during the 1960s and 1970s were drawn to politically active religious groups that opposed feminism, homosexual rights, and the country's perceived secular drift. In all these ways, the 1980s challenged the cultural and political assumptions of the postwar era.

Thatcher's Prescription for a Tired Nation

❖

85 ◆ Margaret Thatcher, *"THE RENEWAL OF BRITAIN"*

Margaret Thatcher, the daughter of a small-town grocer and an Oxford graduate with a degree in chemistry, entered politics at age twenty-five when she ran unsuccessfully as a Conservative for the parliamentary seat in Dartford. After marrying wealthy businessman Dennis Thatcher, she studied law and remained active in the Conservative Party. In 1959, she won a seat in Parliament from the borough of Finchley, which she represented until 1992. She rose in the party's ranks and served as education secretary in the government of Prime Minister Edward Heath. In 1975, she successfully challenged Heath for party leadership, and after the Conservative victory in the 1979 elections became Britain's first female prime minister, an office she held until 1990.

Early efforts to implement her policies were broadly unpopular, and her approval rating fell to 23 percent, the lowest ever recorded for a prime minister. She refused to back down, however, and in 1983, with the economy improving and her popularity soaring after the successful defense of the British-held Falkland Islands against an attempted Argentinian seizure, she led the Conservatives to a landslide victory. There followed a wave of privatizations, a victory over the coal miners' union in a bitterly contested strike in 1984–1985, the lowering of capital gains and inheritance taxes, the deregulation of the private housing market, reduction of subsidies for the unemployed, reduced public support for higher education, and modest reforms in education and the National Health Service. She was forced to resign in 1990 after her popularity was undermined by rising inflation, her opposition to further European integration, and the government-mandated replacement of local property taxes

Source: Copyright Lady Thatcher. Reprinted from www.margaretthatcher.org, the website of the Margaret Thatcher Foundation.

with a highly regressive poll (head) tax, which was the same for all taxpayers regardless of their wealth. After resigning from the House of Commons in 1992, Thatcher wrote her memoirs, sponsored a major charitable foundation, and spoke out on public issues until poor health forced her to limit her activities and end public appearances in 2008.

The following excerpt is taken from a speech delivered in July 1979 by the new prime minister at a meeting in Cambridge sponsored by the Conservative Political Centre, a conservative think-tank. In it, Thatcher provides a blueprint for Britain's revival.

QUESTIONS FOR ANALYSIS

1. What does Thatcher find most disturbing about the events that occurred during Britain's "winter of discontent"? What lessons does Thatcher draw from the events?
2. What does Thatcher mean by the term "collectivization," and how has it contributed in her view to Britain's decline?
3. What are Thatcher's views of the purposes and function of government?
4. According to Thatcher, how have labor unions contributed to Britain's problems?
5. According to Thatcher, what must occur for Britain to experience "renewal"?
6. In what ways do Thatcher's ideas about taxes favor the rich? What is her rationale for such policies?

THE CRISIS IN THE NATION

When we took over the Government on 4th May, we found a nation disillusioned and dispirited.

That was, I believe, the inevitable outcome of the Labour Government's socialist approach. Last Winter,[1] there can have been few in Britain who did not feel, with mounting alarm, that our society was sick—morally, socially and economically. Children were locked out of school; patients were prevented from having hospital treatment; the old were left unattended in their wheelchairs; the dead were not buried; and flying pickets[2] patrolled the motorways. Mr. Bill Dunn[3] seemed to express the spirit of January 1979 when he said, of the ambulance men's pay demands, if "lives must be lost, that is the way it must be"....

We ought to look searchingly at the causes of those events, so as to be able to achieve a more authentic, a more humane and a more successful British way of life. If we take the long view of the antecedents of the events of last Winter, we note the dominance in British intellectual and political life, over a generation and more, of collectivist theory.

Theorists of Socialism,... motivated by a genuine desire for social justice, elevated the State as an instrument of social regeneration.

Simultaneously, Keynes[4] and later various schools of neo-Keynesian economists, exalted

---

[1]A reference to England's "winter of discontent," during which the country experienced fuel shortages and strikes by public service employees. In the midst of the standoff, strikers blocked entrances to a number of schools and hospitals.

[2]Mobile strikers who travel from place to place to join picket lines.

[3]Dunn was a London ambulance driver and a leader of the Confederation of Health Services Employees.

[4]John Maynard Keynes (1886–1941) was a distinguished British economist who advocated the use of government fiscal and monetary policies to mitigate the adverse effects of economic downturns. Economists who later interpreted and refined his theories and developed mathematical models to express them were known as Neo-Keynesians.

the role of Government and humbled the role of the individual in their pursuit of economic stability and prosperity.

The events that we witnessed last winter, mark, I believe, the failure of these collectivist approaches....

I acknowledge, readily, the sincerity and generosity of some Socialists. However, I believe that the Socialist approach is based upon a moral confusion which in practice is profoundly damaging. The moral fallacy of Socialism is to suppose that conscience can be collectivised.... Experience has shown the practical failure of two fundamental Socialist arguments: that nationalisation is justified because it makes economic power accountable to the people whose lives it affects; and that State planning can point to better ways forward than can be charted by free enterprise....

It is certainly the duty of Government to do all it can to ensure that effective succour is given to those in need, and this is a Conservative principle as much as a Socialist one. Where Conservatives part company from Socialists is in the degree of confidence which we can place in the exclusive capacity of a welfare state to relieve suffering and promote well-being. Charity is a personal quality—the supreme moral quality—according to St Paul,[5] and public compassion, state philanthropy and institutionalised charity can never be enough. There is no adequate substitute for genuine caring for one another on the part of families, friends and neighbours.... And yet the collectivist ethos has made individuals excessively prone to rely on the State to provide for the well-being of their neighbours and indeed of themselves. There cannot be a welfare system in any satisfactory sense which tends, in this way, to break down personal responsibility and the sense of responsibility to family, neighbourhood and community. The balance has moved too far towards collectivism....

The imbalance that Socialism has brought about is, I believe, part of the explanation for the irresponsibility and the inhumanity displayed by too many people last winter. The wanton expansion of the State's responsibilities had been accompanied by a great drop in public spirit. Excessive public spending had (as usual) bred great private discontent. Meantime, it was widely assumed that no large enterprise could be managed successfully without the help of the State.... Heavy taxation had lowered fiscal morality.... We seemed to be losing our moral standards as well as our competence.... Foreigners visiting this country shook their heads sadly when they remembered a resolute, industrious and great-hearted Britain which once had seemed to be able to move both "earth and Heaven". Our industrial life seemed marked by petty labour disputes which were often both self-destructive and humiliating. The time spent by works managers upon Trades Union matters of a non-productive nature might be half of their day's work....

What did all this mean for our country? It meant that the 1960s and the early 1970s became the great age of the countries which suffered defeat in the 1939/45 War. The peoples of Germany and Japan, and also of France, worked together to restore their countries, and then to move ahead.... So although we had won the War, we let other countries win the peace. For a long time, too, many leaders of the Labour Party refused to recognise the reality of British decline, to which they had contributed more than their fair share. They seemed blind to the evident truth that, all over the world, capitalism was achieving improvements in living standards and the quality of life, while Socialism was causing economic decay, bureaucracy and, when it took authoritarian or totalitarian forms, cruelty and repression....

---

[5]The Apostle Paul (c. 5 B.C.E.–c. 67 C.E.), by tradition the author of fourteen epistles in the New Testament, wrote frequently and eloquently about the need for Christian charity. Thatcher often included religious references in her writings and speeches.

A NEW CLIMATE OF OPINION

At the heart of a new mood in the nation must be a recovery of our self-confidence and our self-respect.... The foundation of this new confidence has to be individual responsibility. If people come to believe that the State or their employer or their union owe them a living, and that, in turn, the world owes Britain a living, we shall have no confidence and no future.

Governments can animate industry but they should not seek indefinitely to sustain it. Governments can purify the stagnant and corrupt parts of an economy and correct irregularities in the market, but they should not seek to regulate the market itself. Governments may provide certain goods or services which cannot easily be supplied competitively, but they should accept that one of their essential tasks is to define their limitations and those of the State.

We [Conservatives] need ... to create a mood where it is everywhere thought morally right for as many people as possible to acquire capital; not only because of the beneficial economic consequences, but because the possession of even a little capital encourages the virtues of self-reliance and responsibility, as well as assisting a spirit of freedom and independence....

INFLATION

We see it as a first duty of responsible Government to re-establish sound money and to squeeze inflation out of the system. So the Budget set a framework of firm monetary discipline and control of the money supply. That meant a limit on public borrowing and strict control over public expenditure. I am afraid, it also meant high interest rates for a time, until the measures we have introduced take effect.... This framework of Government financial responsibility needs to be matched by private sector responsibility.... In particular, employers and Trade Unions need to understand that this Government will not print money to bail them out if they make irresponsible pay settlements. Higher pay needs to be matched by higher output. If it is not, it will lead only to higher unemployment and higher prices.

DIRECT TAX

The Budget cut income tax in three ways. First, we raised the thresholds so as to take 1.3 million people out of tax altogether. Second, we cut the basic rate of income tax from 33p to 30p in the Pound.[6] Together with the improved personal allowances, this gives benefit to millions of taxpayers, and it reduces tax on every extra pound earned. It is an encouragement to effort.... Thirdly, by reducing the top rate of tax on earned income to 60%, we began to restore to the industrious and to the inventive the encouragement they need to work and to create work for others. Nations depend for their health, economically, culturally and psychologically, upon the achievements of a comparatively small number of talented and determined people, as well as on the support of a skilled and devoted majority. It was not possible for many of these talented people to believe that we valued them and what they could do for our nation, when we maintained penal tax rates, decade after decade, in order to please those who seemed to be motivated mainly by envy. We have given a new sign of appreciation to talent and brought our top tax rates into line with those of other major countries.

THE TRADE UNION MOVEMENT

I believe it is entirely in the interest of the Trade Union movement to play a major part in this national revival and to put all their great weight behind better national economic performance. Like all of us, their members stand to gain from a

---

[6]After the currency was decimalized in 1968, there were 100 pence (p) in a pound, the main unit of the British currency.

stronger, more efficient, more united Britain. We all stand to lose from tactics which make Britain weaker. It is because part of the Trade Union movement seems to have lost sight of this, that the movement has become unpopular with the Electorate, and has lost much of its old moral authority. If some Unions continue to act as an engine of inflation, and a drag on improvements in industrial efficiency, they will go on alienating themselves from the people, including those whom they represent....

CONCLUSION

... we know that the restoration of the confidence of a great nation is a massive task. We do not shrink from it. It will not be given to this generation of our countrymen to create a

great Empire. But it is given to us to demand an end to decline and to make a stand against what Churchill described as the "long dismal drawling tides of drift and surrender, of wrong measurements and feeble impulses". Though less powerful than once we were, we have friends in every quarter of the globe, who will rejoice at our recovery, welcome the revival of our influence, and benefit from the message and from the example of our renewal. Our recovery will give to all the free world a new hope and a new optimism. It will be not only Conservatives and not only British people who will then feel able to say with Tennyson[7]: "We sailed wherever ship could sail, We founded many a mighty state, Pray God our greatness may not fail, Through craven fears of being great."

---

[7]Alfred, Lord Tennyson (1809–1892) was poet laureate of the United Kingdom throughout much of Queen Victoria's reign. The words quoted are from "Hands All Around" (1852).

The Reagan Revolution

❖

86 ◆ Ronald Reagan, *REMARKS AT THE ANNUAL CONVENTION OF THE NATIONAL ASSOCIATION OF EVANGELICALS, MARCH 1983*

Born into the family of a salesman in Tampico, Illinois, and a 1932 graduate of Eureka College in Eureka, Illinois, Ronald Reagan (1911–1994) worked as a sportscaster for a number of Midwestern radio stations before moving to Hollywood in 1937 after an audition won him a seven-year film acting contract with Warner Brothers. After serving in the army in World War II (stateside because of his nearsightedness), he resumed his acting career in film and television while serving as president of the Screen Actors Guild, an actors' union, between 1947 and 1952 and in 1959. Originally a Democrat, Reagan gradually moved to the right and officially became a Republican in 1962. In 1964, while campaigning for Republican presidential candidate Barry Goldwater, he drew widespread attention for his campaign speech, "A Time for Choosing," which was shown as a film at campaign events and reputedly raised $1 million for Goldwater. In 1966, he successfully ran for governor of California on a promise to shrink government, reform the welfare system, and crack down on student disturbances at the University of California at Berkeley. He was reelected in 1970.

Source: Public Papers of the Presidents, Ronald Reagan, 1983 (Washington, DC: Government Printing Office, 1983).

Having launched failed campaigns for the Republican nomination for president in 1968 and 1976, in 1980 he won the nomination and easily defeated the Democratic incumbent, Jimmy Carter. In his eight years as president, he transformed the United States in important ways. Like Prime Minister Thatcher, he slashed spending for social programs, lowered tax rates, especially for the wealthy, reduced government regulations, and battled the unions, most famously in 1981, when he fired over eleven thousand striking air traffic controllers and replaced them with nonunion workers. His administration also reduced the federal government's role in enforcing civil rights, environmental, and workplace safety regulations but lent support to causes dear to the hearts of conservatives and evangelical Christians. These included support for constitutional amendments against abortion and for public school prayer and opposition to the Equal Rights Amendment, affirmative action programs, and busing to achieve racial balance in schools.

Most famously, his foreign and defense policies were based on an unbending opposition to communism and an unwillingness to pursue détente with the Soviet Union. Instead, to counter the Soviet threat, he supported increased defense spending, the buildup of the country's nuclear arsenal, and the development of a space-based anti-missile system. During his second term, however, Reagan steadily moved toward a policy of accommodation with Soviet leaders, conducting a series of summit meetings with Premier Mikhail Gorbachev and signing a major arms control agreement. How much his policies were responsible for bringing about the end of the Cold War continues to be debated among historians, but there is little doubt that they were a major contributor to this world-changing development.

Two years into his term, in March 1983, Reagan discussed some of his most basic convictions about American society and America's role in the world at the annual meeting of the National Association of Evangelicals. Founded in 1942, the association coordinated the activities of thirty-one Protestant denominations in the areas of religious broadcasting, missions, military chaplaincy, and outreach to the poor. Reagan's speech is notable for his characterization of the Soviet Union as a "focus of evil" and its emphasis on the role of religion in American life.

QUESTIONS FOR ANALYSIS

1. According to Reagan, how does secularism weaken and endanger American government and society?
2. When Reagan speaks of "religious values," what religions is he referring to?
3. In what ways, in Reagan's views, is the American experiment in democracy and freedom based on these religious traditions?
4. What is the basis of Reagan's opposition to abortion?
5. For what reasons does Reagan characterize the Soviet Union as the "focus of evil" in the modern world?
6. According to Reagan why is it so important for the United States to maintain its military strength?
7. Reagan is convinced that the United States will win the Cold War. Why is he convinced of this?

... Well, I'm pleased to be here today with you who are keeping America great by keeping America good. Only through your work and prayers and those of millions of others can we hope to survive this perilous century and keep alive this experiment in liberty, this last, best hope of man ...

Now, I don't have to tell you that this puts us in opposition to, or at least out of step with, a prevailing attitude of many who have turned to a modern-day secularism, discarding the tried and time-tested values upon which our very civilization is based. No matter how well intentioned, their value system is radically different from that of most Americans. And while they proclaim that they're freeing us from superstitions of the past, they've taken upon themselves the job of superintending us by government rule and regulation. Sometimes their voices are louder than ours, but they are not yet a majority.

An example of that vocal superiority is evident in a controversy now going on in Washington. And since I'm involved, I've been waiting to hear from the parents of young America. How far are they willing to go in giving to government their prerogatives as parents?

Let me state the case as briefly and simply as I can. An organization of citizens,[1] sincerely motivated and deeply concerned about the increase in illegitimate births and abortions involving girls well below the age of consent, sometime ago established a nationwide network of clinics to offer help to these girls and, hopefully, alleviate this situation. I do not fault their intent. However, in their well-intentioned effort, these clinics have decided to provide advice and birth control drugs and devices to underage girls without the knowledge of their parents.

For some years now, the Federal Government has helped with funds to subsidize these clinics. In providing for this, the Congress decreed that every effort would be made to maximize parental participation. Nevertheless, the drugs and devices are prescribed without getting parental consent or giving notification after they've done so. Girls termed "sexually active"—and that has replaced the word "promiscuous"—are given this help in order to prevent illegitimate birth or abortion.

Well, we have ordered clinics receiving Federal funds to notify the parents such help has been given. One of the Nation's leading newspapers has created the term "squeal rule" in editorializing against us for doing this, and we're being criticized for violating the privacy of young people ... I've watched TV panel shows discuss this issue, seen columnists pontificating on our error, but no one seems to mention morality as playing a part in the subject of sex.

Is all of Judeo-Christian tradition wrong? Are we to believe that something so sacred can be looked upon as a purely physical thing with no potential for emotional and psychological harm? And isn't it the parents' right to give counsel and advice to keep their children from making mistakes that may affect their entire lives? ...

Freedom prospers when religion is vibrant and the rule of law under God is acknowledged. When our Founding Fathers passed the first amendment, they sought to protect churches from government interference. They never intended to construct a wall of hostility between government and the concept of religious belief itself.

The evidence of this permeates our history and our government. The Declaration of Independence mentions the Supreme Being no less than four times. "In God We Trust" is engraved on our coinage. The Supreme Court opens its proceedings with a religious invocation. And the Members of Congress open their

---

[1]The reference is to Planned Parenthood Federation of America, commonly shortened to Planned Parenthood. It is an organization whose roots go back to the American Birth Control League, founded in Brooklyn by Margaret Sanger in 1921. Through its local affiliates it was (and is) the largest provider of comprehensive reproductive health services, including contraception, abortion, and other services, in the United States.

sessions with a prayer. I just happen to believe the schoolchildren of the United States are entitled to the same privileges as Supreme Court Justices and Congressmen.

Last year, I sent the Congress a constitutional amendment to restore prayer to public schools. Already this session, there's growing bipartisan support for the amendment, and I am calling on the Congress to act speedily to pass it and to let our children pray.[2] . . .

More than a decade ago, a Supreme Court decision literally wiped off the books of 50 States statutes protecting the rights of unborn children. Abortion on demand now takes the lives of up to 1½ million unborn children a year. Human life legislation ending this tragedy will some day pass the Congress, and you and I must never rest until it does. Unless and until it can be proven that the unborn child is not a living entity, then its right to life, liberty, and the pursuit of happiness must be protected.

You may remember that when abortion on demand began, many, and, indeed, I'm sure many of you, warned that the practice would lead to a decline in respect for human life, that the philosophical premises used to justify abortion on demand would ultimately be used to justify other attacks on the sacredness of human life—infanticide or mercy killing.

Tragically enough, those warnings proved all too true. Only last year a court permitted the death by starvation of a handicapped infant.[3]

I have directed the Health and Human Services Department to make clear to every health care facility in the United States that the Rehabilitation Act of 1973 protects all handicapped persons against discrimination based on handicaps, including infants. . . .

Now, I'm sure that you must get discouraged at times, but you've done better than you know, perhaps. There's a great spiritual awakening in America, a renewal of the traditional values that

have been the bedrock of America's goodness and greatness.

One recent survey . . . concluded that Americans were far more religious than the people of other nations; 95 percent of those surveyed expressed a belief in God and a huge majority believed the Ten Commandments had real meaning in their lives. And another study has found that an overwhelming majority of Americans disapprove of adultery, teenage sex, pornography, abortion, and hard drugs. And this same study showed a deep reverence for the importance of family ties and religious belief. . . .

Now, obviously, much of this new political and social consensus I've talked about is based on a positive view of American history, one that takes pride in our country's accomplishments and record. But we must never forget that no government schemes are going to perfect man. We know that living in this world means dealing with what philosophers would call the phenomenology of evil or, as theologians would put it, the doctrine of sin.

There is sin and evil in the world, and we're enjoined by Scripture and the Lord Jesus to oppose it with all our might. Our nation, too, has a legacy of evil with which it must deal. . . .

There is no room for racism, anti-Semitism, or other forms of ethnic and racial hatred in this country. . . .

And this brings me to my final point today. During my first press conference as President, in answer to a direct question, I pointed out that, as good Marxist-Leninists, the Soviet leaders have openly and publicly declared that the only morality they recognize is that which will further their cause, which is world revolution. I think I should point out I was only quoting Lenin, their guiding spirit, who said in 1920 that they repudiate all morality that proceeds from supernatural ideas—that's their name for

---

[2]The proposed amendment never received the necessary Senate vote to move forward.

[3]In 1982, with the consent of the parents, water and nourishment were withheld from "Baby Doe," who was born with Down syndrome in a Bloomington, Indiana, hospital.

religion—or ideas that are outside class conceptions. Morality is entirely subordinate to the interests of class war. And everything is moral that is necessary for the annihilation of the old, exploiting social order and for uniting the proletariat.

Well, I think the refusal of many influential people to accept this elementary fact of Soviet doctrine illustrates an historical reluctance to see totalitarian powers for what they are....

This doesn't mean we should isolate ourselves and refuse to seek an understanding with them. I intend to do everything I can to persuade them of our peaceful intent, to remind them that it was the West that refused to use its nuclear monopoly in the forties and fifties for territorial gain and which now proposes 50-percent cut in strategic ballistic missiles and the elimination of an entire class of land-based, intermediate-range nuclear missiles.

At the same time, however, they must be made to understand we will never compromise our principles and standards. We will never give away our freedom. We will never abandon our belief in God. And we will never stop searching for a genuine peace. But we can assure none of these things America stands for through the so-called nuclear freeze solutions proposed by some.[4]

The truth is that a freeze now would be a very dangerous fraud, for that is merely the illusion of peace. The reality is that we must find peace through strength. . . .

A freeze would reward the Soviet Union for its enormous and unparalleled military buildup. It would prevent the essential and long overdue modernization of United States and allied defenses and would leave our aging forces increasingly vulnerable....

A number of years ago, I heard a young father, a very prominent young man in the entertainment world,[5] addressing a tremendous gathering in California. It was during the time of the cold war, and communism and our own way of life were very much on people's minds. And he was speaking to that subject. And suddenly, though, I heard him saying, "I love my little girls more than anything—"... He went on: "I would rather see my little girls die now, still believing in God, than have them grow up under communism and one day die no longer believing in God."

Yes, let us pray for the salvation of all of those who live in that totalitarian darkness—pray they will discover the joy of knowing God. But until they do, let us be aware that while they preach the supremacy of the state, declare its omnipotence over individual man, and predict its eventual domination of all peoples on the Earth, they are the focus of evil in the modern world.

So, I urge you to speak out against those who would place the United States in a position of military and moral inferiority....

I urge you to beware the temptation of pride—the temptation of blithely declaring yourselves above it all and label both sides equally at fault, to ignore the facts of history and the aggressive impulses of an evil empire, to simply call the arms race a giant misunderstanding and thereby remove yourself from the struggle between right and wrong and good and evil....

While America's military strength is important, let me add here that I've always maintained that the struggle now going on for the world will never be decided by bombs, or rockets, by armies or military might. The real crisis we face today is a spiritual one; at root, it is a test of moral will and faith....

I believe we shall rise to the challenge. I believe that communism is another sad, bizarre chapter in human history whose last pages even now are being written. I believe this because

---

[4]The nuclear freeze movement began in 1980 in response to the U.S. Senate's failure to ratify the Salt II disarmament treaty. It advocated a bilateral freeze on nuclear weapons and their delivery systems.

[5]The entertainer was Pat Boone (b. 1934), a successful pop singer of the 1950s and 1960s. He was a born-again Christian well-known for his strong religious convictions.

the source of our strength in the quest for human freedom is not material, but spiritual. And because it knows no limitation, it must terrify and ultimately triumph over those who would enslave their fellow man....

Yes, change your world. One of our Founding Fathers, Thomas Paine,[6] said, "We have it within our power to begin the world over again." We can do it, doing together what no one church could do by itself.

God bless you, and thank you very much.

---

[6]Through his pamphlet, *Common Sense* (1776), which argued that the American colonists sever all ties with Britain, Thomas Paine made an important contribution to the American Revolution. It was strange, however, that Reagan quoted his words in a speech to this particular audience.

Paine's treatise, *The Age of Reason* (1793–1794), affirmed a belief in a supreme being but dismissed organized religions, including Christianity, as superstitions. When he died in 1809, no Christian church would accept his remains, so he was buried on his farm in New Rochelle, New York.

Political Change and Religious Currents in Latin America

In the wake of World War II, Latin America continued to display a bewildering variety of political regimes, with less than perfect democracies maintaining a hold in Mexico, Colombia, Uruguay, Venezuela, Chile, and Costa Rica, and old-style authoritarian rule continuing in Paraguay, the Dominican Republic, Cuba and elsewhere. In the 1960s, however, the region entered a twenty-five year period of political volatility in which democracy was the main victim. In Cuba, Castro's communist revolution of 1959–1960 initiated far-reaching social reforms but established a one-party dictatorship. Right-wing military dictatorships were established in Bolivia and Brazil in 1964, Peru in 1968, Uruguay and Chile in 1973, and Argentina in 1976.

The movement toward military rule resulted in part from the inability of civilian governments to deal with the region's many social and economic problems, which included soaring population rates, rapid urbanization, inflation, growing foreign indebtedness, persistent underdevelopment, and the ever-widening gap between the rich and poor. It also resulted from mounting fear of communism, fueled by the Castro revolution in Cuba, the proliferation of left-wing guerrilla movements, and the election of the Marxist Salvador Allende as president of Chile in 1970. Cold War politics also played a role. In its fight against communism, the U.S. government helped undermine left-leaning democracies in Chile and Bolivia, provided military aid to numerous regimes and provided counterinsurgency training to many hundreds of Latin American military officers at the School of the Americas in Panama and after 1984 in Fort Benning, Georgia.

Although the region's authoritarian regimes prevented the spread of communism and made strides in suppressing terrorists groups, they had no magic formula for solving their countries' chronic economic difficulties. Nor were they able to totally silence critics. As a result, beginning in the mid-1980s the region's military retreated to their barracks and democracy gradually returned.

Opposition to continued military rule had been centered in civic groups, labor unions, and movements such as the Mothers of the Plaza de Mayo, who beginning in 1976 gathered regularly in central Buenos Aires to demand information from the government about their sons and daughters who had "disappeared" into the regime's prisons or had been killed. Added pressure came from within the Roman Catholic Church, an institution that served the poor through its orphanages, hospitals, and other charitable institutions, but throughout most of the region's history had sided with entrenched elites and opposed movements for social reform. In the 1970s and 1980s, however, growing numbers of priests, nuns and bishops, spurred by a new "theology of liberation," dedicated themselves to work among the poor and took up the struggle against social injustice and dictatorship. As a result of their words and actions, no fewer than 850 priests, nuns, and bishops were murdered by right-wing death squads or individual assassins in the 1970s and 1980s.

Argentina's Dirty War

◆

87 ◆ Horacio Domingo Maggio,
LETTER TO THE ASSOCIATED PRESS (1978)
and *ARGENTINE GOVERNMENT REPORT (1983)*

Stability and continuity are not words that come to mind when describing the political history of Argentina in the second half of the twentieth century. Between 1943 and 1976, the country experienced five military coups d'état, witnessed the founding and dissolution of dozens of political parties, and was ruled by a succession of governments that struggled to solve the country's economic problems while balancing the interests of landowners, businesspeople, foreign investors, the Church, the military, and labor unions. Political life was further complicated by the continued popularity of Juan Perón, who was elected president in 1946 and won a devoted following among the working class before he was sent into an eighteen-year exile in 1955.

The nation's political health reached a low point in the 1970s. After troops fired on labor demonstrators in Córdoba in 1969, violence spread throughout the country. Groups such as the People's Revolutionary Army and the Montoneros bombed public buildings, kidnapped foreign businessmen, assassinated politicians, and attacked military installations. With the country facing civil war, the military allowed Perón to return from exile in 1973, hoping that the seventy-nine-year-old politician could restore order. He died in 1974, however, and his wife Isabel, who succeeded him, proved incapable of dealing with the nation's problems. In 1976, the army removed her from power, and military rule resumed.

The new regime turned a crackdown against left-wing groups into the "Dirty War." Death squads broke into homes, kidnapped tens of thousands of "terrorists," and held them in hundreds of detention centers. As many as thirty thousand people were shot, died under torture or other forms of abuse, or were drugged and pushed out of airplanes over the Atlantic Ocean. With loved ones denied information about their fate, they came to be known as *los desaparecidos*, [disappeared ones]. The country's rulers made little effort to cover up the kidnappings, convinced that such acts would frighten the population into submission, but they consistently maintained that their actions targeted terrorists only. This was an increasingly difficult position to defend as the number of victims grew and a few of the arrested were able to describe the horrors of their treatment after they were released or escaped.

One of those who managed to describe his experience to the wider world was Horacio Domingo Maggio, who was thirty years old and the father of two boys when he was kidnapped in late 1977. In March 1978, he escaped from the Navy Mechanics School in Buenos Aires (which had been converted into a detention center), and one month later provided a journalist with a copy of the letter excerpted below. After the letter was published in French newspapers, it drew attention because it provided information about the fate of eleven members of the Mothers of the Plaza de Mayo and two French nuns who supported them, who disappeared in December 1977. The government denied involvement in the women's disappearance, a denial that Maggio's letter contradicts. Maggio was recaptured, and presumably killed, in August, 1978. By then, his wife had also become one of the "disappeared."

Maggio's letter is followed by an excerpt from a report the military junta issued in April 1983, six months before the general elections that ended military rule. At the time, the junta was under intense pressure to justify its actions and to explain why so many Argentines had "disappeared" over the previous seven years.

QUESTIONS FOR ANALYSIS

1. What are Maggio's stated motives for writing his letter?
2. What information does Maggio provide about the reasons why he and the other prisoners he mentions were arrested?
3. On the basis of Maggio's account, what were the motives of his captors in their use of torture?
4. How does the statement issued by the military junta justify the antiterrorist campaign and explain the large number of persons who "disappeared"?
5. In what ways does Maggio's letter contradict specific assertions and general interpretations of the junta's statement?

Buenos Aires, April 10, 1978
Messrs.
Associated Press

Dear Sirs:

The undersigned, Horacio Domingo Maggio, Argentine, National Identity Card No. 6.308.359, ex-delegate general, member of the internal trade union committee of the Provincial Bank of Santa Fé, Main Branch, is writing your office in order to let you know of the bitter experiences that I had to go through when I was kidnapped by the Argentine Navy.

My attitude stems basically from two facts: my being a Christian and also an activist in the Montonero Peronist Movement; as well as my conviction that the press must have at its disposal all the information on what has gone on in our country since March 24, 1976, to be able to inform—as it has always done—the public in spite of the menaces and kidnappings that newspapermen have also suffered.

I was kidnapped in Buenos Aires on February 15, 1977 while I was walking on Rivadavia Street, one block away from Flores Park. The group which kidnapped me identified itself as

Joint Forces. Needless to say, while I was carried away forcefully I was beaten.

From there I was taken to a place which I later learned was the Navy Mechanical [Mechanics] School. I, as well as most of the people there and those who still remain there, was subjected to torture ("electric rod" or "picana" and "the submarine"[1]). Among others there were: Roberto Ahumada, from Santa Fé, national leader of Peronist Youth; Mrs. Osatinsky, widow of a Montonero leader and people's martyr, Marcos Osatinsky, murdered in 1976 in Cordoba City; Alicia Millin de Pirles from Santa Fé; Mrs. Orsci, sociologist, ex-dean of the Tourism School of Mar del Plata. Others who were removed from there were newspaperman Jara; Jaime Dri, the national leader of the Peronista Montonero Movement who had been kidnapped in Uruguay; Mrs. Alicia Eguren, wife of John Williams Cooke. etc.

On March 17, 1978 I was able to escape from that place.[2]

During the 13 months I spent there, I suffered and watched the most brutal and savage activities of this endless dictatorship, which is trying unsuccessfully to reduce to submission our whole country.

Such is the case of the two French nuns Alice Domon and Renée Duquet.

I had a chance to talk personally with Sister Alice, as she was taken, together with Sister Renée, to the third floor where the officer's mess is located, and where I was kept prisoner. This took place around the 11th or 12th of December, 1977.

During these conversations she told me that they had been kidnapped and that they had been made, under torture, to write a letter by hand in French, addressed to the Superior of their Order, and that photographs had been taken of them in what they thought was the basement of the above mentioned building.

She also told me that 11 other persons had been kidnapped with them. They remained at the Navy Mechanical School for about ten days and later were "transferred" with eleven other persons to an unknown place. I use quotation marks because there were many cases like this and later no one knew of their whereabouts. Because of the haste with which they were taken away there were rumors that the 13 people might have been killed.

Something similar happened with Mrs. Norma Esther Arrostito, a leader of the Montonero Movement, who was presumed to be dead, but was actually alive until January 15, 1978, holding up heroicly and stoically during more than one year of detainment and mental and physical pressure of the Navy officers. On that day, she fainted in a peculiar way and was then given an injection and died, according to rumors, in the Navy Hospital. The fact is that she never returned to her cell.

Another similar case was that of Dr. Hidalgo Solá, Argentine Ambassador to Venezuela. According to rumors that were going around on the third floor, the group that operated out of the Navy Mechanical School was responsible for this action.

A young Swedish girl, who disappeared in January 1977, was also there; she was semi-handicapped because of a bullet wound in her head.

The living conditions in that place are similar to those prevailing before the Assembly of 1813.... [3]

We were forced to lie down 24 hours a day on mattresses on the floor. These mattresses were separated from each other by wooden partitions, or we were kept in cells with up to four persons in each cell. We all had shackles on our legs and had hoods or glasses which did not allow you to see. Besides the place was infested with rats.

---

[1]The *picana* is an instrument of torture developed in Argentina in the early 1930s. Based on the cattle prod, an instrument to goad cattle into the slaughter house, it is a wand or prod that delivers high voltage at low current, meaning more shocks can be delivered without the danger of killing the victim. Two people operate the picana, with one controlling the rheostat and the other applying the tip of the instrument to the victim's head, lips, nipples or genitals. The submarine was a form of torture in which an individual's head is covered in a cloth hood and thrust into water to induce asphyxiation. It resembles waterboarding, in which a hooded individual is tied down and has water poured over his or her face, causing gagging and the belief that he or she is drowning.

[2]He escaped while accompanying a guard to make purchases at a local stationery store.

[3]Before the declaration of independence from Spain.

The methods used by these people to rid themselves of the thousands of kidnapped people have changed. At the beginning when this para-military group was formed, whose code name is Task Group 3.3.3. in order to differentiate itself from other groups which report to the Army and the Air Force, they used to get five or six people in a car, shoot them and then set fire to the car in the PanAmerican Highway area. Later, the method was changed and the prisoners were hanged in the Mechanical School and the corpses thrown into the river. At present, they are given a big injection of a sleeping drug and they are wrapped in a piece of canvas and thrown in the sea. For the two latter procedures a helicopter is used....

This followed a certain pattern that some of us had noticed. During the days in which the so-called "transferences" took place, the disciplinary measures and the physical treatment of the prisoners hardened. At times there was corporal punishment with rubber batons or it was prohibited to use the bathrooms.

One time I was able to see by lifting the hood which covered my head, a young man around 20–30 years old being placed semi-concious on a white piece of canvas. Another factor was that after the "transfers" were made, usually on Wednesdays, the noise of a helicopter could be heard.

The people directly responsible for this are those who make up the para-military group which is located inside ESMA[4] and specifically the officers mess which they call "El Dorado." They are, in a hierarchical order:

[A list of 23 names follows, beginning with that of Rear Admiral Jacinto Chamorro, director of the school.]

I am aware that by denouncing all this I put the life of my wife and children, my parents, my sister, parents-in-law and other relatives in danger, as well as that of those who are still in that institution. For that reason should anything happen to my family (kidnapping or death) and/or to the people who remain in prison, I make

the Argentine Military Junta and those Navy officers operating in ESMA responsible.

Sincerely,

Horacio Domingo Maggio
D.N.I. No. 6.308.359

Source: "Kidnapped by Argentine Military," State Department and Other Agencies Declassified Documents, http://foia.state.gov/documents/Argentina/searchable_0000A8FC.pdf.

THE ARGENTINE GOVERNMENT REPORT (1983)

The exceptional conditions in which the country lived during the period of the terrorist aggression caused the essential elements of the state to be affected at levels that made difficult its survival.

The exercise of human rights was at the mercy of violence—selective or indiscriminate—imposed by terrorist activity, translated into assassinations, kidnappings, "Revolutionary Trials," exiles and compulsory taxation....

In that crucial historic moment, the armed forces were summoned by the constitutional government in order to fight subversion....

The actions thus developed were the consequence of decisions that had to be made in the middle of the fight; with a measure of passion that combat and the defense of one's own life generate; in an environment tainted daily with innocent blood and destruction and before a society where panic reigned. In this framework, almost apocalyptic, errors were committed which, as happens in all wars, would, at times, trespass the limits of the respect of fundamental human rights and which are subject to the judgment of God in each conscience and the understanding of men.

The case of the missing is the one which most forcibly strikes the legitimate humanitarian sentiments, the one which is used most insidiously to

---

[4]*La Escuela Superior Mecánica de la Armada* (Naval Mechanics School).

[undermine] the good faith of those who did not know the facts that led us to that final situation.

The experience ... allows us to affirm that many of the disappearances are a consequence of the modus operandi of the terrorists.

They change their authenic names and surnames; they are known among themselves by "War Names" and have abundant fraudulent personal documentation.... Those who decide to become members of terrorist organizations, do it surreptitiously, abandoning their family, work and social milieu. This is the most typical case: family members report a missing person whose disappearance cannot be explained or, knowing the cause, do not want to explain it.

Thus, some of "the missing" whose disappearance had been reported later appeared performing terrorist actions. In other cases, the terrorists abandoned the country clandestinely and lived outside with false identities....

There are cases of deserters from different organizations who live today with false identities in order to protect their own lives, either within the country or outside.

Many of the fallen during confrontations with the police did not have any type of document or had false documents and, in many cases, they had worn off finger prints. Other terrorists, when capture was imminent, committed suicide, generally by ingesting cyanide. In these cases the corpses were not claimed and, since it

was impossible to identify them, they were legally buried as "NN" [not known].

Whenever it was possible, the terrorists would recover the bodies of their dead from the place of conflict. The corpses, as well as the wounded who died as a consequence of the confrontation, were destroyed or clandestinely buried by the terrorists....

Terrorism, hiding under a pseudo-revolutionary code, made mockery of trials and assassinated ... members who defected or who failed on assigned missions. These were buried with false identities or in unknown places and circumstances....

In much the same way, there have been cases of persons reported as missing, who later did appear and led normal lives without the knowledge of the judicial or administrative authorities....

In the same vein, one hears of "missing" persons who might be found detained by the Argentinian government in unknown places in the country. All this is nothing but falsehoods utilized for political aims, since in the republic there are no secret places of detention, neither are there in the jails people who are secretly detained.

Those who gave their life to combat the terrorist scourge deserve eternal, respectful homage and gratitude.

Source: Historic Documents of 1983. Washington DC: Congressional Quarterly Inc. 1984. pp. 459–462 via Copyright Clearance Center.

◆

Catholicism and Liberation Theology

❖

88 ◆ *FINAL DOCUMENT OF THE THIRD GENERAL CONFERENCE OF THE LATIN AMERICAN EPISCOPATE*

When some six hundred bishops gathered in Puebla, Mexico, in 1979 for the Third General Conference of the Latin American Episcopate, they sensed that the Latin American Church, with 35 percent of the world's Catholics, was

Source: From the English translation of the final document of the *Third General Conference of the Latin American Episcopate.* Copyright United States Catholic Conference, Inc. Washington DC. Reprinted with permission. All rights reserved.

at a crossroads. In the 1960s reformist and even revolutionary currents had emerged among the clergy. This was in part a response to the liberal atmosphere in the broader church after the Second Vatican Council of 1962 and in part an expression of the growing conviction that the Church's indifference to social injustice distorted Christ's teachings and threatened to lose the masses to Marxism, religious apathy, or non-Catholic evangelical churches. During the 1960s, bishops spoke out in favor of land reform; young priests went into urban slums to establish clinics, schools, and self-help organizations; and Catholic intellectuals developed a new "theology of liberation," which centered the Church's mission on ministering to and furthering the interests of the poor. Their efforts culminated in decisions made at the second conference of Latin American bishops in Medellin, Colombia, in 1968, by which bishops committed the Church to the task of liberating Latin America's poor from economic and social injustice.

This leftward shift provoked a countereaction in the 1970s. Conservative bishops denounced reformers as more Marxist than Christian, and some members of the laity expressed reservations about the clergy's political activism. Conservatives hoped to regain control of Church policy at the third Catholic bishops' conference in Puebla in 1979. Well-known liberation theologians were excluded, and conservative bishops drafted a working document that, if accepted, would have endorsed capitalism and rejected the clergy's involvement in politics. Remarks by Pope John Paul II, who addressed the opening of the conference, seemed to support the progressives, however, and after two weeks of discussion, the delegates approved a generally progressive statement from which the following excerpts are drawn.

After Puebla, the Latin American Church remained divided. Churchmen in Chile and Brazil continued to speak out against military regimes, and clergy in Central America remained in the forefront of the struggle for social change. Overall, however, conservatives made gains, especially in Argentina and Colombia. This trend was supported by an increasingly conservative Pope John Paul II, who named conservatives as bishops and approved the disciplining of Leonardo Boff, a popular Brazilian liberation theologian, in the mid-1980s. While the Catholic Church struggled to clarify its mission, increasing numbers of Latin Americans abandoned religion or joined one of the many Pentecostal Protestant sects spreading throughout the region.

QUESTIONS FOR ANALYSIS

1. What is the document's overall assessment of the economic and political state of Latin America?
2. What can be gleaned from the document about the bishops' views of the underlying causes of Latin American poverty?
3. Why, according to the Puebla statement, should Latin American poverty not be tolerated by Catholics?
4. What statements in the document seem to confirm the view that it was a compromise between progressives and conservatives?

5. Critics of the Puebla statement contend that it was essentially worthless because it lacked concrete proposals to deal with Latin America's problems. Do you agree with such criticisms?

Viewing it in the light of faith, we see the growing gap between rich and poor as a scandal and a contradiction to Christian existence. . . . The luxury of a few becomes an insult to the wretched poverty of the vast masses. . . . This is contrary to the plan of the Creator and to the honor that is due him. In this anxiety and sorrow the Church sees a situation of social sinfulness, all the more serious because it exists in countries that call themselves Catholic and are capable of changing the situation . . . .

This situation of pervasive extreme poverty takes on very concrete faces in real life. In these faces we ought to recognize the suffering features of Christ the Lord, who questions and challenges us. They include:

- the faces of young children, struck down by poverty before they are born, their chance for self-development blocked by irreparable mental and physical deficiencies; and of the vagrant children in our cities who are so often exploited, products of poverty and the moral disorganization of the family;
- the faces of young people, who are disoriented because they cannot find their place in society, and who are frustrated, particularly in marginal rural and urban areas, by the lack of opportunity to obtain training and work;
- the faces of the indigenous peoples, and frequently of the Afro-Americans as well; living marginalized lives in inhuman situations, they can be considered the poorest of the poor;
- the faces of the peasants; as a social group, they live in exile almost everywhere on our continent, deprived of land, caught in a situation of internal and external dependence, and subjected to systems of commercialization that exploit them;

- the faces of laborers, who frequently are ill-paid and who have difficulty in organizing themselves and defending their rights;
- the faces of the underemployed and the unemployed, who are dismissed because of the harsh exigencies of economic crises, and often because of development-models that subject workers and their families to cold economic calculations;
- the faces of marginalized and overcrowded urban dwellers, whose lack of material goods is matched by the ostentatious display of wealth by other segments of society;
- the faces of old people, who are growing more numerous every day, and who are frequently marginalized in a progress-oriented society that totally disregards people not engaged in production.

We share other anxieties of our people that stem from a lack of respect for their dignity as human beings, made in the image and likeness of God, and for their inalienable rights as children of God.

. . . Our mission to bring God to human beings, and human beings to God, also entails the task of fashioning a more fraternal society here. And the unjust social situation has not failed to produce tensions within the Church itself. On the one hand they are provoked by groups that stress the "spiritual" side of the Church's mission and resent active efforts at societal improvement. On the other hand they are provoked by people who want to make the Church's mission nothing more than an effort at human betterment.

There are other novel and disturbing phenomena. We refer to the partisan political activity of priests—not as individuals, as some had acted in the past . . ., but as organized pressure groups. And we also refer to the fact that some of them are applying social analyses with strong political connotations to pastoral work.

The Church's awareness of its evangelizing mission has led it in the past ten years to publish numerous pastoral documents about social justice; to create [organizations] designed to express solidarity with the afflicted, to denounce outrages, and to defend human rights; . . . and to endure the persecution and at times death of its members in witness to its prophetic mission. Much remains to be done, of course, if the Church is to display greater oneness and solidarity. Fear of Marxism keeps many from facing up to the oppressive reality of liberal capitalism. One could say that some people, faced with the danger of one clearly sinful system, forgot to denounce and combat the established reality of another equally sinful system. . . . We must give full attention to the latter system, without overlooking the violent and atheistic historical forms of Marxism. . . .

To this are added other anxieties that stem from abuses of power, which are typical of regimes based on force. There are the anxieties based on systematic or selective repression; it is accompanied by accusations, violations of privacy, improper pressures, tortures, and exiles. There are the anxieties produced in many families by the disappearance of their loved ones, about whom they cannot get any news. There is the total insecurity bound up with arrest and detention without judicial consent. There are the anxieties felt in the face of a system of justice that has been suborned or cowed. As the Supreme Pontiffs point out, the Church . . . must raise its voice to denounce and condemn these situations, particularly when the responsible officials or rulers call themselves Christians.

Then there are the anxieties raised by guerrilla violence, by terrorism, and by the kidnappings carried out by various brands of extremists. They, too, pose a threat to life together in society. . . .

The free-market economy, in its most rigid expression, is still the prevailing system on our continent. Legitimated by liberal ideologies, it has increased the gap between the rich and the poor by giving priority to capital over labor, economics over the social realm. Small groups in our nations, who are often tied in with foreign interests, have taken advantage of the opportunities provided by these older forms of the free market to profit for themselves while the interests of the vast majority of the people suffer.

Marxist ideologies have also spread among workers, students, teachers, and others, promising greater social justice. In practice their strategies have sacrificed many Christian, and hence human, values; or else they have fallen prey to utopian forms of unrealism. Finding their inspiration in policies that use force as a basic tool, they have only intensified the spiral of violence.

◆

Religion and Politics in the Middle East and India

During much of the twentieth century, it would not have been unreasonable to conclude that religion was a dying force among the world's peoples. Everywhere, it seemed, organized religion was on the defensive. In the West, mainline Protestant churches experienced declining membership and attendance, and the Roman Catholic Church found it increasingly difficult to attract young men to the priesthood. In Muslim Turkey, Iran, Iraq, Egypt, and Indonesia, governments embraced aggressively secularist policies as part of campaigns to modernize their economies, educational systems, and culture. Avowedly atheist regimes in the Soviet Union and communist China sought to obliterate religious belief and practice altogether.

Clearly, however, reports of religion's demise were premature. Martin Luther King, Jr., a Baptist minister with broad support from the nation's religious leadership, led the civil rights movement in the United States. Religious people played important roles in the struggle against apartheid in South Africa, movements on behalf of nuclear disarmament, and events that led to the downfall of communism in Eastern Europe in the 1980s. As we have already seen in this chapter, liberation theology in Latin America and the reiligious right in the United States became important poltical forces.

The most striking examples of religion's vigor in recent history have occurred in the Middle East, North Africa, and India, where affirmation of traditional religious values provided a way to strengthen cultural identity and limit the influence of foreign, Western-inspired values. It also led to conflict and provided the impetus for earthshaking political changes.

Islamic Law in the Modern World

❖

89 ◆ Ruhollah Khomeini, *ISLAMIC GOVERNMENT*

Ruhollah Khomeini, whose name is synonymous with Islamic fundamentalism and Iran's Islamic Revolution of 1979, was born in 1902 in Khumayn, an Iranian village some sixty miles southwest of Tehran. Following the example of his father and grandfather, he became a religious scholar, and by the late 1930s he was director of the prestigious school of Islamic studies in Qom, an important pilgrimage site and the spiritual center for Iran's Shiite Muslims. In the late 1950s, he became a vocal critic of Iran's reigning monarch, Shah Mohammad Reza Pahlavi, attacking him for his pro-U.S. policies, dictatorial rule, and efforts to diminish Islam's role in Iranian life. In 1963, the arrest and imprisonment of Khomeini led to nationwide antigovernment demonstrations and rioting, which were suppressed by army troops at the cost of thousands of lives. Released from prison and sent into exile in 1964, Khomeini continued to denounce the shah, whose secularism, heavy-handed rule, corrupt government, and ill-conceived economic policies continued to cause widespread discontent. In January 1978, rioting again broke out in Qom, this time sparked by the publication of articles in the state-controlled press accusing Khomeini of treason. In the following months, millions of Iranians, spurred on by Khomeini and other religious leaders, took to the streets chanting "death to the shah." In early 1979, events moved quickly. In January, the shah fled the country; in February, Khomeini returned from exile; and in March, a national referendum approved the establishment of the Islamic Republic of Iran.

Iran's new government was a republic in name only. Although it had an elected parliament and president, it was dominated by Khomeini and a small

Source: Ruhullah Khomeini, *Islam and Revolution: Writings and Declarations of Imam Khomeini,* Hamid Algar, ed. and trans. (Berkeley, Cal.: Mizan Press, 1981), 27–31, 33–36, 49–50, 120–121, 131–132.

circle of like-minded Islamic clerics. During the 1980s, they purged the shah's supporters from government, suppressed political and religious opponents, instituted religious courts to enforce Islamic law, and used the army and schools as instruments of religious indoctrination. Although Khomeini had promised to address the problems of poverty and social inequality, his efforts foundered in the face of war with Iraq in the 1980s, inflation, and population growth at the rate of 4 percent a year. Nonetheless, by the time of his death in 1989, millions of Muslims in Iran and elsewhere venerated Khomeini as a heroic defender of their religion against the forces of secularism and imperialism, and his austere, uncompromising version of Islam had become a major force in world politics.

The following selection is an excerpt from *Islamic Government*, Khomeini's best-known work. The book is based on a series of lectures that he delivered while in exile in 1970 to students at a religious school in the Iraqi city of Najaf. It is not a complete exposition of Islamic political philosophy, nor does it provide a detailed outline of what an Islamic state would be like. Khomeini's goal was to inspire his student listeners to actively work for the establishment of an Islamic state and to assume executive and judicial positions within it.

QUESTIONS FOR ANALYSIS

1. According to Khomeini, who are the enemies of Islam and what are their goals?
2. How, according to Khomeini, do the enemies of Islam distort Islamic doctrine and practice? How does he counter their arguments?
3. How does Khomeini characterize the relationship between Islam and modern science and technology?
4. What are the shortcomings of existing governments in the Islamic world according to Khomeini?
5. What benefits will accrue to society if Islamic laws are rigorously enforced?
6. What is the meaning of the term *jihad* as used by Khomeini in this treatise?

[MISCONCEPTIONS ABOUT ISLAMIC LAW]

At a time when the West was a realm of darkness and obscurity—with its inhabitants living in a state of barbarism and America still peopled by half-savage redskins—and the two vast empires of Iran and Byzantium[1] were under the rule of tyranny, class privilege, and discrimination, and the powerful dominated all without any trace of law or popular government, God, Exalted and Almighty, by means of the Most Noble Messenger [Muhammad] (peace and blessings be upon him), sent laws that astound us with their magnitude. He instituted laws and practices for all human affairs and laid down injunctions for man extending from even before the embryo is formed until after he is placed in the tomb.... Islamic law is a progressive, evolving, and comprehensive system of law. All the voluminous books that have been compiled

---

[1]During Muhammad's lifetime, (570-632 C.E.) the region to the north of Arabia was dominated by two large empires, the Byzantine Empire, centered in Asia Minor, and the Sassanid Empire of Persia (Iran).

from the earliest times on different areas of law, such as judicial procedure, social transactions, penal law, retribution, international relations, regulations pertaining to peace and war, private and public law—taken together, these contain a mere sample of the laws and injunctions of Islam. There is not a single topic in human life for which Islam has not provided instruction and established a norm....

The agents of imperialism sometimes write in their books and their newspapers that the legal provisions of Islam are too harsh....

I am amazed at the way these people think. They kill people for possessing ten grams of heroin and say, "That is the law." ... Inhuman laws like this are concocted in the name of a campaign against corruption, and they are not to be regarded as harsh.... When Islam, however, stipulates that the drinker of alcohol should receive eighty lashes, they consider it "too harsh." They can *execute* someone for possessing ten grams of heroin and the question of harshness does not even arise!

Many forms of corruption that have appeared in society derive from alcohol. The collisions that take place on our roads, and the murders and suicides, are very often caused by the consumption of alcohol....

But when Islam wishes to prevent the consumption of alcohol ... stipulating that the drinker should receive eighty lashes, or sexual vice, decreeing that the fornicator be given one hundred lashes (and the married man or woman be stoned), then they start wailing and lamenting: "What a harsh law that is, reflecting the harshness of the Arabs!" They are not aware that these penal provisions of Islam are intended to keep great nations from being destroyed by corruption. Sexual vice has now reached such proportions that it is destroying entire generations, corrupting our youth, and causing them to neglect all forms of work. They are all rushing to enjoy the various forms of vice that have become so freely available and so enthusiastically promoted. Why should it be regarded as harsh if Islam stipulates that an offender should be publicly flogged in order to protect the younger generation from corruption? ...

[SCIENCE, MATERIALISM AND ISLAM]

So far, we have sketched the subversive and corrupting plan of imperialism. We must now take into consideration as well certain internal factors, notably the dazzling effect that the material progress of the imperialist countries has had on some members of our society. As the imperialist countries attained a high degree of wealth and affluence—the result both of scientific and technical progress and of their plunder of the nations of Asia and Africa—these individuals lost all self-confidence and imagined that the only way to achieve technical progress was to abandon their own laws and beliefs. When the moon landings took place [between 1969 and 1972], for instance, they concluded that Muslims should jettison their laws! But what is the connection between going to the moon and the laws of Islam? Do they not see that countries having opposing laws and social systems compete with each other in technical and scientific progress and the conquest of space? Let them go all the way to Mars or beyond the Milky Way; they will still be deprived of true happiness, moral virtue, and spiritual advancement and be unable to solve their own social problems. For the solution of social problems and the relief of human misery require foundations in faith and morals; merely acquiring material power and wealth, conquering nature and space, have no effect in this regard. They must be supplemented by, and balanced with, the faith, the conviction, and the morality of Islam in order truly to serve humanity instead of endangering it....

[THE TIMELESSNESS OF ISLAMIC LAW]

It is self-evident that the necessity for enactment of the law, which necessitated the formation of a government by the Prophet [Muhammad] (upon whom be peace), was not confined or restricted to his time, but continues after his departure from this world. According to one of the noble verses of the Quran, the ordinances of Islam are not limited with respect to time or place; they are permanent and must be enacted until the end of time. They were not revealed merely for the time of the Prophet, only to be abandoned thereafter, with retribution and the penal code of Islam no longer to be enacted, or the taxes prescribed by Islam no longer collected, and the defense of the lands and people of Islam suspended. The claim that the laws of Islam may remain in abeyance or are restricted to a particular time or place is contrary to the essential credal bases of Islam. Since the enactment of laws, then, is necessary after the departure of the Prophet from this world, and indeed, will remain so until the end of time, the formation of a government and the establishment of executive and administrative organs are also necessary. Without the formation of a government ... of law, all activities of the individual take place in the framework of a just system, chaos and anarchy will prevail and social, intellectual, and moral corruption will arise....

In this system of laws, all the needs of man have been met: his dealings with his neighbors, fellow citizens, and clan, as well as children and relatives; the concerns of private and marital life; regulations concerning war and peace and intercourse with other nations; penal and commercial law; and regulations pertaining to trade and agriculture. Islamic law contains provisions relating to the preliminaries of marriage and the form in which it should be contracted, and others relating to the development of the embryo in the womb and what food the parents should eat at the time of conception. It further stipulates the duties that are incumbent upon them while the infant is being suckled, and specifies how the child should be reared, and how the husband and the wife should relate to each other and to their children. Islam provides laws and instructions for all of these matters, aiming, as it does, to produce integrated and virtuous human beings....

[THE FAULTS OF EXISTING GOVERNMENTS]

In order to attain the unity and freedom of the Muslim peoples, we must overthrow the oppressive governments installed by the imperialists and bring into existence an Islamic government of justice that will be in the service of the people....

Through the political agents they have placed in power over the people, the imperialists have also imposed on us an unjust economic order, and thereby divided our people into two groups: oppressors and oppressed. Hundreds of millions of Muslims are hungry and deprived of all form of health care and education, while minorities comprised of the wealthy and powerful live a life of indulgence, licentiousness, and corruption. The hungry and deprived have constantly struggled to free themselves from the oppression of their plundering overlords, and their struggle continues to this day. But their way is blocked by the ruling minorities and the oppressive governmental structures they head....

We must end all this plundering and usurpation of wealth. The people as a whole have a responsibility in this respect, but the responsibility of the religious scholars is graver and more critical. We must take the lead over other Muslims in embarking on this sacred *jihad*,[2] this heavy undertaking; because of our rank and position, we must be in the forefront. If we do not have the power today to prevent these misdeeds from happening and to punish these embezzlers and traitors, these powerful thieves that rule over us, then we must work to gain that power. At the same time, to fulfill our minimum obligation, we must not fail to expound the truth and expose the thievery and mendacity of our rulers. When we come to power, we will not only put

---

[2]*Jihad,* meaning "struggle" in Arabic, is one of the duties of Muslims. Although sometimes interpreted as a "struggle" for righteous living or for a just society, it most frequently is understood in a military sense as a religious struggle against unbelievers as a way of advancing Islam. A *mujahid* is a person who engages in jihad.

the country's political life, economy, and administration in order, we will also whip and chastise the thieves and the liars. . . .

Do you imagine all that bombastic propaganda being broadcast on the radio is true? Go see for yourself at first hand what state our [the Iranian] people are living in. Not even one out of every two hundred villages has a clinic. No one is concerned about the poor and the hungry, and they do not allow the measures Islam has devised for the sake of the poor to be implemented. Islam has solved the problem of poverty and inscribed it at the very top of its program: "*Sadaqat*[3] is for the poor." Islam is aware that first, the conditions of the poor must be remedied, the conditions of the deprived must be remedied. But *they* do not allow the plans of Islam to be implemented.

Our wretched people subsist in conditions of poverty and hunger, while the taxes that the ruling class extorts from them are squandered. They buy Phantom jets[4] so that pilots from Israel and its agents can come and train in them in our country. So extensive is the influence of Israel in our country—Israel, which is in a state of war with the Muslims, so that those who support it are likewise in a state of war with the Muslims—and so great is the support the regime gives it, that Israeli soldiers come to our country for training! . . .

[A FINAL CHARGE TO HIS LISTENERS]

If you present Islam accurately and acquaint people with its world-view, doctrines, principles, ordinances, and social system, they will welcome it ardently. I have witnessed that myself. A single word was enough once to cause a wave of enthusiasm among the people, because then, like now, they were all dissatisfied and unhappy with the state of affairs. They are living now in the shadow of the bayonet, and repression will let them say nothing. They want someone to stand up fearlessly and speak out. So, courageous sons of Islam, stand up! Address the people bravely; tell the truth about our situation to the masses in simple language; arouse them to enthusiastic activity, and turn the people in the street and the bazaar, our simplehearted workers and peasants, and out alert students into dedicated *mujahids*. The entire population will become *mujahids*. All segments of society are ready to struggle for the sake of freedom, independence, and the happiness of the nation, and their struggle needs religion. Give the people Islam, then, for Islam is the school of *jihad*, the religion of struggle; let them amend their characters and beliefs in accordance with Islam and transform themselves into a powerful force, so that they may overthrow the tyrannical regime imperialism has imposed on us and set up an Islamic government.

---

[3] Arabic for charity.

[4] Under the shah Iran purchased more than 200 F-4 Phantom jets, making it the second largest purchaser after Israel of the U.S.-produced planes.

The Place of Hinduism in Modern India

❖

90 ◆ Girilal Jain, *EDITORIALS*

Religious tension between India's majority Hindus and smaller communities of Muslims and Sikhs divided India's political leaders in the 1930s and early 1940s; set off riots that caused the deaths of tens of thousands in 1946; and led to the

---

Source: From Girilal Jain, "On Hindu Rashtra" from the book *Ayodhya and After: Issues Before Hindu Society* by Koenraad Elst. © 1991 Voice of India Publishing. Used with permission.

founding of two separate states, predominantly Muslim Pakistan and predominantly Hindu India in 1947. In the year following independence, as many as fourteen million Muslims, Hindus, and Sikhs crossed borders to escape entrapment in a state that was hostile to their faith. Migrations of such staggering magnitude overwhelmed governments at every level, and violence and slaughter occurred on both sides of the border. As many as five hundred thousand deaths resulted.

Despite partition and the mass-migrations of 1947 and 1948, independent India remained religiously divided among Hindus (approximately 82 percent of the population), Muslims (approximately 13 percent) and smaller communities of Christians, Sikhs, Parsis, Jains, and Buddhists. In 1949, under the leadership of the Congress Party, a constituent assembly that also served as India's first parliament approved a constitution that declared India to be a secular state committed to religious freedom and partiality to no single religious group.

None of India's religious groups has been completely satisfied with the results of India's commitment to secularism. Many Hindus have been convinced that the government has bent over backward to protect Muslims and Sikhs; Muslims and Sikhs, conversely, believed that the government has pandered to Hindus. Religious tensions intensified in the 1980s, as Muslims began to make converts among low-caste Hindus in the south, Sikhs agitated for an independent Punjab, and Hindus in 1982 organized their own political party, the Bharatiya Janata (Indian People's Party), or BJP, whose goal was the "Hinduization" of India.

A leading spokesman for Hindu nationalism was Girilal Jain, a journalist who served as editor-in-chief of the New Delhi *Times of India* between 1978 and 1988. Born into a poor rural family in 1922 and educated at Delhi University, Jain was drawn to Hindu nationalism and the BJP in the 1980s. He wrote the following editorials at a time when Hindu-Muslim tensions were peaking over the Babri mosque, built in the city of Ayodhya in the sixteenth century on a site Hindus believed to be the birthplace of one of the most revered Hindu gods, Lord Rama. Hindus demanded the destruction of the mosque, which was no longer used, so that a temple in honor of Rama could be built. In 1989, Hindu nationalists began laying the foundations for a Hindu temple near the mosque, and in 1990, the year in which Jain wrote his editorials "The Harbinger of a New Order" and "Limits of the Hindu Rashra {Polity}" for the *Sunday Mail,* they attacked and damaged the mosque. In December 1992, 150,000 Hindus stormed the mosque and destroyed it, precipitating a government crisis and causing violence that took two thousand lives. In September 2010, judges from the High Court of Allahabad (the supreme court for the state of Uttar Pradesh) gave control of the main disputed section of the property to Hindus, with the remaining property going to Muslims and a minor Hindu sect. In August 2011, India's Supreme Court agreed to consider an appeal of the verdict.

QUESTIONS FOR ANALYSIS

1. What does Jain mean when he says that the issues that concern the BJP have to do with "civilization," not religion?
2. How does Jain define the West? How does he view the West's role in Indian history?

3. Why, according to Jain, is the controversy over the Ayodhya mosque so significant for India's future?
4. In Jain's view, why have Muslims been satisfied to go along with the secularist policies of the Indian state?
5. What is Jain's vision of India's future?

THE HARBINGER OF A NEW ORDER

A specter haunts dominant sections of India's political and intellectual elites—the specter of a growing Hindu self-awareness and self-assertion. Till recently these elites had used the bogey of Hindu "communalism" and revivalism as a convenient device to keep themselves in power and to "legitimize" their slavish imitation of the West. Unfortunately for them, the ghost has now materialized.

Millions of Hindus have stood up. It will not be easy to trick them back into acquiescing in an order which has been characterized not so much by its "appeasement of Muslims" as by its alienness, rootlessness and contempt for the land's unique cultural past. Secularism, a euphemism for irreligion and repudiation of the Hindu ethos, and socialism, a euphemism for denigration and humiliation of the business community to the benefit of ever expanding rapacious bureaucracy, ... have been major planks of this order. Both have lost much of their old glitter and, therefore, capacity to dazzle and mislead....

The Hindu fight is not at all with Muslims; the fight is between Hindus ... and the state, Indian in name and not in spirit and the political and intellectual class trapped in the debris the British managed to bury us under before they left. The proponents of the Western ideology are using Muslims as auxiliaries and it is a pity Muslim "leaders" are allowing themselves to be so used....

LIMITS OF THE HINDU RASHTRA

The first part of this story begins, in my view, with the mass conversion of Harijans to Islam in Meenakshipuram in Tamil Nadu in 1981[1] and travels via the rise of Pakistan-backed armed secessionist movements in Punjab and Jammu and Kashmir,[2] and the second part with the spectacular success of the Bharatiya Janata Party (BJP) in the last polls....

India ... has been a battleground between two civilizations (Hindu and Islamic) for well over a thousand years, and three (Hindu, Muslim and Western) for over two hundred years. None of them has ever won a decisive enough and durable enough victory to oblige the other two to assimilate themselves fully into it. So the battle continues. This stalemate lies at the root of the crisis of identity the intelligentsia has faced since the beginning of the freedom movement in the last quarter of the nineteenth century....

The more resilient and upwardly mobile section of the intelligentsia must, by definition, seek to come to terms with the ruling power and its mores, and the less successful part of it to look for its roots and seek comfort in its cultural past.... Thus in the medieval period of our history there grew up a class of Hindus in and around centers of Muslim power who took to the Persian-Arabic culture and ways of the rulers; similarly under the more securely founded and far better organized and managed [British] Raj[3] there arose a vast number of Hindus who took to the English language,

---

[1]Hindus were incensed when large numbers of low-caste Hindus, or Harijans, were converted to Islam in 1981. It was believed that Saudi Arabians financed the missionary campaign.
[2]Punjab and Jammu and Kashmir were created at the time of independence. With mixed populations of Hindus,

Muslims, and Sikhs, they have been plagued by religious conflict.
[3]*Raj* is Hindi for reign, or rule; often used to refer to the British colonial administration.

Western ideas, ideals, dress and eating habits; ... they, their progeny and other recruits to their class have continued to dominate independent India.

They are the self-proclaimed secularists who have sought, and continue to seek, to remake India in the Western image.... Behind them has stood, and continues to stand, the awesome intellectual might of the West, which may or may not be anti-India, depending on the exigencies of its interests, but which has to be antipathetic to Hinduism....

Some secularists may be genuinely pro-Muslim.... But, by and large, that is not the motivating force in their lives. They are driven, above all, by the fear of what they call regression into their own past which they hate and dread. Most of the exponents of this viewpoint have come and continue to come understandably from the Left, understandably because no other group of Indians can possibly be so alienated from the country's cultural past as the followers of Lenin, Stalin and Mao, who have spared little effort to turn their own countries into cultural wastelands.

The state in independent India has, it is true, sought, broadly speaking, to be neutral in the matter of religion. But this is a surface view of the reality. The Indian state has been far from neutral in civilizational terms. It has been an agency, and a powerful agency, for the spread of Western values and mores. It has willfully sought to replicate Western institutions, the Soviet Union too being essentially part of Western civilization. It could not be otherwise in view of the orientation and aspirations of the dominant elite of which Nehru

remains the guiding spirit ... Muslims have found such a state acceptable principally on three counts. First, it has agreed to leave them alone in respect of their personal law.... Secondly, it has allowed them to expand their traditional ... educational system in madrasahs[4] attached to mosques. Above all, it has helped them avoid the necessity to come to terms with Hindu civilization in a predominantly Hindu India. This last count is the crux of the matter....

In the past up to the sixteenth century, great temples have been built in our country by rulers to mark the rise of a new dynasty or to mark a triumph.... In the present case, the proposal to build the Rama temple has also helped produce an "army" which can in the first instance achieve the victory the construction can proclaim.

The raising of such an "army" in our democracy, however flawed, involves not only a body of disciplined cadres, which is available in the shape of the RSS,[5] a political organization, which too is available in the Bharatiya Janata Party, but also an aroused citizenry.... The Vishwa Hindu Parishad[6] and its allies have fulfilled this need in a manner which is truly spectacular.

The BJP-VHP-RSS leaders have rendered the country another great service. They have brought Hindu interests, if not the Hindu ethos, into the public domain where they legitimately belong. But it would appear that they have not fully grasped the implications of their action. Their talk of pseudo-secularism gives me that feeling. The fight is not against what they call pseudosecularism; it is against secularism in its proper definition whereby man as animal usurps the place of man as spirit....

---

[4]Madrasahs are advanced schools of learning, or colleges, devoted to Islamic studies.

[5]RSS stands for the Rashtriya Swayamsevak Sangh, a militant Hindu organization founded in 1925 dedicated to the strengthening of Hindu culture.

[6]The Vishwa Hindu Parishad (VHP), or World Hindu Society, was founded in 1964. It is dedicated to demolishing mosques built on Hindu holy sites.

Third World Women Between Tradition and Change

During the twentieth century, political leaders of industrialized nations, revolutionaries such as Lenin and Mao, and nationalists as different as Ataturk and Gandhi all supported the ideal of women's equality. The United Nations Charter of 1945 committed the organization to the same ideal, and the UN Universal Declaration of Human Rights of 1948 reaffirmed the goal of ending all forms of gender-based discrimination. Beginning in the 1960s, powerful feminist movements with agendas ranging from equal educational access to legalized abortion took root in the West and to a lesser degree in Asia, Latin America, and Africa.

Despite this support for gender equality, progress for women worldwide was uneven in the 1970s and 1980s. In developed industrial societies, women undoubtedly made great strides. More women entered professions such as law, medicine, and university teaching; contraception and legal abortions were made available in most nations; and laws forbidding gender-based discrimination were passed. Nonetheless, even in developed countries women still earned less than men for doing the same job, were underrepresented in managerial positions, and played a less significant role in politics than did men. Furthermore, movements for gender equality met strong opposition from individuals and groups who were convinced that women's liberation threatened the family, undermined morality, and would leave women unhappy and unfulfilled.

In less developed parts of the world, attainment of gender faced much greater obstacles. Supporters of feminism were few in number and were mainly middle-class, urban women whose concerns had little appeal or meaning for millions of poor women in urban slums or rural villages. Religious fundamentalists in the Islamic world and elsewhere also sought to keep women in traditional roles. Even in China and India, both of which adopted strong antidiscrimination laws, it proved difficult to modify, let alone eradicate, centuries-old educational patterns, work stereotypes, marriage customs, and attitudes. More so than in almost any other area of modern life, tradition has held its own against those movements and ideologies that sought to liberate Third World women from the burdens of patriarchy and inequality.

Women and Iran's Islamic Revolution

91 ◆ Zand Dokht, *THE REVOLUTION THAT FAILED WOMEN*

Although the Pahlavi rulers of Iran, Reza Shah (1925–1941) and Mohammad Reza Shah (1941–1979), gave women political rights, allowed them to abandon the veil for Western-style dress, and encouraged female literacy and higher

Source: From Miranda Davies, *Third World, Second Sex.* Copyright © 1983. Reprinted by permission of Zed Books Ltd.

education, millions of Iranian women shared in the growing disgust with their government's autocracy, corruption, and secularism in the 1970s. Women played an important role in the massive demonstrations that preceded Mohammad Reza Shah's downfall in 1979 and led to his replacement by an Islamist government led by Ayatollah Ruhollah Khomeini (1902–1989). True to its Islamic principles, Khomeini's government revoked Pahlavi legislation on women and the family and reinstated traditional Islamic practices.

Iranian women who had taken advantage of educational opportunities and had benefited professionally during the Pahlavi years opposed the Islamic republic's effort to turn back the clock. In 1979, representatives from various women's organizations founded the Women's Solidarity Committee, an organization dedicated to the protection of women's rights in Iran. Although banned in Iran itself, Iranian women living in England maintained a branch of the organization in London. Known as the Iranian Woman's Solidarity Group, in the 1980s it published pamphlets and newsletters on issues pertaining to women in Iran. The following selection, written by Solidarity Committee member Zand Dokht, appeared in one of its publications in 1981.

QUESTIONS FOR ANALYSIS

1. In what specific ways did the Islamic Revolution in Iran affect women?
2. According to the author, how do Iran's new leaders envision woman's role in society?
3. How does the author explain the fact that so many Iranian women supported the revolution that toppled the shah?
4. Why, in the author's view, did the shahs' reforms fail to satisfy large numbers of Iranian women?

When Khomeini created his Islamic Republic in 1979, he relied on the institution of the family, on support from the women, the merchants, and the private system of landownership. The new Islamic constitution declared women's primary position as mothers. The black veil, symbol of the position of women under Islam, was made compulsory. Guards were posted outside government offices to enforce it, and women were sacked from their jobs without compensation for refusing to wear the veil. The chairman of the Employment Office, in an interview with the government's women's magazine said, "We can account for 100,000 women government employees being sacked as they resisted the order

of the revolutionary government when it was demanded of them to put the veil on."

Schools were segregated, which meant that women were barred from some technical schools, even some religious schools, and young girls' education in the villages was halted. Lowering the marriage age for girls to 13, reinstating polygamy and *Sighen* [temporary wives] . . . meant that women did not need education and jobs, they only needed to find husbands.

The Ayatollahs[1] in their numerous public prayers, which grew to be the only possible national activity, continuously gave sermons on the advantages of marriage, family, and children being brought up on their mother's lap. They

---

[1]*Ayatollah* is a title of respect for a high Shiite Muslim religious leader.

preached that society would be pure, trouble free, criminal-less (look at the youth problem in the West) if everybody married young, and if men married as many times as possible (to save the unprotected women who might otherwise become prostitutes). The government created a marriage bank at a time when half the working population was unemployed, whereby men were given huge sums—around £3,500—to get married. Another *masterpiece* of the revolutionary Islamic government was to create a system of arranged marriages in prisons, between men and women prisoners, to "protect" women after they leave prison.

Because abortion and contraception are now unobtainable, marriage means frequent pregnancy. If you are 13 when you get married, it is likely that you will have six children by the time you are 20. This, in a country where half the total population is already under 16, is a tragedy for future generations.

Religious morality demands that all pleasures and entertainments be banned. Wine, music, dancing, chess, women's parts in theater, cinema and television—you name it, Khomeini banned it. He even segregated the mountains and the seas for male and female climbers and swimmers.

But compulsory morality, compulsory marriage, and the compulsory wearing of the veil did not create the Holy Society that Khomeini was after; but public lashings, stonings, chopping of hands and daily group executions sank Iran into the age of Barbarism.

Perhaps nowhere else in the world have women been murdered for walking in the street open-faced. The question of the veil is the most important issue of women's liberation in Muslim countries. The veil, a long engulfing black robe, is the extension of the four walls of the home, where women belong. The veil is the historical symbol of woman's oppression, seclusion, denial of her social participation and equal rights with men. It is a cover which defaces and objectifies women. To wear or not to wear the veil, for Muslim women is "the right to choose." ...

Why do women, workers and unemployed, support this regime which has done everything in its power to attack their rights and interests?

The power of Islam in our culture and tradition has been seriously underestimated ... and it was through this ideology that Khomeini directed his revolutionary government. The clergy dealt with everyday problems and spoke out on human relationships, sexuality, security and protection of the family and the spiritual needs of human beings. It was easy for people to identify with these issues and support the clergy, although nobody knew what they were later to do. When Khomeini asked for sacrifices—"we haven't made the Revolution in order to eat chicken or dress better"—women (so great in the art of sacrifice) and workers accepted these anti-materialist ideas....

Women's attraction to Khomeini's ideas was not based simply on his Islamic politics, but also on the way he criticized the treatment of women—as secretaries and media sex objects—under the Shah's regime. Women were genuinely unsatisfied and looking for change. Some educated Iranian women went back to Iran from America and Europe to aid the clergy with the same messages, and became the government's spokeswomen. They put on the veil willingly, defended Islamic virtues and spiritual values while drawing from their own experiences in the West. They said it was cold and lonely, Western women were only in pursuit of careers and self-sufficiency, and that their polygamous sexual relationships had not brought them liberation, but confusion and exploitation. These women joined ranks with an already growing force of Muslim women, to retrieve the tradition of true/happy Muslim women—in defense of patriarchy.

The mosque is not just a place of prayer, it is also a social club for women. It provides a warm, safe room for women to meet, chat or listen to a sermon, and there are traditional women-only parties and picnics in gardens or holy places. Take away these traditional and religious customs from women which the Shah—with his capitalist and imperialist reforms, irrelevant to women's needs—tried to do and a huge vacuum is left. Khomeini stepped in to fill that vacuum. The reason why Khomeini won was that the Shah's social-economic program for women was dictatorial, bureaucratic, inadequate (especially in terms of health education) and therefore irrelevant to women's needs. What little the Shah's reform brought to women was just a token gesture. Women dissatisfied with the Shah's reform felt that they had benefited little from him and would not miss it if it was taken away.

An African Perspective on Female Circumcision

❖

92 ◆ Association of African Women for Research and Development, *A STATEMENT ON GENITAL MUTILATION*

Female genital mutilation, also known as genital cutting or female circumcision, refers to any ritual procedure that involves the partial or complete removal of the external female genitals. The operation, which in different societies may take place from shortly after birth to the onset of puberty, is usually performed by midwives or village women without benefit of anesthesia or antibiotics. It is most widely practiced in sub-Saharan Africa, especially in the Sudan region, but it also takes place in many other parts of the world, including New Guinea, Malaysia, Brazil, Mexico, Peru, India, Egypt, and the Arabian Peninsula. Presumably instituted to encourage chastity by dulling a woman's sexual desire, the practice has come under harsh criticism both from within the societies in which it exists and from outsiders, especially from the West. Efforts to suppress the practice have had little effect, however, among peoples who consider the custom part of their ethnic and religious heritage and a rite of passage into adulthood.

Denunciations of genital mutilation by Westerners and Western-inspired campaigns to end the practice have frequently backfired, especially in Africa, where the custom is most deeply rooted. The following statement reveals that even Africans who oppose the practice resent Western interference. The Association of African Women for Research and Development (AAWORD), which was founded in 1977 in Dakar, Senegal, issued the statement.

QUESTIONS FOR ANALYSIS

1. What is the basis of the authors' assertion that critics of female circumcision are guilty of "latent racism"?
2. How have Western criticisms of female circumcision hindered the efforts of African critics to limit the practice?
3. In the view of the authors, what would be an appropriate Western approach to the issue of female circumcision?
4. How might an ardent Western critic of African female circumcision counter the arguments contained in the AAWORD statement?

Source: From Miranda Davies, *Third World, Second Sex.* Copyright © 1983. Reprinted by permission of Zed Books Ltd.

In the past few years, Western public opinion has been shocked to find out that in the middle of the 20th century thousands of women and children have been "savagely mutilated" because of "barbarous customs from another age." The good conscience of Western society has once again been shaken. Something must be done to help these people, to show public disapproval of such acts.

There have been press conferences, documentary files, headlines in the newspapers, information days, open letters, action groups—all this to mobilize public opinion and put pressure on governments of the countries where genital mutilation is still practiced....

... In trying to reach their own public, the new crusaders have fallen back on sensationalism, and have become insensitive to the dignity of the very women they want to "save." They are totally unconscious of the latent racism which such a campaign evokes in countries where ethnocentric prejudice is so deep-rooted. And in their conviction that this is a "just cause," they have forgotten that these women from a different race and different culture are also *human beings*, and that solidarity can only exist alongside self-affirmation and mutual respect.

This campaign has aroused three kinds of reaction in Africa:

1. the highly conservative, which stresses the right of cultural difference and the defence of traditional values and practices whose supposed aim is to protect and elevate women; this view denies Westerners the right to interfere in problems related to culture;
2. which, while condemning genital mutilation for health reasons, considers it premature to open the issue to public debate;
3. which concentrates on the aggressive nature of the campaign and considers that the fanaticism of the new crusaders only serves to draw attention away from the fundamental problems of the economic exploitation and oppression of developing

countries, which contribute to the continuation of such practices.

Although all these reactions rightly criticize the campaign against genital mutilation as imperialist and paternalist, they remain passive and defensive. As is the case with many other issues, we refuse here to confront our cultural heritage and to criticize it constructively. We seem to prefer to draw a veil of modesty over certain traditional practices, whatever the consequences may be. However, it is time that Africans realized they must take a position on all problems which concern their society, and to take steps to end any practice which debases human beings.

AAWORD, whose aim is to carry out research which leads to the liberation of African people and women in particular, *firmly condemns* genital mutilation and all other practices—traditional or modern—which oppress women and justify exploiting them economically or socially, as a serious violation of the fundamental rights of women....

However, as far as AAWORD is concerned, the fight against genital mutilation, although necessary, should not take on such proportions that the wood cannot be seen for the trees. Young girls and women who are mutilated in Africa are usually among those who cannot even satisfy their basic needs and who have to struggle daily for survival. This is due to the exploitation of developing countries, manifested especially through the impoverishment of the poorest social classes. In the context of the present world economic crisis, tradition, with all of its constraints, becomes more than ever a form of security for the peoples of the Third World, and especially for the "wretched of the earth." For these people, the modern world, which is primarily Western and bourgeois, can only represent aggression at all levels—political, economic, social and cultural. It is unable to propose viable alternatives for them.

Moreover, to fight against genital mutilation without placing it in the context of ignorance, obscurantism, exploitation, poverty, etc., without questioning the structures and social relations which perpetuate this situation, is like "refusing to see the sun in the middle of the day." This, however, is precisely the approach taken by many Westerners, and is highly suspect, especially since Westerners necessarily profit from the exploitation of the peoples and women of Africa, whether directly or indirectly.

Feminists from developed countries—at least those who are sincerely concerned about this situation rather than those who use it only for their personal prestige—should understand this other aspect of the problem. They must accept that it is a problem for *African women*, and that no change is pos-

sible without the conscious participation of African women. They must avoid ill-timed interference, maternalism, ethnocentrism and misuse of power. These are attitudes which can only widen the gap between the Western feminist movement and that of the Third World. . . .

On the question of such traditional practices as genital mutilation, African women must no longer equivocate or react only to Western interference. They must speak out in favour of the total eradication of all these practices, and they must lead information and education campaigns to this end within their own countries and on a continental level.

The Impact of the Indian Dowry System

◈

93 ◆ Editorial on Dowry from Manushi

Although some improvement in the status of Indian women took place under British rule, major steps toward gender equality were taken only after Indian independence in 1947. Women received the right to vote, hold political office, own property, and divorce their husbands; in addition, the government outlawed child marriage and polygamy and eased restrictions on intercaste marriages. In 1961, the government also outlawed dowries, the gifts of property a new bride's family was expected to make to the husband or the husband's family. The intent of the legislation was to lessen the financial burdens of families with daughters and encourage men from higher castes to marry women from lower castes.

As the following editorial shows, however, the practice of dowries continued, often with tragic results for young married women. This anonymous editorial was originally published in 1979 in *Manushi*, an Indian magazine for women.

QUESTIONS FOR ANALYSIS

1. According to the author of this editorial, is the giving and taking of dowries the result of recent developments or of long-standing Indian traditions?
2. According to the author, why have efforts to end the practice of dowries failed?
3. What does the author see as the solution to the problem?
4. According to the author, to what degree do dowry murders fit into a general pattern of mistreatment of women in Indian society?

Source: From Madhu Kishwar and Ruth Vanitar, *In Search of Answers: Indian Voices from Manushi.* Copyright © 1984. Reprinted by permission of Zed Books Ltd.

Most people are not even aware that the giving and taking of dowry is a legal offense. Since the Prohibition of Dowry Act was passed in 1961, the custom has flowered and flourished, invading castes and communities among whom it was hitherto unknown—sprouting new forms and varieties. It is percolating downwards and becoming so widespread even among the working classes that it is no longer possible to consider it a problem of the middle class alone.

With the entire bourgeois mass media oriented towards viciously promoting the religion of mindless consumerism, demands for dowry are becoming more and more "modernized." Marriages are made and broken for such items as cars, scooters, TVs, refrigerators and washing machines, wedding receptions in five-star hotels or an air ticket plus the promise of a job for the son-in-law in a foreign country.

In India, we have a glorious heritage of systematic violence on women in the family itself, sati[1] and female infanticide being the two better-known forms. Today, we do not kill girl-babies at birth. We let them die through systematic neglect—the mortality rate among female children is 30–60% higher than among male children. Today, we do not wait till a woman is widowed before we burn her to death. We burn her in the lifetime of her husband so that he can get a new bride with a fatter dowry.

"Woman burnt to death. A case of suicide has been registered. The police are enquiring into the matter." For years, such three-line news items have appeared almost every day in the newspapers and gone unnoticed. It is only lately that dowry deaths are being given detailed coverage. It is not by accident that fuller reporting of such cases has coincided with a spurt of protest demonstrations.

We, as women, have too long been silent spectators, often willing participants in the degrading drama of matrimony—when girls are advertised, displayed, bargained over, and disposed of with the pious injunction: "Daughter, we are sending you to your husband's home.

You are not to leave it till your corpse emerges from its doors." It is significant that in all the cases of dowry murders recently reported, the girls had on previous occasions left the in-laws' houses where they were being tortured and felt insecure. Their parents had insisted on their going back and "adjusting there."

Death may be slow in coming—a long process of killing the girl's spirit by harassment, taunts, torture. It may be only too quick—fiery and sudden. Dousing the woman with kerosene and setting her on fire seems to have become the most popular way of murdering a daughter-in-law because with police connivance it is the easiest to make out as a case of suicide or accident.

And for every one reported murder, hundreds go unreported, especially in rural areas where it is almost impossible to get redress unless one is rich and influential.…

Why is it that gifts have to be given with the daughter? Hindu scriptures proclaim that the girl herself is the most precious of gifts "presented" by her father to her husband. Thus the money transaction between families is bound up with the marriage transaction whereby the girl becomes a piece of transferrable property. So little is a woman worth that a man has literally to be paid to take her off her father's hands.

The dramatic increase in dowry-giving in the post-independence period reflects the declining value of women in our society. Their only worth is as reproducers who provide "legitimate" heirs for their husbands' property.

Most people opposing dowry feel that the problem can be solved by giving girls an equal share in their fathers' property. This was one of the reasons why daughters were given near-equal rights in the Hindu Succession Act, 1956. And yet the law has been reduced to a farce because in most cases, daughters are pressured to, or even willingly sign away their rights in favor of their brothers. In any case, it is the woman's husband who usually controls

---

[1]Sati is the custom in which a Hindu widow is willingly cremated on the funeral pyre of her dead husband as a sign of devotion to him.

any property she inherits. So the property transaction remains between men, women acting only as vehicles for this transaction.

This will continue to be so as long as the majority of women remain economically dependent on men and as long as this dependence is reinforced by our social values and institutions so that even those women who earn seldom have the right to control their own income....

... We appeal, therefore, to all the women's organizations to undertake a broad-based united action on this issue and launch an intensive, concerted campaign instead of the isolated, sporadic protests which have so far been organized, and which can have only a short-term, limited impact.

Perhaps even more urgent is the need to begin the movement from our own homes. Are we sure that none of us who participated so vociferously in these demonstrations will take dowry from our parents or give it to our daughters in however veiled a form? That we will rather say "No" to marriage than live a life of humiliations and compromises? Do we have the courage to boycott marriages where dowry is given? Even the marriage of a brother or sister or of a dear friend? Will we socially ostracize such people, no matter how close they are to us? All the protest demonstrations will be only so much hot air unless we are prepared to create pressures against dowry beginning from our own homes.

Communism's Retreat

For forty years after the end of World War II the dualisms of the Cold War—communism versus capitalism, the United States versus the Soviet Union, NATO versus the Warsaw Pact—gave clarity, direction, and meaning to international politics. Then, in the late 1980s, the Cold War ended and communism ceased to be a significant force in world affairs. Although communist parties continued to compete for votes in democracies such as India, Australia, Brazil, and South Africa, only five states—China, Cuba, Laos, Vietnam, and North Korea—at present are officially communist. Of these, all except North Korea have loosened strict government economic controls and have introduced elements of the market economy.

Although communism collapsed in Eastern Europe and the Soviet Union in a brief period between 1989 and 1991, it had been losing ground for more than a decade. In the 1960s Hungary developed a mixed socialist-capitalist economy (its "goulash economy") that became the strongest in the region. The Czechoslovakian reform movement of 1968 and the pro-reform demonstrations and strikes in Poland in 1980-1981 were both signs of discontent in the Soviet Union's East European satellites. In Czechoslovakia, the reform movement was crushed by Soviet troops, and in Poland demonstrations ended after the Polish government declared martial law and outlawed Solidarity, the independent organization of labor unions that inspired the protests. The use or threat of force, however, could not hide the fact that communism was losing its appeal, especially among the young.

Chinese communism also underwent significant changes in the late 1970s and 1980s. After Mao Zedong's death in 1976, his successor, the pragmatic Deng Xiaoping, deemphasized ideology and egalitarianism in favor of rapid economic development. He approved the opening of small private businesses, fostered a market economy in agriculture, opened China to foreign investment, supported scientific and technological education, and encouraged Chinese exports of manufactured goods. The results were spectacular, with annual growth rates of 12 percent achieved by the early 1990s. China remained authoritarian and officially communist, but with its commitment to entrepreneurialism and its unique form of state capitalism, it was worlds apart from the isolated, ideology-driven China of previous decades.

Within the Soviet Union, the era of reform began in 1985, when General Secretary Mikhail Gorbachev introduced policies of glasnost and perestroika to rejuvenate the Soviet communist system. But his efforts to save communism by democratization and economic liberalization released forces that he could not control, and by the end of 1991, communist rule had disappeared throughout Eastern Europe, the Soviet Union had broken apart, and the Cold War was over. No one doubted that a new era of world politics had dawned.

China's New Course

94 ◆ Deng Xiaoping, *SPEECH TO OFFICERS AT THE CORPS LEVEL AND ABOVE FROM THE MARTIAL LAW ENFORCEMENT TROOPS IN BEIJING, JUNE 6, 1989*

After emerging as a unified empire in the third century B.C.E., China was the world's most successful state in terms of size, wealth, technological sophistication, and the continuity of its political institutions. This was easy to forget in the nineteenth and twentieth centuries, when China became a pawn of the Western powers and a victim of political breakdown, military defeat, and economic decline. Beginning in the late 1970s, however, China's leaders set a new course for their country, which has turned China into a major world power with an economy second in size only to that of the United States.

The man who launched China on its new path was Deng Xiaoping (1904–1997). Born into the family of a well-off landowner in 1904, Deng studied in China and then in post–World War I France, where he supported himself as a kitchen helper and laborer. He also embraced Marxism, which he studied and observed in Moscow in 1925–1926. On his return to China he joined the Communist Party and became one of Mao's loyal followers in the long struggle against the Guomindang and the Japanese.

After the communists took control of China in 1949 he became a politburo member with responsibilities for overseeing economic development in southwest China. He supported the Stalinist model for China's economic development through investment in heavy industry, agricultural collectivization, and central planning. This was scrapped in 1958, when Mao instituted the Great Leap

Source: From *Chinese Law and Government*, vol. 25, no. 1 (Spring 1992): 31–37. English Translation copyright © 1992 by M.E. Sharpe, Inc. Reprinted with permission of M.E. Sharpe, Inc.

Forward. In the wake of its failure, Deng and other moderates dismantled the communes and reintroduced centralized planning.

This made Deng a prime candidate for vilification during the Cultural Revolution. Having fallen from power, he was paraded through the streets in a dunce cap and put to work in a mess hall and a tractor repair shop. As the Cultural Revolution faded, Deng was reinstated as a party official, and after Mao's death in 1976 he led the moderates in their struggle with the radicals led by Mao's widow, Jiang Qing. Deng's faction won, and in December 1978, at a series of meetings known as the Third Plenum of the Eleventh Central Committee of the Chinese Communist Party, party leaders officially abandoned Mao's emphasis on ideology and class struggle in favor of a moderate, pragmatic policy designed to achieve the "four modernizations" in science and technology, agriculture, industry, and the military.

To encourage economic growth, the government fostered free markets, competition, and private incentives. Rural families were allowed to increase the amount of land they could farm as private plots and sell what they grew on the open market. Industrial mangers were given more control over the operations of businesses and granted the authority to hire and fire workers, award bonuses, and keep more of their business's profits for themselves. In some two dozen Special Economic Zones, foreign investment in new factories was encouraged by offering Western businesses tax incentives, promises of cheap labor, and improved transportation networks. A crash program was undertaken to upgrade the country's educational system through the founding of highly competitive research universities and technological colleges. The people were told, "Do not fear prosperity."

While encouraging economic reform, China continued to be a one-party state in which all major decisions were made by an inner circle of twenty-five to thirty officials in Beijing who were led by the pre-eminent leader Deng Xiaoping. Elections at the local, provincial and national level chose hand-picked party members to be delegates to "peoples' congresses," which routinely and unanimously approved policies decided upon by their leaders. There was no effective mechanism for transferring power and no possibility of meaningful debate on public issues. Individuals who called for a "fifth modernization"—freedom and democracy—were silenced. When in 1986, many thousands of university students and others demonstrated in Hefei and elsewhere for greater democracy, the government arrested the movement's leaders and imposed stricter controls on the press.

Three years later, in 1989, the government faced a graver threat. Against a backdrop of inflation, housing shortages, continuing corruption, cutbacks in university funding, and general uncertainty about the country's future, prodemocracy demonstrations by university students in Beijing began in mid- April, 1989, and soon spread to other cities. By mid-May, Beijing's Tiananmen Square was a tent city with a million inhabitants, including 3000 hunger strikers. With the world looking on, discussions between government officials and student leaders broke down, and early efforts to clear the square by force proved ineffective. By the end of May, government hardliners, led by Deng Xiaoping, decided to crush the prodemocracy movement. On June 3, veteran units of the army entered Beijing, and after breaking through barricades erected throughout city, cleared the square of the few remaining protestors by the morning of June 4. At least several hundred, perhaps as many as 2500, civilians were killed along with several dozen soldiers and police.

On June 9, Deng Xiaoping addressed a gathering of army officers in a speech that became required reading for officials throughout the land and became something of an official interpretation of 1989 prodemocracy movement. There would be no going back, and no major changes. China, he said, must continue on its path of economic development, but there would be no "fifth modernization."

QUESTIONS FOR ANALYSIS

1. How does Deng describe the goals and general characteristics of the prodemocracy movement?
2. How does Deng justify calling the soldiers of the People's Liberation Army the true martyrs of the prodemocracy demonstrations?
3. What does Deng mean when he says that the recent demonstrations were "destined to come?" Why might he have made such an assertion?
4. How, according to Deng, might the recent "incident" help the government correct its mistakes?
5. What specifically does Deng recommend to overcome these "mistakes?"
6. What does Deng see as China's short and long-term future?

We have a group of veteran comrades who are still alive, including those in the army, and we also have groups of backbone cadres[1] who had joined the revolution in various periods. Therefore, it was relatively easy for us to control the state of affairs when the disturbance broke out recently. What is difficult for us to handle in this case is that we have never before faced such a situation. A small number of evildoers were among the vast numbers of young students and the masses of onlookers. For a while the alignment was unclear. All those made it difficult for us to put into effect many measures we should have taken. ... In fact, the opponents are not only the masses who cannot distinguish right from wrong but also a group of reactionaries and a large segment of the dregs of society. They are attempting to subvert our state and overthrow the Communist party, which is the essence of

the issue. If we do not understand this fundamental problem, it means we are not clear about the nature of the issue. After making conscientious efforts in our work, I believe we will be able to win the support from the overwhelming majority in the party for determining the nature and handling of the issue.

It all became clear once the incident broke out. They have two key slogans: one is to overthrow the Communist Party, the other is to topple the socialist system. Their aim is to establish a bourgeois republic totally dependent on the West. We certainly accept the people's demand of opposing corruption. We will even have to accept as fine words the so-called anticorruption slogan by some people with ulterior motives. Of course, this slogan serves merely as a foil, and its crux is to overthrow the Communist Party and topple the socialist system.

---

[1]The term cadre refers to a public official holding a responsible or managerial position, usually full time, in party and government.

In putting down the rebellion, many of our comrades were injured or even killed, and their weapons were stolen. Why did all this happen? It was also because the evildoers were mixed among the good ones, which made it hard for us to put into effect the measures we should have taken resolutely. It was a severe political test for our army to handle this incident. Practice shows that our People's Liberation Army has passed the test. Using the tanks to run over [the demonstrators] would have brought about confusion in the entire country regarding right and wrong. Therefore, I must thank the PLA officers and men for their attitude in handling the incident of rebellion. ...

This incident has impelled us to consider the future, as well as the past, with a sober mind. This incident, bad as it was, may enable us to carry forward our reform and our opening to the outside world more steadily, and to correct our mistakes and better carry forward our strong points. I cannot elaborate on this issue today but only raise a few questions for study.

The first question is whether the lines, guiding principles, and policies, including the "trilogy"[2] of our development strategy, formulated at the Third Plenary Session of the Eleventh Central Committee of the Chinese Communist Party are correct. Are questions raised about the correctness of our lines, guiding principles, and policies because of this turmoil? Is our objective a "leftist"[3] one? Will we continue to regard it as our objective of struggle in the future? We must respond to these major questions with clear-cut and positive answers. We have already accomplished our first objective of doubling the national product; it will take twelve years to accomplish our further objective of doubling the national product for a second time;

in the following fifty years, it will only require a growth rate of little more than 2 percent per annum for us to attain the level of an average developed nation. ... With regard to answering the first question, therefore, we ought to say that, at least up to now, the strategic objective we set is not unsuccessful. It is an extraordinary thing for a country with a population of 1.5 billion to achieve in sixty-one years the level of an average developed nation. We are able to realize this objective. One cannot conclude that our strategic goal is wrong because of this incident that is taking place. The second question is whether "one center, two basic points," set by the Thirteenth National Party Congress, is correct. Or whether the two basic points, namely, adhering to the Four Cardinal Principles[4] and the policies of reforms and opening up,[5] are wrong. Lately, we have been constantly thinking over this issue. We are not wrong. Adherence to the Four Cardinal Principles itself is not wrong. If anything is wrong, it is that we have not been consistent enough in adhering to the Four Cardinal Principles, and have failed to make it a fundamental thinking to educate the people, the students, cadres as a whole, and Communist Party members. The nature of the recent incident is bourgeois liberalization and opposing the four principles. ... The mistake does not lie in adherence to the four principles itself but in the fact that we did not adhere to them all along, and in the poor performance of our educational, ideological, and political work. On New Year's Day of 1980, I made a speech to the Political Consultative Conference in which I talked about the "four guarantees,"[6] including "the pioneering spirit of hard work." Hard work is our tradition. We will attach importance to the education of hard work and plain living for

---

[2]The "trilogy" consisted of reform, stability, and development.

[3]In the context of the 1980s, "leftists" were those who recommended pushing forward with economic reform, while "rightists" recommended a more cautious approach.

[4]These were: the socialist path; the people's democratic dictatorship; the leadership of the Communist Party; and Marxist-Leninist-Mao Zedong thought.

[5]"Opening up" China's economy to the outside world.

[6]The "four guarantees" of the revised constitution of 1978 were "to speak out freely, air views fully, hold great debates, and write big-character posters." In the speech Deng is referring to, he announced that the four guarantees were abolished following a brief period in 1978 and 1979 when intellectuals and others publicly criticized the regime.

another sixty to seventy years. The more developed our country is, the more emphasis will be placed on building the nation through arduous efforts. To advocate the spirit of building the nation through arduous efforts will also help over-come corruption. When life improved after a time, high-level consumption was promoted, and the phenomenon of waste of all aspects was spreading. In addition, the weakness in ideological and political work, the imperfection of the legal system, and the phenomena of lawbreaking, violation of the principles, and corruption all surfaced. I mentioned to foreigners that the biggest mistake over the ten years was made in education; by that I meant the education of the people. We did little to educate the people in terms of building the nation through hard work and about the kind of state China is and will be. That is our big miscalculation.

Is the basic point of reform and opening up wrong? No, it is not. How could we be where we are today if there had been no reform and opening up? The people's living standards have been raised considerably over the past ten years, and we can say that we are now a step further. Despite inflation and other problems, the achievements of our ten years of reform and opening up should be amply evaluated. Of course, along with the reforms and opening up many bad influences of the West inevitably seeped into our country, and this we have never underestimated. In the beginning of the 1980s, when the Special Economic Zones were first established, I talked with the comrades from Guangdong Province on stressing two things simultaneously. On the one hand, I told them to attach importance to reforms and opening up; on the other hand, I told them to emphasize sternly cracking down on economic crimes and also to emphasize ideological and political work. That is the theory of two basic points. Looking back, however, we find there have been obvious shortcomings. We have been strong

on the one hand and weak on the other. . . . Discussion on this point may benefit our future principles and policy making. Moreover, we will continue to keep unchanged the policy of adhering to combining a planned economy with market regulation. . . . We should be more flexible in our work. In the future we will still combine planned economy with market regulation. What is important is that we never build China into a closed nation. It is extremely unfavorable to us to practice a closed-door policy as we would not even have access to information. Now people are talking about the importance of information, and it is important indeed. Without access to information, it is as if those in charge of administration have a stuffed nose, deaf ears, and blind eyes. We will never go back to the old times when the economy was extremely handicapped and tightly controlled. . . . This has been a summary of our work over the past ten years. Some of our fundamental concepts, from our developmental strategies to the guiding principles, including reforms and opening to the outside world, are correct. If anything has been carried out insufficiently, it is in the area of reforms and opening up. The difficulties we have encountered in our reforms are far more than those in opening up. One thing we are sure of is that, in the aspect of reforming the political system, we must adhere to the practice of the system of a congress of people's representatives instead of the system of the American-style tripartite balance of power.[7] In fact, not all the Western nations practice the system of tripartite balance of power. The Americans accused us of suppressing the students, while they themselves sent out police and troops to arrest people and allowed them to shed blood just the same in handling the student upheavals and unrest in their own country. They were really suppressing the students and the people, while we were only cracking down on counterrevolutionary

---

[7]The separation of powers between the legislative, executive, and judicial branches of government.

rebellion. What right do they have to criticize us! Yet, in the future, in handling this type of issue, we must take care to prevent a trend from spreading when it first appears.

What should we do in the future? I believe we should maintain unchanged the basic lines, guiding principles, and policies we formulated before. We should carry our work firmly forward. We need to increase investment in the basic industries for another ten to twenty years, including the industries of raw and processed materials, transportation, and energy. We will do so even at the cost of going into debt. This is also a policy of opening up. We need to be more audacious in these areas, and nothing can

go badly wrong with that. If we generate more electricity, and build more railroads, highways, and ships for transportation, we can do a great many things. Now we have [a yearly production of] nearly 60 million tons of steel and are halfway to our future need of 120 million tons estimated by the foreigners. If we remodel our current plants and increase production by 20 million tons, we will be able to cut down the import of steel. Borrowing foreign money to be used in those areas is also reform and opening up. The question now does not lie in whether reforms and opening up are right and whether we should carry them forward, it lies in how, where, and in which aspects to carry them forward.

A Plan to Save Communism in the Soviet Union

◆

95 ◆ Mikhail Gorbachev, *PERESTROIKA*

The Soviet Union in the 1970s and 1980s was still one of the world's two superpowers. It had an enormous army, what was perceived as an impressive industrial establishment, a solid record of technological achievement, and a seemingly unshakable authoritarian government. No one saw any reason why it would not continue to be the United States' great rival in international affairs. In reality, industrial and agricultural production was stagnating, the people's morale was plummeting, and a fossilized bureaucracy was mired in policies and theories that no longer worked. Against this background, Mikhail Gorbachev became general secretary of the Communist Party in March 1985 and began the task of reviving Soviet communism by introducing reforms based on *glasnost*, or openness, and *perestroika*, or restructuring. Gorbachev, who was fifty-four years old when he took power, was born into a peasant family and had training in law and agricultural economics. He joined the Communist Party in the mid-1950s and steadily advanced in the party hierarchy. In 1979, he became a member of the Politburo, the ultimate power in the Soviet state, and in 1985 was elevated to the position of general secretary of the Communist Party. After serving as the Soviet leader for two years, he published a book, *Perestroika*, from which the following excerpt is taken. In it, Gorbachev outlines his goals for communism in the Soviet Union. He fell from power in 1991, after he had set in motion a series of changes that failed to save the Soviet Union but which transformed the world of the late twentieth century.

Source: Excerpts from pp. 18, 19, 21–5, 30–6 from *Perestroika* by Mikhail Gorbachev. Copyright © 1987 by Mikhail Gorbachev. Reprinted by permission of HarperCollins Publishers.

QUESTIONS FOR ANALYSIS

1. What conditions in the Soviet Union convinced Gorbachev that Soviet society and government were in need of reform?
2. In Gorbachev's analysis, what caused Soviet society to lose its momentum?
3. How, in Gorbachev's view, will the individual in Soviet society be affected by his reforms?
4. To what extent is Gorbachev's idea of perestroika democratic?
5. What similarities and differences do you see between Gorbachev's statements about perestroika and Deng Xiaoping's plans for China?
6. Compare and contrast Gorbachev's views of Soviet society with those of Soviet and Eastern European dissidents from the 1960s and early 1970s (see Chapter 10).

Over the past seven decades—a short span in the history of human civilization—our country has traveled a path equal to centuries. One of the mightiest powers in the world rose up to replace the backward semi-colonial and semi-feudal Russian Empire....

At some stage—this became particularly clear in the latter half of the seventies—something happened that was at first sight inexplicable. The country began to lose momentum. Economic failures became more frequent.... Elements of what we call stagnation and other phenomena alien to socialism began to appear in the life of society. A kind of "braking mechanism" affecting social and economic development formed. And all this happened at a time when scientific and technological revolution opened up new prospects for economic and social progress....

... In the last fifteen years the national income growth rates had declined by more than a half and by the beginning of the eighties had fallen to a level close to economic stagnation. A country that was once quickly closing on the world's advanced nations began to lose one position after another....

It became typical of many of our economic executives to think not of how to build up the national assets, but of how to put more material, labor, and working time into an item to sell it at a higher price. Consequently, for all our "gross output," there was a shortage of goods. We spent, in fact we are still spending, far more on raw materials, energy, and other resources per unit of output than other developed nations. Our country's wealth in terms of natural and manpower resources has spoilt, one may even say corrupted, us....

The presentation of a "problem-free" reality backfired: a breach had formed between word and deed, which bred public passivity and disbelief in the slogans being proclaimed. It was only natural that this situation resulted in a credibility gap: everything that was proclaimed from the rostrums and printed in newspapers and textbooks was put in question. Decay began in public morals; the great feeling of solidarity with each other that was forged during the heroic times of the Revolution, the first five-year plans, the Great Patriotic War,[1] and postwar rehabilitation was weakening; alcoholism, drug addiction, and crime were growing; and the penetration of the stereotypes of mass culture alien to us, which bred vulgarity and low tastes and brought about ideological barrenness, increased.

---

[1]The name for World War II in the Soviet Union.

Political flirtation and mass distribution of awards, titles, and bonuses often replaced genuine concern for the people, for their living and working conditions, for a favorable social atmosphere. An atmosphere emerged of "everything goes," and fewer and fewer demands were made on discipline and responsibility. Attempts were made to cover it all up with pompous campaigns and undertakings and celebrations.... The world of day-to-day realities and the world of feigned prosperity were diverging more and more....

By saying all this I want to make the reader understand that the energy for revolutionary change has been accumulating amid our people and in the Party for some time. And the ideas of perestroika have been prompted not just by pragmatic interests and considerations but also by our troubled conscience, by the indomitable commitment to ideals which we inherited from the Revolution and as a result of a theoretical quest which gave us a better knowledge of society and reinforced our determination to go ahead....

... Here I think it is appropriate to draw your attention to one specific feature of socialism. I have in mind the high degree of social protection in our society. On the one hand, it is, doubtless, a benefit and a major achievement of ours. On the other, it makes some people spongers.

There is virtually no unemployment. The state has assumed concern for ensuring employment. Even a person dismissed for laziness or a breach of labor discipline must be given another job. Also, wage-leveling has become a regular feature of our everyday life: even if a person is a bad worker, he gets enough to live fairly comfortably. The children of an outright parasite will not be left to the mercy of fate. We have enormous sums of money concentrated in the social funds from which people receive financial assistance. The same funds provide subsidies for the upkeep of kindergartens, orphanages,

Young Pioneer[2] houses, and other institutions related to children's creativity and sport. Health care is free, and so is education. People are protected from the vicissitudes of life, and we are proud of this.

But we also see that dishonest people try to exploit these advantages of socialism; they know only their rights, but they do not want to know their duties: they work poorly, shirk, and drink hard.... They give little to society, but nevertheless managed to get from it all that is possible and what even seems impossible; they have lived on unearned incomes.

The policy of restructuring puts everything in its place. We are fully restoring the principle of socialism. "From each according to his ability, to each according to his work," and we seek to affirm social justice for all, equal rights for all, one law for all, one kind of discipline for all, and high responsibilities for each. Perestroika raises the level of social responsibility and expectation....

It is essential to learn to adjust policy in keeping with the way it is received by the masses, and to ensure feedback, absorbing the ideas, opinions, and advice coming from the people. The masses suggest a lot of useful and interesting things which are not always clearly perceived "from the top." That is why we must prevent at all costs an arrogant attitude to what people are saying. In the final account the most important thing for the success of perestroika is the people's attitude to it.

Thus, not only theory but the reality of the processes under way made us embark on the program for all-around democratic changes in public life which we presented at the January 1987 Plenary Meeting of the CPSU[3] Central Committee.

The Plenary Meeting encouraged extensive efforts to strengthen the democratic basis of Soviet society, to develop self-government and extend glasnost, that is openness, in the entire management network. We see now how stimu-

---

[2]A youth organization sponsored by the Soviet regime.

[3]Communist Party of the Soviet Union.

lating that impulse was for the nation. Democratic changes have been taking place at every work collective, at every state and public organization, and within the Party. More glasnost, genuine control from "below," and greater initiative and enterprise at work are now part and parcel of our life....

Perestroika means overcoming the stagnation process, breaking down the braking mechanism, creating a dependable and effective mechanism for the acceleration of social and economic progress and giving it greater dynamism.

Perestroika means mass initiative. It is the comprehensive development of democracy, socialist self-government, encouraging of initiative and creative endeavor, improved order and discipline, more glasnost, criticism, and self-criticism in all spheres of our society. It is utmost respect for the individual and consideration for personal dignity.

Perestroika is the all-around intensification of the Soviet economy, the revival and development of the principles of democratic centralism in running the national economy, the universal introduction of economic methods, the renunciation of management by injunction and by administrative methods, and the overall encouragement of innovation and socialist enterprise....

Perestroika means priority development of the social sphere aimed at ever better satisfaction of the Soviet people's requirements for good living and working conditions, for good rest and recreation, education, and health care. It means unceasing concern for cultural and spiritual wealth, for the culture of every individual and society as a whole.

Perestroika means the elimination from society of the distortions of socialist ethics, the consistent implementation of the principles of social justice. It means the unity of words and deeds, rights and duties. It is the elevation of honest, highly-qualified labor, the overcoming of leveling tendencies in pay and consumerism....

... The essence of perestroika lies in the fact that it *unites socialism with democracy* and revives the Leninist concept of socialist construction both in theory and in practice. Such is the essence of perestroika, which accounts for its genuine revolutionary spirit and its all-embracing scope.

The goal is worth the effort. And we are sure that our effort will be a worthy contribution to humanity's social progress.

CHAPTER 13

The World Since 1990

The world since 1990 has had its share of disappointing, at times appalling, events and developments. Democracy was slow to take root in Russia and the new states formed after the collapse of the Soviet Union; it struggled to survive in Africa and made no discernible progress in China. Despite overall growth in the world economy, poverty remained the lot of millions of human beings, especially in Sub-Saharan Africa, where 50.3 percent of the population in 2010 lived on less than $1.25 a day. Long-standing conflicts between India and Pakistan and between Israel and the Palestinians persisted. North Korea and Iran continued their nuclear weapons programs despite threats and pressures from the international community. Genocides took place in Bosnia, Rwanda, and the Darfur region of Sudan. Religious fundamentalism continued to flourish, especially in the Middle East and parts of Africa, where it destabilized governments and inspired acts of terrorism, including al-Qaeda's attack on the World Trade Center and the Pentagon on September 11, 2001.

It would be a mistake, however, to dwell exclusively on the negatives of the recent past. In South Africa, the dismantling of the apartheid system and the election of Nelson Mandela as the country's first black president in 1994 ended one of the world's most vicious racist regimes. "Intractable" conflicts in Northern Ireland, Bosnia, and Sri Lanka were resolved or contained. Impressive developments in science and technology continued. Advances were made in the fight against HIV/AIDS, cancer, and dozens of other diseases; scientists identified and mapped the 20,000–25,000 genes of the human genome; observations made with the Hubble Space Telescope revolutionized astronomy; researchers using the Large Hadron Collider, a mammoth particle accelerator outside Geneva, Switzerland, deepened our understanding of the minuscule elementary particles that are the building blocks of the universe; and a stream of innovations in computer technology revolutionized how people communicated, shopped, banked, worked, gained information, and entertained themselves.

The world also became more peaceful. Even though world military expenditures since the mid-1990s steadily increased, reaching a historic high of $1.62 trillion in 2010, the number of interstate and civil wars fought around the world declined sharply after 1992 and showed a very modest increase after 2003. Several explanations have been offered for this positive development. These include the worldwide increase in the number of democratic governments (democracies, it is theorized, are less prone to go to war than dictatorships and are less likely to have civil wars); the globalization of the international economy (nations are less likely to go to war with trade partners or nations in which they have extensive investments); the existence of nuclear weapons (which make war too dangerous to contemplate); and changing attitudes toward war itself (few leaders or ideologies any longer glorify violence or justify war as a means of gaining territory, economic advantage, or prestige). Another factor was the end of the Cold War, which between the late 1940s and the late 1980s had led to major wars in Korea, Vietnam, and Afghanistan, and had caused or prolonged dozens of civil wars, especially in Latin America and Africa. The Cold War's end also left the way open for more international activism to prevent, contain, and end wars. Mediation efforts and peace-keeping operations sponsored by the United Nations and other third parties failed in Rwanda and Somalia, but elsewhere were a force for peace.

The human costs of wars also declined. The three wars fought in Southwest Asia (the Persian Gulf War (1991–1992), the Iraq War (2003–2011), and the Afghan War (2001–present) have resulted in approximately 130,500 combat deaths for all sides. This compares to the 2,500,000 battlefield deaths in the Korean War (1950–1953), 1,500,000 battlefield deaths in the Vietnam War (1955–1975), and approximately 125,000 battlefield deaths in the Soviet war in Afghanistan (1979–1989). Although large numbers of civilian deaths resulted from the Persian Gulf, Iraq, and Afghan Wars, (estimates for the Iraq War range from just under 100,000 to 600,000), non-combatant deaths were mainly concentrated in Africa, where anywhere from 2 million to more than 5 million non-combatants died in the two Congo Wars (1996–1997 and 1998–2003) and 300,000 to 400,000 died in the Darfur War (2003–). These deaths resulted from the effects of disease, famine and the disruption of services on populations barely living at the subsistence level even in the best of times. Elsewhere, war-related civilian casualties have followed the downward trend in battlefield deaths. To cite one example, the U.S.-led

Afghan War has led to an estimated 14,000 to 34,000 civilian deaths, far fewer than the most conservative estimate of 600,000 civilian deaths during the Soviet War in Afghanistan in the 1980s.

The world since 1990 not only became more peaceful, it also became wealthier. The market value of all final goods and services produced in the world's economy (gross world product) increased from $20.3 trillion in 1990, to $43.6 trillion in 2000, and to $74.5 trillion in 2010. In actual dollars, most of this growth occurred in the developed economies of Western Europe, the United States, Canada, Australia, and New Zealand. Rates of growth were highest, however, in Brazil, India, Indonesia, Russia, and especially China, nations where millions were lifted out of poverty. Economic underdevelopment continued to plague sub-Saharan Africa, where the number of people living in poverty remains the highest in the world. Nonetheless, Africa showed progress on many fronts. Infant mortality declined, life expectancy increased, and education levels were higher than ever.

Thus, despite evidence of inequality, conflict, injustice, cruelty, and suffering, the story of the recent past has been positive in many ways. But the story of the twenty-first century has just begun, and at this point it is unclear if it will have a happy ending. At the time of this writing, in early 2012, the world is still feeling the aftershocks of the U.S. housing bubble collapse in 2008. The future of the Middle East and North Africa is up for grabs after a wave of protests and demonstrations in 2011 toppled dictators in Tunisia, Egypt, Yemen, and Libya, and threatened them elsewhere. The European Union (EU) and the European common currency (euro) are under pressure as a result of overborrowing by the governments of Greece, Portugal, Spain, Italy, and Ireland. The United States also is at a crossroads. It faces huge government deficits, a sluggish economy, and high unemployment at time of political paralysis. China's Communist rulers have ridden the export-driven economic model to unprecedented growth, but if growth slows, it is unclear how long the Chinese people will accept continued authoritarian rule.

In the long run, the greatest threat comes from the unsustainability of current production and consumption patterns. For two centuries, economic growth has been based on the burning of coal and petroleum-based products. We now know that such dependency is unsustainable because such resources are both finite and harmful. The shrinking Arctic ice cap, melting glaciers, record heat waves, droughts, and increased incidences of severe weather may be foretastes of more damaging climate change unless human-caused emissions of carbon dioxide and other greenhouse gases are reduced dramatically. Prospects of global cooperation to limit global warming, however, were dimmed when President Bush withdrew U.S. support for the Kyoto Treaty in 2001, and the UN Climate Change Conference in Copenhagen in 2009 ended in failure. It remains to be seen if agreements worked out at the most recent international climate conference in Durban, South Africa will be effective.

In the face of these uncertainties, one can take comfort from the world's history since 1900. During these years, human beings planned and carried out genocides, fought wars that killed millions, experienced major economic failures, and tolerated injustices too numerous to mention. Human beings also righted many wrongs, dispelled many illusions, and confirmed in countless ways the awesome power of the human mind. More than a few individuals and nations proved themselves capable of great vision and courage.

◆

The Debate on Free Trade in the 1990s

In July 1944, economists and officials from forty-four nations met in the New Hampshire resort town of Bretton Woods to lay the foundations for the world economy after World War II. Their goal was to create an institutional framework for trade, investment, and finance that would foster economic expansion and strengthen global capitalism, and by doing so would contribute to political stability and peace. The institutions that grew out of the Bretton Woods meeting continue to be the core of the world economy in the early twenty-first century: the International Monetary Fund (IMF), which promotes monetary cooperation and exchange; the World Bank, which makes loans for economic development projects; and the General Agreement on Tariffs and Trade (GATT), which, until its functions were taken over by the World Trade Organization (WTO) in 1995, provided rules for settling trade disputes and negotiating reductions in trade barriers and tariffs.

All three Bretton Woods institutions, especially GATT, were dedicated to encouraging free market capitalism and liberalizing international commerce. Protectionism, universally practiced in the first half of the twentieth century, had, so the planners believed, hindered growth, inflated prices, sharpened national rivalries through trade wars, and contributed to the collapse of international trade during the Great Depression. Liberalizing world trade would unleash capitalism's potential and bring about worldwide economic growth. Not incidentally, it would also open markets for the agricultural and manufactured goods of the United States, whose representatives played a preponderant role in framing the Bretton Woods agreements and later in administering the organizations they created.

To encourage free trade, GATT sponsored seven sets of negotiations, or "rounds," in the 1960s and 1970s in which member nations negotiated reductions in tariffs and other trade barriers. After the seventh round (the Tokyo Round), in 1979, worldwide tariff levels had fallen from about 40 percent to 5 percent, with tariff duties eliminated completely for some commodities. Nevertheless, by the 1990s the world was still not a free trade utopia. In every country, free trade had its critics among economists, consumers, union members, and politicians; it also was opposed by powerful economic interests—Japanese rice farmers, U.S. automakers, and French winemakers, among others—who clamored for protection from foreign competition. Even after having lowered tariffs, therefore, many governments found ways to limit imports through nontariff barriers (NTBs) such as quotas, special labeling and packaging requirements, and complex customs procedures and rules. By the late 1970s, with global recession setting in, many governments took steps to keep foreign products out of their domestic markets, and the prospects for free trade appeared to be dimming.

Beginning in the mid-1980s, however, with the backing of multinational corporations eager to tap into new markets and with the support of newly elected European and U.S. politicians dedicated to free market principles, free trade made a comeback. By 1986 the European Economic Community, or Common Market, which had begun in 1957 with six members, had expanded to twelve nations, creating a powerful free trade zone in Europe; in 1992 the signing of the Treaty of Maastricht and the founding of the European Union held out the promise of opening markets even further. In 1986 the eighth round of GATT-sponsored tariff discussions (the Uruguay Round) got under way. After eight years of bargaining, the final protocol was a breakthrough for free trade. Agricultural products and services such as engineering, accounting, and advertising were included for the first time, and steps were taken to eliminate NTBs. An additional boost to free trade came in 1990, when the leaders of Mexico, Canada, and the United States announced their intention to establish a free trade zone in North America. Three years later, the North American Free Trade Agreement (NAFTA), despite strong opposition in Canada and the United States, was approved and went into effect on January 1, 1994. Free trade was once more ascendant, and its supporters were confident that a new era of capitalist expansion was at hand. But free trade still had opponents, and in the early 2000s the pace of market liberalization faltered after the Doha Round, launched in 2001, was abandoned in 2008 as a result of ongoing disagreements on a wide range of issues, especially the subsidization of agriculture in Europe and the United States.

Free Trade and the "Race to the Bottom"

❖

96 ❖ Ralph Nader,
FREE TRADE AND THE DECLINE OF DEMOCRACY

During the nationwide debate preceding the congressional vote on NAFTA in December 1993, opponents denounced the treaty's economic, political, and environmental implications. A leading critic was Ralph Nader, a lawyer from Connecticut who in the 1960s emerged as a prominent consumer advocate when he published *Unsafe at Any Speed*, about the dangers of flawed automobile design. In the 1970s and 1980s, Nader rallied support for a wide range of consumer and environmental causes, and helped found organizations such as the Center for Study of Responsive Law, the Public Interest Research Group, Congress Watch, and the Tax Reform Group. In 2000, he ran for president on the Green Party ticket, receiving 3 percent of the popular vote. The following article was published in 1993 in an anthology, *The Case Against "Free Trade."*

QUESTIONS FOR ANALYSIS

1. According to Nader, why are multinational corporations so supportive of NAFTA and the new GATT proposals?
2. What will be the economic implications of NAFTA for the U.S. economy, according to Nader?
3. What, in Nader's view, are the potential political dangers of free trade?
4. Why is Nader convinced that there are "no winners" in free trade?
5. What is Nader's alternative to an international economy based on free trade?

Citizens beware. An unprecedented corporate power grab is underway in global negotiations over international trade.

Operating under the deceptive banner of "free" trade, multinational corporations are working hard to expand their control over the international economy and to undo vital health, safety, and environmental protections won by citizen movements across the globe in recent decades.

The megacorporations are not expecting these victories to be gained in town halls, state offices, the U.S. Capitol, or even at the United Nations. They are looking to circumvent the democratic process altogether, in a bold and brazen drive to achieve an autocratic far-reaching agenda through two trade agreements, the U.S.-Mexico-Canada free trade deal (formally known as NAFTA, the North American Free Trade Agreement) and an expansion of the General Agreement on Tariffs and Trade (GATT), called the Uruguay Round.

The Fortune 200's GATT and NAFTA agenda would make the air you breathe dirtier and the water you drink more polluted. It would cost jobs, depress wage levels, and make workplaces less safe. It would destroy family farms and undermine consumer protections such as those ensuring that the food you eat is

---

Source: From Ralph Nader et al., *The Case Against Free Trade.* Earth Island Press, © 1993, pp. 1–2, 6–8, 11–12. Used by permission of North Atlantic Books.

not compromised by unsanitary conditions or higher levels of pesticides and preservatives.

And that's only for the industrialized countries. The large global companies have an even more ambitious set of goals for the Third World. They hope to use GATT and NAFTA to capitalize on the poverty of Third World countries and exploit their generally low environmental, safety, and wage standards. At the same time, these corporations plan to displace locally owned businesses and solidify their control over developing countries' economies and natural resources....

U.S. corporations long ago learned how to pit states against each other in "a race to the bottom"—to profit from the lower wages, pollution standards, and taxes. Now, through their NAFTA and GATT campaigns, multinational corporations are directing their efforts to the international arena, where desperately poor countries are willing and able to offer standards at 19th century American levels and below.

It's an old game: when fifty years ago the textile workers of Massachusetts demanded higher wages and safer working conditions, the industry moved its factories to the Carolinas and Georgia. If California considers enacting environmental standards in order to make it safer for people to breathe, business threatens to shut down and move to another state.

The trade agreements are crafted to enable corporations to play this game at the global level, to pit country against country in a race to see who can set the lowest wage levels, the lowest environmental standards, the lowest consumer safety standards....

Enactment of the free trade deals virtually ensures that any local, state, or even national effort in the United States to demand that corporations pay their fair share of taxes, provide a decent standard of living to their employees, or limit their pollution of the air, water, and land will be met with the refrain, "You can't burden us like that. If you do, we won't be able to compete. We'll have to close down and move to a country that offers

us a more hospitable business climate." This sort of threat is extremely powerful—communities already devastated by plant closures and a declining manufacturing base are desperate not to lose more jobs, and they know all too well from experience that threats of this sort are often carried out.

Want a small-scale preview of the post-GATT and NAFTA free trade world? Check out the U.S.-Mexico border region, where hundreds of U.S. companies have opened up shop during the last two decades in a special free trade zone made up of factories known as *maquiladoras*.... Here are some examples of conditions that prevail in the U.S.-Mexico border region:

- In Brownsville, Texas, just across the border from Matamoros, a *maquiladora* town, babies are being born without brains in record numbers; public health officials in the area believe there is a link between anencephaly (the name of this horrendous birth defect) and exposure of pregnant women to certain toxic chemicals dumped in streams and on the ground in the *maquiladoras* across the border. Imagine the effect on fetal health in Matamoros itself.
- U.S. companies in Mexico dump xylene, an industrial solvent, at levels up to 50,000 times what is allowed in the United States, and some companies dump methylene chloride at levels up to 215,000 times the U.S. standards, according to test results of a U.S. Environmental Protection Agency certified laboratory....
- Working conditions inside the *maquiladora* plants are deplorable. The National Safe Workplace Institute reports that "most experts are in agreement that *maquila* workers suffer much higher levels of injuries than U.S. workers," and notes that "an alarming number of mentally retarded infants have been born to mothers who worked in *maquila* plants during pregnancies."

In many instances, large corporations are already forcing U.S. workers and communities to compete against this Dickensian[1] industrialization—but the

---

[1]Many of the novels of the famous English writer Charles Dickens (1812–1879) focused on the bleakness of early factory life.

situation will become much worse with NAFTA and Uruguay Round expansion of GATT....

Worst of all, the corporate-induced race to the bottom is a game that no country or community can win. There is always some place in the world that is a little worse off, where the living conditions are a little bit more wretched....

... "Non-tariff trade barriers," in fact, has become a code phrase to undermine all sorts of citizen-protection standards and regulations. Literally, the term means any measure that is not a tariff and that inhibits trade—for instance restrictions on trade in food containing too much pesticide residue or products that don't meet safety standards. Corporate interests focus on a safety, health, or environmental regulation that they don't like, develop an argument about how it violates the rules of a trade agreement, and then demand that the regulation be revoked....

... Already, a Dutch and several U.S. states' recycling programs, the U.S. asbestos ban, the U.S. Delaney clause prohibiting carcinogenic additives to food, a Canadian reforestation program, U.S., Indonesian, and other countries' restrictions on exports of unprocessed logs ... the gas guzzler tax, driftnet fishing and whaling restrictions, U.S. laws designed to protect dolphins, smoking and smokeless tobacco restrictions, and a European ban on beef tainted with growth hormones have either been attacked as non-tariff barriers under existing free trade agreements or threatened with future challenges under the Uruguay Round when it is completed....

U.S. citizen groups already have enough problems dealing in Washington with corporate lobbyists and indentured politicians without being told that decisions are going to be made in other countries, by other officials, and by other lobbies that have no accountability or disclosure requirements in the country....

To compound the autocracy, disputes about non-tariff trade barriers are decided not by elected officials or their appointees, but by secretive panels of foreign trade bureaucrats. Only national government representatives are allowed to participate in the trade agreement dispute resolution; citizen organizations are locked out.

... As the world prepares to enter the twenty-first century, GATT and NAFTA would lead the planet in exactly the wrong direction.... No one denies the usefulness of international trade and commerce. But societies need to focus their attention on fostering community-oriented production. Such smaller-scale operations are more flexible and adaptable to local needs and environmentally sustainable production methods, and more susceptible to democratic controls. They are less likely to threaten to migrate, and they may perceive their interests as more overlapping with general community interests.

Similarly, allocating power to lower level governmental bodies tends to increase citizen power. Concentrating power in international organizations, as the trade pacts do, tends to remove critical decisions from citizen influence—it's a lot easier to get ahold of your city council representative than international trade bureaucrats.

Formulas for Economic Success and Failure

❖

97 ◆ David R. Henderson, *ECONOMIC MIRACLES*

David R. Henderson, a Canadian by birth, received his B.A. from the University of Winnipeg and his Ph.D. in economics from the University of California at Los Angeles. He has had academic appointments at the University of Rochester, the University of Santa Clara, and Washington University in St. Louis. During

Source: With kind permission from Springer Science+Business Media and David R. Henderson: "Economic Miracles," by David R. Henderson, *Society*, Vol. 32, No. 59, September 1, 1995. Copyright ©1995 by Transaction Publishers; All rights reserved.

the Reagan administration, he served as a senior economist on energy and health policy for the President's Council of Economic Advisers. Since the mid-1990s, he has held appointments as a research fellow with the Hoover Institution in Palo Alto, California, and as an associate professor of economics at the Naval Postgraduate School in Monterey, California. In his writings he has criticized government spending while promoting the benefits of free markets. In his article, "Economic Miracles," published in the journal *Society* in 1995, he offers his views on the benefits of free trade and economic deregulation.

QUESTIONS FOR ANALYSIS

1. According to Henderson, what explains the contrasting economic experiences of South Korea and India in the post–World War II era? What economic lessons does he draw from the experiences of Chile?
2. How, according to Henderson, does government regulation hamper economic performance?
3. Why does Henderson believe that high marginal tax rates so negatively affect economic performance?
4. How would Nader have responded to Henderson's arguments for free trade and economic deregulation?

Our adventure in looking at economic "miracles" begins with a tale of two countries. Their names are withheld to increase the suspense. For now, they will be called country A and country B. In 1950, these two nations are similar in many ways. Measured in 1990 dollars, country A has a per capita income of $240; country B's is $550. Both countries are so far behind the industrialized world that most observers think neither can ever attain a comfortable standard of living, let alone narrow the gap.

Country A has a number of things going for it: ample natural resources, a huge domestic market, railways and other infrastructure that are good by Third-World standards, and competent judges and civil servants. Country B lacks all of these. Country A's savings rate is 12 percent of its gross national product ... while country B's in an anemic 8 percent.

In the early 1950s, country A's government begins a policy of heavy government intervention in both international trade and domestic business. Not only does the government impose tariffs in excess of a hundred percent, but it also requires all importers to get permission to import, often

refusing to give that permission. Moreover, country A's government imposed detailed regulation on each industry. Let's say that you run a company in country A and you decide that you want to increase production. You cannot just do so without a license from the government. You want to enter an industry, but you cannot do so without a license. You cannot even diversify your product line without a government-granted license. And often the government refuses to grant these licenses.

"Why?" you might ask.

In 1967, one of the bureaucrats answers why. He says that, without the industrial licensing regime, this country would fritter away its resources producing lipstick....

Country A's government also owns and runs entire industries: atomic energy, iron and steel, heavy machinery, coal, railways, airlines, telecommunications, and electricity generation and transmission.

What are the results of all this government intervention? By 1990, country A's income per capita is up from $240 to $350.

Country B's government, with fewer natural resources, less infrastructure, and a lower savings rate, pursues a different policy. It allows much freer trade. And, although it regulates industries, by comparison with country A, it is a model of laissez faire. The result? By 1990, country B's per capita GNP is $5,400, and country B did well in spite of a major war conducted there between 1950 and 1953.

Country A is India. Country B is South Korea....

ECONOMIC POLICIES TO AVOID

... By the mid-1950s, Indian firms had to get permission to import components or capital goods, and the government imposed massive tariff rates on those imports that it did allow. These restrictions, combined with many others, caused massive inefficiency. The Indian Tariff Commission complained that everything made a noise in Indian-made cars except the horn. India's economy stagnated.

Then, in June 1991, in the midst of a foreign-debt crisis, newly elected Prime Minister Narasimha Rao and his finance minister, Dr. Manmohan Singh, an economist who had argued in favor of opening India's economy to the rest of the world, began to free the economy. Import controls, except for those on consumer goods, were dismantled, and in three years the highest tariff rates fell by almost half, to 65 percent. The government planned to lower tariffs to 25 percent within four years....

The results of these and other reforms have already been dramatic. Per capita gross domestic product (GDP) is growing at 2.5 percent a year. Exports in 1993 rose by more than 20 percent, to over $22 billion, and are expected to increase another 20 percent in 1994.... India's middle class, now numbering 150 million, and with incomes of 30,000 rupees ($20,000 in U.S. purchasing power), is growing by 5 to 10 percent a year....

In the 1950s and 1960s, Chile was highly protectionist, with tariffs averaging over 100 percent. By 1972, socialist president Salvador Allende damaged trade by having the government take it over. Between 1961 and 1972, real GDP grew moderately, averaging 4.2 percent.

In 1973, the year of the coup that toppled Allende, economic growth was −5.6 percent.

In desperation, the Pinochet regime turned to the so-called "Chicago boys," native Chileans who had studied economics at the University of Chicago.... From 1974 to 1979, trade was liberalized, with average tariffs falling to 10 percent. After two years of adjustment, 1974 and 1975, in which real GDP grew by 1 percent and 12.9 percent respectively, economic growth took off, averaging 7.2 percent a year between 1976 and 1981....

A new round of trade liberalization began in 1985, bringing average tariff levels down to 11 percent by 1991. Between 1986 and 1991, Chilean economic growth averaged 6.7 percent. Economists Rudiger Dornbusch of MIT and Sebastian Edwards of UCLA, both experts on Chile's economy, wrote, "For the second time in two decades, one speaks of a Chilean "miracle."

What India and Chile learned the hard way is that protectionism stunts growth. Its opposite, an open economy, allows each country to specialize in producing the goods and services in which it has a comparative advantage, and protectionism removes some of the incentive to specialize....

AVOID PRICE CONTROLS

Virtually the whole economics profession rejects price controls.... The reason is simple: If governments keep prices well below their free-market competitive level, suppliers have much less incentive to supply; demanders have an artificial incentive to demand more. The result is a shortage that gets worse the bigger the gap between controlled prices and the price that would have existed in a free market.

A student of mine from Indonesia, when asked what were the major things he learned in my public policy course, focused on one. He said that he had always wondered why so many rice fields in his country were no longer being used to grow rice and why Indonesia had switched from rice exporter to importer. He now knew the answer: price controls on rice. Indonesia's case is familiar in Third World countries. Many of those countries governments, dominated by urban dweller, impose price controls on agricultural crops and cause huge shortages, and then subsidize imports.

AVOID HIGH MARGINAL TAX RATES AT ALL INCOME LEVELS

In 1979, newly elected Prime Minister Margaret Thatcher cut the United Kingdom's top tax rate on earned income from 83 percent to 60 percent and on so-called "unearned" income (income from interest and dividends) from 98 percent to 60 percent. President Ronald Reagan in 1981, along with Congress, cut marginal tax rates by 23 percent of three years and cut the top tax rate from 70 percent to 50 percent immediately. Following their example, many countries around the world cut marginal tax rates at all income levels....

These tax cuts led to economic booms virtually everywhere they were tried....

Why did such cuts in marginal tax rates lead to economic booms? The reason is that the marginal tax rate is the price people pay to the government for earning income. When the price falls, people will find ways of earning more—by working harder, working smarter, working longer, and moving from the underground economy to the above-ground economy. Similarly, a reduction in the marginal tax rate

raises the cost of taking deductions, causing people to take fewer deductions....

DEREGULATE

... One factor that is surprisingly unimportant for economic growth is natural resources. There is little relationship between a country's natural resource base and its degree of economic development. Two of the most resource-rich countries in the world are Russia and Brazil. Both countries, especially Russia, are in terrible economic shape. Hong Kong, on the other hand, which is nothing but a rock at the edge of the ocean—and not even a large rock—is doing quite well economically....

The basic lesson to be learned from the postwar evidence on countries' economic growth is that growth's major enemy is heavy government intervention—whether through tariffs, price controls, high taxes, lavish government spending, or detailed regulation. Therefore, the way to increase economic well-being is to scale back government dramatically. This does not mean that government should do nothing. It has a crucial role to protect its citizens from foreign invasion, to protect them from each other, to maintain and enforce property rights, and to enforce contracts. But most functions that it performs beyond those few hamper not only freedom but also economic well-being.

◆

The New Immigration and Its Critics

Migration has always been a part of human history, but never did it play so prominent a role as it did in the closing years of the twentieth century, when more human beings chose, or were forced, to migrate than ever before. In a series of annual reports, the International Organization for Migration, a Geneva-based agency advocating immigrants' rights, estimated that the number of international migrants, legal and illegal, reached 90 million in 1990, 150 million in 2000, and 214 million in 2010. Since the 1990s, approximately three in every one hundred human beings were international migrants.

The geography of migration also changed. Europe, for example, was transformed from a land of emigrants to a land of immigrants. Between 1500 and the mid-twentieth century, Europe provided most of the millions of immigrants who populated the Americas, Australia, New Zealand, and parts of Africa.

In the late twentieth century, however, this outflow virtually stopped, and Europe became a destination for migrants from the Middle East, the Caribbean, Africa, and Asia. Migration also changed for the United States, Canada, and Australia, when in the late 1900s all three nations abandoned quota systems that had discriminated against non-Europeans. As a result, Asians in Australia; Asians and West Indians in Canada; and Asians, West Indians, and Latin Americans in the United States became the dominant immigrant groups.

Many factors contributed to these changes: growing economic disparities between rich and poor nations; changing demographic patterns, resulting in slow-growing, aging populations in industrialized states and younger, fast-growing populations in Africa, Latin America, and Asia; cheaper and faster means of transportation; new technologies that make instant communication possible between immigrants and family and friends at home; the creation of free trade areas that encourage movements of labor; the liberalization of immigration laws in Canada, Australia, and the United States; and, in developing nations, the weakening of restraints on women's independence and freedom of movement. In other words, increased migration was one part of the transnational revolution that continues to reshape societies around the globe.

Migration can be disruptive, even traumatic, for the migrants themselves, the countries they are leaving, and the countries of their destination. This certainly has been the case with migration since the 1980s, when the number of migrants swelled and most immigrants practiced religions, spoke languages, and came from racial stock different from those of the majority of the population in their new country. Thus, as the number of immigrants rose, so too did the number of individuals and organizations demanding immigration restrictions. Opponents of immigration worried and continue to worry about immigration's economic effects, the difficulty of assimilating newcomers, pressures on government services, and, on a deeper level, the dilution and erosion of distinct national cultures in an era of globalization.

Too Many Immigrants

◆

98 ◆ Roy H. Beck,
THE CASE AGAINST IMMIGRATION

The number of immigrants to the United States diminished dramatically from the 1920s through the 1960s, largely due to restrictive legislation passed in the 1920s. This downward trend was reversed with the passage of the Immigration and Nationality Act in 1965. This law abolished the quota system adopted in 1924 that favored immigrants from Western Europe, limited those from southern and eastern Europe, and excluded Asians. The new law made family reunification and the nation's need for skills more important determinants of who

Source: From *The Case Against Immigration* by Roy Beck. Copyright © 1996 by Roy Beck. Used by permission of the author.

would be admitted than nationality. The law's provision for family reunification meant that if a single family member gained legal immigrant status, it opened the door to his or her spouse, dependent children, adult children, parents, brothers, and sisters. Thus, a single immigrant could begin a chain reaction that enabled a large extended family to immigrate.

After the new legislation, legal immigration, mainly from Asia, Latin America, and the Caribbean, rose to 4.5 million in the 1970s, 7.4 million in the 1980s, and 11.2 million in the 1990s. Millions of illegal immigrants also entered the country. By 2000, immigrants made up 10.3 percent of the population, an increase from 4.7 percent in 1970. Against a backdrop of economic recession, a movement to curb immigration gathered strength in the early 1990s. A leading spokesperson for the movement was the journalist Roy H. Beck, who in 1996 published a widely read book, *The Case Against Immigration*. Deeply concerned about environmental issues and poverty, he became convinced that population growth and immigration were at the root of many social and economic problems in the United States. Since 1997, he has been the director of NumbersUSA, an anti-immigration group that in 2007 successfully lobbied against the comprehensive immigration bill proposed by George W. Bush and in 2011 and the so-called DREAM Act (Development, Relief and Education for Alien Minors Act), which would have provided a path to citizenship through military service or educational achievement for illegal immigrants who had arrived in the United States as minors.

QUESTIONS FOR ANALYSIS

1. According to Beck, what have been the most damaging effects of high immigration on U.S. society?
2. In Beck's view, which groups have been most adversely affected by high immigration? Which groups have benefited?
3. Why, according to Beck, has Congress been slow to react to the "immigration crisis" despite widespread support within the general populace for immigration reform?

Although we often hear that the United States is a nation of immigrants, we seldom ask just what that means. It can be difficult to ask tough questions about immigration when we see nostalgic images of Ellis Island, recall our own families' coming to America, or encounter a new immigrant who is striving admirably to achieve the American dream.

But tough questions about immigration can no longer be avoided as we enter a fourth decade of unprecedentedly high immigration and struggle with its impact on job markets, on the quality of life and social fabric of our communities, and on the state of the environment....

Until recently, policymakers and politicians of every stripe had ignored what public opinion polls found to be the public's growing dissatisfaction with the abnormally high level of immigration. Majority public opinion can be shallow, fleeting, and wrong, but an honest look at major trends during the recent mass immigration shows that ordinary Americans' concerns can hardly be dismissed as narrow and unenlightened:

- Whole industries in the 1970s and 1980s reorganized to exploit compliant foreign labor, with the result that conditions have deteriorated for all workers in those industries.

- Long trends of rising U.S. wages have been reversed.
- Poverty has increased.
- The middle-class way of life has come under siege; income disparities have widened disturbingly.
- Aggressive civil rights programs to benefit the descendants of slavery have been watered down, co-opted, and undermined because of the unanticipated volume of new immigration. A nearly half-century march of economic progress for black Americans has been halted and turned back.
- The culture—and even—language—of many local communities has been transformed against the wishes of their native inhabitants. Instead of spawning healthy diversity, immigration has turned many cities into caldrons of increased ethnic tension and divisiveness.
- A stabilizing U.S. population with low birth rates (like other advanced nations) has become the most rapidly congesting industrialized nation in the world (resembling trends in Third World countries). Vast tracts of remaining farmland, natural habitat, and ecosystems have been destroyed to accommodate the growing population. . . .
- Numerous organized crime syndicates headquartered in the new immigrants' home countries have gained solid beachheads of operations. Law enforcement agencies have been confounded just as they thought they were near victory over the crime organizations that other ethnic groups had brought with them. . . .

. . . Some observers fear that the volume of non-European immigration threatens to swamp America's cultural heritage; others welcome an ever more multicultural society. Nonetheless, the chief difficulties that America faces because of current immigration are not triggered by *who* the immigrants are but by *how many* they are. . . . It is time to confront the true costs and benefits of immigration numbers, which have skyrocketed beyond our society's ability to handle them successfully. . . .

Who wins and who loses? A glance through the roster of immigration winners quickly finds business owners who have followed a low-wage labor strategy. Land developers, real estate agents, home mortgage officials, and others who tend to profit from population growth are winners. Owners of high-tech industries have lowered their costs by importing skilled immigrants who will work at lower wages than college-educated Americans. People who can afford nannies, gardeners, and housekeepers have benefitted from lower costs. . . . Others have won by having the security, prestige, or pay of their jobs enhanced by the high immigrant flow. That would include immigration lawyers, refugee resettlement agency personnel, officials of immigrant-advocacy groups, and educators and other social services employees who work the immigrants.

Unfortunately, the roster of immigration losers is much larger and includes some of America's most vulnerable citizens: poor children, lower-skilled workers, residents of declining urban communities, large numbers of African Americans, the unskilled immigrants who already are here and face the most severe competition from new immigrants, and even some of America's brightest young people, who lose opportunities to pursue science-based careers because of some corporations' and universities' preferences for foreign scientists and engineers. . . .

. . . Finally, it is the local community as a whole that is forced to assume the costs of immigration. . . . Some of the subsidy is monetary: social services to foreign workers who do not earn enough money to rise above poverty; issuance of new school bonds to educate the foreign workers' children; additional infrastructure to handle an expanding population that cannot pay enough taxes to cover the costs; social services to American workers who lose jobs or drop into poverty wages because of the foreign job competition.

. . . We cannot deny that cutting immigration will hurt some citizens. Most immigration lawyers might lose their livelihood and have to enter other specialties. Not surprisingly, they and their organization, the American Immigration Lawyers

Association, have been the most aggressive in fighting any reductions whatsoever.... Also suffering from the change—at least temporarily—would be the businesses which the lawyers represent and which have decided to rely heavily on foreign labor.... A number of national church bureaucracies and other private refugee organizations might have to cut their staffs. On the other hand, the charitable organizations should be able to find plenty of humanitarian work to do overseas—where nearly all refugees are, anyway—as well as among the black underclass and other impoverished citizens here in America.... Then there are the ethnic immigrant organizations that had counted on a continuing flow of their countrymen to boost the power of their budding political machines....

Those few groups that stand to lose money, power, or prestige with a cut in immigration wield tremendous power on Capitol Hill. People representing the broad public interest will have to speak very loudly to be heard. The majority of members of Congress previously earned

their living in self-employed occupations or as executives; they think like employers who love a labor surplus instead of like most Americans who depend on paychecks and benefit from tight-labor markets....

Immigration is so high now that the cuts proposed in Congress reduce the numbers only back to the level of the Great Wave.[1] In fighting that slight reduction, the National Association of Manufacturers[2] proclaimed the great myth about immigration: "Legal immigration strengthens and energizes America. Throughout America's history, legally admitted immigrants have been a source of strength and vitality to our nation. Our current legal immigration policies are specifically designed to reflect American values and serve national interests."

Nothing could be further from the truth, if "national interest" is defined by what is good for the majority of the public. High immigration almost always has reflected the values and served the interest of a small elite at the *expense* of the national interest.

[1]The "Great Wave" of immigration to the United States from the 1890s to the 1910s.
[2]The National Association of Manufacturers, founded in 1895, is an organization of U.S. industrial and business firms joined together to further their trade, business, and financial interests, and to publicize the advantages of free enterprise. Its headquarters is in Washington, DC, where it lobbies extensively.

The Fallacies of Multiculturalism

❖

99 ◆ Paul Scheffer, *IMMIGRANT NATIONS*

How best to integrate millions of new arrivals into European society gained the attention of policy makers, intellectuals, and the general public in the 1970s, when it became apparent that immigration and the existence of large non-Western ethnic minorities were becoming permanent features of European life. During the 1950s and 1960s, it had been expected that most immigrants at some point would return to the country of their birth and that those who stayed would be would be integrated into European society in a process of gradual assimilation. The model was the American "melting pot," in which millions of immigrants through education, intermarriage, and their daily experiences gradually cast off their identities as Germans, Poles, and Italians and became "Americans" in their values and loyalties.

Source: From *Immigrant Nations*, by Paul Scheffer. (Cambridge, Eng. and Malden, Mass.: Polity Press, 2011), pp. 198–202, passim. © 2011 Polity Press. Used by permission of Polity Press.

By the 1980s, however, it was apparent that this model of assimilation was not working in Europe, especially among the millions of immigrants who were Muslims. Members of different ethnic minorities tended to cluster in well-defined neighborhoods or districts, which limited their contacts with other groups in public schools and daily life. Marriage outside one's group was rare. Many individuals returned to their (or their family's) country of origin to find spouses. Furthermore, legal requirements were such that relatively few immigrants sought and received citizenship, and in contrast to the policy in the United States and Latin America, most children of immigrants born in Europe did not automatically become citizens.

As a result, in the 1980s two other approaches to the "immigrant problem" emerged. One approach found expression in the platforms of right-wing nationalist political parties that made opposition to immigration and immigrants' rights a top priority. These parties included the Freedom Party of Austria (1952), the Swiss People's Party (1971), the National Front in France (1972), the Progress Party in Norway (1973), the Flemish Block in Belgium (1979), the British National Party (1982), the Danish People's Party (1995), and the Pym Fortuyn List in the Netherlands (2002). All these parties favored a halt to immigration, the abandonment of efforts to accommodate the unique needs and demands of new ethnic groups, and even incentives to recent immigrants to return to their countries of origin.

Other Europeans advocated an approach that came to be known as multiculturalism. They rejected what they considered to be the underlying racist premises of assimilationism, which took for granted the superiority of Western values and culture over those of newly arrived ethnic groups. Multiculturalists celebrated difference, and claimed that the diversity provided by immigrants enriched and strengthened society. Governments, therefore, should take steps to accommodate Muslims, for example, by subsidizing the building of mosques, providing imams to serve as prison and army chaplains, and even taking into account Islamic law when adjudicating legal cases pertaining to marriage, divorce, and inheritance. Schools should encourage Islamic studies and teach Arabic. Menus in public cafeterias should be changed to reflect Islamic dietary preferences. Businesses should be encouraged to increase minority hiring. Multiculturalists rejected the analogy of the melting pot, and replaced it with the image of a salad bowl, in which each ingredient maintains its integrity while contributing to the whole.

In the early 2000s, criticisms of multiculturalism mounted. In the eyes of its detractors, efforts to protect ethnic minorities' rights, promote their hiring, and make accommodations to their religious needs had done little to eradicate poverty, high levels of crime, and poor academic achievement in ethnic communities. They had not prevented increasing numbers of young Muslims from aligning themselves with fundamentalist imams and their fiery antiwestern ideology. Nor had such efforts made Muslims any more welcome among the non-Muslim majority.

Public discussions of multiculturalism's strengths and weaknesses became more urgent and heated in the wake of Islam-inspired acts of terrorism—the attack on the World Trade Center and the Pentagon in 2001 (in which Muslims living in Hamburg, Germany, played a key role), the train bombings in Madrid in 2004, and the London underground bombings in 2005. In the Netherlands, however, the national debate was set off was by an article, "The Multicultural Drama," published by the Dutch public intellectual and journalist Paul Scheffer in 2000. A graduate of the University of Nijmegen, Scheffer worked as a foreign correspondent in Paris and Warsaw before assuming a position in a think-tank sponsored by the left-leaning Dutch Labor Party in 1986. In the 1990s, he became known for his commentaries on Dutch politics and society in the Dutch press, especially in the *NRC Handelsblad*, the newspaper that published "The Multicultural Drama." Distressed by the poverty, crime rate, and poor academic performance among the approximately one million Muslims who lived in the Netherlands, he declared multiculturalism a failure and called on the Dutch people to explore new ways to fully integrate Muslims into the mainstream of Dutch life. He elaborated on his ideas in his book *Het Land von Aankomst* (2007), which was published in an English translation, *Immigrant Nations*, in 2011. The following excerpts are from Chapter Six "The Cosmopolitan Code."

QUESTIONS FOR ANALYSIS

1. How, according to Scheffer, did decolonization contribute to the rise of multiculturalism?
2. In Scheffer's view, how does multiculturalism have the potential to limit freedom?
3. Scheffer states that not all "cultural manifestations are appropriate to a post-industrial society." How does he develop this line of argument?
4. Scheffer states multiculturalism does not "exhibit any explicatory value to culture." What does he mean by this, and why is it important?
5. How in Scheffer's view does multiculturalism cut off receiving societies from their history?
6. Based on Scheffer's critique of multiculturalism, what can you infer about his recommendations on how Europe can best deal with its "immigrant problem?"

After more than 20 years of debate in the Western world, the tenets of multiculturalism are slowly being abandoned. We are moving in the direction of a renewed emphasis on the ideal of shared citizenship.

Before enumerating the various problems with the notion of a multicultural society, something needs to be said about its history. The first systematic exposition of a multicultural philosophy comes from American author Horace Kallen, who emerged in the 1920s as a fierce critic of the doctrine of the 'melting pot', speaking out against its forceful agitation for the 'Americanization' of the immigrant. His appeal reads like a precursor to what would later become a widely held view, namely the notion of society as an aggregate of cultural minorities. 'For in effect the United States are in the process of becoming a federal state not merely as a union of geographical and administrative unities, but also as a cooperation of cultural diversities, as a federation or commonwealth of national cultures.'[1]

Under the influence of decolonization, a multicultural way of thinking that elaborates on this opposition to the 'melting pot' revealed itself first in America, then in Europe. If taken merely to suggest that worldwide migration

[1]Horace Meyer Kallen (1882–1974) was brought to the United States by his German-born Jewish parents at the age of five. Trained in philosophy at Princeton and Harvard, he was a professor of philosophy for most of his career at the New School in New York. This quote is from his book, *Culture and Democracy in the United States* (1924).

produces multifarious societies, then there's little to be said against it. It's broadly accepted nowadays that such a society must create space for everyone by, for example, adjusting laws about the disposal of the dead or by opening prayer rooms, to allow for the rituals engaged in by Hindus or Muslims. The marking of religious festivals of one kind or another can be seen simply as a reaching out of hands.

Beyond this emphasis on the kind of pluralism that in theory characterizes every open society, and beyond the practical adjustments needed to make room for new religions and lifestyles, a more drastic idea has arisen. It has to do with the belief that society is made up of more or less autonomous cultural communities, which ought to be recognized in a whole range of areas including the administration of justice, education and the jobs market. . . .

To summarize, multiculturalism in its strong or immoderate form tempts us to partition people off into ethnic categories in the name of cultural pluralism. Based on 'integration with the retention of identity', respect for others has in practice meant hampering people's freedom to shape their own lives, with the ultimate result that customs such as honour killing,[2] which claimed many victims, have been ignored for years. We should defend the kind of open society in which all traditions are subjected to critical examination, as opposed to the conservatism of group cultures. . . .

Amartya Sen[3] is decidedly not an adherent of multiculturalism. He quotes Gandhi, who was quick to oppose what he called 'the vivisection of a nation', meaning a division into its cultural or religious components. Sen asks himself where we got the idea that the coexistence of an array of cultures in close proximity will be peaceful in nature. Without a shared foundation, no meaningful exchange is possible and instead we become caught up in permanent miscommunication or worse. An open society should afford plenty of room for disagreement, but without a minimum of common ground disputes cannot be productive, whether in an economic or a democratic sense. . . .

Another shortcoming of multiculturalism is its underestimation of modernity as a shared horizon. It's simply not the case that all cultural manifestations are appropriate to a post-industrial society. In a service economy, cognitive and social skills are of great importance and selection takes place more than ever on the basis of socio-cultural capital. . . . Unless a society exhibits some degree of cultural cohesion it can neither produce nor sustain a modern economy. . . .

Another objection concerns what is perhaps multiculturalism's most curious feature, namely that it does not attribute any explicatory value to culture. All cultures are equal, we're told, so they can't be used to explain disparities between ethnic groups in socio-economic outcomes, say, or in crime figures. Explanations in terms of class, on the other hand, are extremely popular. Multiculturalism celebrates cultural difference and is happy to discuss anything else as long as cultures are spared all criticism. . . .

Yet another objection is that multiculturalism cuts receiving societies loose from their history. It's a conservative concept from the newcomers' point of view—after all, they're expected to cherish their traditions—but from the point of view of the established population it entails profound change, since it requires the setting aside of many prevailing customs. Multiculturalism doesn't explicitly recognize any obligation arising from achievements made by the receiving society through considerable efforts over many generations. It silently accepts this inheritance while at the same time rejecting any suggestion of continuity as merely a way of excluding migrants and their children by regarding them as people who are not part of a shared history and who therefore cannot identify with it.

---

[2]The murder of a member of a family, usually a woman or girl, by other members, due to the belief of those murdered had brought dishonor to the family.

[3]Amartya Sen (b. 1933) is an Indian economist and Nobel Prize winner for his work on the problems faced by society's poorest members.

Recall the telling statement from a Dutch researcher: 'Surely you're not going to bother Turkish children with the years '40-'45?' Why shouldn't children whose parents were born in a village in Anatolia be put in a position to learn about a crucial episode in Dutch history, the Nazi occupation, so that they have a chance to influence the way in which the memory of those events is shaped?

A step further and we see how the denial of a collective memory which newcomers could share fits neatly with a sense of revulsion among orthodox Muslims, who believe their children shouldn't be bothered at school with lessons about the persecution of the Jews. It starts with an enlightened idea—let's look beyond the boundaries of national history—and ends in a form of self-censorship. Once we stop feeling we're part of a continuing history, every attempt to draw upon the past in a way that's open to all as a matter of principle will fail. . . .

Another, final objection is that, taken to its logical conclusion, multiculturalism leads to an undesirable legal pluralism. This occurs when on the basis of a recognition of the equal value of cultures, 'distinct' communities are given the right to live according to their own authority and their own laws, even if their legal institutions deviate from prevailing judicial practice. There are innumerable problems with this approach. When is a community truly 'distinct'?

What demands are to be made of it? Are group rights binding on anyone judged to belong to that group, or can an individual decide whether or not to be counted as a member? . . .

In sum, the main weakness of the notion of a multicultural society is that it is oriented towards the past, as its most common definition suggests: 'integration with the retention of identity'. This formulation was introduced with a view to the eventual return of migrants to their native countries. Education in their own language and culture was judged necessary to ensure that children didn't become divorced from their countries of origin and have great difficulty adapting when they returned. The migrants stayed, but so did the idea of 'integration with the retention of identity'. . . .

This approach not only underestimates the changes thrown up by the transition from one society to another and the generational dynamic that results, it also falls short in a normative sense, since it ignores the shared norms any modern economy and democracy needs to enable it to compete productively and resolve conflicts. In the absence of shared laws, shared public holidays, generally recognized standards of success at school, a level playing field for job interviews and historical references understandable to all, the room for meaningful differences of opinion shrinks and the room for misunderstanding grows.

Dealing with Diversity in France

❖

100 ◆ *The Stasi Report: The Report of the Commission of Reflection on the Application of the Principle of Secularity in the Republic*

Debates about immigration policy and multiculturalism consumed politicians, the press, and the general public across Europe, but nowhere were these debates as tense and divisive as they were in France during the so-called headscarves controversy of the late 1990s and early 2000s. The controversy began

Source: From Bernard Stasi. *Rapport de la Commission de réflexion sur l'application du principe de laïcité dans la République remis au Président de la République le 11 décembre 2003* Paris: La Documentation française 2003 Copyright 2004. Translated by James Overfield.

in the mid-1990s, when a series of disputes occurred over how to deal with the relatively small number of Muslim girls who insisted on wearing the traditional Muslim headscarf, which covered their hair and neck, to school. This was in keeping with the Muslim dress code, which requires women to dress modestly while in public so as not to attract the attention of men. At several schools, officials responded by expelling the girls, claiming that wearing this symbol of their religious affiliation disrupted instruction and violated the cherished French principle of *laicité* (secularity), which required absolute religious neutrality in public institutions such as schools. There followed several years of uncertainty in which the Minister of Education upheld the expulsions, but the Council of State, a body of the national government that provides the executive branch with legal advice and acts as an administrative court, offered the opinion that according to another dimension of secularity, religious freedom, wearing the headscarf was permitted.

In 2003, in the midst of ever-increasing public controversy over the wearing of the headscarf, growing concern over Islamic fundamentalism, and pressures from anti-immigrant political parties of the far right, President Jacques Chirac appointed Bernard Stasi (1930–2011), a career politician and civil servant of moderate political views, to head a Commission of Reflection to report on the "applicability of the principle of secularity" in the Republic. The twenty-person committee, which included only one Muslim, took input from the public and interviewed over one hundred individuals from varying backgrounds. In December 2003, the committee submitted its report to President Chirac. It retraced the history of the principle of secularity back to the French Revolution, and as the following excerpt shows, provided examples of how the need to accommodate the religious concerns of Muslims and other groups were disturbing the country. It also made a number of recommendations, among them the requirement that all teachers sign a "certificate of secularity;" the teaching of "religious facts" in the schools; the founding of a higher school of Islamic studies; the training of Muslim prison and army chaplains; taking into account food requirements of religious minorities in hospitals and penitentiaries; and recognizing as national holidays the Jewish Day of Atonement (Yom Kippur) and the Muslim Festival of Sacrifice (Aid el Kebir). But only one of its recommendations became a topic of international discussion and debate. This was the recommendation that the "wearing or displaying of conspicuous signs and symbols of religious belief, such as large Christian crosses, the Jewish skullcap, or Yarmulke, and Islamic headscarves" should be banned from public schools.

This was also the commission's only recommendation that in the short term was acted upon. In March 2004, the "headscarf ban" was approved by the Chamber of Deputies by a vote of 494 to 36, setting off another protracted and heated discussion of secularity, republican values, what it meant to be French, and what it meant to be a French Muslim.

Subsequently, the government continued to make laws pertaining to the dress of Muslim women. In 2011, it made it a crime for a woman to appear in public wearing a face veil or a burka (a full body cloak), and in early 2012 the Senate approved a law to ban the wearing of headscarves by teachers in nursery schools and nannies, even if they were working in a private home. The Chamber of Deputies, however, decided to table the law pertaining to nannies and nursery school teachers, a step that optimists considered a positive sign that tensions over the religious practices of Europe's seventeen million Muslims were beginning to reside.

QUESTIONS FOR ANALYSIS

1. According to the report, aside from the alleged "disturbances" caused by the wearing of headscarves in schools, in what other ways has the principle of secularity been threatened by Muslim demands and actions?
2. What explanation does the report offer for the isolation and anger of ethnic minorities?
3. French feminists were divided over the issue of the "headscarf ban." What arguments, for and against the ban, might they have made?
4. According to the report, what is the potential of sports in bringing ethnic and religious groups together in France? Why, at the time of the report, were sports failing to achieve this potential?
5. In what ways does the Stasi Report confirm Scheffer's reservations about multiculturalism? (See source 99.)

PUBLIC SERVICES AND THE WORLD OF WORK: SOME DISTURBING ABUSES

New and increasing difficulties have loomed up. They provide evidence that the requirement of secularity in public services, notably in the schools and workplace, is being weakened by demands that tend to make the convictions of one's own community prevail over general rules. The principle of secularity is today being undermined in more sectors than it may appear. The commission is aware that the difficulties we discovered are still in the minority. But they are real, painful, and harbingers of dysfunctions, all the more disturbing due to the recent and rapid spread of these phenomena.... .

AT SCHOOL

In school, the wearing of a conspicuous religious symbol—a large cross, yarmulke,[1] or headscarf— is already enough to disturb the tranquility of daily school life. But the difficulties go far beyond this excessively publicized question.

In fact, the normal course of study is also impaired by the persistent demands for absences one day a week, or by the interruption of instruction or of examinations for reasons of prayer or fasting. Behaviors that challenge the whole curriculum of teaching history or the earth and life sciences disrupt the study of these disciplines. Some young women resort to unjustifiable medical certificates in order to be exempted from physical education and sports. Tests that are part of examinations are disturbed by the refusal of young women to be heard by a male examiner. Teachers and administrators, simply because they are female, see their authority challenged by students or their parents.

Universal access to school is weakened by school withdrawals for religious reasons. . . . Recourse to teaching by correspondence courses has been noted. Moreover, certain private schools under contract[2] only accept students who can provide proof of their allegiance to the institution's own religion; these schools do not offer instruction in those parts of the required

---

[1]A skull cap worn by Jewish males and occasionally females. When and where the yarmulke is worn depends on personal choice and the branch of Judaism to which a person belongs. Orthodox Jews are more likely to wear the yarmulke all the time, while Conservative Jews wear

it while attending synagogue services or participating in events such as a High Holiday dinner.
[2]Private schools that are chartered and funded by the state.

curriculum that in their view do not agree with certain aspects of their worldview.

All these positions are illegal. Even if they are only the actions of an activist minority, they cause serious harm to the principles that govern public service. It is damaged in its very foundations.

AT THE HOSPITAL

The hospital is no longer spared these types of uncertainties. . . . It already has had to come to terms with certain religious prohibitions such as the opposition of Jehovah's Witnesses to blood transfusions.[3] More recently, religiously-inspired refusals have multiplied from husbands or fathers to have their wives or daughters treated or deliver a baby under the care of a male physician. Some women for these reasons have been denied epidurals.[4] Some caregivers have been rejected because of their alleged religious beliefs. More generally, certain religious concerns of the patients can upset the hospital routine: corridors are transformed into private places for prayer; cafeterias parallel to those of the hospital are set up to provide traditional food in defiance of sanitary regulations.

Here again, the foundations of public service are directly affected: principles of equality, continuity, respect for sanitary rules, and health requirements.

IN THE JUSTICE S0YSTEM

In the prisons numerous difficulties have appeared. The Law of December 9, 1905[5] and the code of penal procedure make provisions for the expression of spiritual and religious life among the prisoners. But in an environment where collective pressures are very strong, influences can be brought to bear so that prisoners assent to certain religious practices.[6] At the time of visits from family and friends, prisoners are strongly urged to adopt "religiously correct" behavior. In this tense situation prison administrators are perhaps tempted in the interest of maintaining order in the prison to regroup the prisoners according to their religious background. Such a solution begins a vicious circle by reinforcing group control over the most vulnerable prisoners.

The courts are not spared these issues. A judge was asked to recuse himself because of his alleged religious beliefs. After having been chosen, jurors have expressed the wish to be seated while wearing ostentatious religious symbols. The minister of justice (keeper of the seals) has refused to allow a lawyer to be sworn in while wearing a headscarf....

BEHAVIORS THAT ARE ON THE INCREASE

During Days of Introduction to Defense and the French Military[7], difficulties have been confirmed. Certain girls have not wanted to take part in the course of co-educational first aid and have refused on principle to carry out first aid on males. More generally, the managers of public facilities ... are petitioned to offer time slots to users for non-co-ed use. This way of thinking is dangerous and discriminatory. It opens the door to other forms of discrimination, for example, those pertaining to nationality or ethnic background. Such actions gravely weaken public services, especially for the poorest citizens,

---

[3]Jehovah's Witnesses is a Christian denomination founded in the 1870s by the American Charles Taves Russell, and now centered in Brooklyn, New York. Among its unique beliefs is the conviction that the world is in its "last days" before it will be destroyed by God and replaced by an earthly paradise ruled by God and 144,000 true believers. Members of the church refuse military service and blood transfusions. Jehovah's Witnesses established a presence in France in the early 1900s, but it was not recognized as a true religion by the French government until 2000.

[4]Epidural analgesia is a relatively safe method of relieving pain in labor by introducing drugs through a catheter placed in the lower back.

[5]The law that established separation of church and state in France.

[6]A reference to fundamentalist Islam.

[7]Days on which teen-age boys and girls visit military installations, where they are introduced to the French armed forces and learn certain basic skills related to civil defense.

who should be their main beneficiaries. Public officials have given in to various religious demands. Civil servants have demanded to wear in the workplace a yarmulke or headscarf to show their religious affiliation. Recently medical interns have demanded the same thing.

PRESSURED PUBLIC SERVANTS FACING CHANGE

Confronted with the situations that have been described, public servants find themselves in a confusing situation. There is a state of uneasiness and discomfort that is stirred up in those who are in this position, preventing them from doing their jobs. . . . Hospital personnel exhaust themselves in negotiations with patrons, to the detriment of the care they are to provide on urgent matters. . . .

A WORLD OF WORK WHICH IS NOT SPARED

In the 1960s, large-scale businesses knew how to decide the religious issues they encountered because of the national origins of their employees. They rearranged the menus in their cafeterias; the work schedule was adapted in regard to specific breaks to take into account the time of Ramadan.[8] Lastly, some businesses set aside rooms for prayer on their premises. These steps involved encouraging the integration of the foreign workforce . . . to the extent they did not hinder the success of the business. The situation now is different. Businesses are no longer confronted with the expression of needs, but with demands, mainly as a result of the arrival in the workplace of a new generation of activists. Business managers must deal with employees who wear the headscarf and refuse to shake hands with male colleagues. Some do not recognize the authority of the higher staff when it is a matter pertaining to women.

These demands present a triple menace. They weaken the harmony that must exist among employees, no matter what their sex and philosophical convictions might be. They affect relations with clients. . . . Finally, they cause security risks.

Such behavior sometimes turns against those who embrace it. Business executives have observed that because of the headscarf and the demands that go with it, young women deprive themselves of any chance of being hired, or if they are already employed, any chance of advancement. Some female employees refuse to apply for managerial positions to avoid having to oversee the work of male co-workers; thus they imprison themselves in subordinate positions. Such behavior is a form of "self-discrimination."

COMMUNITY NARROWING MORE IMPOSED THAN SOUGHT AFTER

Field workers interviewed by the commission all drew attention to a social and urban environment favorable to the development community-based reasoning that makes primary allegiance to a particular group more important than a sense of belonging to the Republic. Until the past few years this phenomenon was barely noticeable in France.

A few figures illustrate the gravity of the situation. It was pointed out to the commission that in seven hundred districts, made up of several nationalities, difficulties are growing: unemployment rates of forty percent and acute school attendance problems are social indicators three times more prevalent than in other parts of the country. The inhabitants of these neglected areas have the feeling that that they are the victims of social banishment that condemns them to rely on themselves. This is especially the case with young people. Thirty two percent of the population is under twenty years of age: which is to say this is a mess for themselves and for the Republic.

---

[8]The month in which Muslims refrain from eating, drinking, smoking and sex during daylight hours; its purpose is to teach Muslims patience, spirituality, humility and submissiveness to God.

In certain instances the schools and sport are unable to combat this social narrowing, for they no longer serve the function of being a melting pot. Children withdraw to attend private schools or obtain exemptions from parts of the school curriculum: schools become socially and ethnically homogenous. The growth of sports facilities in the heart of these districts no longer provides opportunities for interactions among persons of different nationalities and cultures on the playing field. The number of community teams has increased, and they no longer participate in competitions organized by sports confederations, which were occasions for intermingling. Sporting activities for women in these districts have notably declined. Females are in fact excluded from the playing fields and swimming pools. Female and co-ed sports clubs are disappearing. . . . On the whole these phenomena undermine confidence in the Republic and identification with the nation.

Activist community groups exploit this real social malaise to make militant converts. They develop an aggressive strategy against individuals to bend them to their preconceived community-based standard. These groups thus act in neglected districts, submitting the weakest part of the population to permanent stress.

A SERIOUS DECLINE IN THE SITUATION OF YOUNG WOMEN

"The situation of girls in the city is approaching the level of a true tragedy," so testified an associate director [official] who brought out that the first victims of the decline in the social situation are young women. Another young woman, who testified behind closed doors because she feared recriminations from her community, put it thusly, "The Republic is not protecting its children."

Young women once more are finding themselves victims of a resurgence of sexism, which is reflected in various pressures and forms of verbal, psychological, and physical violence. Young men force them to wear unrevealing and asexual clothing and to lower their gaze when in view of a man; with failure to conform, they are stigmatized as "whores." Several organizations are alarmed by the increasing resignations of many of their foreign-born female members, who consider themselves forbidden from any social life.

In such a situation some girls and women agree to wear the headscarf, but others wear it under constraint or pressure. This also applies to pre-adolescent girls, on whom wearing the headscarf is imposed, sometimes by force. Once veiled, girls can transverse the stairwells of public buildings and walk on the streets without fear of being insulted, indeed of being abused, as had been the case when their head was uncovered. Paradoxically, the headscarf thus offers them protection that should be provided for by the state. Those who do not wear the veil and consider it a sign of their perceived inferiority because it enfeebles and isolates women are singled out as shameless and even as "infidels."

Young women are victims of other forms of violence: genital mutilation, polygamy, and repudiation by their families. The personal status of women does not always allow women to oppose this; on the basis of bilateral agreements,[9] the laws of the country of origin can be applied to them, including provisions directly contrary to sexual equality and basic rights. Arranged marriages are imposed on them in certain communities, especially Turkish, North African, African, and Pakistani. In bringing in foreigners as future spouses, families try to side-step the autonomy and emancipation chosen by their daughters, and occasionally by their sons. Sometimes a girl is "married" during a visit to the country of origin, which means the end of schooling. . . .

[9]Agreements between France and an immigrant's country of origin.

RACIST AND XENOPHOBIC DISPLAYS

A number of persons heard by the commission made a point about open hostility directed against Muslims. These acts, which sometimes rise to the level of the profanation of tombs and physical violence, indicate the shape of anti-Muslim hatred. In the view of many, all

foreigners, especially if they are North Africans or Turks, are dismissed and reduced to a single religious identity, ignoring all the other aspects of their culture. This stereotyping is accompanied by a perception that identifies Islam with social-political radicalism, thus ignoring the fact that a great majority of Muslims confess to a faith and a credo perfectly compatible with the laws of the Republic.

Racial Reconciliation and Ethnic Hatreds

Modern racism in the West, with its belief in the superiority of white people of European descent and the inferiority of people of color, emerged in the nineteenth century out of a mix of misapplied Darwinian theory, nationalism, American slavery, and the growing disparity between "advanced" Europeans and "backward" Africans, Asians, Aboriginal Australians, and Native Americans. Twentieth-century racism gave comfort to imperialists; justified segregation in the United States and South Africa; inspired restrictive immigration laws; provided the Nazis with their core beliefs; and was a source of injustice and inequality in many societies.

To the credit of the millions who spoke out against racial bigotry and fought to change the institutions it sustained, racism weakened in the second half of the twentieth century. Nazism was defeated and discredited, colonialism ended, segregation laws were eliminated in the United States, and immigration quotas directed against Asians, African, and Latinos were largely eliminated in the United States and elsewhere. Between 1990 and 1994, the world's last avowedly racist regime ended when the white leaders of South Africa bowed to pressures from their own people and the international community and dismantled the apartheid system. By century's end, racism still inspired fringe right-wing political parties and certain anti-immigration groups, but overall, at least for the moment, it was losing its hold.

The same cannot be said for ethnic conflict. With the end of colonialism and the breakup of the Soviet Union, many newly created nations had populations consisting of several ethnic groups that became bitter rivals for political power, economic favors, and cultural ascendancy. In a few cases, such conflicts were resolved, but as the 1990s amply revealed, they also led to civil wars, the disintegration of states, and cruelties of the worst kind. This was the case especially in Africa, where new-state boundaries were based on divisions made during the imperialist scramble without regard for cultural and ethnic realities.

Let There Be Justice and Peace for All

❖

101 ◆ Nelson Mandela,
PRESIDENTIAL INAUGURATION SPEECH,
MAY 10, 1994

During the 1980s, as the South African system of apartheid entered its fourth decade, the Nationalist government under P. W. Botha sought to diffuse black resentment by introducing social and political reforms. In 1979, it legalized black labor unions, and in the mid-1980s it granted blacks greater property rights in cities, established black town councils with limited control over local affairs, revoked the ban on multiracial political parties, ended the prohibition against interracial marriage, and repealed the hated pass laws that had controlled the movement of blacks in designated white areas. With most of the nation's apartheid laws unchanged, however, and with blacks still excluded from participation in national politics, blacks responded with rent strikes, school boycotts, demonstrations, labor strikes, and small numbers of terrorist acts. The government declared a state of emergency, arrested thousands of government opponents, deployed the army in black townships to maintain law and order, and looked the other way when vigilantes attacked black activists.

Faced with a deteriorating economy, almost universal condemnation from the international community, and imminent civil war, President Botha stepped down as prime minister in 1989 and was replaced by F. W. de Klerk. Convinced that South Africa's only hope lay in abandoning apartheid, de Klerk lifted the ban on the African National Congress (ANC) and released its leader, Nelson Mandela, from a twenty-seven-year prison sentence (see Chapter 11, Source 78) in February 1990. In 1991, major apartheid laws were repealed, and the ANC and de Klerk's government began negotiations on a new constitution. Overcoming opposition from white right-wing groups, radical black organizations, and the Inkatha Freedom Party, which represented the interests of Zulus, the two sides drew up a constitution that went into effect in 1994.

In the first election under the new constitution, Nelson Mandela, the heroic black leader who had spent half his adult life in prison for opposing his country's white supremacist government, was chosen as president. His inauguration, on May 10, 1994, with representatives of 150 countries in attendance, was a joyful celebration of a new beginning for South Africa. Coming at the end of a century that often showed humanity at its worst, it was a reminder of the human capacity to right wrongs and overcome even the most extreme forms of injustice.

Source: Nelson Mandela, "Presidential Inauguration Speech, May 10, 1994," as appeared in *Historic Documents of 1994,* Congressional Quarterly Inc. © 1995, pp. 249–251.

QUESTIONS FOR ANALYSIS

1. According to Mandela, who should be credited for bringing about the series of events that led to his inauguration?
2. When Mandela uses the phrase "the people of South Africa," to whom is he referring?
3. According to Mandela, what is the significance of his inauguration as president of South Africa?

Today, all of us do, by our presence here, and by our celebrations in other parts of our country and the world, confer glory and hope to newborn liberty. Out of the experience of an extraordinary human disaster that lasted too long, must be born a society of which all humanity will be proud. Our daily deeds as ordinary South Africans must produce an actual South African reality that will reinforce humanity's belief in justice, strengthen its confidence in the nobility of the human soul and sustain all our hopes for a glorious life for all.

All this we owe both to ourselves and to the peoples of the world who are so well represented here today. To my compatriots, I have no hesitation in saying that each one of us is as intimately attached to the soil of this beautiful country as are the famous jacaranda trees of Pretoria and the mimosa trees of the bushveld.

Each time one of us touches the soil of this land, we feel a sense of personal renewal. The national mood changes as the seasons change. We are moved by a sense of joy and exhilaration when the grass turns green and the flowers bloom.

That spiritual and physical oneness we all share with this common homeland explains the depth of the pain we all carried in our hearts as we saw our country tear itself apart in a terrible conflict, and as we saw it spurned, outlawed and isolated by the peoples of the world, precisely because it has become the universal base of the pernicious ideology and practice of racism and racial oppression.

We, the people of South Africa, feel fulfilled that humanity has taken us back into its bosom, that we, who were outlaws not so long ago, have today been given the rare privilege to be host to the nations of the world on our own soil.

We thank all our distinguished international guests for having come to take possession with the people of our country of what is, after all, a common victory for justice, for peace, for human dignity. We trust that you will continue to stand by us as we tackle the challenges of building peace, prosperity, non-sexism, non-racialism and democracy.

We deeply appreciate the role that the masses of our people and their political mass democratic, religious, women, youth, business, traditional and other leaders have played to bring about this conclusion. Not least among them is my Second Deputy President, the Honorable F. W. de Klerk. We would also like to pay tribute to our security forces, in all their ranks, for the distinguished role they have played in securing our first democratic elections and the transition to democracy, from bloodthirsty forces which still refuse to see the light.

The time for the healing of the wounds has come.

The moment to bridge the chasms that divide us has come.

The time to build is upon us.

We have, at last, achieved our political emancipation. We pledge ourselves to liberate all our people from the continuing bondage of poverty, deprivation, suffering, gender and other discrimination.

We succeeded to take our last steps to freedom in conditions of relative peace. We commit ourselves to the construction of a complete, just and lasting peace.

We have triumphed in the effort to implant hope in the breasts of the millions of our people. We enter into a covenant that we shall build the society in which all South Africans, both black and white, will be able to walk tall, without any fear in their hearts, assured of their inalienable right to human dignity—a rainbow nation at peace with itself and the world.

As a token of its commitment to the renewal of our country, the new Interim Government of National Unity will, as a matter of urgency, address the issue of amnesty for various categories of our people who are currently serving terms of imprisonment.

We dedicate this day to all the heroes and heroines in this country and the rest of the world, who sacrificed in many ways and surrendered their lives so that we could be free.

Their dreams have become reality. Freedom is their reward.

We are both humbled and elevated by the honor and privilege that you, the people of South Africa, have bestowed on us, as the first President of a united, democratic, non-racial and non-sexist South Africa, to lead our country out of the valley of darkness.

We understand it still that there is no easy road to freedom. We know it well that none of us acting alone can achieve success. We must therefore act together as a united people, for national reconciliation, for nation building, for the birth of a new world.

Let there be justice for all.

Let there be peace for all.

Let there be work, bread, water and salt for all.

Let each know that for each the body, the mind and the soul have been freed to fulfill themselves.

Never, never and never again shall it be that this beautiful land will again experience the oppression of one by another and suffer the indignity of being the skunk of the world.

Let freedom reign.

The sun shall never set on so glorious a human achievement!

God bless Africa!

Genocide in Rwanda: 1994

❖

102 ◆ Fergal Keane, *SEASON OF BLOOD*

Their weapons were primitive: iron bars, nail-studded clubs, and machetes were all they had. Nonetheless, in fewer than three months government-trained terrorists, with the help of thousands of their compatriots, carried out the twentieth century's most intense and efficient genocide. The place was Rwanda, a landlocked country in east central Africa about the size of Maryland; the time was April, May, and June 1994. In less than ninety days, Hutus killed an estimated eight hundred thousand Tutsis, at a rate three times faster than that of the Nazis in their murderous campaign against the Jews in World War II.

The Rwandan tragedy was grounded in long-standing ethnic rivalries and resentments, fanned to the point of mass murder by fanatics and desperate politicians. The region of Rwanda and Burundi was settled by Bantu-speaking Hutus around the eleventh century. After 1500, they gradually succumbed to the political authority of the Tutsis, pastoralists who moved into the region from the north and, despite making up only 15 percent of the population, reduced the Hutus to semi-servile status. When the region became part

Source: Fergal Keene, *Season of Blood: A Rwandan Journey,* (Viking, 1995). Copyright © Fergal Keane, 1995. Reproduced by permission of Penguin Books Ltd.

of German East Africa in the late 1800s, the Germans relied on Tutsi chieftains to administer the colony, and the Belgians did the same after they took over the colony following World War I. Under Belgian rule, Tutsis monopolized administrative posts, army commissions, and places in Rwanda's schools. In the late 1950s, with independence approaching and fearing future Tutsi domination, the Hutus rebelled. Belgian authorities did little to halt the violence, and the Hutus killed thousands of Tutsis and forced many thousands more into exile. The Belgians, believing Tutsi power had been destroyed, replaced Tutsi administrators with Hutus, and when independence came, Hutus dominated the new state. Under the dictator Juvénal Habyarimana, Rwanda remained stable in the 1970s and 1980s despite graft, poverty, and population pressures. This changed in 1990 when Rwanda was invaded by the army of the Rwandan Patriotic Front (RPF), a Uganda-based organization of Tutsi refugees which proclaimed as its goal a multiethnic, democratic state to which Tutsi exiles could return. After three years of fighting, the RPF and Habyarimana signed an agreement that provided for power sharing and future free elections. The compromise enraged Hutu extremists, who launched a hate-filled propaganda campaign against the Tutsis and began to train killing squads (*interahamwe*) made up largely of unemployed young men. Then on April 6, 1994, Habyarimana was killed after his plane was shot down, probably by Hutu extremists. Claiming the crash had been the work of Tutsi "cockroaches," these same extremists launched their killing squads against Rwanda's Tutsis.

As the killings, rapes, and maiming continued, and the RPF army once more took the field, the world expressed shock but did little until a small contingent of French troops arrived in late June. By then, the RPF had conquered the country, declared a cease-fire, and instituted a coalition government that included Hutu moderates. With more than one million killed or forced into exile, the Rwandan genocide was over.

When the killing began, Fergal Keane, a young Irish-born television reporter for the British Broadcasting Company (BBC), was dispatched to Rwanda to cover the story. With a Ugandan driver, Moses; another BBC reporter, David; two South African cameramen, Glenn and Tony; and Frank, a soldier from the RPF, Keane made his way across Rwanda, preparing award-winning news reports and recording material for *Season of Blood,* the book he published in 1995.

In the first part of the following excerpt, Keane recounts his visits to an orphanage, to a Rwandan river where thousands drowned, and to a church where three thousand Tutsis were slaughtered. In the second part, he describes his encounter with two Hutu academics, the rector and vice-rector of the National University of Rwanda at Butare.

QUESTIONS FOR ANALYSIS

1. What aspects of the Rwandan massacre particularly disturb Keane?
2. How do the actions he describes differ from those of the Serbs in Bosnia?
3. On the basis of Keane's account, what can you conclude about the ultimate goals of the Hutu extremists?

4. How does Dr. Birchmans view the events in Rwanda?
5. What is the meaning of the episode when Keane was invited to the rector's home to view the World Cup soccer match on television?

[CHILDREN'S STORIES]

A group of children gathered around us. Among them was another girl whose head and right arm were heavily bandaged. I cannot remember her name but her story left me wordless. "The Interahamwe came to our house and they asked all who are *inyenzi* [cockroaches] to step outside. They knew that we were Tutsis, these people, because some of them are our neighbours. When we did not come out they broke down the door. We were inside and could hear them shouting. And then they came through the front door and I followed my parents and brothers and sisters out into the fields at the back and we ran. But they ran fast and caught us and they killed my family members and they thought they had killed me too. They hit me with the machetes and clubs and then threw all the bodies together so that I was lying under my mother who was dead. But I was not dead and at night I crawled away and hid in the fields where the grass was very high. Then after a time the soldiers of the RPF came and they helped me and brought me here." . . .

. . . The militias were always on the alert for the exclamations of small frightened voices. Once caught, children were much easier to kill. The little body frames were clubbed and hacked down within minutes. Some, however, survived their appalling injuries. There were many accounts of children who hid under mounds of bodies until they felt it was safe to crawl out. Rose [the director of the orphanage] said that many of the children called out at night in their sleep. Some called for dead parents; others screamed out in the grip of some nightmare whose depth of terror even she, with her experience of war, could not begin to contemplate. For some children the destruction of their entire family groups had robbed them of the will to live. Frequently as we journeyed through Rwanda, we would hear of little boys and girls who had literally died of sorrow, withdrawing from everyone and refusing to eat or drink, until they finally wasted away. . . .

[DEATH AT THE RIVER]

The Kagera River flows from the highlands of Rwanda, down through the country until it crosses the border into Tanzania and then Uganda, finally filtering out into the vastness of Lake Victoria. The river therefore became an ideal carriageway for the dispersal of evidence of Rwanda's genocide. People were routinely lined up beside the river for execution and then pushed into the flood. An alternative method of killing was to force people to jump into the fast running water. Most drowned within a few minutes. The Interahamwe gangs noted that this was a particularly efficient way of killing small children, who were more easily carried off in the current. . . . There were so many bodies it seemed the earth could not hold them. When the dead finally reached Lake Victoria, Ugandan fishermen went out in their boats to recover them and give them a decent burial. Moses and Edward had heard of many men going out day after day without being paid, to gather in the corpses. Colleagues had seen the bodies of mothers and children who had been tied together and thrown into the water. There were thousands of corpses.

[THE SLAUGHTER AT NYARUBUYE]

. . . As I walk towards the gate, I must make a detour to avoid the bodies of several people. There is a child who has been decapitated and there are three other corpses splayed on the ground. . . . I must walk on, stepping over the corpse of a tall man who lies directly across the path, and, feeling the grass brush against my legs, I look down to my left and see a child who has been hacked almost into two pieces....

... I begin to pray to myself. "Our father who art in heaven ... " These are prayers I have not said since my childhood but I need them now....

... We pass a classroom and inside a mother is lying in the corner surrounded by four children.

The chalk marks from the last lesson in mathematics are still on the board. But the desks have been upturned by the killers. It looks as if the woman and her children had tried to hide underneath the desks. We pass around the corner and I step over the remains of a small boy. Again he has been decapitated. To my immediate left is a large room filled with bodies. There is blood, rust coloured now with the passing weeks, smeared on the walls....

... While we are waiting for Glenn and Tony to pack the equipment away, we hear a noise coming from one of the rooms of the dead.... "What is that? Did you hear that?" I ask. Edward notices the edge of fear in my voice and strains his ear to listen. But there is no more sound. "It is only rats, only rats," says Moses. As we turn to go I look back and in the darkness see the form of the marble Christ gazing down on the dead. The rats scuttle in the classrooms again.

[ENCOUNTERS IN BUTARE]

... It is a beautiful evening. The sun is dipping below the thick garden of trees that surrounds the university. Long, slanting rays of golden light come through the window, illuminating the round face of Mr. Birchmans [the vice-rector] and the full glass of whisky he holds in his chubby fingers. Birchmans is a fat man. He has a moon face and big eyes that bulge when he makes one of his frequent denunciations of RPF....

I fill the glasses again and ask Birchmans what has happened to the Tutsis who lived in Butare. They have all left, he says. But surely he must have known about the massacres? No, he has seen nothing like that. Yes, he knows that people have been killed, but in a war people are killed....

"But did the Tutsis deserve to die?" ...

He pauses. He exhales. "Killing is a terrible thing, but in war people are killed. That is how it happens." ...

The following night the rector [of the university] comes again to our door. "Come with me," he says. "You are Irish, are you not?"

"Yes, I am," I reply.

"You will like this, then," he says, opening the door to his sitting-room, where his wife and several children of all ages are sitting in front of a large television screen. The reception is hazy but I can easily make out the green of the Irish football jerseys. I had forgotten that on the other side of the world, in the middle of the American summer, men were playing in the [soccer] World Cup. "Rwanda has no team in this tournament so we will cheer for you," says the rector.

I am given the most comfortable seat in the room. A deep leather armchair. I notice several family photographs on the wall. There is a portrait of the Pope. When Ireland scores the room explodes into wild cheering. I smile inanely and express my gratitude. While I am sitting watching the game, in a town that has become a citadel of killers, there are thousands of my fellow countrymen cheering and drinking the night away in New York. I wish I was there. I wish I was anywhere but here. "Goodnight, Monsieur Rector, but you will understand. I have a headache. I am not well and must sleep." He gives me a puzzled look. There is an element of hurt in his expression. The rector cannot understand why I would reject the friendship of his family. But he says nothing about it. He only shrugs and bids me goodnight.

... I am not an especially religious person but I went to Rwanda believing in a spiritual world in which evil was kept at bay by a powerful force for good. Sometimes the battle was close but I felt there was enough decency and love around to nourish the gift of hope. There will be many who say that I was foolish, naive to ever have had such faith in man. Maybe they are right. In any event after Rwanda I lost that optimism. I am not sure that it will ever return. For now I can only promise to remember the victims: the dead of Nyarubuye, the wounded and the traumatized, the orphans and the refugees, all of the lost ones whose hands reach out through the ever lengthening distance. At the very outset I asked what it was that dreams asked of us.[1] Perhaps they request something very ordinary: simply that we do not forget.

---

[1] Keane began the book by describing his nightmares in the months after leaving Rwanda. In them "the brothers and sisters, the mothers and fathers and children, all the great wailing families of the night are back, holding fast with their withering hands, demanding my attention."

◆

Terrorism in a Global Age

On the morning of September 11, 2001, four U.S. commercial airliners—two from Logan Airport in Boston, and one each from Dulles International Airport in Washington, DC, and Newark International Airport in New Jersey—were hijacked shortly after departure by members of al-Qaeda, a terrorist organization founded in the 1980s by Osama bin Laden. One of the four jets was commandeered by passengers and crashed in a field in southwestern Pennsylvania without any survivors, but the other three jets found their targets. One was flown to Washington, DC, where it crashed into the Pentagon, the symbol of U.S. military might; the other two were flown to New York City, where they smashed into the twin towers of the World Trade Center, a symbol of U.S. capitalism. The twin towers were destroyed, approximately three thousand people were killed, and the fight against terrorism became the priority of governments around the world.

Terrorism has a long history. Many histories of the subject begin with the first century C.E., when Roman authorities financed dissidents and malcontents to murder enemies in subject territories, and members of a small Jewish sect in Palestine assassinated officials and prominent individuals in and around Jerusalem to bring about the end of Roman rule. Terrorism's history includes the Assassins, an order of Shia Islam that used murder as a weapon against the Seljuk Turks; Catholics who sought to undermine England's Protestant government by plotting to blow up the houses of Parliament in 1605; and European anarchists and radical socialists who assassinated some fifty prominent politicians and heads of state from the late 1800s through the early 1900s.

After subsiding during and after World War I, terrorism revived after World War II. Beginning in the late 1940s, terrorist acts have been carried out in every part of the world, by groups espousing many different causes: anticolonialists in Africa and Asia; left-wing radicals in Europe; Zionists in Palestine; Arabs bent on the destruction of Israel; abortion foes in the United States; religious extremists in India, Northern Ireland, Indonesia, and Africa; enemies of apartheid in South Africa; and Chechen separatists in Russia, to name but a few. They also include obscure religious sects such as Aum Shinrikyo, whose members killed twelve and injured thousands when they released sarin gas in the Tokyo subway system in 1995; alienated individuals such as Theodore Kaczynski, the American opponent of technology whose letter bombs killed three and injured twenty-three before his arrest in 1997; and self-proclaimed patriots like Timothy McVeigh, who sought to strike a blow against U.S. government "tyranny" in 1995 when his truck bomb destroyed the federal building in Oklahoma City and killed 168.

In recent decades, terrorism has been identified mainly with the Middle East, whose peoples are both victims of terrorism and a major source of recruitment, organizational effort, and financing of terrorist activities. Bombings, hijackings, kidnappings, and assassinations related to Middle Eastern political and religious conflict took more than one thousand lives from the 1970s through the 1990s, but it was the attack on the World Trade Center and the Pentagon in 2001 that caused a seismic shift in world politics and made the prevention of terrorism the twenty-first century's first great challenge.

The Worldview of Osama bin Laden

◆

103 ◆ Osama bin Laden, *DECLARATION OF JIHAD AGAINST AMERICANS OCCUPYING THE LAND OF THE TWO HOLY MOSQUES*

Osama bin Laden, the founder of al-Qaeda, was born in 1957 in Saudi Arabia, the son of a billionaire construction company owner and a Syrian woman, who was his tenth or eleventh wife. Raised as a Wahhabi Muslim, young bin Laden led a privileged existence of private schooling, Scandinavian vacations, and English lessons in Oxford. At age 17, he enrolled as an engineering student at King Abdul Aziz University in Jeddah, Saudi Arabia, where he became interested in Islamic theology and forged friendships with Islamic radicals. In 1980, he went to the Pakistani-Afghan border to aid Afghan holy warriors, or mujahideen, who were fighting Soviet troops who had invaded Afghanistan in late 1979 to prop up the pro-Soviet regime. Using his inheritance (perhaps as much as $300 million), he built an organization to provide money and weapons for the Muslim volunteers who had flocked to Afghanistan; from the mid-1980s onward, he joined the fighting. Out of these contacts and activities, al-Qaeda (meaning "the base" in Arabic) took shape under bin Laden's direction.

On his return to Saudi Arabia, bin Laden became an outspoken critic of the Saudi regime, especially its acceptance of the U.S. military presence during and after the first Persian Gulf War. In 1991, he fled to Sudan, where he extended and expanded al-Qaeda to include as many as several thousand agents, who worked in cells ranging from the Philippines to the United States.

Source: Osama bin Laden.

Between 1992 and 1995, al-Qaeda was linked to attacks on U.S. troops in Yemen and Somalia, the bombing of an U.S.-operated Saudi National Guard training center in Riyadh, and unsuccessful plots to assassinate Pope John Paul II, President Bill Clinton, and Egyptian president Hosni Mubarak. Under U.S. pressure, the Sudanese government expelled bin Laden in 1996, forcing al-Qaeda to establish a new base in Afghanistan, which was then coming under the control of the radical Islamic group known as the Taliban. Between 1996 and 2000, al-Qaeda was responsible for more acts of terrorism: the car bombing of an apartment building in Dhahran, Saudi Arabia, that killed nineteen U.S. soldiers; the simultaneous bombings of U.S. embassies in Tanzania and Kenya that killed 234 and injured several thousand; and the attack on the *USS Cole* in Aden, Yemen, that killed seventeen U.S. sailors and wounded thirty-nine. After the attacks on the World Trade Center and the Pentagon on September 11, 2001, the United States invaded Afghanistan, ended Taliban rule, and smashed al-Qaeda headquarters and training camps. Bin Laden eluded capture, however, until May 2, 2011, when in a covert operation ordered by U.S. President Obama, he was shot and killed by U.S. Navy SEALs inside a private residential compound in Abbottabad, Pakistan.

Bin Laden published little, and as leader of a secret organization, gave few interviews or public speeches. One exception is the speech he delivered to his followers in Afghanistan in August 1996 in which he "declared war" on the United States. Printed in Arabic-language newspapers and audiotaped for worldwide distribution, bin Laden's speech describes his motives and priorities.

QUESTIONS FOR ANALYSIS

1. How does bin Laden perceive the Muslims' place in the world? Who are their main enemies?
2. Why does bin Laden oppose the existing government of Saudi Arabia?
3. What are the goals of the "Zionist-Crusaders alliance," according to bin Laden?
4. What lessons can be learned, according to bin Laden, from the U.S. response to terrorist attacks and military setbacks in Beirut, Aden, and Somalia?
5. Why is bin Laden convinced that Muslims will triumph in their struggle with the United States?
6. What do you perceive as bin Laden's ultimate political and religious goals?

It should not be hidden from you that the community of Islam has suffered from aggression, iniquity and injustice imposed on them by the Zionist-Crusaders alliance and their collabo-rators; ... Their blood was spilled in Palestine and Iraq. The horrifying pictures of the massacre of Qana[1] in Lebanon are still fresh in our memory. Massacres in Tajikistan, Burma, Kashmir,

---

[1]In April 1996, the Israelis launched a two-week bombardment of territory in southern Lebanon against the terrorist group Hezbollah. On April 18, one hundred civilians were killed when the Israelis shelled the battalion headquarters of a UN peacekeeping force where some eight hundred Lebanese had taken refuge. The Israelis blamed "technical and procedural errors," an explanation questioned by an official UN report.

Assam, the Philippines, Fatani, Ogadin, Somalia, Eritrea, Chechnya and in Bosnia Herzegovina[2] took place, massacres that send shivers in the body and shake the conscience. All of this and the world watched and listened, and not only didn't respond to these atrocities, but also with a conspiracy between the USA and its allies and under the cover of the iniquitous United Nations the dispossessed people were even prevented from obtaining arms to defend themselves.

The people of Islam awakened and realized that they are the main target for the aggression of the Zionist-Crusaders alliance. All false claims and propaganda about "Human Rights" were hammered down and exposed by the massacres that took place against the Muslims in every part of the world....

Today we work to lift the iniquity that had been imposed on the Umma [the Muslim community] by the Zionist-Crusaders alliance, particularly after they have occupied the blessed land of Jerusalem ... and the land of the two Holy Places.[3] ... We wish to study the means by which we could return the situation [in Saudi Arabia] to its normal path and to return to the people their own rights, particularly after the large damages and the great aggression on the life and the religion of the people. . . .

Injustice [in Saudi Arabia] had affected the people in industry and agriculture. It affected the people of the rural and urban areas. And almost everybody complains about something. The situation at the land of the two Holy Places became like a huge volcano at the verge of eruption that would destroy the Kuffar [non-believers] and the corruption and its sources.... People are fully concerned about their everyday living; everybody talks about the deterioration of the economy, inflation, ever increasing debts and jails full of prisoners.

Through its course of actions the regime has torn off its legitimacy:

(1) Suspension of the Islamic Sharia law and exchanging it with man-made civil law....

(2) The inability of the regime to protect the country and allowing the enemy of the Umma, the American crusader forces, to occupy the land for the longest of years.... As a result of the policy imposed on the country, especially in the oil industry where production is restricted or expanded and prices are fixed to suit the American economy, ignoring the economy of the country. Expensive deals were imposed on the country to purchase arms. People are asking what then is the justification for the very existence of the regime?

But to our deepest regret the regime refused to listen to the people....

The regime is fully responsible for what has been incurred by the country and the nation; however, the occupying American enemy is the principal and the main cause of the situation. Therefore efforts should be concentrated on destroying, fighting and killing the enemy until, by the Grace of Allah, it is completely defeated....

It is incredible that our country is the world's largest buyer of arms from the USA and the area's biggest commercial partner of the Americans who are assisting their Zionist brothers in occupying Palestine and in evicting and killing the Muslims there, by providing arms, men and financial support. To deny these occupiers ... the enormous revenues from their trade with our country is a very important help for our Jihad against them. . . .

---

[2]This is a rather wide-ranging list. The massacres in Assam, a province of northeastern India, were carried out by an Assam separatist group in 1990 and claimed several dozen victims, not all of whom were Muslims. Attacks on Burmese Muslims in the early 1990s were carried out by Buddhists.

[3]Mecca, the birthplace of Muhammad and the site of the Kabah, Islam's holiest shrine, and Medina, the city to which Muhammad and his followers fled in 622 C.E. Both are in Saudi Arabia.

We expect the women of the land of the two Holy Places and other countries to carry out their role in boycotting the American goods. If economic boycott is intertwined with the military operations of the Mujahideen {holy warriors}, then defeating the enemy will be even nearer, by the Permission of Allah. . . .

❖ ❖

A few days ago the news agencies had reported that the Defense Secretary[4] of the Crusading Americans had said that "the explosions at Riyadh and Al Khobar[5] had taught him one lesson: that is, not to withdraw when attacked by coward terrorists."

We say to the Defense Secretary that his talk can induce a grieving mother to laughter! . . . Where was this false courage of yours when the explosion in Beirut took place in 1983? You were turned into scattered bits and pieces at that time; 241 marine soldiers were killed.[6] And where was this courage of yours when two explosions made you leave Aden in less than twenty-four hours![7]

But your most disgraceful case was in Somalia;[8] where you moved an international force, including twenty-eight thousand American soldiers. . . . However, when tens of your soldiers were killed in minor battles and one American pilot was dragged in the streets of Mogadishu you left the area carrying disappointment, humiliation, defeat and your dead with you. Clinton appeared in front of the whole world threatening and promising revenge, but these threats were merely a preparation for withdrawal. You have been disgraced by Allah and you withdrew; the extent of your impotence and weaknesses became very clear. . . .

Since the sons of the land of the two Holy Places feel and strongly believe that fighting against the nonbelievers in every part of the world is absolutely essential; then they would be even more enthusiastic, more powerful and larger in number upon fighting on their own land, the place of their births. . . . They know that the Muslims of the world will assist and help them to victory. I say to you William {Perry} that: These youths love death as you love life. They inherit dignity, pride, courage, generosity, truthfulness and sacrifice from father to father. They are most . . . steadfast at war. They inherit these values from their ancestors. . . .

These youths believe in what has been told by Allah and His messenger about the greatness of the reward for the Mujahideen martyrs. . . .

Those youths know that their reward in fighting you, the USA, is double their reward in fighting someone else. They have no intention except to enter paradise by killing you. . . .

In the heat of battle they do not care, and cure the insanity of the enemy by their "insane" courage. Terrorizing you, while you are carrying arms on our land, is a legitimate and morally required duty. It is a legitimate right well known to all humans and other creatures. Your example and our example is like a snake which entered into a house of a man and got killed by him. The coward is the man who lets you walk, while carrying arms, freely on his land and provides you with peace and security.

Those youths are different from your soldiers. Your problem will be how to convince your troops to fight, while our problem will be how to restrain our youths to wait for their turn in

---

[4]William Perry, secretary of defense between 1994 and 1997.
[5]In November 1995, a car bomb at a Saudi National Guard training center in Riyadh killed five Americans; the bombing of Khobar Towers, a U.S. Air Force housing complex in Dhahran, Saudi Arabia, killed nineteen Americans.
[6]President Reagan ordered the withdrawal of marine peacekeepers after a bomb killed 241 marines and navy seamen in October 1983 in Beirut.

[7]The Pentagon withdrew one hundred army personnel after the U.S. embassy in Aden was bombed in 1993.
[8]President Clinton ordered the withdrawal of U.S. peacekeepers from Somalia by March 1994 after a clash with Somali warlords in Mogadishu in October 1993 resulted in the deaths of eighteen army rangers.

fighting.... The youths hold you responsible for all of the killings and evictions of the Muslims and the violation of the sancties, carried out by your Zionist brothers in Lebanon; you openly supplied them with arms and finance. More than 600,000 Iraqi children have died due to lack of food and medicine and as a result of the unjustifiable aggression imposed on Iraq and its nation.[9]

The children of Iraq are our children. You, the USA, together with the Saudi regime are responsible for the shedding of the blood of these innocent children. Due to all of that, whatever treaty you have with our country is now null and void....

It is a duty now on every tribe on the Arab Peninsula to fight in the cause of Allah and to cleanse the land from those occupiers. Allah knows that their blood is permitted to be spilled and their wealth is a booty to those who kill them.... Our youths know that the humiliation suffered by the Muslims as a result of the occupation of their Holy Places cannot be removed except by explosions and Jihad.

---

[9]The alleged victims of economic sanctions imposed on Iraq after the first Persian Gulf War.

The Final Step Toward Martyrdom

◈

104 ◆ Mohammed Atta, *THE LAST NIGHT*

Mohammed Atta was born in a Cairo suburb on September 1, 1968, and died on September 11, 2001, when he flew a hijacked passenger jet into one of the towers of the World Trade Center in Lower Manhattan. The son of a lawyer, Atta graduated with a degree in architecture from Cairo University. He then moved to Hamburg, Germany, where he was a student at the Technical University and a part-time employee at a Hamburg consulting firm. Devoted to Islam, he made a pilgrimage to Mecca in 1995, and on his return to Hamburg was recruited by al-Qaeda. By the late 1990s his apartment was a meeting place for the Hamburg cell. Late in 1999, it is likely that he met Osama bin Laden at al-Qaeda's base in Afghanistan. In June 2000, Atta entered the United States and attended a flight school in Venice, Florida. In 2001, he briefly visited Germany and Spain and then returned to Florida, where he took additional flying lessons. On the morning of September 11, 2001, he and another conspirator drove from their motel in South Portland, Maine, to Portland International Airport, flew to Boston, and boarded American Airlines Flight 11.

It was later discovered that Atta had left behind a bag containing airline uniforms, flight manuals, and a four-page document in Arabic, copies of which were also found in the effects of two of the other terrorists. The document is a list of Atta's instructions for the nineteen terrorists to review on the night of September 10. Excerpts from these instructions follow.

Source: Translated and © Capital Communications Group, Inc. Washington, DC. Used by permission.

QUESTIONS FOR ANALYSIS

1. According to Atta, how should the participants prepare themselves for what lies ahead of them?
2. Is Atta totally confident about the success of the mission? What might go wrong, and what can be done to prevent failure?
3. What rewards can the participants expect from their anticipated martyrdom?
4. What feelings does Atta express about the victims of their actions?
5. On the basis of this document, what conclusions can be drawn about Atta's and, by extension, the other participants' motives?

1. Make an oath to die and renew your intentions. Shave excess hair from the body and wear cologne. Shower.[1]
2. Make sure you know all aspects of the plan well, and expect the response, or a reaction, from the enemy.
3. Read al-Tawba and Anfal[2] and reflect on their meanings and remember all of the things that God has promised for the martyrs.
4. Remind your soul to listen and obey and remember that you will face decisive situations that might prevent you from 100 percent obedience, so tame your soul, purify it, convince it, make it understand, and incite it.
5. Pray during the night and be persistent in asking God to give you victory, control and conquest, and that he may make your task easier and not expose us.
6. Remember God frequently, and the best way to do it is to read the Holy Quran....
7. Purify your soul from all unclean things. Completely forget something called "this world." The time for play is over and the serious time is upon us. How much time have we wasted in our lives? Shouldn't we take advantage of these last hours to offer good deeds and obedience?
8. You should feel complete tranquility, because the time between you and your marriage [in heaven] is very short [soon to come]. Afterward begins the happy life, where God is satisfied with you, and eternal bliss "in the company of the prophets, the companions, the martyrs and the good people, who are all good company." ...
9. Keep in mind that, if you fall into hardship, how will you act and how will you remain steadfast and remember that you will return to God and remember that anything that happens to you could never be avoided, and what did not happen to you could never have happened to you....
10. Remember the words of Almighty God [lines from the Quran]: ... "How many small groups beat big groups by the will of God." And his words: "If God gives you victory, no one can beat you. And if he betrays you, who can give you victory without Him? So the faithful put their trust in God." ...

12. Bless your body with some verses of the Quran [done by reading verses into one's hands and then rubbing the hands over whatever is to be blessed], the luggage, clothes, the knife, your personal effects, your ID, your passport, and all of your papers.
13. Check your weapon before you leave and long before you leave. (You must make your knife sharp and you must not discomfort your animal during the slaughter.) ...

---

[1]These are ritual acts of self-purification to prepare oneself for martyrdom and salvation.

[2]The ninth and eighth chapters (suras) of the Quran, sometimes referred to as the "war chapters," describe the need for holy war against Islam's persecutors.

THE SECOND STEP

When the taxi takes you to (M) [this initial probably stands for *matar*, airport in Arabic] remember God constantly while in the car....

When you have reached (M) and have left the taxi, say a supplication of place ["O Lord, I ask you for the best of this place, and ask you to protect me from its evils"], and everywhere you go ... smile and be calm, for God is with the believers. And the angels protect you without you feeling anything. Say this supplication: "God is more dear than all of his creation." And say: "O Lord, protect me from them as you wish." And say: "O Lord, take your anger out on them [the enemy] and we ask you to protect us from their evils." And say: "O Lord, block their vision from in front of them, so that they may not see." And say: "God is all we need, he is the best to rely upon." ...

All of their equipment and gates and technology will not prevent, nor harm, except by God's will. The believers do not fear such things. The only ones that fear it are the allies of Satan, who are the brothers of the devil ... [and who] who are fascinated with Western civilization, and have drunk the love [of the West] like they drink water....

Whoever says, "There is no God but God," with all his heart, goes to heaven. The prophet, peace be upon him, said: "If you put all the worlds and universes on one side of the balance, and 'No God but God' on the other, 'No God but God' will weigh more heavily." You can repeat these words confidently, and this is just one of the strengths of these words....

Also, do not seem confused or show signs of nervous tension. Be happy, optimistic, calm because you are heading for a deed that God loves and will accept [as a good deed]. It will be the day, God willing, you spend with the women of paradise....

THE THIRD PHASE

When you ride the (T) [this initial probably stands for *tayyara*, airplane in Arabic], before your foot steps in it, and before you enter it, you make a prayer and supplications. Remember that this is a battle for the sake of God.... When the (T) moves, even slightly, toward (Q) [unknown reference], say the supplication of travel....

And then it takes off.... Pray for yourself and all of your brothers that they may be victorious and hit their targets and [unclear] and ask God to grant you martyrdom facing the enemy, not running away from it, and for him to grant you patience and the feeling that anything that happens to you is for him....

When the confrontation begins, strike like champions who do not want to go back to this world. Shout, "Allahu Akbar" ["God is great"], because this strikes fear in the hearts of the non-believers.... Know that the gardens of paradise are waiting for you in all their beauty, and the women of paradise are waiting, calling out, "Come hither, friend of God." They have dressed in their most beautiful clothing.

If God decrees that any of you are to slaughter, you should dedicate the slaughter to your fathers ... because you have obligations toward them.... If you slaughter, do not cause the discomfort of those you are killing, because this is one of the practices of the prophet, peace be upon him....

Then implement the way of the prophet in taking prisoners. Take prisoners and kill them. As Almighty God said: "No prophet should have prisoners until he has soaked the land with blood. You want the bounties of this world [in exchange for prisoners] and God wants the other world [for you], and God is all-powerful, all-wise." ...

... When the hour of reality approaches, the zero hour ... wholeheartedly welcome death for the sake of God. Always be remembering God. Either end your life while praying, seconds before the target, or make your last words: "There is no God but God, Muhammad is his messenger."

Afterward, we will all meet in the highest heaven, God willing....

And may the peace of the God be upon the prophet.

◆

Internet Freedom: U.S. and Chinese Views

China's astonishing economic growth since the 1990s has been accompanied by an equally amazing explosion of the Chinese people's Internet use. In 1995, just one year after the Internet became available to China's general population, the country had 16 million users, consisting of only 0.4 percent of the population. The number rose to 103 million in 2005 and reached 477 million in 2011, just over 35 percent of the population. This made China the world leader in Internet usage, and created a formidable challenge for China's authoritarian rulers, who understood the Internet's importance for the country's economic and technological development but feared the political dangers of its ease of use and openness.

As a result, beginning in the 1990s, the Chinese government began to institute a series of regulations that now makes China a world leader in Internet repression and control. In December 1997, the government made it illegal to use the Internet for the following: inciting law-breaking, terrorism, and the overthrow of the socialist system; promoting falsehoods that threatened the social order; and damaging the reputation of state organizations. It also banned vaguely defined "other activities" against China's constitution, laws, and administrative regulations. In 2000, the government introduced the Golden Shield Project (also known as the "Great Firewall of China"), a content-filtering system that blocks blacklisted sites and sites that contain certain words or names. Although Internet controls were loosened in the summer of 2008 when China hosted the Olympics, they were reimposed and tightened after the athletes left. It is estimated that the government employs thirty-five thousand individuals to monitor and control Internet content and that more than 1.3 million websites are closed to Chinese users.

Foreign corporations that entered the Chinese market were expected to adhere to the government's regulations. Yahoo!, which entered the mainland Chinese market in 2004, and Microsoft MSN, which entered a year later, also accepted the additional requirement of "self-censorship," which meant that they would not respond to or supply complete information in connection with certain search requests. Both companies have been accused of providing the Chinese government with information leading to the arrest of several Chinese dissidents. When the U.S.-based Internet giant Google entered the Chinese market in 2006, it too accepted government controls and agreed to practice self-censorship, despite its stated goal "to organize the world's information and make it universally accessible and useful."

The efforts of China (and other authoritarian states) to censor the Internet have been criticized by organizations such as Reporters Without Borders and Amnesty International. They also have been a source of tension between China and the United States and other Western democracies, which have criticized China's human rights record, especially after the crackdown against student demonstrators in Beijing on June 4, 1989—the so-called Tiananmen Incident. Since then, the United States has pressured China to end its repressive policies by issuing reports on human rights abuses, threatening trade sanctions, and having China criticized in public forums, such as the annual meetings of the United Nations Human Rights Commission. China has rejected such criticism, claiming that its human rights record has been distorted by foreign governments that have no right to interfere in their internal affairs.

Internet Freedom and Human Rights

◆

105 ◆ Hillary Rodham Clinton, *REMARKS ON INTERNET FREEDOM, JANUARY 21, 2010*

On January 12, 2010, David Drummond, Google's chief legal officer, announced in a blog titled "A New Approach to China" that Google had been the object of "a highly sophisticated and targeted attack on our corporate infrastructure originating from China that resulted in the theft of intellectual property from Google." Theft of intellectual property was only part of the story, however. Drummond also asserted that the main purpose of the cyberattacks had been to access the Gmail accounts of Chinese dissidents. He also claimed that "dozens of U.S.-, China- and Europe-based Gmail users who are advocates of human rights in China appear to have been routinely accessed by third parties." Drummond claimed such attacks "go the heart of a much bigger global debate on freedom of speech" and suggested that Google might be forced to leave the Chinese market unless the government lifted its restrictions on Internet use.

A week later, Secretary of State Hillary Rodham Clinton delivered a sweeping "Internet freedom" speech, in which she called for nations to punish perpetrators of cyberattacks meant to quiet citizens and disrupt businesses abroad. Although China was one of many nations Clinton criticized, those who heard or read the speech (including the Chinese) knew that her speech was a reaction to Drummond's blog and a direct condemnation of Chinese Internet policies.

QUESTIONS FOR ANALYSIS

1. According to the secretary, what motivates the United States to defend Internet freedom?
2. In Clinton's view, how will increased Internet freedom specifically contribute to the spread of democracy and better government?
3. How will economically backward societies benefit from unrestricted Internet usage?
4. According to Clinton, how have authoritarian governments specifically attempted to restrict Internet access and usage?

Source: U.S. Department of State website. http://www.state.gov/secretary/rm/2010/01/135519.htm

The spread of information networks is forming a new nervous system for our planet. When something happens in Haiti or Hunan, the rest of us learn about it in real time—from real people,... And we can respond in real time as well. As we sit here, any of you—or maybe more likely, any of our children—can take out the tools that many carry every day and transmit this discussion to billions across the world.

Now, in many respects, information has never been so free. There are more ways to spread more ideas to more people than at any moment in history. And even in authoritarian countries, information networks are helping people discover new facts and making governments more accountable.

During his visit to China in November [2009], for example, President Obama held a town hall meeting with an online component to highlight the importance of the internet. In response to a question that was sent in over the internet, he defended the right of people to freely access information, and said that the more freely information flows, the stronger societies become. He spoke about how access to information helps citizens hold their own governments accountable, generates new ideas, encourages creativity and entrepreneurship. The United States belief in that ground truth is what brings me here today.

Because amid this unprecedented surge in connectivity, we must also recognize that these technologies are not an unmitigated blessing.... The same networks that help organize movements for freedom also enable al-Qaida to spew hatred and incite violence against the innocent. And technologies with the potential to open up access to government and promote transparency can also be hijacked by governments to crush dissent and deny human rights.

In the last year, we've seen a spike in threats to the free flow of information. China, Tunisia, and Uzbekistan have stepped up their censorship of the internet. In Vietnam, access to popular social networking sites has suddenly disappeared. And last Friday in Egypt, 30 bloggers and activists were detained.[1] ... So while it is clear that the spread of these technologies is transforming our world, it is still unclear how that transformation will affect the human rights and the human welfare of the world's population.

On their own, new technologies do not take sides in the struggle for freedom and progress, but the United States does. We stand for a single internet where all of humanity has equal access to knowledge and ideas. And we recognize that the world's information infrastructure will become what we and others make of it. Now, this challenge may be new, but our responsibility to help ensure the free exchange of ideas goes back to the birth of our republic....

Franklin Roosevelt built on these ideas when he delivered his Four Freedoms speech in 1941.[2] ... And years later, one of my heroes, Eleanor Roosevelt, worked to have these principles adopted as a cornerstone of the Universal Declaration of Human Rights.[3] They have provided a lodestar to every succeeding generation, guiding us, galvanizing us, and enabling us to move forward in the face of uncertainty.

So as technology hurtles forward, we must think back to that legacy. We need to synchronize our technological progress with our principles....

... As I speak to you today, government censors somewhere are working furiously to erase my words from the records of history. But history itself has already condemned these tactics. Two months ago, I was in Germany to celebrate the 20th anniversary of the fall of the Berlin Wall. The leaders gathered at that ceremony paid tribute to the courageous men and women on the far side of that barrier who made the

---

[1]In other words, just months before the beginning of the Arab Spring of late 2010 and 2011, when a wave of demonstrations across the Middle East and North Africa challenged the established political order. Participants in the demonstrations used social media such as Facebook, Twitter, YouTube, and Skype to organize the demonstrations and communicate with one another.

[2]President Franklin Roosevelt delivered the "Four Freedoms" speech on January 6, 1941.

[3]The United Nations Universal Declaration of Human Rights was adopted on December 10, 1948.

case against oppression by circulating small pamphlets called samizdat. Now, these leaflets questioned the claims and intentions of dictatorships in the Eastern Bloc and many people paid dearly for distributing them. But their words helped pierce the concrete and concertina wire[4] of the Iron Curtain.

The Berlin Wall symbolized a world divided and it defined an entire era. Today, remnants of that wall sit inside this museum[5] where they belong, and the new iconic infrastructure of our age is the internet. Instead of division, it stands for connection. But even as networks spread to nations around the globe, virtual walls are cropping up in place of visible walls.

Some countries have erected electronic barriers that prevent their people from accessing portions of the world's networks. They've expunged words, names, and phrases from search engine results. They have violated the privacy of citizens who engage in non-violent political speech.... With the spread of these restrictive practices, a new information curtain is descending across much of the world. And beyond this partition, viral videos and blog posts are becoming the samizdat of our day.

The internet can help bridge divides between people of different faiths. As the President said in Cairo, freedom of religion is central to the ability of people to live together. And as we look for ways to expand dialogue, the internet holds out such tremendous promise....

◆ ◆

There are, of course, hundreds of millions of people living without the benefits of these technologies. In our world, as I've said many times, talent may be distributed universally, but opportunity is not. And we know from long experience that promoting social and economic development in countries where people lack access to knowledge, markets, capital, and opportunity can be frustrating and sometimes futile work. In this context, the internet can serve as a great equalizer. By providing people with access to knowledge and potential markets, networks can create opportunities where none exist.

Over the last year, I've seen this firsthand in Kenya, where farmers have seen their income grow by as much as 30 percent since they started using mobile banking technology; in Bangladesh, where more than 300,000 people have signed up to learn English on their mobile phones; and in Sub-Saharan Africa, where women entrepreneurs use the internet to get access to microcredit loans and connect themselves to global markets.

Now, these examples of progress can be replicated in the lives of the billion people at the bottom of the world's economic ladder. In many cases, the internet, mobile phones, and other connection technologies can do for economic growth what the Green Revolution[6] did for a agriculture. You can now generate significant yields from very modest inputs. And one World Bank study found that in a typical developing country, a 10 percent increase in the penetration rate for mobile phones led to an almost 1 percent increase in per capita GDP [Gross Domestic Product]. To just put this into context, for India, that would translate into almost $10 billion a year.

A connection to global information networks is like an on-ramp to modernity. In the early years of these technologies, many believed that they would divide the world between haves and have-nots. But that hasn't happened. There are 4 billion cell phones in use today. Many of them are in the hands of market vendors, rickshaw drivers, and others who've historically lacked access to education and opportunity. Information networks have become a great leveler,

---

[4]A type of barbed wire formed in large coils that can be expanded or contracted like a concertina, an accordion-like musical instrument.

[5]The speech was delivered in the Newseum, a museum of journalism in Washington DC.

[6]Green Revolution refers to a number of innovations, including irrigation projects, new plant varieties, and the use of chemical fertilizers and pesticides, that increased worldwide agricultural production from the 1940s through the late 1970s.

and we should use them together to help lift people out of poverty and give them a freedom from want.

◆ ◆

The freedom to connect is like the freedom of assembly, only in cyberspace. It allows individuals to get online, come together, and hopefully cooperate. Once you're on the internet, you don't need to be a tycoon or a rock star to have a huge impact on society.

The largest public response to the terrorist attacks in Mumbai [2008] was launched by a 13-year-old boy. He used social networks to organize blood drives and a massive interfaith book of condolence. In Colombia, an unemployed engineer brought together more than 12 million people in 190 cities around the world to demonstrate against the FARC[7] terrorist movement. The protests were the largest antiterrorist demonstrations in history. And in the weeks that followed, the FARC saw more demobilizations and desertions than it had during a decade of military action. And in Mexico, a single email from a private citizen who was fed up with drug-related violence snowballed into huge demonstrations in all of the country's 32 states. In Mexico City alone, 150,000 people took to the streets in protest. . . .

Now, the principles I've outlined today will guide our approach in addressing the issue of internet freedom and the use of these technologies. And I want to speak about how we apply them in practice. The United States is committed to devoting the diplomatic, economic, and technological resources necessary to advance these freedoms.

. . . And I'm proud that the State Department is already working in more than 40 countries to help individuals silenced by oppressive governments. We are making this issue a priority at the United Nations as well, and we're including internet freedom as a component in the first resolution we introduced after returning to the United Nations Human Rights Council.

We are also supporting the development of new tools that enable citizens to exercise their rights of free expression by circumventing politically motivated censorship. We are providing funds to groups around the world to make sure that those tools get to the people who need them in local languages, and with the training they need to access the internet safely . . . . Both the American people and nations that censor the internet should understand that our government is committed to helping promote internet freedom.

Increasingly, U.S. companies are making the issue of internet and information freedom a greater consideration in their business decisions. I hope that their competitors and foreign governments will pay close attention to this trend. The most recent situation involving Google has attracted a great deal of interest. And we look to the Chinese authorities to conduct a thorough review of the cyber intrusions that led Google to make its announcement. And we also look for that investigation and its results to be transparent.

The internet has already been a source of tremendous progress in China, and it is fabulous. There are so many people in China now online. But countries that restrict free access to information or violate the basic rights of internet users risk walling themselves off from the progress of the next century. Now, the United States and China have different views on this issue, and we intend to address those differences candidly and consistently in the context of our positive, cooperative, and comprehensive relationship.

---

[7]FARC refers to the Revolutionary Armed Forces of Colombia, the military wing of the Colombian communist party.

China Responds

106 ◆ *Editorials from the* People's Daily

It did not take long for the Chinese government to respond to Drummond's blog and Secretary of State Clinton's speech. A number of Chinese officials denounced the speech, and the *People's Daily*, a newspaper that is the official organ of the Chinese Communist Party, did the same in a series of editorials. Excerpts from three of these editorials follow.

The Google controversy continued in the following months. On March 23, Google began to redirect all search queries from Google China to Google Hong Kong, which enabled them to bypass Chinese regulators and provide uncensored search results. On March 30, the Chinese government banned searching via all Google search sites in mainland China, but the ban was lifted the following day. On June 30, Google ended the automatic redirect of Google China to Google Hong Kong, and instead placed a link to Google Hong Kong to avoid getting its Internet Content Provider license revoked. Less than a year later, Google announced in June 2011 that suspected Chinese hackers had tried to steal passwords of hundreds of Google email account holders, including senior U.S. government officials, Chinese activists, and journalists. The claim sparked an angry response from Beijing, which said blaming China was "unacceptable."

QUESTIONS FOR ANALYSIS

1. According to the Chinese editorial writers, how is the United States hoping to benefit from the Google controversy?
2. How do the writers justify the Internet restrictions imposed by the Chinese government?
3. According to the editorial writers, what lesson is to be drawn from the breakup of the Soviet Union in the early 1990s?
4. According to the editorial writers, why is the U.S. attack on Chinese Internet policy hypocritical?
5. According to the author of "To Defend 'Freedom' ... ," what may be the true reasons Google is threatening to leave China?

GOOGLE, DO NOT TAKE CHINESE NETIZENS HOSTAGE
January 19, 2010

It is ordinary for a commercial company to enter and exit the Chinese market, but this is not the case for Google. Firstly, it gave the Chinese government an ultimatum, requiring the latter to make a concession, which is obviously political in nature. In addition, Google's move won the collective support from the U.S. government, congress and western media agencies,

Source: From *People's Daily*, January 19, 25, 16.

so this event has completely been politicized. Such politicization was not provoked by China, but imposed by the U.S. and the west onto China....

Of course, the result of the event must be that Chinese government will never violate the rules of the market and laws for the sake of a commercial company, let alone give up its political bottom line and diplomatic principles because of a note from the U.S. government.

It is a lie to claim that the Internet is an absolutely free space without regulations. The truth is that it is the extension of the real world. Therefore, implementing monitoring according to a country's national context is what any government has to do. World countries including the U.S. do not permit the existence of a laissez-faire Internet world either. To combat terrorism after the "9/11" terrorist attack, the U.S. has permitted police to search civilian emails and even monitor their communications without permission. Western countries such as Canada, Australia, New Zealand, the U.K., Germany and Sweden have also passed similar bills.

In recent years, China has sincerely opened up to the outside world. However, China follows its own course while learning from the west and its reluctance to copy the internet control and supervision mode of the U.S. does not contradict its adherence to the "4 Cardinal Principles"[1] released in the early stage of the opening up and reform. At that time, even in China, some people raised doubts about the Chinese government's choice. However, when looking back, we now can find that the government's choice is correct. In contrast, Gorbachev was once widely praised by the west and his political reform even won much admiration in China. But, it was Gorbachev that finally ruined the Soviet Union. Therefore, China must not follow the western world's practice on crucial issues such as Internet control

and supervision. Of course, China is progressing and its Internet industry should advance accordingly. However, China must have its own plan on how to regulate and deregulate the Internet and should not and will not follow orders from Google's CEO and the U.S. Department of State.

Google's CEO Eric Schmidt stated that he "loves China and the Chinese people." The author of this article holds that such love should not be empty talk. Google should show its sincerity by taking practical actions and should first abide by China's laws and not seek any privilege in China, stop launching surprise attacks against China if it really "loves China." At the same time, Google should take the Chinese people's feelings into consideration and stop using Chinese customers as hostage to confront the Chinese government....

By now, a year and a half have passed since the financial crisis, which badly damaged the reputation of the U.S., broke out.[2] From a series of movements that the U.S. government made recently, we can see that the U.S. is trying to recover and maintain its own outlook of values. We do not hope that giant multinational enterprises such as Google will become pure political tools for the U.S. to export its own concepts of values. A lot of Chinese people like Google, but they do not want to become tools being used by Google.

"INTERNET FREEDOM" AND "SMART POWER" DIPLOMACY
January 25, 2010

The United States has lambasted "China's policies to administer the Internet."...

In her speech in Washington D.C., Hillary Clinton mentioned China four times and referred to it as among a number of countries where there has been a "spike in threats to the free flow of information." ...

---

[1]Announced by Deng Xiaoping in 1979, the four cardinal principles could not be questioned or debated. They were the principles of upholding the socialist path, the people's democratic dictatorship, the leadership of the Communist Party of China, and Marxist-Leninist-Mao Zedong thought.

The implication was that political issues other than these four could be debated.
[2]A reference to the collapse of the U.S. housing bubble and the financial crisis that followed.

If the moral high ground is short of real, practical support, however, it can hardly walk on and stand. Take for [example] the attack on Google; the United States urged China to make a thorough-going probe ... but the U.S. should first look into attack problems itself. Not long ago, the largest Chinese search engine Baidu[3] was attacked and the domain name registration service provider was right in the U.S. territory.

Then, let us look at "network freedom" in the U.S.: In order to resist Internet pornography, the U.S. "Children's Internet Protection Act" ... requires all public network resources to curb internet child porn, a serious crime in the country; in order to respond to threats, the Pentagon has developed a new type of troops – cyber troops, and also adopted several measures to beef up the military's cyber warfare capacity; shortly after the September 11, 2001 terrorist attacks, the U.S. Congress approved the Patriot Act to grant its security agencies the right to search telephone and e-mail communications in the name of anti-terrorism ...

It is thus evident that with any freedom, people are not meant to do whatever they want, but they still need the norms of law and order, which constitute the basic premise of "network freedom." On the one hand, you take rigid control of your cyber[space] and on the other, you ask other counties to establish a network of [a] free utopia type. So, this cannot but be called the continued application of double standards.

TO DEFEND "FREEDOM" OR TO DEFEND "HEGEMONY"
January 26, 2010

The "Google case" is a politicized business issue in the final analysis. Google senior vice-president, David Drummond, said on January 13 in the official blog that "Google might have to pull all of its operations out of China." As for the reason, Google said it suffered a "highly sophisticated and targeted attack on our operation ...

On the Google retreat, is it really attributed to the so-called "cyber-attack" and "internet censorship"? Even U.S. internet security experts have acknowledged that Google entered China in 2006 after meticulous, prudent consideration of the decision. At present, Google search engine in China account merely for 35 percent market share, far behind Baidu China's largest search engine; Google's annual income from the country constitutes only less than 2 percent of its total global income.

Some of China's internet industry insiders maintain that Google has been looking for an excuse for its failure due to its "inability to adapt" and loss to Chinese domestic firms.

It is not difficult, however, to see the shadow of the US government behind the highly politicized "Google" case....

As a matter of fact, the U.S.'s international conduct is determined by its "imperial mindset," as the "United Morning News," Singapore's leading newspaper and a major Chinese morning daily, said in a recent commentary that one of its salient features is to direct other nations' policies so as to maximize its own interests.

Around the "Google" incident, the United States has not only focused on the commercial interest of domestic companies and safeguard its own national security . . . but also is trying hard to limit China's cyberspace. This is something totally unacceptable.

To date, Google executives have expressed the hope to go on negotiating with the Chinese government and continue to stay in China, and Google has perhaps come to realize that China could do without it, whereas Google will definitely have no future without China.

---

[3]Founded in 2000, Baidu is a Chinese Web services company. It is publically traded on the NASDAQ stock market, based in New York City.

Human Development in the Era of Globalization

Globalization refers, first of all, to a world of free trade, open markets, and capitalist competition in which goods, services, and capital flow across seamless international borders. It also refers to a world in which a remarkable series of technological breakthroughs—computers, communications satellites, fiberoptic cable, and especially the Internet—have destroyed the barriers of time and space. It refers, finally, to a world of increasing cultural homogeneity, in which tastes in music, art, architecture, personal dress, and countless other areas of life have become increasingly standardized and, for better or worse, Westernized.

Historians agree that globalization represents an acceleration and intensification of trends that go back thousands of years. Where it will take us is impossible to predict. Its supporters see universal benefits from economic growth, strengthened democracies through better-informed citizenry, increased capacity to deal with environmental problems, and even a heightened sense of human community. Its detractors see a widening divide between haves and have-nots, dangerous political transitions, the triumph of an ethos of corporate greed, and a bland uniformity in world culture. Whichever side is correct, understanding globalization and its effects will be a major challenge for the twenty-first century.

107 ◆ World Bank, *WORLD DEVELOPMENT INDICATORS*

The statistics that follow enable us to draw conclusions about short-term economic and social developments during the recent era of intensified globalization. The data were compiled by the World Bank, one of many international organizations concerned with alleviating world poverty by encouraging economic development. Founded at the Bretton Woods Conference in New Hampshire in 1944, the World Bank uses funds subscribed by 187 member nations to make loans to governments and private businesses for projects that further economic development. Although most loans at first were allocated for post–World War II reconstruction projects, since the 1950s the bank has supported projects mainly in developing nations.

Since 1978, the World Bank has annually published its *World Development Report*, which contains commentary on development strategy and statistics on economic, demographic, fiscal, and educational trends. Since 2001, most of the statistical data have been published separately as *World Development Indicators*. The World Bank draws on a wide range of sources for the information in its annual reports, including reports from governments, U.N. agencies, and nongovernmental organizations. Inevitably, in any given year, some data may be missing due to a nation's refusal to cooperate or its inability to do so because of conflict or natural disaster. (In the accompanying tables, the use of a dash [—] shows that no data are available.) Furthermore, many factors affect the reliability of

Source: Data from the World Bank.

the submitted data, including weak statistical methods used by some governments and disagreements over key definitions. Despite such difficulties, the data provided by the World Bank allow us to make broad comparisons over time.

Of the more than one hundred nations covered in the World Bank reports, thirty have been included in the following tables. They represent all the world's regions and range from some of the world's poorest states to the some of the richest. The tables provide data on seven topics:

1. Population.
2. Per capita Gross National Income (GNI), a number calculated by dividing a country's population into the Gross National Income, which is calculated by adding a country's Gross National Product (the value of all goods and services produced within a country in a given time) and net receipts of primary income (compensation of employees and property income) from non-resident sources. In other words, income produced by a U.S-owned company in Mexico counts toward U.S. GNI, but not income produced by a Japanese company in the United States. Per capita GNI gives a broad idea of a country's standard of living, but it is not necessarily an accurate gauge of the prevalence of poverty. For this, information about wealth distribution is needed.
3. Life expectancy.
4. Infant mortality. This measures the number of infants per one thousand who die before their fifth birthday.
5. Maternal mortality rates per 100,000 live births.
6. Percentage of population with access to improved sanitation facilities, defined as those capable of preventing human, animal, and insect contact with human waste. They may range from simple pit latrines to flush toilets connected to a sewer system.
7. Percentage of population with access to an improved water source. This refers to people with access to at least 20 liters of water per person a day from piped water into a building, public tap, tubewell, protected dug well, or rainwater collection, within one kilometer of the dwelling.
8. Literacy of individuals fifteen years or older. Literacy is defined as the ability to read and write simple sentences about one's daily experiences.
9. Per capita energy consumption. This is a number calculated by converting a country's total energy consumption into the energy produced by one kilogram of oil and then dividing it by the country's population.
10. A comparison of the extent of poverty in the world's major regions.

QUESTIONS FOR ANALYSIS

1. What population trends are revealed in the tables?
2. To what extent do the tables reveal uneven development among the world's major regions?
3. Does the information in the tables suggest that the gap between rich and poor nations is getting larger or smaller?
4. For those nations that have not achieved significant economic progress, what insights do the tables provide into reasons for their lack of success?
5. On the basis of the information in the tables, would it appear that things are getting better or worse for humankind?

	Population (Millions)			GNI Per Capita (U.S. dollars)			Life Expectancy at Birth	
	1976	1990	2009	1976	1990	2009	1990	2009
Congo, Democratic Republic	25.4	37.3	66	140	220	121	48	48
Ethiopia	28.7	51.2	83	100	120	330	47	56
Sierra Leone	3.1	4.1	6	200	240	340	40	48
Zimbabwe	6.5	9.8	13	530	640	360	61	45
Haiti	4.7	6.5	10	150	370	420 (2005)	55	61
Uganda	11.9	16.3	33	240	220	460	48	53
Mali	5.8	8.5	13	100	270	680	43	49
Ghana	10.1	14.9	24	580	390	1190	57	57
Nigeria	77.1	115.5	155	380	290	1190	45	48
India	620.4	849.5	115.5	150	350	1220	58	64
Egypt	38.1	52.1	83	280	600	2070	63	70
Indonesia	135.2	178.2	230	240	570	2050	62	71
Syria	7.7	12.4	21	780	980	2410	68	74
Guatemala	6.5	9.2	14	630	900	2650	62	71
China	835.5	1377.7	1331	410	370	3650	68	73
Thailand	43	55.8	68	380	1420	3760	69	69
South Africa	26	35.9	49	1340	2560	5760	61	52
Brazil	110	150.4	194	1140	2680	8070	66	73
Mexico	62	86.2	107	1090	2010	8960	71	75
Russian Federation	—	148.5 (1992)	142	—	2510 (1992)	9340	69(1992)	69
Chile	10.5	13.2	17	1050	1770	9470	74	79
Poland	34.3	38.2	38	2860	1790	12260	71	76
Korea, Rep.	36	42.8	49	670	5400	19830	71	80
Israel	3.6	3.9	7	3920	9700	25790	77	82
Italy	56.2	57.7	60	3050	18520	35160	77	81
Japan	112.8	123.5	128	4910	26930	38080	79	83
Canada	23.2	26.5	34	7510	20440	41980	77	81
United Kingdom	56.1	57.4	62	4020	16190	46040(2008)	76	80
United States	215.1	250	307	7890	22240	46360	75	79
Switzerland	6.4	6.7	8	8850	33160	65430	77	82

	Infant Under 5 Mortality Rate Per 1000 Live Births		Maternal Mortality Rates Per 100,000 Live Births		Access To Improved Sanitation Facilities (% of Population)	
	1990	2008	1990	2008	1990	2008
Congo, Democratic Republic	199	199	900	670	9	23
Ethiopia	210	104	990	470	4	12
Sierra Leone	285	192	130	970	–	13
Zimbabwe	81	90	390	790	43	46
Haiti	152	87	670	300	26	17
Uganda	184	128	670	430	39	48
Mali	129	117	1200	830	26	36
Ghana	120	69	630	350	7	13
Nigeria	212	138	1100	840	37	32
India	118	66	570	230	18	31
Egypt	90	21	220	82	72	94
Indonesia	86	39	620	240	33	52
Syria	36	16	120	46	83	96
Guatemala	76	40	140	110	65	81
China	46	19	110	38	41	55
Thailand	32	14	50	48	80	96
South Africa	62	62	230	410	69	77
Brazil	56	21	120	58	70	77
Mexico	45	17	93(1990)	85(2008)	66	85
Russian Federation	48(1992)	12	74(1992)	39	87(1982)	87
Chile	22	9	56	26	84	96
Poland	17	7	17	6	–	90
Korea, Rep.	9	5	18	18	69	–
Israel	4	4	6	3	100	100
Italy	10	4	6	7	100	100
Japan	6	3	12	6	100	100
Canada	8	6	6	12	100	100
United Kingdom	10	6	28	10	100	100
United States	11	8	12	24	100	100
Switzerland	8	4	8	16	100	100

	Energy Use Per Capita KG of Oil Equivalent		Access To Improved Water Source (% of Population)		Adult Literacy Rate (% Over 15 Years Old)		
	1990	2008	1990	2008	1974	1990	2009
Congo, Democratic Republic	319	346	45	46	15	63	92
Ethiopia	308	393	17	38	–	–	30
Sierra Leone	–	–	–	49	15	21	41
Zimbabwe	889	763	78	82	–	63	92
Haiti	219	281	47	63	20	53	49
Uganda	–	–	43	67	25	48	73
Mali	–	–	29	56	10	32	26
Ghana	353	405	54	82	25	60	67
Nigeria	725	735	47	58	–	41	61
India	375	445	72	88	36	48	63
Egypt	561	867	90	99	40	48	66
Indonesia	576	874	71	80	62	77	92
Syria	895	957	85	89	53	64	84
Guatemala	498	590	82	94	47	55	74
China	1049	1871	67	89	–	77	94
Thailand	742	1591	91	98	82	93	94
South Africa	2581	2756	83	97	–	–	89
Brazil	938	1295	88	97	64	81	90
Mexico	1457	1698	85	94	76	87	88
Russian Federation	5929	4838	93(1992)	96	–	–	100
Chile	1049	1871	90	96	90	93	99
Poland	2705	2567	100	100	98	–	100
Korea, Rep.	217	4669	–	–	92	96	95+
Israel	2462	3011	100	106	84	–	–
Italy	2584	2942	100	100	98	**	100
Japan	3556	3883	100	100	99	**	**
Canada	7509	8008	100	100	98	**	**
United Kingdom	3597	3995	100	100	98	**	**
United States	7672	7503	98	99	99	**	**
Switzerland	3581	3491	100	100	99	**	**

** Presumed to be at 100%

	Regional Poverty Estimates: Percentage Living Under $1.25 A Day		
	1981	1993	2005
	Region or Country		
EAST ASIA & PACIFIC	77.7	50.8	16.8
CHINA	84.0	53.7	15.9
EUROPE & CENTRAL ASIA	1.7	4.3	3.7
LATIN AMERICA & CARIBBEAN	47	47	45
MIDDLE EAST & N. AFRICA	14	10	11
SOUTH ASIA	59.4	46.9	40.3
INDIA	59.8	49.4	41.6
SUBSAHARAN AFRICA	53.4	56.9	50.9
	Percentage Living Under $2 a Day		
EAST ASIA & PACIFIC	92.6	75.8	38.7
CHINA	97.8	78.6	36.3
EUROPE & CENTRAL ASIA	8.3	10.3	8.9
LATIN AMERICA & CARIBBEAN	24.6	20.7	17.1
MIDDLE EAST & N. AFRICA	26.7	19.8	16.9
SOUTH ASIA	86.5	79.7	73.9
INDIA	88.6	81.7	75.6
SUBSAHARAN AFRICA	73.8	75.9	72.9